DATE DUE

5/4/2009			
GAYLORD			PRINTED IN U.S.A.

DISCARD

RED APR 1 3 2006

RODS DOWN
AND
DROPPED FIRES

Illinois Central and the Steam Age
In Perspective

ICLAG02-01

RICHARD P. BESSETTE

RTN Press, LLC
Orland Park 2004

Printed and bound in the United States of America

Published by the RTN Press, LLC
P.O. Box 2333
Orland Park, Illinois 60462
email: rtnpress@comcast.net
Website: www.rtnpress.com

Prepared by the Five Corners Press
5052 Route 100
Plymouth, Vermont   05056
Website: www.fivecorners.com

Cover Design by:
Richard P. Bessette - RTN Press
H. Donald Kroitzsh - Five Corners Press

FIRST EDITION
        First Printing, Spring 2004

Library of Congress Catalog Card Number: 2003099476
ISBN: 0-9747970-0-6

DEDICATION

From a Generation of Builders
For Amedee Savard
Born Les Eboulments on the St. Laurence River, Quebec, Canada 1876; Died 1968
Canadian Pacific Railroad 1898 - 1941

ICLAG21-27

The author's grandfather was a Canadian Pacific employee for 43 years, ending his career as Section Foreman on the Foster to Drummondville branch in the Province of Quebec. He is shown here in two photographs from 1934, at age 58. Above, second from left, he is with part of his summer gang, with their home away from home. Below, he is pictured fifth from right out on the roadway with some of the tools of the trade.

ICLAG21-28

And
Paul Lucien Bessette, M.D.
A.M.D.G.

Steam Engine Nomenclature

(1) Pilot truck, (2) Drive Wheels, (3) Drive Rods, (4) Trailing Truck, (5) Pressed steel pilot, (6) Cylinder, (7) Slide Valves, (8) Piston Valves, (9) Auxiliary Piston Valves, (10) Side Mounted Air Pumps, (11) Pilot Mounted Air Pumps, (12) Pilot Steps, (13) Pilot Ladder, (14) Sand Box, (15) Steam Dome, (16) Smokebox, (17) Cab.

Table Of Contents

List Of Tables And Maps

ACKNOWLEDGMENTS

Many thanks to a number of fine institutions for access to their extensive research collections, both general and specific. Libraries such as the Richard J. Daley Library at the University of Illinois – Chicago (an excellent general collection), the Newberry Library in Chicago (the last word on original documents of the Illinois Central) and the Transportation Library at Northwestern University Deering Library in Evanston (to all things transportation). The author is indebted also to the Chicago Historical Society and The Denver Public Library, sources of many historical photographs.

Thanks to Robert Medina from Rights and Licensing at the Chicago Historical Society who helped unearth informative pictures from the Society's collection, and to Tom Noone who helped rework some old Illinois Central maps to make them more instructive. Thanks also to Philip Bessette who worked his way through early drafts and offered many helpful suggestions, and to Don Kroitzsh at Five Corners Press who lent a big hand in getting this book printed. The author also would like to thank all the people who helped him *learn the ropes* in a 20-year career at the Illinois Central, especially Harry Bruce, Doug Hagestad and Gerry Mohan; ones mentors leave a lasting impression.

Unless otherwise noted, all photographs in this book were printed from negatives or copied from prints and negatives of the Illinois Central Railroad, most of which were made by Illinois Central photographers over the years or taken by professionals engaged by the Illinois Central, such as Hedrich-Blessing and Kaufmann & Fabry; in addition to source photographers, the Illinois Central acquired a number of the original photographs from employees and friends contributions and, where known, suitable credit is given; old friends and family also supplied photographs and are noted were appropriate, as is The Denver Public Library and the Chicago Historical Society. The author developed all materials from the Illinois Central photographic archives during the early 1980's; with ownership of the Illinois Central in a state of flux in the late 1980's, the author's project was put on hold, the photographs and copies stored away for the next 12 years; writing and arranging this record was taken up in earnest in 2000.

Illinois Central has turned over substantially all of its historical photographs to the Illinois Central Historical Society, in Paxton, Illinois; along with the source materials found at Chicago's Newberry Library in its special collection of Illinois Central archive items, these two organizations represent a world of information and data, both written and visual, on the Illinois Central Railroad. In addition, Northwestern University's Deering Library has a complete set of the *Illinois Central Magazine* dating back to 1912. The reader is invited to contact these institutions in order to delve even further into the Illinois Central past.

Company photographers are generally called upon to record the newest, fastest, latest iteration of particular events, such as first crossings or new locomotive types, rather than everyday activities. The author has tried to include both special events and the everyday in this book, that which is not often seen and that which may never be seen again. A number of the photographs reproduced have been published earlier, but many are in print for the first time. In order to allow as many people as possible to access these records, and to further the education of and raise awareness in the history of the Illinois Central Railroad, the author has arranged and commented on over 1,000 photographic views of steam locomotives and/or Illinois Central activities. Rather than publish only photographs that were of the best quality, it was argued that seeing a print of second quality was better than never viewing it in the first place; thus some photos are off-quality, grainy or slightly out-of-focus, but represent the only view available.

Lastly, the author would like to acknowledge how grateful he is to his family for their contributions. Many thanks to my wife Jane who wasn't quite sure what, if anything, might emanate from this project; she remained good humored and stuck it out with me to the end in this basement project; her loyalty is incalculable. Thanks to our children: 15-year old Eliot who had trouble explaining to his friends what exactly his Dad did for a living, and 8-year old Claire who thought it was great fun to have Dad home, and prepared play food day in and day out after school.

ICLAG13-01

Illinois Central land office near the turn of the century. As the signs attest, land in Illinois Central territory, in this case the Yazoo Valley in Mississippi, was going for $8 per acre and the buyer had 6 years to pay.

INTRODUCTION

So why write a book on railroads or steam locomotives, certainly not the subject of current events or interests? Because it is history. Today there are few left who have a clear memory of steam locomotives and their age; this manuscript redresses that by being both a history book and a picture book. It is a history of the Illinois Central, with a focus on the steam age and the machines that propelled it, but with perspective. Many books have been written on railroads, many failing to render a perspective with the dialogue. It is that "from the point of view" that paints the world in which the progress of the Illinois Central took place, an awfully important canvas spanning 1850 to 1950. Thus, the history is American, with a dash of foreign chronicles where it adds to the portrait, and the pictures visually set the time and tempo and technology in development of the Illinois Central.

What makes the period 1850 to 1950 interesting is how many novel and life-changing items arose in that century, especially the middle fifty years: the telephone, automobile, airplane, electric light, phonograph, motion picture, and radio to name just a few. It is an interesting period because it shows the growth of the nascent railroads of the 1850's into the nation's first big business in the 1890's. Many of today's business techniques such as cost accounting and finance, production management, mass production, and labor management were developed by the railroads first; these skills were then incorporated in the next growth industries: steel, oil, tobacco and chemical. As to the photographs, it is fortunate that the development of photography overlaps that of railroading. On viewing the photographs, which show the changes in steam locomotives over the years, the pictures evolve from staged and static engine shots into action scenes of trains; this parallels the development of photography from slow shutters and long exposures into faster shutters and film speeds. Along with the history then, pictures are included to set the time and place, the visual perspective; the pictures focus on steam locomotives, showing the development of these machines that mirrored the advancement of technology during the industrial age; the author purposely chose pictures with people, which give both perspective and proportion. Regarding any particular picture of a locomotive, the reader must remember to differentiate between the time it was built and the date its image was captured.

While the last steam engine on the Illinois Central wasn't scrapped until 1961, the real age of steam was over before 1950, when the construction of new engines stopped; steam locomotives really acted in a supporting role as the changeover to diesel-powered fleets took place during the 1950's, and steam was no longer used in any service in 1959. The primary source for this work was the Annual Reports of the Illinois Central, which listed locomotives and mentioned additions to the fleet in a more general way; the "year ends" of those reports, especially in the early years, were not always comparable; for example, some reports, written in January or February of a particular year, referred to fleet changes for the past year, but included changes that happened in the month of January of the current year. All to say, absolute numbers is not the concern of this work but, rather, showing a pictorial representation of the fleet at different times in its evolution. Records are quoted as they were then, not as they are now when they might be corrected.

While replete with pictures, this volume really cannot begin to represent a compendium on Illinois Central steam locomotives – rosters, names, origins, dates and numbers; for that detail one is referred to the last word, *Railroad History Bulletin # 140*, published by the Railway and Locomotive Historical Society in the Spring of 1979. Illinois Central had the practice, at least in the early days, of reusing roster spots (#'s) as soon as a new unit replaced a retired one, and of renumbering the entire fleet almost regularly; the author relied heavily on *Bulletin # 140* for dating and identifying photographs. In describing particular engines, the terms *Drivers* (diameter of drive wheels), *Boiler Pressure* (pressure of heated engine water), *Total Weight* (weight of engine on all wheels) and *Tractive Force* (calculated figure of pounds of pulling force) are used hundreds of times; for simplicity, they are referred to as D (in inches), BP (in pounds per square inch), TW (in pounds) and TF (in pounds). While quoted data are as accurate as possible, Tractive Force, which is a calculated number based on a percentage of steam pressure, can cause some trouble. The generally accepted calculation utilized an 85% factor, but Illinois Central also used a 90% factor at times. This book reports Tractive Force as it was quoted and makes no effort to reconcile the particular calculations used by the source data; thus, the reported data may vary depending on sources.

In 1850 most commerce in the U.S. moved between the north and south, yet the settling of the frontier moved from east to west – thus there were competing forces at work; the first major railroad development was a north-south railroad, the Illinois Central, but most of the subsequent developments were east/west carriers that opened up the frontier and united the states. Land grants, where a railroad gained title to neighboring property by completing construction of a railroad section, played a large part in the formation of Illinois Central; besides the original State of Illinois grant of 2.6 million acres, five other land grant railroads eventually became a part of the Illinois Central system: Dubuque & Sioux City, Yazoo & Mississippi Valley, Gulf & Ship Island, Mobile & Girard, and the Vicksburg, Shreveport & Texas; ultimately almost five million acres of federal land grants were associated with the Illinois Central System. Through rail companies acquired in later years, the Illinois Central can trace its roots back as far as 1832, the start of construction on the 25-mile long West Feliciana Railroad between Woodville, Mississippi and Bayou Sara, Louisiana; the West Feliciana's locomotive *Mississippi* made its first run in 1837.

The reader will notice that there is not a lot of detail on the construction and operation of steam locomotives, and there is a reason for that. The basic principle of a steam locomotive is simple: steam made in the boiler is transferred to a cylinder where the expansive force pushes a piston connected to a drive rod that turns the wheels; that said, design, mechanics and technology over the years took that basic principle and refined it to the peak of power and efficiency. While the principle is basic, when one looks at the array of valves, dials and levers in the cab and pipes, pumps, siphons, injectors and flues around the firebox one realizes basic is relative. The appendix outlines information on steam locomotives for those new to the subject, and points the reader toward comprehensive sources should the interest be there.

Every railroad had its own look, its own feel that set it apart from the others; whether it was the cab-forward locomotives of the Southern Pacific or the "Big Boys" of the Union Pacific, or the Harvey Houses of the Atchison, Topeka & Santa Fe or the Tuscan Red of the Pennsylvania, each had its own look and feel. The Illinois Central was no different: essentially a water-level route competing with the Mississippi river, operations on the Illinois Central were a long and slow drag from Chicago south to New Orleans; the railroad didn't require prodigious mountain passes or lengthy tunnels, but entailed hundreds of miles of roadway through virgin prairie with thousands of bridges, culverts and trestles spanning rivers, streams and creeks draining the Mississippi river valley; Illinois Central locomotive power was tailored to this purpose, fundamentally slow and powerful.

Remember that dates move around a little bit…when it is said that someone patented an idea on such-and-such a date, he or she may have demonstrated it before that date and/or invented it sometime earlier. Dates are meant to show approximate time and to give context to everything else that was going on in the period being discussed. In addition, there are many ideas mentioned, noted or dated that may have been attempted before; the date shown generally would be the timing of the first practical version of the notion or theory under scrutiny and not necessarily the actual date of conception. A particular date is not meant to represent the final word on carbon-dating innovation, just some perspective. There are two excellent histories on the Illinois Central, one by Carlton J. Corliss and one by John F. Stover; the purpose of this rendering is to provide more perspective, admittedly sacrificing some comprehensiveness and detail.

While care has been taken to describe, date and categorize photographs, some errors are inevitable. Since the photographs were drawn from the Illinois Central files and archives, the author relied on the cataloguing notes and comments that accompanied the prints and negatives and, by default, on those who did the original cataloguing. As errors or omissions are found, future editions will be updated.

Just as the 1893 World's Columbian Exposition in Chicago was a bit late in celebrating the 400-year anniversary of the founding of the New World, this history of the Illinois Central is a year or so late in celebrating the Illinois Central's steam age during the sesqui-centennial of the railroad's founding.

Some readers may view the historical writing as welcome relief from the monotony of hundreds of black & white photographs of steam locomotives, while others might view the photographs as a break from the tedium of the words; regardless of which school of thought one follows, if this feels like an *hommage* to Illinois Central steam, you've figured it out.

Interior view of a steam locomotive cab, showing the pipes, valves, dials and knobs on the engineer's end of the boiler. The fireman peeked out the small window at left, the engineer through a similar one on the right.

ICLAG12-01

FOREWORD

THE DECADE BEFORE THE 1850'S

34-year old Johann Galle found the eighth planet, Neptune. 54-year old Giovanni Maria Mastai-Ferretti was elected Pope by the 50 assembled in the College of Cardinals; Pius IX would lead the Church for 32 years. The French Revolution toppled the monarchy and re-established the republic, King Louis-Philippe abdicating in 1848. Ferdinand I resigned and Francis Joseph I took control. Hungary declared its independence, but Russia interfered (Battle of Temesovar). Karl Marx and Friedrich Engels published the *Communist Manifesto*. 24-year old William Thomson, Lord Kelvin, devised a scale to measure temperature based on absolute zero. Upper and Lower Canada became the single Province of Canada.

The 9th President of the United States was the former Ohio Senator William Henry Harrison; Harrison, renowned for defeating the Indian warrior Tecumseh at the Tippecanoe River, had a campaign slogan of "Tippecanoe and Tyler Too" that proved prophetic; 58-year old Harrison died within 30 days of his 1841 inauguration and 51-year old former Virginia governor Tyler became the first unelected President. In 1845 a compromise candidate would be chosen, U.S. House Speaker 49-year old James K. Polk, elected on a platform of territorial expansion (Manifest Destiny), the 11th President. President Polk declared war on Mexico, and let Major General Winfield Scott and Brigadier General Zachary Taylor lead the offense; Mexican leader General Antonio Lopez de Santa Ana led the defense. West Point graduates Colonel Jefferson Davis (Class of 1828), Captains Robert E. Lee ('29) and Braxton Bragg ('37), 1st Lieutenants P.G.T. Beauregard ('38), George McClellan ('46) and Ulysses S. Grant ('43) learned their trade in the war with Mexico. The Mexican War ended with the 1848 Treaty of Guadalupe-Hidalgo, a $15 million payment from the United States encouraging Mexico to cede New Mexico and California to the U.S., while releasing its claims in Texas. Florida and Texas were admitted to the Union as the 27th and 28th States. Texas' admission to the Union was nine years after the Alamo. The end of the Mexican War brought what would become Arizona, New Mexico, Nevada, Utah and parts of Wyoming and Colorado into the Union as unorganized territories. Virginia-born War veteran Zachary Taylor would go on to represent the Whig Party in 1848. In Baltimore at the 5th Democratic National Convention the Party split, when sitting President Polk chose not to run for re-election; Michigan Senator Lewis Cass ran; former President Martin Van Buren did too, but under the Free Soil party banner. In November, the Taylor/Fillmore ticket won the election, the Free Soil party taking enough votes to give the election to the Whigs. 64-year old "Old Rough and Ready" Zachary Taylor became the 12th President of the U.S.

The U.S. bluffed its way to an agreement with England to split the remote Oregon Country; the Oregon Treaty of 1846 fixed the northwest border of the U.S. along the 49th Parallel, placing Puget Sound in America and Vancouver Island in Canada; what would become Washington, Oregon, and part of Idaho soon were brought into the Union as a Territory; California was claimed, lost and reclaimed by various Americans during the period. Iowa was admitted to the Union as the 29th State, Wisconsin as the 30th. Minnesota, including parts of what would become the Dakotas, was set up as a Territory of the U.S.

What was needed for the development of the country's frontiers was transportation; railroads would prove to be the linchpin, opening up everything west of the Mississippi River. The U.S. population was approximately 20 million. The emigration of what would eventually total more than one million Irish fleeing the potato blight and resulting famine began; thousands would move west to Chicago and help build the Illinois and Michigan Canal, and then move west yet again to help build the transcontinental railroad. Over 15 years more than one quarter million souls would travel the Oregon Trail. The Donner Party of 32 travelers would try a shortcut to California south of the Great Salt Lake across the Wasatch Mountains; most succumbed to winter and hunger in the Sierra Nevada mountain range. Their 38-year old prophet Joseph Smith having been murdered two years earlier, 20,000 Mormons left their *beautiful place* Nauvoo, Illinois and headed west led by 45-year old Brigham Young. 36-year old John C. Fremont, the "pathfinder" from his earlier explorations of the west, conducted an expedition to find a railroad route from St. Louis to the West along the 38th parallel through the Rocky Mountains; the mission ended disastrously.

54-year old Samuel Finley Breese Morse of New York patented an improved version of the telegraph. Morse laid the first telegraph line between Washington and Baltimore along the Baltimore & Ohio Railroad right-of-way in 1843-1844, and sent the first recorded telegraph message (May 24, 1844). 44-year old Charles Goodyear received a U.S. patent on his process of vulcanization of rubber, making raw rubber stable. The forerunner to the U.S. Naval Academy opened in Annapolis, Maryland. 27-year old Boston dentist William T. Morton demonstrated the use of ether as an anesthetic at Massachusetts General, when a doctor removed a neck tumor from a patient. Congress authorized postage stamps. Thomas Alva Edison was born in Milan, Ohio. 38-year old Cyrus H. McCormick began his mechanical reaper business in Chicago, the forerunner to International Harvester. 38-year old Abraham Lincoln took his seat in Congress for his only Term; two years later, Lincoln was granted patent # 6,469 on a device to help steamboats pass over sand bars and shoals. Gold was found at Sutter's Mill in California near Sacramento; the Rush soon began, the population of San Francisco growing from under 1,000 to over 30,000 in two short years. 54-year old Walter Hunt patented (#6,281) the safety pin. The Department of the Interior was created.

The future moral crusader Carry Amelia Moore (Carry Nation from her 2nd marriage) was born; Harriet Tubman escaped slavery in Maryland; freed slave Sojourner Truth (nee Isabella Van Wagener circa 1797) toured the northeast speaking out for equality. 27-year old Herman Melville published *Typee*, based on his experiences in the South Seas. Plagued by alcohol and drugs, Edgar Allan Poe died in Baltimore at age 40. 32-year old Henry David Thoreau published *Civil Disobedience*, passive resistance. Emily Jane Bronte published *Wuthering Heights;* sister Charlotte completed *Jane Eyre*; Emily passed away in 1848 at age 30, sister Charlotte a few years later at age 38.

The 96-mile long Illinois and Michigan Canal connecting Chicago and LaSalle, the missing link in an all-water route between the Great Lakes and the Mississippi River, was completed; until 1854 it would have no rail competitor, and would divert trade away from St. Louis. Cholera soon came up the Illinois and Michigan Canal from New Orleans; Chicago built its first orphanages as a result. The Chicago Board of Trade was founded. John Deere improved his 1837 invention and developed his steel-tipped plow.

The Baltimore & Ohio was chartered in 1827 to build a railroad between Baltimore and the Ohio River; construction started in 1828 and would proceed on-and-off for 25 years; the segment between Baltimore and Ellicott's Mills opened in 1830, the first railroad to open for public passenger and freight business. Construction of the forerunner to the New York Central Railroad (the Mohawk & Hudson Railroad) began in 1829 with tracks from Albany to Schenectady. Completion of the Erie Canal in 1825, connecting Buffalo and Albany, had diverted trade to New York City, from Philadelphia; the response by Pennsylvania was to authorize a canal and railroad across the state; by 1846, the Pennsylvania Railroad Company had the task of connecting Pittsburgh and Philadelphia, and J. Edgar Thomson soon would be its Chief Engineer. Thus continued the great rivalry between Philadelphia and New York City, played out in transportation between the Pennsylvania and the New York Central railroads. The Buffalo, Bayou, Brazos & Colorado Railway became the first in the southwest; it began operations out of Harrisburg, Texas in 1853.

The first locomotive in Chicago was named the *Pioneer* (nee *Alert*); the 11-year old 10-ton locomotive was the 37th built by Matthias W. Baldwin of Philadelphia; its first run was from Chicago to Oak Park on the Galena & Chicago Union Railroad, forerunner to the Chicago & Northwestern. The precursor to the Chicago, Burlington & Quincy, the Aurora Branch Railroad, began operations on 12 miles of track. Anxious to build infrastructure, the Illinois legislature adopted a number of measures in the 1830's, bringing the State near bankruptcy by the end of the decade; the mission to build a great central railroad from LaSalle to the Ohio river with two bisecting lines (a Southern Cross from Alton to Mt. Carmel, and a Northern Cross through Springfield and Quincy) was but one example of the legislatures' unfunded largesse. Four attempts to build a central railroad in Illinois were undertaken before 1850; "An act to incorporate the Illinois Central Railroad" in 1836, an "Internal Improvement Act" in 1837, a private capital venture in 1843 - the Holbrook Company, and an 1849 effort envisioning Federal support – a re-enacted Great Western Railway Company; each effort fumbled around until failure; the Northern Cross ended up a 24-mile long segment between Jacksonville and Meredosia, later extended to Springfield.

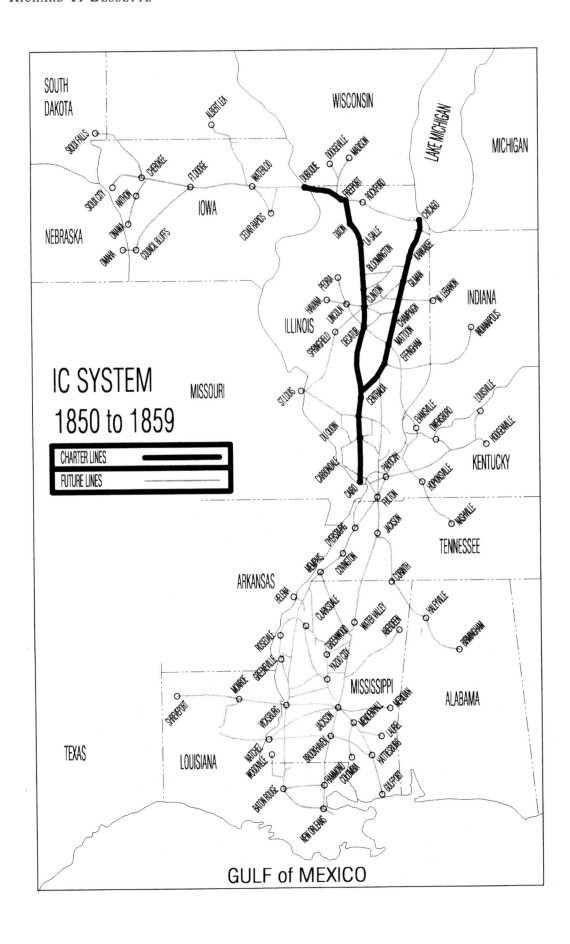

1850's 1860's 1870's 1880's 1890's 1900's 1910's 1920's 1930's 1940's

Destined to play a large role in settling the frontiers of the world, between 1845 and 1855 over two million Irish emigrated to the United States and Australia, with another three-quarters of a million to England.

The Seventh Census of the U.S. population was taken in 1850; there were a little over 23 million people in the U.S., having grown 36 percent from the prior census; the country would add over 8 million people by the end of the decade, one-third through immigration. The Union grew by three States to a total of 33. With the discovery of gold and silver in the West, the entire frontier opened in the 1850's exposing the need for transportation. The settlement of the West during the 1840's brought friction between the South and North, each trying to influence the slavery question – the touchstone of the 1850's. The Missouri Compromise of 1820 had struck a balance, stemming the expansion of slavery in new States; the end of the Mexican War in 1848 reintroduced the question; the 1850 Fugitive Slave Law forced the return of escaped slaves, and the Kansas-Nebraska Act of 1854 modified the Missouri Compromise to allow new States a choice on slavery; in 1856 the anti-slavery Republican Party lost the election, temporarily muffling any discourse; in 1857 the Dred Scott decision upheld the concept of slaves as property, effectively negating the Missouri Compromise; when John Brown and his abolitionists attacked the Federal arsenal at Harpers Ferry, the die was cast; the coup de grace came the next year with the victory of the anti-slavery party of Abraham Lincoln; the 1850's set the stage for resolving the slavery issue.

Presaging the Panama Canal by 60 years, Americans built a railroad across the Panamanian isthmus in the 1850's. Railroads went from an experiment to a business in this decade. By 1852 you could travel from Chicago back to the East coast by rail. In 1850 the major line-haul rail carriers operated a little over 9,000 miles of railroad, up from less than 3,000 miles in 1840; miles of railroad would more than triple to over 30,500 miles by the end of the decade. Between the 1820's and 1850 a lot of small railroads were created; after 1850 a lot of consolidation took place in the industry.

GROWTH OF ILLINOIS CENTRAL RAILROAD BUSINESS

Year (1)	Tonnage (mil/tons)	Lumber (mil/bf)	Grain (mil/bus)	Coal (mil/tons)	Passengers Commuters	Miles/Fare
1850	—				—	
1851	—				—	
1852	—				—	
1853	—				—	
1854	N/A				N/A N/A	
1855	N/A				464,823 N/A	
1856	N/A				653,201 N/A	
1857	.440	71	3.9	.059	714,707 N/A	75/$1.50
1858	.381	59	3.6	.058	568,670 N/A	
1859	.422	59	3.6	.073	609,585 N/A	

Passengers/Commuters = Total Ridership, and Commuter Portion Miles/Fare = Average Passenger Trip and Charge
(1) Fiscal Year bf = Board Feet bus = Bushels N/A = Data Not Available — No Business

1850

65-year old President Zachary Taylor died in office 16 months after his inauguration; 50-year old Vice President Millard Fillmore was sworn in as the 13th President of the U.S. under the rules of succession. Taylor was the second President to die in Office (Harrison and Taylor). Sectional negotiations between the South and North concerning slavery in the new western territory brought some definition to the U.S. map and concessions on both sides, Congress passing the Compromise of 1850: California was admitted as a free state to the Union, the 31st State; its geographical position was uncommon in that California bordered no other State of the Union, only Territories; Utah was organized as a Territory, and Brigham Young was appointed the 1st Territorial Governor; New Mexico also was organized as a Territory; the charters of the two Territories were deliberately silent on slave status; the Fugitive Slave Law, which forced the return to the South of many escaped slaves, was enacted. In September Congress abolished the punishment of flogging in the Navy. Nathaniel Hawthorne published *The Scarlet Letter*.

President Millard Fillmore's Federal Land Grant Act of 1850 was passed, which allocated federal land to the States to encourage development of the country's frontiers; in September the first land grant occurred, the government giving the State of Illinois 2.6 million acres of undeveloped land; over 130 million acres of land eventually would be granted under such land grant acts in the next 21 years. With the westward move of the nation's frontier, interest in a transcontinental railroad heightened; coast-to-coast movement took months via the water route around Cape Horn, while overland on a railroad could take days. 27-year old Thomas A. Scott joined the Pennsylvania Railroad; in ten short years he would rise to Vice President, a preview of a long career in railroads.

31-year old Scotsman Allan Pinkerton founded his National Detective Agency in Chicago, shortly after becoming the City's first detective; Pinkerton would perform independent work for the yet-to-come Illinois Central and thereby meet future notables Lincoln and McClellan.

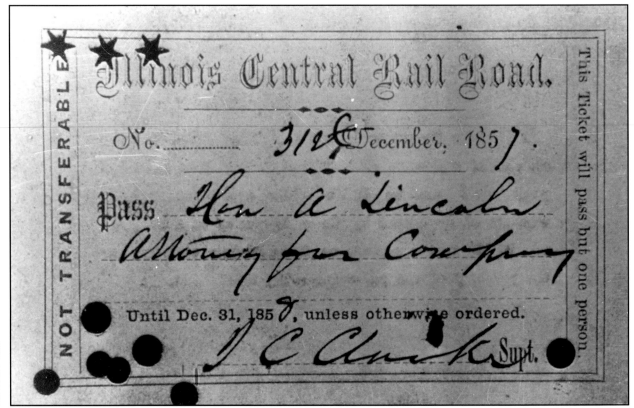

Abraham Lincoln served under retainer for the Illinois Central all through the 1850's, appearing on the Railroad's behalf in a number of counties. Given annual passes to travel on Company business, one is reproduced above.

1851

England staged the London Crystal Palace Exposition, what most believe to be the progenitor of the modern world's fair. Some 250,000 Irish emigrated to the U.S. this year alone, fleeing blight, famine and poverty, persecution.

32-year old Herman Melville published *Moby Dick*, essentially the crowning glory of his writing career; although Melville lived another four decades, he published little of consequence and nothing that could approach the brilliance of *Moby Dick*. 40-year old Isaac M. Singer received a patent on his continuous-stitch sewing machine; Singer was promptly sued by Elias Howe who patented a lock-stitch sewing machine in 1846, when he was 27-years old; while Howe won the patent infringement case, Singer was the name remembered for bringing the sewing machine into every home. The forerunner to the America's Cup Race was held for the first time. The first YMCA opened in the United States, founded by Thomas Sullivan in Boston. Northwestern University was founded by a group of Chicago businessmen, all Methodists. Englishman Frederick S. Archer developed an improved process for producing a photographic image, called the wet-plate process; its claim to fame over daguerreotypes (invented in France in 1839) was that copies could be made from the negative produced; the loss of a daguerreotype plate meant the loss of the image, while an image might now endure even with the loss of the negative. The *New York Times* was published for the first time, one cent per copy; it was called the *New York Daily Times* when first published.

Built entirely within the State of New York, the New York and Erie Railroad was the longest continuous railroad of its day, with over 440 miles of trackage beginning on the outskirts of New York City and reaching west to Dunkirk, New York on Lake Erie; chartered in 1832, this carrier was reorganized out of bankruptcy to become the Erie Railroad in 1861, after extending its reach to Cleveland and Chicago,

Effective March 19, Robert Schuyler was elected the 1st President of the Illinois Central; he would serve until July 28, 1853 and later earn a measure of disgrace being involved in a stock fraud perpetrated with New York & New Haven securities. With less than 100 miles of railroad in operation, Illinois was anxious to grow and develop its part of the frontier. With four efforts to build a central railroad having failed (the first having been chartered in 1836), the second Illinois Central railroad was chartered by act of the Illinois' General Assembly, by a vote of 23 to 2 in the Senate and 72 to 2 in the House, on February 10th. The state of Illinois gave its 2.6 million acres of federal land to the newly chartered Illinois Central Railroad, which became the first land grant railroad; Illinois Central's mission was to build a rail line from Cairo, Illinois (where the Mississippi and Ohio rivers meet) to Galena, Illinois (an area of lead mines in the northwest part of the state) and one to Chicago, Illinois (the growing city on Lake Michigan shore). In order to locate the proposed lines, seven survey parties were organized, one each in Freeport, LaSalle, Bloomington, Decatur, Cairo, Urbana and Chicago beginning in May; while much of the survey was through trackless prairie, the location of the 704 mile long Charter Lines was complete by the end of the year, and construction started at Cairo and Chicago at the same time. Illinois Central would use some of the land grant for right-of-way and facilities, but most would be sold with the proceeds used to fund construction of the railroad. With plans to build so much railroad across so much land with so few people, the venture was really one of settling the prairie; getting sufficient labor crews would be one of the biggest problems, and Irish and German immigrants ended up the solution. Massachusetts-born, Norwich University engineering school graduate, 20-year old Grenville Mellen Dodge hired on in the Illinois Central Engineering Department and soon was laying out track between LaSalle and Dixon. In a storied career, Dodge would progress from the Illinois Central, to a predecessor of the Chicago Rock Island, on to government-sponsored Pacific Railroad survey crews, then distinction in the Civil War at Pea Ridge with appointment to Brigadier General at age 31, and finally fame at the Union Pacific.

1852

44-year old French President Louis Napoleon, showing a weakness for history, declared himself emperor Napoleon III.

Henry Wells and William Fargo joined forces and formed their namesake company in San Francisco. The Studebaker brothers sold their first wagon. In Baltimore at the 6th Democratic National Convention, former U.S. Congressman and New Hampshire Senator Franklin Pierce was nominated for the Presidency on the 49th ballot; the Vice President candidate was Alabama's former Senator William R. D. King. The Whig party candidate for the Presidency was the career military man and hero of the Mexican War Major General Winfield Scott, who beat out the sitting President Millard Fillmore for the nomination on the 53rd ballot; the Vice Presidential running mate was Secretary of the Navy William A. Graham. New Hampshire Senator John P. Hale ran for the Presidency for the Free Soil party. The Pierce/King ticket won the election in a sweep, easily beating the other candidates. Jefferson Davis, from Mississippi, was Secretary of War during the Presidency of Franklin Pierce. Harriet Beecher Stowe published *Uncle Tom's Cabin*, putting a face on slavery and giving abolitionists a touchstone. In September 41-year old Vermont-born mechanic and inventor Elisha Graves Otis invented his safety elevator; he spent the next two years demonstrating it across the land. 39-year old lithographer Nathaniel Currier employed 28-year old artist James Merritt Ives, and they were off to the races; with the print business passing first to their sons, it would see the end of the century, falling to improvements in photography.

The Pennsylvania Railroad spanned Pittsburgh and Philadelphia using connections with other rail carriers. The New Orleans, Jackson & Great Northern and Mississippi Central were chartered to construct railroads in the south, the former between New Orleans and Canton and the latter between Canton and the Tennessee border; while the combination aimed to connect with the Illinois Central at Cairo, both would be finished before and destroyed during the Civil War. Illinois senator Stephen Douglas purchased 70 acres on the south side of Chicago between 31st and 35th streets by the lake for a residence; Douglas sold portions of the property to the Illinois Central for its right-of-way and, even later, an Army training camp was established on part of the property.

By its annual meeting in March, the new Illinois Central land grant railroad reported that its lines had been located, surveyed and six of its twelve divisions were ready to begin letting contracts for grading. The official goal became a 704 mile roadway, joining the upper and lower sections of the Mississippi Valley, in the shape of a "Y": a mainline north from Cairo, Illinois (confluence of the Mississippi and Ohio rivers) to LaSalle, Illinois (a point on the Illinois River where the Illinois & Michigan Canal terminated); a branch line extending north from LaSalle to the east bank of the Mississippi River across Dubuque (Dunleith); and a branch line extending south from Chicago connecting back into the mainline (conveniently, Branch Junction). In June the Chicago City Council granted permission to the Illinois Central "to lay down, construct and maintain…along the margin of the lake…a railroad, with one or more tracks…". Financing for the estimated $17 million project ($353 million in 2002 dollars based on Consumer Price Index) had yet to be secured, but over the next six months the Illinois Central arranged for the sale of $9 million in construction bonds: $4 million at seven percent to American investors and, later, $5 million at six percent to London investors; transfer of about one-third of the Company's stock ownership to these investors facilitated the sales. By the end of the year, the Illinois Central completed its first track, a 14-mile section leading south from the periphery of Chicago at 22nd Street to Lake Calumet Station (now Kensington); this section had two aims: continuing extensions to meet the land grant line building north from Cairo towards Chicago, and to facilitate a rail connection with the Michigan Central Railroad – allowing them access to Chicago and the Illinois Central interchange access to the East; Illinois Central would not begin service on this track segment for a year, leaving the Michigan Central its only tenant. The Illinois Central also began building its double-trestle track and breakwater entrance to the city, along the lake front from 22nd Street north to the heart of the City where the Chicago River meets Lake Michigan; Illinois Central's entrance to the City was a mutual accommodation: Illinois Central gaining access to the inner city like no other railroad, and the city getting shore protection for its irreplaceable Michigan Avenue. The Illinois Central had its Charter amended to allow it to build trackage from 12th Street to the south branch of the Chicago River, the future St. Charles Air Line; construction took four years. Illinois Central's locomotive fleet started with delivery of 3 units, all 4-4-0 American-type wood-burning locomotives built by Rogers, Ketchum & Grosvenor of Paterson, New Jersey (Morris Ketchum was one of Illinois Central's incorporators). With all the rail

IC1852-01

This often-published picture is thought to depict the first Illinois Central steam locomotive - IC #1; a 4-4-0 American-type built by Rogers in 1852 (60 D; 140 BP; 54,000 TW; 7,952 TF), this engine had inclined cylinders and was a wood burner. The picture is heavily retouched and very old, and is thought to be taken in Chicago. This photograph was published in the June, 1925 issue of the Illinois Central Magazine, and a number of other publications and books since that time. Below is a depiction of the 12 working divisions around which construction of the Charter Lines was organized.

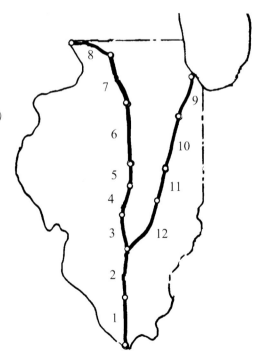

Mainline: Divisions 1 - 6
Dubuque Branch: Divisions 7 - 8
Chicago Branch: Divisions 9 - 12

Division 1 - 60 miles – Cairo to Big Muddy River (N of Carbondale)
Division 2 - 59 miles – Big Muddy River to Mainline Junction (N of Centralia)
Division 3 - 32 miles – Mainline Junction to Ramsay's Creek (N of Vandalia)
Division 4 - 53 miles – Ramsay's Creek to Sangamon River (Decatur)
Division 5 - 43 miles – Sangamon River to Bloomington
Division 6 - 61 miles – Bloomington to La Salle

Division 7 - 78 miles – La Salle to Freeport
Division 8 - 68 miles – Freeport to Dubuque

Division 9 - 56 miles – Chicago to Kankakee River
Division 10 - 72 miles – Kankakee River to Urbana
Division 11 - 48 miles – Urbana to Little Wabash River (Mattoon)
Division 12 - 74 miles – Little Wabash River to Mainline Junction

activity in Chicago, investors Stone, Boomer and Bouten organized the American Car Factory on 13 acres three miles south of Chicago to build rail equipment; with Illinois Central passing right by the factory near 27th Street, this property would one day form the Company's Chicago area car shops.

1853

New Hampshire's favorite son 48-year old Franklin Pierce was sworn in as the 14th President of the U.S. Commodore Matthew C. Perry sailed to Japan to begin discussions aimed at opening up trading relations. In September German immigrant Henry E. Steinway began making pianos in America. 42-year old Isaac Singer marketed his first sewing machine. Even though few European nations paid it any attention and it was mostly an American show, New York staged what some consider to be the first world's fair held in the U.S.; it was called the New York Exhibition of the Industry of All Nations, or the Crystal Palace Exposition, and it lasted through the following year. Vincent van Gogh was born in Holland. Illinois held its first State Fair, in the capital Springfield. Charles Ellet, Jr. published his recommendations for flood control on the lower Mississippi river, calling for a series of diversions, levees and reservoirs; some 75 years later, record floods would force a revisiting of his suggestions.

17-year old Scottish-born Andrew Carnegie started work as a telegraph operator on the Pennsylvania Railroad; he remained with the railroad until 1865, learning much of what would carry him to the top in business and industry. 21-year old Octave Chanute helped design the Chicago & Alton Railroad. The Buffalo Bayou, Brazos & Colorado Railway, the first railroad in Texas, began operations westward out of Harrisburg, Texas; one day this line became the oldest part of the Southern Pacific. With sectional rivalries prohibiting agreement on a single route, the U.S. government under the Pacific Railroad Survey Act commissioned the Army to survey alternative routes to the Pacific Ocean and determine the most practicable; with the hope of building a railroad to connect east and west, five different routes were evaluated under the direction of Secretary of War Jefferson Davis: a "Southern" route around the 32nd parallel from Charleston to San Diego; a route following the 35th parallel; a "Buffalo Trail" route between the 38th and 39th parallels; an "Overland" route between the 41st and 42nd parallels (also called the "Central" or "Mormon" route); and a "Northern" route between the 47th and 49th parallels from St. Paul to Puget Sound (Army Lieutenant George B. McClellan led the west coast portion of this expedition moving east through the uncharted Cascades). The Baltimore & Ohio Railroad completed its original mission of connecting Baltimore to the Ohio River when it sent its first train into Wheeling, Pennsylvania in January. The first major rail consolidation took place when the New York Central Railroad was officially organized; cobbled together by merging ten small regional rail lines constructed during the 1830's and 1840's, it largely followed the path of the Erie Canal between Albany and Buffalo.

Effective July 28th 46-year old William P. Burrall was elected the 2nd President of the Illinois Central; he would serve until January 10, 1855. The Dubuque & Pacific Railroad was chartered. The Illinois Central began its first scheduled train operation (in May), Timetable Number 1 covering Bloomington to LaSalle, Illinois: with stops in Hudson, Kappa, Panola, Minonk, Wenona and Tonica; this sixty-mile span comprised the 6th Division of the Railroad, absent the Illinois River crossing, and was the first portion of the 704-mile Charter Lines then under construction to be completed. As a Committee of the Company's Directors found in touring the construction sites in October, building a railroad through virgin territory witnesses Nature's sense of humor; construction goes from essentially flat prairie for 57 miles of light grading (Bloomington to near LaSalle) into a river valley spanning ¾ th's of a mile and dropping 30 feet or more to low water (Illinois river crossing at LaSalle); it could just as easily go from a steady flat 35-mile long construction site (Freeport west) into a land mass requiring a cut some 1,200 feet long and 50 feet at its deepest point to allow grading of the roadway (Scales Mound). While construction usually took place on either side of such natural hurdles, eventually the pieces of the puzzle had to be connected to make it a railroad. With the southern construction sites supplied with men, material and food by the Mississippi River at Cairo and the northern sites by the Great Lakes through Chicago and the Illinois River, connecting the pieces was a central goal. In June an additional $3 million in Illinois Central construction bonds were arranged, bringing the total to $12 million. Springfield attorney Abraham Lincoln was retained by the Illinois Central as local counsel; the future President remained active on behalf of the railroad and on retainer through his election year. Illinois Central extended its line and began limited train service south from Chicago to Kankakee (in July), still aiming to meet the land grant line building in southern Illinois north toward Chicago. With this service, the Illinois Central effectively put Kankakee on the map, having chosen to build trackage through this settlement rather than nearby Bourbonnais, where they weren't as supportive of a railroad effort; Illinois Central would bridge the Kankakee River and continue south the following year. The Illinois Central completed construction on 118 miles of Charter Line during the year, bringing

IC1853-02

Two Roger's products of 1853, and both 4-4-0 American-type wood burning engines with inclined cylinders. Above, IC #10 (72 D; 54,000 TW) was variously reported as pulling the first train into Kankakee and Cairo; the photograph dates before 1878. Below, IC #24 (72 D; 140 BP; 56,000 TW; 7,644 TF) dates before an 1875 rebuild; it was printed in the January, 1923 issue of the IC Magazine.

IC1853-01

the 704-mile project to 132 miles of roadway. The Illinois Central completed its double-trestle track and breakwater entrance to the city, along and sometimes in the lake front from 22nd Street to the Chicago River; for nearly one mile the breakwater/trestle was in the lake, some 400 feet east of Michigan Avenue and enclosing over 30 acres of area as a lagoon, one day land. The Illinois Central's primary locomotive fleet rose to 24, chiefly work units as construction progressed on the railroad; Illinois Central roster addition of 21 new 4-4-0 American-type wood-burning locomotives were all built by Rogers, Ketchum & Grosvenor of Paterson, New Jersey.

1854

A joint French-British force invaded the Crimea, intending to seize the Russian naval base at Sevastopol; defending the British headquarters at Balaklava, 57-year old James Thomas Brudenell, Lord Cardigan, made his famous but ill-fated charge with the Light Brigade; the Crimean War would last through 1856. The Immaculate Conception became a Catholic article of faith on being proclaimed dogma by Pius IX.

59-year old American Commodore Matthew C. Perry returned to Tokyo Bay, and with the Treaty of Kanagawa, opened Japan to the outside world. Illinois Senator Stephen Douglas' Kansas-Nebraska Act, which proposed two new Territories, passed in Congress; to gain southern support the Act allowed new States to determine their own position on the slavery question on entering the Union, instead of having to follow the Missouri Compromise of 1820 that would have forbade slavery. This Act stirred up dormant passions on slavery, and effectively spelled the doom of the Whig Party and Douglas' chances at the Presidency. The Republican Party was formed from remnants of the Whig Party and some antislavery Democrats. Depression of 1854: crops failed in the Midwest, and another financial crisis swept across the country, with investments in railroad securities attracting a lot of suspicion. 43-year old Elisha Graves Otis' demonstration of his safety elevator at New York's Crystal Palace Exposition brought national attention to the innovation. Henry Wadsworth Longfellow published his *The Song of Hiawatha*. Henry David Thoreau published his reflections on self-reliance and simple living in the woods, *Walden, or Life in the Woods*.

The Chicago & Rock Island became the first railroad to reach the Mississippi River, completed to Rock Island, Illinois; completion of the Rock Island would sound the death-knell for the Illinois and Michigan Canal business. Axed and shoveled through swamps and cypress, the New Orleans, Jackson & Great Northern completed its line from New Orleans northward to the Mississippi border at Osyka.

Although surveyed through Urbana, because of the high prices demanded by a key land-owner, the Illinois Central built track two miles west and formed West Urbana – the future Champaign; 13 years later Illinois Central would donate $50,000 in services to help build a great university. The Company completed construction on 300 miles of Charter Line during the year, bringing system mileage to 432 out of the 704 planned; miles-of-track-laid being a measure of success given the timeframes of the Charter, construction often was primitive, most ballasting and widening of embankments and roadway being left for later. In building its railway, the Illinois Central depended on the other pioneer rail carriers in Illinois to ship material and supplies to staging areas near the construction sites; Illinois Central used the Galena & Chicago Union, the Aurora Branch, and the Chicago & Rock Island railroads for deliveries. The Illinois Central opened four land offices toward the end of the year with an eye to beginning the development of land adjacent to the railroad's new lines. Land development along the lines of the Illinois Central began to show results, especially south of Chicago; settlement and development generally followed communication and transportation, such as allowed by passable rivers; with rail delivery of materials now accessible, the nearby town of Bourbonnais for example, nonexistent two years earlier, sported over 1,000 inhabitants. Similar development would occur at nearly every place the railroad built a station house; thus would the prairies of Illinois be settled and removed from the frontier. Early in the year in its Directors report to Stockholders, the Company reported that it had let contracts for a total of 106 locomotives; by the end of the year, Illinois Central's locomotive roster stood at 56 units, with 32 units delivered that year and more on the way each month; all units were 4-4-0 American-types built by Rogers, Ketchum & Grosvenor out of Paterson, New Jersey; not counted in the above total were second-hand units (maybe 6 units) Illinois Central acquired to supplement the fleet on an as needed basis. Toward the end of the year, the Company announced that the main line was open for travel; other than a few test freight trains, the year's business would be confined to passengers riding the rails.

IC1854-02

Two Rogers-built 4-4-0 American-types, these engines had horizontal cylinders, reflecting the developing state of the art. Above is IC #31 (66 D; 140 BP; 56,000 TW; 8,339 TF) shown at the Chicago Lake Front circa 1862, after it had been rebuilt to burn coal; this photograph was published in the June, 1937 issue of the Illinois Central Magazine. Shown below is IC #32 (60 D; 140 BP; 56,000 TW; 8,339 TF) which was published in the February, 1926 issue of the Magazine. This engine is pictured in front of the original roundhouse in Centralia, Illinois; the roundhouse dates to the early 1850's; David Oxley is pictured between the drive wheels; he was the first Master Mechanic at Centralia, and held the job for 36 years. Machine shop foreman V.P. Bryant is on the ground next to the tender. This picture shows the engine as a wood-burner, and dates to the early 1860's.

IC1854-01

IC1850-01

This 1854 Rogers-built 4-4-0 American (72 D; 56,000 TW) was a high-wheeled locomotive. Pictured here at what is believed to be Amboy, Illinois, the engine is on a manual turntable (sometimes called "armstrong" or "strong arm" turntable). The engine is decorated in honor of General U.S.S. Grant; the story is General Grant was on a trip from Washington, D.C. back home to Galena, Illinois. Illinois Central engine #36 pulled the General's train on the segment from Amboy to Galena. Conflicting dates place the picture in either 1869 or 1879, but agree on the day of November 18th; so the picture dates to either nine months after General Grant's inauguration, or to a time after his retirement from the Presidency. Illinois Central employees in the picture are B.B. Howard (general foreman, shown extreme left), J.B. Adams (Amboy master mechanic, on turntable next to gangway) and Rush Rosier (engineer, in gangway). This engine was renumbered to IC #58 in 1885, before being retired the following year. This picture was published in the December, 1924 issue of the IC Magazine.

IC45x35-26

Illinois Central #44 was a Rogers-built 4-4-0 American (60 D; 56,000 TW), a product of 1854. Shown here in a builder's sketch, it was rebuilt in 1862 at Illinois Central's Weldon Yard shops in Chicago to burn coal; J.J. Hayes was the Superintendent of Machinery and in charge of the rebuild. This engine was renumbered #33 in 1883; #114 in 1885; and #1400 in 1890.

IC1854-03

Illinois Central #1422, an 1854 Rogers-built 4-4-0 American (60 D; 56,000 TW), was originally numbered IC #50; it was renumbered in 1890. It was pictured at the Chicago Lake Front in 1892 in what might be an R.A. Beck photograph. By 1892 the engine already had been rebuilt (1876), note the elongated smokebox.

1855

Bubonic plague raged through China. Paris held an International Exposition; one of the items displayed was the large-scale production of a new metal, aluminum. The Crimean War continued.

Walt Whitman, on his way to becoming an accomplished poet, published his *Leaves of Grass*. Congress revived the rank of Lieutenant General and in a largely honorary gesture bestowed it upon 69-year old Winfield Scott, making him the first to hold that rank since George Washington; Washington had been made Lieutenant General at age 66 in 1798 by then President John Adams.

A chain of individual railroads would span the distance from the East coast to the Mississippi River for the first time. The Mobile and Ohio Railroad, which would form part of the Gulf, Mobile and Ohio 85 years later, completed 170 of the 492 miles of track it intended to build from Mobile, Alabama north to the banks of the Ohio River near Cairo, Illinois; when complete it would form, with the Illinois Central, a two-carrier system linking the Great Lakes to the Gulf of Mexico.

Effective January 10th 32-year old John Noble Alsop Griswold was elected the 3rd President of the Illinois Central; he would serve until December 1st, at which time 34-year old William Henry Osborn was elected the 4th President; Osborn would serve through July 11, 1865, leading the Company through the Civil War. "Old Main" charter line between Cairo and LaSalle, and the branch from LaSalle to the east bank of the Mississippi river across from Dubuque completed (mainline "golden spike" struck near the former Illinois state capital Vandalia); work on the Chicago branch reached Mattoon, and only the 77 miles to Branch Junction outside Centralia remained. Because of the Illinois Central construction, a number of existing towns had more than doubled in population: like Decatur, Bloomington, LaSalle, Dixon, Freeport and Galena; a score of others had sprung up around the new station houses: like Anna, Carbondale, DuQuoin, Centralia, Mendota, Amboy, Polo, Dunleith, Monee, Manteno, Bourbonnais, Loda and Urbana. Overall, Illinois' population had grown from 850,000 in 1850 to an estimated 1,300,000 by the end of 1855 – more than 50 percent. The Illinois Central's Transportation Department was organized around three divisions: Centralia in the south, Amboy in the north, and Chicago for the Chicago Branch; within a short time car and locomotive repair shops would be located in each transportation division headquarters. With no national standard for rail gauge, car transfers oftentimes called for ingenuity; to facilitate movement of Illinois Central cars to St. Louis over the broad-gauge Ohio and Mississippi Railroad and avoid unloading cars or changing out wheels sets, Illinois Central entered into an agreement to lay a third rail between the O & M RR's; while only partially completed, these actions foreshadowed the coming integration of carriers, the Illinois Central's, in particular, by 26 years. Illinois' first underground (shaft) coal mine opened at St. Johns just north of DuQuoin; thus began experiments with Illinois' coal as fuel; Illinois Central made its first conversion of a wood-burning locomotive into coal burner at its Centralia shops. The Company constructed 195 miles of Charter Line during the year, bringing the total to 627 miles of roadway out of the 704 planned; with quantity, rather than quality, still the standard under the Charter, only 188 miles of the 627 had been ballasted to date. With the addition of 19 new Rogers-built units (18 4-4-0's and a single 0-4-0 switcher (#75)), Illinois Central's locomotive fleet rose to 83; 75 of the 83 were new units built by Rogers, Ketchum & Grosvenor of Paterson, New Jersey, but the roster did show some second hand units, some Boston engines and 2 units built by Wilmarth; the 2-driver ex-New Haven Wilmarth units undoubtedly came to the Illinois Central because the Company's Chief Engineer had been Superintendent on the New York and New Haven railroad. Roughly 55 percent of the year's locomotive mileage was for passenger train business; 464,823 passengers were carried; Company revenues exceeded $1.5 million.

IC1855-01

Illinois Central #1425 was another Rogers-built 4-4-0 American (60 D; 56,000 TW), this one a product of 1855, originally as IC #69. It is pictured on the Chicago Lake Front in 1892. This engine sports a shorter smokebox than some rebuilt models, such as IC #1422 shown previously; with the shorter smokebox, the headlamp is carried on extensions. This photograph may be another attributable to R.A. Beck.

ILLINOIS CENTRAL ROADWAY COMPLETION

Date	Segment	Miles
May 24, 1852	Chicago to Kensington	14.27
May 16, 1853	Bloomington to Tonica	50.99
July 11, 1853	Kensington to Kankakee	41.34
November 14, 1853	Tonica to Mendota	24.88
January 6, 1854	Freeport to Nora	20.61
March 14, 1854	Clinton to Bloomington	22.47
May 13, 1854	Kankakee to Ludlow	52.38
July 24, 1854	Ludlow to Champaign	19.57
September 11, 1854	Nora to Apple River	9.47
October 18, 1854	Decatur to Clinton	21.20
October 28, 1854	Apple River to Council Hill	13.67
November 22, 1854	Cairo to Sandoval	118.61
November 27, 1854	Mendota to Amboy	15.94
January 6, 1855	Sandoval to Decatur	86.52
January 15, 1855	Amboy to Freeport	47.51
June 11, 1855	Council Hill to East Dubuque	23.87
June 25, 1855	Champaign to Mattoon	44.51
September 27, 1856	Mattoon to Mainline Junction	77.69

McGrew, Edward W., *Corporate History of the Illinois Central Railroad Company*. Page 12.

1856

43-year old English civil engineer Henry Bessemer received a patent (#16,082) on his process for making steel inexpensively, his steel being an improvement over cast iron and wrought iron. 44-year old Alfred Krupp, son of the scion Friedrich, began manufacturing guns and cannon for a warring Europe; his great-grandson would follow in his footsteps during World War II, and would spend years in prison as punishment. The Crimean War ended.

Tensions would build in Kansas Territory over the slavery issue; abolitionist John Brown with some family and friends committed a massacre at the proslavery settlement at Pottawatomie Creek, which was avenged shortly thereafter with the death of John Brown's son. In Cincinnati at the 7th Democratic National Convention, the first held outside of Baltimore, lawyer, former Ambassador and Secretary of State James Buchanan from Pennsylvania in his fourth campaign for the nomination won it on the 17th ballot over the sitting President Franklin Pierce and Illinois Senator Stephen A. Douglas; Congressman John C. Breckinridge of Kentucky was elected the nominee for Vice President on the 2nd ballot. At the 1st Republican National Convention in Philadelphia John C. Fremont the explorer of and first Senator from California, running on an antislavery platform, was elected the nominee for President on the 1st formal ballot; former Senator William L. Dayton of New Jersey was elected the nominee for Vice President over Illinois' former Congressman Abraham Lincoln. Ex-President Millard Fillmore from New York ran for re-election to the Presidency under the American party banner with former Minister to Germany and Andrew Jackson-nephew Andrew J. Donelson of Tennessee as the candidate for Vice President. In November the Buchanan/Breckinridge ticket won easily, but the nascent Republican Party had made a statement in winning eleven of the sixteen free States. In August 55-year old Gail Borden developed a process for condensing milk; he received a patent the following year. Future playwright George Bernard Shaw was born, the beginning of a 94-year run that would encompass more than 50 plays, including *Pygmalion*, as well as the 1925 Nobel Prize in Literature at age 69. Chicago University was founded on the southside of Chicago; the institution would fail and be resurrected by the Baptists under the name of University of Chicago.

The Sacramento Valley Railroad opened for business, the first on the west coast in California. The first railroad bridge across the Mississippi River south of St. Paul was the Chicago & Rock Island's bridge between Rock Island, Illinois and Davenport, Iowa; the second would be the Chicago & Northwestern's bridge at Fulton 8 years later.

The Illinois Central began operating wood burning trains from Chicago on the Lakefront Line; the first train arrived at Illinois Central's newly finished eight-track Great Central Station (504 feet long and 166 feet wide) between South Water and Randolph streets. In laying out the railroad in 1851 the Illinois Central had negotiated with a lawyer turned real estate developer named Paul Cornell, an associate of Stephen A. Douglas, who had purchased 300 acres of land on the lake on the south side and plated/founded Hyde Park; the parties struck an agreement with the Illinois Central offering daily commuter service to aid Cornell's land development in return for some 60-acres of land deeded to the Illinois Central into the City; Cornell got his rail service and incorporated Hyde Park in 1856; the Illinois Central got its right-of-way and built a passenger station at what is now 53rd Street. Illinois Central dispatched its first commuter train - the Hyde Park Special - to the new suburb of the City (the City limits were at 39th Street) in June beginning regular operation on July 21, with three trains a day in each direction (operating on the wooden trestle between downtown Chicago and 25th Street); while only partly successful at first, the Great Chicago Fire of 1871 would spur on a rebuilding effort that would benefit this new commuter service. Significant funds were spent developing the Chicago terminal near the Chicago River, constructing a freight depot and grain elevator for transshipment to Great Lakes vessels; the first elevator had a capacity of 600,000 bushels, and could lift and transfer 75,000 bushels per day. Taking advantage of market opportunities, in the fourth quarter of the year Illinois Central acquired the car shops of American Car Factory located just south of Chicago near 27th Street on the Illinois Central, adding this facility to its three division shops the following year. Even though train operations would not commence until January, 1857, with construction complete on the 77-mile long last-puzzle-piece between Mattoon and Centralia, the 704-mile Charter Lines were completed; the ceremonial last spike was driven on September 27th near the station house at Mason (named after the 51-year old New York born Chief of Engineering Roswell B. Mason who supervised the construction of the Charter Lines) in Effingham County, 200-some miles south of Chicago and 150-some miles north of Cairo; this completed what was for the time the longest railroad in the world; over 70,000 tons of iron had been used. In five short years the State of Illinois had seen rail lines expand from less

An 1856 Rogers-built 4-4-0 American (60 D; 140 BP; 62,000 TW; 12,411 TF), Illinois Central #79 was captured as a wood burner with the shortened smokebox. The photograph undoubtedly predates the engine's 1872 rebuild, and the location is unknown.

than 100 miles to over 2,100 – and the Illinois Central accounted for one-third of the total. The Illinois Central system now linked Illinois' southernmost city Cairo with Chicago and reached Dunleith (opposite Dubuque) via Freeport and Galena. Illinois Central joined the few other railroads that offered sleeping service, placing six stateroom sleeping cars, known as Gothic cars, in regular service. The largest operating expense on the Illinois Central was for buying and preparing locomotive cordwood, almost 18 percent of expenses. With locomotive wood prices running $4 to $6 per cord and rising, compared to coal prices of $1.25 per ton, the Illinois Central could see where its future lay; as the virgin forests were cleared, wood supplies were located farther and farther from the railheads, whereas coal supplies were growing constantly as new mines and veins were found, especially near LaSalle and DuQuoin; wood was in great demand and diminishing supply, coal was thought to be practically inexhaustible and provided a hotter fire. During the year Illinois Central tested coal from a number of mines and veins near its tracks in an effort to find the cleanest burning material; this accomplished, Illinois Central began the process of putting coal in its future, both in terms of fuel for its locomotives and as a revenue commodity supplying business and industry in the cities it served. By the end of the year, contracts for 36 coal-burning locomotives would be let, Illinois Central becoming an early devotee of coal-fired steam locomotives. With the large grain harvest, low water levels on the rivers and the onset of winter, the Illinois Central decided to experiment with its rate levels, advancing its freight rate schedule 20 percent to offset the expected increase in operating expenses; it intended to keep rates at that winter level until the end of March, when it would return to its summer Tariff. Revenues for the year would total over $2.4 million, slightly less than half of which were attributable to passenger traffic. Feeling winter temperatures reduced elasticity and increased brittleness in the iron rail, the Illinois Central began the practice of lowering train speeds to counteract those forces and increase safety; it lowered passenger train speeds to 20 mph and freight train speeds to 12 mph. Passenger train miles dropped to around 40 percent (653,201 passengers accounting for roughly 45 percent of revenues), as freight operations began building. With the arrival of 12 new Rogers-built 4-4-0 American-type units, the Illinois Central's locomotive fleet rose to 91 units, after adjusting for 3 scrapped and 1 sold unit; the Illinois Central fleet remained a substantially Rogers-built fleet with at least 87 to their credit. Maximum employment during the year hit 3,581. As completion of the Charter Lines neared, land sales boomed; Illinois Central's land sales had brought in almost $5.2 million through 1855 at an ever-increasing average of $9.78 per acre, and over $4.5 million in 1856 alone at an average of $13.52 per acre; all told, the Company had generated over $9.7 million and still retained two-thirds of its original 2.6 million acre land grant; with the Land Department cautious in not selling to speculators, the average sales contract covered only 128 acres; the downside, of course, was that farmers and settlers could pay only 5 percent or so in cash, the rest being notes to the Illinois Central.

IC1856-01

IC1856-03

Two more Roger's products of 1856, Illinois Central #83, above, and #152, below, show few differences in construction. IC #83 was captured at Fort Dodge, Iowa in 1871, when it had to be one of the last wood-burning units on the Illinois Central; a 4-4-0 American-type, it was a smaller drivered engine (56 D; 140 BP; 62,000 TW; 12,411 TF), which allowed it to generate higher tractive force; this engine was rebuilt four years later. IC #152 originally was built (60 D; 55,600 TW) for the Dubuque & Pacific as the Delaware (D&P #2); Illinois Central renumbered the engine to #152 in 1867 when it leased the D&P; it was pictured on a muddy Chicago Lake Front circa 1870, and was published in the February, 1930 issue of the Illinois Central Magazine.

IC1856-02

IC1856-04

Another view of Illinois Central #152, above, was published in the December, 1936 issue of the IC Magazine; it was captured at Lyle, Minnesota in 1880 and purports to be heading up the first train run from Waterloo, Iowa to Lyle; Samuel A. Kier was the engineer. Shown below is Illinois Central #1375, built by Rogers Locomotive in 1856 as #83, as shown on the preceding page; it was pictured here 21 years later on the Chicago Lake Front in 1892, as rebuilt for burning coal; note the rear-facing gas lamp that has been added to allow switching service, and the change from link and pin to automatic coupler.

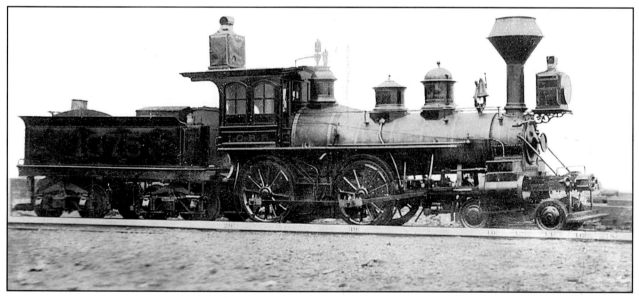

IC1856-05

1857

The 35-year old Austrian monk Gregor J. Mendel began experiments growing peas that would guide him in discerning the basic laws of heredity and inheritance. The end of the Crimean War marked the beginning of the financial slowdown that led to a Panic.

In March 65-year old James Buchanan was sworn in as the 15th President of the U.S. Two days later, the U.S. Supreme Court handed down its Dred Scott decision which affirmed the notion of slaves as property; the Dred Scott decision also declared the repealed Missouri Compromise of 1820 unconstitutional, heightening the friction between the southern and northern States and more clearly defining the differences between the Democratic and Republican political parties. In August a grand Financial Panic began among railroad and real estate speculators, bringing two years of booming economy to an end; 22-year old Andrew Carnegie at the Pennsylvania Railroad learned early lessons in the result.

The process of 'ice packing' perishable meat allowed producers to operate in the summer, as long as ice was available; the Michigan Central Railroad became one of the first, shipping fresh meat from Chicago to the East coast in boxcars equipped with ice compartments.

14-year old William Cornelius Van Horne, who would later gain fame for constructing the Canadian Pacific Railroad through the Rockies, hired on as a telegrapher for the Illinois Central just outside Chicago; the job lasted less than a year, and he moved on to the Michigan Central. The year would mark Illinois Central's first train into Cairo, Illinois. In January, 30-year old U.S. Army Captain George B. McClellan resigned his commission and became Engineer in Chief of the Illinois Central, replacing Roswell B. Mason, who was Illinois Central's first Chief Engineer; Mason would go on to other projects and politics and, in 1871, as the 20th Mayor of Chicago would preside over the Chicago Fire; McClellan would stay with the Illinois Central for 3 ½ years and only leave to join the Ohio and Mississippi Railroad in late 1860, until called to higher duty in the Civil War. At Illinois Central, McClellan organized the Engineering Department: splitting the railroad into four divisions - each with a resident Engineer, each division into 40 to 50 mile long subdivisions – each with its own Supervisor, and each subdivision into 3 to 6 mile long sections - each with its own foreman and labor gang; the titles Division Engineer, Road Supervisor and Section Foreman would endure for more than 100 years. While population increases continued, still much of the Illinois prairie was little inhabited at many places where the railroad coursed through the countryside; to facilitate track maintenance in the more desolate places, where boarding was not available, the Illinois Central built frame houses for use by the section men, eighteen this year alone. Operating a railroad in the north always brought weather into the equation, this year being no exception; during the first two months of the year, despite being cleared nine times, operations were suspended over 130 miles of the branch line north of LaSalle due to drifting snow; it was hoped that completion of board fencing (barbed wire hadn't yet been invented) would alleviate this problem in the future, as well as keeping farm stock off the tracks. Water supply for locomotive boilers, a problem the year before when trains sometimes were detained for lack of water, was relieved in some measure by the construction of 18 wells, 19 tanks, 14 tank houses, 2 pump houses, 1 horse power house and 3 small stationary steam engines. With the Charter Lines completed less than six months, the Master of Transportation had been one of the first to note that linking the upper ends of the "Y"-shaped system, rather than relying on the Galena & Chicago Union and the Aurora Branch railroads for connections, would bring measurable operating benefits to the Company; this was accomplished by yearend as Illinois Central helped the Peoria & Oquawka Railroad complete its east-west line, thus linking the Illinois Central's Main line (at El Paso, just north of Bloomington) and Chicago branch line (at Gilman, just south of Kankakee). The north-south Illinois Central now was crossed by nine different east-west railroads: the Galena & Chicago Union at Freeport and the Chicago, Fulton & Iowa (both one day the Chicago & Northwestern) at Dixon; the Chicago, Burlington & Quincy at Mendota; the Chicago & Rock Island at LaSalle; the Peoria & Oquawka (one day the Toledo, Peoria & Western) at Gilman and El Paso; the Chicago, Alton & St. Louis (one day the New York Central) at Bloomington; the Great Western (Illinois) (one day the Wabash) at Tolono and Decatur; the Terre Haute, Alton & St. Louis (one day the New York Central) at Mattoon and Pana; and the Ohio & Mississippi (one day the Baltimore & Ohio) at Odin and Sandoval. Realizing the potential associated with interchanging traffic and passengers at river points, the Illinois Central made arrangements with a St. Louis steamboat company to establish a line of steamers on an every-other-day schedule between St. Louis and Cairo. The Transportation Master

IC1857-03

Rogers-built in 1857, this 0-4-0 switch engine (43 D; 40,000 TW) was captured on the Chicago Lake Front, sometime before 1885; it appears an equipment record was being made, thus the measuring sticks next to the unit, for perspective.

also suggested equipping locomotives with smaller wheels, aiming for power rather than speed. In July, in order to raise funds for the procurement of rolling stock, the Illinois Central issued an additional 85,000 shares of capital stock, paid partially in cash and with attached optional rights; the financial panic thirty days later would tarnish the monetary affairs of the Company with the market price on the capital stock driven below par, thus negating the impact of the optional rights and forcing a suspension of debt payments; the Illinois Central survived the panic, but prior land sale notes had to be extended for settlers, as the domino-effect on the economy caused lower grain prices and took away their ability to pay. The Land Department sold over 335,000 acres at an average price of $12.11 per acre; with the average sale contract covering less than 100 acres and the economic panic, most sales were paid for in notes, rather than cash; there remained over one half of the original Land Grant acreage available for sale. Illinois Central owned 112 locomotives, having added 24 and dropped 3 from the roster during the year; 21 engines burned coal, 19 of the 24 new arrivals and two that were changed over at Company shops; of the 24 roster additions, 22 were built by Rogers Locomotive Works in Paterson, New Jersey (4 new 0-4-0 switchers; 17 new 4-4-0 American-types; 1 second-hand wood-burning 4-4-0) and the remaining two were coal burning passenger locomotives (#'s 125 *Pluto* and 126 *Lucifer*) newly built by William Mason & Company out of Taunton, Massachusetts; 109 of Illinois Central's 112 unit locomotive fleet were Rogers-built. Passenger revenues for the year accounted for almost one-half the total $2.4 million generated; with 714,707 passengers utilizing the Illinois Central, the western terminus of Dunleith was the busiest station, accounting for almost 20 percent of passenger revenues. Revenue traffic rose to more than 440,000 tons of freight. Toward the end of the year, George McClellan would be promoted to Vice President and Chief Engineer; as the highest-ranking resident officer of the Illinois Central, he Chaired the Executive Committee of local officers, with the authority for day-to-day management of the Company. True control lay in three places: central management of the affairs of the Company, along with its President William Osborn, remained in New York under the Board of Directors; ownership of the Company remained controlled by the majority stockholders located in Holland and Great Britain (Amsterdam and London); local decisions and management of the Company were carried out by the Executive Committee of Illinois resident officers, an arrangement made some years before. McClellan would spar with Company President William Osborn for a greater measure of autonomy; with Osborn located in the Company's New York offices, exercising control over McClellan became increasingly futile.

IC1857-02

Roger's products of 1857, Illinois Central #102 and #106, above and below, were both 4-4-0 American-types (56 D; 62,000 TW). IC #102 was pictured at Amboy, Illinois in 1887, having been rebuilt in 1880; note the rear-facing gas lamp on the cab for switch service. IC #106 was captured just outside the engine house at Bloomington, Illinois in 1884. IC #106 was published in the June, 1936 issue of the Illinois Central Magazine; identified in the picture were: Peter Eich (engineer), Joe L. Irwin (conductor), William Fleming and S. Prince (brakemen), and John Mathey (hostler).

IC1857-01

1858

Sino-American agreement reached in the Treaty of Tientsin signed in 1858, after Britain and France attacked China and took Canton; the Treaty opened additional ports to American trade and allowed travel in China.

In losing an election race for the Illinois Senate seat to 45-year old incumbent Stephen A. Douglas, 49-year old Abraham Lincoln gained a measure of national prominence. Minnesota was admitted to the Union as the 32nd State. The first telegraph cable bridging the Atlantic was completed; it would fail a few weeks later. William H. Rand opened a printing office in Chicago and hired Andrew McNally as a printer, laying the foundation for what would become one of the world's leading mapmakers. A depression settled in over the American economy, a Financial Panic among railroad and real estate speculators begun the preceding year.

The Pennsylvania Railroad connected Philadelphia and Pittsburgh on its own tracks for the first time, completing its original 1846 mission.

The Great Jackson Route (New Orleans, Jackson & Great Northern) completed its 206-mile long line from Canton, Mississippi to New Orleans, Louisiana; 16 years later Illinois Central would take a position in this company. Illinois Central established regular through service to New Orleans, via steamship from Cairo, Illinois to the Gulf. In a reporting relationship replete with symbolism, Illinois Central's Land Department Cashier, Ambrose E. Burnside, owed his position to and reported his work through the Company Vice President, George B. McClellan. In terms of locomotive fleet size, it was a quiet year with a single net addition; scrapped or damaged locomotives were replaced in kind, but no new locomotive orders were let; Illinois Central's locomotive ownership rose by 1 to 113 units, 108 4-4-0 American-type units and 5 0-4-0 switching units, almost all were Rogers-built locomotives; 21 units burned coal. During the year a move was underway to convince the New York-based Board of Directors to move the Company President to Illinois (Board declined), and to promote the Executive Committee of resident officers to Director level and form a quorum in Illinois (Board declined). The impact on Illinois Central of the economic and financial troubles in the country required a call of $20 per share on the stockholders to facilitate debt payments; with shareholders in the same economic straits, they were slow to respond and a complicated assignment of interests had to be arranged; in essence, Company President William Osborn used his personal financial strength and assumed liabilities of the Company to bridge it over the troubled waters; by the end of the year the issues were moot, the assignment released, embarrassment and bankruptcy avoided. Financial troubles would be compounded by the second crop failure in as many years; the Illinois Central, knowing full well that its prosperity rode with that of the settlers, would once again grant credit extensions, rather than cancel land contracts; all along Illinois Central had intentionally sold to farmers on credit, rather than land speculators, at possibly higher per-acre prices - the former's work and produce directly benefiting the Company, the latter's speculative real estate profit or loss bringing nothing to the Illinois Central. Company revenues dropped almost 15 percent to just under $2 million; expenses were reduced in concert; revenue traffic slipped to just over 381,000 tons of freight. Passengers carried dropped over 20 percent to 568,670 for the year. A little over 50,000 Land Grant acres were put under contract in this depressed sales climate, bringing aggregate sales to roughly 1.2 million out of the original 2.6 million Grant. Just shy of his 23rd birthday, Samuel Langhorne Clemens, having worked and trained on steamboats for almost two years, earned his Mississippi River pilot's license in September; early the next year he would begin work as a pilot on steamboats that plied the river from St. Louis, Missouri through Cairo, Illinois to New Orleans, Louisiana; he eventually would adopt the pseudonym Mark Twain, a riverboat term meaning 2 fathoms or 12 feet deep, the minimum depth needed to navigate the river.

1859

50-year old British naturalist Charles R. Darwin published his theory of evolution and findings on natural selection, *The Origin of Species*. Construction began on the Suez Canal to connect the Mediterranean Sea with the Red Sea, a joint French-Egyptian effort. 39-year old French scientist Alexandre Edmund Becquerel pioneered in the exploration of phosphorescence; his seven-year old son Antoine Henri would follow his father in the sciences and would be awarded the Nobel Prize 44 years later for his work with radioactivity. With the dissembling of the Turkish Empire, the ancient territories of Moldavia and Walachia were united, taking the name Romania three years later. Eleven years after being defeated by the Austrian/Hapsburg military (now ruled by 29-year old Emperor Francis Joseph), Italy (backed by 52-year old guerrilla-fighter Giuseppe Garibaldi), in its 2nd War of Independence, fared better when France (under the command of 51-year old Emperor Napoleon III) lent its support; with major battles in the vineyards of Magenta and the hills of Solferino, more than 300,000 troops would take the field; the fact that over 40,000 lost their lives induced Swiss humanitarian Henry Dunant to found the International Red Cross soon after.

Oregon was admitted to the Union as the 33rd State. 40-year old Edwin L. Drake found oil in Titusville, Pennsylvania, creating the world's first oil well of modern times. In September abolitionists led by John Brown raided the Federal arsenal at Harper's Ferry in Virginia to arm themselves to fight slavery; the rebellion lasted two days and was put down by a contingent of marines under Colonel Robert E. Lee; in connection with Brown's subsequent execution, sectional anxiety between the north and south heightened, providing an inkling of the future. 39-year old William Tecumseh Sherman became Superintendent of Louisiana State Seminary of Learning, a forerunner of Louisiana State University. The depression started by railroad and real estate speculators two years earlier ebbed. The Comstock Lode of silver and gold was discovered near Virginia City, Nevada on the eastern slope of the Sierra Nevada range.

Fresh off making a fortune by helping raise Chicago buildings out of the mud, 28-year old George M. Pullman began experimenting with sleeping car designs, converting two passenger coaches of the Chicago & Alton Railroad into prototypes at shops in Bloomington, Illinois; in September these cars made their maiden run from Bloomington to Chicago. The Atchison and Topeka Railroad, the forerunner to the Santa Fe, was chartered in Kansas by Colonel Cyrus K. Holliday; the civil war on the horizon would stall funding and construction for ten years.

The year would prove to be an extraordinary passing of the future, ordinary characters yet to be thrust into history, all on the Illinois Central: 24-year old Samuel Clemens worked as a pilot on Illinois Central steamboats picking up connecting travelers at Cairo, 50-year old Abraham Lincoln was still on retainer as local counsel, 33-year old George B. McClellan was a Company Vice President, and 35-year old Ambrose E. Burnside was Cashier in the Land Department of the Company. Samuel Clemens worked on St. Louis, Cairo & New Orleans Railroad line steamboats and other packets that had contracted with the Illinois Central to provide service from Cairo to New Orleans, such as the *Crescent City, New Falls City, J.C. Swon* and *Philadelphia*; later the *Philadelphia* blew up south of Memphis and Henry Clemens was a casualty, his brother Samuel's recent transfer probably saving Mark Twain's life. After crop failures in 1857 and 1858, the Company's fortunes rebounded with an improved harvest; revenues for the year reached $2.1 million, roughly 40 percent in passenger traffic; revenue traffic rose to more than 422,000 tons of freight. With the opening of rail lines in the South to New Orleans and Mobile (Mississippi Central Railroad + Mobile & Ohio Railroad), migration of settlers and Illinois Central's resulting passenger traffic (609,585 passengers, 86,405 of which were carried only three miles to and from the National Agricultural Fair grounds outside Chicago) began to shift; in 1856 migration was west toward Iowa and Minnesota, and over 22 percent of Illinois Central's passenger revenues were directed over Dunleith across the river from Dubuque, the Company's westernmost and busiest station; by 1859 migration over the Illinois Central moved to a southerly flow and Cairo, the Company's southernmost station, became the second busiest (15 percent), pushing Dunleith (8 percent) to third, both behind Chicago; by the following year, passenger revenues over Cairo (20 percent) would exceed all other stations. With the Dubuque & Pacific and the Dubuque & Western railroads penetrating farther into Iowa, with the completion of Canada's Grand Trunk Railway into Detroit forming a connection with Illinois Central via the Great Lakes, and with southern railroads opening lines from Mobile and New Orleans north toward Cairo, Illinois Central's interchange future brightened every day. In terms of locomotive fleet size, there were no net additions, scrapped or damaged

IC45x35-09

In late 1850's Illinois Central purchased the car shops of American Car Factory near 27th Street, hard by the Illinois Central tracks. Merged into its own shops shortly thereafter, this formed the nucleus of Illinois Central's downtown Chicago car shops in the years that followed. Pictured here is the Old Office of the Car Works at 26th and South Park, one of the few remaining original buildings from that era when this picture was snapped on April 8, 1903.

locomotives were replaced with similar units; Illinois Central's locomotive ownership remained at 113 units, 107 4-4-0 American-type units, 5 0-4-0 switching units and one small tank engine for sale; almost all were Rogers-built locomotives, and 1 had been converted at Company's Amboy shops from wood-burning to coal-burning. Results for the Land Department yielded a little over 28,000 acres put under contract for $415,000, including advance interest; this brought cumulative Land Grant sales to $15.7 million on less than one-half the original 2.6 million acre Grant; of the 1.238 million acres under contract, the average cash payment to secure the contracts amounted to less than $1.12 per acre (half advance interest and half principle); the average pre-interest sale price was $11.52 per acre, $12.76 including interest.

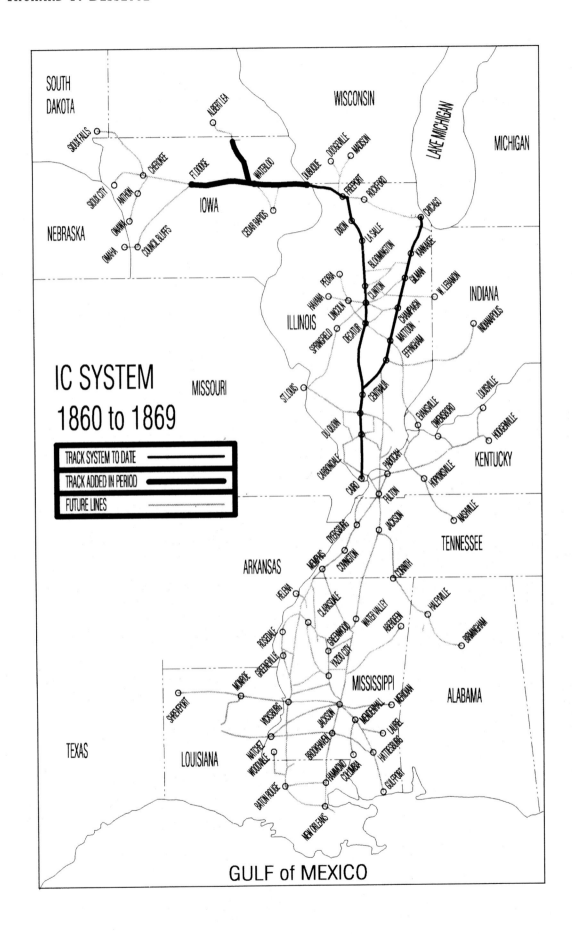

IC SYSTEM
1860 to 1869

TRACK SYSTEM TO DATE	
TRACK ADDED IN PERIOD	
FUTURE LINES	

1850's **1860's** 1870's 1880's 1890's 1900's 1910's 1920's 1930's 1940's

The Eighth Census of the U.S. population was taken; there were almost 31.5 million people in the U.S., having grown 36 percent from the prior census; the country would add over 7 million people by the end of the decade, one-third through immigration. The Union grew by four States to a total of 37; 11 States would join the Confederacy. Many of the Indian Wars took place during the 1860's and not fighting meant the reservation; the white settlement of the West would be at the expense of the Native Americans. The war created fortunes for enterprising souls: such as, Samuel Colt selling to both sides in the War, and the Studebaker family of South Bend producing wagons for the Union. The Conscription Act of 1863 allowed one to avoid the draft by either hiring a substitute or paying a $300 fee; men such as 28-year old Andrew Carnegie, 27-year old Jay Gould, 26-year old J.P. Morgan and 24-year old John D. Rockefeller used this loophole. In the Civil War, what began as a mission to preserve, ended up being a crusade to emancipate. The war consisted of hundreds of small skirmishes, and few major battles. Future Presidents Johnson, Grant, Hayes, Harrison, Garfield, McKinley and Arthur all would see duty in the Civil War as Union officers. A ten-year period of Reconstruction followed the war; the vigilante Ku Klux Klan rose during Reconstruction as a way to maintain white supremacy; former Confederate Lieutenant General Nathan Bedford Forrest became the 1st Grand Wizard. The migration of veterans, deserters, homeless and other wanderers to the western frontier, gave meaning to the moniker Wild West.

During the war, safe passage on the Mississippi river was not a certainty, which pushed tonnage over railroads; business levels surged, but at the expense of plant and property: deferred in the North and destroyed in the South. At War's end, rebuilding of the railroads boomed. A number of Confederate General officers became railroad men after the war: Joseph E. Johnston (commissioner of railroads in Washington, D.C.), Nathan B. Forrest (President of the Selma, Marion & Memphis), John Breckinridge (Vice President of the Elizabethtown, Lexington & Big Sandy (C&0)) and P.G.T. Beauregard (President of the New Orleans, Jackson & Great Northern (IC)). In 1860 the major line-haul rail carriers operated a little over 30,500 miles of railroad, a figure that would surge by 22,000 miles by the end of the decade.

GROWTH OF ILLINOIS CENTRAL RAILROAD BUSINESS

Year (1)	Tonnage (mil/tons)	Lumber (mil/bf)	Grain (mil/bus)	Coal (mil/tons)	Passengers Commuters	Miles/Fare
1860	.590	62	8.7	.061	496,011 N/A	78/$1.70
1861	.720	54	12.7	.050	491,583 N/A	67/$1.64
1862	.806	53	12.7	.061	674,767 N/A	93/$1.97
1863	.952	67	11.8	.069	852,659 N/A	86/$2.10
1864	1.0	91	13.4	.102	1,108.937 N/A	87/$2.12
1865	1.0	118	12.9	.103	1,214,054 N/A	73/$2.25
1866	1.1	111	16.3	.151	1,034,530 N/A	55/$1.92
1867	1.3	135	17.4	.148	1,077,550 N/A	39/$1.53
1868	1.4	166	21.0	.194	1,312,631 N/A	36/$1.42
1869	1.6	181	22.5	.237	1,399,416 N/A	38/$1.50

Passengers/Commuters = Total Ridership, and Commuter Portion Miles/Fare = Average Passenger Trip and Charge
(1) Fiscal Year bf = Board Feet bus = Bushels N/A=Data Not Available

1860

The Pony Express version of overland mail began, inaugurated between St. Joseph, Missouri and Sacramento, California; service over the 2,000-mile route, which might take ten days one-way, would last less than two years, being done in by the transcontinental telegraph; 14-year old William F. (Buffalo Bill) Cody was a Pony Express rider. Phoebe Ann (Annie Oakley) Moses was born in western Ohio. Englishman Frederick Walton received a patent on a process that makes linoleum. In April the Democratic Party regulars met in Charleston to argue issues of political platform and delegation membership; they achieved some harmony, but could not agree on a nominee in 57 ballots. In May the 2nd Republican convention in Chicago nominated downstate Illinois lawyer and former Congressman Abraham Lincoln for President on the 3rd ballot; Senator Hannibal Hamlin of Maine was nominated for Vice President on the 2nd ballot. At the 8th Democratic convention in Baltimore, a continuation of the Charleston meeting, two tickets were nominated because of disagreement concerning secession – a Douglas wing and a Breckinridge wing. At the Democrats' convention Illinois Senator Stephen A. Douglas was elected the nominee for President on the 2nd ballot; the Vice President nominee was Benjamin Fitzpatrick of Alabama, a unanimous first ballot nomination that he later declined, forcing the Party to substitute Georgia's former Governor Herschel V. Johnson. At the Seceders' convention sitting Vice President John C. Breckinridge of Kentucky won the nomination for President on the 1st ballot; Oregon Senator General Joseph Lane was nominated for Vice President on the 1st ballot. A new Constitutional Union party also competed and it slated former House Speaker and Senator John Bell of Tennessee for President on the second ballot and former Harvard President and Senator Edward Everett of Massachusetts for Vice President. Older Whig party supporters of Henry Clay and Millard Fillmore threw their support to the Lincoln/Hamlin ticket; New York Tribune founder Horace Greeley, among others, spoke out in support of Lincoln. In November, with the Democratic Party rift splitting its majority popular vote, Abraham Lincoln easily won the Presidential election. Defeated Illinois Senator Douglas would pass away seven months later at age 47. Almost immediately talk of breaking apart the Union resumed; the South Carolina Legislature called a State Convention in Charleston, and promptly voted for secession, something it had threatened for 30 years; in the next 30 days Mississippi, Florida, Alabama, Georgia, Louisiana and Texas would follow suit; the gauntlet had been thrown.

On the cusp of war, the Nation's railroads consisted of 30,000-some miles of trackage, roughly one-third of that located in the seceding Southern states. There existed only three major railroad connections between North and South: Washington, Louisville and Cairo.

The 236-mile long Mississippi Central, which ran through the grounds of the University of Mississippi in Oxford (102 years later, itself a touchstone in the civil rights movement), was completed to Jackson, Tennessee with the closing of the 86-mile long "Big Gap" in Mississippi south of Water Valley; the Mississippi Central and the New Orleans, Jackson & Great Northern were operated as a single 442-mile long railroad. Illinois Central erected its first metal bridge, a 158-foot long Whipple-truss affair crossing the Cache River at Ullin, Illinois. George B. McClellan left his Vice President's job at the Illinois Central after 3 ½ years to become one of the senior officers of the bankrupt yet recovering Ohio and Mississippi Railroad, a position he soon would leave to rejoin the U.S. Army in the Civil War. With two of the last three harvests a failure, the current year represented a bounty; Illinois Central's revenues exceeded $2.7 million, a 4 percent increase in passenger revenues (496,011 passengers) and a 49 percent increase in freight revenues; revenue traffic rose to over 590,000 tons of freight. Land sales exceeded 71,000 acres placed under contract for $1.1 million, a three-year high; the total accounted for 1,050 purchasers with the average contract covering almost 68 acres. Illinois Central's locomotive fleet consisted of 112 units, 107 4-4-0 American-type units and 5 0-4-0 switching units; while almost all were Rogers-built, the Company acquired a second-hand Niles 4-4-0 engine to replace one that fell out of service; 9 units were converted at Company shops from wood-burning, bringing the coal-burning fleet to 28. In April the shops and engine house in Chicago burned, necessitating their complete rebuild.

1861

The seceding States chose the name Confederate States of America and elected Mississippi Senator Jefferson Davis their President, both before Lincoln was inaugurated. The divided Nation would be led by two Presidents, 52-year old Lincoln and 53-year old Davis, both born in the border state Kentucky. In March Abraham Lincoln was sworn in as the 16th President of the U. S.; on swearing in he set his first record, the first administration to take office in the company of five living ex-Presidents (Van Buren, Tyler, Fillmore, Pierce and Buchanan). In his inaugural address, President Lincoln tried to resolve differences; all became moot on April 13th when 55-year old Army Major Robert Anderson surrendered Fort Sumter in Charleston Harbor to P.G.T. (Pierre Gustave Toutant) Beauregard, then Brigadier General C.S.A. (the first) and formerly Major U.S.A.; Fort Sumter resisted only 36 hours. Virginia then became the 8th State to secede from the Union; within weeks Arkansas, Tennessee and North Carolina seceded making it 11 Confederate States. A number of western Virginia counties refused to secede, and from this would rise the State of West Virginia two years later. As the fighting began there were 34 States in the divided Nation, Kansas having just been admitted; the population of the Union was more than twice that of the Confederacy, one-third of whose residents were slaves. In June President Lincoln created the Civilian Sanitary Commission – one forerunner to the American Red Cross; later in the year 40-year old Clara Barton began organizing medical care for Union soldiers; she would help form the American Red Cross 20 years later. In July came the First Battle of Bull Run Creek (also, First Manassas), 25 miles southwest of the Union capital Washington, D.C. and 75 miles north of the Confederate capital Richmond; Brigadier General Thomas J. Jackson earned the moniker "Stonewall"; Union Brigadier General Irvin McDowell's loss got him fired, being replaced by 34-year old Major General George B. McClellan as head of the Army of the Potomac. 75-year old Lieutenant General Winfield Scott retired in November, leaving this war to younger commanders; the Union grade of Lieutenant General was retired. On the Confederate side, eight men, all graduates of West Point Military Academy, in time would hold the rank of full-general: (Class of 1815, Samuel Cooper; '26, Albert Sydney Johnston; '29, Robert E. Lee; '29, Joseph E. Johnston; '38, P. G. T. Beauregard; '37, Braxton Bragg; '45, E. Kirby Smith; '53, John Bell Hood (temporary rank)). History would count eleven of the Military Academy's Class of '61 reaching the rank of general. A temporary national income tax was enacted to help pay for the Union war effort; it would last ten years. With the help of the Pacific Telegraph Act signed the year before, Western Union cobbled together the first transcontinental telegraph line in October by consolidating a number of existing telegraph companies with new construction filling in the gaps. The first Congressional Medal of Honor was earned by Captain Bernard J.D. Irwin, an Army surgeon, for heroism on the Indian frontier in Arizona; he wouldn't actually receive it until 33 years later. 40-year old New York locksmith Linus Yale received patents on his classic version of a pin-tumbler cylinder lock. 24-year old J.P. Morgan set up in New York as a trade office for securities underwritten by his father's firm. On the demise of unsuccessful presidential candidate Stephen A. Douglas in June, Illinois purchased the remainder of his estate (Okenwald) on the south side of Chicago next to the Illinois Central, adding it to the Army training camp built earlier; Camp Douglas soon was changed into a prisoner-of-war facility to hold Confederate soldiers where it would record its own high death toll; the first southern prisoners arrived at Camp Douglas in February the next year following the Union victory on the Cumberland river; while the prison could hold 12,000 at any one time, over 26,000 prisoners would move through the facility and some 6,000 would perish until closed at the end of the war.

The bankrupt New York and Erie Railroad was reorganized as the Erie Railroad; this iteration would last 17 years.

The year would see a predecessor railroad line completed, the Meridian to Vicksburg line. Through the first quarter of the year, Illinois Central train operations and land sales were favorable enough for the Directors to begin looking for a record year; as the "Southern difficulties" spread to the middle states, those dreams appeared unseemly; yet, even with all the uncertainty, a record was just what the Illinois Central would generate. Within weeks of the surrender of Fort Sumter, the Federal government placed some-8,000 troops at Cairo, effectively shutting off southern markets to Illinois products, the Civil War bringing Illinois Central's regular service to a halt; the Union Army commandeered Illinois Central service for moving men and materials through Cairo, the north-south layout of the Illinois Central making it a vital artery; while freight traffic at Cairo *averaged* $117,000 per month through April, it would total less than $104,000 for the last eight months combined. Passenger revenues fell to $804,769 (491,583

Illinois Central Railroad Co.

REPORT AND ACCOUNTS

For the Year ending December 31st, 1861.

DIRECTORS

HIS EXCELLENCY RICHARD YATES, Governor of Illinois,
Ex-Officio.

THOMAS E. WALKER,
J. N. PERKINS,
} Until May, 1862.

JONATHAN STURGES,
JOS. W. ALSOP,
FREDER'K C. GEBHARD,
} Until May, 1863.

WILLIAM TRACY,
ABRAM S. HEWITT,
W. H. OSBORN,
} Until May, 1864.

L. M. WILEY,
FRANKLIN HAVEN,
JOHN M. DOUGLASS,
} Until May, 1865.

NOTICE IS HEREBY GIVEN, THAT THE ANNUAL MEETING OF STOCKHOLDERS WILL BE HELD AT THE OFFICE OF THE COMPANY, IN CHICAGO, ON THE LAST WEDNESDAY OF MAY, 1862.

W. M. PHILLIPS, Secretary.

ICLAG21-06

passengers, including 70,097 troops), a decline of over 5 percent; total revenues rose to $2.9 million, the entire increase due to that portion billed to but not paid by the government - $207,000. With little market for their farm products, Illinois Central farmers began turning in their grain to the Company as payment against their land contracts; while the Illinois Central was not able to turn a profit on all these exchanges, it mitigated some of the loss buying back construction bonds at a discount; revenue traffic rose to more than 720,000 tons of freight. Land sales exceeded 102,000 acres placed under contract for $1.4 million, a four-year high; the total accounted for 1,402 purchasers with the average contract covering less than 73 acres; after cancellations, 1,358,549 acres of the original land grant remained to be sold. A single new engine was acquired during the year, a coal-burning 4-4-0 American-type built by Rogers Locomotive Works, replacing a sold unit; this kept the locomotive roster at 112 units, 107 4-4-0 Americans and 5 0-4-0 switchers; eighteen units were converted at Company shops from wood-burning to coal-burning, bringing the coal-burning fleet to 52. In spite of the troubled times, the future looked bright for the Illinois Central.

1862

Led by 33-year old Major General Ignacio Zaragoza a small Mexican force held off French invaders outside of Mexico City on May 5th; while France would vanquish Mexico the following year, their rule only lasted four years and *Cinco de Mayo* would not be forgotten.

As the year began there were 34 States in the divided Nation, 11 in the Confederacy and 23 in the Union. Hoping to keep the slave-owning border states of Maryland, Kentucky, Missouri and Delaware from secession, President Lincoln decided against black troops. In March, the revolving turret *USS Monitor* fought to a draw against the *CSS Virginia* (converted from the steam frigate *Merrimac*) in Hampton Roads; more than 50 ironclads would see service, on the Mississippi river and in the Atlantic blockade. In the east, Major General George B. McClellan was in command of the 150,000 strong Army of the Potomac aimed at Richmond. In the Peninsular Campaign, where 22-year old Captain George Armstrong Custer (West Point '61) saw his first action, General McClellan withdrew from battle. The Second Battle of Bull Run (also, Second Manassas) ended as the First; Union forces were led to defeat this time by Major General John Pope, who would see his command merged into the Army of the Potomac. General Robert E. Lee attempted his first invasion of the North, an operation noted for Antietam Creek in Sharpsburg, Maryland; while McClellan stopped Lee's advance, he failed to capitalize and was relieved of command, 38-year old Major General Ambrose E. Burnside replacing him. General Burnside met his match (General Lee) at Fredericksburg and would be replaced by Major General Joseph Hooker, the third head of the Army of the Potomac in 12 months; President Lincoln still sought that special military leader. In the west a number of skirmishes throughout Kentucky and Tennessee led up to Shiloh on the Tennessee River less than 20 miles North of Corinth, Mississippi; Confederate troops retreated. The U.S. Navy's 61-year old Captain David G. Farragut earned the first Admiral's Flag on being promoted to the grade of one-star Rear Admiral after his gunboats overran the Mississippi River defenses and occupied New Orleans, then Baton Rouge; the 100-some miles between Port Hudson and Vicksburg were the last part of the Mississippi River in Confederate hands. Looking beyond the Civil War, Congress passed the Homestead Act that gave 160 acres of land in the West to anyone filing a claim with the promise of living on and improving the land for five years. Congress also passed the Morrill Act that gave public land to individual States to encourage development of agricultural colleges, land grant colleges; 69 land-grant colleges were constructed under the auspices of the Morrill Act. 23-year old John D. Rockefeller invested in his first oil-refining venture with Samuel Andrews and Henry Flagler; the following year, they began refining crude oil in Cleveland. In November 44-year old Richard J. Gatling of Indianapolis received patent #36,836 on his crank-operated machine gun, just in time to add to the horror of the Civil War.

With hope in the future even though engaged in a civil war, Congress passed the Pacific Railway Act (land grants and government-backed bonds) to induce construction of transcontinental lines which would develop the western frontier; this Act authorized the Central Pacific and newly chartered Union Pacific to build a railroad to the Pacific Ocean; because title to the 19 million acres in land grants came with completed track mileage, it eventually became a race. Since studies had determined that slightly over half the U.S. railroad trackage was built on a 4 foot 8 ½ inch gauge, the Pacific Railway Act mandated that gauge for the transcontinental route, effectively creating the standard gauge. Prior federal land grants had been solely to States; the Pacific Railway Act pioneered the granting of land to private enterprises, since much of the western territory to be developed had not yet been officially organized as States in the Union. Congress had debated location of the road, with a northern route thought to be through land too rugged and a southern route too close to seceding States; with the breakaway States withdrawal from Congress, the remaining Union influence settled on a central route for the path of the first transcontinental railroad. The Central Pacific was led by four eastern movers-and-shakers who had followed the Gold Rush west: 38-year old Leland Stanford, 41-year old Collis P. Huntington, 40-year old Charles Crocker and 49-year old Mark Hopkins; Henry Farnum and Thomas C. Durant of the Mississippi and Missouri Railroad, which had been founded in 1852 with the mission to build a railroad across the State of Iowa connecting the namesake rivers, represented the Union Pacific. In January a wartime railroad bill was passed which granted President Lincoln authority to commandeer any railroad property needed for military purposes, something that would become habit.

Gunboats were built and repaired at Illinois Central stations such as Mound City and Cairo, Illinois. Blessed with back-to-back flourishing harvests, Illinois Central followed up its record year with another, total revenues exceeding $3.5 million, 38 percent in passenger traffic (674,767 passengers, including 151,967 military troops); during the last half of the year, the Illinois Central actually had more business than it had cars to handle, a first; revenue traffic rose to more than 806,000 tons of freight. With migration to States in the south and southwest severely pressed because of the War, settlers continued to homestead in the wide-open spaces of the north and northwest; land sales continued, fueled by the unrest in the east and south; 87,600 acres were put under contract for just under $1.0 million. With the second consecutive year of land contract cancellations exceeding sales and the second in which the Company felt forced to accept bushels of grain as payment against existing land contracts, the Company deemed its original plan of financing railroad construction with land sales proved false; the fact that title on more than 2.3 million of the 2.6 million acre land grant remained with the Company, only 271,890 acres having been paid off, drove this point home; to alleviate the problem the Illinois Central raised interest charges from two to six percent, became more guarded against speculators, and kept tract sizes even smaller. The Company's locomotive fleet remained at 112, replacements filling in the roster position of units that dropped out of service; with 15 units converted at Company shops, 67 locomotives now burned coal as fuel; Illinois Central's roster remained at 107 4-4-0 American-types and 5 0-4-0 switch units. Title to Illinois Central's depot property in Chicago finally was settled by the Supreme Court, after years of litigation. Illinois Central's suburban commuter service was extended south from Hyde Park to 63rd Street (Woodlawn).

ICLAG20-07

The Illinois Central's first shops were close in to Chicago, able to quickly build and repair equipment for the new railroad. While commuter/suburban shops were sited with freight facilities for a number of years, after a time they were split up. The shops were built/acquired at Weldon in the early days (they burned down and were rebuilt in the early 1860's); they later moved to 27th Street and, finally, to Burnside at 95th Street in 1893. The three pictures shown (facing SSE above, SSE next page top and NNE next page bottom) are R.A. Beck photographs from January, 1893, just before the move to Burnside. In the bottom perspective seen at left-center, a barely visible triangle shape appears in the distance; this is the roof of the new train shed at the 12th Street station. The above view was published in the September, 1912 issue of the Illinois Central Magazine.

IC45x35-14

IC45x35-15

1863

Home mail delivery began in America's cities. The National Currency Act was pushed through a reluctant Congress; the Act created a national banking system in competition with the state system; it allowed the government to raise money by issuing a national currency, something vital to funding the war. On January 1st President Abraham Lincoln gave his Emancipation Proclamation, making preserving the Union a secondary calling. On the eastern front, Major General Joseph Hooker marked the 130,000-strong Army of the Potomac against General Robert E. Lee, who had but half the force, at Chancellorsville; General Lee would defeat the hesitating Hooker, but lose the irreplaceable Lieutenant General Thomas J. "Stonewall" Jackson, killed by friendly fire at age 39. President Lincoln relieved General Hooker of command, Major General George G. Meade becoming the fourth man in two years to head the Army of the Potomac. Now on a win streak, General Lee began his second invasion of the North, moving through the Shenandoah Valley; five weeks later the raid ended after a three-day battle with General Meade's forces at Gettysburg, the failure of Pickett's charge at Cemetery Ridge being decisive. On the western front the Confederacy controlled Port Hudson, Louisiana and Vicksburg, Mississippi – each overlooking the Mississippi River; while both could be defended, neither could be resupplied. On July 4th, Vicksburg fell to Major General Ulysses S. Grant after a 47-day siege, Port Hudson a few days later, reopening the river. Battle now shifted around strategic Chattanooga; Union Major General William S. Rosecrans' Army of the Cumberland met Confederate General Braxton Bragg's Army of Tennessee at Chickamauga Creek in northwestern Georgia; the Confederate victory would be short-lived as Major Generals Burnside and Sherman finally reopened Tennessee. In mid-July, the all-black 54th Massachusetts stormed Confederate Fort Wagner outside Charleston. West Virginia was admitted to the divided Nation as the 35th State, 11 in the Confederacy and 24 in the Union. Having started out the year with his Emancipation Proclamation, President Lincoln ended it with his Gettysburg Address, dedicating a military cemetery on the Pennsylvania battlefield. Henry Ford was born in Wayne County, Michigan. 38-year old English biologist Thomas H. Huxley published *Man's Place In Nature*.

Cabooses got a cupola, giving trainmen a rooftop view of the train. The Pennsylvania Railroad, experimenting in its Altoona yards, pioneered the use of steel rails made by the process invented by Englishman Henry Bessemer. Cyrus K. Holliday's Atchison and Topeka Railroad received 3 million acres under the federal land grant program with the stipulation that it construct a railroad from Topeka to the Colorado border within ten years, which it did with one year to spare. The Milwaukee and St. Paul Railway was organized in Wisconsin in May; it would add Chicago to its name in 1874 and Pacific in 1909. In December, ground was broken in Omaha for the envisioned transcontinental railroad.

The partial failure of the wheat crop and distress on the corn crop from early frost made for lower yields in Illinois Central territory, yet shipments still notched records as the increased acreage under plow far outweighed the change; revenue traffic rose to more than 952,000 tons of freight; W. H. Osborn noted in the Directors Report that there were insufficient cars and locomotives to handle the increasing traffic levels. Revenue for the year exceeded $4.6 million, a 32 percent gain; passenger revenues accounted for almost 39 percent of the total: 852,659 passengers, including 107,987 military troop movements. The upside of all this was that during the year Illinois Central paid its first stock dividends, amounting to over $775,000. The Land Department changed policy to react with the times: lowering the per acre price on new contracts, and subdividing tracts of existing purchasers with debt in arrears to lower their balance due by spreading the obligation over additional buyers. The results were impressive, with 221,578 acres for $2.4 million placed under contract; for the first time in three years, new sales exceeded cancellations; over half the original Land Grant acres were now under contract, and payments on 383,944 of those acres had been made in full. With delivery of 6 new units (2 IC-built and 4 Smith & Jackson 4-4-0 units built by New Jersey Locomotive and Machine) the locomotive fleet rose to 116; 9 units were converted at Company shops to coal-burning, bringing the total to 82; Illinois Central rolled out its first home-built locomotives - #'s 4 and 110, both 4-4-0 American-types built at the Company's Weldon Yard work shops between 12th/16th Streets in Chicago. Weldon shops date back to 1855 when it was known as Weldon Slip, a harbor to store the marine equipment used to maintain Illinois Central's trestle and breakwater in the City; gradually mechanical facilities were built and when a fire razed the machine shops in 1860, they were rebuilt; eventually Weldon shops would comprise a cab shop, machine shop, storehouse, blacksmith shops, boiler shop and two roundhouses: one for the suburban service engines and the other

Above is Smith & Jackson-built (by New Jersey Locomotive & Machine Company in 1863) Illinois Central #114, a 4-4-0 American (60 D; 62,000 TW) wood-burning engine. Pictured here in front of the original Centralia roundhouse in the early 1860's, this engine blew up in 1876. This picture was published in the February, 1926 issue of the Illinois Central Magazine.

IC1863-01

for road engines; the road engine facility was the old Baltimore & Ohio roundhouse Illinois Central purchased, and it was north and east of the suburban roundhouse; the B&O roundhouse was a 32-stall brick engine house with 3 outlet tracks, 246 feet in diameter at the outside walls and 122 feet diameter at the inside walls. One of sidelights of the war was the increase in raw material prices on needy items, coal being one for the Illinois Central; the per ton cost of coal, loaded on tenders, rose from $1.64 to $2.85 year-to-year, a 73 percent increase. At that time, coal was loaded into tenders by cranes attached to coal bins at appropriately spaced stations on the system.

IC1863-03

Artist's sketch of wood-burning Illinois Central #4, an 1863 IC/Weldon-yard built 4-4-0 American (original IC #4, 60 D; 62,000 TW; later rebuilt, 65 D; 70,000 TW). This was one of Illinois Central's first home-built engines.

IC1863-02

Above is Illinois Central #1104, a rebuilt and renumbered IC #4. This 4-4-0 American previously was numbered IC #167 (1876) and IC #4 (as above); this engine was rebuilt in 1882 (65 D; 140 BP; 70,000 TW; 12,747 TF) and remained on the roster almost to the turn of the century; it was captured here on the Chicago Lake Front in 1892, possibly photographed by R.A. Beck.

1864

In March 42-year old Ulysses S. Grant was promoted to the revived rank of Lieutenant General, the only three-star in the Union Army and only the second since George Washington; General Grant now outranked 344 lesser generals, both brigadier and major. On the eastern front General Grant had his first head-to-head with General Lee, at the Wilderness Campaign; while the Wilderness Campaign would cost the Army of the Potomac twice the casualties of the Confederacy, the Union forces were twice the size; thus did General Grant's strategy of trading casualties unfold. Rather than withdraw, General Grant flanked his enemy toward Spottsylvania Court House, then repeated the maneuver toward a crossroads called Cold Harbor, and once again toward Petersburg, Virginia, a Confederate supply depot 20 miles south of Richmond, beginning a siege that would last into the next year. Major General William Tecumseh Sherman took command of all Union forces in the west and pushed to the outskirts of Atlanta, earning Confederate General Joseph E. Johnston removal from command, General John Bell Hood replacing him; within five weeks General Sherman took Atlanta from General Hood. General Sherman turned east and steamrolled through Georgia on his "March to the Sea", the finale his arrival in Savannah. Having lost Atlanta, General Hood tried to lure the Union out of Georgia, but after the decisive two-day Battle of Nashville, Confederate troops left Tennessee for good. The nascent Union Navy had its day at the Battle of Mobile Bay where one-star Rear Admiral David G. Farragut coined the phrase "Damn the Torpedoes" and earned a second star on his flag, the newly created rank of Vice Admiral. Confederate Lieutenant General Jubal A. Early was detached from General Lee's defense of Richmond for the Confederate States' third and last invasion of the North; while General Early's push North reached within six miles of Washington D.C., he lost the moment when he paused to measure his attack on the Capital, allowing General Grant time to redirect troops. With General Early halted, Union Major General Philip H. Sheridan was placed in command of the Valley Campaign and reclaimed the Shenandoah Valley. At the 3rd Republican convention in Baltimore, incumbent President Abraham Lincoln was nominated for re-election on the 1st ballot; Tennessee military Governor Andrew Johnson was the compromise nominee of Party factions for Vice President on the 1st ballot. At the 9th Democratic convention in Chicago militarily unemployed Democrat Major General George B. McClellan of New Jersey stumped for the nomination on a platform of negotiating a quick peace, the Confederacy's only hope for survival as independent states; McClellan was elected the Democratic nominee for President on the 1st ballot; Congressman George H. Pendleton of Ohio was chosen the nominee for Vice President on the 2nd ballot. In November the Lincoln/Johnson ticket won the election, Lincoln gaining more electoral votes than he had four years earlier and becoming the first sitting President to be reelected since Andrew Jackson 32 years earlier; since the election took place during the Civil War, the eleven Confederate States refused to vote in the election and withheld their 81 electoral votes. Nevada was admitted to the divided Nation as the 36th State; there now were 11 in the Confederacy and 25 in the Union. George Washington Carver was born; years later his experiments with sweet potatoes and peanuts at the Tuskegee Institute in Alabama would bring him fame and improve the lives of southern farmers; Carver worked for forty seven years at Tuskegee, some twenty years with its founder, Booker T. Washington.

George M. Pullman began building sleeping cars for real; his first was named the *Pioneer*, and would be placed in service the next year; anecdote would claim it was used to transport Lincoln's family to Springfield for the burial of the assassinated President. The Northern Pacific Railroad was chartered with the task of building a road from Lake Superior (Duluth) to Puget Sound on the west coast; some 39 million acres of federal land, the largest grants ever made, were approved to facilitate construction of this railroad. Locating and surveying were begun on the projected transcontinental railroad.

With the demand on Illinois Central locomotives and freight cars for normal business increasing, the Government's stepped-up usage put operations off plan; even with many customers up in arms because of the government priority, the Railroad still managed a record year; revenues exceeded $6.3 million, with passenger traffic accounting for 37 percent of the total (a record 1,108,937 passengers, including 175,200 for the government); revenue traffic rose to more than 1.0 million tons of freight; for the second consecutive year, stock dividends were paid, this time amounting to almost $1.7 million. Land sales continued apace, 265,520 acres being placed under more than 3,500 contracts totaling $2.9 million; sales again exceeded cancellations, with purchasers paying an average of $10.96 per acre on the average tract of just over 75 acres. The locomotive roster rose to 126, 10 new 4-4-

0 American-types having been received (3 IC-built and 7 Norris-built), and a few second-hand Rogers-built units acquired; in addition to the ten new units 15 units were converted over to coal-burning, which fleet now numbered 107. Allan Pinkerton, rich from his Pinkerton Detective Agency, purchased a 264-acre estate where Illinois Central tracks cut across the property near Onarga, Illinois.

LINCOLN FUNERAL CAR ON THE OLD TRACKS OF THE ILLINOIS CENTRAL R. R.
BY LAKE MICHIGAN, CHICAGO, 1865

ICLAG04-02

LINCOLN FUNERAL TRAIN 1865
I.C.R.R. CHICAGO ILL

ICLAG04-01

Top of page is the Lincoln Funeral car, as it was set out on the Illinois Central tracks as it paused in Chicago. Shown above and on the next page is the Lincoln Funeral train from the same period. It was captured on the old Illinois Central trestle entrance to the city of Chicago, in a photograph dated 1865. The train was on its way to Springfield, Illinois.

1865

In November 52-year old Henry Bessemer patented a method for removing impurities from molten iron, his second revolution for the conversion of iron into steel. 32-year old Swedish-born chemist Alfred B. Nobel invented the detonating cap, making explosives less precarious; thirty-one years later he would establish the Nobel Prizes.

As the year began there were 36 States in the divided Nation, 11 in the Confederacy and 25 in the Union. To formalize his Emancipation Proclamation, President Lincoln began the constitutional process on a proposed 13th Amendment to the U.S. Constitution; ratification by the States was completed by the end of the year as Georgia became the 27th State to ratify and slavery was banned; Lincoln's home state of Illinois was the 1st to ratify, his birth state of Kentucky would be the 35th and last some 111 years later, and Mississippi rejected the proposal and never did ratify. On the war front, there now were two major thrusts by the Union armies: at Savannah, Georgia with Major General Sherman moving north, and at Petersburg, Virginia just to the south of Richmond under siege by Lieutenant General Grant. General Lee abandoned Petersburg on April 2nd; on April 3rd Union soldiers walked unopposed into Richmond, the capital of the

Confederate States of America. General Lee escaped west of the city, with Generals Sheridan and Meade in pursuit; the Civil War officially ended on April 9th at Appomattox Court House, Virginia when Robert E. Lee surrendered to Ulysses S. Grant; over 500,000 Union and Confederate soldiers gave their lives in the four year struggle, the most costly war Americans would ever endure. 56-year old Abraham Lincoln's 2nd Term as President would end, 41 days after his inauguration and 6 days after Lee's surrender, at the hands of John Wilkes Booth in the Ford's Theatre; 56-year old Vice President Andrew Johnson, who had been a U.S. Congressman and Governor of Tennessee before Vice President, would finish out the remaining 3 years and 10 months of the slain President's Term. Lincoln was the third President to die in Office (Harrison, Taylor and Lincoln), and the first to be assassinated. Congress established the Secret Service, at the beginning a force against counterfeiting. Major Henry Wirz commander of the infamous Andersonville, Georgia prisoner of war camp, where at one time almost 33,000 prisoners were

jammed onto its 26 acres, became one of the few to be tried as a war criminal; he was tried, sentenced and executed for allowing prisoner mistreatment. Surgeon, Union spy and Confederate prisoner of war 32-year old Mary Edwards Walker became the only woman to earn the Medal of Honor; the Medal of Honor was granted in 1865, revoked in a 1917 purge, and reinstated 60 years later. Midway through his life, 33-year old English scholar Charles L. Dodgson reduced one of his tall tales to writing and published *Alice's Adventures in Wonderland*; the author, writing under the pseudonym Lewis Carroll, was an Oxford University mathematician. Vassar opened as a women's college in New York. Looking for adventure after the war, 47-year old P.G.T. Beauregard began employment with the New Orleans, Jackson & Great Northern railroad; he made President the following April and remained there until outmaneuvered by Colonel Henry S. McComb five years later. By 1861 some 300 miles of levees had been built by private landowners and local governments to reclaim portions of the Yazoo Delta from the Mississippi river between the high bluffs of Memphis and Vicksburg; the triumph over nature was temporary, as the war destroyed most of the improvements, which would not be rebuilt for years. On its way to replacing Cincinnati as the livestock slaughter capital of the country, Chicago opened its Great Union Stock Yard at the end of the year.

James J. Hill began his quest, signing the Milwaukee and Mississippi railroad to an essentially exclusive contract, and matching it with similar contracts with a steamship company. George M. Pullman's first sleeping car, the *Pioneer*, was placed in service; the car allegedly was part of slain President Abraham Lincoln's funeral train between Chicago and his final resting place in Springfield, Illinois; the actual funeral car was an armored car that had been built for President Lincoln and his Cabinet members at United States Military Car Shops in Alexandria, Virginia in 1863/1864. The Southern Pacific Railroad was organized with the mission of building a line to connect San Francisco and San Diego. In July the first trackage was laid for the anticipated transcontinental railroad.

Effective July 11th 45-year old John M. Douglas was elected the 5th President of the Illinois Central; he would serve until April 14, 1871. With the end of the war, Illinois Central knew its vanished southern business would return in time, but it would not be in the current year, since the return of peace came too late in the season. Still, the Company chalked up record revenues for the year, reaching $7.2 million; revenue traffic rose to more than 1.0 million tons of freight. Passenger traffic accounted for over 37 percent of revenues (1,214,054 passengers, including 121,267 for the military). Returning servicemen fueled land sales: 155,056 acres put under 2,364 contracts valued at almost $1.9 million with an average tract size of roughly 65 acres; with sales exceeding cancellations for the third consecutive year, the balance of original land grant acres available for sale dropped under one million for the first time. The Illinois Central's locomotive roster grew to 148, with new 4-4-0 units (5 IC-built, 3 Norris-built, 10 Hinkley-built) and a few second-hand Rogers-built units; all but 9 of the 148 were coal-burning units. For the third consecutive year, Illinois Central paid stock dividends, this time at the rate of $10 per share or more than $2.2 million. Fresh off the war, Ambrose E. Burnside rejoined the Company, this time as a Director, instead of as Cashier for the Land Department, his original position.

1866

Having developed something of a bad attitude as a teen-age raider for the Confederates, Jesse James started making armed withdrawals from banks. Winslow Homer was born. American Society for the Prevention of Cruelty to Animals was organized in New York. A 5-cent coin was authorized, soon-to-be-called a nickel. The first successful telegraph cable across the Atlantic was laid, making up for failed and short-lived attempts in 1857 and 1858. Congress passed the Civil Rights Act granting citizenship to all native-born Americans, except Indians; it would be another 58 years before Indians would be granted the same status. While George Washington held a similar rank in 1775 under the auspices of the Continental Congress, the first four-star full Army general under the U.S. Constitution was Ulysses S. Grant who achieved that grade in July by act of Congress for his victory in the Civil War; both William Tecumseh Sherman and Philip H. Sheridan would, in turn, be promoted to four-star rank; Congress also created and conferred the Navy grade of three-star Admiral on David G. Farragut, the third time a new rank was created for Farragut.

James J. Hill signed exclusivity contracts with the Saint Paul and Pacific railroad. With the Civil War over the Central Pacific/Union Pacific 1862 mandate to build a railroad to the Pacific Ocean could begin in earnest; by 1866 less than 100 miles had been built; Chief Engineer for the Central Pacific was Samuel S. Montague, Union Army Major General Grenville M. Dodge performing that function for the Union Pacific. The Atlantic & Pacific Railroad was chartered with the task of constructing a railroad along a southerly route from Missouri west to the Colorado River; the Southern Pacific was authorized to build a railroad east from San Francisco to meet up with the Atlantic & Pacific on the Colorado River; federal land grants of some 12 and 7 million acres were granted to these rail companies to fund construction.

Illinois Central became one of the first to transport fresh produce under refrigeration, shipping strawberries from Cobden, Illinois to the Chicago market in wooden chests equipped with ice compartments. Revenues for the Illinois Central fell a little over $600,000 to $6.5 million, the entire shortfall attributable to the decline in passenger related traffic; the number of passengers carried dropped from 1,214,054 (including 121,267 military) to 1,034,530 (including 39,361 military); revenue traffic rose to more than 1.1 million tons of freight. The fact that the southern economy was not yet reconstructed also played a part in limiting Illinois Central's fortunes for the time being. Illinois Central's locomotive fleet grew by two (IC-built, coal-burning passenger units) to 150; with five additional units converted to coal-burning service, only a handful of the 150 roster burned wood. Land sales to 2,218 purchasers yielded almost $1.7 in contracts, covering 158,015 acres at an average of $10.65 per acre; land sales were five times the number of cancellations; the inventory of unsold acres numbered 868,841, roughly one-third of the original Land Grant. For the second year in a row, the Illinois Central paid a stock dividend exceeding $2.2 million. During the year Company forces worked to reduce the grade at Scales Mound; with the excavation of almost 5,000 cubic yards, the grade was reduced from 85 feet per mile to 40 feet.

This Rogers-built 4-4-0 American-type (60 D) was built in 1866 for the Dubuque & Sioux City as #14, the Manchester. *It was re-numbered by the Illinois Central upon lease in 1867 to #164. This picture predates 1888, and was published in the June, 1942 issue of the IC Magazine.*

1867

19 years after his *Communist Manifesto*, Karl Marx published *Das Kapital*, his treatise on the evolution of capitalism. 34-year old chemist Alfred B. Nobel of Sweden discovered how to turn unstable nitroglycerin into a manageable solid by soaking an inert substance in it; he named his invention dynamite and became a multi-millionaire. Diamond fields were discovered in South Africa. In April under the British North America Act, Great Britain's Parliament decreed Ontario, Quebec, New Brunswick and Nova Scotia united as the Dominion of Canada.

The Reconstruction Act passed in Washington DC which sent U.S. Army occupation forces into the South; the Reconstruction Act changed the national focus from one of preserving the Union to one of remaking the South. Nebraska was admitted to the Union as the 37th State. In March Secretary of State William H. Seward paid $7.2 million or about 2 cents an acre to Russia for the Alaska territory; the Alaska Purchase Treaty gave the Nation its first noncontiguous territory; Seward also secretly hoped that citizens of British Columbia, located between Alaska and Washington Territory, would opt to join the States instead of the newly forming Dominion of Canada. Illinois Industrial University, the future University of Illinois, was founded on February 28th; school opened the next year. Frank Lloyd Wright was born in Wisconsin. 39-year old Norwegian playwright Henrik Ibsen wrote *Peer Gynt* and gained national attention. Swiss pharmacist Henri Nestle introduced the first baby formula. The end of the War brought a return to the pursuit of "Manifest Destiny", toward the vanishing American frontier in the West as railroads and settlers came across the Plains; the government subsidized four geographical and geological surveys of the West in the next 12 years, two by the War Department and two by the Department of the Interior; Congress would consolidate all four Great Surveys into the United States Geological Survey in 1879.

George M. Pullman incorporated his Pullman Palace Car Company (in partnership with Andrew Carnegie) and introduced sleeping cars equipped with kitchen and dining facilities. With the Central Pacific Railroad building east from Sacramento through the Sierra Nevada's and the Union Pacific Railroad laying track west from Omaha, Nebraska on the Missouri River across from Council Bluffs, Iowa, construction of the first transcontinental rail line continued. Working west from Omaha, the Union Pacific charted a course though Indian territory and the Black Hills via a crossing it named Sherman Pass (above what would become Cheyenne) in honor of the military commander of the Division of the West General William Tecumseh Sherman; hero of the Civil War, General Sherman now commanded the Army patrols that protected railroad construction parties. The Chicago & Northwestern Railroad completed its line into Council Bluffs, Iowa thus forming a connection back to the east for the Union Pacific. 73-year old Commodore Cornelius Vanderbilt assumed the Presidency of the New York Central Railroad, topping off a second career for the old financial baron of ferry and steamship renown.

Company fortunes experienced a slight rebound during the year, with revenues on the original Charter Lines rising to almost $7.0 million, just $0.2 million short of the Civil War record set two years earlier; passenger business, although down for the second consecutive year, represented 24 percent of total, 1,077,550 passengers in all. Revenue traffic rose to more than 1.3 million tons of freight. Revenues allowed a third consecutive annual stock dividend, once again exceeding $2.2 million. The big news of the year occurred in October with the 20-year operating lease of the 143-mile long Dubuque & Sioux City railroad (created from the ruins of the Dubuque & Pacific seven years earlier), the first line extension for the Company since building the Charter Lines and the first venture outside Illinois; the Dubuque to Iowa Falls line became the fifth engineering section on the railroad, was promptly dubbed the Iowa Division, and came with shop facilities at Dubuque; the lease required Illinois Central to pay 35 percent of annual revenues to the owners for the first ten years and 36 percent for the second decade, meaning operations at anything better than a 65 or 64 percent operating ratio was profit for the Illinois Central; Illinois Central had the option to make the lease arrangement perpetual at the higher percentage; the lease also brought interchange with one of its connections, the Cedar Falls and Minnesota railroad (chartered in 1858), 15 miles of track from Cedar Falls to Waverly, one day part of Illinois Central's Albert Lea District. With the Chicago & Northwestern having just completed its line into Council Bluffs, Iowa, the Illinois Central's lease agreement with the Dubuque & Sioux City had a defensive posture to it; Sioux City and Council Bluffs competed to be the gateway to the West, the Missouri river crossing for the transcontinental railroad, and the contest was not yet settled. The line extension covered approximately 158 miles of track in Iowa, bringing the total under operation to 862 miles by yearend; connections between the two railroads was via steamboat transfer at the Mississippi river crossing at Dubuque and Dunleith;

Illinois Central #166 originally was Dubuque & Sioux City #16, the C.W. Place. It was Rogers-built in 1867 and cascaded into Illinois Central ownership when the property was leased by the IC in 1867. This 4-4-0 American (60 D) was the last built for the Dubuque & Sioux City. It was captured here at an unknown time and place.

IC1867-01

Illinois Central joined with others in forming the Dunleith & Dubuque Bridge Company to build a river crossing spanning those points; the construction price was estimated at $1.0 million. With the addition of 16 Rogers-built and 1 William Mason-built wood-burning locomotives from the Dubuque and Sioux City lease, one an 0-4-0 switcher and the rest 4-4-0 Americans, Illinois Central's roster rose to 167 units, 20 wood-burners in total. Land sales continued to rise with the resettlement of civil war soldiers and families, 203,834 acres being sold to some 2,633 purchasers for almost $2.2 million, with the average tract size of almost 80 acres exchanged at an average of $10.67 per acre

1868

Astronomers gained evidence of a new element in the solar spectrum during a solar eclipse; it would be 27 years before helium was reproduced in the laboratory. In May the U.S. celebrated its first Memorial Day. The impeachment trial of President Andrew Johnson finally came to a head after months of investigation and testimony and debate; the Senate, voting first on the general Article 11 of the Articles of Impeachment, acquitted President Johnson on that charge when it failed to gain the required two-thirds vote by a single vote – 19 against to 35 for impeachment. In July the 14th Amendment to the Constitution was enacted as South Carolina became the 28th State to ratify; Connecticut was the 1st to ratify and Kentucky would be the 37th and last, some 108 years later; aimed at giving newly enfranchised blacks the same rights many whites took for granted, it guaranteed equal protection under the laws and due process for all citizens. At the 4th Republican convention in Chicago, Ohio-born war hero Ulysses S. Grant of Illinois was unanimously elected the nominee for President on the 1st ballot; Speaker of the House Schuyler Colfax from Indiana was chosen the nominee for Vice President on the 6th ballot. At the 10th Democratic convention in New York, ex-Governor of New York Horatio Seymour was elected the nominee for President on the 22nd ballot; once Congressman and future Senator Major General Francis P. Blair of Missouri was the unanimous choice as the nominee for Vice President on the 1st ballot. The Grant/Colfax ticket carried the day in November, swamping the democratic challengers by winning all but eight states; because of Reconstruction, Mississippi, Texas and Virginia did not vote their 23 electoral votes in the election. Evaporated milk was patented. Ohio inventor Charles Fleischmann invented compressed fresh yeast. 36-year old Louisa May Alcott published the first volume of *Little Women*.

George M. Pullman's first all-dining car, the *Delmonico*, was placed in service on the Chicago & Alton Railroad. Former C.S.A. Major Eli Hamilton Janney patented the first automatic coupler for railroad cars, a vast improvement over link and pin couplers. Construction of the missing link in the first transcontinental rail line continued with thousands of Chinese laborers on the Central Pacific racing thousands of Irish laborers on the Union Pacific to see who could lay more rail in a day; the fact that federal land grants were tied to miles of track laid pushed this contest. The Union Pacific began work on a bridge to span the Missouri River and connect Omaha, Nebraska to Council Bluffs, Iowa; construction lasted, on-and-off, for four years. Central Pacific owners Stanford, Crocker, Hopkins and Huntington added the budding Southern Pacific Railroad to their growing empire. 33-year old financier Jay Gould, partner James Fisk, and company insider Daniel Drews' control of the Erie Railroad facilitated their scheme of printing counterfeit stock certificates and selling them on the market; Commodore Cornelius Vanderbilt's effort to expand the New York Central's presence was taken in by the Gould/Fisk/Drew conspiracy; when arrest warrants were issued later, Gould and Fisk simply fled – Gould moving first to New Jersey and then west with his brand of entrepreneurship, eventually entering management at the Union Pacific in 1873.

Revenues for the 862 miles of owned and leased lines, reported on a consolidated basis for the first time, exceeded $7.8 million, a record; passenger traffic accounted for 24 percent of the total, 1,312,631 passengers (including 140,269 on the Dubuque & Sioux City and connections). Revenue traffic rose to more than 1.4 million tons of freight. The Cedar Falls & Minnesota railroad, which connected with the leased Dubuque & Sioux City, extended its reach by 28 miles, from Waverly to Charles City, thus attracting additional business. Land sales rang up $2.2 million for 207,351 acres to 2,776 purchasers, the average tract selling for $10.76 per acre; with a structure for draining lands adopted under governmental authority, over 55 percent of the acreage sold was between Champaign and Kankakee on the Chicago branch, previously unmarketable flat land. The locomotive fleet rose to 170, with the addition of 3 new IC-built passenger locomotives; having converted 12 wood-burners, the coal-burning fleet now numbered 162. The Mississippi river bridge connecting Dubuque and Dunleith was completed by the end of the year, ending 13 years of ferry service across the river; the single-track bridge spanning the river, built by Andrew Carnegie's Keystone Bridge Company of Pittsburgh, used wrought iron instead of cast iron, saw the first crossing of a train on December 28th and opened for general traffic on New Years Day 1869. The fourth consecutive annual stock dividend exceeding $2.2 million was paid during the year. Ambrose Burnside left the Board of directors of the Company to focus on politics, and was replaced by Jonathan Sturges. Illinois Central inaugurated the *Thunderbolt Express* between Centralia and Chicago, a refrigerated fruit train.

Absent mountain passes and major tunnels, Illinois Central's particular engineering difficulty was bridges, large and small. Over one hundred years of bridge building, Illinois Central grew up with technology; Howe truss, Pratt truss, Whipple truss, pony truss spans, I-beam spans, through pin spans, 2-deck plate girders, Warren truss, Bollman iron truss, lattice girder, pile ridge, Murphy Whipple Patented Iron truss, Fink through truss bridge, and on and on. One of the first and most significant for its time was the Mississippi river crossing between Dubuque and Dunleith, which was completed by Keystone Steel in 1868. Bridges at Cairo (1889) and Thebes (1905) also were major undertakings. The photograph shown below was published in the April, 1936 issue of the Illinois Central Magazine.

Photo Courtesy of Chicago Historical Society; Chicago (ICHi-09070)

1869

New York Herald reporter Henry Morton Stanley began an African expedition to search for missionary David Livingstone. 64-year old French engineer Ferdinand de Lesseps finished his ten-year project and the Suez Canal opened for business; the French-Egyptian venture linked the Mediterranean and Red seas and brought the Orient 3,500 miles closer to the U.S. While others had postulated a pattern in the known chemical elements, it was 35-year old Russian-born Dmitri I. Mendeleev who first published an understandable table showing the order or periodicity of the elements; his Table included 63 of the 90 elements eventually found in nature.

63-year old German-born American engineer John A. Roebling began construction on the East River Bridge in New York City, a project his 34-year old son Washington A. Roebling would finish; completed in 1883, it would later be renamed the Brooklyn Bridge. In February a general amnesty was declared by lame duck President Andrew Johnson for all former confederate soldiers, including Jefferson Davis. In March 46-year old Ulysses S. Grant was sworn in as the 18th President of the United States. The forerunner to the vacuum cleaner was patented (#91,145); Ives W. McGaffey was the inventor. In September the plot by financiers/hoarders Jay Gould and James Fisk to corner the gold market backfired when President Grant allowed the sale of government bullion and the market price of gold collapsed on Black Friday, bringing Wall Street down with it. Chewing gum was invented. Having adopted the pseudonym Mark Twain, 34-year old Samuel L. Clemens published his first book, *Innocents Abroad*. 25-year old Henry J. Heinz from Sharpsburg, Pennsylvania organized his earliest food company; the first of his later "57" varieties is prepared horseradish. Joseph Campbell began canning tomatoes and soups in Camden, New Jersey. Having tried unsuccessfully to have women specifically included in the 14th Amendment's equal protection guarantee, Susan B. Anthony began organizing the women's suffrage movement; Elizabeth Cady Stanton independently founded the National Woman Suffrage Association; while this was but the beginning of a fifty year quest, these early efforts would coalesce with others to form a united front 21 years later, with each woman having a turn serving as President. 35-year old science teacher John Wesley Powell set out in a party of ten to map one of the last unexplored areas of the U.S.; his party became the first white explorers to investigate the Grand Canyon.

With two 4-4-0 American-type steam locomotives built the year before (the Schenectady-built wood-burning Jupiter for the Central Pacific and the Rogers-built coal-burning No. 119 for the Union Pacific) meeting at Promontory Point, in the Utah Territory on the northeast side of the Great Salt Lake outside of the city of Ogden, on May 10th the first transcontinental line was forged with a golden spike, as the Union Pacific and the Central Pacific railroads completed their route between the Missouri River and Sacramento. Civil War financier Jay Cooke's firm was employed by the Northern Pacific for the purpose of promoting the 39 million acres granted under the Northern Pacific charter, which called for construction of a railroad spanning the Great Lakes to Puget Sound; Cooke's involvement would last until his bankruptcy four years down the road. 22-year old George Westinghouse, who would eventually receive over 350 patents, invented (patent #88,929) the air powered brake for stopping trains, which he would further improve and automate over the next four years; powered-brakes allowed railroads to operate longer trains and greatly improved safety; the formation of Westinghouse Air Brake would follow in the years to come. The forerunner to the Santa Fe operated its first train in Topeka, Kansas. The Baltimore & Ohio Railroad purchased the Central Ohio Railroad to extend its reach to Sandusky on Lake Erie, more than half way to its goal of Chicago. Vanderbilt's New York Central Railroad began construction of its first Grand Central depot on Manhattan in New York City; construction would last two years.

Considered by some the Great Land Steal of 1869, the Illinois Central was granted title to property in the 400-foot wide strip between its breakwater and Michigan Avenue; four years later it was repealed and then the litigation started, more steps in the continuing saga of the lake front. With the south rising, Illinois Central's fortunes followed; with low wheat prices and a failed Illinois corn crop more than made up for by Iowa's agricultural success, revenues from both leased and owned trackage exceeded $8.8 million, a record; passenger traffic accounted for 24 percent of revenues (1,399,416 passengers). Revenue traffic rose to more than 1.6 million tons of freight. With the nation focused on the golden spike in the west, Illinois Central worked to keep pace gaining trackage with two extensions of the leased lines Iowa division: Illinois Central leased the 49-mile long Iowa Falls & Sioux City, which connected at Iowa Falls with the Dubuque & Sioux City and extended west to Fort Dodge on the Des Moines river; the Company also leased 54 miles of the Cedar Falls & Minnesota, from Waverly to St. Ansgar; with the 103 mile

Illinois Central-built in 1869, this 4-4-0 American (60 D; 66,000 TW) was rebuilt in 1888 (65 D; 140 BP; 70,000 TW; 12,747 TF). Originally numbered #170, it was renumbered to #1107 in 1890, and #2107 in 1912. It was pictured here at Scovel, Illinois in 1894. This picture appeared in the November, 1927 issue of the Illinois Central Magazine; identified in the picture were, left to right, William Fox (farmer), unidentified, Daniel Tonrey (conductor), Ruben Scovel (agent), and Peter Eich (engineer).

IC1869-01

addition, total owned and leased lines now operated by the Transportation department reached 965 miles. Land sales approached $0.9 million in 1,521 contracts covering 85,860 acres at an average per acre price of $10.48 and tract size of 56 acres; with sales far outstripping cancellations, the remaining inventory of unsold Land Grant property dipped under 500,000 for the first time. The Company's locomotive roster gained 7 to 170, all seven built at Company shops; with five more units converted, all but 3 now burned coal. The fifth consecutive stock dividend exceeding $2.2 million was paid during the year.

IC1869-02

Illinois Central #1111 was a 4-4-0 American (60 D; 66,000 TW) built in IC shops as #174 in 1869; it was renumbered to #1111 in 1890 after being rebuilt (65 D; 70,000 TW); its final roster number was #2111, which was applied in 1912. The picture was captured at McComb, Mississippi in 1895; it was published in the May, 1929 issue of the Illinois Central Magazine. Identified in the picture were: P.H. Geary (engineer) and R.C. Ricks (fireman, in the gangway). This engine regularly pulled trains #24 and #25 between New Orleans and Canton.

IC45x35-53

Illinois Central #1144 was another Illinois Central-built 4-4-0 American from 1869; originally #122, it was renumbered #1144 in 1890 and #2144 in 1912. The time and place of the picture were unidentified.

IC1869-04

Two views of Illinois Central-built #1115; built as #178 in 1869 (60 D; 66,000 TW), this engine was rebuilt in 1888 (65 D; 70,000 TW). Renumbered to #1115 in 1890, its final number was #2115 in 1912, and it was retired two years later. The picture above was by Company photographer by C.B. Medin and appeared in the May, 1950 issue of the Illinois Central Magazine; the picture dates to 1905 and shows a passenger train on a Cherokee to Sioux Falls run. The view below is very late in the engine's service life, at an unidentified time and place.

IC45x35-55

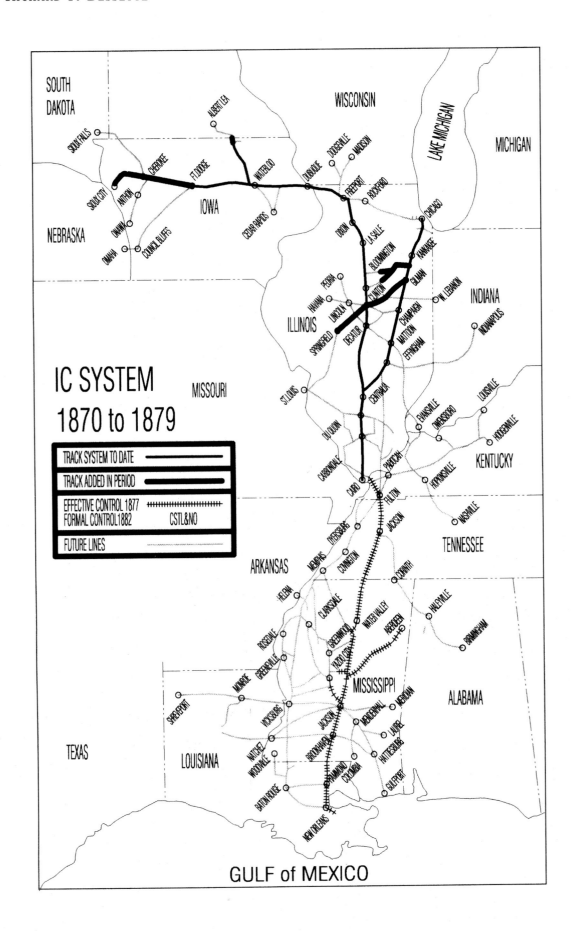

IC SYSTEM
1870 to 1879

TRACK SYSTEM TO DATE

TRACK ADDED IN PERIOD

EFFECTIVE CONTROL 1877
FORMAL CONTROL 1882   CSTL&NO

FUTURE LINES

GULF of MEXICO

1850's 1860's **1870's** 1880's 1890's 1900's 1910's 1920's 1930's 1940's

The Ninth Census of the U.S. population was taken; there were a little over 38.5 million people in the U.S., having grown 23 percent from the prior census; the country would add over 11.5 million people by the end of the decade, one-quarter through immigration. The Union grew by one State to a total of 38. With the Civil War buckling the South's economy, Reconstruction ran from 1867 to 1877. There were many civil rights advances during Reconstruction, but most of those gains eroded with the end of the protective umbrella of Reconstruction. Chaffing under Republican leadership, Southerners joined with Northern Democrats to rebuild a power base during Reconstruction; this culminated in the election of 1876, where a Democrat finally garnered enough votes to challenge a Republican candidate and win the popular vote. After the Civil War the troops were used to chase the Indians out of the West, with Indian Wars continuing on through the decade: the Northern Plains Indians raiding homesteaders in Montana, Wyoming and Nebraska with the resulting Stand at the Little Big Horn being just one example. There occurred a tremendous building of telegraphs and railroads, and mass immigration to fuel the industrial age on the horizon. This was a time when America changed from an agricultural to an industrial-based economy.

After the Civil War, railroads proved to be a leading factor in stimulating and reshaping the nation's economy; railroads were the biggest industry in the country. The 7-mph horsecar business in Chicago was big up to the early 1870's, when a horse disease felled many of the horses and put a crimp in that business. In 1870 the major line-haul rail carriers operated almost 53,000 miles of railroad, a figure that would swell by 40,000 more miles by the end of the decade. The postwar boom period came to a sudden end with the Financial Panic in 1873 followed by a recession in business; what had been a building boom in railroads and trackage soon became a buyers market, as a smorgasbord of bankrupt small carriers became available.

With the growth of suburbs south of Chicago, spurred by the Chicago Fire, Illinois Central's suburban service grew from 6 daily trains to 36 a day by the end of the decade.

Growth Of Illinois Central Railroad Business

Year (1)	Tonnage (mil/tons)	Lumber (mil/bf)	Grain (mil/bus)	Coal (mil/tons)	Passengers Commuters	Miles/Fare
1870	1.6	175	23.0	.221	1,376,585 N/A	39/$1.54
1871	1.8	133	24.0	.259	1,286,584 250,000est	39/$1.48
1872	2.0	134	25.5	.372	1,352,156 382,900	38/$1.30
1873	2.1	144	24.2	.347	1,472,005 487,319	33/$1.17
1874	2.1	176	21.5	.300	1,586,637 508,636	32/$1.05
1875	2.0	201	18.0	.367	1,648,541 539,012	31/$1.01
1876	1.9	155	18.4	.350	1,815,788 600,481	28/$0.89
1877	1.8	161	15.6	.355	1,711,398 648,931	27/$0.84
1878	2.1	121	21.6	.414	1,725,236 673,762	25/$0.80
1879	2.3	150	23.7	.423	1,807,744 802,703	25/$0.76

Passengers/Commuters = Total Ridership, and Commuter Portion Miles/Fare = Average Passenger Trip and Charge
(1) Fiscal Year bf = Board Feet bus = Bushels N/A = Data Not Available

1870

Otto von Bismarck took charge to unify Germany. Napoleon III picked a fight, and the Franco-Prussian War exploded. Manitoba was added as a Province of the Dominion of Canada. Popular novelist 58-year old Charles Dickens was laid to rest in Westminster Abbey. At the 4th Solemn Session of the Vatican Council called by Pius IX, papal infallibility became a dogma of the Catholic Church.

In February the 15th Amendment to the Constitution, the last of the reconstruction era, became law as Iowa was the 29th to vote for ratification; Nevada had been the 1st to ratify, Kentucky would be the 34th and last 106 years later, while Tennessee rejected the proposal and never did ratify; specifically upholding a citizen's voting rights regardless of race or color, it ostensibly enabled blacks to vote but still not women. Daniel C. Stillson of Charlestown, Massachusetts patented an improved monkey wrench. 31-year old John D. Rockefeller, and partners Samuel Andrews and Henry M. Flagler, founded Standard Oil Company of Ohio, the first block in his empire, only eight years after the partners' first oil refining venture. 47-year old William Marcy "Boss" Tweed's political career came to a screeching halt after 20 years of wheeling and dealing; Tweed, who ran New York City's Tammany Hall Democratic machine, ended up in and out of prison over the next eight years, until he died of natural causes broken but unrepentant.

Transcontinental train service was inaugurated; passengers had to change trains in Chicago and a number of other cities along the way, and had to be ferried across the Missouri River. Colonel Henry S. McComb wheedled his way into the Presidency of the 442-mile long New Orleans, Jackson & Great Northern/Mississippi Central that spanned New Orleans to Jackson, Tennessee, pushing out the aging P.G.T. Beauregard.

With the Golden Spike at Storm Lake completing the last 134 miles of the Iowa Falls & Sioux City from Ft. Dodge into Sioux City on the Missouri River, engine #144 (a Hinkley 4-4-0 from 1865) was the first into Sioux City that September; combined with a few additional miles on the Cedar Falls & Minnesota railroad from St. Ansgar to the Minnesota border at Mona, Illinois Central now operated a little over 1,107 miles of track, 402 in Iowa and almost 706 in Illinois. Illinois Central revenues, including leased lines, approached $8.7 million, just short of the prior year's record, which allowed for the sixth consecutive stock dividend exceeding $2.2 million; 1,376,585 passengers accounted for 24 percent of total revenues. Revenue traffic rose to more than 1.6 million tons of freight. Land sales accounted for $0.6 million, on 60,858 acres divided among 1,124 purchasers; the average tract was 54 acres at a per acre price of $10.28; of the 415,610 remaining land grant acres in inventory, most were located in the southern portion of the state, in heavily wooded areas rather than the prairies settlers found more suitable for farming and homesteading. During the year, one unit was sold and eleven new Company-built locomotives were added to the roster, bringing the total to 187 units, almost all coal burning 4-4-0 American-types. Requiring a more central location, Illinois Central moved the shop facilities acquired with its lease of the Dubuque & Sioux City railroad from Dubuque to Waterloo.

Illinois Central #70 was an 1870 product of the Illinois Central engine shops (60 D; 56,000 TW); originally #185, it later became #21, then #70 and then #1452 in 1890. It was dropped from the roster sometime before the turn of the century.

IC1870-01

Illinois Central #1123 was an IC product of 1870 (60 D; 66,000 TW), built originally as #186; it was renumbered to #1123 in 1890, after being rebuilt (65 D; 140 BP; 70,000 TW; 13,313 TF), and later #2123 in 1912. This picture appeared in the October, 1928 issue of the Illinois Central Magazine, and was referred to as the locomotive and crew of a pile driving outfit. Identified in the photograph were, right to left, unidentified (on the pilot), C.M. Murphy (brakeman, on steam chest), Bill Cornish (conductor, left of bell), Billy Bell (engineer, in the right seat), Jim Reardon (fireman, in the gangway), and unidentified (on ground). The picture was captured on a bright day, with glare off the snow, near Argyle, Wisconsin, on the Dodgeville branch; the date was December, 1898.

IC45x35-107

Illinois Central #2119 was a 4-4-0 American-type built at Illinois Central shops in 1870 (60 D; 66,000 TW); originally #182, it was renumbered to #1119 in 1890, and then #2119 in 1912; this engine was rebuilt in 1891 (65 D; 70,000 TW), and had a long service life, remaining on the roster until scrapped in 1928.

1871

Russian-born Dmitri I. Mendeleev continued his development of the periodic table of chemical elements by postulating (correctly) that the gaps in the chart would be filled in by discoveries of new elements. Paris fell in January, and the Franco-Prussian War ended in May; as a result, a number of independent German states joined to form a united German Empire with Prussian king William I as Emperor. 62-year old British naturalist Charles R. Darwin published his thesis about man and primates in *Descent of Man*. British Columbia was added as a Province of the Dominion of Canada.

In the midst of a drought, the Great Chicago Fire leveled most of the city in October; generally conceded to have started in O'Leary's barn, it's uncertain whether the cow was to blame for the flame. An unrelated fire in the logging town of Peshtigo, Wisconsin took the lives of over 1,100. One month later Joseph Medill, one of the owners of the Chicago Tribune newspaper, was elected Mayor of Chicago. Due to the deepening of the Illinois and Michigan Canal, an engineering feat was made possible; the flow of the Chicago River was reversed, sending Chicago sewage down the Illinois River instead of into Lake Michigan; in 1900 the Chicago Sanitary and Ship Canal would take over this function. The National Association of Base-Ball Players was founded with nine charter teams; thus began the 1st official professional baseball season. Orville Wright was born in Dayton, Ohio. Samuel L. Clemens, having settled in Hartford, Connecticut, invented a clothing improvement, his first patent (#121,992). The city of Birmingham, Alabama, founded the year before, was incorporated mainly to develop its rich iron ore deposits, which led to steel production years later. New York Herald reporter Henry Morton Stanley asked his famous question in Central Africa, "Dr. Livingstone, I presume?".

The New York Central Railroad's original Grand Central depot in New York City opened for business, arguably one of the grandest stations in the nation; the tracks from upper Manhattan into Grand Central were at grade level down Fourth Avenue – now called Park Avenue; over the next three years, the tracks would be lowered below grade to pass under Fourth Avenue. 34-year old J.P. Morgan formed a New York finance house, Drexel, Morgan and Company; it was renamed after its founder in 1895. Smith College for women was founded in Northampton, Massachusetts; instruction started four years later.

Effective April 14th 41-year old John Newell was elected the 6th President of the Illinois Central; he would serve until September 11, 1874. The Chicago Fire occurred in October and devastated the City; during the 15 months after the Fire over 425,000 cubic yards of debris would be used as fill: on the shoreline of Lake Michigan up to Illinois Central's trestle bridge entrance to the city, and on property east of the Weldon yard engine house between 12th/16th Streets. The Lake Michigan shoreline fill became new land, the future Lake Park, later renamed Grant Park. Besides Illinois Central's Great Central Station passenger depot between Randolph and South Water streets (where the stone walls remained but the collapsed trainshed roof was never rebuilt, remaining roofless for 22 years), the freight depot, the Land Office and other buildings were destroyed by the Fire; many records were lost in the Fire, presenting reporting difficulties at the end of the year; after the Fire the Land Office was moved to Centralia, where it remained for a single year before returning to Chicago. The bigger picture showed Illinois experiencing large harvests, with Iowa's coming in less than average; revenue traffic rose to more than 1.8 million tons of freight. Illinois Central revenues, including leased lines, approached $8.5 million; 1,286,584 passengers (one-fifth being commuters riding between Chicago and Hyde Park) accounting for $1.9 million, or 22 percent of revenues. Land sales accounted for almost $460,000 - 48,927 acres at an average of $9.38 per to 855 purchasers in average tracts of a little over 57 acres; the remaining original land grant acreage dropped to 379,210. Even with all the difficulties, the Company paid its seventh consecutive annual dividend exceeding $2.2 million to shareholders. With no significant track additions, the Transportation department continued to operate a little over 1,107 miles of track, almost 706 in Illinois and the rest in Iowa. Illinois Central's locomotive roster rose by six units, all built in Company shops, to 193 total units. Illinois Central's suburban commuter service was extended south from 63rd Street to 71st Street. 49-year old real estate developer Paul Cornell, having laid out Hyde Park, laid out Grand Crossing (Lake Shore & Michigan Southern + Pittsburgh & Fort Wayne + Illinois Central intersection) by situating a hotel and his watch factory there.

The big news of 1871 was the big fire in Chicago. Illinois Central's Great Central Station for passenger service, between South Water and Randolph streets, saw its roof razed in the Fire. The photograph of the roofless station was captured by R.A. Beck in April, 1893, exhibiting the "see through" appearance of the station. This picture was taken just before the remaining walls were torn down at the opening of the Central Station at 12th Street.

IC45x35-28

Illinois Central #195 was an 0-6-0 switch engine with a long and varied history. Baldwin-built (44 D; 47,000 TW) in 1871, it was originally constructed for the New Orleans Jackson & Great Northern as the Hercules; renumbered #10 by the Chicago St. Louis and New Orleans, it then became IC #255 in 1883, and finally IC #195 in 1890; it was dropped from the roster shortly thereafter. This previously published photograph was captured by R.A. Beck.

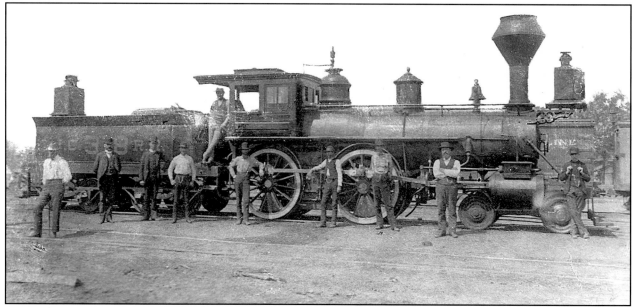

IC1871-01

Shown above is what is presumed to be Illinois Central #338, an 1871 Rogers-built 4-4-0 American (62 D; 67,000 TW) that came to the Illinois Central by way of the Chicago St. Louis & New Orleans; from CStL&NO #71 to IC #338 in 1883 to IC #1358 in 1890, this engine served until the turn of the century. Note the rear-facing lamp on the tender, making this engine/ tender combination perfect for switching duty. This photograph was published in the June, 1930 issue of the Illinois Central Magazine; J.A. Weathersford was credited with snapping the original negative at Canton, Mississippi in 1890. Identified in the picture were, left to right, O.S. Miller (roundhouse foreman), Mr. Holt (agent), Jim O' Shea (section man), Jim Smith (fireman), Lon Ramsey (engineer, in the gangway), Jim Owens (helper), Max Purviance (day caller), John Crawford (foreman), Mr. O'Shea (section foreman), and J.C. Cowan (night caller).

IC45x35-250

Illinois Central #1462, above, and #1464, below, were two 4-4-0 American-type locomotives originally built for the Gilman Clinton & Springfield. Baldwin-built in 1871 (60 D; 69,450 TW), IC #1462 (original GC&S #1) was acquired in 1877 and renumbered to IC #203, then to the number shown in 1890. IC #1462 is pictured on the 50-foot wooden gallows-style turntable at West Lebanon, Indiana. Illinois Central #1464 shown below also was Baldwin-built (61 D; 71,500 TW) in 1871 (as GC&S #3); acquired by Illinois Central in 1877, it was renumbered IC #205, then to IC #1464 in 1890, and finally to IC #1498 in 1899. This engine produced a tractive force of less than 10,000 pounds, and remained on the roster until retired in 1909. It was pictured here on the turntable at Cherokee, Iowa in 1895.

IC1871-02

1872

His Majesty King Christian opened the World's Fair in Copenhagen, Denmark. 55-year old British chemist Robert A Smith became the first to use the term "acid rain", in a published paper on "…Climatology".

The National Park System was formed; Yellowstone National became the first set aside as a public reserve. At the 5th Republican convention in Philadelphia, incumbent President Ulysses S. Grant was nominated for re-election on the 1st ballot unanimously; Massachusetts Senator Henry Wilson was chosen the nominee for Vice President on the 1st ballot over the sitting Vice President Schuyler Colfax who was accused of accepting bribes in return for political favors in the Credit Mobilier scandal. At a deeply divided Democratic convention (11th) in Baltimore, New York Tribune publisher Horace Greeley - who had been elected the Reform candidate at the breakaway Liberal Republican convention in Cincinnati - was transformed into a Democrat and elected the nominee for President on the 1st ballot; Missouri Governor Benjamin Gratz Brown, also a nominee from Cincinnati, was chosen the nominee for Vice President. In November, the Grant/Wilson ticket won easily over the divided Democratic Party candidates: Horace Greeley (official Democratic Party nominee), Charles O'Connor (Straight Democrat), Thomas A. Hendricks (Indiana Democrat), B. Gratz Brown (Democrat), Charles J. Jenkins (Democrat), and David Davis (Democrat); with the untimely demise of Horace Greeley late in November, the vote of Arkansas and Louisiana and part of Georgia representing 17 electoral votes were withheld in the election. Pre-empting suffrage by 48 years Susan B. Anthony defied the law and voted in a New York election. Mail order service was originated by Montgomery Wards & Company. Popular Science, founded by Edward L. Youmans to increase interest in science, was published for the first time. The great Apache leader Cochise surrendered to U.S. troops.

The Credit Mobilier scandal erupted when it was revealed that Union Pacific officials including founder Thomas C. Durant had established a sham construction company and distributed the stock to Company insiders and influence-peddling Congressmen; kickbacks arrived in the form of stock dividends. After almost 3 ½ years of work, the Union Pacific completed its Missouri River bridge connecting Omaha and Council Bluffs in March; now one could take the train from east to west without being ferried across the river. Built largely on the backs of Civil War veterans, the Atchison and Topeka Railroad reached the Colorado border, one year ahead of schedule; its arrival in Colorado set it in competition with the two-year old Denver & Rio Grande, particularly for rights to mountain crossings through the lofty Raton Pass and up the Grand Canyon of the Arkansas (Royal Gorge). 35-year old Marvin Hughitt, an Illinois Central trainmaster at Centralia during the Civil War, began a 55-year association with the Chicago & Northwestern, where he would help cobble together some 200 smaller roads into the C&NW System.

Elizabethtown & Paducah completed spanning the named points, with a spur to Louisville built two years later; eventually all was absorbed by Collis P. Huntington's Chesapeake, Ohio & Southwestern. Illinois Central commuter service trains reached south all the way to Kensington, 115th Street, and a new downtown station was built at Van Buren Street. Revenues for the year dropped to less than $8.1 million, 22 percent of which was attributable to passenger service; 1,352,156 passengers were carried, 382,900 of which were commuters moving between Chicago and Hyde Park at approximately 10 cents per ride. The decline in business levels was caused by two factors, the inadequate supply of Great Lakes vessels and lack of elevator space in the Chicago terminal, both areas Illinois Central would address during the year. First was the tightening supply of Great Lakes vessels caused by increased ore shipments to Ohio and Pennsylvania mills: to partially alleviate it's dependence on the Great Lakes as a conduit for Chicago terminal business, the Company was determined to access another outlet, and it looked south to New Orleans; work began on a freight transfer and car ferry facility in Cairo to facilitate freight interchange between the Illinois Central and the Mississippi Central, along with its sister railroad the New Orleans, Jackson & Great Northern, both controlled by Henry S. McComb; a contract was signed between the companies calling for the Mississippi Central to complete construction 22 miles north from its terminus to East Cairo, Kentucky on the south side of the Ohio river; this joint operation would compete with the current rail/river combination and would directly access New Orleans for the first time via an all-rail route from Chicago; with five steamship lines serving the New Orleans to Europe corridor, it was felt that Illinois/Iowa grain could be exported to Europe faster and cheaper via an all-rail route through New Orleans than a rail/lake/canal route through the Atlantic Seaboard. The second factor that weighed heavily on revenues was the lack of elevator space at the Chicago terminal's sole remaining grain warehouse: by the end of the year Elevator "A" was rebuilt, out of the ashes of the Chicago Fire, with a capacity of one million

IC1896-05

Illinois Central #294 was an engine that went from Tinkers to Evans to Chance; originally Pennsylvania G1a-class engine #845, it was acquired by the Indiana & Illinois Southern and renumbered to I&IS #16; later a part of the St. Louis Indianapolis & Eastern, it fell under Illinois Central control and was renumbered IC #294. A Baldwin-built (51 D; 75,800 TW; 18,777 TF) 4-6-0 of 1872, this engine saw service until retired in 1914. This picture dates to 1901, and was published in the October, 1923 issue of the Illinois Central Magazine. Identified in the picture were E.C. Donoghue (engineer) and James Grady (fireman).

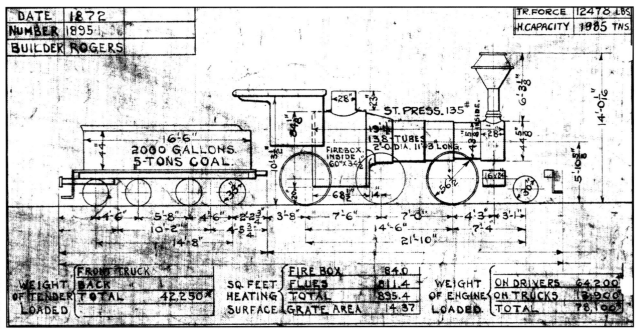

IC1999-27

Illinois Central received its first 2-6-0 Mogul-type engines in 1872; they were Rogers-built engines IC #194 and #195, later renumbered IC #895/896 and, finally, IC #1895/1896. The equipment diagram above shows the facts and figures for these first units (56 1/2 D; 78,100 TW; 12,478 TF).

bushels, giving the Chicago terminal 2.75 million bushel capacity. Revenue traffic rose to more than 2.0 million tons of freight. With the sale of 41,677 land grant acres for almost $340,000 (average $8.08 per acre) the balance available from the original 2.6 million acres dropped to 344,367; the current year's sales were to 850 purchasers with an average tract size of almost 72 acres. The Company paid stockholders their eighth consecutive annual dividend exceeding $2.2 million. With the purchase of four new locomotives, two of which were the Company's first 2-6-0 Mogul-type engines, the Illinois Central roster rose to 197 units, mostly coal-burning 4-4-0 American-types. System mileage remained at 1,107, almost 706 miles in Illinois and the rest in Iowa.

1873

51-year old French chemist Louis Pasteur received a patent (#135,245) for a sterilization process in making beer, later named pasteurization. Prince Edward Island was added as a Province of the Dominion of Canada. The North West Mounted Police, the forerunner to the Royal Canadian Mounted Police, was formed in Canada.

In March 50-year old Ulysses S. Grant was sworn in for his 2nd Term as President of the U.S. Sinking a cable (like his father's patented wire rope) beneath the street, 37-year old Andrew S. Hallidie began operating his cable car system in San Francisco, the Clay Street Hill Railroad cable car that operated over Nob Hill.

In September Civil War financier Jay Cooke's effort to develop the Northern Pacific charter of some 39 million acres under the federal land grant program ended with the bankruptcy of his brokerage firm, the leading American banking company; the resulting failure of a few banks ignited the Panic of 1873; the shock caused a ten-day shutdown of the New York Stock Exchange, many railroad companies to teeter toward bankruptcy and the worst recession in memory followed by a monetary contraction. Congress investigated Credit Mobilier, a financial kickback scheme with the Union Pacific construction company building the transcontinental rail line; political personages such as past, present and future Vice Presidents Colfax, Wilson and Morton, House Speaker Blaine and future President Garfield were dragged into the fray; Henry S. McComb, while a small player, was an early investor in Credit Mobilier. The Southern Pacific/Central Pacific moved its headquarters from Sacramento to San Francisco. Railroad worker and living legend "Big John" Henry, the "steel drivin' man", worked on the Chesapeake & Ohio's Big Bend Tunnel near Talcott, West Virginia; legend and ballad claim he breathed his last proving a man could beat a machine (steam drill). On gaining ownership of the Lake Shore & Michigan Southern and control of the Michigan Central, the Vanderbilt's New York Central offered the first single-system train service between New York and Chicago, albeit neither direct nor non-stop. Armed construction gangs faced each other for the rights to build across the 8,000-foot Raton Pass, the Atchison and Topeka getting the better of the Denver & Rio Grande; it would be five years before the Atchison and Topeka would drive a train through the Pass to reach New Mexico.

Illinois Central rolled out its first Sunday suburban passenger train. With high levels of traffic during the first 9 months of the year, Illinois Central prepared for large increases during the fourth quarter as the harvest proved abundant; but the financial Panic of 1873 would change that perspective, causing a severe fall off during the last three months; since the Company paid its ninth consecutive annual dividend exceeding $2.2 million before the bottom dropped out of the markets, Illinois Central was stretched financially, but escaped insolvency. Revenue traffic rose slightly to just under 2.1 million tons of freight. Illinois Central booked $8.3 million in revenues during the year, the first rise after three years of diminishing results; a little over 20 percent of revenues were generated by 1,472,005 passengers, of which 487,319 were commuters moving among Chicago, Hyde Park and Grand Crossing. The Land department sold 23,580 acres to 535 purchasers for almost $205,000, an average of $8.62 per acre on the average tract of 44 acres; 325,171 acres remained from the original Land Grant. Illinois Central completed the rebuilding of its Illinois River bridge at LaSalle, changing it over from wood to iron; the bridge was 2,883 feet long and would serve as practice for what would come 16 years later in crossing the much broader Ohio River at Cairo. Illinois Central instituted through rail service from Chicago to New Orleans as it finished its freight transfer and car ferry facility at Cairo, and the Mississippi Central completed its line north to Fillmore, Kentucky two miles short of East Cairo and just across the Ohio river; service began the day before Christmas, as cars and passengers were ferried across the Ohio River from the Illinois side to the Kentucky side by means of a brand new 200' long double-track first-class steamer with the capacity for six passenger cars or twelve freight cars; ferry service would last to 1889. Since the track gauge on the Mississippi Central was 5 feet (broad gauge) and the Illinois Central's was 4' 8 ½" (standard gauge), each car transferred between the railroads had to have its wheel sets changed out, or the lading transferred between cars. During the year, Illinois Central built 40 new boxcars and modified 10 others to allow for the wheel set change-out, and constructed three sets of 6-wheel broad gauge trucks to be used under the Company's passenger sleeper cars intended for through service to New Orleans. As grain and other freight began using this corridor, Illinois Central proved to have a viable alternative to the Great Lakes route and also offered competition to the Eastern carriers such as the Pennsylvania and New York Central that had built line extensions west into Illinois and now moved traffic directly from interior Illinois points to the Atlantic. During the year Illinois Central renewed rail at various points along its corridors; almost 68 miles of rail now had been renewed since 1871 with steel replacing

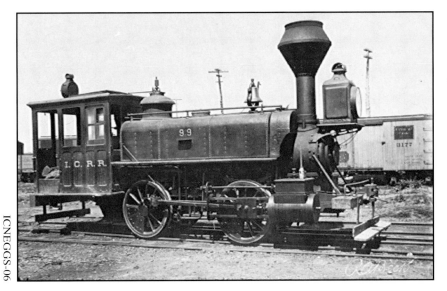

Grant-built in 1873 for the Chicago St. Louis & New Orleans (#11), Illinois Central #99 was an 0-4-0 switch engine (48 D; 54,600 TW); this R.A. Beck photo dates between 1890 and 1898.

Illinois Central #1156 was a Rogers-built 4-4-0 American (56 D; 64,000 TW), this unit also built for the CStL&NO (#88) in 1873. This picture was captured at Water Valley, Mississippi between 1890 and 1899; it was published in the May, 1950 issue of the Illinois Central Magazine.

ICNEGGS-06

IC45x35-73

the original iron; another 230 miles were scheduled for renewal in steel over the next three years. System mileage remained at a little over 1,107. Illinois Central's locomotive roster remained at 197, the same as the prior year. With no track extensions, system mileage remained at a just over 1,107, with almost 706 of those in Illinois.

IC1873-01

Illinois Central #1312 was an 1873 Rogers-built 4-4-0 American (63 D; 64,000 TW; 10,362 TF); as new #82 for the Chicago St. Louis & New Orleans, the Illinois Central gained ownership in 1882. The picture dates to 1902 and was snapped at Brilliant, Alabama on the Illinois Central's "Orphan Line". The five men in the picture were identified as, left to right, R.E. Moore (engineer), A.L. Stevens (conductor), Mr. Hill (brakeman), Ellis Parker (fireman, astride car), and George W. McDonald (flagman, on ground).

IC1870-04

Taunton-built in 1870, this 4-4-0 American-type was owned by the Belleville & Southern Illinois division of the St. Louis Alton & Terre Haute. B&SI #11 (65 D; 66,900 TW) supposedly was the first engine to cross the Eads bridge in St. Louis, and the picture here is said to be a view of the engine decorated for just such crossing.

1874

Winston Churchill (England) and Ehrich Weiss (Hungary) are born; one would become a statesman and world leader, the other would make watching him wiggle out of tight places a national pastime, as Houdini.

49-year old American inventor Christopher L. Sholes with Carlos Glidden and Samuel Soule collaborated to invent the forerunner to the typewriter in 1868 (patent # 79,265); Philo Remington, a New York gun manufacturer looking for new products after the Civil War, helped design a practical version, and manufactured and sold the Remington No. 1 typewriter with the familiar QWERTY keyboard of Sholes. Blue jeans with copper rivets at stress points appeared for the first time thanks to 45-year old Levi Strauss; they were made of a durable French fabric called serge de Nimes, or denim for short. 61-year old farmer Joseph F. Glidden patented (#157,124) his version of barbed wire; while not the first, his concept became the standard and helped tame the prairies of America. The Women's Christian Temperance Union began its fight against liquor. American engineer 54-year old James B. Eads completed the first bridge at St. Louis across the Mississippi River; the first train across is led by Belleville & Southern Illinois engine #11, an Illinois Central predecessor railroad. Gold was discovered in the Black Hills of Dakota Territory, setting off yet another rush, which would swell the population over the next two years.

Building from Sandusky, the Baltimore & Ohio Railroad reached Chicago, spanning some 800 miles from Baltimore. Shady financier Jay Gould, having been run out of the Eastern railroad establishment, gained control of the Union Pacific; before finished he would have power over rail carriers that controlled almost one-half of the nation's rail trackage.

Effective September 11th 70-some year old Wilson G. Hunt was elected the 7th President of the Illinois Central; he would serve until January 28, 1875. Illinois Central invested in the mortgage bonds of the New Orleans, Jackson & Great Northern and the Mississippi Central railroads, hedging its bet on the Chicago to New Orleans corridor; Illinois Central would force those carriers into receivership two years later and gain control of operations. Land sales saw 34,523 acres put under contract for a total of $267,652, less than 300,000 Land Grant acres remained in inventory. Revenue traffic steadied at just under 2.1 million tons of freight. Total revenues for the year, down from the prior year's because of the lingering effects of the Financial Panic, still exceeded $7.9 million; roughly 21 percent of revenues were attributable to passenger traffic (1,586,637 passengers). Even with the decline in revenues, Illinois Central was able to pay a substantial annual dividend to stockholders, just under $2.2 million. Having sold one engine, Illinois Central's roster dropped to 196 units. System mileage remained at 1,107, with some 706 miles in Illinois.

1875

37-year old French-born Paul-Emile de Boisbaudran discovered the element Gallium, the first of three new elements predicted to exist by Dmitri I. Mendeleev's periodic table four years earlier. Command of the Suez Canal passed from French-Egyptian to British, with England's purchase of a controlling share of stock; the British Empire would station troops in the Suez seven years later to protect its interests, and would remain there for 74 years. 37-year old Georges Bizet composed his four-act opera about the cigarette girl *Carmen*, Bizet died during the opera's first season.

President Ulysses S. Grant's administration became mired in scandal with exposure of the Whiskey Ring, a number of distillers and Federal officials diverting tax revenues to their own uses. Toward the end of the year with the death of Andrew Johnson, President Grant became only the second Chief Executive to hold office with no living ex-President (John Adam's administration 75 years earlier was the first). In March the Roman Catholic Church named its first American Cardinal – John McClosky of New York. The Kentucky Derby was held for the first time, *Aristides* was the winner; Colonel M. Lewis Clark had built a track and named it after the people from whom he bought the land, the Churchill Brothers.

Opened in February by the Troy & Greenfield railroad (eventually, Boston & Maine) with the first train movement after construction on and off since 1851, the Hoosac Tunnel in Massachusetts under the Berkshires was the first major railroad tunnel in the U.S., at a little over 4½ miles in length. The Atlantic & Pacific effort to build a transcontinental line went bankrupt after reaching St. Louis

Effective January 28th 56-year old John M. Douglas was re-elected President of the Illinois Central; this was Douglas' second term in office, as he had been the 5th President when elected in 1865, and his second term would last until October 17, 1877. With competition from other carriers serving the Illinois grain market coupled with overall depressed business levels, Illinois Central booked a second consecutive year of lower revenues – just over $7.8 million; passenger traffic (1,648,541 passengers) accounted for 21 percent of total revenues. Revenue traffic barely reached 2.0 million tons of freight. Illinois Central paid annual dividends exceeding $2.3 million during the year. With the price of steel rails down by 50 percent, Illinois Central stocked up for the future, placing 12,000 tons in inventory. With business to New Orleans growing, a double-track barge was built to handle an additional ten freight cars each crossing in ferry service at Cairo. System trackage renewed with steel replacing the original iron rose to a cumulative 218 miles. Having sold one unit and scrapped another, Illinois Central's locomotive roster rose to 202 with the net addition of eight units, 5 new 4-4-0 American-type freight engines built by Brooks Locomotive Works and three used Hinkley Locomotive Works 0-6-0 switching units. System mileage remained at slightly over 1,107, roughly 706 miles in Illinois.

IC1875-01

Illinois Central #124 was a 4-4-0 American-type. It is thought that this engine was originally built by Norris in 1865 with 60-inch drivers, and totally rebuilt with 65-inch drivers at Illinois Central shops in 1875. It was pictured here at Sioux Falls, South Dakota in 1888.

IC1875-04

Illinois Central #199 was an 0-6-0 switch engine built by Hinkley (48 D; 62,000 TW) in 1875. It was constructed for the Chicago Danville & Vincennes as CD&V #74; Illinois Central renumbered the unit to IC #199 in 1890, then IC #1567 in 1898. The picture dates 1890 to 1898, and was captured by R.A. Beck on the Chicago Lake Front.

IC45x35-72

IC1875-03

IC1875-02

A trio of Brooks-built 4-4-0 Americans, quite possibly R.A. Beck photographs, all appear to be posed on the Chicago Lake Front circa 1892. On top, Illinois Central #1151 was constructed as IC #199, renumbered as shown in 1890, and one last time in 1912 (IC #2151). The middle photograph shows IC #1303, originally IC #201, and later IC #1325. Bottom picture exhibits IC #1304, originally IC #202. The two bottom engines were mirrors of each other when built (60 D; 66,000 TW). Note the engine in the middle has a shorter smoke-box and balances the headlamp on armatures, while the other two units (probably rebuilt) have different headlamp and smokestack configurations.

1876

In March 29-year old Scottish-born American inventor Alexander Graham Bell telephoned his assistant Thomas A. Watson in the next room and founded a new industry; Bell beat Elisha Gray to the U.S. Patent Office with this invention by only a few hours; Bell originally was trying to invent a hearing aid. In June Lieutenant Colonel (brevet Brigadier General at age 23 in the Civil War) 36-year old George Armstrong Custer and his Seventh Cavalry regiment (264 men) made a stand at Little Big Horn in Montana Territory against followers of Sioux Chiefs Sitting Bull (Lakota) and Crazy Horse (Oglala). Such was the time of America in transition, celebrating its centennial in the east, while Custer was scalped in the west. The Sioux victory was short lived, as both Sitting Bull and Crazy Horse would be forced into submission later in the year. Melvin R. Bissell of Grand Rapids, Michigan improvised enough improvements to make the first practical carpet sweeper. In order to distance itself from the corruption of the Grant administration, the 6th Republican convention in Cincinnati selected Ohio Governor Rutherford B. Hayes (Major General during the Civil War) the nominee for President on the 7th ballot; New York Congressman William A. Wheeler was chosen the nominee for Vice President on the 1st ballot. At the 12th Democratic convention in St. Louis, New York Governor Samuel J. Tilden was elected the nominee for President on the 2nd ballot; Indiana Governor Hendricks was chosen the nominee for Vice President on the 1st ballot. In November with both sides claiming election irregularities, the election was too close to be made official. Samuel L. Clemens published *The Adventures of Tom Sawyer*, under the pseudonym Mark Twain. America's Centennial Exposition opened in Philadelphia, celebrating 100 years since the Declaration of Independence; this Exposition competed with 1853's New York Exhibition for title to the first world's fair held in the United States; the typewriter was introduced at the Exposition, and Bell demonstrated his telephone. Colorado was admitted to the Union as the 38th State. Milton S. Hershey started in the candy business. In January, breakaway teams from the National Association of Base-Ball Players formed the National League of Professional Base Ball Clubs; the defection was led by William Ambrose Hulbert, owner of the Chicago White Stockings (renamed Chicago Cubs in 1898), and future sporting goods magnate Albert G. Spaulding, who managed and pitched on the team; the White Stockings won the pennant that first year. Baltimore's John Hopkins University opened its doors.

Tilden was considered a "railroad lawyer" when that term was used as a pejorative, for his practice had been involved in a number of railroad reorganizations and he had been on the Boards of other rail companies. The St. Louis and San Francisco Railway (FRISCO) assumed the assets of the failed Atlantic & Pacific Railroad; Jay Gould and Collis P. Huntington owned a controlling interest. The Southern Pacific completed its line connecting San Francisco in the north with Los Angeles in the south, uniting California.

IC's 25th anniversary. The year would prove to be a pivotal one for the Illinois Central. With restrictive legislation forcing lower rates on the leased lines coupled with a failed wheat crop in Iowa and untimely rain in the Illinois corn fields, the Company reported its third consecutive revenue decline, to just under $7.1 million; 23 percent of revenues were accounted for by 1,815,788 passengers. Revenue traffic dipped to just under 1.9 million tons of freight. While the bulk of central Illinois grain traditionally moved via rail to Chicago and thence via the Great Lakes and canals to the eastern seaboard, a growing portion now moved east on all-rail routes of the Baltimore & Ohio, the Pennsylvania and the New York Central; Illinois Central's Chicago terminal handled just under 11 million bushels of grain and over 90 million board feet of lumber, both numbers in decline; business south via Cairo continued to grow, having quadrupled to almost $600,000 since 1873; the Company discerned its future and set course on two fronts. On one front, having invested some $5.0 million in the mortgage bonds of the Mississippi Central and its sister the New Orleans, Jackson and Great Northern, the Illinois Central forced those carriers into receivership in March when they missed interest payments, and the Company positioned itself to gain outright ownership of the southern connections, planning to buy the failed mortgage bonds from the Trustee. On the second front, in November Illinois Central began looking at 25 failed or near bankrupt carriers in Illinois that operated some 3,000 miles of track, much adjacent to or extensions of Illinois Central's core lines; with an eye toward bargain-priced acquisitions, the Company began a study of this smorgasbord of opportunity. With dividends declared and paid before the autumn falloff in business, over $2.3 million in dividends went to shareholders during the year. The Company's locomotive roster remained the same, 202 units. With only groundwork laid for the future, system mileage remained at slightly over 1,107 with roughly 706 of those in Illinois. By year's end, the cumulative mileage changed over to steel from iron had risen to a little over 352 miles of track. Taking effect in July, Illinois Central signed its first formal agreement with labor, setting out a schedule of wages for Locomotive Engineers and Firemen; over the years numerous labor agreements with operating and non-operating organizations would be inked, such as: Boilermakers, Sleeping Car Porters, Yardmasters, Telegraphers, Ushers, Signalmen, Patrolmen, Conductors, Maintenance of Way Employees, Carmen, Firemen and Oilers, Engineers, Dispatchers, Blacksmiths, Clerks, Dining Car Employees, Firemen, Sheet Metal Workers, Electrical Workers, Machinists, and other crafts and groups.

ILLINOIS CENTRAL RAILROAD COMPANY.

REPORT OF THE DIRECTORS TO THE SHAREHOLDERS.

The results of working your property for the year 1876, have been affected by three causes:

First. Restrictive legislation, and the failure of the wheat harvest in Iowa.

Second. The serious injury to the corn crop of Illinois, by the copious rains of July.

Third. The competition of the Trunk Lines in extending their contest for Western business, to points upon and West of your road.

The general business of the country is still suffering from the evils of an irredeemable currency. The shrinkage of values of every description of property increases, as the value of the currency approximates to the gold standard. There has been a wide-spread feeling that legislation might find a cure for this, and hence the Legislatures of some of the States have adopted measures, which are not only restrictive, but fatal to commercial enterprise, and from which no benefit has been derived by the people.

These remarks apply with special force to Railways, which can only be kept in existence by continued expenditures of money. The legislation of the State of Iowa, affecting our Company from the lease of the Iowa Lines, compelled a reduction of 25 to 40 per cent. from the tariff in force in Iowa prior to our submission to the Law. This came at a most unfortunate season, when we were suffering from a bad harvest and consequent short crops. The average production of wheat in Northern Iowa last year, was four to six bushels per acre. Thus, the volume of traffic diminished, while the compensation was also reduced.

Unless sounder opinions prevail, and protection is afforded to the Railways in Iowa, it will not be long before we shall witness applications to the Legislature for appropriations to assist some of the Railways to continue operations in order to secure means of transportation for the agricultural products of the regions traversed by them.

ICLAG21-08

Copied from the 1876 Directors Report to the Shareholders, the Company celebrated its 25th Anniversary with poor results, increased competition and an anti-business, especially railroad business, climate in Iowa.

1877

Russia declared war on Turkey, ostensibly to help solve a dispute between Serbia and Turkey. England's two party leaders, Liberal William E. Gladstone and Conservative Benjamin Disraeli, continued to spar over Irish grievances; Gladstone would push for Free State status 9 years later, roughly 35 years ahead of its time.

Beginning in January Congress busied itself with settling the Hayes/Tilden election, vote totals and the qualifications of electors being challenged in various States; lawsuits, counter suits and filibusters all contributed to an agonizingly slow decision process. As the March inauguration approached, a settlement had to be negotiated between the two National Parties to elect someone. In the end the Hayes-Tilden Compromise shifted enough electoral votes to give Rutherford B. Hayes the Presidency in return for the withdrawal of occupation troops from the South and yielding control of three southern states to the Democrats – essentially ending the period of Reconstruction. The election would officially go down as 185 electoral votes for Hayes and 184 electoral votes for Tilden; Tilden had actually won the popular vote total. In March 54-year old Rutherford B. Hayes was sworn in as the 19th President of the United States. US Army occupation forces recalled from the southern states. The great Sioux war chief Crazy Horse died at Fort Robinson, Nebraska. Georgia-born Henry O. Flipper became the first black man to graduate West Point Military Academy; it would be 103 more years for the first woman.

In February the locomotive engineers and firemen of the Boston and Maine Railroad went on strike against pay cuts and work rule changes; spreading to the Baltimore & Ohio, Pennsylvania Railroad and others, it ended up being called the Great Railroad Strike of 1877. The Pennsylvania Railroad, which had enjoyed some 65% of Standard Oil business (the New York Central, Erie and Baltimore & Ohio sharing the remainder) had lost it because it tried to compete with John D. Rockefeller/Henry M. Flagler; the 1877 Panic pushed the weakened Pennsylvania Railroad over the edge and the Pennsylvania had to negotiate a costly truce with Standard Oil, regaining 47% of the business but granting significant concessions. The negotiations/concessions left Standard Oil with its monopoly of oil production and oil transportation in the East. Gustavus F. Swift introduced wet-ice refrigerator cars, using ideas patented by Chicagoan Joel Tiffany, and pioneered rail shipments of fresh meat. Commodore Cornelius Vanderbilt, first a ferry and steamship magnate and then of New York Central Railroad fame, passed away at age 83. Jay Gould continued his worrisome ways and gained control of the Texas Pacific Railroad. English-born 42-year old Frederick H. Harvey, utilizing his restaurant experience gained in St. Louis and Kansas, opened the first Harvey House in Topeka, Kansas on the Santa Fe Railway.

Effective October 17th 45-year old William K. Ackerman, with 25 years of Company service, was elected the 8th President of the Illinois Central; he would serve until August 15, 1883. While ripples of the Great Railroad Strike were felt in the Chicago area, the Illinois Central was largely untouched by the labor strife. With the falloff in business the prior year and with similar prospects for the current year, the Company cutback spending, lowering Maintenance of Way expenditures alone over $400,000; shareholder dividends were cut in half for the year, less than $1.2 million being paid out; the retrenchment strategy proved prescient in that revenues fell for the fourth year in a row, to just under $6.7 million. A little over 21 percent of revenues were attributable to passenger traffic (1,711,398 passengers). Revenue traffic dropped to just over 1.8 million tons of freight; business south via the Cairo gateway grew for the fifth consecutive year. With its first expansion in seven years, Illinois Central took effective control of the financially troubled former Gilman, Clinton & Springfield Railroad which dated back to 1867, connecting Gilman on the Chicago Division and the State Capital Springfield via Clinton on the mainline; with this rail link - the Springfield Division - the Illinois Central realized a desire first verbalized back in 1857 when the Master of Transportation noted that linking the upper ends of the "Y"-shaped system would bring measurable operating benefits to the Company; historically the connection was over the Toledo, Peoria and Warsaw railroad, but foreclosure efforts saw it looking to join the competing Wabash railway; with the impetus of Illinois Central's bankers pressuring it to help rescue floundering foreign bondholders, Illinois Central acted to protect its Gilman gateway. Since these 112 miles would not be consolidated into the Illinois Central structure until the following year, reported system mileage remained at slightly over 1,107 with some 706 miles of the total in Illinois. With final decrees issued by the Courts late in the year, the Illinois Central also gained effective control of the former Mississippi Central and New Orleans, Jackson & Great Northern properties, and would begin operating them on an unconsolidated basis as the Chicago, St. Louis and New Orleans at the start of the new year; formal possession with the Illinois Central as lessee would follow in 1882, with reporting on a consolidated basis the next year. The locomotive roster rose to 212, with the net addition of ten leased units from the Gilman, Clinton & Springfield railroad; nine were 4-4-0 American-types and the tenth would be Illinois Central's first 4-6-0 ten-wheeler (built 1871), all products of Baldwin Locomotive Works; through succeeding Company reports this ten-wheeler was confusingly referred to as either a ten-wheeler or a 10-wheel switch engine; while it was undoubtedly the former, since it was an older light ten-wheeler, it was probably used as the latter. Cumulative system trackage renewed with steel replacing iron rails rose to 375. Majority ownership of the capital stock of Illinois Central still lay in Europe: Great Britain and Holland having over 80 percent; control would remain in Europe until the 1890's.

ILLINOIS CENTRAL RAILROAD.

FREIGHT TARIFF

To take Effect October 1, 1878.

This Tariff succeeds all others.   The Company reserves the right to make, at its pleasure, any change in the Rates or Classification.

HENRY L. SHUTE,
Ass't Gen'l Freight Agent,
CHICAGO, ILLINOIS.

HORACE TUCKER,
Gen'l Freight Agent,
CHICAGO, ILLINOIS.

JOSEPH F. TUCKER,
Traffic Manager,
CHICAGO, ILLINOIS.

ICLAG21-05

1878

With July's Treaty of Berlin taking away some of the territory Russia gained in March's Treaty of San Stefano, Turkey received its comeuppance, while Serbia and Romania gained independence and a measure of autonomy, a least for a while. 46-year old British scientist William Crookes built a glass tube and sent an electric current through a vacuum to investigate cathode rays, and the forerunner to the CRT or television tube was invented.

31-year old Thomas Edison received patent #200,521 on the *Phonograph or Speaking Machine*, which he developed the prior year in his research laboratory/converted barn in Menlo Park, New Jersey; he sold his patents for $10,000 plus a royalty and turned his attentions to other interests. Proctor & Gamble shipped out a bad batch of a white soap, and inadvertently developed a soap that floats - Ivory Soap. The *St. Louis Post-Dispatch* was formed by the merger of two papers by Hungarian immigrant Joseph Pulitzer, the beginning of a publishing empire; Pulitzer Prizes lay 33 years away. Pope Pius IX died in Rome, having led the Church for 32 years, longer than any other; 61 Cardinals assembled and elected 68-year old Gioacchino Vincenzo Raffaele Luigi to replace him; the new Pope took the name Leo XIII and would lead the Church for 25 years.

Canadians George Stephen, Donald A. Smith, R.B. Angus and James J. Hill acquired the Saint Paul and Pacific Railway from its Dutch owners and later renamed it the Saint Paul, Minneapolis and Manitoba Railroad, the forerunner to the Great Northern Railway; all four men became millionaires and would participate in founding the Canadian Pacific Railway three years in the future. Jay Cooke's bankrupt Northern Pacific was reorganized with new owners led by 55-year old Frederick Billings for another effort to develop a railroad from Lake Superior to Puget Sound using some 39 million acres under the federal land grant program. Vanderbilt's New York Central Railroad finally gained complete access to Chicago all the way from New York City, the "Water Level Route" was created. Having suffered irreversibly from the Jim Fisk/Jay Gould/Daniel Drew brand of management, the Erie Railroad was reorganized once again, this time as the New York, Lake Erie and Western Railroad; on bankruptcy three years earlier (its second), it had been auctioned off for $6 million to former New York governor Edwin Morgan; the latest version of the Erie would last for 17 years.

Showing the first rise in revenues in five years, Illinois Central booked a little over $7.1 million; just under 20 percent of revenues were passenger traffic (1,725,236 passengers). With low rates on the Erie Canal and Great Lakes, business volumes were attracted across the Chicago terminal, rather than via all rail routes from the Illinois interior to the Atlantic Seaboard; the Chicago terminal alone handled upwards of 15 million bushels of grain, almost double the prior year. Overall revenue traffic jumped to just under 2.1 million tons of freight. With no additions, Illinois Central's locomotive fleet remained at 212 units; cumulative track miles renewed with steel replacing iron rails rose to 466. As an entrée to another link between its mainline and the Chicago Division, Illinois Central constructed a 37-mile branch line from Otto, just south of Kankakee, south and west to Chatsworth; the Company used iron rails salvaged from the main line renewal over to steel on this new branch – the Kankakee & South Western, dubbed the Middle Division. To enhance the north-south interchange of traffic at the Ohio river crossing, Illinois Central extended the southern lines it controlled through the Chicago, St. Louis and New Orleans from Fillmore, Kentucky a little over 3 miles to East Cairo on the south side of the river facing Illinois Central's terminal at Cairo, Illinois; this extension would cut the transit time from New Orleans to East Cairo by five hours; the Chicago, St. Louis and New Orleans held ownership of the bankrupt Mississippi Central (nee 1855), the Mississippi Central & Tennessee (nee 1856), the New Orleans, Jackson & Great Northern (nee 1858) and the New Orleans, St. Louis & Chicago (nee 1874) properties. Adding the 112 miles of Gilman, Clinton & Springfield track and the 37-mile branch line built out of Otto to the system raised the total to almost 1,256 miles, roughly 855 in Illinois with the rest in Iowa. With an outbreak of yellow fever moving up the Mississippi to Cairo, quarantines were established virtually suspending passenger traffic from the South for a time.

1879

39-year old Swedish-born Lars F. Nilson discovered the element scandium, the second of three new elements predicted to exist by Dmitri I. Mendeleev's periodic table in 1871. The elements thulium, holmium and samarium also were discovered.

On his second try at creating a discount shopping store, 27-year old Frank W. Woolworth opened his successful five and dime store, in Lancaster, Pennsylvania. American Thomas A. Edison and Englishman Joseph W. Swan created a practical incandescent lamp independent of each other. The first cash register was invented by Dayton, Ohio restaurant owner James J. Ritty. The first off-reservation residential school for Indians was opened in Carlisle, Pennsylvania; the United States Indian Training and Industrial School would gain fame over 30 years later with a student named Jim Thorpe. Mary Baker Eddy established the Christian Science Church in Boston.

James J. Hill's railroad built a line north to the Canadian border. It was a very good year for railroad pirate Jay Gould; he gained control of the Kansas Pacific, Missouri Pacific, Western Pacific and Denver Pacific properties during the year.

Havana, Rantoul & Eastern Railroad, organized six years earlier, opened for operations in February; with name changes to the Rantoul Railroad and the Rantoul Narrow-Gauge, it would be folded into the Illinois Central eight years later. With a cumulative 543 miles of track now renewed with steel replacing iron, Illinois Central neared its goal of an all-steel roadway from Chicago to Cairo. The Middle Division spur line built from Otto to Chatsworth was extended in two places: almost 19 miles from Chatsworth to Anchor (the Kankakee & South Western heading for Normal Jct. 24 miles away), and 12 miles from the middle of the spur line (Saxony near Kempton) to Eylar (the Kankakee & Western on course for Minonk Jct. 32 miles away); the effect of these 31 miles was to raise system trackage to almost 1,287, roughly 886 in Illinois. With demand high, revenue traffic rose to over 2.3 million tons of freight; it was prosperous times for the country served by Illinois Central. The Company recorded revenues of over $7.2 million, 19 percent in passenger traffic (1,807,744 passengers). Illinois Central's locomotive roster remained at 212 units. The Company continued to operate, improve and rebuild the 550-mile long Southern Lines under its control of the Chicago, St. Louis and New Orleans railroad; Illinois Central re-laid track with steel replacing iron, ballasted roadbed and reduced grades, all with an eye to increase capacity and reduce operating expenses.

IC45x35-251

Illinois Central # 1303, and not the first IC 4-4-0 American to hold that number, was eased out of the Leroy, Illinois engine house onto the 52-foot long wooden gallows-style turntable on January 20, 1903 when this picture was captured. Originally IC #5, then IC #9, then IC #51, it was renumbered to IC #1132 in 1890, and IC #1303 in 1899. A product of the Illinois Central shops in 1879, it saw service until retirement in 1909.

ICLAG14-01

Illinois Central's first Van Buren Street station was built in 1879, right in the middle of Lake Park (future Grant Park) between Lake Michigan and Michigan Avenue, and all on street level. This photograph, which appeared in the January, 1937 issue of the Illinois Central Magazine, was snapped on April 27, 1896.

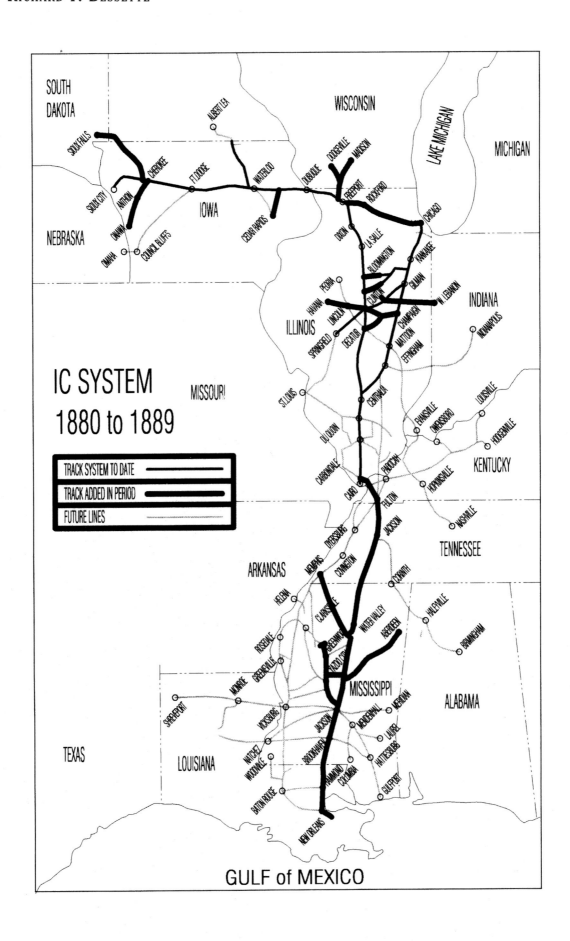

IC SYSTEM
1880 to 1889

TRACK SYSTEM TO DATE	———————
TRACK ADDED IN PERIOD	━━━━━━
FUTURE LINES	

GULF of MEXICO

1850's 1860's 1870's **1880's** 1890's 1900's 1910's 1920's 1930's 1940's

The Tenth Census of the U.S. population was taken; there were a little over 50 million people in the U.S., having grown 30 percent from the prior census; the country would add almost 13 million people by the end of the decade, over one-third through immigration. The Union grew by four States to a total of 42. This decade experienced a period of economic expansion in the U.S., the beginning of the 20-year industrial age that would encounter six recessions and six expansions. John D. Rockefeller formed his Standard Oil Trust; Andrew Carnegie assembled his steel empire encompassing iron ore to finished products - now called vertical integration. Indian Wars continued as the U.S. cavalry worked to tame the West: for example, Apache raids led by Geronimo, until his surrender in 1886.

E. H. Harriman and James J. Hill (Empire Builder of the Northwest) began their battles for control of the railroad industry, which would persist on-and-off for the next 30 years. Because railroads profited from heavy tonnage, they bent over backwards to secure the business of large shippers – including predatory pricing, rebates and other anti-competitive actions. 14-mph cable cars came to Chicago transportation in 1881; cable cars did away with 7-mph horse cars but were expensive, noisy and unreliable in winter; this iteration of transportation was gone by 1906. In 1880 the major line-haul rail carriers operated a little over 93,000 miles of railroad, a figure that would rise by 70,000 more miles by the end of the decade.

With the rapid growth of suburbs south of Chicago, Illinois Central's suburban service grew from 36 daily trains to 114 by the end of the decade.

GROWTH OF ILLINOIS CENTRAL RAILROAD BUSINESS

Year (1)	Tonnage (mil/tons)	Lumber (mil/bf)	Grain (mil/bus)	Coal (mil/tons)	FFV (mil/tons)	Cotton (mil/tons)	Aggregates (mil/tons)	Passengers Commuters	Miles/Fare
1880	2.7	174	27.6	.533	N/A	N/A	N/A	2,753,544 1,394,912	23/$0.58
1881	2.9	214	26.0	.655	N/A	N/A	N/A	4,008,047 2,537,141	20/$0.44
1882	2.9	192	26.7	.753	N/A	N/A	N/A	4,340,211 2,694,309	20/$0.47
1883	3.5	237	21.5	.817	.036	.124	N/A	4,354,033 2,376,466	26/$0.63
1884	3.4	192	19.9	.723	.044	.113	N/A	4,848,140 2,777,266	25/$0.57
1885	3.6	188	24.1	.868	.047	.120	N/A	5,312,759 3,347,613	24/$0.54
1886	4.1	195	30.0	.877	.046	.138	N/A	6,112,110 4,218,955	19/$0.41
1887	4.9	254	36.7	1.1	.064	.152	N/A	6,949,852 4,828,128	18/$0.40
1888	5.3	275	39.6	1.3	.098	.124	N/A	7,184,691 4,813,695	19/$0.40
1889	5.5	613,500*	1.0 mil*	1.1	.144	.148	.184	7,444,111 N/A	20/$0.41

FFV = Fresh Fruit & Vegetables Passengers/Commuters = Total Ridership, and Commuter Portion
Miles/Fare = Average Passenger Trip and Charge (1) Fiscal Year bf = Board Feet bus = Bushels
N/A = Data Not Available * = Reporting Measurement Changed to Tons

1880

21-year old French physicist Pierre Curie discovered the piezoelectric effect, where some substances, when subjected to pressure, produced electric charges. 40-year old Peter Tchaikovsky inked his flashy *1812 Overture*; commissioned to commemorate the 70th anniversary of Russia's victory over Napoleon, it premiered at the Moscow Exhibition two years later.

At the 7th Republican convention in Chicago, ex-President U. S. Grant had accumulated enough support to block anyone's nomination but not enough to gain it himself; to break the stalemate and to insure General Grant did not gain the nomination for a 3rd Term, Presidential aspirants Maine Senator James G. Blaine and Secretary of Treasury John Sherman (brother of William Tecumseh) from Ohio directed their support to Ohio Congressman and Civil War General James A. Garfield who was elected the nominee for President on the 36th ballot (Republican Party record); New York lawyer and Republican political activist Chester A. Arthur was chosen the nominee for Vice President by a worn out Convention. At the 13th Democratic convention in Cincinnati, Major General Winfield Scott Hancock of Pennsylvania was elected the nominee for President on the 3rd ballot; ex-Congressman William H. English of Indiana was chosen the nominee for Vice President. In November the Garfield/Arthur ticket won the election by a sizable margin of electoral votes but a slim margin in popular votes. In September 25-year old John Philip Sousa began leading the U.S. Marine Corps Band. Thomas Edison received patent #223,898 for *An Electric Lamp for the Giving of Light by Incandescence*, the light bulb. Former Civil War Union General Lew Wallace, now governor of New Mexico Territory, published *Ben-Hur*. 35-year old Sarah Bernhardt, one of the great actresses of her time, made her U.S. stage debut.

Canadian James J. Hill became an American citizen. Fraud and bribery was charged in the original Texas Pacific Railroad grant; Colonel Thomas A. Scott, President of the Texas Pacific, was accused of bribing Senators and Congressmen. The Denver & Rio Grande avenged its loss of the Raton Pass to the Atchison and Topeka, gaining exclusive rights through the Grand Canyon of the Arkansas – the Royal Gorge Canyon route through the mountains west of Pueblo.

George M. Pullman began his "model city" on a little over 4,000 acres of land around the Pullman rail car factory on the outskirts of Chicago in May; in response, Illinois Central extended commuter trains to reach the site and built a station dubbed Pullman with train service increased to 36-daily trains. Illinois Central began regular service of refrigerated boxcars of imported bananas from New Orleans to Chicago-St. Louis-Detroit-Cincinnati. Prosperity continued as Illinois Central revenues surged to over $8.3 million, just over 19 percent in passenger traffic (a record 2,753,544 passengers, 1,394,912 of which were commuters riding the Chicago, Hyde Park, Kensington line. While traffic via the Cairo gateway continued to grow, the Chicago terminal still reigned supreme with over 17 million bushels of grain and over 85 million board feet of lumber handled. Overall revenue traffic rose to more than 2.7 million tons of freight. Illinois Central's locomotive fleet climbed to 213 units with the addition of six new 2-6-0 Moguls and 4 new 4-4-0 Americans, all built in Company shops, filling in the roster for scrapped and worn out units; one Rogers-built 2-4-4T was purchased for commuter service, the first locomotive built expressly for commuter service (Rogers #213, IC #221). On its Middle Division, Illinois Central track gangs finished the last 31 miles of the Kankakee & Western branch line from Otto to Minonk Jct. via Saxony, and an additional 3 between Anchor and Colfax on the Kankakee & South Western segment. Illinois Central continued its operation of the 550-mile long Southern Lines with its controlling interest in the Chicago, St. Louis & New Orleans; with heavy capital improvements and rebuilding essentially the entire line over the last few years, transit time from Chicago to New Orleans was expected to drop to 36 hours even with the delays in changing gauge and crossing the Ohio river. Plans were underway on both of those fronts: resetting the track gauge on the Southern lines to the standard 4' 8 ½" and construction of a bridge over the Ohio river. System mileage grew to a little over 1,320 with the completed branch line, a bit over 918 miles located in Illinois and 402 miles in Iowa. Cumulatively, almost 660 miles of track had been re-laid with steel replacing the iron.

IC45x35-149

IC45x35-154

Illinois Central suburban 2-4-4T, an 1880 Rogers-built locomotive tailored for IC's commuter service; numbered IC #213 by Rogers for the Illinois Central on delivery in 1880, the engine was renumbered IC #221 in 1884, IC #201 in 1890, and finally IC #1401 in 1900. These four pictures highlight the history of the first suburban engine. Clockwise from upper left, the original Builder's Photo from Roger's Paterson, New Jersey plant; in service and as renumbered to IC #1401 sometime after 1900; refurbished and in a staged shot commemorating the first electric commuter train and the last steam run in 1926; lastly, as refurbished and renumbered yet again, back to IC #201, for exhibition at the Chicago Railroad Fair on July 7, 1948. The top picture was published in the July, 1926 issue of the Illinois Central Magazine; the third photograph was published in the October, 1933 issue. This engine (56 1/2 D; 140 BP; 107,600 TW; 11,862 TF) was sold in 1928 to the Rosenwald Industrial Museum, now called the Museum of Science and Industry.

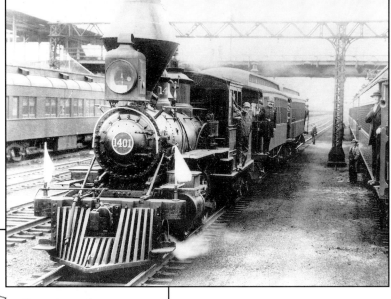

IC1880-04

IC1880-02

IC1880-03

Illinois Central #731 was a 2-6-0 Mogul (56 1/2 D; 95,900 TW) built at Company shops in 1880 as original IC #6; this engine saw roster numbers IC #466, IC #731 (1890), IC #1731 (1903), and IC #2731 (1915), before being scrapped in 1916. Pictured here, a previously published C.W. Witbeck photograph, between 1890 and 1903, it had been fitted with a snowplow for clearing the roadway. Illinois Central #1149, below, was an 1880 IC-built 4-4-0 American, originally rostered as IC #127; it was posed in a staged shot on Chicago's Lake Front circa 1890's.

IC45x35-54

IC1880-01

Baldwin-built in 1880 as St. Louis Alton & Terre Haute #5, it became Illinois Central #1401 in 1895, and then IC #1497. A 4-4-0 American (54 D; 62,000 TW; 10,246 TF), this engine saw service as an old pay car locomotive, and, as shown here, suburban unit (the sign on the engine states Grand Crossing). This photograph dates to 1897 on the Chicago Lake Front, and appeared in the July, 1937 issue of the Illinois Central Magazine. Identified in the picture was J.C. Leahan (engineer, on left); the fireman was not identified.

IC45x35-82

Illinois Central #1727 was a 2-6-0 Mogul-type (56 1/2 D; 95,900 TW) produced by the IC shops in 1880; originally IC #2, it was renumbered to IC #462, IC #727, and finally IC #1727; it was scrapped in 1914.

IC45x35-100

Illinois Central #1798 was a 2-6-0 Mogul built by Baldwin (52 D; 79,400 TW) in 1880 for the Paducah & Elizabethtown (P&E #18); after a stint with the Chesapeake Ohio & Southwestern, this engine came into Illinois Central ownership as IC #798 in 1896; it was renumbered IC #1798 in 1904, and scrapped in 1914.

1881

59-year old French chemist Louis Pasteur developed the anthrax vaccine, immunization by artificial means. French colonialists established a protectorate over Tunisia, the site of ancient Carthage, something they would battle for in World War II. Pablo Picasso was born in Spain.

In March 49-year old James A. Garfield was sworn in as the 20th President of the United States. President Garfield named his convention rival Maine Senator James G. Blaine Secretary of State. 120 days into his Term, President Garfield was shot as he passed through the Baltimore and Potomac Railroad depot in Washington, D.C. by a disgruntled office seeker, Charles Guiteau; the President struggled on for 11 weeks but lost his battle on September 19th. 50-year old Vice President Chester A. Arthur assumed the fallen President's office – becoming the 21st President of the U. S. Garfield was the fourth President to die in Office (Harrison, Taylor, Lincoln and Garfield), and the second to do so by assassination. In late March Phineas T. Barnum teamed up with James A. Bailey forming the forerunner to the Barnum & Bailey Circus. In May Clara Barton formed the American Red Cross in Washington, D.C.; she would be its president for the next 23 years. The Wild West still was: the shootout at O.K. Corral took place in Tombstone, Arizona when good guys Virgil and Wyatt Earp along with Doc Holliday outshot Billie Clanton and the McLowery Brothers; in July 21-year old William H. Bonney, nee Henry McCarty (Billy the Kid), was shot dead by Sheriff Pat Garrett in New Mexico. Typhoid fever felled more than 200,000 in Chicago; sewage in the Lake Michigan drinking water was the cause. 25-year old Booker T. Washington founded the Tuskegee Normal and Industrial Institute; George Washington Carver would join him 15 years later.

46-year old Henry Villard gained financial control of the Northern Pacific line and began extending it westward, heading for the coast. In February the Canadian Pacific Railway Company was created by government, and organized by: 51-year old Scotch-born Canadian émigré George Stephen (former President Bank of Montreal); 42-year old James J. Hill of St. Paul (who would gain fame with the Great Northern Railway); R.B. Angus (former General Manager Bank of Montreal); banker John Stewart Kennedy of New York (another Scottish immigrant); Duncan McIntyre (a Montreal investor); Kohn, Reinach & Company (a Paris investment house); and Morton, Rose & Company (a banking firm in London founded by Levi P. Morton); having run afoul of Canadian Prime Minister Macdonald, Stephen's cousin 60-year old Scotsman Donald Alexander Smith (President of the Hudson Bay Company) would be a silent investor. Illinois-born 38-year old William Cornelius Van Horne would be hired away from the Chicago, Milwaukee and St. Paul Railroad to be the Canadian Pacific's General Manager of Construction with the mandate to find a way through the mountains to the west coast; with the railroad committed to a southern route, American-born Yale graduate civil engineer 52-year old Major A. B. Rogers would locate the linchpin path through the Selkirk Mountain Range the following year at a Pass that would one day bear his name; it would take four years to build the railroad across the mountains at three passes: Kicking Horse Pass through the Rockies, Rogers Pass through the Selkirks and the Eagle Pass through the Gold Range. The second transcontinental line in the U.S. was formed when the Atchison and Topeka Railroad building west from Topeka to Albuquerque turned south to meet the Southern Pacific building east from California; the two roads met and opened the route at Deming in Territory that would become New Mexico in March; while holding title to formation of the second transcontinental route, its construction was so poor it was not operated for years. The New York, Chicago & St. Louis (Nickel Plate) was organized in February; in less than two years it would become a 500-some mile long line between Buffalo and Chicago via Cleveland and Fort Wayne; Jay Gould and William H. Vanderbilt would grapple for control.

Even with short wheat and corn crops, revenues for the year approached $8.6 million, the fourth consecutive year of growth; almost 21 percent of revenues, and most of the year-to-year growth, were from the 4,008,047 passengers; six locomotives and 50 cars were dedicated to commuter service. Revenue traffic rose to almost 2.9 million tons of freight. To solve Illinois Central's gauge disparity (4' 8 ½" north of Cairo and 5' south), at the end of July, more than 3,000 men worked to regauge the entire 550 miles of track from East Cairo, Kentucky to New Orleans, Louisiana in a single day; this improvement enhanced service between Chicago and New Orleans, and more than doubled the throughput of the Cairo ferry service; efforts to resolve the car ferry routine also were underway, with test borings in the Ohio river to site a vital bridge. The locomotive roster grew to 224 units, with the net addition of 10 new Company-built 2-6-0 Mogul's and the purchase ($8,000) of a single (IC's second) Rogers-

IC45x35-40

Illinois Central #752 was a 2-6-0 Mogul built by the IC in 1881 (56 1/2 D; 95,900 TW), originally rostered as IC #217. This previously published photograph shows the engine posed on the Chicago Lake Front circa 1890's.Illinois Central #1315 was built at the Water Valley shops of the Chicago St. Louis & New Orleans in 1881 (56 D; 69,000 TW), and rostered as CStL&NO #16; acquired by IC in 1882, it was renumbered IC #346 in 1883, IC #1161 in 1890 and finally IC #1315 in 1899. This picture was captured at DuQuoin in June, 1900; the four men standing next to the 4-4-0 American-type locomotive were unidentified.

IC1881-01

built 2-4-4T for the suburban commuter service (IC#222). System mileage remained a little over 1,320, a little over 918 miles in Illinois and 402 miles in Iowa. Cumulatively, almost 764 miles of track had been re-laid with steel replacing the iron.

Published in the May, 1930 issue of the Illinois Central Magazine, IC #1322 was an 1881 Chicago St. Louis & New Orleans-built (original CStL&NO #9) 4-4-0 American (58 D; 69,000 TW; 10,362 TF). It was pictured here at Rocky Cut, Alabama on the Orphan Line at Brilliant in 1902. Identified in the picture were, left to right, J.E. Dollohite (flagman), A.L. Stevens (conductor), R.E. Moore (engineer), George W. McDonald (brakeman), and Mr. Harris (fireman).

IC1881-02

IC1999-29

ICNEGGS-40

Illinois Central #1402, an 1881 Rogers-built 2-4-4T suburban (56 1/2 D; 140 BP; 107,600 TW; 11,862 TF) as shown from the driver's side and the fireman's side; sign says Van Buren. These are Gerald M. Best negatives from 1926 in Chicago.

Illinois Central #1506 is an 1881 IC-built 0-4-0 switch engine (48 1/2 D; 125 BP; 60,000 TW; 13,460 TF), originally rostered as IC #16. This picture appeared in the May, 1940 issue of the Illinois Central Magazine; identified in the photo were, left to right, Joe Michaels (engineer), unidentified (fireman), John Williams (switchman), Thaddeus Mitchell (engine foreman), and John White (switchman). The picture dates to the mid 1890's, and shows the old Decatur, Illinois station house in the background.

IC1881-03

1882

38-year old German researcher Robert Koch identified the microorganism that caused tuberculosis – TB; Koch was awarded the Nobel Prize in Physiology 23 years later. British forces occupied Egypt and the Suez, the start of a 74-year love/hate relationship; it would be 40 years before England would allow partial independence.

43-year old John D. Rockefeller re-organized his Standard Oil affiliates into a Trust to circumvent anti-monopoly laws; this Trust eventually would control 90 percent of the U.S. oil; Rockefeller's success was attributable to his control of the transportation and because he concentrated on refining oil instead of on drilling wells. Leaving the way he lived, Jesse James was felled by a bullet in St. Joseph, Missouri. With the demand for Chinese labor lessened and the competition for jobs heightened, the push for immigration restriction turned toward these people; President Chester A. Arthur signed the Chinese Exclusion Act suspending their immigration for ten years; over time the Act was renewed, and it would be 61 years before barriers to Chinese immigration were rescinded.

James J. Hill was named President of the Saint Paul, Minneapolis and Manitoba Railroad, the forerunner to the Great Northern Railway. The 513-mile long New York, Chicago & St. Louis Railroad opened for business in October, having been put together in 21 months; at the beginning, the Nickel Plate accessed Chicago over the Illinois Central from Grand Crossing into the City; in a battle for ownership, William H. Vanderbilt got the better of Jay Gould as his New York Central Railroad won control by the end of the month. Collis P. Huntington gained control of the St. Louis & San Francisco Railway (the FRISCO), a railroad that would never quite reach California.

When numerous breaks in the Mississippi levee system overwhelmed local governments, preserving the Delta between Memphis and Vicksburg became a Federal enterprise. For the fifth consecutive year revenues gained ground, this time exceeding $8.9 million; passenger traffic accounted for almost 23 percent of total revenues (4,340,211 passengers). Revenue traffic exceeded 2.9 million tons of freight. System mileage increased by ten to a little over 1,330 with the construction of a ten-mile spur from Buckingham, Illinois on the Middle Division into nearby Essex coal fields; Illinois mileage now exceeded 928, while that in Iowa topped 402. The 550 miles of track on the Chicago, St. Louis & New Orleans, the southern lines connecting East Cairo and New Orleans, operated by the Company for the last five years, were formally assumed into the Illinois Central system under a 400-year lease arrangement; consolidated operations would begin at the turn of the year. A cumulative 855 miles of track now had been re-laid with steel replacing iron; for the first time, one could ride the entire Chicago to New Orleans corridor over steel. With the addition of nine Company-built locomotives replacing worn out engines, the roster remained at 224. To accommodate the expansion in South Chicago since the location two years earlier of the Illinois Steel Company (the future U.S. Steel) at the mouth of the Calumet River, Illinois Central's began construction of a South Chicago commuter branch to expand its suburban service.

IC45x35-47

Illinois Central-built in 1882 (65 D) and originally rostered as IC #54, IC #1135 was a 4-4-0 American-type that was numbered as shown in 1890; it was renumbered one last time in 1912, to IC #2135, and then retired three years later. It was captured here at the Weldon Yard car shops on September 19, 1891. Note the arrangement on the old-fashioned cow-catcher pilot for link and pin coupling.

*1882 Schenectady-built Illinois Central #1189, a 4-4-0 American-type (63 D; 150 BP; 71,000 TW; 14,037 TF) was originally
Chesapeake Ohio & Southwestern #34; it became IC #1189 in 1896. This picture appeared in the March, 1941 issue of the
Illinois Central Magazine; identified in the picture were, left to right, Robert Moore (conductor), William Reed (engineer), John
Smith (flagman), F.B. Warren (fireman), and unidentified (express messenger). The photograph was snapped at Horse Branch,
Kentucky in the mid 1890's.*

*Illinois Central #1534 was an 1882 Brooks-built 0-4-0 switch engine (47 D; 130 BP; 60,000 TW); built originally for the
Peoria Decatur & Evansville (PD&E #29), IC acquired and renumbered the engine in 1900. Since this engine was renumbered to
IC #2534 in 1912, this picture, taken at an unknown location, dates between 1900 and 1912.*

1883

A volcano erupted on the island of Krakatoa in Indonesia, west of Java in the Sunda Strait killing over 30,000.

43-year old American Hiram S. Maxim invented the first practical automatic machine gun, using the recoil energy from each fired bullet to eject the spent cartridge and load and fire the next; Maxim would be granted patent #436,899 seven years later on his automatic gun; ten years after the patent he would become a British citizen. In November a General Time Convention was held in Chicago to recommend and implement a Standard Time System; the U.S. was divided into a series of time zones (Eastern, Central, Mountain and Pacific) patterned after railroad timetables; Standard time became effective in U.S. New York City's East River Bridge was completed and opened in May, linking Brooklyn and Manhattan; it would later be renamed the Brooklyn Bridge. 24-year old Chicago-born Yale graduate Francis S. Peabody formed his coal company in Chicago. The *Ladies Home Journal* was founded. Cashing in some of his eastern assets, Jay Gould sold his *New York World* newspaper to Joseph Pulitzer; in the coming years Pulitzer's *World* would stage circulation wars with William Randolph Hearst's *New York Journal*. Woman's rights advocate Isabella Baumfree passed away at age 86, Sojourner Truth.

Forging a much-improved transcontinental link compared to their Deming route of 1881, the Southern Pacific joined rails with the Santa Fe, building west from Albuquerque using a portion of the defunct Atlantic & Pacific land grants, at a second location - Needles, California. The pioneering Northern Pacific transcontinental route from the Great Lakes to Puget Sound in the northwest was completed in September with the last spike driven at Gold Creek, Montana; Henry Villard had finished the work others started 19 years earlier and was credited with completing this third major transcontinental line spanning the U.S.; this line to the coast was via Portland on the Columbia River, the direct route through the Stampede Pass in the Cascades lay five years away. James J. Hill (and John Stewart Kennedy) sold their Canadian Pacific holdings, concentrating on their Great Northern venture. 53-year old Henry M. Flagler, a partner in John D. Rockefeller's Standard Oil adventures from 1867 to 1911, began visiting Florida; while becoming rich and famous at Standard, Flagler would turn his business acumen toward nurturing parts of tropical Florida from wetlands to paradise, eventually putting together the Florida East Coast Railway and a string of luxury hotels.

Effective August 15th 59-year old James C. Clarke was elected the 9th President of the Illinois Central; he would serve until May 18, 1887. 31-year old Stuyvesant Fish was elected second vice president of the Illinois Central. 34-year old Edward Henry Harriman was elected a Director of Illinois Central, beginning a 26-year involvement in Illinois Central affairs. As of the first of January, Illinois Central consolidated its operations with the 550-mile long Chicago, St. Louis & New Orleans, dubbed the Southern Division; with the building of 20 miles of track from Colfax, Illinois to Normal Jct., construction of the Kankakee & South Western was completed; another 28 miles of track were built on the Southern Division on the Kosciusko and Lexington branches; with these additions, system mileage grew to 1,928; this comprised roughly 948 miles of track in Illinois, 402 in Iowa and 578 south of Cairo in the Southern Division. Illinois Central also set in motion two track extensions through sister companies; the Canton, Aberdeen & Nashville was projected over 87 miles from Kosciusko to Aberdeen, Mississippi; the Yazoo & Mississippi Valley was laid out for a little over 47 miles from Jackson to Yazoo City, Mississippi. With Spring floods in the Ohio river valley, the Company worked to strengthen embankments and raise grade above flood levels in the Cairo and East Cairo depot areas. With a full year operating the Southern Division, revenues would soar almost 50 percent to a little over $13 million; passenger traffic accounted for 21 percent of total (4,354,033 passengers). Revenue traffic leaped to over 3.5 million tons of freight. With the addition of 11 new Company-built locomotives, the purchase of 6 Rogers-built 2-4-4T suburban commuter units, and 106 engines from the Southern Division, Illinois Central's roster rose to 340, almost 300 of the 4-4-0 American-type, after netting against worn out units; the commuter fleet stood at eight-specially built dedicated suburban units, supplemented by the existing fleet of 4-4-0 Americans. Illinois Central's suburban commuter service opened for business on the 4.7-mile long South Chicago branch with the first train in September. The year would end on a rocky note: Cawood Patent # 15,687 issued in 1856 covered an improvement to swedge-blocks used to reform and weld the shattered ends of cast iron rails; feeling the Illinois Central's use of this idea infringed those patent rights, Cawood's interests sued the Company and won a judgment which, by the October Term, had worked its way through the U.S. Supreme Court (110 US 301), where it was affirmed; the following year Illinois Central paid out a little over $115,000 in damages for its infringement from 1856 to 1872.

IC1883-01

Illinois Central #206 was an 1883 Rogers-built 2-4-4T suburban engine (56 1/2 D; 140 BP; 117,000 TW: 11,862 TF); originally rostered as IC #228, it was renumbered as shown in 1890, and renumbered again to IC #1406 in 1900. The picture above was captured at South Chicago in 1896, while the view below was at the Weldon turntable on September 6, 1897. The Weldon turntable was a manual disk, 66 feet long and constructed out of iron by Chicago Forge & Bolt.

IC1883-03

IC1883-04

There are conflicting records whether the engine shown above is Illinois Central #228 or #229 but, in either event, it was an 1883 Rogers-built 2-4-4T suburban (56 1/2 D; 140 BP; 117,200 TW; 11,862 TF); this picture has been published many times, probably first in the November, 1925 issue of the Illinois Central Magazine. This picture dates to 1884, when the locomotive was nearly new, and was captured at Randolph station (note the entranceway of the old Great Central station that had been rendered roofless in the Chicago Fire of 1871). Identified in the photograph was the young engineer, 26-year old J.W. Miller leaning on the pilot; Miller was born in England and emigrated to the United States as a four-year old during the Civil War; he hired on with the Illinois Central in 1875 as a 17-year old, became an engineer, and retired in 1922 with 47 years of service. Shown below is IC #1403, another 2-4-4T suburban with the same performance statistics as above; IC #1403 was Rogers-built in 1883 as IC #225, then renumbered IC #203 in 1890, and IC #1403 in 1900.

IC45x35-151

IC45x35-152

Suburban engine IC #1408 above was another 1883 Rogers-built 2-4-4T (56 1/2 D; 140 BP; 117,200 TW; 11,862 TF); originally rostered as IC #230, it was renumbered to IC #208 in 1890 and to the number shown in 1900; this picture was snapped at an unidentified location, sometime after 1900; the signage on the engine states Woodlawn.

Illinois Central #1743 shown below was a 2-6-0 Mogul-type (56 1/2 D; 150 BP; 95,900 TW; 17,547 TF) built by the IC in 1883, and originally rostered as IC #44; it was renumbered IC #743 in 1890, IC #1743 in 1903, and IC #2743 in 1915. The photograph was captured in the yard at Pana, Illinois in 1903; it appeared in the March, 1926 issue of the Illinois Central Magazine. Identified in the picture were, left to right, Charles Barnett (engine foreman), unidentified (fireman), John P. Meehan (engineer), Lute Penwell (superintendent, Powell Coal Mine), and switchmen Syd G. McGavic and R.C. Haddow.

IC1883-02

1884

Englishman Charles Parsons developed an alternative method for converting the linear motion of a piston into rotary motion; instead of a connecting rod and crankshaft, Parsons simply directed the jet of steam at vanes on a wheel, thus creating the steam turbine.

New Orleans hosted the Cotton Centenary through the following year. In August 30-year old German immigrant Ottmar Mergenthaler found a way to replace time-consuming manual typesetting with his invention of the linotype machine. 28-year old Croatian-born American engineer Nikola Tesla invented the electric alternator. A crisis in the financial centers in the east would see over 100 banking firms close before some confidence returned. At the 8th Republican convention in Chicago, former Secretary of State and Maine ex-Senator James G. Blaine was elected the nominee for President on the 4th ballot; Illinois Senator Major General John A. Logan was chosen the nominee for Vice President on the 1st ballot. At the 14th Democratic convention in Chicago, New York Governor Stephen Grover Cleveland was elected the nominee for President on the 2nd ballot; ex-Governor Thomas A. Hendricks of Indiana was chosen the nominee for Vice President. In November the Democratic ticket of Cleveland/Hendricks swept to victory in a close race. Samuel L. Clemens, as Mark Twain, published *The Adventures of Huckleberry Finn.* Charles Dow published his first indicator of stock market prices – the Average of American Stocks – the forerunner to the Dow Jones Average; it contained eleven stocks. The 1st roller coaster in the U.S. appeared, built by LaMarcus Thompson; it was called the Switchback Railway and was built at New York's Coney Island. Insurance salesman Lewis E. Waterman improved the fountain pen and established a new brand name.

Wall Street and railroad tycoon Jay Gould supported Blaine for President. The Railway Panic of 1884 occurred; it was caused by rate wars among the railroads. While conceived by others 16 years earlier, Canadian Orange Jull designed the first practical rotary snow plow and had it built by the Leslie Brothers; tested in the winter of 1883/1884, it proved to be a quantum leap over older wedge plows like the V-shaped "pilot plow" and Congdon "bucker plow"; the Leslie Brothers eventually bought the manufacturing rights. Frank J. Sprague developed the direct-current or DC electric motor; he intended it for use in electric locomotives. French engineer Anatole Mallet designed an articulated locomotive where two sets of driving wheels were placed under a single boiler rigidly attached to the rear engine frame; while altered and refined over the years, this articulated design would forever bear his name.

32 years in the making, the Vicksburg, Shreveport & Pacific was completed as the first train rolled into Shreveport, Louisiana on July 1st; Shreveport was accessed by crossing west over the Red River from Bossier City and was 20-some miles from the Texas border. The second consecutive year of Spring flooding in the Ohio river valley necessitated additional work on strengthening embankments and raising grade above flood levels at Illinois Central's river crossing between Cairo and East Cairo. Illinois Central booked slightly lower revenues for the year at $12.2 million; over 22 percent of revenues were attributable to passenger traffic (4,848,140 passengers). Revenue traffic dipped to just under 3.4 million tons of freight. In the prior year, Illinois Central Directors reminded stockholders that the Company's 20-year lease of the Dubuque & Sioux City, the linchpin to the Iowa Division, would lapse in less than four years if not renewed; the Directors issued the same reminder again and, partly as posturing, added the veiled caution that the Iowa lines had suffered a "steady diminution in…value". System mileage grew by almost 138 miles to 2,066 with the completion of over 87 miles on the Canton, Aberdeen & Nashville, the opening of over 45 miles on the Yazoo & Mississippi Valley and the inclusion of almost 5 miles on the South Chicago railroad; the System was comprised of roughly 953 miles of track in Illinois, 402 in Iowa and 711 south of Cairo. The Company finished construction on a transfer steamer, with a hull length of 285 feet, for Cairo traffic; the latest had capacity for 18 freight cars, compared to the 12-car capacity of the older transfer steamer in use. Illinois Central's locomotive roster rose to 346 units with the completion of 6 new Company-built 2-6-0 Mogul units and the addition/replacement of a few 4-4-0 American-types; the fleet was composed of 8 suburban passenger engines, 284 eight-wheeled passenger and freight engines, 1 ten-wheeled passenger engine, 33 2-6-0 Mogul-type freight engines, and 20 switching engines: 16 four-wheeled and 4 six-wheeled.

Just a short hop from the knackerman, Illinois Central #1757, a 2-6-0 Mogul-type (56 1/2 D; 95,900 TW) rests easy while awaiting dismantling in this photograph; indeed this locomotive had seen much action. Built in 1884 at Illinois Central shops as IC #233, it was renumbered to IC #757 in 1890, and then IC #757 in 1903. As part of its Indianapolis Southern Railway subsidiary, which was constructing an 89-mile long section between Effingham and Switz City, the Illinois Central renumbered seven of its 2-6-0 Moguls for Indianapolis Southern service; IC #1755 through IC #1761 were renumbered IS #71 through IS #77; in 1908 the numbering was reversed, and the seven Moguls were rerostered on the Illinois Central with their old numbers. The picture captured the engine (with smokebox door open, cylinder covers removed and the steam dome atop the cab) at an unidentified location; Illinois Central #1743, another 2-6-0 Mogul, keeps old IC #1757 company.

IC45x35-96

IC1884-01

IC1884-03

Three views of the same engine, at three different periods in its service life. Above, Illinois Central #11, an 1884 IC-built (48 D; 60,000 TW; 12,800 TF) 0-4-0 switch engine posed at Broadway Crossing in Centralia in the Fall of 1884; middle photograph shows the engine renumbered in 1890 to IC #1 on the Chicago Lake Front from an R.A. Beck negative; bottom view shows the engine rerostered in 1898 as IC #1501, during a snowstorm; this engine would be renumbered a final time, to IC #2501 in 1912, and serve five more years. The top picture was published in the October, 1926 issue of the Illinois Central Magazine; identified in the photograph were, left to right, on the engine, David Oxley and Henry McMillan, on the ground, Willis McNamee, C.B. Fletcher, unidentified, William Linton, William Davis, Harry Newell, Ben James, John Green, Charles Parkhurst, Marion Hunt, Frank McCoy,

IC45x35-078

and unidentified; all but the last man in the picture were current or former Illinois Central employees; for example, David Oxley, shown in the gangway, was the same Master Mechanic pictured between the drive wheels of IC #32, an 1854 engine in front of the Centralia roundhouse (Page 9), but 30-some years later.

1885

The British introduced the modern version of the bicycle. 46-year old German-born Clemens A. Winkler discovered germanium, the third of three new elements predicted to exist by Dmitri I. Mendeleev's periodic table in 1871.

In March 47-year old Grover Cleveland, the second bachelor to live in the White House (James Buchanan was the other), was sworn in as the 22nd President of the United States; Cleveland married the next year, and became the first to wed in the White House. The completed Washington Monument was dedicated, 38 years after the cornerstone was laid. The copper-clad Statue of Liberty, designed by 51-year old Frenchman Frederic Auguste Bartholdi and given by France to the U.S. as a centennial gift, was erected in New York City Harbor on Bedloe's Island; President Cleveland dedicated the Statute the following year, fully ten years after the Centennial. 53-year old William Le Baron Jenney saw his design of the 10-story Home Insurance Building built in Chicago and invented the skyscraper. Terre Haute resident 30-year old Eugene V. Debs began his political career on entering the Indiana legislature. Arguably the first world's heavyweight boxing championship went to 27-year old John L. Sullivan, the last of the bare-knuckle brawlers; he would retain the title for seven years. Illinois Industrial University changed its name to the University of Illinois.

The first electrification of mainline railroads in North America was completed on the 3.6-mile tunnel in Baltimore on the Baltimore & Ohio Railroad in August. In November the Canadian Pacific became Canada's first transcontinental railroad, and thereby the first to span the Canadian Rockies, with a connection between east and west at Craigellachie in British Columbia in the Eagle Pass; 42-year old William Cornelius Van Horne was the Canadian Pacific's General Manager of Construction, and would be its next President. Under common ownership since 1868, the Central Pacific and Southern Pacific solidified the relationship by merging operations.

In Chicago over 330 people were killed in grade crossing accidents in one year. Illinois Central's fortunes rebounded somewhat with revenues exceeding $12.6 million; over 22 percent of revenues were passenger traffic: 5,312,759 passengers of which 3,347,613 were commuters riding the Chicago to Kensington and South Chicago lines; there now appeared 32 daily suburban trains each way. Revenue traffic rose to almost 3.6 million tons of freight. New Orleans celebrated the Cotton Centennial & Industrial Exposition. Matching replacements to retirements, Illinois Central's locomotive roster was maintained at 346 units; 14 Company-built units (eight 4-4-0 Americans, four 2-6-0 Moguls and two 2-4-4T suburbans) were received, most having twice the power of the unit replaced; the locomotive fleet was composed of 10 suburban passenger engines, 278 eight-wheeled passenger and freight engines, 1 ten-wheeled passenger engine, 37 2-6-0 Mogul-type freight engines, and 20 switching engines: 16 four-wheeled and 4 six-wheeled. System mileage remained at 2,066, comprised of roughly 953 miles of track in Illinois, 402 in Iowa and 711 south of Cairo. With an eye toward Memphis, Illinois Central laid plans for extending the Yazoo & Mississippi Valley from Yazoo City to the Yalobusha river near Parsons, together with a spur connecting Gwin to the West & East at Lexington; the 70-mile extension would bring it within 90 miles of Memphis. The Iowa lines, once a large contributor to Illinois Central's prosperity, continued in decline with a second consecutive year of operating losses; while posturing to some extent, Illinois Central exhibited less and less interest in extending its lease with the Dubuque & Sioux City two years hence. Predecessor companies to the Illinois Central established rail service across the Mississippi river with a car ferry connecting Vicksburg, Mississippi and Delta Point, Louisiana in October; ferry service would continue until a bridge spanned the river 43 years later; as proven during the Civil War, Vicksburg was a strong river point on high bluffs overlooking the Mississippi River, and this fact of nature required steep grades to make land once on the Vicksburg side of the River.

IC1885-03

Illinois Central #1409 and #1410, the first two 2-4-4T suburbans built at Illinois Central's Weldon Yard shops, both products of 1885 (56 1/2 D; 140 BP; 117,200 TW; 11,862 TF). In the photograph above, IC #1409 is shown near the Chicago Lake Front in a picture that appeared in the June, 1926 issue of the Illinois Central Magazine; originally rostered as IC #223, it was renumbered IC #209 in 1890, and IC #1409 in 1900; it is shown tagged as a 67th Street Express. IC #1410 shown below had the same engine dimensions as its sister; labeled for service on the Blue Island branch, this engine originally was rostered IC #224, then renumbered IC #210 in 1890 and IC #1410 in 1900.

Shown on the facing page are front and rear views of IC #1410; since these pictures date after 1900, they exhibit the more modern appliances, such as automatic couplers and brakes, and steam heat lines. Also seen are the headlamps at each end, allowing push or pull service. The water catch on the rear of the tender shows where the boiler water was loaded.

IC45x35-142

1950 GAL.
1410

1410

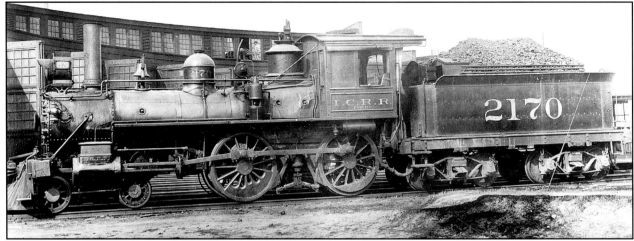

IC1885-02

IC45x35-108

IC1885-01

Three Illinois Central-built 4-4-0 American-types from 1885; all three photographs date to sometime after a 1912 renumbering. These locomotives had identical dimensions (65 D; 140 BP; 83,400 TW; 12,747 TF), and each notched over 35 years of service, IC #2170 over 45 years. Original roster numbers of IC #32/252/254, respectively, became IC #1170/1174/1176 in 1890, and the numbers shown in 1912.

1886

The elements gadolinium and dysprosium were discovered. While aluminum had been produced for decades, production economies were needed to extend its use; independently, American Charles M. Hall and Frenchman Paul L. T. Heroult experimented with direct electrolysis and helped push the acceptance of aluminum. England's Prime Minister William E. Gladstone proposed home rule for Ireland, but free state status lay 35 years away.

48-year old Charles Tyson Yerkes began assembling his monopoly in public transportation with the purchase of North Chicago City Railway. Labor unrest consumed the country: rail labor struck Jay Gould's southwestern rail system in March and April; strikes in support of the 8-hour day broke out in April and May; two workmen having been killed the previous day while protesting outside McCormick Harvester Works in Chicago, over 1,000 laborers gathered in Chicago's Haymarket Square to stage a protest; riots took place, someone threw a bomb, police opened fire and it went down in history as a massacre with 8 police and three civilian fatalities; 31 anarchists were rounded up and indicted, eight on murder charges, of which all would be found guilty and four would face the gallows in 1887. Dr. John S. Pemberton, a Confederate veteran of the Civil War and a druggist in Atlanta, Georgia, invented a syrup headache remedy; when carbonated water was added it became what now is recognized as Coca-Cola. The condition of appendicitis was theorized to be a cause of unexplained abdominal disorders. In November the American Federation of Labor (AFL) was organized with 36-year old Samuel L. Gompers as its first head, a position he would retain until his death in 1924; the AFL was organized craft by craft. A ranch in California's Cahuenga Valley began subdividing land into town lots and adopted the name *Hollywood*, Los Angeles' latest subdivision. The great Apache war leader Geronimo surrendered to U.S. troops; he would live another 23 years, going on to his reward from Fort Sill, Oklahoma in 1909 at age 80. 56-year old Emily Dickinson passed away having composed in seclusion for years; little of her work was published ere her death, and it would be years before her 1,500-some poems would be available to the public.

Canadian Pacific Railway began through transcontinental train service on June 28th, Train No. 1 the *Pacific Express* leaving Montreal on its 2,900-mile adventure.

Illinois Central annual revenues dipped to slightly over $12.5 million, roughly $100,000 less than the prior year; 20 percent of revenues were attributable to passenger service (6,112,110 passengers); service on the commuter line was extended to Riverdale. Revenue traffic approached 4.1 million tons of freight. Illinois Central's locomotive roster rose to 365 units with the completion of 10 Company-built units (including three 2-4-4T suburbans), and a number of additional units constructed for and dedicated to the branch lines; 24 switchers (20 0-4-0 and 4 0-6-0), 13 suburban engines, 58 2-6-0 Moguls, 269 8-wheeled passenger and freight units and one ten-wheeler. System mileage rose to 2,149 in six states with two additions: the 12-mile spur from Gwin to Lexington, and 71 miles on the Yazoo & Mississippi Valley from Yazoo City to Parsons; now just 15 miles shy of Grenada on the way to Memphis, it would be another 15 years before the Yazoo & Mississippi Valley's future Greenwood District would be linked back to Grenada through Ransom, Holcomb and Dubard. There now were 953 system miles in Illinois, 402 in Iowa and 794 on the lines south of Cairo. The Company set in motion plans to shape the future: the year-end foreclosure-acquisition of the 13-year old Chicago, Havana & Western (Champaign to Havana and its spur from White Heath to Decatur, all in Illinois) and the 7-year old Rantoul Narrow-Gauge (West Lebanon, Indiana to Le Roy, Illinois) would be consolidated into operations the following year; the acquisition of a majority position in the stocks and bonds of the financially-troubled almost 30-year old Mississippi & Tennessee (Grenada, Mississippi to Memphis, Tennessee) would be consolidated three years later; and construction was begun on the planned 170-mile long Chicago, Madison & Northern (segment one: Freeport, Illinois to Madison, Wisconsin; segment two: Freeport to Chicago) to connect the northern-most ends of the system. Posturing for the end game, Illinois Central reiterated its lack of interest in renewing its lease of the Iowa lines – the Dubuque & Sioux City.

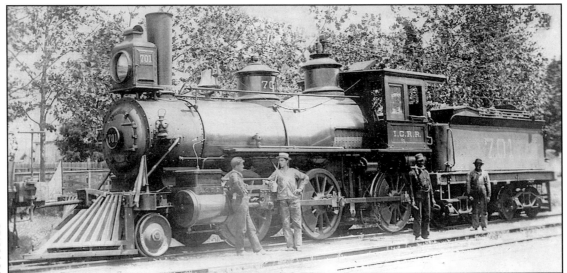

IC1886-04

IC1886-03

IC1886-02

IC1886-06

Illinois Central #1413 and #1415 were two of the three suburban engines produced in 1886 at IC's Weldon Shops (56 1/2 D; 140 BP; 117,200 TW; 11,862 TF); IC #1413 originally was rostered IC #58, then IC #213 in 1890, and finally IC #1413 in 1900; IC #1415 originally was numbered IC #60, then renumbered to IC #215, and finally to IC #1415. IC #1413 was tagged for Gary, and was pictured at an unknown location; IC #1415 was shown listed for 67th Street, and was captured at 23rd Street in July, 1914.

IC1886-01

On the previous page top, Illinois Central #701 was an 1886 IC-built 2-6-0 Mogul-type (56 1/2 D; 150 BP; 95,900 TW; 17,547 TF); it was captured at Grenada, Mississippi in 1897 with everyone posed for the picture; this engine originally was rostered as IC #238, and was renumbered to IC #701 in 1890. Middle photograph on the previous page shows another IC-built 2-6-0 from 1886; this engine arrived as IC #242 and was renumbered to IC #705 in 1890; this engine had dimensions identical to IC #701, and was captured at Fulton, Kentucky. The lower picture opposite page shows Illinois Central #1197, a Pittsburg-built 4-4-0 American (63 D; 140 BP; 82,000 TW; 13,101 TF) that was constructed for the Ohio Valley in 1886 (OV #3); IC renumbered the unit to IC #1197 in 1897. This photograph appeared in the September, 1928 issue of the Illinois Central Magazine; identified in the picture were, right to left, John Ross and John Burke (firemen), J.C. Patterson (engineer, in gangway), L.L. Click (baggageman), A.J. Goepfert (flagman), and Edward Hegler (conductor). This picture was taken on May 5, 1904 at Benton, Illinois; it showed IC #1197 pulling Train #624.

IC1904-01

In the early 1900's Illinois Central needed to expand its suburban locomotive equipment and it did so, for the first time, with rebuilt engines. Previously, the IC either had built new suburban engines or purchased them from Rogers; for this expansion IC took some lighter-weight 4-6-0 Schenectady-built 10-wheelers (56 D; 86,700 TW) that it had acquired with the Chesapeake Ohio & Southwestern and converted them into 4-6-4T suburban engines (56 1/2 D; 150 BP; 155,130 TW; 17,548 TF). Illinois Central #1437 above and IC #1440 below were 1886 Schenectady-built 4-6-0's that were converted in 1904 to 4-6-4T's. IC #1437 (tagged for South Chicago) was pictured in 1925 in a negative credited to E.B. Adams and as published in the July, 1926 issue of the Illinois Central Magazine; IC #1440 (headed for Gary) was captured under the coal tipple at 27th Street in Chicago in 1915.

IC1904-02

IC1886-05

Illinois Central #1514 was an IC-built 0-4-0 switch engine, constructed in 1886 (48 1/2 D; 140 BP; 60,000 TW; 15,075 TF); it originally was rostered as IC #24, was renumbered to IC #14 in 1890, then IC #1514 in 1898 and finally IC #2514 in 1912; it was pictured here at Dixon, Illinois right around the turn of the century; this picture appeared in the October, 1926 issue of the Illinois Central Magazine; identified in the photograph were, left to right, Joe Carney (fireman, in gangway), Henry Davis (engineer, in the right seat), Mr. Ruggles (yardmaster), Milt Stahl (retired employee), and M.J. Reilly (switchman). This engine supposedly was the first yard engine at Dixon. Pictured below is Illinois Central #2518, an 0-4-0 saddle-tank switching unit, also called a shop-goat; this unit began its service life as IC #28, an 0-4-0 switcher in 1886 (48 1/2 D; 60,000 TW); renumbered to IC #18 in 1890, IC #1518 in 1898, IC #2518 in 1912, it was rebuilt into an 0-4-0T saddle-tank in 1917 (67,000 TW; 15,232 TF), and retired 18 years later. This unit saw service at IC's Burnside shops.

IC1886-07

1887

The Kingdoms of Cambodia and Vietnam were combined by colonial France into French Indochina, Laos would be added six years later; the amalgamation would last over 50 years.

The U.S. leased Pearl Harbor from Hawaii for a naval base. Richard W. Sears and Alvah C. Roebuck joined in offering a mail order business to compete with Aaron Montgomery Wards' service. 36-year old German-born American-inventor Emile Berliner improved on Edison's tin-foil phonograph and Alexander Graham Bell's wax cylinder graphophone and made it a flat disk, the gramophone arrived. The game of softball was invented in Chicago, but as an indoor sport.

In spite of increasingly anti-competitive behavior by railroads, a court ruling found that individual states had no jurisdiction over interstate trade; in response, Congress passed the Act to Regulate Commerce (now Interstate Commerce Act) to regulate rates; even though this signaled the dawn of rail regulation, it would be almost 20 years before enforcement power was attached to the Act. Former C.S.A. Major Eli Hamilton Janney's invention of a vertical plane automatic coupler for railroad cars became the standard. The Northern Pacific reached Seattle. The Pullman vestibule appeared, the enclosed porch making movement between cars in motion a much less risky maneuver. The Santa Fe Railway began construction of a line between Chicago and Kansas City to meet up with its mainline to the west coast; the line was completed and service would begin the next year.

Effective May 18th 35-year old Stuyvesant Fish was elected the 10th President of the Illinois Central; he would serve for 19 years. Revenues jumped to a little over $13 million; almost 21 percent of revenues were from passenger traffic (6,949,852 passengers). Revenue traffic leaped to over 4.9 million tons of freight. Making the short hop from posturing to pressuring, in March Illinois Central renounced its option to renew the lease of the Iowa lines, forcing the owners of the Dubuque & Sioux City into the position of owing the Illinois Central for past improvements (betterments) to the tune of almost $1million, an unreachable sum; in its end game, Illinois Central purchased control of the Iowa Falls & Sioux City, the western connection and feeder to the Dubuque & Sioux City, for fifty cents on the dollar; squeezed thusly, the Dubuque & Sioux City folded its hand along with that of its sister company the Cedar Falls & Minnesota, all at ever lower prices; in this fashion the Iowa lines became a permanent part of the Illinois Central system, even though lawsuits from the Cedar Falls & Minnesota would drag on for years. System mileage grew by 206 miles to 2,355 with the addition of the 130-mile long Chicago, Havana & Western and the 76-mile long Rantoul Narrow-Gauge, whose three foot gauge had been changed over to Illinois Central's standard 4' 8 ½"; there now existed 1,159 miles in Illinois, 402 in Iowa and 794 south of Cairo. To increase business on the Iowa lines, Illinois Central constructed the 155-mile long Cherokee & Dakota from Cherokee, Iowa to Sioux Falls and to Onawa; and the 42-mile long Cedar Rapids & Chicago between Manchester and Cedar Rapids; both would be consolidated into operations the next year. Illinois Central crews continued work on the Chicago, Madison & Northern from Freeport to Madison and to Chicago; construction was expanded to include a 57-mile long branch off the Madison segment leading up the Pecatonica river valley to Dodgeville, Wisconsin; it would be two years before this railroad would be completed and consolidated into operations. As traffic levels between the southern and northern portions grew, the ferry transfer at Cairo became a jam in the system; Illinois Central's affiliate the Chicago, St. Louis & New Orleans, *defacto* owner of the Southern lines, entered into a contract to have a $2.5 million bridge built across the Ohio River at Cairo; with Illinois Central guaranteeing funds, completion was expected in two years. Illinois Central's locomotive roster grew to 402 units with the net addition of 26 Company-built freight units (mostly 2-6-0 Moguls) including 4 IC-built 2-4-4T suburban units, a few locomotives purchased for the branch lines and some 5 units acquired with the Chicago, Havana & Western; the locomotive fleet stood at 28 switchers (24 0-4-0 and 4 0-6-0), 17 suburban engines, 87 2-6-0 Moguls, 269 8-wheeled passenger and freight units and one ten-wheeler.

Illinois Central suburban engine # 211 was an IC-built 2-4-4T from 1887 (56 1/2 D; 140 BP; 117,200 TW; 11,862 TF); originally rostered as IC #56, it was renumbered to IC #211 in 1890 (picture above) and renumbered yet again in 1900, to IC #1411 (see picture below). In the top photograph, IC #211 is captured at an unknown time and place, with its placard calling for Riverdale. IC #1411, shown below, catches its breath with another engine in between rush hours at an unidentified suburban station.

IC45x35-150

IC45x35-13

With its placard reading *South Chicago, Illinois Central #216, a 2-4-4T built in 1887 by the IC (56 1/2 D; 140 BP; 117,200 TW; 11,862 TF), is posed on the Chicago Lake Front; originally IC #62, it later became IC #1416. The two photographs below show IC #1417, another Weldon Yard shops 2-4-4T built in 1887, with dimensions as above; posed at two different stations, one unidentified and the other by the Chicago Lake Front, this engine had roster numbers of IC #63 and IC #217 in its earlier life.*

IC45x35-173

IC1887-03

IC45x35-101

Having feigned losing money for years, Illinois Central positioned itself for the demise and takeover of the leased Iowa Lines in 1886/1887; when the Iowa Lines fell under IC control, the Illinois Central could execute its plan of connecting the upper ends of the Charter Line "Y" to bring marketing and operating efficiencies to bear. The Company formed a subsidiary (the Chicago Madison & Northern) for just this purpose, and ordered up ten 2-6-0 Mogul-type engines (CM&N #354 to #363) to be used as construction equipment. Pictured on this page are Illinois Central #1806 and #1810, former CM&N #359 and #363; both were 2-6-0 Mogul-types built by Brooks Locomotive (56 1/2 D; 92,900 TW) in 1887; they became Illinois Central #806 and #810 in 1890, and were rerostered to the numbers shown in 1904. While the top photograph shows an engine ready to go and the lower picture shows one that looks worn out, both pictures date after 1904.

1888

Scottish-born Irish veterinarian John Boyd Dunlop patented the first practical pneumatic tire. 44-year old Nickolai Rimsky-Korsakoff composed his orchestral piece *Scheherazade*.

The time clock was invented. Great Blizzard of 1888; started in the west in January and worked its way to the east by March. 34-year old George Eastman marketed his first Kodak camera; it was a point and shoot camera, preloaded with film for 100 shots; you mailed the camera to Rochester, New York and received prints and the camera back in the mail. Nikola Tesla invented the alternating current or AC induction motor; he also received patent #381,968 on his *Electromagnetic Motor*, the AC synchronous motor; in total, Tesla received seven patents on May 1st. In August William S. Burroughs patented an adding machine. At the 15th Democratic convention in St. Louis, incumbent President Grover Cleveland was nominated for re-election by acclamation; ex-Senator Allen G. Thurman of Ohio was chosen the nominee for Vice President on the 1st ballot. At the 9th Republican convention in Chicago, ex-Senator General Benjamin Harrison of Indiana was elected the nominee for President on the 8th ballot; on the 4th ballot for President, Frederick Douglass of the District of Columbia received one vote, a first; New York former-Congressman and Minister to France Levi P. Morton was chosen the nominee for Vice President on the 1st ballot. In the election, the Republican ticket of Harrison/Morton unseated incumbent Grover Cleveland in November, the Republicans taking 20 States to 18 for the Democrats; the Republican ticket lost the popular vote, but won the electoral college vote total. The National Geographic Society was formed in Washington, D.C. by Clinton M. Merriam. Wallace C. Abbott invented the measurement of medicine in pill form and, twelve years later, organized Abbott Laboratories.

With completion of its Chicago to Kansas City line, the Santa Fe (ATSF) completed its own route from Chicago to California in May; this formed the first single-carrier route from Chicago to the coast. Fred Harvey operated his first dining car on the Santa Fe. Henry M. Flagler, of Standard Oil fame and fortune, acquired two small rail carriers in Florida and began laying rail south in constructing what would become the Florida East Coast Railway. The Northern Pacific completed its direct route to Puget Sound, constructing trackage through the Cascade Range at Stampede Pass on the line between Yakima and Tacoma; Stampede Pass was 40-some miles northeast of and two miles below 14,410-foot Mt. Rainier.

64-year old Levi Parsons Morton, a member of the Illinois Central Board in 1886 and 1887, resigned his directorship to run on the Republican ticket. In March John Luther "Casey" Jones from Cayce, Kentucky began his 12 years of Illinois Central service as a locomotive fireman. System mileage grew by 197 miles to slightly over 2,552 with the consolidation of the Cherokee & Dakota from Cherokee, Iowa to Sioux Falls, South Dakota (96 miles) and Onawa Jct. to Onawa (59 miles); and the 42-mile long Cedar Rapids & Chicago between Manchester and Cedar Rapids; Illinois Central had 1,159 miles of track in Illinois, 599 west of the Mississippi River and 794 south of the Ohio River. Illinois Central now had two interchange points close by the Missouri River (Sioux City and Onawa, with Sioux Falls on a tributary), one on the Illinois River (at LaSalle, about 100 miles from Chicago), one at the navigable limit of the Wabash River (West Lebanon, about 100 miles from Chicago), and three on the Mississippi River (Dubuque, Cairo (technically on Ohio River) and New Orleans). Illinois Central merged all its interests west of the Mississippi River into a single company, the Dubuque & Sioux City. Revenues rose slightly to $13.7 million, just under 21 percent of which were attributable to passenger traffic (7,184,691 passengers). Revenue traffic rose to almost 5.3 million tons of freight. The Chicago terminal remained the busiest, handling over 24 million bushels of grain and 129 million board feet of lumber. Illinois Central's locomotive fleet rose to 436 with the net addition of 30 freight units (some Company-built and some purchased outside) and the purchase of switching units; the fleet stood at 34 switchers (29 0-4-0 and 5 0-6-0), 17 suburban engines, 116 2-6-0 Moguls, 268 8-wheeled passenger and freight units and one ten-wheeler. Construction of the Chicago, Madison & Northern was essentially complete by yearend; operations on this 222-mile long segment would begin at the turn of the year; building the last few miles to effect an actual connection to its own lines in Chicago would take almost three more years of wrangling with the carriers whose lines had to be crossed, such as the Chicago, Burlington & Quincy and the Belt Railway. Work on the Ohio River bridge-crossing at Cairo continued apace; ten of the eleven principal piers had been constructed and the two 518 ½ -foot long main channel spans erected.

Illinois Central #199 was an 1888 Schenectady-built 0-6-0 switch engine (51 D; 99,000 TW). Built originally for the Paducah Union Passenger Depot (PUPD #1). Illinois Central acquired this engine in 1896. This engine carried numbers IC #191 and IC #193 before being rostered as IC #199; the picture shown dates between 1896 and 1919. After Illinois Central acquired the engine in 1896, the locomotive did not stray far from its roots; it spent years working the ferry between Paducah and Brookport on the Ohio river. It was captured here, with eight men posed, at an unknown location.

IC1888-10

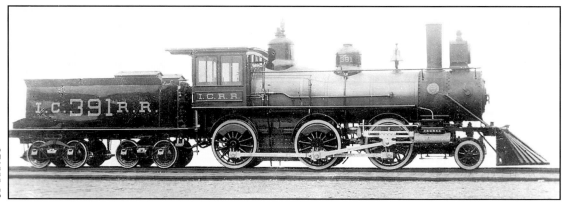

IC1888-02

IC1888-03

IC45x35-97

This page shows three 1888 Brooks-built 2-6-0's (56 1/2 D; 150 BP; 100,000 TW; 17,547 TF); as part of a group of 48 Brook's Moguls, these engines went through a series of number changes: from the original roster position when built 1886 to 1889, to a #500-series in 1890, to a #800-series in 1896, to a #1800-series in 1904 until a few were renumbered into the #2800-series. The top picture was a Builder's Photo from Dunkirk, New York (in the rods-down position). The middle picture dates to Central City, Illinois in 1900, and appeared in the May, 1938 issue of the Illinois Central Magazine; IC #847 was the engine on the Centralia to Effingham local and was shown with her crew: left to right, Mr. Duncan (brakeman), J.J. Cavanaugh (conductor), J.M. Daugherty (engineer), J.F. McNally (fireman), and brakemen Charles Maxfield and Mr. Toller. The bottom view dates to after 1917, at an unknown location.

On the facing page are five pictures of Hinkley-built 2-6-0 Moguls, from a series of ten Hinkley made for the Illinois Central in 1888. These engines (56 1/2 D; 150 BP; 92,900 TW; 17,547 TF) saw a variety of service, and all were retired by 1929. Top photograph shows IC #506, posed on the Chicago Lake Front between 1890 and 1896. The second picture shows IC #872 at Fordham Yard near Chicago in 1899; this picture appeared in the Illinois Central Magazine in September, 1941; identified in the photo were, right to left, Ole Lindrew (engineer, at the drivers), John Perry Smith (fireman, in the gangway), John Blake (lead brakeman), Mr. Blodger (conductor), and unidentified (extra brakeman). The next two photographs show IC #1871, first at Tutwiler, Mississippi in 1915 and, second, pulling a log train around the same time. The last view was IC #2877 captured at 27th Street in Chicago on May 12, 1917.

IC1888-14

IC1888-04

IC1888-07

IC45x35-201

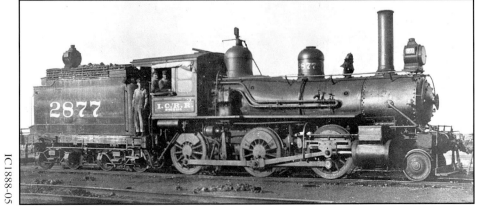

IC1888-05

IC1888-08

IC45x35-192

IC1888-15

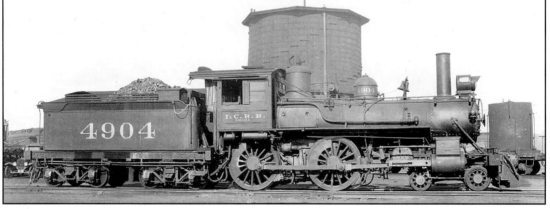

IC1888-01

Shown are four views of Illinois Central-built 4-4-0 American-type locomotives; these engines were built in 1888 (69 D; 150 BP; 69,100 TW; 14,369 TF). Topmost is IC #903 (original IC #163); it was captured here on the Chicago Lake Front between 1890 and 1906, and appeared in the September, 1925 issue of the Illinois Central Magazine. The two photographs in the middle show IC #1901 (original IC #161) backing by and around the station house and coupling up a baggage car at Beulah, Mississippi. The bottom photograph shows IC #4904 (original IC #164) at Paducah, Kentucky on April 22, 1927, two short years before its retirement after 41 years of service.

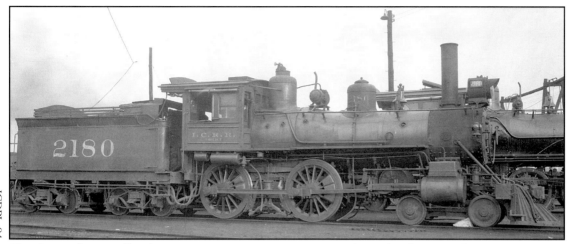

ICDPL-04

Photo Courtesy of Denver Public Library, Western History Department, Otto C. Perry Photograph Collection (DPL#12281), Denver.

IC1888-06

Illinois Central #2180 was an 1888 Pittsburg-built 4-4-0 American (64 D; 88,600 TW); originally constructed for the St. Louis Alton & Terre Haute (StLA&TH #40), it became IC #1180 when acquired in 1895; in 1912, it was renumbered IC #2180; it was pictured here at Memphis, Tennessee on October 19, 1929. Shown next was IC #2338, another unit built for the StLA&TH in 1888; this engine (originally #20) was a Pittsburg-built 4-6-0 10-wheeler (56 D; 165 BP; 105,000 TW; 21,699); this picture was captured in Chicago in the 1920's.

Illinois Central #2527, as shown, was an 0-4-0T saddle-tank switch engine, or shop goat. Originally an 1888 IC-built 0-4-0 switch engine (48 1/2 D; 60,000 TW), it began on the roster as IC #410; it subsequently had roster numbers of IC #27, IC #1527, and IC #2527. This engine was rebuilt into a saddle-tank, with its total weight raised to around 72,000. It remained in service until scrapped in late 1927.

IC45x35-111

1889

67-year old French engineer Gustave Eiffel's Tower was completed in time for the Paris Exposition of 1889/1900, the centennial of the French Revolution; at over 980 feet, it was the tallest free-standing structure when completed. While various levels of service dated as far back as 1883, through-train service was inaugurated between France and Turkey via Paris, Munich, Vienna, Budapest, Belgrade, Sofia and Istanbul; the service was renamed the *Orient Express* two years later.

In March 55-year old Benjamin Harrison was sworn in as the 23ʳᵈ President of the United States. In April, the Oklahoma Land Rush began, the public homesteading of the last piece of western frontier - a two million acre swatch of Oklahoma in the middle of Indian Territory as yet "unassigned" to any particular Indian nation; trying to beat others to a claim tagged you as a "Sooner"; this was the first of six rushes in the Oklahoma District. Over 2,200 people perished in the Johnstown Flood in western Pennsylvania when rain-swollen Lake Conemaugh broke through its earth-fill dam in May. The Dakota Territory, unable to agree on a single capital city, was split in half and brought into the Union as two States; North Dakota, South Dakota, Montana and Washington were admitted to the Union as the 39ᵗʰ, 40ᵗʰ, 41ˢᵗ and 42ⁿᵈ States. In September social reformers and college friends 29-year old Jane Addams and Ellen Gates Starr kick-started the settlement-house movement in America when they opened Hull House in Chicago; Addams would receive the Nobel Peace Prize in 1931 for her life's work, the first American woman to be so honored. The first coin-operated public telephone debuted, as did the first Singer Sewing Machine. American Thomas A. Edison and Englishman William K. Dickson worked on moving-pictures: a camera called a kinetograph and a viewing machine called the kinetoscope; halving George Eastman's 70mm camera roll film, they produced a celluloid-based 35mm movie film to play on it by 1891. Andrew Carnegie purchased the H.C. Frick Coke Company in Pennsylvania, beginning the vertical integration of his steel business into a personal empire; Henry Clay Frick, who had developed the monopoly in coke and coal, came along with the deal to be Carnegie's main colleague and collaborator. Future astronomer Edwin Powell Hubble was born in Missouri; over 100 years later they would name a space telescope in his honor; between these moments, Hubble determined that there were other galaxies besides our own, and that the universe was expanding. Dentist Edward H. Angle received a patent on his device that corrects an imperfect "bite" and founded the field of orthodontics. Walter Camp selected the first college All-America football team, comprised mostly of Ivy League players. The *Wall Street Journal* hit the streets for the first time; it was published by Dow Jones and Company, a news agency founded seven years earlier by Charles H. Dow and partners.

James J. Hill, by this time, had built branch lines south to the Great Lakes and westward into Montana; Hill's chief engineer now found the Marias Pass in Montana, a more direct and lower crossing of the Northern Rockies than that used by Hill's adversary the Northern Pacific; Hill's railroad empire officially assumed the name Great Northern Railway. In November the first through rail service spanning the coasts was instituted. 1,860 locomotives were produced in the U.S.

To satisfy Federal and State requirements, Illinois Central changed its annual reporting basis from a December 31ˢᵗ calendar year to a June 30ᵗʰ fiscal year; this mid-year convention would remain through 1916, when the Interstate Commerce Commission ordered all carriers back on a common calendar year basis; Illinois Central also began reporting business levels on the common basis of tons. After testing bridge strength with ten coupled 2-6-0 Moguls crossing, Illinois Central opened its four-mile long Cairo Bridge (2 miles of steel bridge and 2 miles of wooden trestle approaches) on October 29ᵗʰ with the passing of the first regularly scheduled train (IC-built 2-6-0 engine #215) from north to south not needing to be ferried across the Ohio River; the ferry had been used from 1873 to 1889; as part of a system-wide program later to reduce the miles of bridging that had to be maintained, the wooden trestle approaches were filled in as embankments. The suburbs of Hyde Park and Pullman were annexed into the city of Chicago, along with other communities; this 100-square mile annexation more than doubled the size of Chicago. The Mississippi & Tennessee, which spanned the 100 miles between Grenada and Memphis, was formally consolidated into the operations of the Chicago, St. Louis & New Orleans, becoming the Memphis Division on Illinois Central's leased Southern lines; the recently-completed 222-mile long Chicago, Madison & Northern also was consolidated into operations, as the Wisconsin Division; together, these raised system mileage to just over 2,874: 1,381 north of the Ohio River, 599 west of the Mississippi River and 894 south of the Ohio River. Illinois Central's locomotive

From a photograph that appeared in the October, 1935 issue of the Illinois Central Magazine, a Directors and Management meeting is shown being held on the road, in this particular case, at Rockford, Illinois in 1889. It was the custom of the time to venture out on the property every so often and view the actual operations of the Illinois Central, up close and personal.

J.B. Kemp	*46-year old Memphis Division Superintendent*
T.J. Hudson	*43-year old Traffic Manager*
Judge James Fentress	*General Solicitor*
Henry Schlacks	*Superintendent of Machinery*
Benjamin F. Ayers	*64-year old General Counsel*
Stuyvesant Fish	*38-year old President*
Horace W. Clarke	
Edward T. Jeffrey	*46-year old General Manager*
E.H. Harriman	*41-year old Vice President*
D.B. Morey	*General Freight Agent, Southern Lines*
William Waldorf Astor	*41-year old Board Member*

fleet size rose to 470 units with the addition of 12 Rogers-built 4-4-0 units from the Mississippi & Tennessee and 23 new units (2-6-0 Moguls, 4-4-0 Americans, 4-6-0 ten-wheelers and a few switching units; some Company-built and some purchased) filling in for worn out units and increasing the roster; the fleet stood at 40 switchers (33 0-4-0 and 7 0-6-0), 17 suburban engines, 135 2-6-0 Moguls, 274 8-wheeled passenger and freight units and 4 ten-wheelers. With average cotton crops in the South and good corn harvests in Illinois, business levels jumped; revenues rose to $14.7 million, almost 21 percent of which was generated by 7,444,111 passengers. Revenue traffic rose to over 5.5 million tons of freight. In December in order make management of the Company less variable, the Directors adopted a written code of conduct for all officers and employees.

IC1889-04

Three Baldwin-built engines, all original equipment on the Ohio Valley as OV #9, OV #10 and OV #11; the units became Illinois Central assets in 1897 and eventually had roster numbers of IC #2574, IC #4953 and IC #4954. IC #2574 was an 0-6-0 switch engine (51 D; 76,000 TW; 16,184 TF), pictured at the Henderson, Kentucky yards between 1912 and 1916; identified in the picture were, left to right, William McKinney, T.E. Stith and L. Dunning. IC #4953 was a 4-4-0 American-type (65 D; 150 BP; 94,550 TW; 16,834 TF), captured at Princeton, Kentucky on June 12, 1925 in a L.P. Blattner negative; IC #4954 was a twin of IC #4953 and was snapped at Evansville, Indiana on the same date. The last two photos appeared in the IC Magazine in July, 1925 (the first in July, 1929); these engines began their careers running the new Evansville to Princeton line of the Ohio Valley.

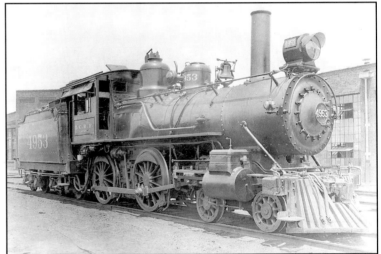

IC1889-01

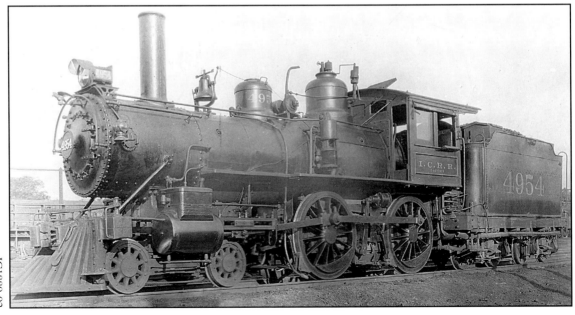

IC1889-02

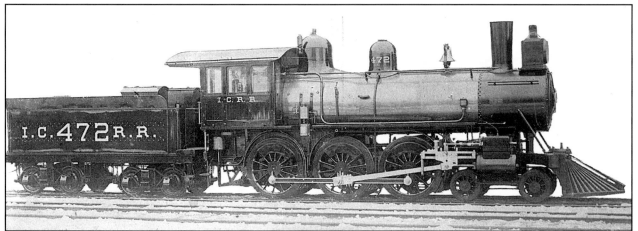

IC1889-03

IC45x35-249

Three Schenectady-built engines of 1889, originally rostered as IC #472, IC #459 and IC #447. IC #472 is shown in a Builder's Photo from Schenectady, New York; the engine was a 4-6-0 10-wheeler (65 D; 165 BP; 123,500 TW; 18,766 TF); this photo appeared in the April, 1926 issue of the Illinois Central Magazine. IC #864 was rostered as such in 1890; it was a 2-6-0 Mogul (56 1/2 D; 100,800 TW) captured coming off the turntable at Canton, Mississippi in February, 1898; the turntable was a 54-foot long cast iron product of William Sellers & Company. IC #1866 was another 2-6-0, with dimensions identical to that of IC #864. It was pictured at an unknown location, sometime between 1904 and 1916.

IC1889-07

IC1912-01

Illinois Central #1443 and #1444 were 2-6-4T suburban engines (56 1/2 D; 150 BP; 163,300 TW; 17,548 TF) converted from 1889 Schenectady-built 2-6-0 (56 1/2 D; 92,900 TW) Moguls; IC #1443 (pictured at Burnside in 1927) was rebuilt by Lima Locomotive, while IC #1444 (captured at 27th Street in Chicago in 1926) was rebuilt by IC shop forces at Burnside. The photograph of IC #1444 appeared in the July, 1926 issue of the Illinois Central Magazine. These 1912 conversions saw duty in suburban and other service until sold in 1928 and 1934, respectively.

IC1912-02

IC1920-07

Another 2-6-4T suburban, Illinois Central #1447 had the same dimensions as those noted on the facing page; this unit also was rebuilt from a 1889 Schenectady-built 2-6-0. Pictured in a Gerald M. Best negative in Chicago in 1926, this engine was rebuilt into the 2-6-4T in 1920/1921. Signage on the engine notes it's a Special to Kensington. This photograph appeared in the July, 1926 issue of the Illinois Central Magazine.

IC45x35-260

An unidentified Illinois Central 4-4-0 American took on water at Council Hill, Illinois in this photograph dated 1889/1890.

ICLAG08-04

The big news of the year was the opening of the Cairo bridge crossing over the Ohio river, connecting with rail the north and south parts of the Illinois Central for the first time. Union Bridge Company erected the bridge, which consisted of nine through truss spans (two - 518' 6" long and 7 - 405' long) and three deck spans (each 250' long), all supported on 13 masonry piers. The bridge was engineered by George S. Morison (Chief Engineer) and E.L. Corthell (Assistant Chief Engineer). On the opposite page, the top picture shows a view of the bridge from the north side of the river; note the light gauge of steel, compared to modern day bridgework; the picture, with Illinois Central track and cars in the foreground, dates to July 15, 1896. The bottom photograph shows a view from the south side of the river, illustrating the south approach; note the train headed north; this picture dates to May, 1903. The picture on this page, taken from the north side of the river, dates to the 1950's, when the Illinois Central was replacing the superstructure of the old Cairo bridge; this photograph is from the Final Report on Reconstruction, Illinois Central Railroad Cairo Bridge over the Ohio River, *published by Engineers Modjeski and Masters for the Illinois Central Railroad in June, 1953; this view shows reconstruction of the piers before replacing the bridgework; note the lower water level, comparing this photograph to the previous page.*

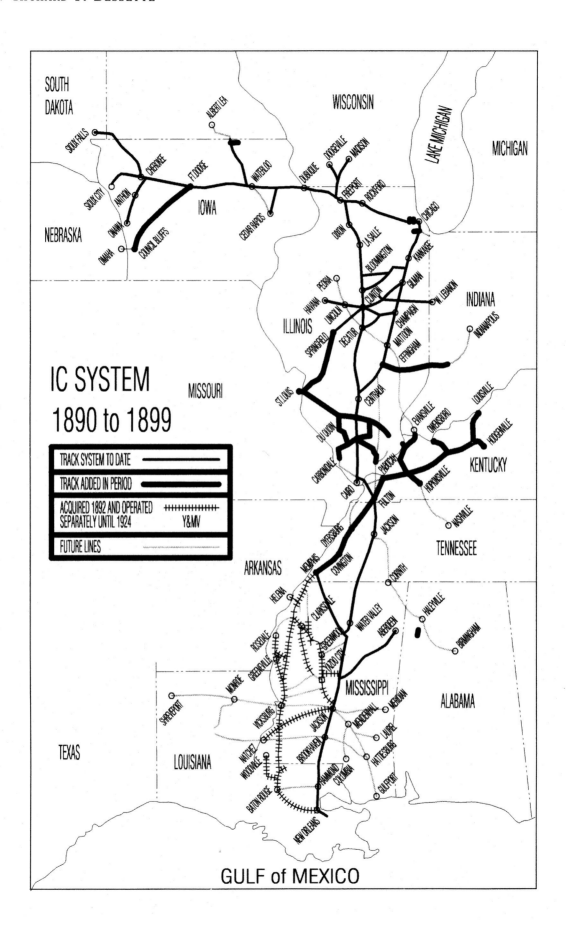

1850's 1860's 1870's 1880's **1890's** 1900's 1910's 1920's 1930's 1940's

The Eleventh Census of the U.S. population was taken; there were almost 63 million people in the U.S., having grown 26 percent from the prior census; the country would add over 13 million people by the end of the decade, one-quarter through immigration. The Union grew by three States to a total of 45. The Indian Wars effectively ended with the massacre of Big Foot and his band of Sioux at Wounded Knee Creek, South Dakota in 1890. While the 1890's continued the industrial age with another decade of economic expansion, it also was a period of depression and social unrest…labor unions, activists, settlement houses, child labor laws. During the 1890's there were newspaper wars where each tried to increase circulation at the expense of the other – such as yellow press wars between William Randolph Hearst and Joseph Pulitzer. John D. Rockefeller, Andrew Carnegie, Jay Gould, James J. Hill, J. Pierpont Morgan, James Buchanan Duke and many others made fortunes in this period of tremendous growth, emerging technologies and few restrictive laws on how business was conducted; many became large and monopolistic and, with little competition, unfriendly to labor. The 1890's brought the Sherman Antitrust Act and the Interstate Commerce Act. The Sherman Antitrust Act was used more to bust the unions than to curb big business. The mid-1890's would see the rise of Populism, and then Progressivism.

In 1890 Chicago, 14-mph cable cars met the competition, 25-mph electric trolleys; trolleys were not allowed inside the City limits for years because of people's innate fear of electricity. In 1890 the major line-haul rail carriers operated over 163,500 miles of railroad, a figure that would swell by almost 30,000 more miles by the end of the decade.

GROWTH OF ILLINOIS CENTRAL RAILROAD BUSINESS

Year (1)	Tonnage (mil/tons)	Lumber (mil/tons)	Grain (mil/tons)	Coal (mil/tons)	FFV (mil/tons)	Cotton (mil/tons)	Aggregates (mil/tons)	Passengers Commuters	Miles/Fare
1890	6.4	.628	1.1	1.5	.144	.150	.144	8,207,213 5,464,267	19/$0.40
1891	6.9	.780	1.2	1.8	.137	.200	.176	10,108,375 6,778,436	18/$0.38
1892	7.5	.963	1.2	1.9	.177	.203	.191	11,912,463 7,945,937	18/$0.37
1893	8.1	1.2	1.2	2.3	.164	.129	.303	17,661,828 11,292,517	15/$0.29
1894	7.4	.715	1.2	2.3	.178	.156	.159	22,897,476 11,961,690	14/$0.27
1895	7.9	.943	1.3	2.2	.192	.226	.209	11,391,733 8,007,141	17/$0.34
1896	9.7	1.1	1.6	3.1	.234	.175	.156	12,812,206 9,132,227	17/$0.34
1897	9.9	.920	2.0	3.0	.199	.235	.185	12,827,205 9,156,901	17/$0.33
1898	12.7	1.4	2.2	4.0	.239	.317	.158	13,772,221 9,393,116	19/$0.37
1899	13.5	1.5	2.0	4.4	.225	.319	.221	14,401,234 9,616,064	19/$0.38

FFV = Fresh Fruit & Vegetables   Passengers/Commuters = Total Ridership, and Commuter Portion
Miles/Fare = Average Passenger Trip and Charge   (1) Fiscal Year

1890

Tortured 37-year old Vincent van Gogh took his own life, ending one of the greatest, albeit short, careers in art. Starting a once-every-hundred-years-or-so tradition, Baring Brothers & Company failed in November; it would repeat the feat 105 years later.

Louisiana passed the "Separate Car Act" which required "separate but equal" rail accommodations, using a distinction to neutralize the ideals of the Civil War in 25 short years. Financial centers in the New York area suffered through a banking crisis when insufficient reserves met head on with cash hoarding. Dwight D. Eisenhower was born in Kansas. Idaho and Wyoming were admitted to the Union as the 43rd and 44th States. Congress acted to add Yosemite National in California to the National Park System roster. Seven Merritt family members discovered iron ore on the Mesabi Range in Minnesota, and launched commercial development; the ore range would turn out to be over 100 miles long and up to three miles wide at points; John D. Rockefeller would gain control in a financial panic three years later. Sponsored by Ohio Senator and Judiciary Committee Chairman John Sherman (the younger brother of William Tecumseh), Congress passed the Sherman Antitrust Act to combat monopolistic business practices and restraint of trade. The Chicago Symphony was formed. 59-year old Lakota-Sioux Chief Sitting Bull was killed by his own people, the Indian police in December on the Standing Rock Reservation. The last official battle between federal troops (the U.S. Seventh Cavalry) and American Indians (Big Foot's Miniconjou Sioux) took place at Wounded Knee Creek, South Dakota in late December; Native Americans finally were beaten into submission. In November Navy won the first Army-Navy football game 24-0, at West Point. Through cagey pricing and cornering raw materials, James Buchanan Duke forced competitors to join his American Tobacco Company, eventually controlling 90 percent of the market; his monopoly would last through 1911 when the Supreme Court dismantled his empire; Duke's involvement in Southern Power in 1905, and Duke Power and later Duke University would effectively diversify his investments. The University of Illinois from Urbana played its first intercollegiate football game, losing 16 to 0 to Illinois Wesleyan at Bloomington; undeterred, the University of Illinois would help found the Western Intercollegiate Conference (one day the "Big Ten") six years later.

The Santa Fe Railroad claimed a speed record: from La Junta, Colorado to Chicago, Illinois averaging 78.1 mph. Chicago opened its Grand Central Station.

Illinois Central Chicago-area suburban commuter service was extended to Harvey on March 9th; by mid-summer service was extended to Homewood. There were 17 locomotives and 97 coaches dedicated to suburban service, running a total of fifty daily trains in each direction, thirty on Sunday. To cut down on grade crossing accidents, the Chicago City Council called for elevating railroad tracks. In February John Luther "Casey" Jones was promoted from locomotive fireman to engineer. Consolidated revenues approached $16.5 million, 20 percent from passenger traffic (8,207,213 passengers). Revenue traffic rose to almost 6.4 million tons of freight. System mileage remained at approximately 2,875: 1,381 north of the Ohio River, almost 600 west of the Mississippi River and 894 south of the Ohio River. Due to a rift in the levee on the east bank of the Mississippi River near Baton Rouge, some 20 miles of Illinois Central track between New Orleans and Ponchatoula were inundated with water from the flooding Mississippi River, remaining submerged for more than two months. In its maintenance of way programs, after testing for one year Illinois Central settled on 75-pound rail (weight of 75 pounds per yard) as the standard of the future. Illinois Central's locomotive roster rose to 473 units available for service, netting retirements against the addition of 26 units (including 2 IC-built 2-4-4T suburban units): 6 passenger units, 18 Mogul freight units and 2 switching engines. The fleet was composed of 19 suburban passenger engines, 137 eight-wheeled passenger engines, 7 ten-wheeled passenger engines (6 from Schenectady and 1 from Baldwin), 130 4-4-0 American-type freight engines, 141 2-6-0 Mogul-type freight engines, and 41 switching engines: 34 four-wheeled and 7 six-wheeled. In mid year, in what would be only one of many fleet renumberings, Illinois Central renumbered its entire locomotive roster, basically according to cylinder size: 1 to 100 was reserved for 4-wheel switch engines, 101 to 200 for 6-wheel switchers, 201 to 300 for Suburban equipment, 301 to 500 for 10-wheelers with 19" by 24" cylinders, 501 to 600 for Moguls with that cylinder size, 601 to 700 for Consolidations with 21" by 24" cylinders, 701 to 900 for Moguls with 18" by 24" cylinders, 901 to 1100 for similar sized 8-wheelers, 1101 to 1300 for 8-wheelers with 17" by 24" cylinders, 1301 to 1369 for 8-wheelers with 16" by 24" cylinders, 1370 to 1404 for 8-wheelers with 16" by 22"

IC45x35-34

IC1890-10

A pair of 1890 Brooks-built 0-6-0 switch engines (51 D; 84,000 TW); Illinois Central #108, above, and IC #110, below. IC #108 is pictured on the Chicago Lake Front, around the 1890's; IC #110 was shown switching a solid trainload of raw cane sugar in Mill, Louisiana, probably in 1895.

cylinders and 1405 to 1478 for 8-wheelers with 15" by 22" cylinders and smaller. The renumbering revealed Illinois Central still had a few of its oldest units in service: IC #158 was a Rogers-built 4-4-0 from 1854 (original #31 renumbered in 1885) that was renumbered to 1436; IC #77 (original 1854, and renumbered from #55 in 1884) was a Rogers-built 4-4-0 renumbered to 1370; IC #95 was a Rogers-built 0-4-0 switch engine from the 1850's.

IC1890-11

Illinois Central #305 began its service life as Schenectady-built #474; it was a product of 1890 and IC promptly renumbered it to that shown. A 4-6-0 (65 D; 123,500 TW) 10-wheeler, it was captured most likely on the Chicago Lake Front in the 1890's; this engine would also be rostered as IC #2305, in a 1917 renumbering.

ICNEGGS-53

Illinois Central #323 was an 1890 Cooke-built 4-6-0 (65 D; 123,500 TW) 10-wheeler. It was pictured on the south-side of Chicago picking up a trainload of farm implements. The sign on the sides of the cars proudly states, "FC Austin, Mfg. Co. Harvey, Ill's". The date of the picture is unknown, but is between the engine's 1890 construction and its 1917 renumbering (to IC #2323).

IC1890-04

IC45x35-43

IC1890-05

Three views of Illinois Central #905, a product of Brooks Locomotive in 1890; this 4-4-0 American (64 D; 175 BP; 119,700 TW; 15,422 TF) holds the distinction of being one of the last two 4-4-0's on the Illinois Central roster; it was renumbered to IC #1905 in 1906 and IC #4905 in the 1920's, all the while remaining in service until scrapped in 1940. The topmost photograph shows the engine as new in a Builder's Photo from Dunkirk, New York. The middle picture captures the engine in a yard shot. The bottom photograph, which appeared in the June, 1927 issue of the Illinois Central Magazine, was snapped at Clinton, Illinois in 1895/1896; identified in the picture were, left to right, William Deto (fireman, in gangway), Eli Perkins (engineer, in right seat), Edward J. Young (roundhouse foreman, at rear driver), Robert Goddall (general foreman, at front driver), and J.H. Bannerman (master mechanic, at pilot). This engine saw a lot of service pulling the Daylight *and the* Diamond.*

IC45x35-44

IC1890-01

A pair of Brooks-built 4-4-0 Americans (64 D; 175 BP; 119,700 TW; 15,422 TF), both products of 1890; both shown in two views, one when nearly-new and the other in 1914 at 27th Street in Chicago when the units were being used in suburban service (note they were tagged for Matteson). IC #906/1906 above was (along with IC #905) one of the last two 4-4-0's on the IC roster, remaining in service until 1940.

IC1890-02

IC45x35-45

Brooks-built in 1890, Illinois Central #1907 was originally rostered as IC #907; it was renumbered to IC #1907 in 1906, and one last time (to IC #4907) in the early 1920's. This 4-4-0 American-type (64 D; 175 BP; 119,700 TW; 15,422 TF) remained in service until 1935. It was pictured here being used in suburban service, tagged for Matteson.

Illinois Central #909 was another Brooks-built 4-4-0 American (64 D; 175 BP; 119,700 TW; 15,422 TF) from 1890 that saw long service, in this case until 1935; similar to others in this series, the engine was renumbered regularly, this particular unit to IC #1909 and IC #4909. It was pictured here in a relatively rare shot; captured on January 8, 1894 at Martin, Tennessee pulling a train carrying the Columbian Liberty Bell, an artifact from the World's Columbian Exposition in Chicago, it was on a promotional tour around the countryside. This picture was published in the Illinois Central Magazine in the 1950's. The writing on the car behind the tender states "International Columbian Liberty Bell."

IC1890-03

Two more 1890 Brooks-built 4-4-0's (64 D; 175 BP; 119,700 TW; 15,422 TF). IC #1910, above, was captured at Divernon, Illinois on November 5, 1913 by Company photographer J.K. Molton. IC #1912, below, was snapped in March, 1911 on the turntable at Paducah, Kentucky.

IC1890-14

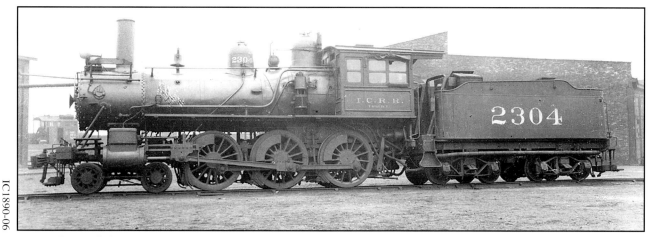

1890 Schenectady-built 4-6-0 (65 D; 165 BP; 123,500 TW; 18,766 TF) 10-wheeler (originally rostered as IC #473) pictured at the Illinois Central's Burnside shops outside Chicago in April, 1927, one year before being sold for scrap.

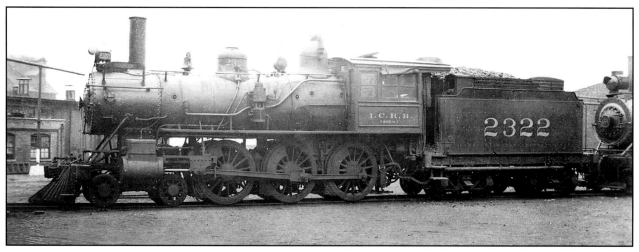

A product of Cooke Locomotive in 1890, this 4-6-0 (65 D; 165 BP; 123,500 TW; 18,766 TF) 10-wheeler was captured at the same location, Burnside shops in April, 1927. It too was sold for scrap the following year.

Captured at an unknown location, 1890 Pittsburg-built 2-6-0 Mogul-type (56 D; 165 BP; 115,000 TW; 21,699 TF) was constructed for the St. Louis Alton & Terre Haute (original StLA&TH #27). Illinois Central acquired this engine in 1896 and renumbered it to IC #880, then IC #1880 in 1904 and finally IC #2880 in 1917; it was retired in 1929.

IC1890-06

IC1890-07

IC1890-08

1891

Congress approved a Copyright Act to protect authors. Thomas A. Edison demonstrated his Kinetoscope – a peep show machine that ran short movies on celluloid film. 30-year old Canadian James A. Naismith, working as a physical education instructor at the Springfield, Massachusetts YMCA Training Center (now Springfield College), saw the need for an indoor wintertime activity and invented the game of basketball; while any number could play, nine players on each side was suggested. American novelist 72-year old Herman Melville passed away with little ceremony; it would be years before his literary value was acknowledged. Leland Stanford founded Stanford University in Palo Alto, California. Pope Leo XIII issued his encyclical on social doctrine – *Rerum Novarum* – laying out the Church's standing on modern issues such as capitalism, labor unions and socialist movements.

The Elgin, Joliet and Eastern, stitched together through acquisitions, formed a 130-mile long belt around Chicago roughly 40 miles outside the city limits; control would pass to the new U.S. Steel empire ten years later. 16-year old Walter Chrysler hired on as an apprentice machinist with the Union Pacific.

A second daily Chicago-New Orleans limited passenger service commenced, with running time reduced from 35 hours to 29. A new passenger through train, the *Diamond Special*, began overnight service between Chicago and St. Louis in October; its day-time companion, the *Daylight Special*, followed two years later. In spite of floods in the south (Big Black River) and the north (Onawa, Sioux Falls and Sioux City lines), earnings surged; revenues for the year approached $17.9 million, with over 21 percent attributable to passenger traffic (10,108,375 passengers); eighteen suburban trains - nine each way - were added to schedule, and 24 suburban coaches were built to handle traffic loads. Revenue traffic rose to over 6.9 million tons of freight. Illinois Central's locomotive availability rose to 532 with the addition of 25 8-wheeled passenger engines, 26 Cooke-built 10-wheeled passenger and freight engines, 2 Rogers-built Consolidation-type freight units and 21 6-wheeled switch units (plus 2 IC-built 2-4-4T suburban units); the roster composition was 21 suburban passenger engines, 162 eight-wheeled passenger engines, 33 ten-wheeled passenger and freight engines, 112 4-4-0 American-type freight engines, 140 2-6-0 Mogul-type freight engines, two Rogers-built 2-8-0 Consolidation-type freight engines (IC's first, #601 + #602), and 62 switching engines: 34 four-wheeled and 28 six-wheeled. While the older lower capacity engines were being replaced by higher capacity units, some very old equipment remained in use: 29 units from the 1854-1856 period alone; motive power remained in short supply. As the carrying capacity of freight cars rose, the pulling capacity of locomotives was increased in lock-step; heavier engines and train consists required stronger rail (thus the move to a 75-pound rail standard) which called for more ties per mile in the roadbed; taken together, train weights and train lengths rose. System mileage remained approximately 2,875: 1,381 north of the Ohio River, almost 600 west of the Mississippi River and 894 south of the Ohio River.

IC1891-02

Above and below are 1891 Brooks-built 0-6-0 switch engines (51 D; 150 BP; 84,000 TW; 19,440 TF). IC #119 was captured at Harahan Junction, Louisiana on February 2, 1926 with John F. Marshall (engineer) at the head end; it was reported that Marshall was somewhat famous for never wearing overalls, he was pictured in his normal working attire. IC #119 had Stephenson slide valves, and the tender held 4 1/2 tons of coal and 3,000 gallons of water; note the little generator, right behind the bell, which powered the electric lamp. The picture was in the April, 1926 IC Magazine. IC #132 was snapped at an unknown location.

IC45x35-36

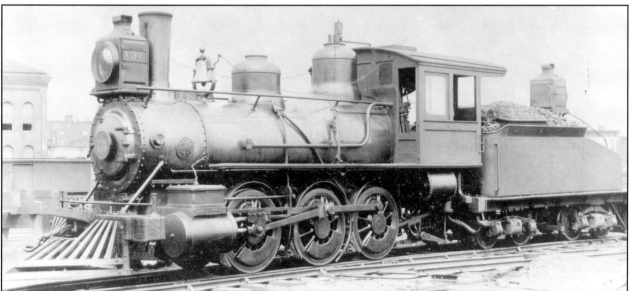

IC1891-01

Pictured in Chicago in 1893, this Brooks product of 1891 was another 0-6-0 switcher (dimensions as above). This particular engine (IC #130) was tested for suitability in suburban service; note the signage near the bell called out for Blue Island.

IC1891-03

IC1891-04

IC1891-08

Three Rogers-built 2-8-0 Consolidations. The top two pictures show units (51 D; 165 BP; 135,000 TW; 29,106 TF) late in their service lives, probably in the 1920's, at unknown locations (IC #601 possibly at Chicago). The bottom photograph shows a unit (saturated, Stephenson valve gear) with slightly different dimensions (56 1/2 D; 165 BP; 137,300 TW; 26,272 TF) and nearly new; this photograph probably dates in the 1890's and on the Chicago Lake Front.

IC1891-06

ICDPL-05

Photo Courtesy of Denver Public Library, Western History Department, Otto C. Perry Photograph Collection (DPL#12307), Denver.

IC45x35-52

1891 Brooks-built (saturated, Stephenson valve gear) 4-4-0 Americans (65 D; 119,400 TW), originally rostered as, top to bottom, IC #923, IC #924, IC #925. All were renumbered to the 1900-series in 1906, and then the 4900-series in the early 1920's. The topmost picture shows IC #4923 in Chicago suburban service; note the signage stating Matteson. Middle photograph of IC #4924 was snapped at Waterloo, Iowa on September 18, 1931 when the engine was stored. Bottom picture of IC #925 is a posed shot on the Chicago Lake Front in the 1890's.

IC1891-09

IC45x35-143

IC45x35-207

IC1891-10

0-6-0T saddle-tank switch engines, Illinois Central #2501 and #2502, began their service lives as 1891 Brooks-built 0-6-0 switchers (51 D; 84,000 TW); these engines (original roster numbers IC #123 and IC #129) were rebuilt in 1925 into the configuration shown (51 D; 112,500 TW). IC #2501 served as a shop goat at Burnside shop for years, while IC #2502 held the same position at the Paducah roundhouse. The photograph of IC #2502 appeared in the June, 1927 issue of the Illinois Central Magazine.

IC1891-11

Illinois Central #3285 was an 1891 product of Schenectady that saw many numbers; originally Newport News & Mississippi Valley #506, as an 0-6-0 switch engine (51 D; 99,000 TW) it held roster numbers of IC #192 and IC #198 before being renumbered to IC #200. This engine was rebuilt in 1918 into 0-6-0T saddle-tank IC #3285 (51 D; 165 BP; 127,000 TW; 25,000 TF).

On the facing page, Illinois Central suburban engines IC #1420 and IC #1421 are the top two views; these engines (56 1/2 D; 140 BP; 117,200 TW; 11,862 TF) were the last two Illinois Central-built 2-4-4T suburbans to be built from start to finish at Weldon Shops. IC #1420 was shown tagged as a Local, 67th Street. IC #1421 is shown headed for Matteson; the photograph includes Peter Schlax, an IC suburban engineer with 34 1/2 years service when this picture was snapped.

IC1891-12

The lower picture shows a 4-6-0 Schenectady-built 10-wheeler; this engine was built for the Newport News & Mississippi Valley (as #614) when that railroad leased the Chesapeake Ohio & Southwestern; eventually this engine (56 D; 119,700 TW) reached the Illinois Central where it was renumbered IC #369 in 1896 and then IC #2369 in 1914. The unit was captured pushing a cut of cars at an unidentified location, sometime after 1917.

1892

34-year old French-born mechanical engineer Dr. Rudolf Diesel built his first model of a diesel engine, a rudimentary engine he would continue working on through 1897. Peter Tchaikovsky completed his composition *The Nutcracker*.

At the 10th Republican convention in Minneapolis, incumbent President Benjamin Harrison of Indiana was nominated for re-election on the 1st ballot; Minister to France and New York Tribune Editor Whitelaw Reid of New York was chosen the nominee for Vice President. At the 16th Democratic convention in Chicago, ex-President Grover Cleveland was elected the nominee for President on the 1st ballot; General Adlai E. Stevenson of Illinois was chosen the nominee for Vice President on the 1st ballot. In November the Cleveland/Stevenson ticket won the election beating the Republican incumbent Benjamin Harrison and the Populist nominee from Iowa James B. Weaver; Grover Cleveland became the only man to serve two non-consecutive Terms in the Presidency. In October just before leaving office, President Harrison's vice president Levi P. Morton dedicated the World's Columbian Exposition buildings in Chicago; the Fair, celebrating the 400th anniversary of the discovery of America, would open in May 1893. Louisiana's Separate Car Act was struck down for interstate passenger traffic, but "separate but equal" was left standing for intrastate movement. The Sierra Club was formed. Overcapacity in steel, lower prices and reduced wages caused the Homestead Strike, pitting labor against Pinkerton Agents at Andrew Carnegie's Homestead Steel Mill in Pennsylvania; plant manager Henry Clay Frick, the former coal king, used the strike as a means to drive out the union, but more than a dozen people lost their lives in the ensuing fray; with troops needed to quell the disturbance, this arguably represented the dawn of the organized labor movement. Market Hall, in Chicago's Pullman District, burned for the first time. Ellis Island opened as an immigration station, within sight of the Statue of Liberty; little did anyone know that 20 million immigrants would pass through the Great Hall over the next 62 years. Even though acquitted, 33-year old Lizzie Borden gained infamy wielding her hatchet against her parents in Fall River, Massachusetts. In September the first world's heavyweight boxing championship was contested with gloves; 26-year old James J. Corbett beat 33-year old John L. Sullivan in the 21st round in New Orleans; Corbett would retain the title for five years. The bottle cap was invented. The shared effort of biblical scholar William Rainey Harper and oil magnate John D. Rockefeller, the second and current University of Chicago opened its doors for the first time. In a devious plot to enhance his credit worthiness, streetcar utility tycoon Charles Tyson Yerkes promised one million dollars to the newly-founded University of Chicago to fund an astrophysical observatory; organized three years later, the Yerkes Observatory opened its 40-inch refracting telescope in 1897; Yerkes and his business ethic would be serialized in Theodore Dreiser's trilogy – *The Financier* (1912), *The Titan* (1914) and *The Stoic* (1947). The distinguished man of letters, Walt Whitman, passed away at age 72. Connecticut dentist Washington W. Sheffield moved toothpaste from jars into flexible metal tubes; on creating the first toothpaste tube, he increased hygiene and beget arguments about rolling up the tube. The Ohio Supreme Court ordered J.D. Rockefeller to break up his Standard Oil Trust monopoly in the oil industry, to little effect; Rockefeller would rebuild through the use of holding companies by 1899; in 1911 the U.S. Supreme Court broke that up too

The 1892 railroad station in St. Louis was the largest train shed in the world. In May predecessors to the FRISCO opened their bridge across the Mississippi river at Memphis, the first bridge across south of St. Louis. The first Chicago elevated train service was built by the Chicago and South Side Rapid Transit Company for the Chicago World's Columbian Exposition; it was a steam-powered train that went down alleys on elevated tracks from 12th Street to the fairgrounds nine miles away, and charged 5 cents for the trip. The unrepentant railroad pirate 56-year old Jay Gould, having managed to control half the nation's rail trackage, moves on to his reward having schemed for the last time.

In a deal that both extended its reach and lessened the competition, Illinois Central acquired the 807-mile long Louisville, New Orleans & Texas, which was owned by Collis P. Huntington of Central Pacific fame, for less than 60 cents on the dollar; the Louisville, New Orleans & Texas formed a mainline from Memphis to New Orleans, via Vicksburg and Baton Rouge, with a number of feeder lines and ferry access to Helena, Arkansas (begun in 1889) across the Mississippi river; the 807-mile line included 13 miles of track in Tennessee, 624 in Mississippi and 170 in Louisiana; in October the acquisition was merged into Illinois Central's subsidiary, the Yazoo & Mississippi Valley, which operated as a separate entity until 1924; one of the feeder lines was the 25-mile long West Feliciana branch

IC1892-07

IC1892-06

Illinois Central 2-6-4T suburban engine #232, Rogers-built in 1892 (56 1/2 D; 160 BP; 160,000 TW; 17,158 TF); note the signage heralds Blue Island. It is shown here in an R.A. Beck photograph, probably in the 1890's on the Chicago Lake Front. This engine was renumbered to IC #1423 in 1900, and sold in 1926 after electrification of the suburban service.

which dated back to 1832 and represented Illinois Central's oldest antecedent. With the World's Columbian Exposition on the horizon, Illinois Central prepared for the surge in passenger traffic to and from the Jackson Park site with the addition of suburban locomotives and passenger cars. Illinois Central completed its Adler & Sullivan designed New Orleans Passenger Station; Frank Lloyd Wright was an Adler & Sullivan assistant on the design. Even with floods for the second year in a row in Illinois and Iowa and especially the Mississippi River valley, revenues rose handsomely, to $19.3 million; almost 23 percent of revenues were from passenger traffic (11,912,463 passengers). Revenue traffic rose to over 7.5 million tons of freight. Illinois Central and its sister companies would deliver more than 10 percent of the entire U.S. cotton crop to New Orleans, almost one million bales. System mileage (not including the 807-mile Yazoo & Mississippi Valley) rose to 2,888 with the construction of 13 miles: the 4-mile long branch to Blue Island on the commuter line, and the 9-mile connector line into Chicago from the west on the Chicago, Madison & Northern line; there now were 1,394 miles north of the Ohio River, 600 west of the Mississippi River and 894 south of the Ohio River. The Company began construction of new shop facilities at Burnside, on the far southside of Chicago, with the intent of consolidating most Machinery Department work at one location; eventually the car works (former American Car Factory bought in 1856) were relocated from 27th Street (January, 1896) and the locomotive shops from 16th Street (March, 1893). A new "scientific" freight car classification yard was constructed at Fordham between 82nd and 90th Streets on the East side of the mainline, less than 11 miles south of Randolph street; this yard would perform Chicago Terminal yard operations for the next 34 years. Locomotive availability grew to 572 with the addition of 27 Rogers-built 2-8-0 Consolidation-type freight units, a number of switch engines and 3 8-wheeled Passenger units; the fleet roster was now composed of 23 suburban passenger units (with the delivery of two Rogers-built 2-6-4T suburban units), 273 8-wheeled passenger and freight units, 33 10-wheeled passenger and freight units, 145 2-6-0 Mogul-type freight locomotives, 29 2-8-0 Consolidation-type freight units and 71 switching units: 34 4-wheeled and 37 6-wheeled. To improve roadbed and operations, Illinois Central adopted the standard of 18-foot wide embankments as measured at the bottom of the ballast, up from the original 12 to 14-foot single-track embankments of the past.

Illinois Central #416, a 2-6-0 Mogul-type (56 1/2 D; 165 BP; 126,000 TW; 24,500 TF) built by Rogers in 1892, was captured at Effingham, Illinois circa 1901 in a negative by A.A. Loomis. This engine would retain its roster number for 30 years and then, in 1922, be rebuilt into 2-6-4T suburban engine IC #1454 (211,070 TW; 23,299 TF).

IC1892-05

Illinois Central #424 was another Rogers-built 2-6-0 Mogul with the same dimensions as IC #416, with one exception; this engine was built as a compound, specifically: 20, 29 x 26 inch cylinders. This engine was scrapped in 1926. This view was captured on the Chicago Lake Front probably when the engine was new in 1892.

IC1892-08

IC45x35-216

Illinois Central #633 was a Rogers-built 2-8-0 Consolidation (56 1/2 D; 165 BP; 137,300 TW; 26,272 TF); this engine was one of a series that were sold to the National Railroads of Mexico after the Illinois Central determined these units were underpowered for IC's needs; the engines were transferred to Mexico around 1921. IC #633 is shown pulling a work train.

Not every operation on the railroad was automated, as the pictures on the right will attest; in fact, labor was a major part of the equation. Coal loading spanned automated gravity dumps to inclined chutes to bucket brigades. Pictured at Wildwood Yard outside Chicago in 1916, a crew used buckets, albeit bigger than household, to load out IC #634.

Illinois Central #634 was a Rogers-built 2-8-0 Consolidation (56 1/2 D; 165 BP; 137,300 TW; 26,272 TF), a product of 1892. This engine was another in that series sold to the National Railroads of Mexico in 1921.

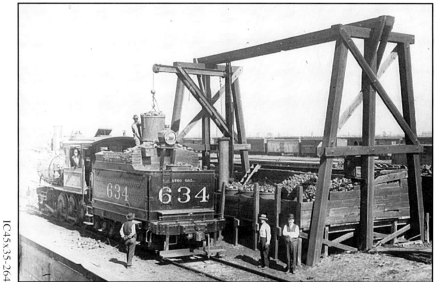

IC45x35-264

IC45x35-265

IC45x35-60

Illinois Central #930 was a Rogers 4-4-0 American-type product of 1892 (69 D; 165 BP; 110,200 TW; 15,805 TF). Renumbered IC #1930 in 1906, it was renumbered for the last time in the early 1920's to IC #4930; this engine saw service until retirement in 1928.

IC1892-04

Illinois Central #1932 was a similar 4-4-0 American-type (69 D; 165 BP; 110,200 TW; 15,805 TF) built by Rogers Locomotive in 1892; originally rostered as IC #932, it gained its markings as shown in 1906 and was renumbered once again in the early 1920's to IC #4932. This engine was retired in 1929. This photograph was captured near Haleyville, Alabama in June, 1911; it was a special train advertising development in the countryside. On the first car behind the tender there is a three-line sign posted on the side; it read: "Drain the Swamps," "Exterminate the Mosquito," and "Make Homes on the Land."

Three Cooke-built 4-4-0 Americans, products (63 D; 165 BP; 103,000 TW; 17,311 TF) of 1892. All three originally were built for the Newport News & Mississippi Valley railroad, when that railroad leased the Chesapeake Ohio and Southwestern; these engines had roster numbers of NN&MV #541, #542 and #543. They were rostered on the Illinois Central as IC #948, #949, and #950 in 1896; they were renumbered into the 1900-series in 1906, and the 4900-series in the early 1920's. The picture of IC #4948 appeared in the December, 1928 issue of the IC Magazine; this engine was snapped at Memphis, Tennessee on November 2, 1928; the engine often worked an employee train between McLemore Avenue at Memphis and Nonconnah Yard a few miles away. IC #4949 was captured at 27th Street in Chicago, in suburban service in 1926 (note signage for Matteson). IC #4950 was caught at New Orleans in 1926.

IC1892-02

IC1892-01

IC1892-03

1893

The Montreal Amateur Athletic Association Hockey Club won the first trophy, donated by Canada's Governor-General Lord Preston of Stanley.

In March 55-year old Grover Cleveland was sworn in as the 24th President of the United States. Coca-Cola registered its trademark in the U.S. Patent Office. With farm prices dropping in the south and west, investors began hoarding cash which caused deposits to shrink; the resulting Panic would see over 350 banking institutions fail throughout the south and west; to help quell the Panic, the U.S. decided to remain on the gold standard. Colorado granted women's suffrage rights. The U.S. sent out its first ambassador ever – former Senator and Presidential aspirant Thomas F. Bayard of Delaware to Great Britain. Oklahoma Land Rush continued with the largest section of land – over six million acres – opened up to homesteading; this "rush" was the last of six that populated the former Indian Territory. Hawaii was declared under U.S. protection. The World's Columbian Exposition - the White City – was officially opened by newly-returned-to-office President Grover Cleveland in May in Chicago; the Fair included more than 150 buildings spread over 600 acres, with adult daily admission set at 50 cents. The Ferris Wheel (designed by 34-year old American bridge builder George Washington Ferris), zipper (invented by Whitcomb L. Judson) and fiberglass would all debut at the White City, and Pabst Beer would earn its blue ribbon. At a time when the U.S. population was less than 70 million, the Fair would draw over 25 million visitors in its six short months. Bicycle designers Charles E. and J. Frank Duryea demonstrated their internal combustion gasoline-powered automobile in Massachusetts, the first to do so in the U.S. Henry Morrison Flagler purchased land in Florida for the first time, and added an interest in resort hotels to his railroads that would last until his death in 1913.

With an overbuilding of railroads causing a crash in the stock market, the U.S. suffered the Panic of 1893; almost 500 banks and 15,000 businesses would fail; only one transcontinental railroad would survive the depression – Hill's Great Northern Railway. The Great Northern completed its line between the Great Lakes and Puget Sound arriving at Everett, Washington, in January, crossing the Cascade Range at Stevens Pass; this would form the fourth major transcontinental route in the U.S. The Panic caused by the railroads and the stock market would spread into a national depression in the Spring affecting the entire populace. The Northern Pacific was bankrupt by the depression and this, its second bankruptcy, would open the way for J. J. Hill to take control three years later. The American Railway Union, the largest union of railway workers yet organized, was begun. New York Central & Hudson River engine No. 999, (a 4-4-0 American with 86" drivers built at their West Albany Shops), broke the 100-mph barrier setting a claimed speed record of 112.5-mph in May pulling the *Empire State Express*, a record it would argue for eight years. In one of his last official acts, President Harrison signed the Safety Appliance Act requiring air brakes and automatic couplers on all trains.

The *Nancy Hanks* set a speed record with a solid consist of bananas. Illinois Central completed it's Chicago passenger facility at 12th Street and Michigan Avenue – Central Station, built near the old Weldon Yard and locomotive shops between 12th/16th Streets that had been there almost 40 years; Company offices adjoined the passenger facility, and the Weldon shop activities were relocated to the new Burnside Shops. Illinois Central revenues crossed another milestone in approaching $20.1 million for the fiscal year, effectively all of the increase attributed to passenger service; almost 26 percent of revenues were from passenger traffic: 17,661,828 passengers, of which 11,292,517 were commuters and 1,848,822 were travelers using Illinois Central's service to the World's Columbian Exposition Fair grounds. To facilitate passenger traffic to the Jackson Park site, the suburban tracks had been elevated between 51st and 67th Streets an average of ten feet, on a 130-foot wide embankment, calling for 12 new bridges where the intersecting street would be lowered two to four feet for clearance, and 31 suburban coaches had been added to help handle passenger loads; the grade returned to the old level at 47th and 71st Streets; in the end, 41 locomotives (some suburban and some brought in for special duty), 300 passenger cars and two tracks were dedicated to the World's Fair traffic; express service during the Fair left Randolph Street every fifteen minutes. During the Fair's six-month run from May 1st to October 30th which spread over two of the Company's fiscal reporting periods, Illinois Central handled a total of 8,780,616 passengers on Special World's Fair Trains at a fixed rate of ten cents each for the nine mile trip; Illinois Central hauled all-time one-day record of over 505,000 passengers on Chicago Day at the World's Fair, October 9th the 22nd Anniversary of the Chicago Fire; Chicago Mayor Carter Harrison was assassinated a few days later, just before the Fair closed on October 30th. With the completion of the World's Fair, Illinois Central

IC45x35-153

Illinois Central #147, a Brooks-built 0-6-0 (51 D; 94,000 TW) switch engine of 1893. It was captured shuffling passenger cars at an unknown location and time.

suburban service began express train service; with no stops between Van Buren and Hyde Park, the commuter run between Randolph and Grand Crossing went from 32 minutes to 20. Locomotive availability grew to 595 with the addition of 8 2-8-0 Consolidation-type freight units and 24 2-6-0 Mogul-type freight engines (10 units were purchased outside); the fleet roster was now composed of 31 suburban passenger units (with the delivery of 8 Rogers-built 2-4-6T suburban units), 254 8-wheeled passenger and freight units, 33 10-wheeled passenger and freight units, 169 2-6-0 Mogul-type freight locomotives, 37 2-8-0 Consolidation-type freight units and 71 switching units: 34 4-wheeled and 37 6-wheeled. Illinois Central purchased a controlling interest in Collis P. Huntington's Chesapeake, Ohio and Southwestern Railroad and affiliates; with a mainline from Memphis to Louisville via Paducah, the acquisition provided Illinois Central a direct connection between Memphis and Fulton, Kentucky, obviating the need for cars headed north from Memphis to first be backed 100 miles south to the Illinois Central mainline at Grenada; Illinois Central also gained trackage and access to terminals in Evansville, Indiana (via ferry to the north side of the Ohio River) and Louisville, Kentucky (on the south side of the Ohio River); these 456 miles of track would be consolidated into operations four years later, after a number of legal hurdles. System mileage (not including the 807-mile Yazoo & Mississippi Valley nor the 456-mile Chesapeake, Ohio and Southwestern) remained steady at 2,888: 1,394 miles north of the Ohio River, 600 west of the Mississippi River and 894 south of the Ohio River. The Directors of the Company provided for an Improvement Fund to upgrade freight car capacity, deciding to replace 10 and 12-ton capacities with 20-ton and higher cars. Revenue traffic rose to over 8.1 million tons of freight; freight tonnage on the unconsolidated Yazoo & Mississippi Valley for the eight months under possession exceeded 813,000 tons. Placed in operation on January 1st two new brick engine roundhouses at 27th Street: one with 20 stalls intended for the suburban "teakettle" steam locomotives and the other with 23 stalls for passenger and freight steam locomotives.

CYLS.		BOILER PRESS.	FIREBOX		GRATE AREA	HEATING SURFACES				WEIGHTS			TRACTIVE EFFORT	DIA. DRIVER
D.	S.		L.	W.		FIREBOX	TUBES	TOTAL	SUPER.	DRIVER	TRUCK	TOTAL		
18"	24"	150	78"	33⅞"	18.19	117.70	1034.3	1152.0	-	84000	-	84000	19440	51"

Illinois Central #141 was an 1893 Brooks-built 0-6-0 (51 D; 150 BP; 84,000 TW; 19,440 TF) switch engine. The photograph above had an engine dimensions chart attached; the picture below highlights the two-man crew with tender loaded and ready for work. Time and place of the view were unidentified.

Rogers products of 1893, these photographs show 2-6-0 Moguls (56 1/2 D; 165 BP; 126,000 TW; 24,500 TF). IC #433 was captured in storage, with parts removed and its smoke door open. IC #442 was snapped as it finished at the water tipple, with its fireman and engineer ready for duty. While these photographs date to an unidentified time and place, the picture of IC #447 probably is the oldest, maybe dating back to when nearly-new. IC #447 was snapped with its crew ready to couple on to a string of cars; this picture appeared in the November, 1922 Illinois Central Magazine. IC #442 might have been the longest-lived 2-6-0 Mogul, built in 1893 it saw service until 1954...61 years.

IC1893-01

Illinois Central #638, an 1893 Rogers-built 2-8-0 Consolidation (56 1/2 D; 165 BP; 137,300 TW; 26,272 TF); two views, same engine, 30 years apart. The photograph above was famous and often-published, appearing in the March, 1929 issue of the Illinois Central Magazine. While there is disagreement as to where the picture was captured - Hunter's Cut just north of Water Valley, Mississippi or Halls, Tennessee between Fulton and Memphis - there was a consensus as to who appeared in the picture - Casey Jones (engineer, in the right seat) and J.W. McKinney (fireman, in the gangway). This picture was believed to be the only photograph of Casey Jones at the throttle of an Illinois Central steam engine; the photograph dates to 1898, or two years before Casey Jones death. The view below of IC #638 shows many changes, not the least of which is a steel cab. The 2-8-0's in this series from Rogers were thought to be underpowered and, as such, were sold to the National Railroads of Mexico in 1921; the photograph shows old IC #638 at Sabinas, Mexico on October 17, 1928, still carrying its Illinois Central markings. This was the only Illinois Central engine to ever carry #638.

ICDPL-10

Photo Courtesy of Denver Public Library, Western History Department, Otto C. Perry Photograph Collection (DPL#20609), Denver.

These Baldwin-built 4-6-0 (51 D; 165 BP; 120,000 TW; 23,826 TF) 10-wheelers were two such engines produced for the St. Louis Alton & Terre Haute in 1893; they originally were rostered as StLA&TH #32 and #33. When Illinois Central took control of the StLA&TH in 1896, it acquired these engines and promptly renumbered them IC #344 and #345; they were renumbered in 1917 to the 2300-series shown. Note both engines have front and rear headlamps for switching service. IC #2344 above was captured at Markham Yard in May, 1927. IC #2345 was snapped at an unknown location.

On these two pages, seven views of 2-4-6T suburban engines, all Rogers-built in 1893 (56 1/2 D; 160 BP; 166,000 TW; 16,695 TF); all pictures were from the Chicagland area, where IC had its commuter service. Counter clockwise, from right, IC #1424 is shown with, left to right, Jack Keeler (conductor), Frank Bellows (engineer), Garrett Orth (fireman), and George Kern (hostler); this photograph dates to Homewood, Illinois on July 10, 1902; the engine was marked for Flossmoor. Next was IC #1426, tagged for Grand Crossing and posed with her crew. Bottom is IC #1427 working a run to Addison. IC #1431, opposite, was caught in Chicago on September 23, 1930 marked up for Addison. IC #1430 was tagged for Grand Crossing. IC #1429 pushed a string of cars and headed for South Chicago. Lastly was IC #1428, coupled and ready for Addison.

IC1893-04

IC45x35-144

IC1893-11

IC1893-12

IC1893-13

IC45x35-145

ICDPL-03

Photo Courtesy of Denver Public Library, Western History Department, Otto C. Perry Photograph Collection (DPL#12259), Denver.

IC1893-08

Original 1893 Rogers-built 2-6-0 Mogul-type (56 1/2 D; 165 BP; 126,000 TW; 24,500 TF) is shown above, captured at Kankakee, Illinois on March 11, 1943. IC #431 was in service on the Illinois Central from 1893 to 1915, when it was lent to the Engineering School of Purdue University in West Lafayette, Indiana; the engine was used for demonstrations in Purdue's testing labs. The engine stayed at Purdue from 1915 to 1943; due to a shortage of locomotive power during the War, the unit was returned to the Illinois Central. Upon return in 1943, IC rebuilt the 2-6-0 into an 0-6-0T (IC #3291) saddle-tank engine (same dimensions); the rebuild began service at the Mattoon roundhouse, and then finished at Markham Yard, replacing IC #3289.

IC1893-14

ICLAG06-01

This oft-published photograph shows the roundhouses at 27th Street on the Illinois Central mainline, hard by Lake Michigan's shoreline. Illinois Central moved most of the locomotive work to 27th Street in 1893, freeing up space at Weldon Yard closer in to the City; 27th Street housed both suburban and freight engines. These photographs date to August, 1917 after additions had been made to the roundhouses. In the close-up picture below, since the view is to the north-northeast, Navy Pier can be seen just above and to the right of the rightmost smokestack.

ICLAG06-03

Part of the news in 1893 was completion of the Illinois Central passenger facility at 12th Street on the near southside of Chicago. The replacement for the old Great Central Station was opened in time for the World's Columbian Exposition. The station was constructed as a through-station, where trains could literally drive straight through the open-ended train shed and station. When new, the east side of the station butted right up against Lake Michigan. In time, this area would be filled in as Lake Park (later, Grant Park), created out of submerged land; Soldier Field and a number of museums would be located on this land in the future.

ICLAG07-11

The photograph above dates to October 23, 1893, one week before the closing of the World's Columbian Exposition; note the horse-and-buggies lined up awaiting customers; this view is toward the east-southeast. The picture bottom right, a view straight south, shows the through-tracks, and waiting platforms for suburban trains. Opposite page top is a view west-northwest looking back across 12th Street Station from the water's edge; this photograph dates to August 10, 1894 and shows passenger and freight trains at work, and Lake Michigan lapping at the edge of the tracks; this photograph was published in the January, 1937 issue of the Illinois Central Magazine. Opposite page bottom is a view looking straight down the center of the train shed, showing the open-on-all sides design; the train shed rose 62 1/2 feet over the rails and was 610 feet long, covering six tracks, four under roof and two under the wings.

IC45x35-01

ICLAG07-12

ICLAG07-13

1894

Japan feuded with China in the Sino-Japanese war, a preview of the future; Japan would force the Chinese to renounce their control of Korea. 42-year old English chemist William Ramsey and a partner produced argon in a laboratory; Ramsay would generate helium the next year.

Milton Hershey began marketing his new chocolate bar. Jacob S. Coxey led his army of unemployed men to Washington D.C. demonstrating for a public works program – jobs. Labor unrest spread to the coal miners, lowering shipments and putting a crimp in locomotive fuel supplies. While the new American Railway Union launched its first strike ever against Hill's Great Northern, it's action against Pullman really served notice. In May industrial magnate George Pullman, squeezed by the economic depression, responded by cutting wages while maintaining rent levels in his 13-year old utopian village on the outskirts of Chicago; the resulting Pullman Strike, led by 39-year old Eugene V. Debs and the American Railway Union, was staged to protest those wage cuts and other grievances; when railroad employees in Chicago supported the Pullman workers and refused to move cars with Pullman equipment, a boycott quickly spread to take in 27 states, seven of which would call out troops; fires caused by the labor unrest in Chicago destroyed most of the buildings left over from the Columbian Exposition, and torched many rail yards in the City, including the destruction of 70 some freight cars near Illinois Central's Fordham Yard; federal troops were called in by President Grover Cleveland, over the protests of Illinois' 47-year old pro-labor governor John Peter Altgeld, which stopped the union in July. Coca-Cola began marketing its drink in bottles. Having built railroads and designed the Chicago Union Stockyards as a civil engineer, Paris-born 62-year old Octave Chanute began writing about and experimenting with his flying machines. Three years after ascending to her brother's throne, Queen Liliuokalani lost control and her Monarchy when Hawaii was turned into a Republic; Sanford B. Dole was its first President. The Lowell Observatory, built to study the planet Mars, opened in Flagstaff, Arizona. Born a slave in Holly Springs, Mississippi during the Civil War, 32-year old Ida B. Wells became an activist and journalist, and founded the first black woman's club in Chicago.

The Santa Fe introduced an oil-burning steam locomotive. St. Louis opened its vast Union Station. In July the Southern Railway was formed out of the financial ruins of the Richmond & Danville Railroad. In May Dr. John Harvey Kellogg and his brother Will Keith Kellogg stumbled into flaked cereals, corn flakes following soon after.

IC revenues set another record, approaching $20.7 million for the fiscal year; with the depression in business conditions throughout the country, all of the revenue increase was attributed to passenger service, more than 29 percent of revenues from passenger traffic: 22,897,476 passengers, of which 11,961,690 were commuters and 6,931,794 were travelers using Illinois Central's service to the World's Columbian Exposition Fair grounds, with two-thirds of the Fair's passenger traffic falling in this fiscal reporting period. Revenue traffic dropped to just under 7.4 million tons of freight; freight tonnage on the unconsolidated Yazoo & Mississippi Valley exceeded 1.1 million tons. System mileage (not including the 807-mile Yazoo & Mississippi Valley nor the 456-mile Chesapeake, Ohio and Southwestern) remained 2,888: 1,394 miles north of the Ohio River, 600 west of the Mississippi River and 894 south of the Ohio River. With the addition of a single 2-8-0 Consolidation-type unit and 49 purchased units replacing retirements, locomotive availability grew to 598: composed of 31 suburban passenger units, 218 8-wheeled passenger and freight units, 33 10-wheeled passenger and freight units, 194 2-6-0 Mogul-type freight locomotives, 38 2-8-0 Consolidation-type freight units and 84 switching units: 32 4-wheeled and 52 6-wheeled.

Destruction of railroad cars in the Pullman Strike of 1894 was widespread, and touched the Illinois Central along with many other railroads. Above and below are photographs showing the fire damage to some of the Illinois Central freight cars in that disruptive strike; the freight equipment that was destroyed had been set out on side tracks between Burnside Crossing and 104th Street. The above picture was taken from the southern end of the damaged cars, looking back north toward downtown Chicago. The lower photograph shows another view of the destruction. The strike happened on July 5th and 6th, 1894; these pictures were snapped on July 15, 1894 after Federal troops stopped the destruction.

IC1894-02

Illinois Central #292, an 1894 Baldwin-built 4-6-0 (55 D; 109,200 TW; 18,026 TF) 10-wheeler was constructed for the Ohio Valley railroad (originally rostered as OV #24); when Illinois Central acquired the OV in 1897, this engine was part of the transaction. IC #292 was captured at Henderson, Kentucky on June 17, 1900. This photograph, which appeared in the February, 1927 issue of the Illinois Central Magazine, showed the engine pulling a solid 35-car trainload of tobacco. The signage on the car behind the tender reads: "Solid Train of Tobacco, From Henderson, Ky. to Liverpool Eng & Belfast, Ireland, via ICRR to New Orleans."

Illinois Central #452 was an 1894 Rogers-built 2-6-0 Mogul-type (56 1/2 D; 165 BP; 126,000 TW; 24,500 TF), caught right next to Lake Michigan in an R.A. Beck photograph; the engine was hauling a solid trainload of refrigerator cars. This picture, which dates to the 1890's, appeared in the Illinois Central Magazine in the 1950's.

IC45x35-195

Illinois Central #458 was another Rogers-built 2-6-0 Mogul-type (56 1/2 D; 165 BP; 126,000 TW; 24,500 TF); since the picture dates from June 14, 1938, it shows a modernized version of that 1894 engine. While this engine never sported any other roster position, it stayed in service until 1949. This picture was taken at Freeport, Illinois. The tender held 15 tons of coal and 7,000 gallons of boiler water.

Illinois Central #1940 (originally rostered as IC #940) was a Brooks-built 4-4-0 American (69 D; 118,800 TW) constructed in 1894. Renumbered from IC #940 to IC #1940 in 1906, it was renumbered yet again in the early 1920's to IC #4940. It was captured working at Paducah in March, 1911; the engine was retired in 1928.

1895

Cuban nationalists began skirmishing against Spanish colonial authorities. German physicist 50-year old Wilhelm Konrad Roentgen discovered electro-magnetic rays which he named "X-rays"; in 1901 he would be awarded the first Nobel Prize in Physics for his work. With both the English and Italian governments showing no interest in his work, 21-year old Italian electrical engineer Guglielmo Marconi developed his concept of wireless radio transmissions or telegraphy; these theories would hasten the day of television, radar, wireless telephone and radio; they would also earn him the Nobel Prize in Physics in 1909. French inventors 33-year old Auguste and 31-year old Louis Lumiere invented the cinematograph, a machine that reduced the jumpiness in moving pictures being played on Edison's kinetoscope. Italian criminologist Cesare Lombroso developed a crude but scientific lie detector, measuring pulse rate and blood pressure. The Sino-Japanese war ended with Japan taking control of the island of Formosa from China; this war was simply the first in a series for imperialist Japan. 29-year old English author Herbert George "H.G." Wells published *The Time Machine*, Morlocks and Eloi in time without ever leaving Earth.

Pennsylvanian John Mast built the first mousetrap. Chicago held America's first automobile contest, six cars racing the 54 miles to Evanston and back; Frank Duryea, in one of the two cars to finish, won the race with an elapsed time of just under 10 ½ hours; the Duryea brothers became the first to market a gasoline-operated automobile. 40-year old King Camp Gillette came up with the idea of a disposable safety razor, thus no re-sharpening. In October eleven golfers, one an amateur, got together and played the first U.S. Open; the match was four rounds of nine holes in one day at Newport Golf Club in Rhode Island. The U.S. Patent Office issued its first patent on a gasoline-powered engine; Henry Ford later would successfully challenge the validity of this patent. 30-year old German-born mathematician Charles P. Steinmetz working at the General Electric laboratory in Schenectady, New York received a patent for the AC power system. 24-year old Stephen Crane published *The Red Badge of Courage*, his classic on baptism by fire during the Civil War. 27-year old Massachusetts-born William Edward Burghardt (W.E.B.) DuBois became the first black to receive a Ph.D. from Harvard.

The Santa Fe, bankrupt in the panic two years earlier, was reorganized for operation; the New York, Lake Erie and Western Railroad having suffered similarly, was reorganized for the third time, on this occasion as the Erie Railroad. Henry M. Flagler changed the name of his Jacksonville-St. Augustine-Indian River Railroad to the Florida East Coast Railway.

Even with record freight revenues, without the World's Fair passenger business total revenues dropped to less than $19.1 million; over 20 percent of revenues were attributable to passenger traffic (11,391,733 passengers). Revenue traffic rebounded to 7.9 million tons of freight; tonnage on the unconsolidated Yazoo & Mississippi Valley almost reached 1.2 million tons. During the fiscal period, system mileage (not including the 807-mile Yazoo & Mississippi Valley nor the 456-mile Chesapeake, Ohio and Southwestern) remained 2,888: 1,394 miles north of the Ohio River, 600 west of the Mississippi River and 894 south of the Ohio River; toward the end of the year, Illinois Central leased 239-miles of track from the St. Louis, Alton & Terre Haute (former Cairo Short Line); these tracks connected the St. Louis area back to Illinois Central's Land Grant mainline, and would be included in the next fiscal reporting period. With 19 purchased units replacing retirements of smaller locomotives, roster availability was 597: composed of 33 suburban passenger units (with the receipt of 2 Rogers-built 2-4-6T units), 207 8-wheeled passenger and freight units, 34 10-wheeled passenger and freight units, 204 2-6-0 Mogul-type freight locomotives, 38 2-8-0 Consolidation-type freight units and 83 switching units: 31 4-wheeled and 52 6-wheeled. On the commuter line, platforms were constructed at all stations north of Kensington to match the floor level of the passenger cars. In an October 21st City Ordinance, Illinois Central and City of Chicago authorities hammered out an agreement settling lake front property disputes dating back to restrictions imposed in 1852; Illinois Central was granted ownership of certain land between the Chicago River and 16th Street (some of it underwater) amounting to roughly 55 acres, and in return Illinois Central agreed to relocate its operation below grade so that stations and equipment were not visible from street level of the City; this agreement resulted in Illinois Central's below-grade Van Buren Street station (completed 1897), one of it's two in-town passenger stations for the Chicago commuter service.

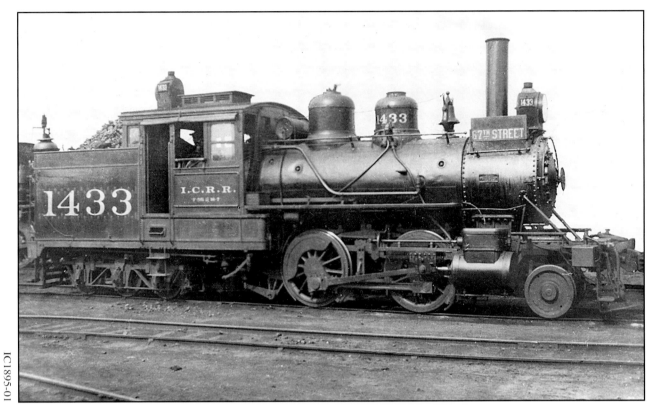

Illinois Central suburban engine #1433 was an 1895 Rogers-built 2-4-6T (56 1/2 D; 160 BP; 166,000 TW; 16,695 TF); pictured at 27th Street in Chicago in July, 1914 this engine originally was rostered as IC #250, then renumbered as shown in 1900. This photograph appeared in the February, 1946 issue of the Illinois Central Magazine.

Illinois Central #464 was an 1895 Rogers-built 2-6-0 Mogul (56 1/2 D; 165 BP; 126,000 TW; 24,500 TF). This unit, captured at an unknown time and place, saw duty until 1928.

IC1895-04

IC4x4-03

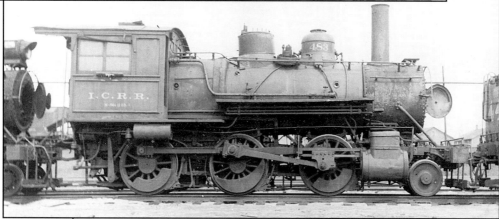

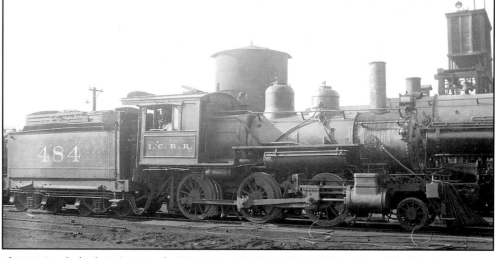

These two pages, five views of 1895 Brooks-built 2-6-0 Moguls (56 1/2 D; 165 BP; 126,000 TW; 24,500 TF). IC #473 on opposite page saw service until 1955. IC #479 on top appeared in the April, 1939 issue of the IC Magazine; the photograph from 1907 shows the engine being used as a switch engine in Centralia's old North Yards; identified in the picture were: Charles E. Barr (engineer, on steam chest) and switchmen W.H. Jones and Charles Sargent; the tender held 7 1/2 tons of coal and 3,850 gallons of water. IC #483 is shown in storage, missing parts. IC #484 was caught at Freeport in July, 1944.

1896

The Olympics returned after a 1,500-year sabbatical; the men-only summer games were held in Athens, 13 nations showed up. Cuban independence efforts continued, with severe reprisals from Spanish overlords. Gold was found in the Yukon Territory of Canada in August; the Klondike Gold Rush would peak two years later. On his death, 63-year old bachelor Alfred B. Nobel of Sweden donated his fortune to a foundation that would acknowledge contributions in science, literature and peace; the first Prizes would be handed out in 1901. In Paris, 44-year old Antoine Henri Becquerel discovered radioactivity; he would share the Nobel Prize in Physics in 1903 for his research.

The U.S. Supreme Court upheld Louisiana's Separate Car Act for intrastate passenger business (on the East Louisiana Railroad), thus allowing "separate but equal" segregation to apply within individual States; while struck down for interstate traffic, it was just the beginning of the long road to desegregation; it would be 58 years before the Supreme Court would reverse this ruling. The Post Office began Rural Free Delivery in sparsely populated areas. One of the first successful comic strips – the Katzenjammer Kids – appeared in the Hearst newspaper the New York Journal. American aviation pioneer 62-year old Samuel Pierpont Langley conducted the first unmanned, heavier-than-air powered airplane flight in May. German glider builder Otto Lilienthal, whose pioneering study of lift on curved surfaces influenced future aviators work, had a fatal crash in one of his gliders. Henry Ford assembled his first automobile in Detroit. Austrian immigrant Leo Hirshfield hand-rolled his first Tootsie Roll, named after his daughter. The Dow Jones Industrial Average appeared in the *Wall Street Journal*. At the 11th Republican convention in St. Louis, Ohio Governor William McKinley was elected the nominee for President on the 1st ballot; New Jersey civil servant and former state legislator Garret A. Hobart was chosen the nominee for Vice President on the 1st ballot. At the 17th Democratic-Populist convention in Chicago, former Congressman William Jennings Bryan of Nebraska was elected by the Silver-Democrats the nominee for President on the 5th ballot; businessman and Democratic National Committee member Arthur Sewall of Maine was chosen the nominee for Vice President on the 5th ballot. At the breakaway National Democratic convention in Indianapolis, Illinois Senator General John M. Palmer was elected by the Gold Democrats the nominee for President on the 1st ballot; former Governor of Kentucky and C.S.A. General Simon Bolivar Buckner was chosen the nominee for Vice President on the 1st ballot. Despite William Jennings Bryan's famous "Cross of Gold" speech, the Republican ticket of McKinley/Hobart won the election on a "sound money" platform. Utah and Idaho granted women's suffrage rights. Utah was admitted to the Union as the 45th State. Former Bureau of the Census worker 36-year old Herman Hollerith founded the Tabulating Machine Company, which became IBM in 1924 after a number of name changes. 32-year old George Washington Carver joined 40-year old Booker T. Washington at Tuskegee Institute where the two educators would make history. Tennessee was the first State to stop the practice of convict leasing, the trade in free labor to generate State funds; convict leasing would be replaced by chain gangs at the County level, and over the next 50 years every State in the Union save Rhode Island would have some such work program.

With the help of J. P. Morgan at reorganizing and developing restrictive alliances, James J. Hill gained control of the Northern Pacific Railroad, even though he owned less than 50% of the stock. The Baltimore & Ohio Railroad went bankrupt and into receivership. The East Chicago Belt Railroad was incorporated; its name was changed eleven years later to Indiana Harbor Belt Railway.

IC revenues rose to a record $22 million, with 20 percent attributable to passenger traffic (12,812,206 passengers). Revenue traffic notched a record in reaching almost 9.7 million tons of freight; tonnage on the unconsolidated Yazoo & Mississippi Valley almost reached 1.2 million tons. System mileage (not including the 807-mile Yazoo & Mississippi Valley nor the 456-mile Chesapeake, Ohio and Southwestern) rose to 3,127 with the inclusion of the 239 miles of St. Louis, Alton & Terre Haute trackage; the composition now was: 1,633 miles north of the Ohio River, 600 west of the Mississippi River and 894 south of the Ohio River; toward the end of the year the 3-mile long Mound City Railway, a separately operated subsidiary since 1882, was combined into Illinois Central operations to be included in the next fiscal reporting period. With 40 units received with the lease of the St. Louis, Alton & Terre Haute (8 switchers, 10 8-wheel, 16 10-wheel and 6 Moguls) and 45 purchased units replacing retirements and scrapped units, roster availability rose to 626: composed of 33 suburban passenger units, 162 8-wheeled passenger and freight units, 50 10-wheeled passenger and freight units, 249 2-6-0 Mogul-type freight locomotives, 38 2-8-0 Consolidation-type freight units and 94 switching units: 33 4-wheeled and 61 6-wheeled. The Company began

IC45x35-248

Illinois Central #2003 was captured coming off the turntable at Paducah in a photograph dated between 1907 and 1922. This engine was a Rogers-built 4-6-0 (69 D; 158,300 TW) 10-wheeler; constructed in 1896, it originally carried the roster number IC #373; it was renumbered to IC #203 in 1900, to IC #2003 in 1907 and to IC #5003 in 1922. This engine saw 40 years of service, retiring in 1936.

paying wages to employees with checks drawn on local banks, rather than cash; first started with employees north of the Ohio river, it spread to all employees six years later; so began the demise of wages paid cash-in-hand from the Paymaster visiting monthly in his pay car. Capitalizing on its control of the Chesapeake, Ohio and Southwestern, on June 1st Illinois Central began operating Chicago to New Orleans passenger trains via Memphis instead of Jackson, providing Memphis through train service while adding only ten miles to the distance. A group of Illinois Central workers, mostly Burnside shop employees, formed the Illinois Central Railroad Union Band and Orchestra. Illinois Central began implementing its part of the Lake Front Improvement project.

IC 1896-02

These two views highlight the changes to an engine over the years as they were modernized, maintained and modified; as depicted, the difference in age between the two engines shown was 30 years. Both of the engines were from a series of 40 built by Rogers Locomotive for the Illinois Central in the late 1890's; this series included the engine in which Casey Jones rode into fame (IC #382). These particular 4-6-0 10-wheelers were built in 1896 (69 D; 180 BP; 158,300 TW; 21,922 TF) and retired 39 years later.

The photograph at top is a Builder's Photo taken at the Roger's plant in Paterson, New Jersey in 1896. The view in the bottom picture was snapped at Memphis, Tennessee on December 7, 1926. The engines in this series had economy steam chests, Baker valve gear and were superheated. In noting 30 years of changes between the two pictures, the celestory disappeared, the steam chest was modernized, and the headlamp improved, along with other alterations.

IC 1896-03

On the opposite page, three 2-6-0 Moguls, the top one a Brooks product and the other two Rogers-built, all in 1896 (56 1/2 D; 165 BP; 126,000 TW; 24,500 TF). IC #488 was caught with its switch crew on a run between Webster City and Fort Dodge, Iowa; this picture, which dates to 1924, appeared in the January, 1925 issue of the IC Magazine; identified in the photo were, left to right, A. Fisher (engineer), P.J. Reidy (fireman), J.S. Pyle (conductor), and brakemen A.R. Mead and H. Coffey. IC #495 (with IC #479 behind it) was seen pushing through the periodic high water from the Mississippi river on the Cleveland district in Mississippi. IC #499, which appeared in the June, 1930 issue of the IC Magazine, was caught in the yard at Council Bluffs, Iowa in 1907; identified, left to right, were C.L. Rankin, Sr. (engine foreman), M.A. Doran (switchman), F.G. Slusher (engineer, in cab), and F.G. Alexander (engineer, on ground).

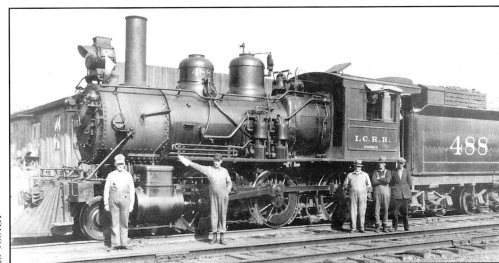

IC1896-07

IC45x35-196

IC1896-04

IC1896-06

IC1896-01

These engines represent another of Illinois Central's experiments, here at engineering a sleeker and lighter passenger engine. What resulted was a series of nine Brooks-built 4-4-0 American-types (75 D; 200 BP; 121,000 TW; 19,094 TF). Originally rostered as IC #961 to IC #969, they were renumbered into the 1900-series in 1906, and then the 4900-series in the early 1920's. The experiment proved less than perfect as the units were a little too light, and with high drivers, generated too little tractive force. For appearances, the experiment included moving the air pumps and sand box underneath the boiler. This series also was Illinois Central's first try at 200 pound boiler pressure.

The photograph on top shows a Builder's view of the first in the series, Illinois Central #961; this photograph was taken at the Brooks Locomotive Works, in Dunkirk, New York, and was published in the January, 1924 issue of the Illinois Central Magazine. In the bottom photograph, IC #1966 was captured at 27th Street in Chicago on November 30, 1907. Only 11 years old, and already the sandbox experiment had been changed back to the old reliable. All of the engines in this series were retired between 1922 and 1926.

As part of its agreement with Chicago in the Lake Front Improvement Ordinance, Illinois Central worked to build a retaining wall and backfill the park area between that retaining wall and Michigan Avenue. These two pictures from May, 1896 show that work underway. The top picture shows a view north from 12th Street Station toward South Water Street; the hole in the retaining wall on the left allowed trainloads of backfill to enter the parkside. This picture appeared in the January, 1937 issue of the Illinois Central Magazine. The lower photograph was taken from the Station facing north and shows a bird's-eye view of the work area. The West retaining wall bisects the picture from the bottom to the Art Institute near the left horizon. Note the two South Water Street grain elevators on the right horizon.

Ever since it first entered Chicago over the Lake Front, Illinois Central had bargained, negotiated and fought with the City powers; in allowing IC to build to the Chicago river over trestle on the lakefront, both parties had benefits: the City did receive protection from Lake erosion on Michigan Avenue and Illinois Central did get the most direct entrance into the City center, but past that the parties had trouble agreeing on the particulars. The City of Chicago, the South Park Commissioners and the Illinois Central would hammer out a number of agreements over the years, especially the 1895 Lake Front Ordinance, and similar pacts dating 1912 and 1919.

In the 1895 Ordinance, Illinois Central agreed to backfill Lake Park (the future Grant Park) between Michigan Avenue and a retaining wall the railroad would build near its tracks; the practical effect of this would be to make the tracks invisible from Michigan Avenue. In addition, the IC was to allow bridges to be built over its right-of-way, in the event the City filled in portions of the Lake on the east side of the IC tracks; this would allow the City to connect both sides of the Park. In the later agreements amending and expanding the Lake Front Ordinance, Illinois Central's role would be enlarged to include complete grade separation, electrification of the commuter service, and even sandy beaches for the public.

Another item in the 1895 Ordinance allowed the Illinois Central to purchase approximately 55 acres of submerged land, with permission to backfill it and locate facilities on the reclaimed property. These 55 acres of lagoon had been formed when the IC built its trestle entrance to South Water Street; the two pictures on the opposite page highlight the 55 acres of submerged land. The photograph on top faces north-northeast toward South Water Street and shows the lagoon formed by the trestle; note the grain elevators A and B in the photo. The lower picture was taken from the opposite vantage point, at the north end of the lagoon, looking back south-southwest toward 12th Street Station; note the buildings that front on Michigan Avenue. These two photographs date to April/May, 1896.

The photograph at the bottom of this page showed results; it dated to July, 1896, just a few months after the pictures on the opposite page. This picture was from the same vantage point as the one at the bottom of the previous page; the reader can visually line up the buildings on Michigan Avenue to get a perspective. The picture shows that the backfilling of the submerged land was well on its way by July, 1896.

1897

Cuban nationalists, aided by gringo mercenaries, continued the internal struggle to be free of Spanish domination. 39-year old French-born mechanical engineer Dr. Rudolf Diesel built his first successful engine, a 25-horsepower single-cylinder model. Guglielmo Marconi received a patent on wireless radio transmissions. 41-year old physicist Professor J. J. (Joseph John) Thomson at Cambridge in England discovered the electron, the first particle found to be smaller than the atom, or subatomic; for this discovery he would be awarded the Nobel Prize in Physics in 1906; Thomson's assistant was the 26-year old New Zealand-born Ernest Rutherford who would discover the second subatomic particle in 1914.

In March 54-year old William McKinley was sworn in as the 25th President of the United States; McKinley Republicans continued their control in both Houses. New gold ore strikes were found in Alaska and South Africa stimulating the American economy. The Yerkes Observatory opened in Williams Bay, Wisconsin; it remains the world's largest refracting (two convex lenses) telescope (40 inch). Bob Fitzsimmons took the world's heavyweight boxing championship, something he would retain for only two years. Elijah Poole was born in Georgia; from Pullman porter to devotee of Marcus Garvey's planned exodus to Africa to follower of Wallace Fard's Nation of Islam in the Wilderness, the future Elijah Muhammad would rise to become its last prophet.

Passenger car impresario George Pullman succumbed to a heart attack. The Union Pacific Railroad went bankrupt and into receivership in 1893, having been run into the ground by Jay Gould and associates; it was reorganized and reincorporated in 1897 and sold to railroad tycoon Edward H. Harriman, the Illinois Central Director, who assumed operations in 1898; Harriman spent the next decade rebuilding, relining, relocating and reconstructing the Union Pacific's part of the original Overland Route.

IC revenues rose slightly to $22.1 million, a new record; 19 percent of revenues were from passenger traffic (12,827,205 passengers). Revenue traffic notched its second consecutive record in reaching over 9.9 million tons of freight; tonnage on the unconsolidated Yazoo & Mississippi Valley exceeded 1.3 million tons. System mileage (not including the 807-mile Yazoo & Mississippi Valley nor the 456-mile Chesapeake, Ohio and Southwestern) rose to 3,130 with the inclusion of the 3-mile long Mound City Railway; the composition now was: 1,636 miles north of the Ohio River, 600 west of the Mississippi River and 894 south of the Ohio River; toward the end of the year 678 miles of trackage that had been operated separately began combined operations to be included in the next fiscal reporting period; this included the Chesapeake, Ohio & Southwestern, the Ohio Valley, the Chicago & Texas and the Stacyville Railroad. With 51 used units (5 passenger, 42 freight and 4 switching) purchased at a foreclosure sale of the Chesapeake, Ohio & Southwestern, plus 25 new locomotives (eight of which were special Brooks 8-wheelers) purchased to replace retirements and scrapped units, roster availability rose to 693: composed of 33 suburban passenger units, 166 8-wheeled passenger and freight units, 98 10-wheeled passenger and freight units, 256 2-6-0 Mogul-type freight locomotives, 38 2-8-0 Consolidation-type freight units and 102 switching units: 33 4-wheeled and 69 6-wheeled. The special-built Brooks 8-wheelers were an attempt to mimic the clean lines of English locomotive art; while a total of nine were built to this radical design standard (air pumps and sand boxes under the boiler, and the first with 200 pounds steam pressure), not much came of the effort. Illinois Central continued its program of reducing grades to attain operating efficiencies, grade reductions effectively increasing the tonnage rating of locomotive power; Illinois Central reduced the ruling grade (ruling = maximum demand on locomotives) between East Cairo and Fulton, Kentucky to a maximum of 38 feet per mile, an improvement but still higher than the desired one-half of one percent (26.4 feet per mile). In March Illinois Central opened its riverside Stuyvesant Docks facility in New Orleans, including scales, conveyors, elevators and warehouses on the Mississippi River. Illinois Central inaugurated dining service on its trains, adding two café cars on the *Daylight Special* between Chicago and St. Louis. In September an epidemic of yellow fever struck in New Orleans; since it was years before Walter Reed's discovery, quarantines were established in a number of towns, virtually suspending passenger traffic until November frosts brought a respite and a return to normalcy.

IC1897-01

Pictured at Cairo, Illinois in 1899, Illinois Central #379 was an 1897 Rogers-built 4-6-0 (69 D; 180 BP; 158,300 TW; 21,922 TF) 10-wheeler; renumbered to IC #209 in 1900, then IC #2009 in 1907, this engine had its final roster position of IC #5009 in 1922. This picture was published in the January, 1939 issue of the Illinois Central Magazine; identified in the photograph were, William Edwards (engineer, in the cab), and Lon Brown (fireman, in the gangway).

IC45x35-66

Illinois Central #969 was another one of those lightweight, streamlined 4-4-0 Americans the Illinois Central experimented with in the late-1890's; the locomotives in this series had sandboxes and air pumps hidden underneath the boiler for appearances, and were the first units on the IC to utilize 200 pound boiler pressure. IC #969 was the last in the series of nine engines; this engine was Brooks-built in 1897 (75 D; 200 BP; 121,000 TW; 19,094 TF); it was renumbered IC #1969 in 1906 and IC #4969 in the early 1920's. It was not noted why the engine was decorated in this photograph.

1898

With Cuba fighting for independence from Spain, the U.S. sent one of it's second-string battleships to Havana Harbor on a neutral yet not altruistic visit; within 30 days the *USS Maine* mysteriously exploded and sank. Lusting to annex Cuba, the U.S. declared war on Spain in April to begin the Spanish-American War. The 1ˢᵗ U.S. Volunteer Cavalry Regiment (*Rough Riders*) with Lieutenant Colonel Teddy Roosevelt took Kettle Hill and San Juan Hill near Santiago in Cuba, and Commodore George Dewey leading nine American warships defeated the Spanish Navy at Manila Bay in the Philippines. Within months Spain relinquished Cuba, sold the Philippines, ceded both Puerto Rico and Guam, and ceased to be a sea power. The Treaty of Paris signifying peace with Spain was signed in December. This represented America's start of a period of colonialism/imperialism as an emerging world power. Ohio Judge and future president William Howard Taft was named the first governor of the Philippines. Russian Czar Nicholas II summoned an International Peace Conference, which, in turn, led to The Hague Peace Conference (1899), the Permanent Court of Arbitration (1902), the Permanent Court of International Justice (1922 – League of Nations auspices) and finally the International Court of Justice (1946 – United Nations auspices), which located in The Hague, Holland. English chemists 46-year old William A. Ramsay and his 26-year old student Morris W. Travers discovered the elements krypton, xenon and neon; Ramsay would be awarded the Nobel Prize in Chemistry six years later for these discoveries and those of helium and argon; separately, the Curies discovered the elements polonium and radium. English author H.G. Wells' published *War of the Worlds*, the Martian invasion of Earth, which Orson Welles would make even more famous in a 1938 radio broadcast. 29-year old Danish engineer Valdemar Poulsen patented his method of recording messages on a magnetized steel wire and a crude tape recorder, the telegraphone, was born.

Joshua Slocum became the first man to sail around the world alone when he docked his boat – the *Spray* – at Newport, Rhode Island; the trip took three years. In another example of labor unrest, a bloody mine incident occurred in Virden, Illinois as four miners were shot by hired guards. The Morgan Athletic Club formed a football team that later became the Chicago Cardinals, the St. Louis Cardinals and then Arizona Cardinals. Schwinn opened a bicycle factory. 56-year old British scientist James Dewar liquefied hydrogen, expanding scientific study. The outer boroughs of the Bronx, Brooklyn, Staten Island, and Queens joined with the island of Manhattan under a common government to give New York City its present arrangement. The Trans-Mississippi and International Exposition was held in Omaha, Nebraska, exhibiting the development of the West; an Indian Congress was held as part of the exposition with over 20 tribes represented by 450-some Native Americans, the old Apache war chief Geronimo being but one. Under U.S. protection since 1893 and declared a Republic in 1894, Hawaii is annexed by the U.S. Government.

The Southern Pacific went international when it began operations in Mexico via the Sonora Railroad at Nogales on the Arizona border.

With consolidated operations showing a 20 percent increase in trackage, revenues jumped to $27.3 million, almost 19 percent attributable to passenger traffic (13,772,221 passengers). Revenue traffic cruised to its third consecutive record in reaching almost 12.7 million tons of freight; tonnage on the unconsolidated Yazoo & Mississippi Valley approached 1.8 million tons. System mileage (not including the 807-mile Yazoo & Mississippi Valley) rose to 3,808 with the inclusion of 678 miles of track formerly operated separately (the 456-mile long Chesapeake, Ohio & Southwestern from Memphis to Louisville via Paducah, the 139-mile long Ohio Valley from Evansville, Indiana south across the Ohio River through Kentucky to Hopkinsville, the 75-mile long Chicago & Texas from Gale to Johnson City via Carbondale and the 8-mile long Stacyville Railroad from Mona to Stacyville in Iowa); the Illinois Central system now served 10 states of the Union: 1,612 miles in Illinois, 15 in South Dakota, 11 in Minnesota, 581 in Iowa, 91 in Wisconsin, 14 in Indiana, 506 in Kentucky, 252 in Tennessee, 638 in Mississippi and 88 in Louisiana. At mid-year Illinois Central reclassified some 140-miles of trackage to Yazoo & Mississippi Valley accounts, thus lowering Illinois Central's reported system miles for the next year, with no change in its effective control. With 60 used units added to the roster through acquired lines (30 passenger, 22 freight and 8 switching units) plus 18 new locomotives (13 Moguls (8 Rogers and 5 Brooks), 1 8-wheeled Brooks and 4 10-wheeled Rogers units) purchased to replace retirements and scrapped units, roster availability rose to 754: composed of 33 suburban passenger units,

ICNEGGS-01

Illinois Central #1, one of six engines to carry that roster position over the years, was a 4-6-0 (62 D; 180 BP; 159,394 TW; 27,639 TF) 10-wheeler built by Rogers in 1898. Shown in a Builder's Photo, it was one of many that Illinois Central felt underpowered after a period of time, and it was sold to the National Railroads of Mexico in 1921.

187 8-wheeled passenger and freight units, 116 10-wheeled passenger and freight units, 272 2-6-0 Mogul-type freight locomotives, 38 2-8-0 Consolidation-type freight units and 108 switching units: 32 4-wheeled and 76 6-wheeled. Reviewing its freight equipment, the Illinois Central found that 64 percent of its freight equipment (18,333 of 28,719 cars) were equipped with automatic couplers and 46 percent (13,243 cars) with air brakes (the figures were 52 percent (1,707 of 3,286 cars) and 14 percent (460 cars) on the Yazoo & Mississippi Valley). Continuing its effort to constantly upgrade plant and property, Illinois Central increased its track standard to 85-pound rail on most of the system; the Company also increased the standard single-track embankment width to 20 feet from 18 feet. In its grade reduction program, the Company began work on the 61-foot ruling grade between Fulton and Memphis; reducing the ruling grade from 61-feet per mile to 26.4 feet would effectively double the tonnage rating of locomotives over this section of track; discounting the 38-foot ruling grade on the 99 miles between Carbondale and Fulton, once the Fulton to Memphis work was complete Illinois Central would have a 942-mile route from Chicago to New Orleans at the preferred one-half of one percent (26.4 feet per mile) ruling grade. The Company increased its coal car capacity standard from 30-tons to 40-tons, with receipts of the first 40-tonners in February. While not the Wild West anymore, train robberies still were attempted; on April 26th three men were prevented from robbing a southbound Illinois Central passenger train near Louisville and, after conviction, were sentenced to two years in the penitentiary.

IC1898-02

Illinois Central #171 and #172 were a pair of 0-6-0 switch engines built by Brooks Locomotive in 1898; these engines (51 D; 165 BP; 115,600 TW; 25,811 TF) served the switching needs of the Company well into the 1930's. IC #171 shown above was captured at 27th Street in Chicago on July 25, 1914. IC#172 shown below was snapped at Paducah, Kentucky; note horse transportation still was commonplace and caught in the picture; the people were not identified.

IC1898-04

IC1898-08

Illinois #2015, shown above, was a Rogers-built 4-6-0 (69 D; 180 BP; 158,300 TW; 21,922 TF) 10-wheeler; constructed in 1898 and originally rostered as IC #385, this engine was renumbered IC #215, IC #2015 and IC #5015 over the years; it was retired in 1940. The undated photograph shows it on point, of a double-headed passenger job.

IC1898-03

Illinois Central #2296 was a Brooks-built 4-6-0 (56 D; 165 BP; 115,800 TW; 19,475 TF) 10-wheeler. This engine was built in 1898 for the Indiana & Illinois Southern (later the St. Louis Indianapolis & Eastern), originally rostered as I&IS #40; this unit became IC #296 in 1899, and then was renumbered to IC #2296 in 1914. IC #2296 was captured at an unknown time and place.

IC1897-02

IC1898-05

Work long enough in a darkroom and the details get sharper and sharper, as do the differences. Illinois Central #380 shown at top was a 4-6-0 (69 D; 180 BP; 158,300 TW; 21,922 TF) 10-wheeler; built by Rogers in 1897, this engine was one of a series of 40 constructed over a five year period; the engine Casey Jones road into immortality (IC #382, built 1898) came from this series. The photograph of IC #380, taken at Cairo when nearly-new, was published in the February, 1926 issue of the IC Magazine; identified in the picture were, right to left, J.W. Shepherd (engineer), E.C. Brown (fireman), and Walter Boone (flagman). Shown under IC #380 is IC #382, supposedly another in the series and supposedly the actual engine Casey Jones wrecked. This view of IC #382 has appeared before, but never right next to the picture of IC #380. Note how IC #382 appears to be retouched, the flagman being air-brushed out and the roster number changed in three places on the engine; all the while the pose of the engine crew is the same, as is the background seen between the pilot wheels at rail height.

Opposite page, four more views of the Casey Jones engine, as it passed through a series of renumberings. Top to bottom, IC #382 probably right after being repaired at the Water Valley shops in the Fall of 1900; this photograph was published in the IC Magazine in the 1950's; identified in the picture were W.H. Hartwell (in gangway), Bob Davis (in cab), engineers John Brown and Bob Moore (on ground) and firemen Ed Kennedy and Lorin Rogers. IC #2012, renumbered as such in 1907. Another as IC #2012, snapped at Chicago's 27th Street in August, 1914. Lastly, as IC #5012, to which it was renumbered in 1922.

IC1898-06

IC1898-07

IC1898-01

IC1898-09

1899

The Spanish-American War officially ended in February. Having escaped Spanish rule, Filipino insurgents now fought for the same independence from U.S. territorial ambitions – the Philippine Insurrection was on and would last three years. Nationalist sentiments rose in China, as nationalists rebelled against foreign encroachments. The Boer War began in South Africa as England sought to unite the two Boer republics (South African Republic (Transvaal) and Orange Free State) under its flag; the battle between imperialism and nationalism would be marked by sieges at Mafeking, Kimberley and Ladysmith; as a sign of how small actions can foreshadow great events, the Boers captured a young soldier, 25-year old Winston Churchill, who escaped prison a few weeks later. The U.S. began discussions aimed at building a Panama Canal. Hermann Dreser synthesized acetylsalicylic acid – aspirin; his employer was Friedrich Bayer & Company.

Carry Nation began the women's temperance assault by tearing apart a saloon in Kiowa, Kansas. The American Chicle Company was incorporated and Chicklets were chewed for the first time. Coca-Cola put bottle caps on their bottles. J.D. Rockefeller formed the Standard Oil Company of New Jersey; this was a holding company used to control the separate entities, and to skirt the Ohio Supreme Court's 1892-ordered dissolution of Rockefeller's Trust; the U.S. Supreme Court would break up this charade in 1911. 25-year old James J. Jeffries took the world's heavyweight boxing title; he would retain it for six years.

The Baltimore & Ohio Railroad was brought out of bankruptcy, receivership ending after three years. Wanting it to link up with his interests in the Union Pacific and the Illinois Central, Edward H. Harriman's group outbid the Gould's in acquiring the Chicago & Alton Railroad for almost $40 million; after leveraging its capital structure, control would pass to the Rock Island five years later.

Illinois Central constructed an 8-mile branch from Winfield to Brilliant, Alabama to access coal mines in Brilliant; this isolated segment connected back at Aberdeen, Mississippi via the Kansas City, Memphis & Birmingham Railroad – the future FRISCO; Illinois Central's desire to build its own connecting link back to Aberdeen never materialized, yet it retained the Orphan Line over 50 years. With the return of 140-some miles of track to Yazoo & Mississippi Valley operation, Illinois Central's grasp in miles of track dropped, while its effective reach remained the same; system mileage declined to 3,679 spread over 11 states, while that of the Yazoo & Mississippi Valley rose to 969 in three states. Toward the end of the year Illinois Central effectively gained control of three new segments: via purchase at foreclosure, the 89-mile long St. Louis, Indianapolis & Eastern Railroad (nee Indiana & Illinois Southern) spanning Effingham, Illinois and Switz City, Indiana; acquired through the Dubuque & Sioux City, the 131-mile long Fort Dodge & Omaha Railroad between Tara and Council Bluffs, Iowa; and through lease arrangements, the 98-mile long St. Louis, Peoria & Northern from Springfield to East St. Louis, Illinois; all three segments would be consolidated into operations in the next fiscal reporting period. Revenues for the fiscal period rose to $28.1 million, a little over 19 percent of which was passenger traffic (14,401,234 passengers). Revenue traffic set its fourth consecutive record in exceeding 13.5 million tons of freight; tonnage on the unconsolidated Yazoo & Mississippi Valley exceeded 1.8 million tons. With 26 new locomotives (16 10-wheeled freight units (9 Rogers and 7 Brooks), 5 10-wheeled Rogers-built passenger units, and 5 6-wheeled switch units) purchased to replace retirements and scrapped units, roster availability rose to 763: composed of 33 suburban passenger units, 171 8-wheeled passenger and freight units, 136 10-wheeled passenger and freight units, 272 2-6-0 Mogul-type freight locomotives, 38 2-8-0 Consolidation-type freight units and 113 switching units: 32 4-wheeled and 81 6-wheeled.

Illinois Central #25, a Brooks-built 4-6-0 (62 D; 180 BP; 159,394 TW; 27,639 TF) 10-wheeler, was a product of 1899; this engine was one in a series sold to the National Railroads of Mexico in the early 1920's; it was captured on the turntable at an unknown location and time. IC #36 shown below was another 4-6-0, but one built by Rogers in 1899; this engine was caught in a similar pose, had similar dimensions and met a similar fate.

IC1899-03

IC45x35-31

IC1899-04

Brooks-built in 1899, Illinois Central #181 was an 0-6-0 (51 D; 165 BP; 118,900 TW; 25,811 TF) switch engine. Circa 1905, this engine was converted from an 0-6-0 unit into an 0-6-0T engine; it was changed into a shop switcher (IC #3294), but not as a saddle-tank unit as many others were in later years. Conversion included footboards and eventually a new cab, among other things, but retained the single-truck under the short tender. This unit saw service into 1946.

IC1905-08

The battle for biggest - at Illinois Central it became an experiment to see which wheel arrangement, a 2-8-0 Consolidation-type or a 4-8-0 12-wheeler-type, would be the most efficient on the road. In 1899 Illinois Central purchased two new units to find out: IC #639, a 2-8-0 (57 D; 203,000 TW; around 49,000 TF) from Rogers Locomotive, and IC #640, a 4-8-0 (57 D; 210 BP; 221,750 TW; 49,698 TF) from Brooks Locomotive. Both pictures shown were captured at Pullman, Illinois on the IC upon delivery of the engines; both were published in the January, 1926 issue of the Illinois Central Magazine. When delivered, IC #640 was considered the biggest engine in the world, and it was advertised as such; the tender for IC #640 held 15 tons of coal and 7,000 gallons of boiler water. The only person identified in the two pictures was the man standing by the pilot, Fred Ehrestman, IC #640's engineer. While built and received in 1899, these engines were reported in Illinois Central's results for 1900, due to the Interstate Commerce Commission's mandated mid-year reporting periods. Illinois Central never bought another 4-8-0 engine; both units were sold to the Peoria & Pekin Union railroad in 1917.

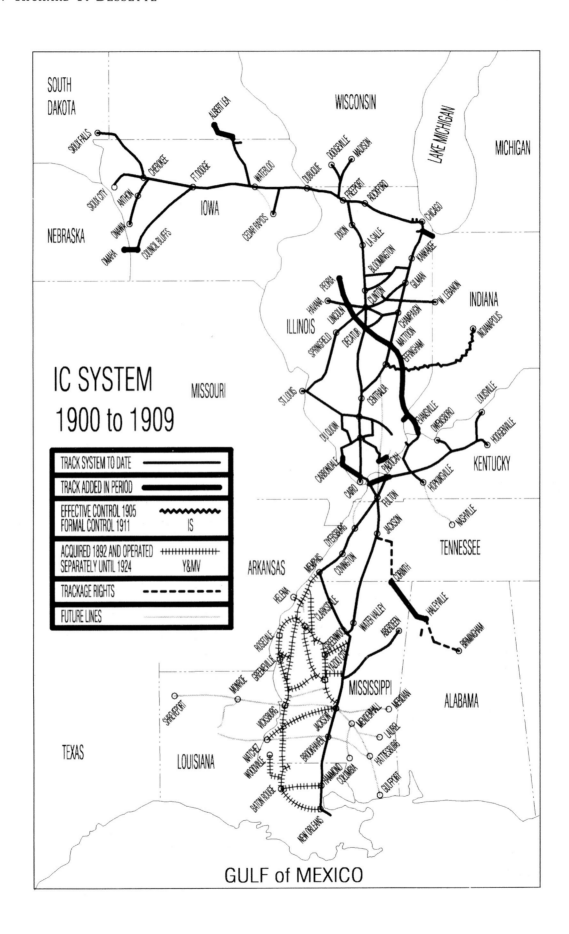

1850's 1860's 1870's 1880's 1890's **1900's** 1910's 1920's 1930's 1940's

The Twelfth Census of the U.S. population was taken; there were a little over 76 million people in the U.S., having grown 21 percent from the prior census; the country would add over 16 million people by the end of the decade, over one-half through immigration. From 1900 to 1914 (the floodtide years), millions of Italians, Greeks, Poles, Russians, and others from the Austria-Hungarian empire would pour through Ellis Island, fleeing southern and eastern European farms and villages; the first decade of the century alone would see more than eight million immigrants come to the U.S., the highest of any ten-year period in history. The Union grew by one State to a total of 46. The 1900's became a period of trust busting and antitrust legislation. Overall it was a prosperous time during the first half of the decade; when a short depression hit in 1907, a lot of Americans went to work on the Panama Canal; this labor shift would be repeated in the Great Depression years. At the start of the century in 1900, 95 percent of the population still lived on farms.

In 1900 the major line-haul rail carriers operated a little over 193,000 miles of railroad, a figure that would increase by almost 47,000 miles by the end of the decade. The "trust busting" brought to bear on mounting industrial empires would not skip railroads; the decade would see a number of railway systems engaged, some forced apart and some held together, as the national rail network continued to evolve. The principal rail organizations of the period were: the independent Atchison, Topeka & Santa Fe and Chicago, Milwaukee & St. Paul roads; the Gould-aligned Missouri Pacific and Denver & Rio Grande; Harriman's Union Pacific, Southern Pacific and Illinois Central roads; J. J. Hill's Northern Pacific, Great Northern and Chicago Burlington & Quincy; the Southern, Erie, Atlantic Coast Line and Louisville & Nashville roads of Morgan; the Pennsylvania's alliance, which included the Baltimore & Ohio and the Chesapeake & Ohio; and Vanderbilt's New York Central and Chicago & Northwestern;

25-mph electric trolley cars finally invaded the inner city of Chicago; by 1906 just about everything was electrified. By 1907 there were two million people in Chicago and only 50,000 horses.

GROWTH OF ILLINOIS CENTRAL RAILROAD BUSINESS

Year (1)	Tonnage (mil/tons)	Lumber (mil/tons)	Grain (mil/tons)	Coal (mil/tons)	FFV (mil/tons)	Cotton (mil/tons)	Aggregates (mil/tons)	Passengers Commuters	Miles/Fare
1900	16.0	2.3	2.5	5.2	.253	.265	.220	16,245,007 10,641,869	19/$0.38
1901	17.7	2.2	2.9	5.7	.370	.231	.318	17,865,439 10,869,200	21/$0.41
1902	19.1	3.0	2.3	6.2	.475	.263	.370	19,006,204 11,683,023	21/$0.42
1903	21.9	N/A	N/A	N/A	N/A	N/A	N/A	21,231,607 12,996,289	21/$0.42
1904	22.4	3.4	2.5	7.7	.550	.297	.605	22,563,613 14,094,656	22/$0.42
1905	23.1	3.4	2.7	7.7	.600	.354	.782	21,645,601 12,954,919	27/$0.50
1906	25.6	4.1	3.2	8.1	.540	.264	.990	22,052,673 13,439,354	23/$0.45
1907	26.9	4.3	3.1	8.5	.700	.289	.845	23,441,337 13,964,621	24/$0.48
1908	25.0	3.7	2.8	8.6	.600	.315	.691	23,357,184 12,631,166	25/$0.47
1909	24.9	3.6	2.6	9.3	.525	.365	.725	22,666,383 11,716,987	26/$0.48

FFV = Fresh Fruit & Vegetables Passengers/Commuter s= Total Ridership, and Commuter Portion
Miles/Fare = Average Passenger Trip and Charge (1) Fiscal Year N/A = Data Not Available

1900

The Philippine Insurrection blazed on with Filipino insurgents continuing the fight for independence – this time from the U.S. General Arthur MacArthur (a Medal of Honor winner in the Civil War and father of Douglas) led troops in the Philippines. Sigmund Freud published *Interpretation of Dreams*. 31-year old Victor Emmanuel III, Head of the House of Savoy, became King of Italy in July upon the assassination of his father (Humbert I); Emmanuel would rule for 46 years, joining the Allies in World War I and the Axis in World War II, until pressured into abdicating the throne. Trying to eject foreigners from their country, Chinese nationalists waged the short and savage Boxer Rebellion by trying to seize foreign embassies in Peking and Tientsin; in the end England, the U.S., France, Russia, Germany and Japan sent in thousands of troops to put down the two-month old disturbance. Boer War in South Africa advanced from large-scale battles into guerilla skirmishes. German Count Ferdinand von Zeppelin floated his first dirigible, a few days before his 62nd birthday. Croatian-born 44-year old American engineer Nikola Tesla speculated that radio reflections could be used to locate moving ships, foretelling the invention of radar 35 years later. The second edition of the Modern Olympics was held in Paris; women (11) competed in events for the first time. Begun in 1891 at the direction of Tsar Alexander III, passenger service was inaugurated on the world's longest train journey, the soon-to-be-named *Trans-Siberian Express*. 32-year old Austrian physician Karl Landsteiner drew a distinction and discovered the first three blood groups: A, B and O; his work with blood would lead to the Nobel Prize in Medicine thirty years later.

Packard sold an automobile, the Ohio, which debuted with the first steering wheel. As the year began there were 45 States in the Union; there were only 38 cities with a population exceeding 100,000. The 28-mile long Chicago Sanitary and Ship Canal was completed; this canal took over for the Illinois and Michigan Canal in facilitating the reversal of the flow of the Chicago River from east (into Lake Michigan) to west (toward the Mississippi River); the Illinois and Michigan Canal had performed this function since 1871. The first Brownie Box camera was a marketing hit for Kodak. AM (amplitude-modulation) radio was conceptualized; with no practical radio amplifiers or home radio receivers in existence, the process was essentially theory, for the next six years. The *Holland*, named after Irish schoolmaster 60-year old John P. Holland because of his development work, became the U.S. Navy's first submarine; the first non-military submarine was the *Argonaut*. The American Baseball League was formed, beginning operation and fielding teams the following year. 42-year old German-born Max Planck formulated the quantum theory; he would be awarded the Nobel Prize in Physics in 1918 for his work. In March Congress made gold the standard for U.S currency. In May at the Populist convention in Sioux Falls, William Jennings Bryan was elected the nominee for President by acclamation; Charles A. Towne of Minnesota was chosen the nominee for Vice President in similar fashion. At the 12th Republican convention in Philadelphia, incumbent President William McKinley was nominated for re-election on the 1st ballot unanimously; New York Governor Theodore Roosevelt was chosen the nominee for Vice President on the 1st ballot, after Convention Chairman and Ohio Senator and industrialist Mark Hanna withdrew. In an effort to close ranks and heal the Party rift, at the 18th Democratic convention in Kansas City, the Populist nominee William Jennings Bryan was elected the Democratic party nominee for President by acclamation, Admiral of the Navy George Dewey the hero of Manila having decided not to make it a race; ex-Vice President Adlai E. Stevenson of Illinois was chosen the nominee for Vice President on the 1st ballot. 45-year old Eugene V. Debs ran for President as the nominee for the Socialist party, something he would do five times with increasing success. In November the McKinley/Roosevelt ticket carried the day and earned continued majorities in both Houses. The International Ladies Garment Workers Union was established. The seismograph, a practical means of measuring the strength of earthquakes, first appeared. New York City held the first National Auto Show. L. Frank Baum published *The Wizard of Oz*; the 1939 movie starring Judy Garland became the classic adaptation.

Lionel trains arrived and allowed kids to mimic their elders. The U.S. rail system consisted of 190,000 miles of roadway. The Pennsylvania Railroad gained control of 40% of the stock in the Baltimore & Ohio Railroad, a position "trust-busting" Theodore Roosevelt would later force the Pennsylvania to sell. With the death of Collis P. Huntington of Central Pacific fame, Edward H. Harriman's Union Pacific set to buying up Huntington's stock in the Southern Pacific Railroad, gaining effective control of it and the Central Pacific by the next year.

36-year old John Luther "Casey" Jones, a locomotive engineer on the Water Valley District working the Memphis to Canton segment, rear-ended freight train No. 83 (engine #'s 870 and 871) and hurtled off the tracks and into lore

IC1900-02

Illinois Central #196 was one of three 0-6-0 (51 D; 165 BP; 118,900 TW; 25,811 TF) switch engines Brooks built for the IC in 1900. It is shown above near the end of its service life in the late-1930's.

at Vaughan, Mississippi piloting southbound passenger Train # 1 (engine #382, a 4-6-0 Ten-Wheeler built by Rogers in 1898); he was the only casualty; it will forever be a question whether he was a hero or cause of the wreck. Illinois Central commuter trains extended their reach to Flossmoor on April 29; weekday suburban service rose to 110 trains each way. With the addition of 317 miles of track (the 89-mile long St. Louis, Indianapolis & Eastern, the 131-mile long Fort Dodge & Omaha, and the 98-mile long St. Louis, Peoria & Northern), system mileage grew to 3,996 spread over 11 states; mileage on the separately-operated Yazoo & Mississippi Valley rose by 32 to 1,001 with the addition of trackage on the Greenwood District and two sections of the Lake Dawson Division. During the last half of the year, provisions were made on an additional 270 miles of track: construction of the 19-mile long Albert Lea & Southern Railroad; purchase of the 244-mile long Peoria, Decatur & Evansville; purchase of the 6-mile long New Harmony to Stewartsville branch; and a short segment of track in the Charles City, Iowa area. All 270 miles would be consolidated into operations in the next fiscal period. Revenues rose to $32.6 million, passenger traffic making up almost 19 percent (16,245,007 passengers). Revenue traffic exceeded 16.0 million tons of freight, the fifth consecutive record; tonnage on the unconsolidated Yazoo & Mississippi Valley almost reached 2.1 million tons. Locomotive availability rose to 813 units with the purchase of 47 new units (20 Brooks 10-wheeled, 19 Rogers 10-wheeled, a single Brooks 12-wheeled, a single Rogers Consolidated and 6 Brooks 6-wheel switch units) and the addition of 17 used locomotives (8 8-wheeled, 8 10-wheeled and 1 Mogul) from acquired lines; the fleet consisted of 119 switching units (32 4-wheel and 87 6-wheel), 33 suburban units, 180 10-wheel locomotives, 271 2-6-0 Mogul-types, 170 8-wheel types, 39 2-8-0 Consolidations and the Illinois Central's first 12-wheel arrangement. The Brooks Locomotive 4-8-0 12-wheel (#640) and the Rogers 2-8-0 Consolidation (#639) were specially built freight units with heavy duty features; scheduled for head-to-head comparison, the competition was intended to rule out the need for helper units on trains making Makanda Hill between Centralia and Mounds in southern Illinois: both had 8,472 tons traction versus the fleet average of 3,216 tons, 23" by 30" cylinders, 57" drivers and each cost $15,700; the heavy 2-8-0 apparently won out, as Illinois Central never purchased another 4-8-0 12-wheel arrangement.

ICDPL-08

Photo Courtesy of Denver Public Library, Western History Department, Otto C. Perry Photograph Collection (DPL#20607), Denver.

IC45x35-27

ICDPL-09

Photo Courtesy of Denver Public Library, Western History Department, Otto C. Perry Photograph Collection (DPL#20608), Denver.

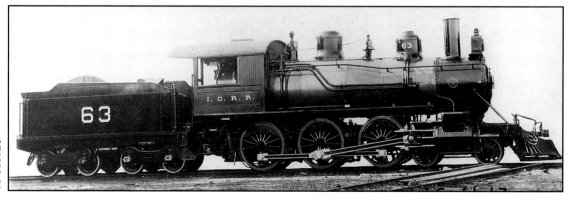

IC1900-01

IC45x35-49

Part of a group of 14 2-6-0 Mogul-types (56 D; 200 BP; 167,200 TW; 30,222 TF) built by Rogers and Brooks for the Illinois Central in 1900, these pictures represent one of each. IC #552 shown above was a Rogers Locomotive 2-6-0, while IC #555 shown below was a Brooks product, depicted in a Builder's Photo. Both engines were retired in 1938.

IC45x35-48

Rogers, Brooks and Baldwin combined to build 64 4-6-0 (62 D; 180 BP; 159,394 TW; 27,639 TF) 10-wheelers for the Illinois Central over a four-year period from 1898 to 1901, all but seven of which were sold to the National Railroads of Mexico in 1921/1922. On the facing page four views are presented, two Brooks-built 4-6-0's and two Baldwin-built engines. Top to bottom: Brooks-built IC #49 is captured in Mexico at Monclova on October 17, 1928; even though years after being sold to the Mexican railways, the engine still carries the IC roster numbers. IC #59 (another Brooks) was snapped at an unknown time and place. IC #62 was a Baldwin product and was caught at Lampacitos, Mexico on October 17, 1928, still dressed for IC service. IC #63 was shown in a Builder's Photo as it was released from Baldwin; this view shows what IC #61 to #63 looked like when new and was made in the classic rods-down pose.

IC1900-03

IC1900-04

The picture of IC #2024 above appeared in the IC Magazine in November, 1919; it showed the engine and crew (engineer E.L. Fortin and fireman J.B. Graham) that pulled the Federal Manager's Safety Special over the Illinois Division during World War I.

IC #2025 was captured at Waterloo, Iowa pulling Train #527; this picture was in the November, 1922 issue of the IC Magazine. Engineer Hackett and Fireman Sciles were identified in the photograph.

All four engines on this page were 1900 Rogers-built 4-6-0 (69 D; 180 BP; 158,300 TW; 21,922 TF) 10-wheelers, from a series of 40. These engines were renumbered into the 2000-series in 1907 and the 5000-series in 1922.

IC #2036 was captured at the Grenada, Mississippi depot on July 30, 1913, horses still working.

IC #5034 was caught at Sioux Falls, South Dakota in 1930 pulling a passenger train.

IC45x35-20

IC1900-05

On the facing page are two views of the bridge crossing at Dubuque, Iowa. The top photograph shows the scene in November, 1894 with the rail bridge on the right and the highway bridge on the left; this picture appeared in the April, 1936 issue of the Illinois Central Magazine. The renewal of the 1868 rail bridge began in 1900, and is shown in the lower photograph. This view shows the west end span being erected on January 22, 1900; this picture was snapped from the highway bridge, looking back over the rail crossing.

1901

The guerrilla war called the Philippine Insurrection essentially ended with the capture of the rebel leader Emilio Aquinaldo by American Brig. Gen. Frederick Funston. The Hay-Pauncefote Treaty, which gave the U.S. control of the Panama Canal Zone, was signed; shortly thereafter the U.S. Canal Commission purchased the French holdings of engineer Ferdinand de Lesseps' company that had tried to dig a canal fourteen years earlier. Enrico Fermi (the future father of fission) was born in Rome, Italy. Eugene Demarcay discovered the chemical element europium. Boer War in South Africa continued as guerilla warfare. English Queen Victoria passed on to her reward.

In March, the first President to succeed himself since U.S. Grant, 58-year old President McKinley was sworn into office for his 2nd Term; in September, a little over six-months later, President McKinley was assassinated by anarchist Leon Czolgosz while attending the Pan-American Exposition in Buffalo, New York, and 42-year old Theodore Roosevelt became the 26th President. McKinley was the fifth President to die in Office (Harrison, Taylor, Lincoln, Garfield and McKinley), and the third to do so by assassination. Guglielmo Marconi received the first wireless telegraph message, the letter S in Morse code (…), sent as a radio signal across the Atlantic Ocean; it would be a different pioneer and five years later before two-way transmissions were made. The first great Texas oil strike occurred when drillers struck oil at Spindletop field near Beaumont, Texas. 63-year old J.P. Morgan bought out 65-year old Andrew Carnegie's steel interests for $480 million; Morgan followed up by adding a number of smaller companies and other interests, such as holdings in the Mesabi ore range, and organized the consolidation into the U.S. Steel Corporation, the first billion dollar company. 49-year old German-born American chemist Herman Frasch developed a Process to recover sulfur from deep deposits in Louisiana. Working with volunteers in Cuba, 50-year old Walter Reed completed his determination that a virus carried by mosquitoes caused yellow fever. New York became the first State to require license plates. Chicago held its first Auto Show. Beatrix Potter published *Peter Rabbit*. King C. Gillette filed for a patent on his disposable safety razor.

Edward H. Harriman and James J. Hill, each having amassed an enormous western railroad network, began their battle for control of the Chicago, Burlington and Quincy Railroad – a key rail link into Chicago. Hill and his Great Northern Railway were backed by J. P. Morgan; Harriman and his Union Pacific Railroad were backed by William Rockefeller (John D. Rockefeller's brother) and banker Jacob Schiff. When the Hill partnership gained control of the Chicago, Burlington and Quincy, Harriman and his partners went after Hill's Northern Pacific Railroad where Hill had control but not majority ownership. This battle took place on the New York Stock Exchange, and the Hill-Harriman spat drove the price of Northern Pacific stock up by a factor of 10, and initiated a panic on Wall Street. Finally, Hill and Harriman reached a compromise – a $400 million holding company named Northern Securities. While Harriman didn't gain control of the Chicago, Burlington and Quincy or the Northern Pacific, the effect of the compromise was to lower competition between Hill and Harriman. Frank Norris published *The Octopus*, describing the struggle between California farmers and the Southern Pacific Railroad.

Illinois Central, celebrating its 50th anniversary, reported that 60 percent of its stock now was American-owned, the Company shedding much of its English influences. With the consolidation of an additional 270 miles of track (the Albert Lea & Southern; the Peoria, Decatur & Evansville, and the New Harmony branch), Illinois Central system mileage grew to 4,266 spread over 11 states; mileage on the separately-operated Yazoo & Mississippi Valley rose by 90 to 1,091 including the purchase of the Yazoo Delta Railroad and the line extension from Parsons linking back to Grenada. At the end of the year, Illinois Central added the 18-mile long Kentucky Western, spanning Blackford to Dixon, to its holdings; this segment would be consolidated into operations the following year. Revenues topped $36.9 million, almost 20 percent from passenger traffic (17,865,439 passengers); commuter service was extended to newly-opened Flossmoor. With general business levels strong, revenue traffic rose to a sixth consecutive record, 17.7 million tons of freight; tonnage on the unconsolidated Yazoo & Mississippi Valley almost reached 2.5 million tons. Locomotive availability rose to 891 units with the purchase of 63 new units (23 10-wheel freights (3 Baldwins and 14 Brooks and 6 Rogers, all 56" drivers), 14 Moguls (12 Brooks and 2 Rogers, all 49 ½" drivers), 10 10-wheel passengers (all Rogers with 62" drivers) and 16 0-6-0 switchers) and the addition of 20 used locomotives from acquired lines; the fleet consisted of 136 switching units (32 4-wheel and 104 6-wheel), 33 suburban units, 212 10-wheel locomotives, 285 2-6-0 Mogul-types, 185 8-wheel types, 39 2-8-0 Consolidations and one 12-wheel

The last of four Baldwin-built 4-6-0 (62 D; 180 BP; 187,880 TW) 10-wheelers in 1900/1901, Illinois Central #64 was the only one to have a Vanderbilt boiler. The rods-down pose was a 1901 Builder's Photograph from Baldwin's plant.

Richmond-built in 1901 for the New Orleans & Northeastern (rostered as NO&NE #205), this 4-4-0 American-type (68 D) came to the Illinois Central by way of the Alabama & Vicksburg in 1926, when it was rostered as IC #4970. Note the drive-wheel tires or rings in the foreground. This engine was retired a year after being rostered.

arrangement. With rising fortunes on all fronts, track capacity neared on a number of single-track segments; as a result, the Directors ordered the completion of the double-track from Chicago to Fulton, and the construction of a second track from Jackson, Mississippi to New Orleans; while the former would be complete by year-end 1902, the latter would take until 1907.

Three 1901 Pittsburg-built 2-6-0 Mogul-types (63 D; 200 BP; 177,750 TW; 30,222 TF; - some rebuilt to 3700-series in 1937/ 1938 as 53 1/2 D; 215 BP; 42,500 TF). This was the last year IC bought new Moguls, and these were the heaviest.

Illinois Central #541 seen pulling a passenger train, possibly in the Chicago area. This engine was scrapped in 1938.

Caught at Jackson, Mississippi in January, 1932 (near Asylum Shops and before being rebuilt), this unit eventually was rebuilt and renumbered IC #3728.

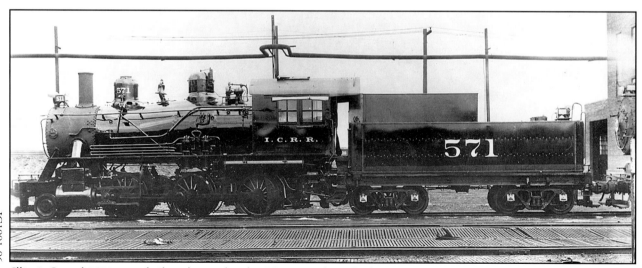

Illinois Central #571 was rebuilt and renumbered to IC #3730, then rebuilt once again in a conversion into an 0-6-0 (53 1/2 D; 215 BP; 181,500 TW; 40,194 TF) switch engine (IC #391) in 1942.

IC1901-07

A product of Baldwin Locomotive in 1901, this 2-6-0 Mogul (63 D; 200 BP; 173,232 TW; 30,222 TF) saw long service, as it wasn't sold until 1953. This engine was rebuilt (53 1/2 D; 215 BP; 42,500 TF) and renumbered to IC #3746 in 1937-1938; it was renumbered one last time in 1943 to IC #3711.

IC1901-08

Pittsburg-built in 1901, this 2-6-0 Mogul (63 D; 200 BP; 173,232 TW; 30,222 TF) saw service until being scrapped in 1946. This engine was rebuilt (53 1/2 D; 215 BP; 42,500 TF) and renumbered to IC #3733 in 1937/1938; it was renumbered one last time in 1943 to IC #3708. This photo is thought to date to that 1943 renumbering.

1902

Philippine Insurrection officially ended early in the year. 53-year old Russian physiologist Ivan Petrovich Pavlov played with dogs and laid down the law, demonstrating learning by conditioning; Pavlov would win the Nobel Prize in Physiology two years later for his work in an unrelated field, digestion. Robert Bosch invented the spark plug; Louis Renault invented the brake drum. Boer War in South Africa ended in May with a peace treaty signed at Vereeniging; unknown to all was that many future military leaders had served their apprenticeship, for a war that lay on the horizon.

Morris Mitchtom named a stuffed bear after sitting President Theodore Roosevelt and the Teddy Bear was invented. Crayons and Animal Crackers were introduced. J.P. Morgan, on a roll with his giant U.S. Steel, formed International Harvester Company in August. First issue of *Popular Mechanics* was published. 61-year old Oliver Wendell Holmes was appointed to the U.S. Supreme Court, where he would remain seated for 29 years. The first Rose Bowl was played early in the year, the University of Michigan beating Stanford 49 to 0. After calculating the census of the U.S. twelve times, a permanent Census Bureau was organized by act of Congress. The Locomobile debuted as the first American car with a four-cylinder water-cooled gas engine. 26-year old Willis H. Carrier developed an air conditioner, the beginning of a creative span that would lead to 80 patents. 45-year old Ida M. Tarbell began publishing her series of stories about Standard Oil Company in *McClure's*, exposing big business and crusading for reform – muckraking like Henry Demarest Lloyd's *Wealth Against Commonwealth.*

President Teddy Roosevelt would initiate 42 antitrust suits during his administration, but he began to earn his reputation as a "trust buster" by taking on James J. Hill's Great Northern railroad empire - the Northern Securities Company, which controlled the Great Northern, Northern Pacific and Chicago, Burlington and Quincy. In June the New York Central Railroad inaugurated its *20ᵗʰ Century Limited* service with a schedule of 20 hours between New York City and Chicago (later reduced to 18 hours); sprints against the Pennsylvania Railroad's *Broadway Limited* lay on the horizon ten years away. Edward H. Harriman cobbled together five of his railroad interests under an "Associated Railroads" umbrella; while ordered broken up in 1912, it provided the venue for establishing "Harriman Standards" to bridges, equipment and structures; locomotive design would be made uniform along seven wheel arrangements: 0-6-0, 2-8-0, 2-8-2, 4-4-2, 4-6-0, 4-6-2, and 2-8-8-2 types.

With the addition of the Kentucky Western, system mileage grew to 4,284 spread over 11 states; mileage on the separately operated Yazoo & Mississippi Valley grew to 1,096 with the addition of five miles of track in Mississippi. The 17-mile long St. Louis & Ohio River railroad from Reevesville to Golconda, Illinois was acquired; it would be consolidated into operations the next year. With completion of extensive track work, Illinois Central now had a double-main all the way from Chicago to Fulton, Kentucky, with the sole exception of the single-track Cairo river bridge crossing; the single-track Kankakee river bridge crossing was within yard limits, and would be double-tracked 16 years later. Illinois Central began its part of a three-year engineering/construction project on a Mississippi river bridge crossing at Thebes, Illinois. Revenues exceeded $40.8 million, almost 20 percent due to passenger traffic (19,006,204 passengers). With general business levels steady, revenue traffic rose to its seventh consecutive record, 19.1 million tons of freight; tonnage on the unconsolidated Yazoo & Mississippi Valley exceeded 2.7 million tons. Locomotive availability rose to 947 units with the purchase of 66 new units (5 10-wheel (1 Baldwin + 4 ALCO-Pittsburg), 44 Moguls (30 ALCO's + 14 Baldwins), one Atlantic, one Prairie, 10 Consolidations by Rogers, and 5 ALCO 6-wheel switcher units) and 1 used locomotive; the fleet consisted of 138 switching units (31 4-wheel and 107 6-wheel), 34 suburban units, 211 10-wheel locomotives, 329 2-6-0 Mogul-types, 183 8-wheel types, 49 2-8-0 Consolidations, one 12-wheel arrangement, and two new models for experimentation: engine # 1000, a 4-4-2 Atlantic-type (Baldwin Locomotive Works, rated 4,020 tons tractive effort with 79" drivers) and engine # 1001, a 2-6-2 Prairie-type (Rogers Locomotive, rated 4,233 tons tractive effort with 75" drivers). To supplement the locomotives in commuter service, Illinois Central began a program of converting light 4-6-0's into suburban units; over four years seven Schenectady-built ten-wheelers (original 1882-1886), acquired with the Chesapeake, Ohio & Southwestern, were converted into 4-6-4T's at the Company's Burnside Shops; the first unit was received in late-1901 (1902 reporting period) and the last in late-1904, bringing the suburban fleet to 40 units.

A pair of 1902 Rogers-built 2-8-0 Consolidations (57 1/2 D; 200 BP; 199,210 TW; 32,243 TF). Illinois Central #668 shown above had been modernized, as can be seen when compared to IC #669 shown below. IC #668 saw long service, until sold sometime before the 1943 renumbering. IC #669 was renumbered in 1943 to IC #710; this unit remained on the roster until scrapped in 1955, a 53-year service life. None of the four people in the photograph below were identified, although the picture of IC #669 is an older view.

ICLAG17-01

The river bridge crossing at Thebes, Illinois was a major engineering project, and one in which the Illinois Central played a major role; this rail crossing of the Mississippi river was not completed until May, 1905 when the bridge opened for business to Cape Girardeau, Missouri.

This page, top to bottom, the Railroad Hotel built in Thebes to house workers (photograph dated May 22, 1902). A picture of the Resident Engineering Force, dated August 11, 1902. Grading on the Illinois approach to the bridge, viewed south toward the bridge from "Big Cut" (July 23, 1902). The last photograph shows how much work was still not mechanized.

Most grading work on the Illinois Central approach was contracted out to companies such as: Shugart & Blythe Brothers, A. Guthrie & Company, Dominion Construction and H.W. Nelson Company.

Facing page, upper picture, shows a general view of the riverfront on the Illinois side (October 20, 1902); note the caissons for piers already dug in the ground. The lower photograph shows the launching of the caisson for Pier #3 by the steamboat FORDYCE, the barge being sunk in place (December 17, 1902).

ICLAG17-02

ICLAG17-03

THEBES BRIDGE IN. 40
GENERAL VIEW ILL APPROACH
OCTOBER 20, 1902

THEBES BRIDGE No. 47
LAUNCHING CAISSON FOR PIII
BARGES BEING SUNK
DEC. 17, 1902. 2-30 P.M.
LAUNCHING FINISHED AT 3-45 P.M.

1903

The first Tour de France bicycle race took place. Panama escaped Columbian ownership, when the U.S. recognized the Republic of Panama; conveniently, the U.S. was granted perpetual control of an expanded Canal Zone. Pierre and Marie S. Curie and Antoine Henri Becquerel shared the Nobel Prize in Physics for their research in radioactivity; 36-year old Marie, the first female laureate, would win another, the Nobel Prize in Chemistry in 1911; the Curies' daughter Irene and son-in-law Frederic would be awarded the Nobel Prize in Chemistry in 1935. Pope Leo XIII died in Rome; 68-year old Giuseppe Melchiorre Sarto would replace him, take the name Pius X, and would lead the Church for 11 years; the new Pope, the 258th in line, would one day become the latest to reach Sainthood.

Frederick Law Olmsted, landscape designer of New York's Central Park, passed away at age 81. The economy suffered through a short banking panic in the year. King C. Gillette sold his first disposable safety razors. Crayola brand crayons hit the street. 43-year old Dutch physiologist Willem Einthoven invented the forerunner to the electrocardiograph. The modern era of professional baseball arrived with the older National and upstart American leagues reaching a peace; the first World Series: two-year old American League representative Boston Pilgrims (future Red Sox) beat the National League's Pittsburgh Pirates 5 games to 3 in the best-of-nine series. On December 17th, having flown gliders for two years, 36-year old Wilbur and 32-year old Orville Wright flew a 625-pound powered biplane 120 feet on the sands of Kill Devil Hill near Kitty Hawk, North Carolina; the secret was solving the problem of control, not lift; their "Flying Machine" was awarded patent No. 821,393 in 1906. At Chicago's new Iroquois Theatre, in an era before safety codes and regulations, a fire during a packed show caused over 550 fatalities. Hollywood was incorporated in California's Cahuenga Valley. Henry Ford incorporated Ford Motor Company. 30-year old Italian opera singer Enrico Caruso made his American debut. 27-year old Californian Jack London published *The Call of the Wild*; thirteen years later he would overdose on drugs, some say intentionally. North Carolina-born William Sydney Porter began writing weekly short stories for the *New York World*, ending each with a surprise, a style he would carry to his end at age 48; O. Henry would write for seven more years, publishing collections such as *Cabbages and Kings* in 1904 and *The Four Million* in 1906, the latter including *Gift of the Magi* and *The Furnished Room*. Coca-Cola replaced the cocaine in the formula with caffeine.

On April 9th, the U.S. Circuit Court of Appeals in Saint Paul decided against Hill's Northern Securities Company and called for its break up; Hill appealed. Edward H. Harriman's Southern Pacific completed its Lucin Cutoff across the Great Salt Lake, shaving 40-some miles of trackage, lopping hundreds of feet in elevation and hundreds of degrees in curvature from the original alignment through Promontory Point to Ogden; operations began the following year.

With the addition of the St. Louis & Ohio River railroad, system mileage grew to 4,301 spread over 11 states; mileage on the Yazoo & Mississippi Valley grew to 1,162 with the completion of the over 66-mile long Lake Cormorant to Tutwiler branch. Toward the end of the year, a net 36 miles of track was in the process of being added to the system, chiefly the 32-mile long segment between East Cairo and Paducah; this trackage would be consolidated into operations the next year. Revenues approached $45.2 million, almost 20 percent attributable to passenger traffic (21,231,607 passengers). With general business levels steady, revenue traffic set its eighth consecutive record, 21.9 million tons of freight; tonnage on the unconsolidated Yazoo & Mississippi Valley almost reached 3.6 million tons. Locomotive availability rose to 1,003 units with the purchase of 63 new units (48 Consolidations (12 ALCO and 36 Rogers), 10 Rogers-built Atlantics, and 5 Rogers 6-wheel switch units); the fleet consisted of 142 switching units (31 4-wheel and 111 6-wheel), 36 suburban units, 207 10-wheel locomotives, 328 2-6-0 Mogul-types, 180 8-wheel types, 97 2-8-0 Consolidations, one 12-wheel arrangement, 11 4-4-2 Atlantic-types and a single 2-6-2 Prairie-type. Outgrowing the old north yard (575 car capacity) and the Iowa Avenue yard (990 car capacity), a new classification yard was built just south of Memphis; named Nonconnah after a nearby creek, the twin-hump switching facility had a capacity exceeding 6,000 cars and was used by the Yazoo & Mississippi Valley. For the second year, construction on a Mississippi river crossing at Thebes, Illinois continued, and Illinois Central's part of the effort would remain a major engineering endeavor for the Company, until opened in 1905.

IC1903-05

Four views of three different 1903 Rogers-built 0-6-0 switch engines (51 D; 165 BP; 118,900 TW; 25,811 TF), each of which saw service well into the 1930's.

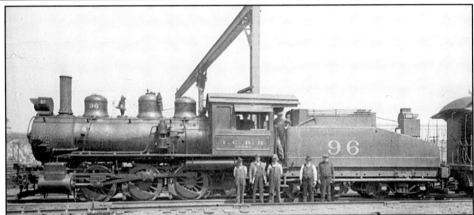

IC45x35-32

IC1903-04

IC #96 was captured at 27th Street in Chicago on July 25, 1914. The second view of IC #96 appeared in the June, 1926 issue of the IC Magazine; the picture is from Randolph Street in Chicago where the engine made up suburban trains; identified in the picture were Leo Fossler (engineer, in gangway) and, left to right on the ground, switchmen W.C. Fieffer and J.C. Horton, V. Jones (fireman), W.W. O'Keefe (conductor) and E. Gorman. IC #97 was snapped at 27th Street in Chicago on November 2, 1927. IC #98 was caught with its switch crew, at an unknown time and place.

IC45x35-33

Three 1903 Rogers-built 2-8-0 Consolidations (57 1/2 D; 200 BP; 199,210 TW; 32,243 TF), most superheated, with Baker valve gear and Economy steam chests. Units were either scrapped or rebuilt into 0-8-0 switchers in the 1940's.

IC45x35-46

IC #671 was scrapped in 1941; note men standing on flatcar behind tender.

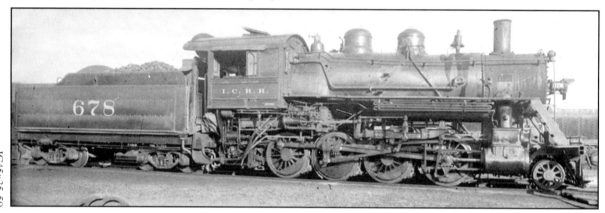

IC45x35-50

IC #678, rebuilt in 1941 into 0-8-0 switch engine IC #3305 (53 1/2 D; 220 BP; 201,600 TW; 43,160).

ICDPL-01

Photo Courtesy of Denver Public Library, Western History Department, Otto C. Perry Photograph Collection (DPL#12221), Denver.
IC #683 (taking on water at Rockford, Illinois in 1919) was rebuilt in 1942 into 0-8-0 switch engine IC #3319 (53 1/2 D; 220 BP; 201,600 TW; 43,160), after swapping boilers with another unit.

From the top, three 2-8-0 Consolidations (57 1/2 D; 200 BP; 199,210 TW; 32,243 TF). Alco/Schenectady-built IC #692 shown pulling a stock train; this picture appeared in the February, 1918 issue of the Illinois Central Magazine; this engine rebuilt in 1941 into 0-8-0 switcher IC #3306 (53 1/2 D; 220 BP; 201,600 TW; 71,346 TF). Rogers-built IC #700 was captured at Nonconnah Yard outside of Memphis in April, 1940; it was renumbered to IC #735 in 1943 and scrapped in 1949. IC #713, another product of Rogers, was caught at an unknown location with six unidentified people on the ground; it was scrapped in 1939.

Three 1903 Rogers-built 2-8-0 Consolidations (57 1/2 D; 200 BP; 199,210 TW; 32,243 TF), most superheated, with Baker valve gear and Economy steam chests. Last two units were rebuilt into 0-8-0 switchers in the 1940's.

ICDPL-02

Photo Courtesy of Denver Public Library, Western History Department, Otto C. Perry Photograph Collection (DPL#12222), Denver.

IC #719 was caught at Council Bluffs, Iowa on May 18, 1925; this unit saw service to 1951 with same wheel arrangement.

IC1903-07

IC #728, on a turntable, was rebuilt as 0-8-0 switch engine (53 1/2 D; 220 BP; 201,600 TW; 43,160) IC #3322 in 1942.

IC1903-08

IC #733 was rebuilt as 0-8-0 switch engine (53 1/2 D; 220 BP; 201,600 TW; 43,160) IC #3330 in 1942.

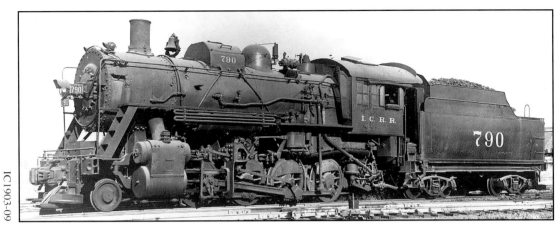

IC1903-09

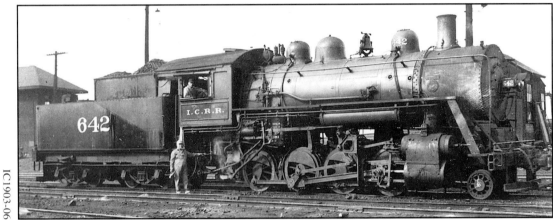

IC1903-06

IC1903-10

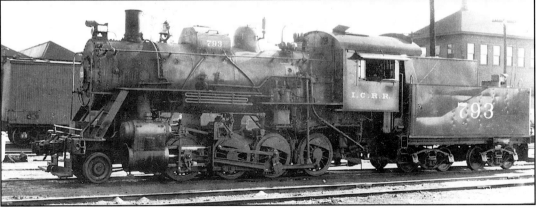

IC1903-11

Four Alco/Cooke 2-8-0 Consolidations (51 D; 190 BP; 183,100 TW; 41,946 TF) built for the Chicago Union Transfer as CUT #100-103 in 1903. IC acquired these units in 1904 and renumbered them IC #641-644; they were renumbered IC #790-793 in 1943; the last three had boiler pressure boosted to 230 pounds later, yielding 51,000 tractive force; the tender held 8 tons of coal and 5,000 gallons of water. IC #642 was captured at Nonconnah Yard in November, 1935.

IC1903-12

IC45x35-186

IC1903-14

IC45x35-187

IC45x35-62

IC45x35-63

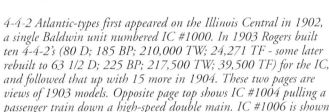

4-4-2 Atlantic-types first appeared on the Illinois Central in 1902, a single Baldwin unit numbered IC #1000. In 1903 Rogers built ten 4-4-2's (80 D; 185 BP; 210,000 TW; 24,271 TF - some later rebuilt to 63 1/2 D; 225 BP; 217,500 TW; 39,500 TF) for the IC, and followed that up with 15 more in 1904. These two pages are views of 1903 models. Opposite page top shows IC #1004 pulling a passenger train down a high-speed double main. IC #1006 is shown at ease picking up passengers. Lastly two pictures of IC #1009, one on a double main and the other on branch line. This page shows two views of IC #1006 with a friend, and a single shot of the running gear of IC #1008. Highlighted in IC #1008, besides the 80" drive wheels, are the slide valve cylinders and Stephenson valve motion, which was changed over to piston valve cylinders and Baker valve gear in the 1920's.

IC1903-13

IC1903-15

IC1903-01

This page, the last two 1903 Rogers-built 4-4-2 Atlantics, IC #1010 and IC #1011. The two views of IC #1010 were snapped at Clinton, Illinois in June, 1938. The view of IC #1011 was caught at the coal chute at McComb, Mississippi on an unknown date. These units (80 D; 185 BP; 210,000 TW; 24,271 TF) were rebuilt into IC #2002 and IC #2004 (63 1/2 D; 225 BP; 217,500 TW; 39,500 TF) in 1942.

IC45x35-257

Facing page shows two 1903 views of the work in progress on the Mississippi river bridge crossing at Thebes, Illinois. The upper photograph dates to April, 1903 and shows how trestle was put up and backfilled to create an embankment; note the head of a culvert facing in place on right. The lower picture illustrates the construction of the bridge on the Illinois side of the river, with forms being laid up for concrete work; this view dates to March, 1903.

THEBES BRIDGE No. 65,
BR. 0-08 & FILLING OF TRESTLE.
APRIL 22, 1903.

ICLAG17-04

THEBES BRIDGE No. 60.
ILLINOIS CONCRETE APPROACH.
MARCH 12, 1903.

ICLAG17-06

1904

The Russo-Japanese war began as aggressive Japan, fearing Russia's ambitions in China and Korea, attacked Russia to protect its own aims for territorial expansion.

St. Louis put on the Louisiana Purchase Exposition – the St. Louis World's Fair, celebrating 100 years since the Louisiana Purchase; the third edition of the Modern Olympics Games, the first ever held in the U.S., was held during the Fair; the Apache war chief Geronimo, a U.S. prisoner, was paraded around the Fair, earning small change for signing his autograph. Construction on the Panama Canal began; the biggest hurdle would be conquering yellow fever and malaria, not busting through mountainsides and rock. Fire raged through the steamer *General Slocum* in New York's East River with the loss of over 1,000 lives. American astronomer 36-year old George E. Hale, having helped establish the Yerkes Observatory's 40-inch refracting telescope years earlier, was a prime mover in envisioning a newer, bigger, better observatory on Mt. Wilson in California; eventually Mt. Wilson opened up the heavens with both 60-inch (1908) and 100-inch (1917) reflecting (concave mirror) telescopes. The Thermos vacuum bottle was invented. Helen Keller, already a publishing celebrity because of her autobiography, graduated from Radcliffe College. In June at the 13th Republican convention in Chicago incumbent President Theodore Roosevelt was nominated for re-election unanimously on the 1st ballot; Indiana Senator Charles Warren Fairbanks was elected the nominee for Vice President by acclamation. At the 19th Democratic convention in St. Louis, New York Judge Alton Brooks Parker was elected the Presidential nominee on the 1st ballot over publisher William Randolph Hearst. Ex-Senator Henry G. Davis from West Virginia was selected the nominee for Vice President by acclamation. Eugene V. Debs represented the Socialist Party for the 2nd time. In November the Roosevelt/Fairbanks ticket was swept into office taking 32 of the 45 voting States – Arizona, New Mexico and Oklahoma having no Electoral College votes. In September New York City opened its subway transit trains, the first underground and underwater system – the Interborough Rapid Transit (IRT). King C. Gillette received two patents on his disposable safety razor. New York City began the tradition of marking the New Year in Times Square. Postmaster General Henry Clay Payne initiated Permit Mail. 55-year old Englishman John Ambrose Fleming invented the electronic vacuum tube, a diode (two electrodes) that acted like a rectifier and detected radio waves; he received a patent the following year. General Motors was started with the Buick nameplate. There would be no 1904 World Series as the National League champion New York Giants simply refused to play the American League title-holder Boston Pilgrims; the fact that the Pilgrims won the inaugural World Series may have weighed heavily in the decision. Cy Young of the Boston Pilgrims pitched the first perfect game in major league baseball; 52 years later Brooklyn's Don Newcombe would be the first to win an award named after Young. A dentist from Zanesville, Ohio became an author on publishing his first novel, *Betty Zane*; 32-year old Pearl Zane Gray soon gave up dentistry for writing full-time and changed the spelling to Grey; *Riders of the Purple Sage* with the hero Lassiter arrived eight years later.

In March the U. S. Supreme Court decided against Hill's Northern Securities Company, ordering the railroad amalgamation dissolved. Facilitated by its acquisition of the Long Island Railroad four years earlier and the resulting access to Brooklyn, the Pennsylvania Railroad would defeat New York Central's isolation effort and gain access to New York City's Manhattan; from the New Jersey side two tunnels under the Hudson River into Manhattan were started and holed through within two years; from the Long Island side, work started on four tunnels to be bored under the East River into and under Manhattan to connect with the Hudson tunnels to form a through-station; after design considerations, construction of the passenger station over the six tunnels began in 1906, with the first full day of operation on November 27, 1910.

With the net addition of 73 miles of track (including the East Cairo to Paducah segment), system mileage grew to 4,374 spread over 11 states; mileage on the Yazoo & Mississippi Valley grew to 1,175 with the addition of 13 miles of track in Mississippi. Seeing the advantage of balanced trackage rights agreements, the Illinois Central's Yazoo & Mississippi Valley exchanged rights with the St. Louis & San Francisco's Kansas City, Memphis & Birmingham; the FRISCO gained access to New Orleans over the Baton Rouge line, and the Illinois Central gained part of what it needed for access to Birmingham via Jasper. Revenues exceeded $46.8 million, a little over 20 percent of which was due to passenger traffic (22,563,613 passengers). With general business levels steady, revenue traffic rose to a ninth consecutive record, 22.4 million tons of freight; tonnage on the unconsolidated Yazoo & Mississippi

IC1904-03

IC1904-04

A 1904 product of Alco/ Brooks, Illinois Central #81 was an 0-6-0 switch engine (51 D; 200 BP; 142,000 TW; 31,287 TF) deployed, at the time of this picture, in the Indianapolis, Indiana terminal facilities. This photograph appeared in the October, 1915 issue of the Illinois Central Magazine; this view dates to between 1904 and 1915.

Valley exceeded 3.6 million tons. Locomotive availability rose to 1,086 units with the purchase of 84 new units (65 2-8-0's (51 Rogers and 14 ALCO's), 9 Rogers Atlantic 4-4-2's and 10 ALCO 0-6-0 switch units); the fleet consisted of 152 switching units (31 4-wheel and 121 6-wheel), 36 suburban units, 207 10-wheel locomotives, 328 2-6-0 Mogul-types, 179 8-wheel types, 162 2-8-0 Consolidations, one 12-wheel arrangement, 20 4-4-2 Atlantic-types and a single 2-6-2 Prairie-type.

IC1904-05

IC45x35-168

IC45x35-68

IC45x35-69

Opposite page, top to bottom: Illinois Central #381 was a 1904 Baldwin-built 0-6-0 switch engine (51 D; 200 BP; 144,000 TW; 38,220 TF) originally erected for the Alabama & Vicksburg (as A&V #420); when IC acquired the A&V it renumbered this unit to IC #3333, and renumbered it in 1942 to IC #381; this picture dates between 1942 and 1948. Illinois Central #1014 was caught waiting for a signal, stopped with its passenger train; IC #1014 was a 1904 Rogers-built 4-4-2 Atlantic (80 D; 185 BP; 210,000 TW; 24,271 TF); this unit was later rebuilt (63 1/2 D; 225 BP; 217,500 TW; 39,500 TF) and renumbered to IC #2008. IC #1017, another Rogers 4-4-2 of 1904, had similar original dimensions and was improved in the 1930's yet never renumbered; instead, this unit was retired by 1939. Another view of IC #1017, this one from an earlier time, is shown on this page; note the slide valve cylinders on the older view on this page, versus the piston valve cylinders on the same unit, after modernization, on the facing page.

IC1904-07

Illinois Central #1018 is shown above, having received the improvements most of the 4-4-2 Atlantic fleet did in the 1920's. This unit was a 1904 Rogers-built 4-4-2 (80 D; 185 BP; 210,000 TW; 24,271 TF) that was rebuilt (63 1/2 D; 225 BP; 217,500 TW; 39,500 TF) and later renumbered (to IC #2001 in 1942).

IC1904-08

Illinois Central #1019 directly above and IC #2009 below are the same engine, after renumberings. While exhibiting the upgrades this series of 1904 Rogers-built 4-4-2 Atlantics received in the 1920's (piston valves swapped for slide valves; Baker valve gear swapped for Stephenson motion; 63 1/2 inch drivers swapped for 80" drivers; a 40 pound boost to boiler pressure) IC #2009 shows a later modernization, the square sandbox on top of the engine. The result of these changes to the 4-4-2's was that it took an underpowered engine and made it slippery; IC's fleet never exceeded 26 units.

IC1904-13

IC1904-06

Illinois Central #1018, shown above and on the facing page at top, was another Rogers 4-4-2 Atlantic. It was captured above at an earlier time, before the improvements of the 1920's. This passenger train was called the Taft Special, as it carried William Howard Taft; the picture was taken in September, at Webster City, Iowa. It is not known whether Mr. Taft was Secretary of War, the Republican Nominee, President or ex-President at the time this photograph was snapped.

Illinois Central #1025 was caught on a turntable in the picture below. The next-to-last 1904 Rogers-built 4-4-2 Atlantic, this unit had the same dimensions as the rest of the series, and was modernized in the 1920's; this unit was retired in 1939 and, as such, was never renumbered.

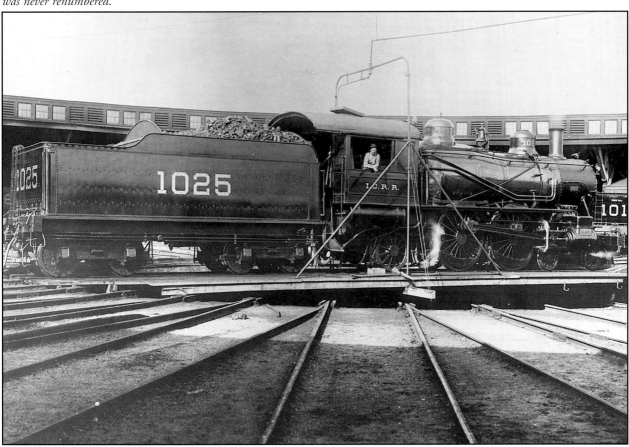

IC1904-09

IC1904-10

IC1904-11

IC1904-12

Illinois Central #2000 was a 1904 Rogers-built 4-4-2 Atlantic (original IC #1015), rebuilt and renumbered in the photograph above. While this 4-4-2 had the same dimensions as the others in this series when built, it was rebuilt with slightly larger cylinders (22 1/4 x 28, instead of 21 x 28) which yielded tractive force of 44,000 pounds rather than the 39,500 pounds the other modernized units were given. This unit saw service until the late-1940's.

IC1904-14

Shown on the facing page are two views of the last 4-4-2 Atlantic built for the Illinois Central - IC #1026. These two pictures show the 1904 Rogers-built engine on release from the shops after being superheated in the early 1920's; superheating allowed the engine to be run at lower pressure while maintaining efficiency; superheating supposedly saved 20 percent in coal and 25 percent in water, when compared to saturated steam. The head-on photograph was published in the August, 1922 issue of the Illinois Central Magazine. The photograph directly above on this page shows this unit renumbered to IC #2010 in 1943 and with the addition of a square sandbox; this engine was retired in 1946.

1905

Moroccans under French rule revolted; Germany offered support to Morocco, thus hinting at its objectives and setting the stage for a larger conflict. While taking on a geographically superior nation, the Russo-Japanese War ended with Japan taking territory from Mother Russia and the Czarists; U.S. President Theodore Roosevelt would be awarded the 1906 Nobel Peace Prize for helping broker the peace, signified by the Treaty of Portsmouth; Japan would continue its aggression on and off for 25 years, when it would get serious in China. 26-year old German born Albert Einstein earned his Ph.D. at Berlin University, and published theories on the photoelectric effect, Brownian motion and special relativity; $E = mc^2$ was first used. Guglielmo Marconi invented the directional radio antenna. French psychologist Alfred Binet developed a series of mental tests, the foundation for classifying children by mental age or intelligence level. Alberta and Saskatchewan were added as Provinces of the Dominion of Canada. Essentially a protectorate of Sweden since 1814, Norway gained its independence. Farmers pressed into navy service on the Russian cruiser *Potemkin* mutinied because of inhumane treatment; Hollywood fodder 20 years later.

Having been elected President for the first time in his own right, the 26th President of the U.S. 46-year old Theodore Roosevelt was sworn in to office in March. The Industrial Workers of the World, the Wobblies, began their work to organize less-skilled workers. Novocain was introduced as a local anesthetic. The second edition of the World Series, having skipped 1904, was held with the New York Giants defeating the Philadelphia Athletics 4 games to 1. The University of Minnesota's Bob Marshall became the first black named a college football All-American, as another brick in the wall fell. The Institute of Musical Art, antecedent to the Juilliard School of Music, was established.

Both the Pennsylvania and the New York Central initiated 18-hour service between New York and Chicago. The Santa Fe Railway set the record of just under 45 hours for a 2,267-mile steam-powered run from Los Angeles to Chicago, paid for by the wealthy miner Walter Scott – nicknamed Death Valley Scotty; this record lasted over 30 years until the age of diesel power, when *The Super Chief* service was introduced with a 39 ½ hour schedule on substantially the same route. The Great Northern Railway inaugurated its *Oriental Limited* service between Puget Sound and Chicago.

System mileage remained steady at 4,374 spread over 11 states; mileage on the Yazoo & Mississippi Valley grew to 1,210 with the addition of 35 miles of track in Mississippi, consisting of new branch lines to Belzona, Stover and Murphy. Toward the end of the year, Illinois Central executed a 3-year lease with the option to acquire the Tennessee Central line from Hopkinsville to Nashville; results of this 85-mile segment would be included in the next fiscal reporting period, but this proved temporary as the lease was not renewed in 1908; it would be 63 years before this line was acquired and consolidated into operations. During the 1905 fiscal reporting period the Illinois Central gained control of the Indianapolis Southern Railway, a planned 89-mile long road to connect Indianapolis with Switz City; construction would drag into 1906 and the line would not be consolidated into operations until 1911. Early in the year a fire at the Yazoo & Mississippi Valley facilities in New Orleans caused significant damage: elevators and warehouses at Stuyvesant Docks on the Mississippi River were destroyed, along with over 200 freight cars; fire losses would exceed $600,000. Revenues exceeded $49.5 million, almost 22 percent of which was due to passenger traffic (21,645,601 passengers). With general business levels steady, revenue traffic set its tenth consecutive record, 23.1 million tons of freight; tonnage on the unconsolidated Yazoo & Mississippi Valley approached 4.1 million tons. Locomotive availability rose to 1,158 units with the purchase of 72 new units (56 Consolidations (30 ALCO and 26 Rogers), 6 Rogers Atlantic 4-4-2's, and 10 Rogers 0-6-0 switch units); the fleet consisted of 162 switching units (31 4-wheel and 131 6-wheel), 40 suburban units, 203 10-wheel locomotives, 328 2-6-0 Mogul-types, 179 8-wheel types, 218 2-8-0 Consolidations, one 12-wheel arrangement, 26 4-4-2 Atlantic-types and a single 2-6-2 Prairie-type. There were 40 locomotives and 178 coaches dedicated to suburban service, with 123 daily trains in each direction, 43 on Sunday. In light of its importance to rail operations, Illinois Central began a two-year project upgrading the Cairo River bridge approaches with double-track embankments, leaving out the more expensive double-tracking of the bridge. On May 25th, the Mississippi river crossing at Thebes, Illinois over to Cape Girardeau, Missouri was tested with 18-coupled 800-Class 2-8-0 Consolidations venturing their way across without incident; this bridge replaced the Grays Point ferry service.

IC1905-02

IC45x35-24

Four Alco/Brooks-built 0-6-0 switch engines (51 D; 200 BP; 142,000 TW; 31,287 TF), all products of 1905. IC #65 would be rebuilt as an 0-6-0T (230 BP) switcher (IC #3290) in 1943.

Illinois Central #66 was captured at Memphis in December, 1926. IC #71 also was snapped at Memphis, but ten years later on November 11, 1936.

IC1905-01

IC1905-03

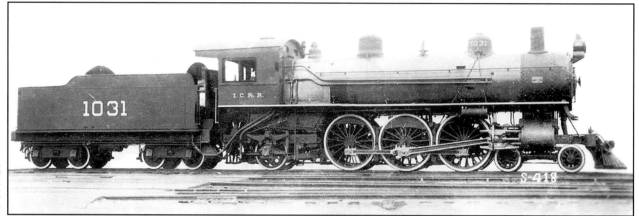

IC1905-04

IC1905-06

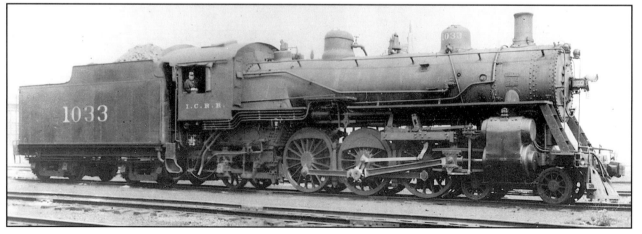

IC1905-05

Facing page, top to bottom: Illinois Central #1031 is shown in a 1905 Alco/Schenectady Builder's Photograph; this engine (75 1/2 D; 215 BP; 224,000 TW; 39,334 TF) was the first 4-6-2 Pacific-type acquired by the IC and came equipped with Stephenson valve gear and piston valve cylinders; the engine was received late in 1905, and commented on in the 1906 reporting period; this photograph appeared in the Illinois Central Magazine in the 1950's. In the middle picture, IC #1033 is shown in its original configuration, pulling a passenger train at speed. In the bottom view, this same engine is shown after some improvements have been added, especially in the valve gear. IC #1031 was renumbered to IC #1003 in 1942/1943; IC #1033 was renumbered to IC #2085 and rebuilt (61 D; 215 BP; 248,733 TW; 48,683 TF) in the same period.

ICNEGGS-50

The picture of Illinois Central #3288, which was published in the December, 1942 issue of the IC Magazine, shows an 0-6-0T (230 BP; 35,228 TF) saddle-tank switch engine built from IC #72, a 1905-model 0-6-0 switcher (51 D; 200 BP; 142,000 TW; 31,287 TF) from Alco/Brooks; the conversion was made by shop forces at Clinton Shops in 1942, and this engine served the Clinton Roundhouse. This unit held less than a ton of coal in its bunker and 1,000 gallons of boiler water in the tank above the boiler. This unit was scrapped in 1954.

IC1905-09

Illinois Central #5060 was a 1905 Baldwin-built 4-6-0 (68 D; 180 BP; 146,070 TW; 25,000 TF) 10-wheeler, originally erected for the New Orleans & Northeastern (as NO&NE #289); when the Vicksburg Shreveport & Pacific gained control of the NO&NE, this engine became VS&P #308; IC acquired the VS&P and this engine in 1926, renumbering it as shown. This engine saw duty until after World War II, being retired in 1946.

1906

Picasso invented cubism. The Sorbonne in France installed its first female professor, Nobel laureate Marie Curie. Having paired Charles Roll's sales with Henry Royce's manufacturing for the last two years, the two formalized their partnership with a merger.

The first jukebox appeared. The San Francisco earthquake leveled much of the city in April and some 700 people perished; what survived the earthquake would fall to the fires that followed. Upton Sinclair published *The Jungle*, exposing deplorable conditions in Chicago's meat packing industry; this would create enough commotion that a Pure Food & Drug Act would be rushed through Congress in the same year. The third World Series took place, the first and only all-Chicago Series; Charles A. Comiskey's White Sox won their first Series trophy upsetting the favored Cubs in six games. Willis H. Carrier received a patent on the forerunner to air conditioners. 33-year old physicist Lee De Forest invented the Audion tube, his version of the triode, a 3-electrode vacuum tube; he received a patent two years later. 40-year old Canadian-born American physicist Reginald A. Fessenden broke new ground twice: the first transatlantic two-way wireless transmission and the first public radio broadcast, amplitude-modulation in radio broadcasting; Fessenden had previously worked as Chief Chemist for Thomas A. Edison and in electrical engineering at Purdue University and the University of Pittsburgh, where he did some of his conceptual work on AM radio. United States Steel commenced development of a site on Lake Michigan for a new steel plant, and so began the city of Gary, Indiana.

Edward H. Harriman set a transcontinental record of 71 hours and 27 minutes in covering the 3,344 miles from Oakland to New York City; this record would stand for 28 years. Working together the Union Pacific and Southern Pacific created the Pacific Fruit Express as a venture to speed fresh produce to eastern markets. Congress passed the Hepburn Act that empowered the Interstate Commerce Commission to regulate rail rates, and pipelines and terminals; the authority granted by the 1887 Act finally had enforcement power; the Commission began investigating Harriman's empire. The Canadian Pacific pioneered the use of vista dome-type observation cars for its scenic routes in the west through the Rockies.

Ending a spat between long-time Illinois Central President Stuyvesant Fish and Board Chairman Edward H. Harriman, James T. Harahan was elected the 11th Illinois Central President, serving until 1911; the ouster of Fish was under the pall of some shady financial dealings, while Harriman's powerplay was rumored to be an effort to subjugate Illinois Central to his Union Pacific empire. On consolidating the Tennessee Central's 85-mile long Nashville line into Illinois Central's operations, system mileage rose to 4,459; mileage on the Yazoo & Mississippi Valley rose to 1,239 with the addition of 29 miles of track in Mississippi. The 89-mile long Indianapolis Southern was completed with the driving of the golden spike near Bloomfield, Indiana; this road would not be consolidated into Illinois Central operations until 1911; in fact, toward the end of the year Illinois Central split off its 89-mile long Effingham to Switz City segment and folded it into the Indianapolis Southern property; the loss of these 89 miles would be reported in the next fiscal period. During the year Illinois Central advanced construction funds to a number of other carriers, with an eye toward acquiring the finished product at a later time; funds were advanced to the Memphis & State Line (building a 16-mile route around congested Memphis from Woodstock to East Junction) and the Bloomington Southern (constructing a 27-mile long road from Bloomington to Bedford, Indiana to access stone quarries). The Company also completed negotiations with the Mobile & Ohio, the Southern and the Northern Alabama railroads which would eventually give Illinois Central access to Birmingham via Jackson, Tennessee; in addition to the trackage rights gained two years earlier from the FRISCO, to complete the puzzle Illinois Central advanced funds to build a 3-mile stub into Perry, Tennessee and an 80-mile long track from Corinth, Mississippi to Haleyville, Alabama; service on this pieces-and-parts route began in 1908, when the construction was finished. Revenues exceeded $51.6 million, a little over 19 percent of which was due to passenger traffic (22,052,673 passengers). With general business levels rising, revenue traffic grew to its eleventh consecutive record, 25.6 million tons of freight; tonnage on the unconsolidated Yazoo & Mississippi Valley approached 4.4 million tons. Locomotive availability rose to 1,193 units with the purchase of 40 new units from ALCO (25 Consolidations, 5 Pacifics, and 10 0-6-0 switch units) and the acquisition of 10 used locomotives through line extensions; the fleet consisted of 172 switching units (31 4-wheel and 141 6-wheel), 40 suburban units, 203 10-wheel locomotives, 328 2-6-0 Mogul-

Illinois Central #899 was a 1906 Alco/Brooks-built 2-8-0 Consolidation (63 D; 200 BP; 203,500 TW; 39,180 TF); it is shown in a Builder's Photograph. This engine was one in a series of 40 received from Brooks in 1906, all of which were scrapped, sold or rebuilt by the mid-1930's.

Illinois Central #1036 was a 1906 Alco/Schenectady 4-6-2 Pacific (75 1/2 D; 215 BP; 224,000 TW; 39,334 TF); this unit was renewed and then rebuilt in the 1940's, becoming IC #2030 (61 D; 215 BP; 248,733 TW; 48,683 TF). It was pictured at an unknown place, after the improvements, dating it to post-1940.

types, 171 8-wheel types, 246 2-8-0 Consolidations, one 12-wheel arrangement, 26 4-4-2 Atlantic-types, a single 2-6-2 Prairie-type and 5 new 4-6-2 Pacific-types (IC's first (Schenectady-built in November, 1905) was #1031, rated at just under 40,000 lbs. tractive effort with 75" drivers). Similar to actions in 1893, Directors of the Company provided for an Improvement Fund to upgrade freight car capacity, this time deciding to replace 20-ton capacities with 40 and 50-ton cars.

IC45x35-42

IC1906-03

1907

French inventor Louis Lumiere invented color photography.

In December President Theodore Roosevelt sent 16 of the newest Navy battleships - the Great White Fleet - on a good will tour around the world, a fourteen-month project that would end in early 1909. The Jamestown Exposition, celebrating 300 years since the founding of the Jamestown settlement, was held at Hampton Roads, Virginia. 43-year old Belgian-born chemist Leo Hendrik Baekeland of Yonkers, New York announced his development of the compound Bakelite, one of the world's first synthetic plastic substances. Construction on the Washington National Cathedral began, the start of an 83-year project. Set aside as Indian Territory in 1834, opened for Homesteading in 1889, and organized as a Territory in 1890, Oklahoma was admitted to the Union as the 46th State. The Panic of 1907 - the Rich Man's Panic - occurred when the Dow Jones Industrial Average crashed 36 percent between March and November; President Theodore Roosevelt asked J.P. Morgan to help bail out and stabilize the brokerage firms and major banks, which he did. In the year Sweden's King Oscar passed away, the Swedish Academy notched a few firsts: German-born 54-year old University of Chicago Professor Albert A. Michelson became the first American to win the Nobel Prize in Physics, and the first of 73 laureates attributed to the University of Chicago; 42-year old Rudyard Kipling became the first Englishman to win the Nobel Prize in Literature. The Chicago Cubs won the fourth edition of baseball's World Series, gaining their first Series trophy; the Cubs swept the Tigers with four wins and a tie in the Series, the first Series sweep. 40-year old Florenz Ziegfeld rolled out the first of 22 musical revues under his own name, *The Ziegfeld Follies*.

Washington's Union Station, jointly owned by the Pennsylvania and Baltimore & Ohio Railroads was completed in the nation's capital; the station was designed by famed Chicago architect Daniel H. Burnham and extended 620 feet in length with 33 tracks on two levels. Virginia's Tidewater and West Virginia's Deepwater railroads combined to form the Virginian, a 435-mile long coal hauler from Norfolk to Charleston.

While adding 7 miles of track in the Illinois coal fields between Zeigler and Herrin, on splitting off its 89-mile long Effingham to Switz City segment, system mileage dropped to 4,377; mileage on the Yazoo & Mississippi Valley remained at 1,239 with no new additions. Revenues for the year topped $56.6 million, almost 20 percent due to passenger traffic (23,441,337 passengers). With general business levels steady, revenue traffic set its twelfth consecutive record, 26.9 million tons of freight; tonnage on the unconsolidated Yazoo & Mississippi Valley almost reached 5.0 million tons. Locomotive availability rose to 1,240 units with the purchase of 47 new ALCO units (40 Consolidations, 5 Pacifics, and 2 0-6-0 switch units); the fleet consisted of 174 switching units (31 4-wheel and 143 6-wheel), 40 suburban units, 203 10-wheel locomotives, 328 2-6-0 Mogul-types, 171 8-wheel types, 286 2-8-0 Consolidations, one 12-wheel arrangement, 26 4-4-2 Atlantic-types, a single 2-6-2 Prairie-type and 10 4-6-2 Pacific-types. During the year Illinois Central continued advancing construction funds to a number of carriers, eyeing acquisition when finished; funds were advanced to the Kensington & Eastern (building a 7-mile double-track line into Hammond, Indiana in order to access trackage to the new United States Steel plant site under construction in Gary), the Memphis & State Line (a 16-mile route from Woodstock to East Junction, 6 miles of which were put in operation during the year), the Mississippi & Alabama and the Alabama Western (the 80-mile long puzzle piece from Corinth, Mississippi to Haleyville, Alabama to allow access to Birmingham) and the Bloomington Southern (a 27-mile long road from Bloomington, Indiana, 2 miles of which were put in operation during the year). During the year Illinois Central continued its track elevation project, elevating its tracks between 67th Street and 79th Street. Edward H. Harriman enlarged his empire by buying control of the 1,915-mile long Central of Georgia Railroad, which he then turned over to the Illinois Central for operation; the Central of Georgia had rail operations in Alabama, Georgia and Tennessee, and both passenger and freight steamship operations through its Ocean Steamship Company from its terminus at Savannah to New York and Boston.

IC1907-01

Illinois Central #202 was an 0-6-0 switch engine (51 D; 200 BP; 142,000 TW; 31,287 TF) built by Alco/Brooks in 1907; this engine was one of seven Brooks built for the IC in 1907. This photograph appears to be in the Chicago area and date before the 1926 electrification. This unit was converted in 1943 into an 0-6-0T saddle-tank switch engine (230 BP; 35,288 TF) and numbered IC #3292; this was the only one of the seven 1907 Brooks 0-6-0's to be converted. This engine saw service until 1956.

IC1907-03

Illinois Central #205 was another one of the seven Alco/Brooks-built 0-6-0 switch engines received in 1907; this unit had identical dimensions as IC #202 shown on top. This unit was not converted, and saw service until 1944.

IC1907-04

Illinois Central #798 was built by Alco/Brooks for the Indianapolis Southern (as IS #6) in 1907; IC acquired this 2-8-0 Consolidation (63 D; 200 BP; 203,500 TW; 39,180 TF) and renumbered it to IC #798 in 1912. This unit was renumbered (IC #3761) and renewed (225 BP; 43,731 TF) in 1937; in 1942 it was renumbered to IC #851, and sold five years later.

IC45x35-51

Another Alco/Brooks 2-8-0 Consolidation of 1907, IC #928 was erected for the Illinois Central. This unit had identical dimensions as IC #798 on top, but a much shorter service life; it was sold in 1927.

IC1902-03

Funny as it sounds, this 4-6-2 Pacific was the only 2-6-2 Prairie Illinois Central ever owned. In 1902 IC acquired a Rogers-built engine with a 2-6-2 wheel arrangement (75 D; 201,800 TW) for a test; this Prairie-type (IC #1001) was run head-to-head against a Baldwin-built 4-4-2 Atlantic (IC #1000); the railroad chose to go with the Atlantic type, and IC's only Prairie was converted at Burnside shops in 1907 into a 4-6-2 Pacific-type (75 D; 180 BP; 231,070 TW; 33,150 TF), and swapped roster numbers with the Baldwin Atlantic-type. IC #1000 was rebuilt once again with larger cylinders (61 D; 69,000 TF) and renumbered to IC #2099 in 1942/1943, as shown on the bottom of the facing page in a C.W. Witbeck photograph. IC #1000 was superheated and had Baker valve gear; the tender held 15 tons of coal and 9,000 gallons of boiler water.

IC1907-07

IC45x35-59

Three pictures of Alco/
Schenectady-built 4-6-2
Pacific-type (75 1/2 D; 215
BP; 224,000 TW; 39,334 TF)
engines, each constructed in
1907. Each was renumbered in
1942/1943: IC #1042 to IC
#1006, IC #1045 (caught at
Memphis on December 7,
1926) to IC #2037, and IC
#1047 to IC #2063. IC #1045
and IC #1047 were rebuilt (61
D; 215 BP; 248,733 TW;
48,683 TF) during the early
part of World War II.

ICNEGGS-37

IC1902-04

1908

Austria-Hungary's expansionism escalated into an invasion of Bosnia, increasing tension with Serbia. The basis of "sulfa" drugs (sulfanilamide) was determined, although its properties would not be known and perfected and used commercially until 1935. Working in England 37-year old Ernest Rutherford and his assistant 26-year old German physicist Hans Geiger developed an apparatus to detect energized alpha particles; it would be some 20 years before Geiger would perfect the radiation detector that bears his name; for his work involving radioactive substances, Rutherford would be awarded the year's Nobel Prize in Chemistry. The fourth edition of the Modern Olympics was held in London; a record number of nations and athletes participated in 21 different sports.

The Ford Model T, the first mass market automobile, debuted; 15 million copies would be produced in the years to come. The first paved road was constructed out of concrete outside Detroit. Congress established the Army Reserve. In December 30-year old Texan Jack Johnson broke the color line in heavyweight boxing, but not in the U.S.; he did it in a fight in Sydney, Australia, knocking out Canadian champion Tommy Burns; Jackson would cross the line in the States the following year in California, knocking out Stanley Ketchel in the 12th round; Jackson retained the title for seven years. The NCAA was formed; the Bureau of Investigation (forerunner to the FBI) was created. At the 14th Republican convention in Chicago, the Roosevelt Administration's Secretary of War William Howard Taft, a former Ohio Judge, was nominated for President on the 1st ballot; New York Congressman James Schoolcraft Sherman was elected nominee for Vice President. The sitting President Theodore Roosevelt did not seek a third Term because he felt it unbecoming, and handpicked Taft as his successor; with the passing of Grover Cleveland, Roosevelt became the third Chief Executive to hold office with no living ex-President. At the 20th Democratic convention in Denver, William Jennings Bryan won the Party nomination for President for the third time, this occasion on the 1st ballot; twice-defeated Gubernatorial candidate John Worth Kern of Indiana was chosen the nominee for Vice President from a dearth of candidates vying for the dubious honor. Eugene V. Debs represented the Socialist party for the 3rd time. Having lost to McKinley in 1896 and 1900, William Jennings Bryan now lost to the Taft/Sherman ticket, being swept 2 to 1. At the fifth World Series in baseball, the Chicago Cubs won their second and last Series trophy, over the Detroit Tigers in five games. The *Christian Science Monitor* was founded by Mary Baker Eddy, 29 years after founding the church.

Edward H. Harriman took a position in the troubled Erie Railroad, essentially bailing it out of a fourth bankruptcy. The government deemed Harriman's western railroad empire combination in restraint of trade and initiated court proceedings to force the Union Pacific to divest its holdings in the Southern Pacific, which it had held for seven years; Union Pacific would win round one, but lose at the Supreme Court four years later.

While adding 217 miles of track in reaching Birmingham via Jackson, Tennessee, system mileage jumped to 4,594; mileage on the Yazoo & Mississippi Valley rose by 132 to 1,371 with the addition of three small roads (the Helm & Northwestern, the Sunflower & Eastern and the Baton Rouge, Hammond & Eastern) plus other short trackage. Effective July 1, 1907 the Interstate Commerce Commission proscribed changes in the classification of revenues and expenses for reporting purposes; on the new basis the prior year's revenues of $56.6 million would approximate $55.5 million. Revenues for the year, on the new basis, approached $52.8 million, a little under 21 percent due to passenger traffic (23,357,184 passengers). With a general weakening in the economy and a six-week shutdown of the coal mines, revenue traffic levels broke the string of twelve consecutive records and dropped to 25.0 million tons of freight; tonnage on the unconsolidated Yazoo & Mississippi Valley almost reached 5.2 million tons. The locomotive fleet rose to 1,273 units with the purchase of 50 new ALCO units (35 Consolidations, 7 6-wheel switchers and 8 4-6-2 Pacifics), netted against retirements and replacements; the fleet consisted of 179 switching units (29 4-wheel and 150 6-wheel), 40 suburban units, 201 10-wheel locomotives, 321 2-6-0 Mogul-types, 165 8-wheel types, 321 2-8-0 Consolidations, one 12-wheel arrangement, 26 4-4-2 Atlantic-types and 19 4-6-2 Pacific-types. During the year Illinois Central continued advancing construction funds to a number of carriers, eyeing eventual acquisition; funds were advanced to the Kensington & Eastern (building toward Hammond, Indiana) and the Bloomington Southern (building out of Bloomington, Indiana).

ILLINOIS CENTRAL RAILROAD COMPANY

Diagram No. 1.—GROSS TRANSPORTATION RECEIPTS AND MILES OF RAILWAY OPERATED.

Showing by years the per cent of increase over the year ended June 30, 1899, in gross transportation receipts of the Illinois Central Railroad Company, and the per cent of increase in the average miles of railway operated during the year.

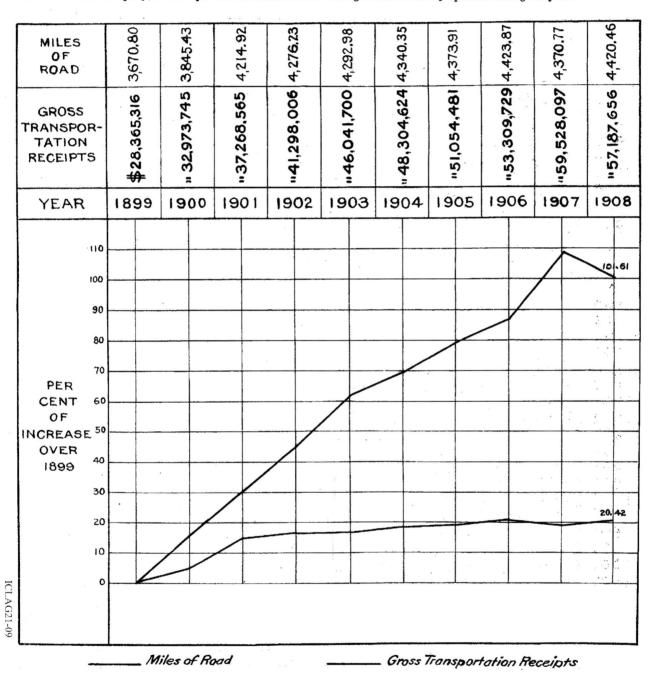

MILES OF ROAD	3,670.80	3,845.43	4,214.92	4,276.23	4,292.98	4,340.35	4,373.91	4,423.87	4,370.77	4,420.46
GROSS TRANSPORTATION RECEIPTS	$28,365,316	"32,973,745	"37,268,565	"41,298,006	"46,041,700	"48,304,624	"51,054,481	"53,309,729	"59,528,097	"57,187,656
YEAR	1899	1900	1901	1902	1903	1904	1905	1906	1907	1908

———— *Miles of Road*   ———— *Gross Transportation Receipts*

Shown above is a page from the Annual Report for the Year Ending June 30, 1908. It shows how Illinois Central reported on its rise in revenues over the past years, certainly a time of growth for the Company, having doubled over ten years.

ICLAG21-09

1909

Sicily's Mount Etna, one of the most active volcanoes and the tallest in Europe, erupted again, this time accompanied by earthquakes.

33-year old American inventor Charles F. Kettering formed Dayton Engineering Laboratories Company. Leo Baekeland received a patent on his compound Bakelite, a synthetic plastic substance. Sears, Roebuck and Company began selling homes by mail order; it would continue sales until 1937. The 2 ½-mile long Indianapolis Motor Speedway was completed. The United States stepped on stage as a world power when the 16-ship Great White Fleet completed its circumnavigation of the globe by sea. In April 53-year old Lieutenant Commander Robert Edwin Peary led an exploration party that is generally credited with being the first to reach the North Pole; 43-year old Dr. Frederick Albert Cook's claim of having been there in 1908 being discredited. Ole Evinrude introduced an outboard motor. Plastic was invented. In March 51-year old William Howard Taft was sworn in as the 27th President of the United States. The first film studio in California was opened by the Selig Company in Los Angeles. The Cadillac nameplate joined the ranks of General Motors. Still very much a wilderness, President Taft opened up 700,000 acres of government land in Washington, Montana and Idaho to settlement. Plans for a National Association for the Advancement of Colored People (NAACP) were formed in New York by a biracial group including 41-year old W.E.B. DuBois and Jane Addams; formal organization followed the next year. The Alaska-Yukon-Pacific Exposition was held in Seattle.

The Chicago, Milwaukee & St. Paul Railroad completed its transcontinental route with the driving of the last spike on its Pacific Coast Extension at Garrison, Montana in May; this road formed the fifth major transcontinental route in the U.S. and it would be the last of any significance; addition of Pacific to the Milwaukee's name also marked the turning point for the road from a cash-rich granger railroad to one entangled in lawsuits and past its peak. The Canadian Pacific completed its upper and lower spiral tunnels, moderating the 4.4% grade (232 feet per mile) temporarily constructed 25 years earlier in the valley of the Kicking Horse River to the original desired maximum 2.2% grade found on the rest of the system.

Edward H. Harriman ended his run as a railroad magnate, passing away at age 61 in September; Harriman, unlike the robber barons and pirates of his day, understood the impact he could have in railroading. Upgrading through sleeping car service established the year before, the first run of *Seminole Limited*, the first daily, year-round passenger train between Chicago and Florida was inaugurated. While adding 60-some miles of track across the system, discontinued operations (such as the 85-miles on the Tennessee Central between Hopkinsville and Nashville) outweighed those gains causing system mileage to drop to 4,551; mileage on the Yazoo & Mississippi Valley remained at 1,371. Revenues for the year topped $53.7 million, just over 20 percent due to passenger traffic (22,666,383 passengers). With general business levels slow to recover from the prior year's depression, revenue traffic dropped slightly to 24.9 million tons of freight; tonnage on the unconsolidated Yazoo & Mississippi Valley dipped to 4.9 million tons. The locomotive fleet, which dropped slightly due to the return of engines to the Tennessee Central, stood at 1,267 units; the fleet consisted of 179 switching units (29 4-wheel and 150 6-wheel), 40 suburban units, 199 10-wheel locomotives, 321 2-6-0 Mogul-types, 164 8-wheel types, 318 2-8-0 Consolidations, one 12-wheel arrangement, 26 4-4-2 Atlantic-types and 19 4-6-2 Pacific-types. During the year Illinois Central continued advancing construction funds to a number of carriers, notably the Kensington & Eastern; completed during the year, this line was turned over to the lessee, the Chicago, Lake Shore & South Bend railway (the former Chicago & Indiana Airline) on April 4th, service between South Bend and Kensington began two months later. Illinois Central purchased Edward H. Harriman's controlling interest in the 1,915-mile long Central of Georgia Railway out of his estate; the Illinois Central connected with this line at Birmingham, giving it a direct route into the southeast all the way to the coast at Savannah; Illinois Central would operate the Central of Georgia as a subsidiary for 33 years, entering receivership in the depths of 1932, and being written off in 1942. Electrification of Chicago-area terminal activities, with an eye toward reducing smoke and noise in the City proper, was considered during the year; while many points of view would be pondered over time, interchange with non-electrified carriers was thought to be a major impediment to any plans.

IC1909-03

Illinois Central #947, one of 50-some (IC series 941-993) Baldwin-built 2-8-0 Consolidations (63 D; 200 BP; 238,200 TW; 39,180 TF) erected to the Harriman Common Standard; the picture shown is a Builder's Photograph, the 1909 engine was saturated and carried Stephenson valve gear. Many of these units saw long service and were rebuilt over the years.

IC1907-05

Illinois Central #908 was another of the 1909 Baldwin-built 2-8-0 Consolidations (original IC #944) from the IC #941-993 series. This unit began with the same dimensions as IC #947, but was rebuilt in 1943 (62 D; 235 BP; 249,000 TW; 70,460 TF) with stoker; note the pilot-mounted dual air-pumps, Baker valve gear, pilot ladders and low-profile sandbox in comparison to the Builder's Photograph on top. IC #908 held the distinction of being the last 2-8-0 on the Illinois Central, not retiring until 1960.

IC1909-04

IC1909-01

ICNEGGS-30

IC1909-05

IC1909-05

Illinois Central #1050, shown taking on water at Kankakee, Illinois, was another of those 1909 Baldwin-built 4-6-2 Pacific engines with the large diameter drivers (77 1/2 D). This particular unit, not yet modernized in this photograph, saw service until retired in 1941.

Three views on the facing page of the same 4-6-2 Pacific-type. Top photograph shows Illinois Central #1049, one of a short series (IC #1049-1053) of Baldwin-built 4-6-2's erected with unusually large diameter drive wheels (77 1/2 D). The five engines (77½ D; 240 BP; 242,150 TW; 42,453 TF) were built to Harriman Common Standards with Baker valve gear, and all saw service into the 1940's, only IC #1049 being rebuilt. IC #1049 was rebuilt (61 D; 215 BP; 248,500 TW; 48,317 TF) in 1942/1943, and scrapped in 1949. The top picture shows a nearly-new IC #1049 pulling a passenger train out of IC's Central Station in Chicago. The middle view shows the same engine after a renewal in the 1920's, but before the rebuilding of the 1940's. The bottom picture shows the engine rebuilt in 1942 and renumbered to IC #2098.

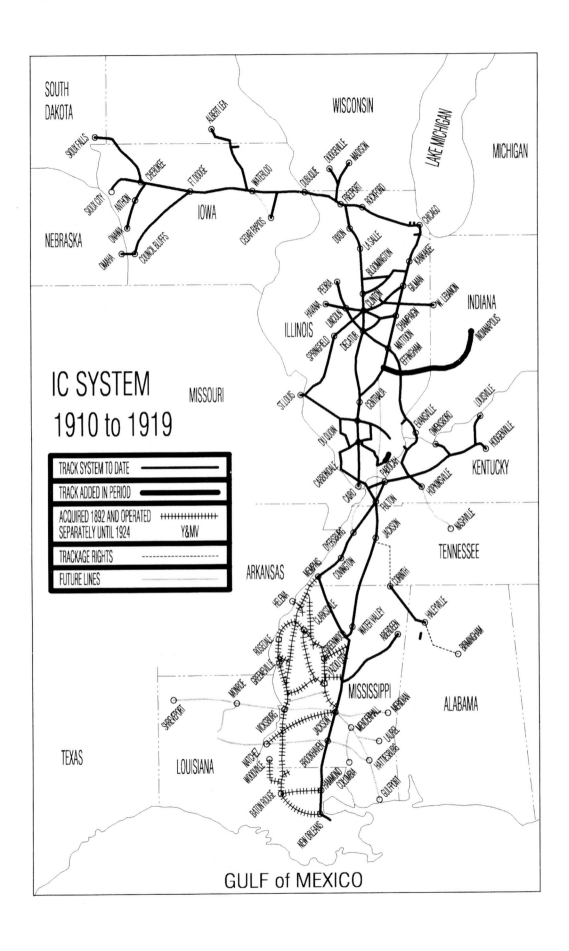

1850's 1860's 1870's 1880's 1890's 1900's **1910's** 1920's 1930's 1940's

The Thirteenth Census of the U.S. population was taken; there were a little over 92 million people in the U.S., having grown 21 percent from the prior census; the country would add almost 14 million people by the end of the decade, over one-third through immigration. The Union grew by two States to a total of 48. In the 1910's there were no cures for infectious diseases like smallpox, scarlet fever and diphtheria; influenza struck in 1918 and killed over 20 million in under a year. World War I ended in 1918; rather than working to rebuild war torn Europe, the Allies choose to exact revenge and reparation, a plan that would frame a future war. In 1918, the US was training 2 million new troops to help end the war. With millions of men drawn from the labor pool for the War effort, a great migration of blacks to the industrial north took place and continued on through the 1920's. A war economy built up momentum during the decade of the 1910's, and ended with the beginning of a period of stimulation and high spirits – the onset of the Roaring 1920's. The groundwork for the suffrage movement was laid. The subject of "wet" versus "dry" party platforms and States began…leading to Prohibition.

In 1910 the major line-haul rail carriers operated a little over 240,000 miles of railroad, a figure that would increase by only 12,500 more miles by the end of the decade, signaling the peak in the national railroad structure. During this period railroads reinvested in their plant, double-tracking many former single-track sections in order to handle increased business levels.

In conjunction with the Agricultural and Mechanical College at Starkville (the future Mississippi State University) Illinois Central put on a number of educational programs for Mississippi farmers, an effort that soon spread throughout the Illinois Central system; as the program grew Illinois Central provided information on topics such as the Boll Weevil, helped establish demonstration farms and instruction on dairy farming, even supplying Company-owned pedigreed bulls to help improve dairy herds.

GROWTH OF ILLINOIS CENTRAL RAILROAD BUSINESS

Year (1)	Tonnage (mil/tons)	Lumber (mil/tons)	Grain (mil/tons)	Coal (mil/tons)	FFV (mil/tons)	Cotton (mil/tons)	Aggregates (mil/tons)	Passengers Commuters	Miles/Fare
1910	27.6	4.8	3.0	8.7	.700	.288	1.0	25,244,516 N/A	26/$0.47
1911	27.5	4.6	3.1	8.2	.758	.279	1.1	26,801,511 N/A	26/$0.48
1912	26.4	4.2	3.1	8.6	.792	.244	1.0	27,005,956 N/A	26/$0.49
1913	30.4	4.8	3.5	10.5	.980	.216	1.3	27,537,947 N/A	26/$0.49
1914	32.3	4.8	3.3	12.1	1.1	.304	1.3	27,522,774 N/A	26/$0.50
1915	31.3	3.9	3.6	12.4	1.1	.290	1.4	26,019,820 N/A	25/$0.49
1916	35.0	4.7	3.5	14.1	1.3	.246	1.5	27,300,134 N/A	25/$0.49
1917	42.5	6.2	3.1	17.5	1.2	.263	2.0	28,382,898 N/A	30/$0.60
1918	45.9	6.0	3.7	20.4	1.3	.268	1.4	27,181,219 N/A	32/$0.75
1919	38.2	5.0	3.5	14.5	1.4	.312	1.9	31,002,734 N/A	31/$0.77

FFV = Fresh Fruit & Vegetables Passengers/Commuter s= Total Ridership, and Commuter Portion
Miles/Fare = Average Passenger Trip and Charge (1) Fiscal Year N/A = Data Not Available

1910

The neon lamp, which glowed red, was invented by 40-year old French chemist Georges Claude. Dutch designer Anthony Fokker began building airplanes. Halley's Comet returned on schedule and passed through the firmament; in 1705, then 49-year old British astronomer Edmund Halley correctly predicted the comet he viewed 23 years earlier would reappear in 1758; after it did, it was immortalized with his name; the comet appears about every 76 years. With the passing of English King Edward VII, his 45-year old son rose to become George V, King and Emperor of Great Britain, Ireland and the British Empire. Imperial Japan officially annexed the Kingdom of Korea, daring anyone to do something about it. 82-year old Leo Tolstoi, the author of both *War and Peace* and *Anna Karenina*, passed away and was buried at his ancestral home in Russia.

In his second official title defense, Jack Johnson fought 35-year old James J. Jeffries on July 4th in Reno, Nevada; in retaining the heavyweight boxing crown with a 15th round KO, Johnson handed Jeffries his only professional defeat, prompting Jeffries to retire from the game. Woodrow Wilson, lawyer and former President of Princeton University, was elected Governor of New Jersey for the first time. The first practical electric washing machine appeared. Octave Chanute died. Buick innovated with a model that had a six-cylinder gasoline engine. 24-year old Eugene Ely made history when he took off in an aircraft from a ship at sea, from the cruiser *USS Birmingham*; the next year he would make the first landing. The 6-4-3 double-play combination of Tinkers to Evers to Chance was made famous when Franklin P. Adams coined the sobriquet to fill space in his newspaper column. Cy Young won his 500th game, the only player to ever do so. Joy Morton founded his Salt Company. A corollary of Robert Baden-Powell's work in England three years earlier, the Boy Scouts of America was incorporated. 19-year old Fannie Brice (nee Fannie Borach) debuted in the *Ziegfeld Follies* musical; she would star in the *Follies* six more times over the next 13 years.

The Pennsylvania Railroad completed construction of its New York City passenger station in mid-town Manhattan; today the site of Madison Square Garden.

System mileage remained at 4,551; mileage on the Yazoo & Mississippi Valley rose by barely one mile to 1,372. Even with a strike by coal miners during the last two months of the fiscal year, revenues leaped to over $57.9 million, almost 21 percent due to passenger traffic (25,244,516 passengers). Even with a 16.7 percent drop in coal revenues, overall business levels surged almost 8 percent; revenue traffic tonnage rose to 27.6 million tons of freight; tonnage on the unconsolidated Yazoo & Mississippi Valley exceeded 5.3 million tons. Locomotive availability rose slightly to 1,272 units with the purchase of 23 new Baldwin units (18 Consolidations and 5 Pacifics) and the retirement of 18; the fleet consisted of 176 switching units (26 4-wheel and 150 6-wheel), 40 suburban units, 199 10-wheel locomotives, 320 2-6-0 Mogul-types, 150 8-wheel types, 336 2-8-0 Consolidations, one 12-wheel arrangement, 26 4-4-2 Atlantic-types and 24 4-6-2 Pacific-types. Washing its laundry in public, the Company, in its annual report, disclosed an internal scandal; in an era when a million could really buy something, collusion between a number of Illinois Central officials and certain car repair companies resulted in the Company being swindled in an amount upwards of $1.5 million; expenses for freight train cars under Maintenance of Equipment went from $5.0 million in 1908 to $7.8 million in 1910, an increase of 56 percent; investigated, caught and prosecuted, this expense fell back to $4.9 million the following year.

IC1910-01

Illinois Central #1009 (original IC #1062) was one of a series of fifteen (IC #1054-1068) 1910 Alco/Brooks-built 4-6-2 (75 1/2 D; 215 BP; 224,000 TW; 39,334 TF) Pacifics; the photograph above shows the engine as modernized in the 1920's, showing updated valve gear and twin air-pumps. This engine was scrapped in 1952, and this photograph dates to the last ten years of its service life.

IC1910-02

Illinois Central #1056 was from the same series of Alco/Brooks-built 4-6-2 Pacific's; this engine had the same dimensions as IC #1009, when both were new. In the photograph above it is shown as delivered in all its simplicity, as was the whole series when built, with saturated steam and Stephenson valve gear. This engine would be rebuilt (61 D; 215 BP; 248,733 TW; 48,683 TF) in the early 1940's and renumbered as IC #2049; it was retired in 1946.

IC45x35-58

Illinois Central #1068 was the last in the series of fifteen Alco/Brooks-built 4-6-2 Pacific's, and is shown in near-new condition in the photograph above. This engine had identical original dimensions as the other engines, and was rebuilt to the same dimensions mentioned for IC #1056; this unit was renumbered to IC #2073, and sold for scrap in 1952.

IC1910-03

Illinois Central #1057, shown above, was a 1910 Alco/Brooks-built 4-6-2 Pacific; the photograph shows this unit in almost-new condition, before any improvements or upgraded parts were added. The engine (75 1/2 D; 215 BP; 224,000 TW; 39,334 TF) was rebuilt (61 D; 215 BP; 248,733 TW; 48,683 TF) in the early 1940's and was renumbered to IC #2090. This unit saw service until 1952. The picture is thought to show IC #1057 being eased off the scales, with an engineer and one groundman in the view.

In the lower picture, Illinois Central #2068 is shown pulling a string of cars from the yard; this engine (original IC #1059) was a 1910 Alco/Brooks-built 4-6-2 Pacific with the same dimensions, original and rebuilt, as above. This photograph appeared in the April, 1950 issue of the Illinois Central Magazine in a story on the Memphis Division.

IC4x5-50

1911

Germany sent warships to Morocco, giving at least visible support to rebels fighting French rule and heightening anxiety in Europe. The Mexican Revolution began as Porfirio Diaz, military dictator for the last 35 years, was forced out; Francisco I. Madero took control of government. 39-year old Norwegian explorer Captain Roald E. Amundsen became the first to reach the South Pole in December. 44-year old Polish-born Marie Sklodowska Curie won the Nobel Prize in Chemistry; this was her second Nobel Prize, the first being a shared Prize in physics in 1903; Curie was the first of six people/organizations to be honored more than once.

Ray Harroun became the first Indy 500 winner. Eugene Ely made the first aircraft landing on a ship at sea, onto a platform above the afterdeck of the *USS Pennsylvania*, matching his feat of being the first to take-off; he would die later in the year barnstorming in Georgia. A Wright-brothers airplane (the *Vin Fizz*) flew across the country, making 70 stops on the way into the record books. 35-year old Charles Kettering invented the electric self-starter for Cadillac, doing away with handcranks. Henry Ford was granted a patent on an automobile transmission. Standard Oil lost the antitrust suit in the U.S. Supreme Court and 72-year old J.D. Rockefeller's holding-company monopoly was broken up into smaller units, for the second time; the Supreme Court also forced James Buchanan Duke (one day the source of Duke University's arrival in the top echelon) to dismantle his 90 percent monopoly of the tobacco market, American Tobacco. On his death, Joseph Pulitzer left a $500,000 endowment to Columbia University for annual awards, Pulitzer Prizes. Sixteen years after the first U.S. Open, 19-year old John J. McDermott became the first American to win it; he also won it the following year. 58-year old Heike K. Onnes discovered superconductivity, a condition of zero electrical resistance. The future of gospel music was born in New Orleans; Mahalia Jackson would move to Chicago at 16, make her first recording at 23, and be celebrated at Carnegie Hall at 39.

50-year old Charles H. Markham was elected the 12th President of Illinois Central; Markham would serve until 1918, resign to become a Director of the U.S. Railroad Administration during the war, and be re-elected in 1919. In February the *Chicago-New Orleans Limited* was renamed the *Panama Limited* in honor of the canal being constructed in Latin America; Illinois Central ran the *Panama Limited* for nearly 60 years. On July 1st, Illinois Central's Indiana division absorbed the Indianapolis Southern Railroad, through foreclosure purchase; results would be consolidated in the following year's report of operations. While adding 25 miles of track, chiefly the Brookhaven & Pearl River between Brookhaven and Monticello, Mississippi, system mileage rose to 4,576; mileage on the Yazoo & Mississippi Valley remained at 1,372. Revenues for the year reached just under $61.0 million, slightly over 21 percent due to passenger traffic (26,801,511 passengers). With steady business conditions, revenue traffic levels over Illinois Central dipped ever-so-slightly to 27.5 million tons of freight; tonnage on the unconsolidated Yazoo & Mississippi Valley exceeded 5.6 million tons. Locomotive availability rose to 1,321 units with the addition of 51 units (49 net). Illinois Central recorded two firsts: delivery of its first 2-8-2 Mikado-type engine (Baldwin-built # 1601), and purchase of its first superheated engine – a small Pacific-type 4-6-2 (Alco-Brooks-built # 1069).

Baldwin Locomotive erected 50-some (series IC #941-993) 2-8-0 Consolidations (63 D; 200 BP; 238,200 TW; 39,180 TF) for the Illinois Central between 1909 and 1911, a number of which were rebuilt with larger cylinders and higher boiler pressure to boost tractive effort. These two pages show six 1911 units, some as original and some as rebuilt/renumbered.

IC1906-01

This page, three rebuilt units. Shown top and bottom, IC #904 (original IC #983) and IC #909 (original IC #972) were rebuilt from 22" x 30" cylinders to 27" x 30" cylinders (62 D; 235 BP; 249,000 TW; 70,460 TF) with stoker, yielding much higher tractive force. IC #905 (original IC #985) was not rebuilt with such a large increase in cylinders (62 D; 235 BP; 244,000 TW; 48,930 TF) with stoker.

IC1906-02

IC1907-06

IC #909 shown on the facing page at bottom was captured at Evansville, Indiana in 1952 as crews changed; the tender held 17 tons of coal and 9,000 gallons of boiler water. This page, top to bottom, shows three more 1911 Baldwin-built 2-8-0's. IC #966 (later IC #902, rebuilt to 48,930 TF), in the first two views, is shown early in its service life; note the air-pump still is side-mounted, the lack of pilot ladders and the tender is the original Vanderbilt-type. IC #977 (later IC #903, rebuilt to 48,930 TF) is shown with those three items improved. IC #981 (later IC #911, rebuilt to 70,460 TF) was caught with some modifications.

IC45x35-65

IC45x35-64

IC1911-04

IC1911-05

IC45x35-67

Three views of the same engine, at different periods in its service life. Top picture shows Illinois Central #990, a 1911 Baldwin-built 2-8-0 Consolidation (63 D; 200 BP; 238,200 TW; 39,180 TF) when nearly new; note Vanderbilt tender. Picture below shows same engine with a few changes, notably the headlamp arrangement and the pilot wheels; this picture was snapped at Vicksburg, Mississippi on August 29, 1933 in a negative by C.B. Medin.

IC1911-06

Illinois Central #990 was rebuilt into an 0-8-0 (61 D; 235 BP; 225,500 TW; 50,844 TF) switch engine (IC #3481) in 1938; it was renumbered to IC #3406 in 1942 and remained in service until being dropped from the roster sometime between 1943 to 1951. The tender held 12 tons of coal and 7,000 gallons of boiler water.

ICNEGGS-22

A pair of views of two 1911 Alco/Brooks 4-6-2 Pacifics (75 1/2 D; 215 BP; 245,000 TW; 39,334 TF), IC #1072 and IC #1074, both rebuilt (61 D; 215 BP; 248,733 TW; 48,683 TF) in the 1940's. IC #1072 is shown top with five men crawling over her to turn and return to service. Next shows the same engine later in its service life pulling a passenger train by IC's 12th Street Central Station; this engine was renumbered to IC #2036 in 1942/ 1943, and saw duty until the 1950's.

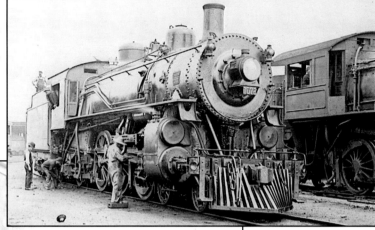

IC45x35-57

IC1911-01

IC45x35-169

IC #1074 (which would be renumbered to IC #2072) is shown taking on water with its passenger train, and in a sideview awaiting duty. This engine served into the 1950's.

IC1911-07

IC45x35-170

IC1911-08

On top, Illinois Central #1081, a 1911 Alco/
Brooks-built 4-6-2 Pacific (75 1/2 D; 215 BP;
45,000 TW; 39,334 TF), is shown hustling its
passenger train toward Chicago from the
outskirts; this unit was renumbered to IC
#2091 in 1942/1943 and was scrapped in
1949. IC #1082, shown in the middle picture,
was another 4-6-2 Pacific-type with similar
dimensions; it was captured with its crew
sometime before its renumbering (to IC #2034)
in 1942/1943; identified in the picture were,
left to right, F. Reidiman, J. Baum, E.
Rosenbaum, and O. Doyle (in gangway). Both
IC #1081 and #1082 were rebuilt (61 D; 215
BP; 248,733 TW; 48,683 TF) at the time of
renumbering. On the bottom is IC #1082
again, but in its renumbered life; this view
shows the old Pacific far from the mainline
service to which it had become accustomed; this
unit retired in 1960.

IC1911-12

IC4x5-47

These pictures all date to Decatur, Illinois in October, 1949.

In 1911, Illinois Central accepted delivery of its first 2-8-2 Mikado wheel-arrangement (IC #1601) from a series of 150 units (IC #1551-1700) that Baldwin built (63 1/2 D; 185 BP; 282,700 TW; 54,158 TF) for IC in 1911/1912. Over the years, a number of these units would be modernized and improved, giving the Mikado wheel arrangement a very long service life on the Illinois Central.

IC1911-09

IC1999-25

In the two views at top, Illinois Central #1612, a 1911 Baldwin-built 2-8-2 Mikado (original IC #1606, renumbered in 1944) worked to pull an elevator; this unit would be renumbered yet again, in 1951 to IC #1757; it was scrapped the following year; this 2-8-2 was long past its prime in this 1949 shot. Shown below was another 2-8-2 in the same circumstance, IC #1725 (original IC #1637, renumbered in 1944); it was scrapped in 1950.

IC1911-10

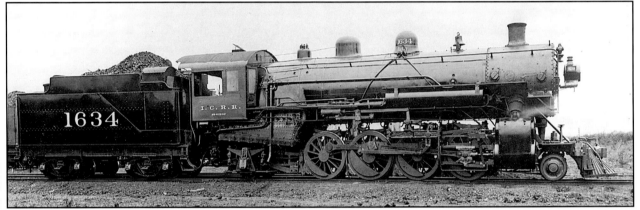

IC1999-17

IC1999-18

Three more views of Mikados from that first series of Baldwin-built 2-8-2's (63 1/2 D; 185 BP; 282,700 TW; 54,158 TF) received in 1911 (IC #1601-1664); all of these engines were built to the Harriman Common Standard, were superheated and came with Walschaerts valve gear; the tender held 15 tons of coal and 9,000 gallons of boiler water. IC #1619, on top, was captured at an unidentified time and place, as was IC #1634; IC #1634 was rebuilt in 1942 into an 0-8-2 switch engine (IC #3690), and it served until sold in 1955. IC #1643, shown on the bottom, was renumbered twice: to IC #1618 in 1943 and to IC #1762 in 1951; this unit served until sold for scrap in 1952.

Illinois Central #1657 was a 1911 Baldwin-built 2-8-2 Mikado (63 1/2 D; 185 BP; 282,700 TW; 54,158 TF); a Harriman Common Standard locomotive, IC experimented with a Coffin Feed Water Heater on this unit. In 1942 this unit was rebuilt into another 2-8-2 wheel arrangement (IC #2134), but with the chassis from a 2-10-2 locomotive yielding an impressive Mikado unit (64 1/2 D; 225 BP; 336,000 TW; 85,395 TF). This unit was sold for scrap in 1955.

Illinois Central #2081 was a 1911 Alco/Brooks 4-6-2 (61 D; 215 BP; 248,733 TW; 48,683 TF) Pacific; originally rostered as IC #1080 (75 1/2 D; 215 BP; 245,000 TW; 39,334 TF), it was rebuilt and renumbered in 1942/1943 and scrapped in 1957. This picture dates to June 18, 1951.

Illinois Central #3336 was a 1911 Baldwin-built 0-6-0 (51 D; 200 BP; 141,300 TW; 38,220 TF) switch engine; erected for the Alabama & Vicksburg (as A&V #423), IC acquired the engine in 1926 and renumbered it as shown. This picture was captured at Vicksburg, Mississippi on August 29, 1933.

1912

In April, Britain's White Star liner *Titanic* left Southhampton, England for New York City on its maiden voyage; more than 1,500 passengers were lost on the "unsinkable" in the North Atlantic. Queen Nefertiti's statue was found. Swiss chemist Dr. Jacques Brandenburger introduced his 1908 invention of cellophane by beginning large-scale production on specially-developed machines. Tension between Austria-Hungary and Serbia boiled over into the Balkan Wars, which would represent Europe's powder keg until overshadowed by a larger conflict. The revolution in Mexico continued as rebel leader Francisco I. Madero struggled to remain in control of the revolutionary government he established the prior year. 44-year old English explorer Robert Falcon Scott, in his second expedition to the Antarctic (1st 1901-1904), became the second to reach the South Pole, one month after Norwegian Roald E. Amundsen; Scott and his party of four perished on the return trip. Stockholm, Sweden hosted the fifth edition of the Modern Olympics; American James Francis Thorpe took temporary custody of gold medals for wins in the pentathlon and decathlon.

In March, the first troop of Girl Guides, the future Girl Scouts of America, was organized by 51-year old Georgia-born Juliette Gordon Low. Having pioneered work in AM-radio broadcasts, Reginald Fessenden developed the heterodyne radio receiver. The first successful parachute jump from an airplane occurred in the U.S. Columbia University Professor Herschel Parker, on his third attempt in 10 years, became the first to scale the highest peak in the U.S., Mt. McKinley at 20,320 feet. S.I. Russell invented the electric heating pad for patients with TB; years later, the heating pad would evolve into the electric blanket. At the 15th Republican convention in Chicago both incumbents - President William Howard Taft and Vice President James Schoolcraft Sherman - were re-nominated to the national ticket, the first time this had happened in Republican Party politics. Ex-President Theodore Roosevelt, like ex-President Ulysses S. Grant in 1880, returned from travel abroad and, after four years out of office, thirsted for a return to the White House; refused the nomination for a third term at the Republican convention Roosevelt, unlike Grant, broke away from the Party and formed a new Progressive branch which, in Chicago at its first National Convention, promptly chose him its nominee for President by acclamation; California Governor Hiram W. Johnson was the Third Party nominee for Vice President, also chosen by acclamation. At the 21st Democratic convention in Baltimore, New Jersey Governor Thomas Woodrow Wilson was nominated for President on the 46th ballot; the Vice Presidential candidate was Indiana Governor Thomas R. Marshall, selected after two ballots. Eugene V. Debs ran for President for the 4th time on the Socialist party ticket. With the rift in the Republican Party set off by Theodore Roosevelt's new Progressive wing, the Democratic ticket of Wilson/Marshall swept into office in November on a reformist platform they called New Freedom; Roosevelt and Taft together had actually garnered more popular votes, showing how expensive the schism was. New Mexico and Arizona were admitted to the Union as the 47th and 48th States. 21-year old Katherine Stinson of Canton, Mississippi became the fourth woman to receive a pilot's license and began a career as pilot/barnstormer; she helped her brother Eddie found Stinson Aviation the following year. Max Sennett debuted his *Keystone Cops*.

Henry M. Flagler's nine-year construction push to have his Florida East Coast reach Key West was completed. The Pennsylvania Railroad's *Pennsylvania Special* was renamed the *Broadway Limited*, connecting New York City with Chicago in 18 hours (later reduced to 16 hours); famed races with the New York Central's *20th Century Limited* lay in the future. The Pennsylvania Railroad's two-year old passenger station in Manhattan had been designed to be a through-station; to make it such, trains needed to regain the mainland after passing from New Jersey to Manhattan to Long Island; construction began on a bridge to cross back over the East river, and the Gustav Lindenthal-designed East River Arch Bridge (one day the Hell Gate Bridge) would be completed five years later with the passing of the first Pennsylvania train over the four-track span. In December the Supreme Court ordered the breakup of Edward H. Harriman's "Associated Railroads" and forced the Union Pacific to divest its holdings in Southern Pacific Railroad; partners since the 1901 acquisition by Harriman, the divestiture made them competitors once again; no one could foresee this would come full-circle 84 years later.

Illinois Central commuter service from Chicago reached Matteson, thirty miles from downtown Chicago; the Chicago, Lake Shore & South Bend railway (the future Chicago, South Shore & South Bend) extended its operations from Kensington into Randolph station using Illinois Central steam locomotives. System mileage grew to 4,763, chiefly due to the addition of the Indianapolis Southern's 179 miles of track; mileage on the Yazoo & Mississippi

1912 Alco/Brooks built 0-6-0 (51 D; 200 BP; 166,000 TW; 38,220 TF) units, part of a series of superheated switch engines. IC #211 on top is shown at Nonconnah Yard on December 1, 1944. IC #217, middle left, was captured at Vicksburg, Mississippi on September 4, 1939 with O.M. Teate (engineer) in the right seat. IC #3295 on the bottom shows a conversion of one of these 0-6-0's (IC#215) into an 0-6-0T saddle-tank switcher; the conversion to saddle-tank was done in 1947. As original 0-6-0 switch engines, these units held 9 1/2 tons of coal and 5,500 gallons of water in the tender. The picture of IC #217 appeared in the September, 1941 IC Magazine.

Valley edged upward to 1,374. Revenues were under pressure all year: a strike by Company shop men in the Fall which spread to over 10,000 employees, followed by spring floods in the south (reaching nine feet over the 45' flood stage on the Cairo gauge, it was the highest in 28 years), and ending with severe winter in the north; revenues for the year dropped to $58.7 million, almost 23 percent due to passenger traffic (27,005,956 passengers). Revenue traffic levels over Illinois Central dropped to 26.4 million tons of freight; tonnage on the unconsolidated Yazoo & Mississippi Valley dipped to almost 4.8 million tons. Locomotive availability rose to 1,458 units with the addition of 127 units (net 117) and the inclusion of 20 units from the Indianapolis Southern. Having proven its hand at converting light 4-6-0's into 4-6-4T's, Illinois Central turned its attention to 2-6-0's to supplement the suburban service locomotive fleet; eight Schenectady-built light Moguls (original 1889) were converted into 2-6-4T's, three at Lima Locomotive Works and five at the Company's Burnside Shops; the first four units were received during 1912 and the last in 1920/1921.

IC1912-06

A pair of 1912 Alco/Brooks 4-6-2 (75 1/2 D; 215 BP; 245,000 TW; 39,334 TF) Pacific passenger engines. IC #1088, shown above, was captured in a picture dated 1928, supposedly at East Dubuque (formerly Dunleith); identified in the picture were, left to right, Charles Wing (engineer), brakemen L. Dankley and Oscar Blume, Henry Kleth (fireman), and Martin Buckley (conductor, on the pilot); this engine was rebuilt (61 D; 215 BP; 248,733 TW; 48,683 TF) and renumbered to IC #2069 in 1942/1943 and served until 1960. IC #1093, shown below, was another 4-6-2 Pacific with the same dimensions; it was captured at an unknown time and place; this unit was renumbered IC #2045 (also rebuilt to the same dimensions as IC #2069) in 1942/1943 and scrapped in 1952.

IC1912-07

IC1912-08

IC1912-09

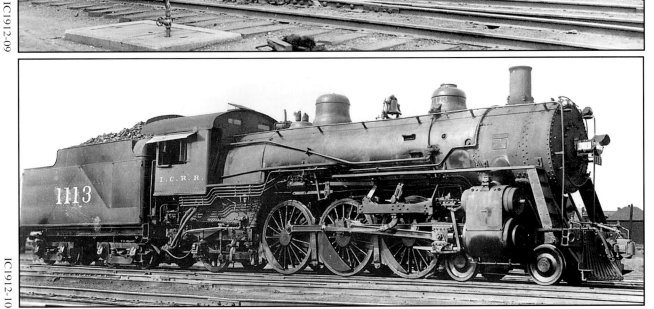

IC1912-10

Three more 4-6-2 Pacifics, all products of Alco/Brooks during 1912, each with slightly different dimensions as Illinois Central tried to fine-tune its 4-6-2 protocol. IC #1101 (75 1/2 D; 215 BP; 245,000 TW; 39,334 TF), shown on top and published previously, was rebuilt and renumbered to IC #2062 (61 D; 215 BP; 248,733 TW; 48,683 TF) in 1942/1943 and sold for scrap in 1952. IC #1103 (75 1/2 D; 235 BP; 250,000 TW; 44,041 TF) was photographed at an unknown time and place, and appears to have retained its roster number until scrapped in 1949. IC #1113 (75 1/2 D; 215 BP; 247,500 TW; 39,334 TF) was renumbered in 1942/1943 to IC #1014 and scrapped by 1952.

IC45x35-199

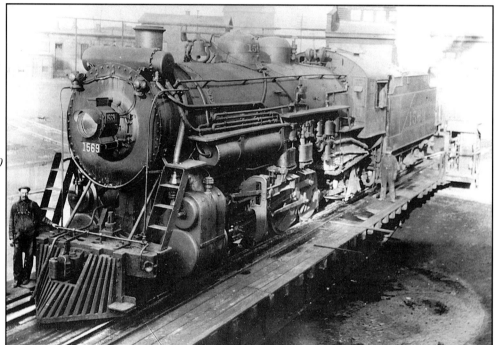

The Mikado 2-8-2 wheel arrangement was versatile, producing engines that were rebuilt for many services. Top photo shows IC #1568, which was converted into an 0-8-2 hump switcher (IC #3688) in 1942. IC #1569, on the turntable, was converted into a 2-10-0 Decapod switch engine (IC #3623) in 1940. IC #1576, on the bottom, kept its wheel arrangement, but was rebuilt and improved nonetheless; with its boiler pressure raised to 225 pounds, its tractive force exceeded 70,000.

IC1999-05

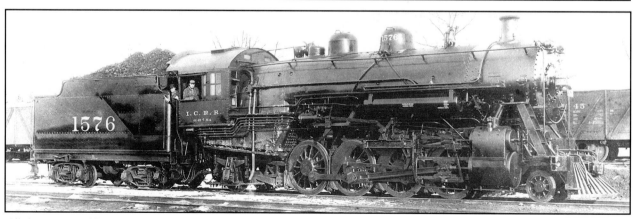

IC1999-08

All three engines (63 1/2 D; 185 BP; 282,700 TW; 54,158 TF) were 1912 Baldwins; the engines in the IC #1551-1599 series were superheated and had Walschaerts valve gear; a few, as IC #1569 shown, had Elesco Feed Water Heaters installed. IC #1568, on top, was pulling a trainload of Baby Ruth candy, as told in a story in the June, 1927 IC Magazine.

IC1912-11

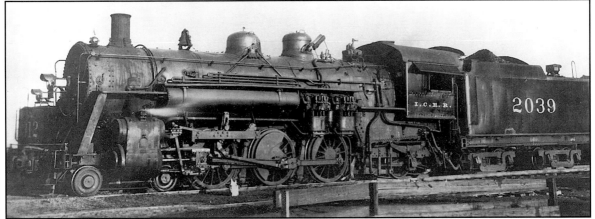

IC1912-12

IC1912-13

On top, 1912 Baldwin-built 2-8-2 (63 1/2 D; 185 BP; 282,700 TW; 54,158 TF) Mikado captured on August 2, 1934 at Chicago, Illinois; the boiler from this engine would be used with a 2-10-2 Central chassis to cobble together a bigger and better 2-8-2 (64 1/2 D; 225 BP; 336,000 TW; 74,078 TF) in 1941; the unit was scrapped in 1956. Middle and bottom, two 1912 Alco/Brooks-built 4-6-2 (75 1/2 D; 215 BP; 245,000 TW; 39,334 TF) Pacifics, originally rostered as IC #1085 and IC #1098, respectively; both were rebuilt (61 D; 215 BP; 248,733 TW; 48,683 TF) in the 1940's.

1913

The Mexican revolution evolved yet again as Francisco I. Madero lost control of his two-year old government to a new military dictator, Victoriano Huerta. 31-year old Fyodorovich (Igor) Stravinsky premiered his ballet *Rite of Spring*, about primitive man and the forces of nature.

The *Domelre* – the first functional household refrigerator – was marketed in Chicago. The Post Office began Parcel Post service. Henry Ford started his moving assembly line in the plant's magneto department in Highland Park, Michigan. The crossword puzzle was invented in London; twelve years later, the *Sunday Times* would be the first newspaper to publish one. "Big Storm" on the Great Lakes sent 11 ships and 250 men to a watery resting place. In February the 16th Amendment to the Constitution became law as New Mexico was the 36th to ratify; Alabama had been the 1st, New Hampshire the 38th and last, while Connecticut, Rhode Island and Utah rejected the proposal and never did ratify; giving Congress the power to collect income taxes, the first income tax was set at a flat rate of 1 percent over a small exemption level for most taxpayers. 56-year old Woodrow Wilson took the oath and became the 28th President of the U.S. in March. In April the 17th Amendment to the Constitution became law as Connecticut became the 36th State to ratify; Massachusetts had been 1st, Louisiana the 37th and last, and Utah rejected the proposal and never did ratify; instituting popular election of senators and discontinuing the practice of appointment by State Legislatures, the Amendment established the two Senator/six-year term representation for each State. Notre Dame made football history when it invented the forward pass, beating Army 35 to 13 at Army. Congress established the Federal Reserve System of 12 district banks by passing the Federal Reserve Act in December, the first significant banking and currency reform since the Civil War. Los Angeles finally got its water as the vision of 58-year old Irish-born architect William Mulholland was opened after six years of construction; over 5,000 men had worked to build aqueducts, sluiceways, tunnels and siphons from the Owens River some-250 miles through the Sierra Nevada and across the Mojave into the San Fernando Valley outside Los Angeles. A. C. Gilbert's Erector set debuted, mirroring the age of engineering and builders.

Henry M. Flagler passed away in Florida. The New York Central Railroad completed its second Grand Central depot replacing the original on Manhattan in New York City; with only an above ground terminal building, train and yard operations and the rest of the facility were on two-levels underneath the city; in the coming years the right to build over the New York Central underground facilities were sold, thus pioneering "air rights".

Congress ordered the Interstate Commerce Commission to make a "valuation of the physical property of common carriers," a project that would begin at the Illinois Central two years later. With no additions during the year, system mileage remained at 4,763; mileage on the Yazoo & Mississippi Valley dipped slightly to 1,372. Effective July 1, 1912 the Interstate Commerce Commission proscribed changes in the Income Account format for reporting purposes; under these new guidelines revenues for the year approached $64.3 million, almost 21 percent due to passenger traffic (27,537,947 passengers); despite floods washing out the Evansville bridge and trackage between Mounds and Cairo, which effectively cut the railroad in two for nine days, the Company set records in both freight and passenger business. With a strong year across the board, revenue traffic levels over Illinois Central surged to 30.4 million tons of freight; tonnage on the unconsolidated Yazoo & Mississippi Valley rebounded to a record of almost 6.1 million tons. Locomotive availability rose to 1,460 units with the addition of 136 new units (50 2-8-2 Mikados, 45 4-6-2 Pacifics, and 41 switching units); with 134 units disposed of via lease, the net gain was 2 locomotives.

IC45x35-193

IC1913-01

During the first half of 1913 Illinois Central took delivery of thirty Alco/Pittsburg 0-6-0 (51 D; 200 BP; 166,000 TW; 38,200 TF) switch engines; some of these engines later were upgraded with higher boiler pressure.

IC #220, shown on top, was captured switching a trainload of Pacific Fruit Express ventilated refrigerator cars out of downtown Chicago.

IC #221 was caught in Jackson, Mississippi on September 14, 1948; note the improved sandboxes on top of the engine, sporting the newer square design.

IC #222 is shown in the last two photographs; it was snapped early in its service life, as can be seen by the old-fashioned headlamp (on which one of the train crew appears to be working); the picture comes from an unknown location, but undoubtedly in the north, as snow covers the landscape.

IC45x35-37

IC45x35-30

IC1913-02

IC1913-03

IC1913-18

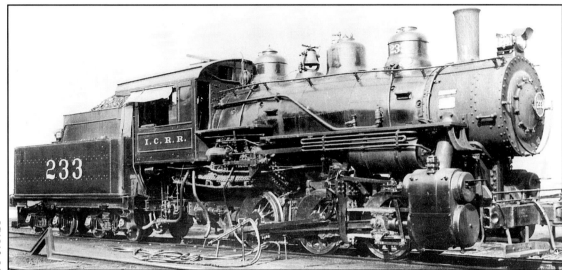

IC1913-04

IC1913-05

On the facing page, IC #226, at top, is shown on a short hop with a small consist. Lower two photographs depict the same engine, but a few decades apart; IC #232 was a typical 0-6-0 switch engine from that series; it was converted into an 0-6-0T saddle-tank switch engine (IC #3298) in 1954, at age 41; it retired in 1960.

This page, top to bottom, IC #233, IC #234, IC #236 and IC #238; IC #236 has the improved square sandboxes.

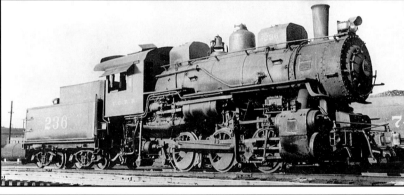

IC1913-06

IC1913-07

IC1913-08

IC1913-09

IC45x35-29

Alco/Pittsburg 0-6-0 switch engines from 1913, part of the series of 30 such units. IC #242, on top, was captured at an unknown time and place. IC #243 looks nearly new in the middle photograph. IC #248, shown on the bottom, probably is the oldest snapshot of the three; it has the old headlamp style, indicating an early stage in its service life; this picture also highlights the dual air-pumps on the left side of the engine.

Another major purchase of 1913 was a series of 25 (IC #1114-1138) Alco/Richmond built 4-6-2 (75 1/2 D; 215 BP; 247,500 TW; 39,334 TF) Pacifics that Illinois Central received in the first quarter of the year; most of these units were renumbered into the 2000-series and rebuilt (61 D; 215 BP; 248,733 TW; 48,683 TF) in the 1940's. On top is IC #1030, which originally was the last unit delivered to the IC (IC #1138); this engine was renumbered to IC #1030 in 1937, and then renumbered to IC #2064 in 1942/1943. IC #1116 was never renumbered, and was retired in 1941. IC 1117, on bottom, was renumbered to IC #2077 in the 1940's.

IC45x35-171

IC1913-12

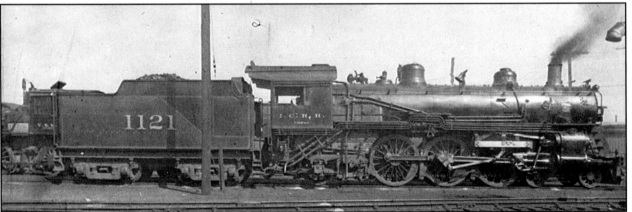

IC45x35-71

These two pages, six views of Alco/Richmond 4-6-2's from the series of 25 received in 1913. This page, top to bottom, IC #1118 stopped at a station after fueling, snapped while the oiler walked around to make sure everything was just right; IC #1119 posed in a yard on a run-out track; IC #1121 caught at an unknown location. These engines were renumbered to IC #1016, IC #1017 and IC #2079, respectively. Facing page, IC #1123 caught as IC #1118 above; IC #1125 was captured ready to make way, apparently at Chicago; lastly, IC #1131, at ease, fueled and ready for its next assignment. These engines were renumbered IC #1018, IC #1019 and IC #2054, respectively, in the 1940's.

These two pages, five more views of the 1913 Alco/Richmond 4-6-2 Pacifics from the series IC #1114-1138; all of the engines in this series were superheated and had Walschaerts valve gear.

Facing page shows, at top, IC #1133 loading its passenger train under the vaulted trainshed at IC's 12th Street Central Station. Below, IC #1137 posed in nearly-new condition; note the pilot steps (later replaced with a ladder) and the old fashioned headlamp. IC #1133 was renumbered to IC #2056 in the 1940's; IC #1137 was renumbered to IC #1029 in 1937, and IC #2093 in the 1940's.

This page, top to bottom, IC #2057 (original IC #1114) at Jackson, Mississippi roundhouse on June 28, 1948. IC #2065 (original IC #1124) seen at Owensboro, Kentucky; this engine was posed with, left to right, J.B. Warren (flagman), C.L. Gregory (brakeman), H.M. House (engineer), R.V. Hundley (fireman), J.H. Kennedy (conductor), J.P. Flowers (Owensboro agent), and A.T. Zigler (Commercial agent); this picture preserved the preparation of the last steam engine out of Owensboro. IC # 2096 (original IC #1128) is shown with its square sandbox.

1914

A territorial conflict between Austria-Hungary and Serbia led to the assassination of the Hapsburg heir Archduke Franz Ferdinand on June 28th by 19-year old Bosnian-Serb nationalist Gavrilo Princip in Sarajevo. Over time, England, France, Russia, Italy and the United States would be drawn into the *guns of August* against Austria-Hungary, Germany and the Ottoman Empire; the War would develop along fronts in France, Russia and in the Mediterranean. On the western front Germany's chief of staff General Von Moltke made a classic mistake in splitting his troops in the conquest of France; at the Battle of the Marne, French and British commanders stopped the German army outside Paris; the war settled into a seesaw battle for the next three years with neither side able to gain a sustainable edge. On the eastern front, Russia took the offensive to Germany until defeated at the Battle of Tannenburg and driven back out of Poland and Lithuania. On the southern front, the Austrians continued to battle for control in Serbia. Pope Pius X died in Rome, Sainthood lay 40 years away; 60-year old Giacomo Della Chiesa would replace him, take the name Benedict XV, and lead the Church for 8 years; the latest Pope would promulgate a new Code of Canon Law. In Mexico the revolution continued, Venustiano Carranza becoming the fourth government leader in as many years, as military dictator Victoriano Huerta was driven out with the help of U.S. forces at Veracruz. 43-year old New Zealand-born British physicist Ernest Rutherford discovered the proton, the second subatomic particle. Edgar Rice Burroughs brought *Tarzan of the Apes* to market.

The 51-mile Panama Canal was completed, marked by the first official passage – the steamer *USS Ancon*; it was dedicated at precisely midnight January 1, 1915; the 51-mile long canal shaved 6,000 some miles off the route around Cape Horn between the Atlantic and Pacific oceans. Construction of the Lincoln Highway began. 35-year old Oskar Barnack, a development manager at Leica in Germany, made the first high-quality photographs on 35mm film; the Leica 35mm camera (prototype 1913) would be mass-produced and sold eleven years later, being delayed by the coming world war. In May President Woodrow Wilson began a new tradition by proclaiming the first national Mother's Day. In September the Federal Trade Commission was created with the task of regulating interstate business; the Clayton Antitrust Act was passed to facilitate government control of competition, such as outlawing price discrimination and 'tying' agreements. 25-year old Charlie Chaplin debuted as *The Tramp*. Cadillac led design innovation with the first American eight-cylinder gas engine. 32-year old American engineer Robert H. Goddard began experimenting with rockets. Heavyweight boxing champion Jack Johnson defended his title against another in the long line of Great White Hopes, beating Frank Moran in a 20 round fight in Paris.

While adding 6 miles of track on the Indiana division's Bloomington Southern, system mileage rose to 4,769; mileage on the Yazoo & Mississippi Valley rose slightly to 1,378 as trackage was added toward Swan Lake. Revenues for the year approached $65.9 million, almost 21 percent due to passenger traffic (27,522,774 passengers). With the steady business conditions, revenue traffic levels over Illinois Central exceeded to 32.3 million tons of freight; tonnage on the unconsolidated Yazoo & Mississippi Valley grew to almost 6.9 million tons. Locomotive availability dipped to 1,448 units with the addition of 72 units (50 2-8-2 Mikados and 22 switching units) netted against 84 disposals. The elimination of grade crossings in the Chicago area continued with the elevation of tracks between 79th Street and 116th Street started. After Illinois Central's formal application to double-track the Cairo river bridge was rejected by a board of government engineers, work to strengthen the bridge members was begun to permit heavier locomotives such as Mikados to utilize the crossing. A major grade reduction program began on the Central City to Paducah line on the Kentucky division; the Princeton to Paducah segment would be finished before a world at war stopped expenditures.

Alco/Schenectady produced a series of 22 (IC #250-271) 0-6-0 (51 D; 200 BP; 169,000 TW; 38,200 TF) switch engines for the Illinois Central in 1914; shown here are four of those engines.

IC1914-01

IC1914-02

IC1914-03

All of the engines on this page were captured after they had been in service a while, denoted by the dual square sandboxes, a later improvement. IC #257 is shown with C.S. Terrill (engineer, wearing tie) and L.E. Barron (fireman); the photograph dates to Rockford, Illinois in 1950. IC #270 was caught at McComb, Mississippi on February 20, 1952.

IC1914-04

IC1915-10

IC1914-05

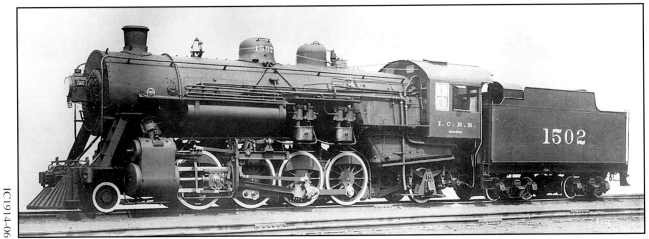

The two units on this page were 2-8-2 Mikados from Baldwin in 1914; the pictures depict these units before improvements. IC #1502 above was captured in a Builder's Photograph. IC #1509 was snapped in a yard shot, but with an oddity; note the lady dressed in "flapper" style to the left of the engineer's-side pilot ladder? These units began service with dimensions similar to most 2-8-2's of the time, but both were rebuilt into 0-8-2 hump switchers (62 D; 225 BP; 294,000 TW; 72,551 TF) in 1942, IC #3695 and IC #3687, respectively.

Facing page on top, Illinois Central #1206 was a Baldwin-built 2-8-2 Mikado (63 1/2 D; 185 BP; 282,700 TW; 54,158 TF); this unit was a 1914 product and saw extensive service, renumbering and rebuilding. Originally rostered as IC #1503, it was renumbered to IC #1516 in 1944, to IC #1702 later on in 1944, and to IC #1206 in 1951; sometime during the renumberings this unit was rebuilt (63 1/2 D; 225 BP; 308,500 TW; 70,837 TF). It was captured on the Kentucky Division near Paducah, hauling a coal train on May 5, 1953; this picture appeared in the Illinois Central Magazine. The lower photograph shows IC #1463 (IC #1538 when new in 1914), another 2-8-2 with similar dimensions, also rebuilt to similar dimensions; this unit was renumbered as shown in 1944, and to IC #1689 in 1954; the epitome of "full steam ahead."

IC4x5-17

Ever since the original construction of the railroad, the effort went on to improve the layout: reducing curvature, lowering grade, removing bridges and grade crossings, increasing embankments, and the like. The importance of lowering grade impacted efficiency of operations at all levels, reducing fuel consumption and allowing longer trains, and reducing wear and tear on equipment. One such grade reduction program worked its way to the Mattoon area by 1914; the photograph above shows the work gang, with heavy steam shovel doing the hardest removal work, proceeding through the center of Mattoon; the Essex House is visible at upper center, on the right side of the lowered grade. Grade reduction in Mattoon brought with it the removal of all grade crossings through town, another efficiency. The work in Mattoon proper extended through 1915, and was reported on in the Illinois Central Magazine.

One of the major engineering projects for the Illinois Central over the years was the Lake Front Improvement program, which program consisted of numerous parts. One was the rearrangement of the at-grade intersection at Grand Crossing, the crossing of the Illinois Central at right angles to the Pennsylvania and New York Central railroads. On the facing page, at top, the situation at Grand Crossing was obvious in a picture from August 14, 1902; the Illinois Central tracks ran from the lower left to the upper right, crossing the other railroads. The grade separation program was completed by 1914, as shown in the lower photograph dated November 7, 1914; the tracks of the Pennsylvania and New York Central were made to run over those of the Illinois Central, underpasses allowing movement of pedestrians and automobiles through the maze. The lower photograph appeared in the March, 1922 issue of the Illinois Central Magazine.

GRAND CROSSING, ILL.
Aug. 14, 1902
Looking N.W. from Gate Tower

IC1850-06

Grand Crossing Nov. 7, 1914

ICNEGGS-57

1915

In May Germany raised the stakes when one of its submarines torpedoed the British Cunard liner *Lusitania*; enroute from New York to Liverpool with a cargo of passengers and war material, ten percent of the 1,200 casualties were American; Woodrow Wilson's pacifist Secretary of State William Jennings Bryan resigned his cabinet post, unwilling to chance war over the sinking. World War I settled into a pitched battle concentrated in the northwest of France; on the southern front, Austria finally conquered Serbia; in the east Russia turned its attention to Austria-Hungary. Turkish extremists, using the war as a cover, started their own atrocities and exterminated more than 1.5 million Armenians over the next eight years. Mexico continued to experience turmoil, rebel Francisco "Pancho" Villa making a name by fighting government forces with hit-and-run tactics across the Mexican countryside. 43-year old French scientist Paul Langevin began using the echo of sound waves to detect underwater objects; this would lead to the invention of sonar – SOund Navigation And Ranging. Japan forced an ultimatum on China, the Twenty-one Demands that gave Japan effective control; protested for the next 15 years, it would be fought over for another 15. 53-year old William Henry Bragg and 25-year old William Lawrence Bragg were awarded the Nobel Prize in Physics for their work on the structure of crystals, the only father-son team ever so honored.

The U.S. would experience economic expansion, partially due to the growing conflict overseas. San Francisco hosted the Panama-Pacific International Exposition, commemorating the completion of the Panama Canal; one of the highlights: 39 years after pioneering the telephone, Alexander Graham Bell (now 68 years old) and Thomas A. Watson repeated their tag-team performance, this time making the first transcontinental telephone call, New York to San Francisco. The Great Lakes steamship *USS Eastland*, only yards from the dock, rolled over in the Chicago River causing over 800 fatalities. Although invented in 1878, it wasn't until 1915 that the first practical commercial phonograph – the Victrola – was rolled out. Heat-resistant glass, Pyrex cookware, debuted. Willis H. Carrier formed the Carrier Engineering Corporation producing air conditioning and refrigeration equipment. The Coast Guard was formed. J.L. Kraft started making processed cheese, for which he received a patent one year later. The Dodge brothers - Horace and John - rolled-out their all-steel body automobile. Seven years after Jack Johnson broke the color line in boxing, 34-year old Jess Willard lived up to the racist title of Great White Hope when he defeated Johnson for the heavyweight championship with a 26th round KO in Havana, Cuba; Willard would retain the title for four years. West Point graduated 164 cadets, 59 of which would achieve the rank of General, including two that rose to five-star - Bradley and Eisenhower.

The visionary Canadian Pacific Railroad builder William Cornelius Van Horne passed away. The Canadian Northern Railway completed its competing line across the Canadian Rockies to Vancouver, thus becoming the second Canadian transcontinental road; bankrupt in 1919, it would become part of the Canadian National Railways. The Canadian government's National Transcontinental would form a third transcontinental line, yet it too would be folded into the Canadian National Railway a few years later.

The Illinois Central donated a site to the Chicago Park District on which they built the Field Museum of Natural History over the next six years; Illinois Central hoped the contribution would bolster its negotiating position with the South Park commissioners and the City of Chicago in the lake front controversy. ICC Valuation Project began on Illinois Central, dividing the System into 240 sections. With a net reduction of two miles, system mileage dipped to 4,767; mileage on the Yazoo & Mississippi Valley rose to 1,382 with extension of the Lambert to Murphys, Mississippi line all the way to Swan Lake. With business reversals on the southern lines leading the way to a decline of 900,000 tons in lumber shipments and 1.5 million fewer passengers, revenues for the year dropped over six percent to $61.7 million, over 20 percent from passenger traffic (26,019,820 passengers). With the malaise in business spreading, revenue traffic levels over Illinois Central dropped to 31.3 million tons of freight; tonnage on the unconsolidated Yazoo & Mississippi Valley rose to almost 7.3 million tons, the third consecutive record. Locomotive availability rose to 1,455 units with the addition of 75 new units (50 2-8-2 Mikados and 25 switching units) netted against the disposal of 68 units. During the year Illinois Central advanced construction funds to a number of carriers, building branch lines and yard tracks in southern Illinois; funds were advanced to the Herrin Northern, the Fredonia & Reeds, the Benton Southern, and the Johnston City Southern railroads; (these short lines would account for less than 10 miles of mainline trackage when complete).

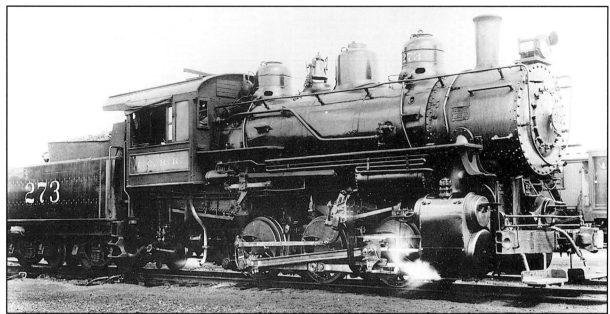

IC1915-03

IC4x5-18

Alco/Schenectady-built 0-6-0 switch engines were one of the two major types received by the Illinois Central in 1915. These switch units (51 D; 200 BP; 169,000 TW; 38,200 TF) were part of a series (IC #272-296) of 25 delivered that year; these units saw service into the 1950's. IC #276 is shown in an October 6, 1953 picture, pulling a mixed consist. IC #285 was taking water, bristling with dual New York air-pumps and larger sandboxes.

IC1915-04

Three views of 1915 Alco/ Schenectady-built 0-6-0's. IC #289 is shown at left as it worked a wood yard on the Memphis Division. IC #294, shown fueling with coal and water in the middle photograph, was a switcher that worked the Jackson, Mississippi to Meridian, Mississippi run; the picture dates February 2, 1948. IC #295 was caught in the yard with its crew, getting ready for work.

IC1915-05

IC1915-06

IC45x35-38

The other large delivery of steam locomotive equipment was a series of 50 (IC #1701-1750) Lima-built 2-8-2 Mikados, the first such engines produced by Lima for the Illinois Central. These units would be renumbered into the IC 1200-series during the late 1930's-early 1940's as they were renovated; some of these would be renumbered once again, about ten years later, into the IC 1500/1600-series.

As built (63 1/2 D; 185 BP; 282,700 TW; 54,158 TF), these 50 engines were just the beginning of scores that Lima would erect for the Illinois Central over the next eight years. A number of original units would be renovated during the massive upgrade programs Illinois Central scheduled in the 1930's, adding to the engine's life span.

Shown on this page, at bottom, IC #1200 (the first Lima 2-8-2, originally IC #1701); it was caught from the top of another train, and was published in the April, 1950 issue of the Illinois Central Magazine in a story on the Memphis Division. The photograph right is a snapshot of IC #1201 captured at Fulton, Kentucky in March, 1952.

IC1915-08

IC1915-07

IC1915-09

IC4x5-23

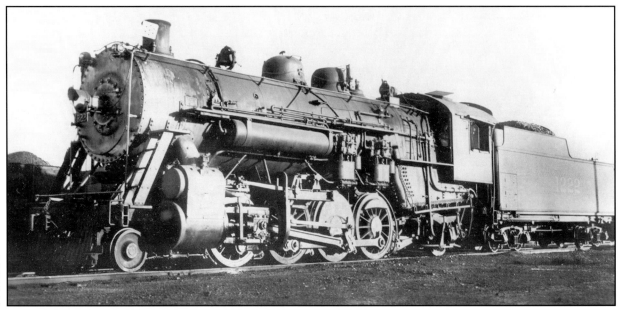

IC1915-12

These two pages, all 2-8-2 Mikados from Lima in 1915. This page top, IC #1203 fueled and ready in the yard. IC #1207 was caught as it rolled through Hammond, Louisiana past the station and water tipple on September 2, 1953. IC #1222 was snapped at ease, waiting orders and crew. Facing page, two views of IC #1208, both of which appeared in the IC Magazine. Top, IC #1208 is shown huffing a local on June 11, 1947 into Clarksdale, Mississippi from the south, crossing the Sunflower river (October, 1947 Magazine). On bottom was the same engine on a different day and mission (Magazine story on CN-3).

IC4x5-24

IC1915-11

IC1915-13

Two pages of Lima 2-8-2's from 1915, all with the dimensions standard for this series. This page, top to bottom, Illinois Central #1224, shown left and middle, was snapped at McComb, Mississippi on February 20, 1952; the tender on this unit held 16 tons of coal and 13,000 gallons of boiler water; this particular engine had been modernized (63 1/2 D; 185 BP; 284,000 TW; 54,158 TF) by the time this photo was taken. IC #1225, on bottom, was caught passing through Rockford, Illinois.

Facing page top, IC #1531 steams out of Iowa Falls, Iowa in late-1950; this photograph, from a negative by Paul, appeared in an Illinois Central Magazine story in the 1950's on Iowa Division Steam. On bottom, IC #1542 was captured hauling a solid meat train through Rockford, Illinois on May 16, 1951.

ICNEGGS-39

IC1915-14

IC4x5-28

IC4x5-44

IC1915-15

IC1915-16

IC1999-23

The 2-8-2 Mikado on this page was Baldwin-built (57 1/2 D; 200 BP; 217,500 TW; 40,418 TF) in 1915 for the Vicksburg Shreveport & Pacific (as VS&P #352); VS&P subsequently renumbered this unit to VS&P #362. Illinois Central acquired the VS&P in 1926 and fell heir to this engine, which it renumbered IC #3962. While the top view shows the right side of the engine before it was rebuilt, the bottom view shows the left side after rebuilding (57 D; 220 BP; 217,500 TW; 62,097 TF); note the square sandbox on the rebuilt model. The tender held 21 tons of coal and 7,500 gallons of boiler water.

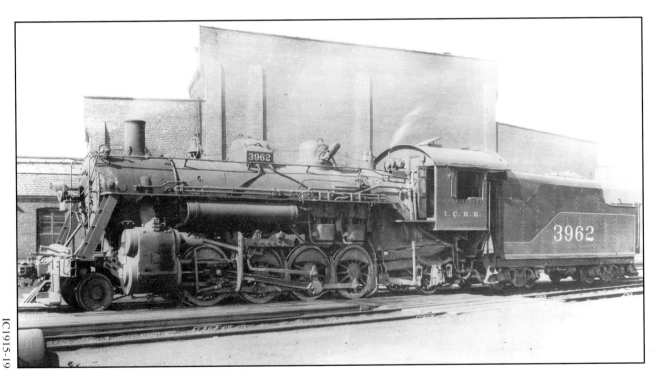

On the facing page, three more Illinois Central 2-8-2's from Lima in 1915. IC #1229, on top, was caught fueling for an assignment; this engine was rebuilt (63 1/2 D; 185 BP; 284,000 TW; 54,158 TF) and saw service until 1955; the tender held 16 tons of coal and 13,000 gallons of boiler water. IC #1248, another unit that had been modernized, was snapped at rest in a picture dated June 18, 1951. IC #1711 shows a 2-8-2 from the series before rebuilding or renumbering; IC #1711 was an original number from the Lima group, which were superheated and came with Baker valve gear. This picture was captured at Vicksburg, Mississippi on June 3, 1937; the engine was rebuilt (64 1/2 D; 225 BP; 336,000 TW; 74,078 TF) in July, 1937 by patching the 1711's boiler to a 2-10-2 chassis to form a much more powerful 2-8-2; this produced IC #2100, the first engine so modified. The picture shows IC #1711 with a 6000 Mallet-class tender.

1916

The sixth edition of the Modern Olympics, to be held in Berlin, was canceled because of the war in Europe. In a presage of things to come, Irish rebels defied British rule in the Easter Rebellion. World War I continued the massive human loss as opposing generals launched thousands of soldiers out of the trenches against each other on the western front; on July 1st at the Battle of the Somme, England would lose over 60,000 soldiers in a single day; intended to relive pressure on Verdun, it would take another four months; the Battle of Verdun lasted eleven months into December and was the longest sustained battle of the War, the English and French claiming over 625,000 casualties and the Germans one half million. Germany, with its back to the wall, began chemical warfare. War on the southern front continued with Austria-Hungary invading Italy and conquering Romania. The eastern front saw Russia suffer considerable losses against Austrian forces. In May in what turned out to be the crucial naval battle of the war, the Battle of Jutland took place off the Danish coast with Great Britain and Germany facing each other in mass formation; both sides would claim victory and lose a combined 24 ships. At Berlin University, Albert Einstein floated his general theory of relativity; worked on since 1911 and completed in 1915, it was presented in 1916. Mexico continued embroiled in a war of its own, a revolution for control of the government; Mexican rebel Francisco "Pancho" Villa crossed the border into New Mexico and started shooting; in response an American military expedition under Brigadier General John J. "Black Jack" Pershing rode into Mexican territory in an unsuccessful attempt to find the revolutionary. 28-year old Englishman Thomas Edward Lawrence, the future *Lawrence of Arabia*, began helping Arabs rise up against their Turkish oppressors; the Suez Canal and oil fields being the real importance.

Social justice advocate 59-year old Louis D. Brandeis became the first Jewish member of the U.S. Supreme Court on winning a contentious six-month long confirmation in the Senate; he would serve on the Court for 22 years. The U.S. economy was in a boom period, caused in large measure by the war overseas; the industrial surge would see the U.S. become a creditor nation in foreign trade for the first time, and would set the stage for the U.S. emergence as a world power; along with the boom came the inevitable inflation. Jeanette Rankin of Montana became the first U.S. Congresswoman. The U.S. purchased the Virgin Islands from Denmark. At the 16th Republican convention in Chicago, U.S. Supreme Court Justice Charles Evans Hughes, former Governor of New York, won the Presidential nomination on the 3rd ballot; ex-Vice President Charles Warren Fairbanks of Indiana was selected the Vice Presidential candidate on the 1st ballot. At the Progressive convention in Chicago, former President Theodore Roosevelt was nominated the Third Party candidate for President – an honor he refused. At the 22nd Democratic convention in St. Louis, incumbent President Woodrow Wilson was nominated for re-election by acclamation; Vice President Thomas R. Marshall was similarly honored. In November one of the closest elections ever took place. Needing at least 266 of the 531 votes in the Electoral College, Wilson slipped by with 277 votes to Hughes' 254. Woodrow Wilson was reelected to a 2nd Term on the promise of keeping America out of the war, a promise he would keep for a few months. 35-year old Bill Boeing formed a company and began flying. Kelvinator manufactured and marketed one of the first practical electric refrigerators. Standardized IQ test was developed by Stanford psychologist Lewis M. Terman based on the original work of French psychologist Alfred Binet from 1905. President Wilson signed the Federal Road Act. The National Park Service was formed by Congress, bringing management and funding to the 44-year old National Park System. As a measure of war preparedness, Congress doubled the flat income tax rate from 1 percent to 2 percent. Harry F. Sinclair formed Sinclair Oil and Refining Company. Clarence Saunders opened his Piggly Wiggly grocery in Memphis and set in motion the age of self-service. Stainless steel was introduced. 56-year old U.S. Army Colonel (later Brigadier General) John T. Thompson invented a new machine for destruction – the submachine gun; continuing development through 1918, he received a patent on it in 1920. Polio arrived in the U.S. 24-year old John Lloyd Wright, the son of architect Frank Lloyd Wright, invented Lincoln Logs as a building playtoy for children. 22-year old Norman Rockwell prepared his first cover illustration for the *Saturday Evening Post*; he would create 320 more over the next 47 years.

In May brothers and Drs. Charles H. and William J. Mayo traveled from Rochester, Minnesota to St. Paul to operate on railroad magnate James J. Hill who suffered from a serious infection; sometime later the "Empire Builder" James J. Hill died at age 77. Toward the end of the year the Adamson Act was passed by Congress in order to avert a threatened railroad strike; the Act mandated the eight-hour workday for most railroad workers, with time-and-a-half for overtime. The U.S. rail system peaked at 254,000 miles of road in 1916. Cleveland real estate developers

IC45x35-188

(Shaker Heights) 37-year old Oris and 35-year old Mantis Van Sweringen gained control of the Nickel Plate Road, buying out the New York Central interests.

Panama Limited re-equipped as a luxury all-Pullman express service. Other than reclassifying some trackage, there were no changes in the number of miles operated by the Company and system mileage remained at 4,767; mileage on the Yazoo & Mississippi Valley remained steady at 1,382. With the return of prosperous times, revenues for the year rebounded to almost $69.1 million, a little over 19 percent due to passenger traffic (27,300,134 passengers); some income account items were reclassified in this reporting period, in accordance with ever-changing Interstate Commerce Commission rules. Revenue traffic levels over Illinois Central rose to 35.0 million tons of freight; tonnage on the unconsolidated Yazoo & Mississippi Valley exceeded 8.4 million tons. With the addition of 51 locomotives (48 2-8-2 Mikados and 3 switching units), netted against the retirement of 72 units and the transfer of 15 saddle-tank switch units to work equipment, locomotive availability dropped to 1,419 units; during the year the Company converted one 4-4-2 Atlantic and 2 4-6-2 Pacifics into superheated locomotives. After 27 years of reporting on a June 30 fiscal year basis because of Federal requirements, Illinois Central returned to a December 31 calendar year convention when the fickle Interstate Commerce Commission, on November 24th, ordered all carriers back on a common calendar year basis. In its second annual report for 1916 (this one a calendar year), Illinois Central reported $73.7 million in revenues, 27,974,948 passengers, and 37.0 million tons of freight, while system mileage dropped less than one mile to 4,766. During the last six months of the period, the locomotive fleet rose to 1,437 units, a net increase of 18 (20 4-6-2 Pacifics added with 2 units retired); two additional 4-6-2 Pacifics and one 4-4-2 Atlantic were converted to superheated engines. Due to the increased weight of locomotives and cars, the suburban service elevation and bridge building for the Columbian Exposition 23 years earlier required complete replacement, the start of a three-year project. Preliminary surveys aimed at relieving congestion in southern Illinois were begun; twelve years later a second mainline to Fulton, Kentucky would be opened. In September Illinois Central sent a proposal for a major new Chicago Terminal Facility to the Chicago City Council; the Plan would be tentative for over eight years, and then become terminal.

IC1916-01

Previous, facing and this page, all 4-6-2 Pacifics from Alco/Brooks in 1916; the first of the heavy Pacifics (75 1/2 D; 190 BP; 278,000 TW; 41,000 TF), where the total weight of the engine exceeded 125 tons. All in this series (IC #1139-1158) were superheated and had Walschaerts valve gear; most would be rebuilt (75 1/2 D; 215 BP; 285,500 TW; 45,816 TF). The oiler standing next to the 75 1/2 drivers on IC #1141 gives perspective.

IC1916-02

IC1916-16

(Photos this page courtesy Judy Schutter, Engineer McCormick's grand-daughter)

Man and his machine. Daniel James McCormick worked for the Illinois Central for 45 years, many of them as engineer on the City of New Orleans. Engineer McCormick is seen in his work clothes and off duty garb, proudly visiting his office (4-6-2 Pacific-type #1142).

IC1916-18

IC1916-17

IC1916-03

Two 4-6-2 Pacifics from the IC #1139-1158 series. IC #1151, below, was snapped at Hattiesburg, Ms. on May 3, 1950.

IC1916-04

IC1916-05

Illinois Central #1155, a 4-6-2 heavy Pacific, had identical dimensions (original and rebuilt) as those on the previous pages; it is shown below in a Builder's Photograph from Alco/Brooks depicting how these engines looked new in 1916. IC #1158, the last of the series, is shown on bottom in a picture that appeared in the December, 1951 issue of the Illinois Central Magazine; this photograph shows IC #1158 pulling the Panama Limited *out of Chicago, right on the Lake Front, sometime before 1939.*

IC45x35-89

IC1916-06

IC4x5-04

IC4x5-26

Besides the 20 heavy Pacifics, Illinois Central also took delivery of almost 50 Lima-built 1916 model (63 1/2 D; 185 BP; 282,700 TW; 54,158 TF) Mikado 2-8-2 wheel arrangements (series IC #1751-1797); these units would be renumbered into the 1200-series in the 1930/1940's, and then the 1500/1600-series after that.

IC #1259, above, is shown driving through the snow, like an apparition. IC #1261, right, is shown on the head end of CC-2, taking on coal; the picture dates to October 12, 1948.

Illinois Central #1265, above with its bell clanging through the crossing, was captured at Crystal Springs, Mississippi on August 1, 1948 by C.W. Witbeck; with engineer V.L. McCaskill leaning out the right window, this short consist was headed to Canton to pick up a second section of Train #3, the Louisiane; *this photograph appeared in the January, 1949 issue of the IC Magazine. Another 2-8-2 Mikado from that series is shown on bottom, IC #1270 (original IC #1776).*

IC1916-07

IC1916-08

IC4x5-27

1916 Lima-built 2-8-2 Mikados IC #1271, IC #1273 and IC #1276 (original IC #'s 1777/1779/1784), each with dimensions similar to those in the series. IC #1271, on top, is shown motoring through Webster City, Iowa on September 2, 1947 with CC-2. IC #1273 is pictured with Work Extra #1273 (repairing communication lines) at Cloverdale, Illinois on January 5, 1948; this photograph appeared in the February, 1948 issue of the IC Magazine. IC #1276 is shown in a stock photograph.

IC1916-09

IC1916-10

IC #1282 and IC #1285 (original IC #'s 1794 and 1797) are pictured after being modernized in the IC's rebuild programs.
IC #1565 (original IC #1788), on bottom, also was modernized and was captured in Waterloo, Iowa on November 7, 1947;
the tender for this unit held 16 tons of coal and 13,000 gallons of boiler water; this unit was sold for scrap in 1956.

IC1916-11

IC1916-12

ICNEGGS-33

IC4x5-32

IC1916-13

IC1999-26

ICNEGGS-31

IC45x35-200

These two pages, all 1916 Lima-built 2-8-2 Mikados. Facing page top, IC #1568 (original IC #1770) hustles through the crossover, with the coal tipple in the background; this was an April, 1950 snapshot used in a story on Mississippi Division Steam. Lower photograph shows another picture, different location, same train and for the same story on Mississippi Steam. This page, top to bottom, three views of 2-8-2's with their original roster numbers, before renovating; the OEM placement of the air-pumps on the side indicates these engines as original; in the renovation and rebuilding, the air-pumps usually were moved to the pilot, and a higher-capacity sandbox was placed on top of the engine. IC #1753 was snapped at Markham Yard on April 22, 1937, the other two at unknown locations.

IC1916-14

IC1916-15

Two photographs above, IC #1778 from the original series of 2-8-2's built by Lima in 1916; this engine was captured before renovation or rebuilding; a Worthington Feed Water Heater is located just to the right of the twin side-mounted air-pumps. Below, IC #3811 is another 2-8-2 Mikado, but it was not always so; Alco/Brooks built in 1904 as a 2-8-0 Consolidation (IC #811), this engine was the first in a series of 33 2-8-0's converted into 2-8-2's over the years (63 D; 185 BP; 268,140 TW; 46,830 TF); it was renovated in 1937; the tender held 15 tons of coal and 7,000 gallons of water.

IC1904-19

1917

World War I struggled on another year, trench warfare and no man's land a battle of numbers on the western front; Germany pioneered an atrocity, mustard gas. Spurred on by the massive military losses on the eastern front, Russians revolted (the *February Revolution* drove out Czar Nicholas II) and instituted a new Republic; unable to stabilize its rule, the infant Republic was overthrown and the Bolshevik Revolution (the *November Revolution*) ended with Communists under 46-year old Nikolai Lenin taking power; by the end of the year Russia would no longer be in the war. On the southern front, Italy was invaded again and Greece joined the Allies. In Mexico the revolution finally died down after over five years of internal struggle; Mexican President Venustiano Carranza successfully established a new, moderate national constitution. Dutch-born, French-living, German-spy 41-year old Margaret G. Zelle was executed by a French firing squad; Mata Hari's career spanned exotic dancing to espionage.

In March 60-year old Woodrow Wilson was sworn in for his 2nd Term as President of the United States. Re-elected on the promise of keeping America out of the war, President Woodrow Wilson on April 2nd called on Congress to declare war on Germany; Congress began debating the President's request and, four days later on April 6th, approved the declaration. Recently seated 37-year old Republican Jeanette Rankin of Montana, the first woman to sit in Congress, voted against the war declaration, just as she would do in 1941. U.S. joined the world at war in April; Congress passed the Selective Service Act in May to facilitate raising troops for the war effort; all told, almost three million American men would be drafted, two million shipped across the Atlantic Ocean, and one million actually would see action of some sort. Chanute Field in central Illinois opened and began training pilots for the War. In October, General John. J. "Blackjack" Pershing was promoted to the rank of four-star full general, the first since the Civil War commanders Grant, Sherman and Sheridan. With the diversion of millions of men from the labor pool into the armed forces, the great migration of blacks from the agrarian south to the industrial north began; the movement would last through the 1920's. Gypsum board arrived in construction. The first portable electric drill was introduced by Black & Decker. While the "signature" of basketball pro Chuck Taylor would not be added for six years, Converse Rubber Company debuted its All-Star sneaker. Chicago White Sox won the World Series (their 2nd and last) over the New York Giants in six games. Mt. Wilson Observatory in California installed its 100-inch reflecting telescope. 19-year old Italian immigrant Antonio Pasin came out with a wooden wagon for kids – the *Liberty Coaster*; his little red wagons soon would be of stamped metal and his empire renamed to Radio Flyer.

In December partially to defuse the possibility of threatened rail strikes and partially with the hope of augmenting the nation's response to wartime transportation demands, the US Railroad Administration (USRA) took operational control of all railroads for the duration of World War I; control would last for 26 months and be a very unsuccessful experiment; President Woodrow Wilson named his Treasury Secretary (and son-in-law) William G. McAdoo the Director General of Railroads. With an inadequate Merchant Marine to move supplies and material, war operations found severe bottlenecks at embarkation ports with thousands of rail cars used as rolling storage, instead of transportation. USRA standardized locomotive designs; 12 wheel arrangements were developed: 0-6-0, 0-8-0, 2-6-6-2, 2-8-8-2, and a heavy and light version each of a 2-8-2, 2-10-2, 4-6-2, and 4-8-2. Train crew unions won the eight-hour day.

With limited reclassification of trackage, system mileage remained at 4,766; mileage on the Yazoo & Mississippi Valley remained at 1,382. With buoyant business levels, revenues for the year surged to over $87.1 million, over 19 percent from passenger traffic (28,382,898 passengers). With the prosperous business conditions, revenue traffic levels over Illinois Central rose to almost 42.5 million tons of freight; tonnage on the unconsolidated Yazoo & Mississippi Valley exceeded 11.1 million tons. Locomotive availability rose to 1,447 units with the addition of 14 0-6-0 switch engines netted against the retirement of four units; 18 units were converted into superheated engines. Illinois Central built and opened a new facility for its accounting forces at 63rd and Dorchester on Chicago's southside.

IC45x35-39

Alco/Cooke delivered a series of twenty 0-6-0 switch engines (51 D; 200 BP; 169,000 TW; 38,200 TF) to the Illinois Central in 1917, two of which are shown on this page. IC #308, above, was captured with eight men on the ground and one in the cab, some crew members and some onlookers; the tender for this unit held 9 1/2 tons of coal and 5,500 gallons of boiler water. IC #315, shown below, had the same original dimensions but was rebuilt (61,093 TF) with bigger cylinders (25" x 26" in place of the OEM 21" x 26"); the increased power required additional fuel, and the tender shown held 11 tons of coal and 5,500 gallons of boiler water; this picture was captured after the rebuilding, as can be seen in the square high-capacity sandboxes.

IC1917-01

Illinois Central #316, shown above, was another in the 1917 series from Alco/Cooke; this particular picture appeared in the June, 1950 issue of the Illinois Central Magazine in a story on IC's Memphis, Tennessee Operations. IC #316 was captured leading a work detail, with Burro crane #3681 in tow.

Illinois Central #2510, an 0-4-0T saddle-tank (48 1/2 D; 140 BP; 72,000 TW; 15,075 TF) switch engine, started its service life as IC #20, a simple 0-4-0 switcher built by IC in 1882; this engine went through a number of roster changes (IC #20, #10, #1510, and #2510). One of a dozen or so saddle-tanks IC fashioned out of older 0-4-0 switch engines, this unit was converted in 1917 into the saddle-tank pictured; the photograph dates to April 4, 1927 at Markham Yard outside Chicago. Units of this type were variously called shop goats, shop switchers, or saddle-tanks; with boiler pressure as low as 125 pounds in some units, they served at major yards and shops, such as Burnside, Markham and Paducah.

IC45x35-19

Growing and expanding through the turn of the century, Illinois Central looked for more space; its decision was to relocate all the Accounting forces to an office building of their own, and outside the city center; Illinois Central built a new office building on IC property at 63rd and Dorchester, immediately behind the commuter station at 63rd Street. In the photograph above the new office building rises like an Erector Set, dwarfing the suburban station that lies at its feet. This picture dates to February 9, 1917; the office building was completed that year. Note the commuters standing on the platform waiting for a suburban train. Obviously the snow, covering part of the station roof and on the ground, did not stop construction.

ICLAG07-01

Illinois Central's work on the Lake Front Improvement might seem like a seamless transition or a project confined to a small area, but in reality it was a huge undertaking, argued in the Courts for years and decades to be implemented in all its parts. Whether it was the lowering of suburban tracks in the City to make them invisible from Michigan Avenue, or the electrification of service to make it environmentally palatable, many supporting projects had to be accomplished, pieces of the overall puzzle.

One major work was the complete grade separation of the suburban lines heading south out of the City. This part of the project would entail a number of bridges, pedestrian walkways and viaducts to allow removal of all grade crossings. Captured on July 6, 1917 the photograph shows work on the grade separation in progress at Kensington or 115th Street south of Chicago. On the right was the elevated portion of the grade separation under construction and not yet ready for use; on the left was the current ground level commuter operation, station and trains, at the intersection of 115th Street; note the crossing guard shack in the lower left of the picture. The train at the station is thought to be an electric from the Chicago Lake Shore & South Bend (the future Chicago South Shore & South Bend), operating into Kensington from Indiana points; the CLS&SB handed off its customers to the Illinois Central at Kensington for the final mileage into Chicago using steam locomotives; IC would electrify its route by 1926.

1918

The last German attempt to end the war before Americans arrived in force ran out of gas in the spring, and the Allies planned their counterattack. Led by the Twenty-eighth Infantry Regiment of the First Infantry Division (Big Red One, under the command of Major General Robert L. Bullard) U.S. forces went on offense in May, facing off against German troops at Cantigny, 40 miles north of Paris; the Americans' first offensive would be their first victory; the defense of Chateau-Thierry followed, and then a costly victory at Belleau Wood; in July on the western front the Allies began the Aisne-Marne offensive, culminating in the Meuse-Argonne operation in October, involving over one million American troops and driving the Germans into retreat between the river and the forest. In April Germany's top fighter pilot with over 75 victories in less than 20 months of flying, 26-year old Manfred von Richthofen (the "Red Baron") received his comeuppance when his Fokker tri-plane was shot down by English Sopwith Camels. The eastern and southern fronts drew together as the war came to Austria-Hungary, causing the monarchy to collapse and speeding along the closing stages. With the Armistice on November 11, World War I came to an end, having exhausted all of Europe and slaughtered over 11 million worldwide, over 100,000 of those from the U.S.; agreement on an actual peace accord - the Versailles Treaty - lay months away. Harsh terms and reparations imposed on Germany at the end of the war would set the stage for another. 28-year old Ohio-born Eddie Rickenbacker retired from the U.S. Army Air Service as America's ace with a record 26 confirmed enemy kills (22 airplanes and 4 balloons) shot out of the sky; he received the Medal of Honor 13 years later and his record would stand until the next world war. Closer to the ground, Tennessee-born Alvin York had earned his Medal of Honor for heroism in fighting near Chateau Thierry. The end of the war would bring about the reshaping of Europe: the Kingdom of Serbs, Croats and Slovenes was formed out of the nationalities between the Danube and the Adriatic, one day Yugoslavia; Poland, Czechoslovakia, Lithuania, Latvia, Estonia would each find new boundaries, some based on politics and some on ethnicity. Germany's 50-year old Fritz Haber received the Nobel Prize in Chemistry for his process producing synthetic ammonia (U.S. patent # 971,501).

In March as a wartime fuel-saving measure, Congress adapted Standard Time to provide for a Daylight Saving Time, and clocks jumped ahead one hour. Knute Rockne became head coach of Notre Dame football where in 13 years his teams would lose only 12 games. In May the US Post Office began airmail service between New York and Washington D.C. using a "Jenny" bi-plane (number 38262); the Post Office issued a 24-cent stamp to commemorate the event, but printed one sheet with the vignette upside down or inverted, creating a philatelic treasure. Started during the Spring of the final year of the war and probably spread by returning servicemen, an influenza epidemic - the Spanish flu - struck killing over 20 million worldwide, twice as many as died in World War I; over 550,000 of the 25 million infected in the United States would perish, more than the U.S. would ever lose in any war. 23-year old Babe Ruth and the Boston Red Sox beat the Chicago White Sox for the World Series. Walter Jacobs began a car rental company with twelve Model-Ts, one day Hertz. The forerunner to Zenith Radio Corporation was founded by Ralph Mathews and Karl Hassel, two developers of amateur radio equipment. General Electric scientist 38-year old Albert W. Hull invented the magnetron, a vacuum tube utilizing magnetic fields to control power output; a key device for producing high frequency short wavelength radio waves (microwaves), the magnetron would be the power tube to drive radar equipment and microwave ovens.

With the addition of 16 miles of trackage rights between Metropolis, Illinois and Paducah, Kentucky, system mileage rose to 4,782; mileage on the Yazoo & Mississippi Valley remained steady at 1,382. The Illinois Central was operated under government control for the entire year; as such, results were measured and managed under Section 1 of the Federal Control Act as certified by the Interstate Commerce Commission. Revenues for the year advanced to over $107.3 million, almost 19 percent due to passenger traffic (27,181,219 passengers). Mirroring revenues, traffic levels over Illinois Central rose strongly to almost 45.9 million tons of freight; tonnage on the unconsolidated Yazoo & Mississippi Valley exceeded 12.2 million tons, the sixth consecutive increase. Locomotive availability rose to 1,570 units with the addition of 123 new units (68 2-8-2 Mikados, and 20 4-6-2 Pacifics; the rest in switching equipment, mostly 0-6-0 units); one Consolidation unit was converted into a Mikado, while 14 other units were converted to superheated engines. During the year, 605 acres were purchased between Harvey and Homewood, Illinois for the purpose of constructing a new yard and division terminal facility...to be named Markham Yard; longtime Illinois Central President Charles H. Marham had resigned from the Company in May to serve as Regional

IC45x35-185

Alco/Cooke-built 0-6-0 switcher IC #317 takes point on this double-header leading through high water at an unknown location. The four men on the front check the roadbed as the passenger train eases over the tracks.

Director of Railroads for the U.S. Railroad Administration during the war, a position he would retain for 16 months until re-elected President of the Illinois Central; Director Charles A Peabody acted as President, the 13th in succession, in the interim. The War's end brought an accounting for the Illinois Central as well: of the 8,775 employees who served in the armed forces during the conflict, 55 gave it their all.

IC1918-03

IC4x5-10

IC1918-04

These two pages, all Alco/Cooke-built 0-6-0 switch engines (51 D; 200 BP; 169,000 TW; 38,200 TF) from a series of 25 delivered to Illinois Central in 1918. Facing page, top down, IC #318 after rebuilding (230 BP; 45,500 TF); its tender held 11 tons of coal and 5,500 gallons of water. IC #319 was captured on October 26, 1944 switching the John Morrell 40-acre meat packing plant in Sioux Falls, South Dakota; this plant processed 2 million live head per year; the crew was pictured spotting Morrell reefers, part of a fleet of 300 reefers and tank cars Morrell owned. IC #324 was caught switching a mixed consist. This page, top, IC #339 rumbles through an unidentified station headed for employment in this winter shot. Yet to be rebuilt or renovated, IC #341, bottom, posed with its crew in an unknown yard.

IC45x35-90

1918 was a year of 0-6-0 switchers, 4-6-2 Pacifics and 2-8-2 Mikados. These two pages show some of the series of 20 Alco/Brooks-built 4-6-2's (75 1/2 D; 190 BP; 278,000 TW; 41,000 TF); many of these were rebuilt (215 BP; 285,500 TW; 45,816 TF) in the modernization years. This page, top, IC #1160 is shown fueled and ready for action. Bottom, IC #1162 was caught on May 25, 1950 hustling its passenger train by the IC shops at 27th Street in Chicago. Facing page, top to bottom, IC #1164 was captured in a yard shot. IC #1165 was snapped at work on the head end of the first Chickasaw, *the Memphis to St. Louis non-stop overnight in a picture dated January 13, 1924. On bottom, IC #1169 is shown leaving Greenville, Mississippi in a picture that appeared in the* Illinois Central Magazine *in the 1950's in a story about the Memphis Division; this photograph shows IC #1169 on lead with the* Delta Express *between Vicksburg and Memphis; Thomas W. Lane (train baggageman) worked the crossing.*

IC4x5-21

IC1918-07

IC45x35-190

IC1918-08

IC1918-01

IC1918-11

Illinois Central #1174 is shown in three views. In the top two photographs, IC #1174 is shown with different sandboxes on top of the boiler, indicating renovation of some sort. Actually, engines such as this went through many renovations, improvements, and an occasional re-building, during its service life; both pictures on top appear to show a rebuilt engine, with the new sandbox being a simple improvement at some later point. The lower photograph, a picture dating to 1950, shows the same engine posed with Art Riegard (engineer), Lee Mayer (fireman) and an interested onlooker, Ricky Axelson.

IC1918-10

Two more 4-6-2 Pacifics from Alco/Brooks in 1918. IC #1173, shown above, was caught blowing fuel up the stack as it left town with its passenger train, at an unknown location. IC #1178, below, was snapped fueled and ready to go in a yard shot. IC #1173 had the improvement of pilot-mounted air-pumps, while IC #1178 had yet to see that change. IC #1178 was the last of the series from Alco/Brooks in 1918.

IC1918-09

IC1918-12

IC1918-13

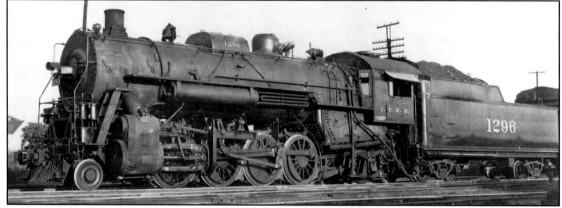

IC1918-14

IC1918-15

Mikados were quickly becoming the engine of choice, and the Illinois Central accepted delivery of many 2-8-2's during 1918; dimensions for most units (63 1/2 D; 185 BP; 282,700 TW; 54,158 TF) were standardized, and many were rebuilt (usually increasing BP 40 pounds to 225, TW to over 300,000 and TF to around 70,000) in the modernization programs that followed; the engines of 1918 from Baldwin and Lima were rostered in as IC-series #1798-1882; these units would be renumbered into the 1200/1300-series in the late-1930's/early-1940's, and renumbered yet again in the 1940's/1950's into the 1500/1600-series; three would be renumbered one last time, into the 1800-series. This page, top, IC #1322 (Lima original IC #1834) was snapped getting the once-over after coupling up to a string of cars. IC #1323 (Lima original IC #1835) was caught at Mays Yard outside New Orleans on July 23, 1946; IC #3797 (a 2-8-2 fashioned out of a 2-8-0) was in the background, getting all the attention.

Facing page, top down, IC #1287 (Baldwin original IC #1799) was caught on the ready track on June 18, 1951. IC #1296 (Baldwin original IC #1808) was fueled and ready for assignment. IC #1301 (Baldwin original IC #1813) was captured on June 18, 1951 in the yard. All three views give a good perspective of the pilot-mounted air-pumps.

IC1918-18

Lima-built 2-8-2 IC #1334 (original IC #1846) appeared in a story on the Memphis Division in the April, 1950 issue of the Illinois Central Magazine. It was captured at rest and at work, in photographs top and bottom. The picture above shows the engine waiting at the water tipple; the lower photograph shows IC #1334 steaming past Sidon, a station eight miles from Greenwood on the Tallahatchie District.

IC4x5-51

IC1918-19

Same engine, different times and places. IC #1851, shown below in a pre-1938 picture, shows what these Lima-built 2-8-2's looked like as original equipment; note the differences when compared to IC #1339 above, to which number this unit had been changed in 1938. The dual air-pumps have been moved from the left side to the pilot; the sandbox has been enlarged and is box-like; the pilot has been changed over to a pressed-steel unit; the pilot wheels went from spoked to solid, and these are just the changes one can see. Undoubtedly, the total weight of the engine was increased, as was the boiler pressure and the tractive force.

IC45x35-11

IC1918-20

These two pages, all Lima-built 2-8-2's from 1918. This page, IC #1350 (original IC #1862) at top was snapped at rest on the station approach, hostling a caboose. IC #1351 (original IC #1863), shown below, appeared in a story on the Memphis Division in the April, 1950 issue of the IC Magazine; the photograph posed the crew with the engineer having train orders handed up at the start of the day.

IC4x5-52

IC #1353 (original IC #1865) at top was pictured before improvements. IC #1358 (original IC #1870) was captured at McComb, Mississippi on February 20, 1952, three years before it was scrapped. On bottom, IC #1362 (original IC #1874), captured before many of the improvements of modernization, showed its OEM superheating and Baker valve gear.

IC1918-21

IC1918-22

IC1918-23

IC1918-24

IC4x5-06

IC4x5-30

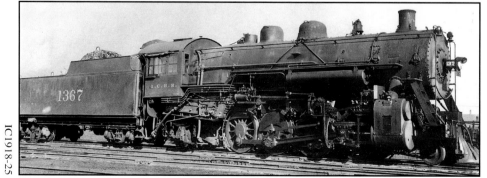

IC1918-25

IC4x5-37

Illinois Central #1505 (original Baldwin IC #1806), above, appeared in an article on the Indianapolis District in the August, 1954 issue of the IC Magazine; it was pictured pulling a string of cars out onto the mainline. IC #1597 (original Lima IC #1845) also appeared in an IC Magazine story, this one on Mississippi Division Steam, in a picture dated April, 1950.

IC1999-14

On the facing page, two views of IC #1363 (original Lima IC #1875) and two views of IC #1367 (original Lima IC #1879). IC #1363 in the top two photographs was caught pulling the same train but at different locations, neither of which were identified. In the lower pictures, IC #1367 was snapped in two different times: rebuilt in the first and cruising through Applington, Iowa (30 miles from Waterloo) on April 4, 1946 and, in the second, before improvements at an earlier time.

IC4x5-48

The September, 1950 issue of the Illinois Central Magazine featured a story on the Kentucky Division; 1918 Lima-built 2-8-2 IC #1811 (original IC #1841) as shown above appeared in that article. IC #1836 was the original roster number for the engine shown below; this whole series of Limas (IC #1833-1882) came with Baker valve gear and superheating.

IC1918-26

On the facing page are two 1918 Lima-built 2-8-2 Mikados, IC #1857 (top two photographs) and IC #1880 (bottom picture), both original roster numbers. While the first view of IC #1857 was a posed shot with crew before fueling the unit, the second shot of IC #1857 shows it hard at work; this picture is thought to show IC #1857 on point of a double-header pulling a solid trainload of feed from East St. Louis; this picture was published in the May, 1924 issue of the Illinois Central Magazine. IC #1880 was preserved in a Builder's Photograph, from Lima Locomotive Works.

ICNEGGS-28

Illinois Central #2104 was an example of the IC taking a 1918 Lima-built 2-8-2 (IC #1815) Mikado (63 1/2 D; 185 BP; 282,700 TW; 54,158 TF) and rebuilding it into a much more powerful (64 1/2 D; 225 BP; 336,000 TW; 85,395 TF) Mikado (IC #2104); Illinois Central converted 41 smaller Mikados into these more powerful versions, and 11 of the 41 were given 30" x 32" cylinders instead of 28" x 32" cylinders, yielding 85,395 TF instead of 74,078 TF; the conversions were made between 1937 and 1942. The photograph above shows the converted 1918 Lima.

IC45x35-125

Illinois Central #3285 was an 0-6-0T saddle-tank engine (51 D; 165 BP; 127,000 TW; 25,000 TF) converted by IC in 1918; originally an 1891 Schenectady-built 0-6-0 switcher (51 D; 99,000 TW), IC acquired the unit in 1896 and eventually converted it into the saddle-tank shown; note the little hopper on the back end for coal.

Illinois Central #3771 was originally a 1904 Alco/Brooks-built 2-8-0 Consolidation (63 D; 200 BP; 203,500 TW; 39,180 TF) rostered as IC #837; in 1918 Illinois Central converted this 2-8-0 into a 2-8-2 Mikado (63 D; 185 BP; 268,140 TW; 46,830 TF) wheel arrangement; this was the second such conversion; this unit had one further renovation in 1937 (210 BP; 52,706 TF). The photograph at top shows the unit prior to the 1937 renovation; the lower picture shows the engine after that improvement in boiler pressure and resulting tractive force.

1919

Armed violence between Irish gangs, and police and government employees erupted; Britain and Ireland would war over independence. Students led protests in May calling for modernization of China. World War I was over with the Armistice, yet the Allies dickered over points in the Versailles Peace Treaty; German naval officers, interned with their High Seas Fleet for over six months, scuttled 52 of their capital ships in Scapa Flow in the Orkneys, rather than turn them over to the Allies.

44-year old Walter Chrysler was elected first vice president, of General Motors. Short-wave radio was invented. 29-year old Edwin Howard Armstrong blended the work of Reginald Fessenden's heterodyne radio receiver and Lee De Forest's Audion tube in developing the super heterodyne High Vacuum radio tube, which amplified weak radio signals without causing distortion; Armstrong sold his new circuit to Westinghouse. 48-year old Ernest Rutherford artificially split the atom. In January with Wyoming the 36th State to ratify, prohibition was enacted in the form of the 18th Amendment to the U.S. Constitution, scheduled to begin one year later; five states voted for ratification on the day it reached the 3/4th's majority required, Wyoming generally credited with pushing the proposal over the top; Mississippi was the 1st to ratify, New Jersey the 45th and last, while Rhode Island rejected the proposal and never did ratify. The U.S. Senate would refuse to ratify the Treaty of Versailles peace agreement, failing to muster the required 2/3rd majority by nine votes (55 to 39); this was a direct rebuff of Woodrow Wilson's Presidency, especially so because it was his own Party's recalcitrance that cratered the vote, led by Foreign Relations Committee chairman Senator Henry Cabot Lodge. Because of Wilson's work to promote the League of Nations, he was awarded the Nobel Peace Prize. 24-year old J. Edgar Hoover began work with the General Intelligence Division of the Justice Department collecting information on suspected radicals, the "Red Scare". The Black-Sox Scandal ended the Chicago White Sox dynasty after eight players threw the 1919 World Series to the Cincinnati Reds; the White Sox, who won the 1917 World Series and finished second in 1918 and 1919, would never win another. 24-year old Jack Dempsey arrived on the scene and gained his first heavyweight boxing title, knocking out Jess Willard in the third round in a fight staged in Toledo, Ohio; Dempsey would retain the title for seven years. Patterned after Navy observation blimps, a commercial version was assembled by Goodyear at White City on Chicago's Southside; in flight it crashed through the roof of the Illinois Trust & Savings building in downtown Chicago in July. Malcolm Lockheed perfected 4-wheel hydraulic brakes and set up business in Detroit to supply the auto industry. Conrad Hilton began his hotel empire with a small Inn in Texas. As usually happens immediately after a war, it would turn out to be a rough year in labor/management relations; first steelworkers and then miners struck for a shorter workweek and higher pay; eventually 4 million workers would walk off the job in various industries throughout the year. *Sir Barton* became the first to win horse racing's Triple Crown, accomplished before the series-name ever took hold. *Man o' War* began his two-year run of beating all comers; ineligible to the Kentucky Derby and, therefore, the Triple Crown series, he settled for one career loss and later sires a Triple Crown winner in *War Admiral*.

The Canadian government organized the Canadian National Railway to bring together over 200 bankrupt or near-bankrupt public and private railroads under an umbrella of public ownership.

While a good neighbor and model citizen, the Illinois Central's smoky, sooty operation of steam locomotives in the downtown commuter service and its virtual control of the Chicago lake front because of its location continued to disturb the City fathers; after long negotiations with the Illinois Central, the City reached an agreement and passed the Lake Front Ordinance in January which returned control of the lake front to the City, and among other things required the Illinois Central to electrify its commuter service into the City and eliminate its grade crossings within City limits by elevating or lowering the track; Chicago regained control of Lake Park/Grant Park and got the right to fill in and develop to the east of the Illinois Central tracks, thus extending the park even further into Lake Michigan; the commuter system was electrified by 1926. With the addition of 18 miles of track in southern Illinois (13 on the Golconda Northern and 5 on the Benton Southern), system mileage rose to 4,800; mileage on the Yazoo & Mississippi Valley was unchanged at 1,382. Still under government control and with strong passenger traffic balancing weak freight results, revenues for the year steadied at $107.9 million, over 22 percent from passenger traffic (31,002,734 passengers). With a 29 percent decline in coal tonnage, revenue traffic levels over Illinois Central dropped to 38.2 million tons of freight; tonnage on the unconsolidated Yazoo & Mississippi Valley approached 11.5

IC45x35-138

ICNEGGS-19

Illinois Central #3100, a 2-10-2 (58 D; 185 BP; 274,720 TW; 51,318 TF) Central-type built in 1919 by Baldwin, represented some of the earliest big power on the IC, even though it wasn't built for the IC. Erected for the Alabama & Vicksburg (as A&V #470) this unit cascaded to IC ownership in the 1926 combination; IC renumbered the unit as shown and, in 1937, converted the 2-10-2 into an 0-10-0 (55 D; 225 BP; 264,720 TW; 68,374 TF) switch engine (renumbered to IC #3602); the Vanderbilt-tender on IC #3602 held 10 tons of coal and 7,000 gallons of boiler water.

million tons. Locomotive availability rose to 1,587 units with the addition of 17 2-8-2 Mikados; seventeen locomotives were converted to superheated engines. Construction of the 4-track reinforced-concrete bridge over the Kankakee River was finished.

ICI1919-05

These two pages, all 1919 Baldwin-built 2-8-2 (63 1/2 D; 185 BP; 282,700 TW; 54,158 TF) Mikados, some of which are shown rebuilt (usually 40 additional pounds of boiler pressure and tractive force approaching 70,000 pounds). Shown above is IC #1314 (original IC #1826) in a yard shot dating between 1940 and 1947, before all the improvements. Below is IC #1550 (original IC #1819) captured crossing over with the Waterloo to Dubuque local on May 10, 1949; note the extended coping on the tender to increase coal capacity. On the facing page, at top, IC #1563 (original IC #1825) was caught working past an elevator in a late-1950 photograph featuring Iowa Division steam. On bottom, IC #1593 (original IC #1822) was snapped at McComb, Mississippi on February 20, 1952. IC #1563 and IC #1593 weren't retired until 1960.

ICNEGGS-09

IC4x5-29

IC1999-13

IC1919-03

Illinois Central acquired three Baldwin-built 4-6-2 Pacifics (68 D; 200 BP; 217,500 TW; 33,800 TF) with the Vicksburg Shreveport & Pacific in 1926. VS&P #380-382 were renumbered to IC #1300-1302 in 1926, renumbered once again in 1937 to IC #994-996, and for a last time in 1943 to IC #1000-1002; these units were rebuilt (220 BP; 52,052 TF) in 1943 with larger cylinders. IC #1000 is shown above as rebuilt; the tender held 17 tons of coal and 7,500 gallons of boiler water. IC #995 is shown in the middle picture (in what is thought to be a C.W. Witbeck photo), dating it to between 1937 and 1943. IC #1001 is that same unit as rebuilt in 1943. IC #1000 and #1001 were built in 1919 and acquired in 1926.

IC45x35-61

IC1919-04

The heaviest (438,000 pounds) steam engines Illinois Central would ever own, these 2-6-6-2 Mallet-type engines (57 D; 220 BP; 438,000 TW; 92,700 TF) were acquired in a swap with the Central of Georgia; IC traded 10 2-8-0 Consolidations to the CofG for 10 of these mallets (series IC #6000-6009); these units were built for the CofG in 1919 by Alco/Richmond and traded away in 1926. The engines were superheated, had Duplex stokers and Walschaerts valve gear; the tender held 17 tons of coal and 9,000 gallons of boiler water; they were in hump-yard service only ten years, at places such as Markham and Nonconnah. IC #6003, on top, was the first mallet delivered to IC (January 27, 1926), and supposedly the first one over the Markham Yard hump (March 12, 1926) with Engineer L.J. Dailey. IC #6007 was snapped at an unidentified location. On bottom, IC #6008 was captured in between, with the IC roster number, but CofG still on the cab.

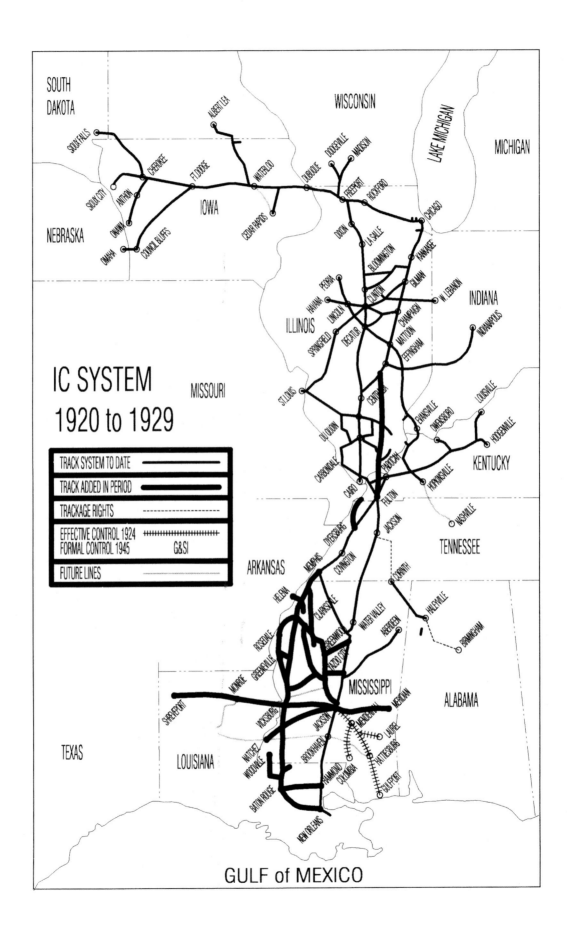

IC SYSTEM
1920 to 1929

TRACK SYSTEM TO DATE	
TRACK ADDED IN PERIOD	
TRACKAGE RIGHTS	
EFFECTIVE CONTROL 1924 FORMAL CONTROL 1945	G&SI
FUTURE LINES	

Literally wiped off the map for 120-some years when divided among Russia, Prussia and Austria, Poland returned, achieving independence after World War I. The former Allies of World War I would experience a period of peace and prosperity, while Germany would suffer through financial ruin and disgrace; the disparity would set the stage for another struggle. Between the two world wars, Italy, France, Germany, the U.S., Japan and England would build fleets of ever-larger battleships, the new linchpin in the arm's race. France would build its 200-mile long series of fortified tunnels and gun emplacements and a false sense of security – the Maginot Line.

The Fourteenth Census of the U.S. population was taken; there were a little over 106 million people in the U.S., having grown 15 percent from the prior census; the country would add over 17 million people by the end of the decade, one-quarter through immigration. Quotas would be placed on immigration through Ellis Island. During the 1920's America went sports crazy. It was the Jazz Age. So began the Roaring 1920's; the economy charged ahead for eight years from 1921 until the Crash in 1929, industrial output almost doubling, mostly in consumer goods. Gains in the agricultural sector would not match those in the industrial sector, a portent of the future; for the first time over half the population lived in city centers, instead of on farms. The decade ended with the stock market crash, bank runs, and a credit crunch; the Stock Market Crash and the Dust Bowl worked together to fuel the Great Depression. Calvin Coolidge inherited an economy on the rebound from World War I and handed off an economy on the brink of collapse; Herbert Hoover didn't cause the depression, he simply couldn't stop it.

In 1920 the major line-haul rail carriers operated a little over 252,500 miles of railroad, a figure that would decline by almost 4,000 miles by the end of the decade, indicating the national railroad system had reached its peak.

Business levels on the Illinois Central were strong, as locomotives were put into service as soon as they were delivered, almost 2,000 in use. Illinois Central conducted fuel saving programs and contests, inasmuch as coal was the second largest expense in maintenance and operation of the railroad.

Growth Of Illinois Central Railroad Business

Year (1)	Tonnage (mil/tons)	Lumber (mil/tons)	Grain (mil/tons)	Coal (mil/tons)	FFV (mil/tons)	Cotton (mil/tons)	Aggregates (mil/tons)	Passengers Commuters	Miles/Fare
1920	49.2	4.2	3.5	22.4	1.2	.228	2.6	35,036,448 N/A	28/$0.76
1921	40.4	3.2	4.1	17.3	1.2	.220	3.0	32,612,358 19,885,466	25/$0.76
1922	47.7	4.6	4.1	19.6	1.4	.236	3.5	33,454,751 22,117,028	24/$0.73
1923	55.1	5.5	3.5	21.9	1.4	.189	5.0	33,944,305 22,731,965	26/$0.80
1924	55.6	5.6	3.3	17.6	1.5	.406	6.4	36,339,704 23,399,360	27/$0.80
1925	58.2	5.8	3.1	18.9	1.3	.573	5.2	34,490,871 23,978,647	28/$0.82
1926	61.9	5.7	2.9	21.4	1.3	.674	6.1	34,110,874 24,555,138	28/$0.83
1927	63.3	5.3	2.8	22.6	1.5	.611	6.7	38,089,266 29,192,020	25/$0.71
1928	61.9	5.1	3.1	20.5	1.5	.560	7.1	40,473,220 33,208,557	23/$0.62
1929	62.8	5.1	3.0	20.6	1.5	.695	6.1	42,712,964 36,069,535	22/$0.56

FFV = Fresh Fruit & Vegetables Passengers/Commuters = Total Ridership, and Commuter Portion
Miles/Fare = Average Passenger Trip and Charge (1) Fiscal Year N/A = Data Not Available

1920

51-year old Mohandas K. Gandhi began leading nonviolent protests in India, a 27-year project that would lead to independence from Great Britain. In March, Thomas MacGurin, Lord Mayor of Cork and a member of the Sinn Fein, was assassinated by masked gunmen, fueling violence between opposing factions in Ireland's war for independence from Great Britain. The seventh edition of the Modern Olympics was held in Antwerp, Belgium; wanting to put the war years behind, a record number of athletes competed in over 150 events, while Russia began a 32-year boycott of the Games.

The U.S. Supreme Court ruled that giant United States Steel Corporation was an allowable combination under rules the Court had set down nine years earlier in dissolving Standard Oil Company of New Jersey. Cuts and scrapes met Band-Aids brand for the first time; Earle Dickson of Johnson & Johnson got the credit. First regularly scheduled U.S. commercial radio broadcast took place; the station, KDKA in Pittsburgh, was the first to be licensed on a frequency outside the amateur bands; they would break ground with the first baseball broadcast the following year, a Pirates-Phillies game. Financier Charles Ponzi pioneered a new money-losing pyramid scheme, bilking over 35,000 investors out of some $12 million. Chanel No. 5 hit the perfume shelves for the first time. Donald Wills Douglas began designing airplanes on his own. Coast-to-coast airmail service was started. In January in what would be called a "noble experiment", prohibition began when the Volstead Act became effective. In another rejection of Woodrow Wilson's policies, the U.S. Senate voted against U.S. participation in the League of Nations. In April, Italian immigrants and supposed radicals Nicola Sacco and Bartolomeo Vanzetti robbed a payroll and murdered two in Massachusetts; justice would consume seven years of controversy, with the lasting question of whether they were punished for their politics or their crime. Having become ill, incumbent President Woodrow Wilson decided not to run for the nomination of his Party. Ohio proved a pivotal state in the Presidential election – claiming both presidential nominees. At the 17th Republican convention in Chicago, Ohio Senator Warren Gamaliel Harding gained the nomination for President on the 10th ballot; Massachusetts Governor Calvin Coolidge was chosen nominee for Vice President. At the 23rd Democratic convention in San Francisco in July, former Ohio Governor James M. Cox won the nomination for President on the 44th ballot; Assistant Secretary of the Navy Franklin Delano Roosevelt of New York was chosen the Vice President nominee. The Socialist party candidate Eugene V. Debs ran for the Presidency for the fifth and last time, this time from a prison cell in Atlanta where he had been sent on being convicted of sedition in speaking out against World War I. The 19th Amendment to the U.S. Constitution was enacted in August when Tennessee became the 36th State to ratify; Illinois had been the 1st, Mississippi would be the 48th and last; Mississippi, the first to ratify prohibition and the last to ratify suffrage, would take 64 years to make it unanimous; the Amendment gave women full voting rights and would add almost ten million first-time women voters to the election results; suffrage was one hallmark of the progressive era. In November the Republican ticket of Harding/ Coolidge won the election in a runaway. After the 1919 season started, the New York Yankees bought out 24-year old Babe Ruth's contract from the Boston Red Sox for $125,000 in one of the all-time great deals; Ruth then hit 54 home runs, beating the old record (his) of 29, and provided an immediate payback on the investment; the Boston Red Sox, who had won the World Series in 1915, 1916 and 1918 with Ruth, would never win another; the New York Yankees, who had never won a pennant, won seven with Ruth and added four World Championships. Ford sold a million automobiles. The Decatur Staley's George Halas and nine other team representatives formed the American Professional Football Association, the forerunner to the National Football League, in a Canton, Ohio auto showroom. Tennis great Bill Tilden became the first American to win at Wimbledon. Douglas Fairbanks and Mary Pickford wed and moved into Pickfair. Edith Wharton was awarded the Pulitzer Prize for her novel *The Age of Innocence*. 24-year old Minnesota-born F. Scott Fitzgerald published his novel about student life at Princeton *This Side of Paradise* and rocketed to fame. Gangster Johnny Torrio shot his way to the top of the Chicago crime scene, knocking off his uncle, top dog Big Jim Colosimo. In September the Miss America contest was held for the first time, in Atlantic City, New Jersey.

USRA operational control of all U.S. railroads was eliminated in March; 1920 Transportation Act was enacted to form a regulatory framework centered on the authority granted the Interstate Commerce Commission (ICC). Railroad employment set its all-time record in topping two million.

IC1920-01

IC45x35-147

Illinois Central converted a few 2-6-0 Mogul-types into 2-6-4T suburban engines in 1920/1921; shown above are IC #1449 and IC #1450. IC #1449 was converted from an 1896 Brooks-built 2-6-0 (IC #485), while IC #1450 was converted from an 1893 Rogers-built unit (IC #438). As rebuilt (56 1/2 D; 165 BP; 211,070 TW; 23,299 TF), these suburban units were the heaviest and most powerful used in commuter service on a permanent basis; a total of eight units would be converted into this class by 1923. IC #1449 was the only suburban engine to have a steel cab; its picture was in the July, 1926 IC Magazine. Both these engines had tenders that held 6 1/2 tons of coal and 3,000 gallons of water.

With the shortening of track and construction of a cutoff, system mileage dipped by a single mile to 4,799; mileage on the Yazoo & Mississippi Valley was steady at 1,382. Freed from war and government operation, revenues for the year topped $145.5 million, over 18 percent from passenger traffic (35,036,448 passengers). With the resurgent economy, revenue traffic levels over Illinois Central set a record of 49.2 million tons of freight; tonnage on the unconsolidated Yazoo & Mississippi Valley exceeded 11.6 million tons. Locomotive availability rose to 1,594 units with the addition of 25 new 4-6-2 Pacifics netted against 18 retirements; three 2-8-0 Consolidation units were converted to 2-8-2 Mikados; 12 locomotives (3 Pacifics and 9 others) were superheated. In September Illinois Central began a public relations campaign with advertisements in local newspapers; these monthly messages reached out to customers for more than 25 years.

IC1913-13

IC1913-14

IC1913-15

Illinois Central received a series of 25 (IC #1179-1203) 4-6-2 heavy Pacifics (75 1/2 D; 190 BP; 280,000 TW; 41,000 TF) in 1920 from Alco/Schenectady; most of these units would be renovated/rebuilt, including an increase of 25 pounds in boiler pressure to kick up the tractive force (45,816 TF versus 41,000 TF). IC #1136/1137/1138 shown above were renumbered in 1937 from the original IC #1201/1202/1203; note the 7,000-class tender on IC #1136 and IC #1138. All of the engines in this series came with superheaters and Walschaerts valve gear as original equipment.

On the facing page are two more 4-6-2's from the same series with the same dimensions: IC #1181 and IC #1185; these were two of only a few that had the old IC Diamond insignia on the tender and the roster number on the cab. Two views of IC #1185 are shown: the first at rest and waiting for additional cars to be coupled on; the second shows the train starting to make way, it's consist now lengthened. Note the children running away at lower right, as power comes up things get serious.

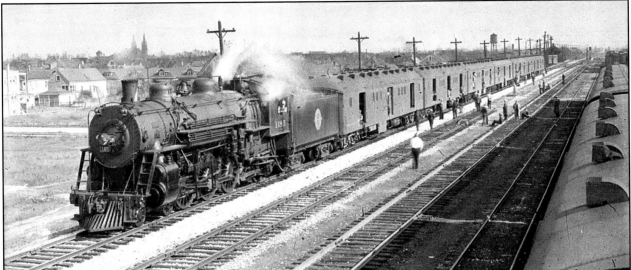

IC1920-02

IC1920-03

IC1920-04

IC1920-05

On this page, two more 4-6-2's from that series with the same dimensions as listed are shown on top. IC #1192 was pictured with the newer square sandbox. IC #1194 was captured sticking out of the Central Station trainshed at 12th Street in Chicago; note the employee on the left makes the cardinal sin of standing on the railhead. At bottom of this page is IC #3773, one of IC's conversions. This engine is a 2-8-2 Mikado (63 D; 185 BP; 268,140 TW; 46,830 TF) fashioned out of a 1904 Alco/Brooks-built 2-8-0 (IC #839) Consolidation (63 D; 200 BP; 203,500 TW; 39,180 TF).

On the facing page, two more Alco/Schenectady 4-6-2's from 1920. IC #1187 is shown in the top two pictures, one at rest in the yard and the other at work pulling its passenger train over the short bridge span at an unknown location; note how the sandbox changed between the two pictures. IC #1188 on the bottom was caught being hostled in the yard.

IC45x35-91

IC45x35-130

1921

British Premier Lloyd George met with 39-year old Eamon de Valera, defacto President of the Irish Republic, to discuss peace; by December, an agreement to establish an Irish Free State excluding Ulster and five other counties in the north of Ireland had been reached; the Free State would have constitutional status in the British Empire similar to Canada, a Dominion. The Free State Agreement was signed by 47-year old Winston Churchill and 31-year old Michael Collins, among others; thus began the partition of northern and southern Ireland. In December, European exchange markets began rising sharply, causing money centers to start scrambling. Albert Einstein was awarded the Nobel Prize in Physics for his 1905 discovery of the photoelectric effect. The Chinese Communist Party was formed, and soon fashioned an alliance with the Nationalist party Kuomintang.

Unprecedented race riots erupted in Tulsa as a Ku Klux Klan-driven white mob burned down the entire prosperous black section of the city, Black Wall Street, with many fatalities resulting. In March 55-year old Warren G. Harding was sworn in as the 29th President of the United States. President Harding appointed former President William H. Taft to the U.S. Supreme Court. The economy slipped into a recession in mid-year. 71-year old Samuel L. Gompers was re-elected President of the American Federation of Labor (AFL) over John L. Lewis, continuing his reign that began in 1886. 30-year old Canadian-born physiologist Frederick G. Banting and 22-year old American-born Charles Best isolated a pancreatic extract (one day called insulin) and developed a crude therapy for diabetes; they would publish their findings the following year and direct the first human trial; Banting shared the Nobel Prize in Physiology two years later with the man who originally dismissed Banting's ideas. 28-year old Canadian-born American medical student John A. Larson improved the crude lie detector, developing the forerunner of today's instrument. 37-year old Swiss-born psychiatrist Hermann Rorschach broke new ground with his famous inkblot test. In July in the first million dollar gate, 26-year old American Jack Dempsey defended his world championship heavyweight boxing title by knocking out the 27-year old French challenger Georges Carpentier in the 4th round in front of 90,000 fans in New Jersey. 26-year old Babe Ruth raised the bar by 5, smashing 59 home runs for the year, a figure that exceeded the total home run production of eight teams. The Black-Sox Scandal officially ended; eight players deemed guilty of throwing the 1919 World Series were acquitted in court but new baseball czar Judge Kenesaw Mountain Landis banned all eight from baseball for life; 55-year old rookie Landis would remain Commissioner until his death in 1944; Landis earned the moniker Judge when appointed to the Federal Bench in Chicago by President Theodore Roosevelt in 1905, where he remained for 17 years, the last two years performing as both Judge and Commissioner. The Decatur Staley football team moved to Chicago; they were renamed the Chicago Bears the next year. The first *Reader's Digest* was published; Clarence W. Barron published the first edition of his weekly magazine *Barron's*. White Castles debuted in Wichita, Kansas. Rudolph Valentino starred in *The Sheik*; 6-year old John Leslie "Jackie" Coogan debuted in *The Kid* with Charlie Chaplin, who wrote, directed and starred in the silent film. Naples-born Enrico Caruso brought the curtain down for the last time, passing away at age 48. 34-year old black leader Marcus Garvey gave up hope of achieving true freedom in the U.S. and prepared his Back to Africa movement with some 500,000 followers; his departure was interrupted for a stint at the Atlanta penitentiary, on being convicted of mail fraud; pardoned in 1927, he was deported to his native Jamaica and lived another 13 years. In May the new Field Museum of Natural History opened, having moved to its new building from the old Palace of Fine Arts, a relic from the 1893 Columbian Exposition which had not yet breathed its last.

With no substantive changes in trackage, system mileage remained at 4,799; mileage on the Yazoo & Mississippi Valley was unchanged at 1,382. The falloff in business, from the prior year, continued; revenues for the year dipped to $141.1million, almost 18 percent due to passenger traffic (32,612,358 passengers). With the general depression in business, especially in coal traffic, revenue traffic levels over Illinois Central dropped to 40.4 million tons of freight; tonnage on the unconsolidated Yazoo & Mississippi Valley crashed to less than 7.4 million tons, a decline of over one-third. Locomotive availability rose to 1,611 units with the addition of 125 new units (100 2-10-2 Lima-built Centrals and 25 Baldwin 0-8-0 switching units) netted against 108 retirements; three Consolidations were converted into Mikados and eight Moguls into suburban units; a total of 37 additional units were superheated. The last conversion program to increase the suburban locomotive fleet involved the conversion of eight Mogul-type units: six Rogers-built (original 1892-1896) and two Brooks-built (original 1893 and 1895); all eight light 2-6-0's were rebuilt at the Company's Burnside Shops into 2-6-4T's; the first four units were received in 1920/1921, the

IC1921-10

Illinois Central accepted delivery of 100 (original series IC #2901-3000) Lima-built 2-10-2 Central-types in 1921, IC's first venture into big power. While the Company had tried out 2-10-2 wheel arrangements as far back as 1916, it wasn't until five years later that IC made a significant investment in this type of power. The 100 units were part of a total order for 125; 100 were delivered in 1921, five more in 1922 and the last 20 in 1923. These units served the IC long and hard over the years, and formed the platform for a number of mechanical efforts, such as conversions into 4-8-2's, or renovations into the most powerful engines on the System. The original series was IC #2901-3025 (64 1/2 D; 190 BP; 382,000 TW; 72,112 TF); most were converted/rebuilt/ renovated during the late-1930's early 1940's into one of three series: 56 were converted into the 2500-series of 4-8-2 Mountains, 49 were modernized into the 2700-series of Centrals (240 BP; 404,500 TW; 91,088 TF) and 20 were renovated into the 2800-series of 2-10-2's (275 BP; 416,000 TW; 104,322 TF). The 2800-series had higher boiler pressure and tractive force than any other units on the Illinois Central. IC #2706 (original IC #2963), shown above, was captured on the Winnfield District next to IC #1599, a 2-8-2 Mikado.

next two in 1922 and the last two in 1923. Illinois Central's first suburban service composed of all-steel cars (Train #329, Engine #1448) was initiated; it would be five years until all-steel electrified service was inaugurated; the original 20 all-steel cars were moved via steam power, and later retrofitted with electric equipment for self-propulsion. The Kentucky grade reduction program begun seven years earlier and halted by wartime exigencies was restarted between Dawson Springs and Princeton; the finished project would turn a ruling grade of 1.25 percent with 6 degrees of uncompensated curves into a one-half percent maximum grade southbound with a maximum curve of 2 degrees. In August the Interstate Commerce Commission proposed a consolidation of the Nation's railroads into 21 major systems; hearings would consume the rest of the decade.

IC1943-12

IC4x5-41

IC1943-06

On the facing page, two views of IC #2711 (original IC #2977): the upper view was snapped May 19, 1953 near Paducah; the lower view (a picture that appeared in the IC Magazine in the 1950's) on May 20, 1953 near Madisonville, Kentucky. This page, IC #2713 (original IC #2931) was captured in the fashion of O. Winston Link, in this night shot by Gibson at Birmingham Yard (BC-4) on April 5, 1949. IC #2717 (original IC #2951) was shot by Gibson on the St. Louis Division.

ICNEGGS-10

IC1943-08

Three views of 2-10-2 units on the Kentucky Division. Above and right, IC #2728 (original IC #2994) works a coal train on the P&I in pictures dated May 19, 1953. The lower view of IC #2731 (original IC #2986) shows similar action; IC #2731 had a very long service life, reaching the 1960's.

IC1943-09

IC1944-01

Illinois Central #2738 (original IC #2981) is shown above fueled and ready for action; the tender held 19 tons of coal and 12,000 gallons of boiler water. IC #2741, shown below, was caught at Paducah on August 21, 1958; this engine held the distinction of being the last steam locomotive overhauled at Paducah Shops.

Facing page shows three 2800-series units, most of which were equipped with an auxiliary tender to provide for extra boiler water; these units had been fitted with new boilers, and were the most powerful locomotives on the IC. Top to bottom, IC #2806 (original IC #2914) is shown cruising through Independence, Iowa on May 10, 1949 with westbound freight #96; IC #2808 (original IC #2939) was captured hauling a steam freight out of Dubuque, Iowa on August 2, 1951; lastly, IC #2809 (original IC #2915) was snapped in a static yard shot, giving a good view of the extra tender.

ICNEGGS-42

This page, three pictures, two engines. Above and right is IC #2743 (original IC #2991); it was caught pulling a coal train in the first view at an unknown location (a previously published photo); in the second view, it was snapped working a mixed consist over the Gilbertsville Dam crossing the Tennessee River (a Hedrich & Blessing negative for the IC); the picture caught the train moving by the lifting mechanism of the Dam. This latter picture appeared in the 1947 IC Shareholders Report. The lower photograph shows IC #2750 (original IC #2997) in a posed shot in the yard; this engine was notable for the fact that it was the only 2-10-2 modernized to 260 pounds of boiler pressure (260 BP; 417,500 TW; 98,678 TF), rather than 240 or 275 pounds.

IC4x5-79

IC1943-10

IC1945-02

Illinois Central #2818 (original IC #2938), one of the twenty 2-10-2's with 104,322 pounds tractive force, was captured at Paducah Shops on August 21, 1958; the pressed steel pilot and pilot-mounted air-pumps are visible in the photograph.

IC4x5-74

IC #2819 (original IC #2902) is shown streaming through the countryside with its extra tender on the Iowa Division in this May 29, 1951 picture; over 100 auxiliary tenders would be produced in the 1940's and 1950's to help balance coal and water consumption in powerful locomotives, such as these 2-10-2 Centrals and the 4-8-2 Mountains on the horizon.

Shown below is the same engine over two renumberings; IC #2850 (original IC #2936) was renumbered in 1943, and then again in 1945 (to IC #2814). The engine had a Type-A superheater and an enlarged cab; the tender held 19 tons of coal and 12,000 gallons of boiler water. This unit was retired in December, 1959.

IC1943-11

IC1945-01

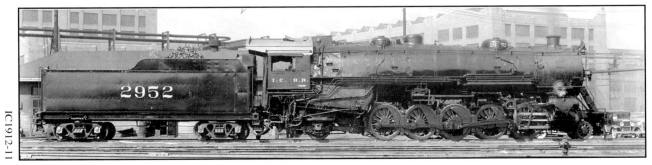

Illinois Central #2985, shown above, would be rebuilt and renumbered to IC #2720, shown below. The top photograph was published in the October, 1926 issue of the Illinois Central Magazine; it showed a solid trainload of iron ore which IC moved from Chicago to Granite City; the picture was snapped at Hazelcrest, near Chicago. The lower photograph was captured at East St. Louis, Illinois in July, 1950.

On the facing page are four shots of 1921 Lima 2-10-2's, the first three from the original series. Top to bottom, IC #2921 was shown in a Builder's Photograph. IC #2950 was captured at Central City, Kentucky in September, 1928, after being overhauled and painted; this picture appeared in the February, 1929 issue of the IC Magazine. IC #2952 was snapped at an unknown location, and was the precursor to IC #2704, to which it was renumbered in 1943. IC #2704 was published in the IC Magazine in July, 1950 in a story on the East St. Louis Division.

The other large delivery of steam locomotives in 1921 was of 25 (series IC #3500-3524) Baldwin-built 0-8-0 switch engines (53 D; 175 BP; 221,500 TW; 49,115 TF); most of these were later rebuilt (190 BP; 56,500 TF); all were superheated, and most had tenders that held 9 tons of coal and 9,000 gallons of water. On the facing page in the middle view, IC #3504 was caught in a Kaufmann & Fabry photo for the IC, and published as the October, 1937 IC Magazine cover; identified in the picture were, left to right, William Griffen (machinist), Paul Tribbett (crane operator), Harry Forbes (pipe fitter), and R.W. Russell (fire chief); the picture was taken at Markham Yard and advertised the fact that IC had equipped 350 of its switch engines with fire-fighting apparatus; with the injector pump, these units could pump water directly from the engine's tender, and help reduce fire damage in shops and yards. This page top, IC #3511 is shown working a cut across the Kankakee river bridge (completed in 1918) on June 11, 1954. All the other photographs are 3500-series engines in unidentified yard shots.

1922

In January, the Irish ruling body - the Dail Eireann - voted 64 to 57 to accept Irish Free State; the close vote exemplified the division between northern and southern Ireland, and the fight for control of the Irish Republican Party; ending their war with Great Britain, the Irish started fighting each other; in the end, 32-year old Michael Collins was assassinated late in the year by Sinn Fein extremists. In January, Pope Benedict XV succumbed to influenza; 65-year old Achille Ratti would replace him, take the name Pius XI, and lead the Church for 17 years. Gandhi was arrested in March on charges of sedition. The Tomb of Tutankhamen was discovered in the Valley of the Kings in Egypt by Englishman Lord Carnarvon and American Howard Carter. Fascists having gained seats in Parliament for the first time the prior year, 39-year old Benito Mussolini garnered power in Italy, the beginning of his 21-year rule.

The Lincoln Memorial was dedicated in Washington, D.C. In April it was alleged that Secretary of the Interior Albert B. Fall leased the military's Naval Reserve No. 3 (Teapot Dome) oil field in Wyoming to oilman Harry F. Sinclair; disgraced and run out of office, Fall would be convicted of fraud in 1929. 57-year old George O. Squier, chief signal officer of the Army, unveiled the forerunner to Muzak, founded on his invention for transmitting music through electrical wires. Emily Post published her first book on etiquette. 40-year old Irishman James Joyce published *Ulysses* in the U.S. Hollywood established a morals code and blacklisted over 100 of its own. *Our Gang* appeared in the first of what would total over 200 comedy shorts in the next 22 years. Charles Atlas won one of his world titles, a body-building contest. *Better Homes and Gardens* appeared for the first time. 21-year old Louis Armstrong left New Orleans and arrived in Chicago in July at Illinois Central's Central Station; he came north to play the cornet in Joe "King" Oliver's Creole Jazz Band.

On the heels of the second 12 percent pay cut in two years, railroad shop craft workers made history when they went out on strike and commenced the first national railroad strike; the strike would collapse the next year under the weight of Federal injunctions.

Illinois Central inaugurated its deluxe all-Pullman *Floridan* from Chicago to Jacksonville and beyond. At its annual meeting in April, the Company received authority to issue up to $50 million in preferred shares to fund the electrification of Illinois Central lines within Chicago, under the City's Lake Front Ordinance; an Electrification Commission was appointed to determine the best system and, upon its recommendation, a 1,500-volt D.C. overhead system was adopted and construction started. With the release of 15 miles of trackage rights and little else changed, system mileage dropped to 4,785; mileage on the Yazoo & Mississippi Valley dipped to 1,380. With the return of prosperous business conditions, even the Interstate Commerce Commission's mandated rate reduction couldn't undermine results; revenues for the year approached $154.9 million, less than 16 percent from passenger traffic (33,454,751 passengers). In spite of labor strikes during the year by coal miners and railroad shop men, with the overall business environment, revenue traffic levels over Illinois Central rebounded strongly to 47.7 million tons of freight; tonnage on the unconsolidated Yazoo & Mississippi Valley exceeded 7.8 million tons. Locomotive availability dipped to 1,602 units with the addition of 10 8-wheeled switch units outnumbered by the 19 retirements; an additional 43 locomotives gained superheaters.

IC45x35-140

IC1922-05

Illinois Central accepted delivery of 15 additional Baldwin-built 0-8-0 (53 D; 175 BP; 221,500 TW; 49,115 TF) switch engines in 1922/1923; most would be rebuilt (190 BP; 56,500 TF) in the ensuing years. Three of the 1922 products are shown on this page. IC #3525, at top, was a Builder's Photograph in OEM configuration. IC #3529 was caught in a yard shot; the tender held 9 tons of coal and 9,000 gallons of boiler water. IC #3536 was snapped switching one of the early TOFC (Trailer On Flat Car, now Intermodal) shipments.

IC1922-06

Illinois Central received 25 Lima-built 2-10-2 (64 1/2 D; 190 BP; 382,000 TW; 72,112 TF) Centrals in 1922/1923; of the five delivered in 1922, three are shown on these two pages. On the facing page at top is IC #2705 (original IC #3003), captured dragging a coal train through the switches. IC #2816 (original IC #3001) was caught at rest after being rebuilt (275 BP; 416,000 TW; 104,322 TF) with a new boiler and equipped with an auxiliary tender; the units main tender, with its high coping, held 19 tons of coal and 12,000 gallons of boiler water. On this page, at top, another 2-10-2 is shown, this one IC #3002, an original roster number; this unit (as did all in the IC #3001-3025 series) came with a superheater and Baker valve gear; IC #2705 at top on the previous page and IC #3002 were rebuilt (240 BP; 404,500 TW; 91,088 TF) to a slightly powered-down standard, as they did not receive new boilers.

Illinois Central #1002, a Baldwin-built 4-6-2 Pacific (68 D; 200 BP; 217,500 TW; 33,800 TF) from 1922, originally was erected for the Alabama & Vicksburg (as A&V #480); renumbered to Vicksburg Shreveport & Pacific #382, this unit came to IC ownership in 1926, and it was rostered in as IC #1302; renumbered twice more, to IC #996 in 1937 and IC #1002 in 1943, this unit was rebuilt (220 BP; 52,052 TF) and remained in service until sold for scrap in 1955.

1923

Japan was rocked by an earthquake in September, the death toll was estimated between 200,000 and 300,000. Relations between Italy and Greece deteriorated. France and Belgium took control of the Ruhr to force Germany into paying its war reparations; taking advantage of their neighbor when down would lead to another war. While London to Edinburgh service dated back to 1862, the *Flying Scotsman* only settled on its name in 1923.

Patented and produced in Switzerland since 1912, Dupont began American production of cellophane. Vaccines for whooping cough and tuberculosis were developed. RCA debuted the Radiola. 34-year old Russian immigrant physicist Vladimir K. Zworykin patented the iconoscope, the forerunner to the television camera; the next year he patented the kinoscope, the television receiver tube. 50-year old Lee De Forest demonstrated sound on moving film, or talking pictures, recording sound directly on film; the first commercial use would be three years later. Clarence Birdseye developed quick freezing of food products; he concluded the crux of food preservation wasn't extreme temperature but fast freezing. Colonel Jacob Schick patented the first electric shaver. In August, having served as President for 2 ½ years, President Warren G. Harding died of complications from a stroke after a short illness; on taking the oath of office, 51-year old Calvin Coolidge became the 30th President of the U.S. Harding was the sixth President to die in Office (Harrison, Taylor, Lincoln, Garfield, McKinley, and Harding). *Time* magazine was published for the first time, founded by Henry R. Luce and Briton Hadden. Hollywood outside Los Angeles put up its first landmark sign – *Hollywoodland*. Walter Chrysler became President of Maxwell Motors, later renaming it Chrysler Motors. The first non-stop transcontinental flight, from New York to San Diego, was completed in 27 hours by Army Lieutenants Oakley G. Kelly and John A. Macready; having failed twice to complete the coast-to-coast flight starting in the west because the fuel-heavy airplane couldn't scale the mountains, the route was switched to an east to west configuration. Kahil Gibran published his poetry *The Prophet* in the U.S. Knocked out of the ring in the 1st Round, Jack Dempsey returned with a vengeance to KO Luis Firpo in the 2nd Round of their heavyweight boxing title fight. 20-something year old blues singer Bessie Smith cut her first record, *Down Hearted Blues*.

Power-operated car retarders, used to slow moving cars when being classified in rail yards, was first tried in 1923 on the Indiana Harbor Belt-operated Gibson Yards of the New York Central; E.W. Wilcox and George H. Hannauer were credited with the concept of car retarders. Caboose design evolved to a bay window instead of a cupola, giving trainmen a side view instead of roof-top view of the train. The financially challenged Grand Trunk Railway ceased operating as a private company and was folded into the Canadian National Railway, giving the CNR its current shape. The Van Sweringen brothers consolidated their Nickel Plate with the Erie and the Toledo, St. Louis & Western forming a 1,695-mile long system; the New York, Chicago & St. Louis finally gained access to St. Louis, something planned 42 years earlier.

With the addition of a net 60 miles of track, most notably the Deer, Tennessee to Hickman, Kentucky branch, system mileage grew to a little over 4,845; mileage on the Yazoo & Mississippi Valley remained steady at 1,380. With an expansive economy and increased passenger traffic, revenues for the year topped $165.6 million, a little over 16 percent due to passenger traffic (33,944,305 passengers). Revenue traffic levels over Illinois Central rose strongly to 55.1 million tons of freight; tonnage on the unconsolidated Yazoo & Mississippi Valley grew to over 9.6 million tons, continuing its recovery. Locomotive availability rose to 1,768 units with the addition of 165 new units (15 4-8-2 Mountains (IC's 1st Mountains, built by ALCO/Schenectady), 120 2-8-2 Mikados, 25 2-10-2 Centrals and 5 8-wheeled switchers) netted against 24 retirements; 21 Consolidations were converted into Mikados and two Moguls into suburban units; 55 locomotives were converted into superheated units. In line with the Chicago Lake Front Ordinance, Illinois Central continued work on electrification of its lines within the city; the grading for depression and elevation of the roadbed for viaducts between 29th and 51st streets progressed rapidly; elevation of the main tracks through Harvey was started.

Illinois Central would accept delivery on more than 150 steam locomotives in 1923: a majority as 2-8-2 Mikado-types, the tag-end of orders for 2-10-2 Centrals and 0-8-0 switchers, and the first of a new breed, 4-8-2 Mountain-type wheel arrangements. The Mikado-types (63 1/2 D; 185 BP; 298,000 TW; 54,158 TF) were the first new 2-8-2's in five years, and came from three builders: Alco/Schenectady (series IC #1883-1907), Lima (series IC #1908-1982) and Baldwin (series IC #1983-2017). The 2-10-2's (64 1/2 D; 190 BP; 382,000 TW; 72,112 TF) were the end of an order from Lima, and the switchers (53 D; 175 BP; 221,500 TW; 49,115 TF) were the same from Baldwin Locomotive. The 15 new 4-8-2 Mountain-type locomotives (73 1/2 D; 230 BP; 362,500 TW; 58,389 TF) came from Alco/Schenectady and were rostered in as IC-series 2400-2414. Most of these steam engines, in all four wheel arrangements, would be rebuilt in the massive upgrade programs of the 1930's/1940's.

Shown above is IC #1375 (original IC #1887), an Alco/Schenectady-built 2-8-2 that appeared in the IC Magazine in a story on Mississippi Division Steam; the picture dates to April, 1950; this unit would be renumbered to IC #1675.

These two pages, all 2-8-2's from Alco/Schenectady in 1923. Below, IC #1380 (original IC #1892) hides underneath all that steam and smoke. IC #1383 (original IC #1895) below was caught at McComb, Mississippi on February 20, 1952; in earlier days it looked like the view at bottom. On the facing page, IC #1386 at top originally was rostered in as IC #1898. IC #1387 at middle appeared in the December, 1946 issue of the IC Magazine; the view showed a through freight rushing by a local, as the local crew gave the one a look by and the other rear end protection, at Charles City, Iowa. On bottom, IC #1501 (original IC #1894) was captured at Paducah on February 4, 1944 sporting a gadget: an auxiliary piston valve, which let more steam in to the cylinder over a longer duration to increase efficient use of steam.

IC4x5-33

IC1923-02

IC45x35-003

IC1923-03

IC1923-04

IC45x35-077

IC4x5-45

IC45x35-104

IC1923-14

IC1923-15

On the facing page, three Alco/Schenectady 2-8-2's; this page, three by Lima. Opposite page at top, IC #1567 (shown with original IC #1891) was caught at Fulton, Kentucky moving a local freight to Jackson, Tennessee on February 15, 1949. IC #1889 was shot before being renumbered. On bottom, original roster number IC #1903 was snapped crossing a bridge. This page at top, IC #1398 (original IC #1910) was captured parked by the water tipple at Mays Yard outside New Orleans on November 14, 1951. IC #1403 (original IC #1915), at middle, was viewed on March 14, 1950 coupling up its train in the New Orleans area. On bottom, IC #1411 (original IC #1923) was snapped being hostled into the yard tracks.

IC1923-05

IC4x5-34

IC45x35-083

IC45x35-083

IC45x35-085

IC1923-07

Five Lima-built 2-8-2's on these two pages. On opposite page at top, IC #1414 (original IC #1926) was snapped at an unrecorded time and place. At middle, IC #1421 (original IC #1933) was posed outside the roundhouse. At bottom, IC #1439 (original IC #1951) was captured at an unknown yard in a photograph dated June 18, 1951. This page at top, IC #1446 (original IC #1958) was caught hauling a St. Louis Division freight train in a negative by Gibson. IC #1451 (original IC #1963) was snapped, fueled and ready for assignment, in a yard shot.

IC4x5-39

Two Lima-built 2-8-2's. Above, IC #1564 (original IC #1955) was handling the Waterloo to Fort Dodge local when captured on August 6, 1952; this appeared in an IC Magazine story series entitled A Day In The Life Of...; Engineer Deberg was in the picture. IC #1683 (original IC #1923), at bottom, was caught as the train orders were being handed up at Evansville, Indiana and was published in the April, 1958 issue of the Illinois Central Magazine.

IC5x7-02

IC1923-01

IC1923-06

A single Lima (IC #1415 at far left), in a sea of Baldwins, all 2-8-2's. At top, IC #1302 (original IC #2015) was shot at an unrecorded time and place. At left, IC #1474 (original IC #1986) was caught easing past the Lima (original IC #1927) at Reevesville, Illinois in late-1950. IC #1986 was shot in a Builder's Photograph; note the side-mounted twin air-pumps, an item generally relocated to the pilot when the engine was rebuilt. At bottom, IC #1472 (original IC #1984) was stopped on December 14, 1950 in New Orleans, fueled and ready for action.

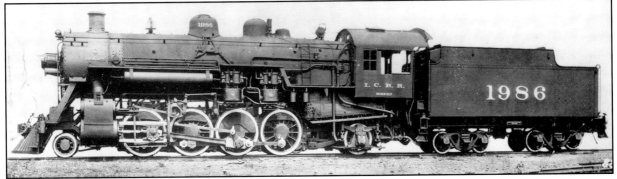

IC1923-16

IC1923-08

IC1923-09

Two pages of Baldwin-built 2-8-2's, all products of 1923. This page from top to bottom, IC #1476 (original IC #1988) was caught at Mays Yard outside New Orleans on November 14, 1951. IC #1486 (original IC #1998) was snapped at Freeport, Illinois in October, 1945 in this previously published photograph; the tender held 16 tons of coal and 13,000 gallons of boiler water. IC #1491 (original IC #2003) was shot at McComb, Mississippi on February 20, 1952. IC #1492 (original IC #2004) is shown in two views, a static side pose in the yard and working hard to get a string of reefers up to speed.

ICNEGGS-34

IC1923-10

IC1923-11

IC45x35-180

IC1923-12

Illinois Central #1493 (original IC #2005) shown above was captured in a C.W. Witbeck negative on August 1, 1948; the picture caught NC-4 raising dust through Crystal Springs, Mississippi and Operator Vernon O. Holmes handing up train orders as it sped northward; this photograph was published in the January, 1949 issue of the Illinois Central Magazine. Shown below is another view of IC #1493, this one at McComb, Mississippi on February 20, 1952. At bottom, IC #1513 (original IC #2000) was snapped sometime between 1944 and 1949, when it was renumbered to IC #1813.

IC1923-13

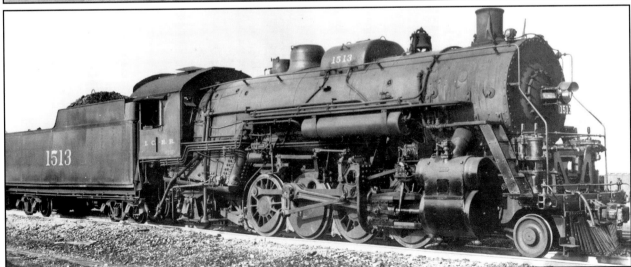

IC1999-03

IC 1999-12

Two pages of Baldwin-built 2-8-2's from 1923. This page, top, caught IC #1590 (original IC #2010) making its way out of North Yard at Jackson, Mississippi in May, 1950. Below, IC #1591 (original IC #2008) was stopped at Mendenhall, Mississippi on June 9, 1953. Facing page, top to bottom, IC #2009, an original roster position, was snapped riding a string of refrigerator cars around Lake Pontchatrain (one of the longest curved sections of rail trackage) with the Pass Manchac bridge in the background. IC #2011 was caught in a yard shot with its crew; IC #2016 waiting for a signal.

IC 4x5-46

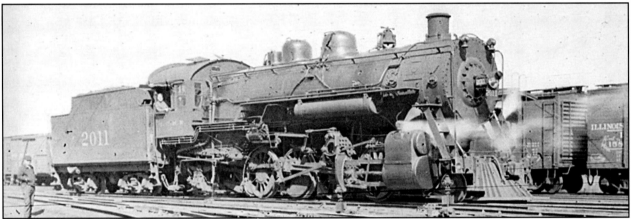

And then there were Mountains, 4-8-2 Schenectady-built Mountains in 1923. On the facing page at top, IC #2303 (original IC #2413) was snapped on January 6, 1955 as the crew made a final walk-around; the train was NC-2 preparing a night-time departure from New Orleans; the engine was rebuilt (73 D; 275 BP; 384,500 TW; 69,813 TF) with a new boiler. Shown at bottom, IC #2306 (original IC #2406) was captured bringing the bad weather with it in a December, 1950 picture; this photograph was used in an IC Magazine story on St. Louis Division steam. This page, at top, IC #2401, an original roster number, is shown in a yard shot; this engine was rebuilt with Boxpok drivers and 245 pounds of boiler pressure; the tender, with its high coping, held 22 tons of coal and 10,000 gallons of boiler water. At bottom, IC #2403 was caught outside the roundhouse framed in a window; this photograph was published in the Illinois Central Magazine in the 1950's.

Two pages of 4-8-2 Mountain wheel arrangements built by Alco/Schenectady in 1923. On facing page at top, IC #2407 pauses in Birmingham, Alabama next to FRISCO #3741. At bottom, IC #2410 was caught south of Carbondale, Illinois in a negative by Gibson. Both of these engines were rebuilt with boiler pressure boosted to 245 pounds. This page, three views of IC #2411. At top is a picture showing the engine trimmed out to pull the Panama Limited, *including striped shade on the cab window; the picture dates to the 1933/1934 Chicago Century of Progress Fair where this engine was displayed; this engine came equipped with dual No. 5 New York air-pumps, Dupont stoker (the first IC passenger power with this) and a Delta one-piece trailer truck (first IC engine with this), superheater and Walschaerts valve gear; the tender held 18 tons of coal and 10,000 gallons of boiler water; this photograph appeared in the December, 1934 IC Magazine. The middle view shows this engine pulling a passenger train out of Central Station in Chicago. The bottom picture shows the engine toward the end of its service life, after having been rebuilt and outfitted with a higher capacity tender.*

IC45x35-109

IC1923-24

IC1923-25

IC1923-26

IC1923-27

On the facing page are two 4-8-2 Mountains. IC #2412 at top was shown being readied in Chicago for assignment; note the tender was the greater-capacity type with high coping. On bottom, IC #2414 was caught at the Carbondale, Illinois coal chute at dusk, in a picture from the 1949 Annual Report; this unit was rebuilt with higher (245 lbs) boiler pressure.

IC's large order of 2-10-2 Centrals was completed with the delivery of 20 units in 1923 (series IC #3006-3025). Above is IC #2807 (original IC #3013), one of the units rebuilt (275 BP; 416,000 TW; 104,322 TF) with a new boiler; the tender held 19 tons of coal and 12,000 gallons of boiler water. Original roster number IC #3008, shown below, came with superheat and Bakers valve gear (as did all units in series IC #3001-3025); this photograph was published in the September, 1925 issue of the Illinois Central Magazine. IC #3025, the last of the lot, was snapped in a Builder's Photograph. These last two units had their boilers used to fashion 4-8-2 Mountain-types, IC #2509 and IC #2545, respectively.

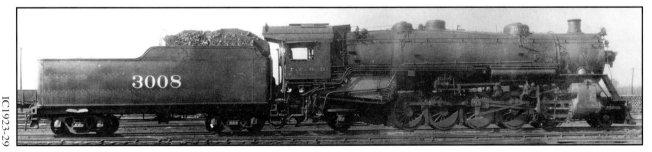

ICNEGGS-55

IC1923-29

IC45x35-137

IC45x35-129

IC45x35-128

IC1906-04

Illinois Central fashioned 2-8-2 Mikado wheel arrangements out of other engines, notably 2-8-0 Consolidations; these two pages depict four examples. On this page at top, IC #3768 (original IC #3816) was caught at an unidentified crossing; this engine was converted into a 2-8-2 from IC #816, a 1904 Alco/Brooks built 2-8-0. At middle, IC #3780 (original IC #3875) was fashioned out of IC #875, a 1906 Alco/Brooks built 2-8-0. At bottom, IC #3787 (original IC #3894) was a conversion of IC #894, another 1906 Alco/Brooks built 2-8-0. All three engines were converted (63 D; 185 BP; 268,140 TW; 46,830 TF) in 1923 and then renovated (63 1/2 D; 210 BP; 287,500 TW; 52,706 TF) in 1937; the tender held 10 tons of coal and 7,000 gallons of boiler water.

Illinois Central #3817 is shown in two views on this page. This engine was originally IC #817, a 1904 Alco/Brooks built 2-8-0. In 1923, it was converted (63 D; 185 BP; 268,140 TW; 46,830 TF) into a 2-8-2 Mikado wheel arrangement. It would be renovated in 1937 to the dimensions mentioned on the previous page, and renumbered to IC #3769.

1924

53-year old Vladimir Ilyitch Ulianov (Nikolai Lenin) passed away in January after almost 7 years in control; 44-year olds Yosif Vissarionovich Djugashvili (Joseph V. Stalin) and Lev Davidovich Bronstein (Leon Trotsky) would vie to replace him in office, Stalin outlasting the competition. The eighth edition of the Modern Olympics Games was held in Paris, Johnny Weismuller of the U.S. won two golds in swimming; the Olympics inaugurated winter games, in Chamonix, France – 16 countries showed up. Canadian hockey clubs formed the National Hockey League and vied for a trophy donated by Lord Preston of Stanley; the League expanded into the U.S. by granting the first American franchise to the Boston Bruins in 1924; then followed Pittsburgh in 1925 and Chicago, Detroit and New York in 1926. Mountaineer George Mallory died trying to climb Mt. Everest. Dutch physiologist 64-year old Willem Einthoven was awarded the Nobel Prize for his development of the electrocardiograph, which measured electrical currents from the heart. The Leitz Company, known for building precision microscopes, began mass-producing the Leica 35mm camera, which would be offered for sale the following year.

Showing their expansive prejudice, over 35,000 Klu Klux Klan supporters poured into South Bend demonstrating against Irish Catholics. Loudspeakers were introduced. Zenith Radio Corporation invented the portable radio. Kleenex arrived. Masonite board was introduced. Young and rich teenagers Leopold and Loeb attempted the perfect murder as thrill killers of 13-year old Bobby Franks; in their defense, 67-year old Clarence Darrow, in one of his last celebrated trials, had his clients plead guilty in order to avoid a public jury trial; with only a sentencing hearing in front of a single judge, they avoided the death penalty. In June native-born Indians were granted citizenship - in their own country. In June at the 18th Republican convention in Cleveland, incumbent President Calvin Coolidge was nominated for re-election on the 1st ballot; Brigadier General Charles G. Dawes of Illinois was chosen nominee for Vice President. At the 24th Democratic convention in New York, Wall Street lawyer John William Davis of West Virginia was chosen the party's Presidential nominee on the 103rd ballot (Democratic Party record); Nebraska Governor Charles W. Bryan (brother of William Jennings) was chosen nominee for Vice President. In November, the Coolidge/Dawes Republican ticket won the election defeating both the Democratic nominees and the Progressive candidate La Follette, who carried only his own state of Wisconsin. Samuel L. Gompers, President and Founder of the American Federation of Labor, died at age 74. U.S. Attorney General and future U.S. Supreme Court Justice Harlan Fiske Stone appointed J. Edgar Hoover to the Bureau of Investigation, the forerunner of the Federal Bureau of Investigation. Grant Park Stadium, renamed Soldier Field when dedicated one-year later, opened in Chicago. A.T.& T. and General Electric formed Bell Laboratories. Four Douglas World Cruiser aircraft left Seattle, Washington on April 6th attempting to be the first to circumnavigate the globe by air; two of the U.S. Army Air Service aircraft finished the journey; it took them 175 days, but they are generally credited with the record of first. Edna Ferber's novel *So Big* was awarded the Pulitzer Prize; Lowell J. Thomas published his *With Lawrence in Arabia*. 51-year old German psychiatrist Hans Berger invented the electroencephalograph, measuring the electrical impulses of the brain for the first time.

IC's non-stop passenger service between Memphis and St. Louis debuted as the *Chickasaw*. For the first time since gaining control of the Yazoo & Mississippi Valley 32 years earlier, the Company reported results on a consolidated basis. Blending the Illinois Central's 4,845 miles of track with the Yazoo & Mississippi Valley's 1,380 miles, system mileage began the year just shy of 6,226; with a few additional miles acquired during the year, total system mileage rose to 6,243. Consolidating reports masked a general malaise in the economy; revenues for the year topped $173.8 million, almost 17 percent due to passenger traffic (36,339,704 passengers). Revenue traffic levels over the Illinois Central system grew to 55.6 million tons of freight. Adding the Illinois Central's 1,768 locomotives to the Yazoo & Mississippi Valley's 132, the system fleet began the year at 1,900 units; availability rose to 1,909 units with the addition of 18 2-8-2 Mikados netted against the retirement/reclassification of nine engines; 27 additional units were converted to superheaters during the year. Work under Chicago's Lake Front Ordinance and on Chicago terminal improvements continued throughout the year: track elevation, separation of grades, relining tracks, relocating utilities, bridging sewers, forming concrete and steel viaducts, building overhead walkways, tunneling under Michigan Boulevard at Van Buren Street, bridging the Calumet River at Riverdale, filling submerged lands between 16th and 26th Streets, and the initial work and foundations for an overhead catenary system for the suburban electrification were just some of the parts involved. Toward the end of the year the Company acquired control of the 307-mile long Gulf & Ship Island (built between 1886 and 1906) that operated a line between the Mississippi capital of Jackson

IC45x35-131

IC1924-20

Illinois Central completed its 33-engine program of converting 2-8-0 Consolidations (63 D; 200 BP; 203,500 TW; 39,180 TF) into 2-8-2 Mikados (63 D; 185 BP; 268,140 TW; 46,830 TF) with the last three units in 1924; each would be renovated (63 1/2 D; 210 BP; 287,500 TW; 52,706 TF) in 1937 to extend their useful service lives. At top, IC #3778 (original IC #3857) was caught outside its roundhouse; this engine was converted from IC #857, a 1905 Alco/Brooks built 2-8-0. The lower photograph snapped IC #3972, a 1924 Baldwin-built 2-8-2 (57 1/2 D; 200 BP; 217,500 TW; 40,418 TF) at Vicksburg, Mississippi on August 4, 1931; this unit was erected for the Alabama & Vicksburg (as A&V #463) and came into IC ownership in 1926, when it was renumbered as shown; it was rebuilt into an 0-8-0 switcher in 1941 and renumbered to IC #3499.

and Gulfport, Mississippi along with assorted branch lines; effective control would change to formal 21 years later. The long-term lease of the 313-mile long Alabama & Vicksburg and Vicksburg, Shreveport & Pacific also was arranged; these roads connected Meridian, Mississippi and Shreveport, Louisiana, crossing the Mississippi river at Vicksburg, Mississippi by car ferry to Delta Point, Louisiana; this trackage was along the "32nd Parallel route" espoused by Jefferson Davis' Pacific Railway Survey 70 years earlier. Approval of these deals was sought from the Interstate Commerce Commission.

Illinois Central accepted delivery on the last of its new 2-8-2 (63 1/2 D; 185 BP; 298,000 TW; 54,158 TF) Mikado wheel arrangements, receiving 12 units (series IC #1971-1982) from Lima at the beginning of 1924. IC #1467 (original IC #1979) shown at top was rebuilt (225 BP; 299,215 TW; 65,868 TF) in 1937 and equipped with a stoker and extended tender. At middle, IC #1468 (original IC #1980) was captured in an undated picture at Jackson, Mississippi. On bottom, IC #1470 (original IC #1982) was caught hauling Local #91 westbound out of Elmhurst around noon on March 26, 1952.

IC4x5-42

After stopping the train, setting up a posed shot (left) and taking the actual photograph (below) were both recorded on film in this instance. On point, IC #1527 (original IC #1973) was captured with its coal consist near Madisonville, Kentucky on May 20/21, 1953; this 2-8-2 engine remained in service until early 1960.

Shown on bottom is IC #1540 (original IC #1981), the penultimate 2-8-2 received from Lima Locomotive. This picture was taken on May 21, 1953 and was used in a story on Louisiana Division steam.

ICNEGGS-41

IC4x5-43

IC45x35-110

IC1924-09

Illinois Central continued in the 4-8-2 Mountain business in 1924, accepting delivery of 17 (series IC #2415-2431) units. The 1924 engines (73 1/2 D; 230 BP; 362,500 TW; 58,389 TF) were products of Lima Locomotive; this was IC's first order from that manufacturer of the 4-8-2 wheel arrangement, and it was Lima's first effort at heavy passenger power. Above are two views of the first of the 1924 series, IC #2415. The topmost picture is a Builder's Photograph from Lima, showing the delivered condition; the second view was snapped at an unknown time and place, but after the bell had been moved; this engine was rebuilt and renumbered to IC #2350 in 1944/1945. The picture on bottom is that of IC ##2416, caught in a publicity photo crossing a bridge while viewed by a bystander underneath.

ICLAG19-04

IC1924-11

IC's 4-8-2 Mountains would be rebuilt/renovated in a number of ways; some of the units had boiler pressure boosted from 230 pounds to 245 pounds; other units had complete overhauls, to one of two standards: the 2300-class (73 D; 275 BP; 384,500 TW; 69,813 TF) or the 2350-class (70 D; 275 BP; 390,500 TW; 73,303 TF), both centered around a new boiler.

This page, three views of IC #2421. On top, IC #2421 pulls it's consist, including its auxiliary tender, by the Cloverdale, Illinois station on January 5, 1948. Right, in a photograph by IC's Mechanical Department Inspector John S. Ingles, the same engine was caught working up a head of steam near the south end of the Champaign, Illinois station in a picture dated to 1932. At bottom, the engine was photographed in like-new condition, sporting the Green Diamond on the tender and the roster number on the cab, a rarely used and short-lived convention.

IC1924-10

IC45x35-122

IC4x5-57

IC1924-12

Illinois Central #2423, at top, was snapped in a yard scene, ready to be fueled and assigned; note the high coping on the tender, which allowed it to hold 22 tons of coal and 10,000 gallons of boiler water; this engine eventually had its boiler pressure raised to 245 pounds. IC #2425 above was caught in another yard view, fueled and ready for work.

On the facing page are two views of Illinois Central #2422, another Lima-built 4-8-2 of 1924. In the top view, IC #2422 was captured crossing over with its passenger train in Fulton, Kentucky. The lower view caught the engine, bell clanging, apparently as it prepared to make way.

IC1924-13

IC1924-14

Three views of IC #2426, one of the Lima-built 4-8-2 Mountains. At top, IC #2426 was caught on lead of Train #16 at Rockford, Illinois in 1949. At middle, the same engine was seen hustling by warehouses in April, 1950; this picture was used by the IC Magazine in a story on Memphis Division steam. At bottom, IC #2426 was captured taking on water at Paducah Shops on August 21, 1958; this view shows the high coping on the tender; this engine was retired in 1960.

IC1924-15

Lima-built 4-8-2 IC #2428, shown above, was captured at Paducah, Kentucky in 1944 just before being rebuilt and renumbered to IC #2300. This unit also had the high-coping on the tender, increasing its capacity.

IC #2429, at left and bottom, was caught in two views, after and before rebuilding, respectively. Note how the air-pumps moved to the pilot, the bell was relocated to the head end, the ladders were changed, a pressed-steel pilot was installed, and the drivers were upgraded to the Boxpok product; an unseen improvement, the boiler pressure was boosted to 245 pounds.

IC1924-01

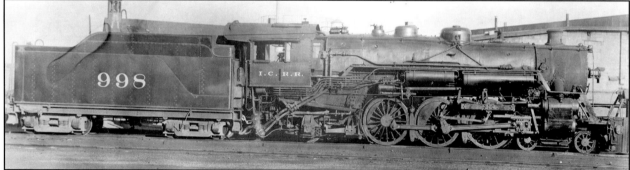

IC1924-02

Illinois Central #998, a 4-6-2 Pacific (later rebuilt to: 230 BP; 293,500 TW; 47,478 TF) began its service life as Alabama & Vicksburg #481 (74 1/2 D; 210 BP; 279,780 TW; 42,212 TF); IC acquired ownership of this unit in the 1926 merger of railroads, and rostered it in as IC #1311; the engine was renumbered in 1937, to IC #998. The top photograph caught the engine stopped at Cherry Street in Vicksburg, Mississippi on July 7, 1941. The lower picture comes from a C.W. Witbeck negative. This engine was superheated; these pictures date 1937 to 1943, the last renumbering (to IC #1131).

IC1924-03

IC #1310, at left, shows another A&V 4-6-2 Pacific (A&V #480) that was acquired by IC in 1926. This engine was rostered in as IC #1310, dating the photograph to between 1926 and 1937, when it was renumbered to IC #997; this unit was renumbered one last time, in 1943, to IC #1130; this engine had the same original dimensions as IC #998 above. The units on this page were Baldwin products of 1924.

Along with its acquisition of the Alabama & Vicksburg, Illinois Central fell heir to a pair of 1924 Baldwin-built 0-10-0 oil-burning switch engines, A&V #430-431. These engines (58 D; 220 BP; 308,300 TW; 92,855 TF) had been erected for the A&V for the specific duty of working the incline at the Mississippi river ferry crossing at Vicksburg. These units were rostered in as IC #3400-3401 in 1926, renumbered to IC #3600-3601 in 1942, and both served until the mid-1950's. They remained oil-burning engines until changed over in 1934; original equipment was Young valve gear and a pair of high-capacity sand domes. The top photograph shows the unit converted to coal, with a tender that held 14 tons of coal and 7,000 gallons of boiler water; the lower picture shows a new tender and higher-capacity sand domes.

ICLAG07-18

ICLAG07-19

Breakwater between 26th St. Shop & 31st St.

ICLAG07-20

Illinois Central work on its part of the Lake Front Improvement agreement continued in earnest. Expenditures on filling in submerged land from 35th Street back north received a lot of attention; the three pictures on these pages illustrate those efforts. All three pictures look north, back toward downtown Chicago, from varying distances beginning at about 35th Street and moving closer to the 27th Street roundhouses of the railroad. On the facing page at top, the building of a breakwater to isolate the submerged lands is shown; the 27th Street roundhouses are noted by the three smokestacks in the middle distance. The lower photograph on the facing page shows a slightly closer view, with emphasis on how the breakwater was filled in with rip-rap. This page shows the closest view to the roundhouses, and depicts the breakwater being filled in.

1925

Field Marshall Paul von Hindenburg was elected President of Germany in April, the first presidential election by popular vote. The Locarno Treaties among the World War I combatants settled the borders of Germany. Greece invaded Bulgaria.

In March 52-year old Calvin Coolidge the 30th President of the U.S. was sworn in for his first full Term. The first national highway – the Lincoln Highway – connected San Francisco and New York, crossing over 3,000 miles through 13 different States. Walter Chrysler renamed Maxwell Motors after himself, Chrysler Motors. There were 950,000 housing starts. Highlighted by appearances of William Jennings Bryan for the prosecution and Clarence Darrow for the A.C.L.U.-led defense, creation and evolution squared off in the trial of Tennessee high school biology teacher 25-year old John T. Scopes – the celebrated Monkey Trial; while convicted and sentenced, the $100 fine was later overturned on a technicality; for an exhausted Bryan, this would be his last public engagement as he would not live to see the end of the year. In September newly-demoted military maverick 46-year old Colonel William "Billy" Mitchell pushed too hard for a separate military branch dedicated to the growing field of aviation – an Air Force; his vision would come true the following year, but so would his five year suspension of rank and pay from the service on being convicted of insubordination; he was posthumously restored to the rank of Major General 17 years later. President Coolidge signed the Contract Mail Act transferring airmail from the U.S. Post Office to private carriers, in essence starting the airline industry. The oldest antecedent of Trans World Airlines was founded in July as Western Air Express. In November Harold E. "Red" Grange, the football superstar of the 1920's, played his last year of football at the University of Illinois, having set numerous records; on leaving college he toured with an all-star team and then promptly signed a contract with the Chicago Bears. Notre Dame's Four Horsemen (Miller, Layden, Crowley and Stuhldreher) played together for the last time, beating Stanford 27 to 10 in the Rose Bowl. The Chicago Cardinals won their first (of two) NFL Championship, beating the Pottsville Maroons. Chicago's first professional basketball team, the Chicago Bruins, was formed. Wally Pipp took a day off from 1st base and was replaced by rookie Lou Gehrig, forever. *New Yorker* magazine was published for the first time. Eliot Ness graduated from the University of Chicago's School of Commerce and Administration. 29-year old F. Scott Fitzgerald published *The Great Gatsby*; he would live but fifteen more years and *The Last Tycoon* would be published after his death. Theodore Dreiser published his classic *An American Tragedy*. 42-year old Lon Chaney starred on the big screen in *The Phantom of the Opera*. Wyoming became the first State to elect a female governor when Nellie Ross was voted into the Statehouse. Having played with King Oliver in Chicago and Fletcher Henderson in New York, 24-year old Louis Armstrong made his first recording with his own band. Lawrence Welk formed a band in North Dakota. Bill Tilden won his fifth straight U.S. Tennis Open, and his sixth overall; he would win one more, a seventh, in 1929. James Buchanan Duke, who was forced by the U.S. Supreme Court to dismantle his tobacco monopoly in 1911, contributed $40 million to Trinity College, which promptly changed its name to Duke University. Chicago gangster Johnny Torrio retired back to Italy and turned over his empire to 26-year old bodyguard Al Capone. Caterpillar rolled out its first tractor. Charlie Chan hit the big screen. Malcolm Little was born in Omaha; in 40 short years on the way to legend he would go from X to El-Shabazz, from Black Muslim to Sunni Muslim, from separatist to integrationist, yet always champion personal integrity and racial pride. The Juilliard Graduate School, a precursor to the Juilliard School of Music, was formed as a legacy to Augustus D. Juilliard. In September the largest hotel in the south opened in Memphis, the 12-story 625-room Peabody Hotel.

Superpower 2-8-4 prototype A-1, with a 4-wheel trailing truck and booster, rolled out of Lima's Ohio works; the A-1 would eventually be purchased by Illinois Central and renumbered IC #7050. Centralized Traffic Control – CTC – was introduced. Diesel-electric power arrived for the first time; a switch engine on the Central Railroad of New Jersey.

Illinois Central broke ground for a major steam locomotive manufacturing facility on 83 acres in Paducah, Kentucky. System mileage remained at 6,243 including the Yazoo & Mississippi Valley. Revenues for the year topped $178.2 million, almost 16 percent due to passenger traffic: 34,490,871 passengers, of which 23,978,647 were commuters riding the suburban service in its last year of steam operation. Rebounding from the previous year, freight tonnage rose to 58.2 million. The locomotive roster rose to 1,915 units with the purchase of 25 4-8-2 Mountain-type locomotives from Lima (Lima's first attempt at heavy passenger units), more than replacing the 19

Lima Locomotive was coming on with a rush, a rush to get into heavy power. Having been a factor with 2-8-2 Mikado wheel arrangements ever since 1915, Lima's first foray into heavy passenger power arrived with its 4-8-2 Mountains in 1924 (delivered in 1924, reported on in 1925); that success was followed with a wheel arrangement that just flipped the 4-8-2 into a 2-8-4, and created the engine that put Lima on the map - Superpower. Lima rolled out its 2-8-4 Berkshire wheel arrangement in 1925 (called simply a Lima on the IC), the A-1 demonstrator; the demonstrator was assigned to the Boston & Albany for tests, and then was shown around the country to potential buyers. As fate would have it, Illinois Central eventually purchased the original demonstrator, and rostered it in as IC #7050, one of 51 units the IC would acquire. IC #7050 was renumbered to IC #8049 in 1941. The original 2-8-4 configuration (63 1/2 D; 240 BP; 388,000 TW; 70,259 TF) later would be boosted with additional boiler pressure (265 BP; 393,500 TW; 77,578 TF). The tender held 20 tons of coal and 15,000 gallons of boiler water.

retirements; 25 locomotives were converted into superheated engines. To relieve pressure on the congested mainline between Carbondale, Illinois and Fulton, Kentucky (steep grades and excessive curves, albeit double-tracked) and the single-track Cairo bridge river crossing, construction of a second main from central-Illinois to the south was undertaken; the 163-mile long Edgewood, Illinois to Fulton line was laid out with a lower ruling-grade (3/10th's of 1% maximum); the Southern Illinois & Kentucky railroad was the subsidiary building the Edgewood Cutoff and, to achieve the desired grade and alignment, would construct three tunnels: #1 at 803 feet long and #2 at 6,994 feet long, both near Ozark, Illinois, and #3 at 2,623 feet long near Grantsburg, Illinois, all three in southern Illinois sandwiched between the Mississippi and Ohio rivers deep in what soon became the Shawnee National Forest; the new line would cross the Ohio river at Metropolis over the Chicago, Burlington & Quincy's 8-year old double-track bridge in which Illinois Central had a one-third interest. The Interstate Commerce Commission approved the Company's acquisition of control in the Gulf & Ship Island. Work under Chicago's Lake Front Ordinance and on Chicago terminal improvements continued throughout the year.

IC1925-01

Eight (series IC #2432-2439) Lima-built 4-8-2 Mountains were received in 1925, following the 17 delivered in 1924 and completing the order of 25 engines. Five of these eight units (73 1/2 D; 230 BP; 362,500 TW; 58,389 TF) would have a 15 pound boost in boiler pressure (to 245 pounds) and one was rebuilt (73 D; 275 BP; 384,500 TW; 69,813 TF) with a new boiler. Above is IC #2433 in a typical yard shot. Below, IC #2435 was captured hauling the Iowan into Iowa Falls, Iowa in an August, 1949 photograph. On the facing page, at top, IC #2436 was caught stopped at Waterloo, Iowa in August, 1949. On the bottom, IC #2438 was snapped in a scene at an unidentified location on the Memphis Division.

IC1925-02

IC1925-03

IC1925-04

July 11. 1923

ICLAG16-01

ICLAG16-06

ICLAG16-02

The pictures on this page all flow from the first, at left; this photograph was captured on June 15, 1925; it shows a section of roadway laid out in all its particulars: from the graded land in the distance, moving to the as yet un-backfilled falsework to create an embankment, to the backfilling operation, to cleared land in the foreground. Two close-ups, below, focus in on the work train with dump cars, showing it to be a double-headed train; the picture also caught the crew on the ground, trying to rerail the apparently derailed second engine. The view at bottom brings the falsework and future bridge opening into sharper relief.

ICLAG16-03

ICLAG16-04

Construction of the Edgewood Cutoff began before 1925 and continued after, but a substantial part of the work was done in 1925. On the facing page is shown an example of the construction method used in building track and its embankment through virgin territory. The upper picture shows preliminary work on the Edgewood Cutoff from 1923; note the raw wood and limbs used, and the unsupported ties spiked directly to the rail sections. This later would be filled in to create the embankment, as shown in the lower photograph; note the bend in the rails where the weight of the dump cars rests, as yet unsupported; as the cars are pulled by a certain point, the man on the ground releases a lever on the cars to dump the fill.

ICLAG16-05

These two pages show different views of the tunnel construction on the Edgewood Cutoff. This page, the top two pictures are of the south portal of Tunnel #1; the first dated August 19, 1925 and the second dated October 13, 1926, showing what the finished product was. The bottom photograph captured the north portal of Tunnel #1 on August 19, 1925.

ICLAG16-07

ICLAG16-08

ICLAG16-09

On the facing page are two views of construction activity on Tunnel #3. The upper view showed early work on the south portal and was dated June 15, 1925; the picture was captured from the steam shovel and showed digging to the portal face. The lower picture showed the same portal but 60 days later, on August 18, 1925; this view showed the beginning of the tunnel at the portal face.

No. From Sta. 1516
Rds 11   6-15-25

So. Portal Tunnel #3

ICLAG16-10

ICLAG16-11

1926

In May, the North Pole was crossed by air for the first time; first by 38-year old naval aviator Lieutenant Commander Richard E. Byrd and 36-year old pilot Floyd G. Bennett in an airplane, and a couple days later by adventurer Lincoln Ellsworth and Norwegian explorer Roald E. Amundsen in the dirigible *Norge* which also crossed the Arctic ice cap on the trip. Labor management disputes in England became an industrial crisis when they escalated into a nation-wide general strike. In August, 19-year old American Gertrude Ederle became the first woman to swim the English Channel. Italian-born motion picture heartthrob Rudolph Valentino passed away in New York at age 31 from acute peritonitis. Hirohito became Emperor of Japan. Chiang Kai-shek rose to head the revolutionary party in China, the Kuomintang.

America would celebrate its sesquicentennial, 150 years since the Declaration of Independence. Route 66 – connecting Los Angeles and Chicago – opened for business. The first coast-to-coast radio-broadcasting network was formed by linking stations, by the newly formed National Broadcasting Company (NBC), a subsidiary of RCA. With the invention of single-strip color film, albeit two-color process, the first successful color movie was made, *The Black Pirate* starring Douglas Fairbanks. Antifreeze was developed for the automobile industry, facilitating driving in winter weather in the North. Thomas M. Rivers showed some distinctions do have a difference when he contrasted viruses and bacteria, launching the field of virology. Moving pictures became talkies with the addition of sound in the first commercial demonstration; it was called the Vitaphone sound system. Congress passed the Air Corps Act and created the Air Corps, an air force separate from the Army. Municipal Airport, renamed Midway Airport after World War II, opened in Chicago (there were a lot of WPA projects at Midway during the depression). The all-metal Ford Tri-Motor aircraft began passenger service. In March 43-year old American physics professor Robert H. Goddard, who already held two patents on rockets, demonstrated the first liquid-fuel rocket, sputtering roughly 40-feet into the sky; his pioneering work was largely ignored by the U.S. government, until the success of German V-2 rockets during World War II. The Book-of-the-Month Club began operations. Boxing's first amateur Golden Glove competition was organized by the New York Daily News, the first bouts held the following Spring. Changing hands for the first time by decision, ex-marine 29-year old Gene Tunney took the heavyweight championship away from Jack Dempsey in ten rounds in front of more than 120,000 in a rainy Philadelphia in September; Tunney would hold the title for two years. In an effort to lower unemployment and check overproduction, Henry Ford instituted the 8-hour day and the 5-day week, thus the 40-hour workweek. 16-year old Benny Goodman debuted with a band in Los Angeles. 27-year old Ernest Hemingway published *The Sun Also Rises* and *The Torrents of Spring*. 41-year old Sinclair Lewis refused the Pulitzer Prize for his novel *Arrowsmith*; four years later he would accept the Nobel Prize for his life's work and become the 1st American to receive the Literature prize. 52-year old Harry Houdini found no means of escape, succumbing to a ruptured appendix.

The Railway Labor Act was passed, a durable and formal mechanism for management and labor to settle disputes. The Chicago, Milwaukee, St. Paul and Pacific Railway auctioned off its assets in November to satisfy creditors; the auction brought $140 million, but eight years later (1934) the new company also would founder.

IC's 75th anniversary. With over 110 miles of track Markham Yard, on the outskirts of Chicago, was completed after eight years of work; locomotive # 6003 a 1919 2-6-6-2-mallet from the Central of Georgia, on its maiden work run on the Illinois Central, was the first engine to push across the Markham yard hump. Charles H. Markham, President since 1911, was moved up to Chairman and 54-year old Lawrence Aloysius Downs was hired as the 14th President of the Company. Illinois Central completed electrification of its suburban lines along the Chicago lake front; the first electric commuter train was put in regular service in August; having eliminated grade crossings by elevating the track south of 50th Street, commuter service now sped along connecting 53 stations. On consolidating the now 330-mile long Alabama & Vicksburg and Vicksburg, Shreveport & Pacific into operations in June, system mileage rose to 6,573. Revenues for the year topped $186.6 million, over 15 percent due to passenger traffic: 34,110,874 passengers, of which 24,555,138 were commuters riding the suburban service in its first year of electric operation. Chiefly due to operation of the increased trackage, freight tonnage rose to almost 61.9 million. Locomotive availability rose to 1,964 (IC's all-time peak; a total tractive force of 81,236,880 pounds, average 41,364 pounds per engine) units with 70 new units purchased (20 ALCO-built 4-8-2 Mountain-type passenger units and 50 freight) in addition to 10 units from the Central of Georgia (7-year old ALCO-built 2-6-6-2 mallets acquired in trade for a

IC1926-08

IC1926-09

Illinois Central #3570 was a 1926 Baldwin-built 0-8-0 (53 D; 175 BP; 221,500 TW; 49,115 TF) switch engine; erected originally for the Chicago & Illinois Western (as C&IW #801), this unit was acquired by the IC in 1950/1951; it was rebuilt (190 BP; 56,500 TF) and remained in service until 1960. It was captured at work, pushing and pulling.

similar amount of Illinois Central 2-10-2's) and 72 engines received from acquired lines, netted against the retirement/reclassification of 103 engines; seventeen engines received superheat during the year. Of the 70 new units, 50 were the first-generation superpower 2-8-4 Lima's (Berkshires in the East) received at the end of the year, the last new road steam power Illinois Central would purchase from outside builders; the 1925-built A-1 LIMA demonstrator was purchased the following year, for a total of 51 of this class; Lima's fit right between two other classes, pulling heavier trains than a Mikado and faster than a Central. Work under Chicago's Lake Front Ordinance and on Chicago terminal improvements continued throughout the year: Markham Yard and suburban electrification being prime examples. Work on the new and improved locomotive facility in Paducah continued, with completion expected the following year.

IC45x35-176

IC45x35-259

IC45x35-209

Three views of the same engine: IC #2456 at top, and as renumbered to IC #2301 in the bottom two pictures. In the lower views, as rebuilt, the pilot is the newer pressed-steel version with new ladders and relocated air-pumps; the sandbox has been refashioned and the cylinders equipped with auxiliary piston valves, allowing in more steam over a longer period to have more efficient utilization of steam; coal capacity of the tender was raised 4 tons to 22 by extending the sides of the tender; water capacity remained at 10,000 gallons. Note in the lower views, one was taken for PR purposes and had the background deleted, while the other was for practice and included two crew members on the ground.

IC accepted delivery of 20 (series IC #2440-2459) Alco/Schenectady-built 4-8-2's (73½ D; 230 BP; 362,500 TW; 58,389 TF), the last new Mountain types to be purchased from outside builders; nine of these units would be upgraded with additional boiler pressure (245 pounds), and three would be rebuilt (two to: 73 D; 275 BP; 384,500 TW; 69,813 TF and one to: 70 D; 275 BP; 390,500 TW; 73,303 TF) with new boilers.

At top, two views of IC #2307 (original IC #2455); in the first, with more than enough supervision, the big 4-8-2 was eased over the turntable at 27th Street shops in Chicago in 1950; in the second picture, the engine was captured dragging MS-1 southbound through North Yard at Memphis in a photograph that appeared in the July, 1952 issue of IC Magazine. In the bottom picture, IC #2351 (original IC #2444) was the 1926 unit rebuilt to 73,303 tractive force; note the 8,000-class tender with extended rear to hold more water. This engine worked between Nonconnah and Bluford, Illinois; this picture dates to November 26, 1947 at Memphis and appeared in the January, 1948 issue of the IC Magazine.

IC1926-05

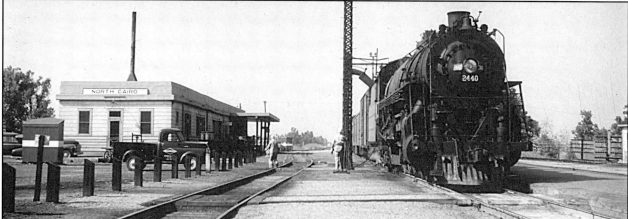

IC4x5-58

IC45x35-121

These two pages, all 4-8-2 Mountains from Alco/Schenectady. This page at top, IC #2440, the first of the 1926 deliveries is shown in two views. Uppermost, the engine was caught hustling its mixed consist through the switch points; the second captured this engine taking on water at North Cairo, Illinois. At bottom, IC #2441 was snapped in near-original condition, with air-pumps still side-mounted. Both engines remained in service until 1960.

On the facing page, the top two views capture the same scene of a trio of Mountain-led Specials at IC's 12th Street station. On top, the view was from the west side of the tracks and caught IC #2443 at ready; after the track to the west filled, the photographer went to the front of the trio and captured a head-end shot of, left to right, IC #2443, IC #2452 and IC #2453; all three were lined and loaded and ready for dispatch. The bottom two pictures show IC #2447 and IC #2452, respectively; the former was caught getting a hosedown at Chicago's 27th Street shops, while the latter was snapped near Carbondale, Illinois in a negative by Gibson. Note the changes in IC #2452 between the second photograph and the last; the pilot has been changed over to pressed-steel and the air-pumps relocated, among other modifications and improvements.

IC45x35-174

IC45x35-175

IC4x5-14

IC4x5-59

IC1926-07

IC4x5-60

IC45x35-132

ICDPL-06

Photo Courtesy of Denver Public Library, Western History Department, Otto C. Perry Photograph Collection (DPL#12311), Denver.

IC1926-10

While the Alco/Schenectady 4-8-2's of 1926 were the last new Mountains from outside builders, the Lima-built 2-8-4 Berkshire-types (simply Lima's on the IC) were the last new road power Illinois Central would acquire from any outside builder; IC accepted delivery on 50 units (series IC #7000-7049) of the 2-8-4 wheel arrangement in October/November, 1926. These 2-8-4 Limas (63 1/2 D; 240 BP; 388,000 TW; 70,259 TF) were the first generation of Lima Superpower; the A-1 demonstrator would be purchased by IC later and rostered in as IC #7050, bringing the fleet to 51 engines. All but one of the 51 units would be rebuilt (265 BP; 393,500 TW; 77,578 TF) and renumbered into the 8,000-series (IC #8000-8049) between 1939 and 1943. All 50 original units came with Type-E Superheaters, Chambers throttle, Baker valve gear, Dupont stokers and Nicholson siphons; the first 40 were equipped with Elesco feedwater heaters, and the last 10 with Worthington feedwater heaters. When renovated in later years, the feedwater heater was removed. The six-axle tender carried 20 tons of coal and 15,000 gallons of boiler water.

IC #7000 at top, the first of the lot, was preserved in a Builder's Photograph; the picture on bottom also was a Builder's Photograph, but of IC #7008 and previously published in the September, 1933 issue of the IC Magazine. The picture at middle caught IC #7004 at Memphis, Tennessee on October 19, 1929.

On the facing page at top, 4-8-2 Mountain IC #2457 was captured near Fulton, Kentucky in March, 1952. IC #2458, on bottom, was caught hustling down a straight piece of track (Allen Richards negative) in a previously seen picture.

IC45x35-133

IC1926-11

ICNEGGS-14

Illinois Central #7011, at top, appeared in the December, 1926 issue of the IC Magazine; it showed the unit as delivered. Note the shields on the pilot that protect the pilot-mounted air-pumps; the air-pumps had been relocated to the pilot when the feedwater heater pump received the side-mount position. The picture at middle caught IC #7015 in the yard; note the air-pump shields had been removed. At bottom, IC #7016 was captured in a standard side view.

ICDPL-07

Photo Courtesy of Denver Public Library, Western History Department, Otto C. Perry Photograph Collection (DPL#12357), Denver.

IC45x35-246

IC1926-12

From the top, three more Lima-built 2-8-4's. IC #7028 was caught on a southbound caboose hop near Ferber, Illinois on August 15, 1940. At middle, IC #7039 was snapped at Paducah shops on October 30, 1932; note the offset bell position, due to the location of the feedwater heater. At bottom, IC #8001 (original IC #7001), one of the first renumbered units, dating to December, 1939; these rebuilt units had feedwater heaters removed and injectors installed in place.

IC1926-13

IC1926-14

Three views of IC #8005 (original IC #7019) on this page. Above IC #8005 was captured at Reevesville, Illinois in a picture dated late-1950; this photograph was used in the Illinois Central Magazine in 1950.

The two views of IC #8005 on bottom caught the same engine months later in a winter scene. Even in winter, the crew had to perform grate shakedowns, as in the picture directly above. In addition, bad weather often made getting locomotive coal out of the car a difficult task, as shown, frozen in place, on right.

IC1926-15

Three 2-8-4 Limas, all rebuilt and renumbered into the 8,000-series. Top to bottom, IC #8012 (original IC #7034) was captured in a static yard shot. IC #8017 (original IC #7010) was caught drifting through an unidentified station; note the relocated bell, with the feedwater heater removed; the pressed-steel pilot also was in view. On bottom, IC #8020 (original IC #7012) was stopped, fueled and ready for assignment.

IC1926-19

ICLAG19-05

IC1926-01

Two pages of 2-8-4 Limas from 1926. This page, top to bottom, IC #8022 (original IC #7009) and IC #8026 (original IC #7040) both caught in standard pose side shots. IC #8029 (original IC #7003), at bottom, was captured at Paducah, Kentucky in August, 1941, three months after being rebuilt. At top on the facing page, IC #8030 (original IC #7046) was caught cruising through a cut on the Edgewood Cutoff leading to the north portal of Tunnel #2 near Abbott, Illinois; this photograph, from a Henry H. Gibson negative, was published as the cover of the November, 1948 issue of the IC Magazine. The picture on bottom was from another Gibson negative; IC #8037 (original IC #7007) was caught in a long cut on the Edgewood Cutoff.

ICLAG19-02

ICNEGGS-44

2-8-4 Lima IC #8039 (original IC #7047) was snapped on the Edgewood Cutoff signal line and published in the December, 1952 issue of the IC Magazine; this photograph was highlighted in a story on IC's ABS (automatic block signal) signal system. The lower picture captured IC #8041 (original IC #7043) just past a major bridge. On the facing page at top, IC #8045 (original IC #7045) was stopped in a June 18, 1951 photograph.

IC1926-20

IC45x35-267

Since a classification yard outside Chicago would remove most railroad operations out of the City center, Markham Yard became an important piece of the Lake Front Improvement plan; the Yard was opened for business late-1926 with a starting capacity of 8,785 cars; final capacity was to be 13,285 cars. The photograph above shows a bird's-eye view of the setup in two of the processing yards with the initial layout, taken from one of the hump towers.

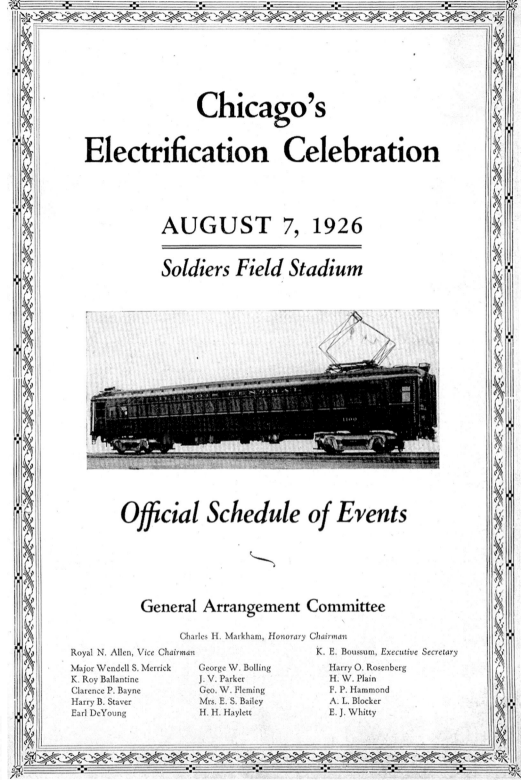

Chicago's Electrification Celebration

AUGUST 7, 1926

Soldiers Field Stadium

Official Schedule of Events

General Arrangement Committee

Charles H. Markham, *Honorary Chairman*

Royal N. Allen, *Vice Chairman*   K. E. Boussum, *Executive Secretary*

Major Wendell S. Merrick	George W. Bolling	Harry O. Rosenberg
K. Roy Ballantine	J. V. Parker	H. W. Plain
Clarence P. Bayne	Geo. W. Fleming	F. P. Hammond
Harry B. Staver	Mrs. E. S. Bailey	A. L. Blocker
Earl DeYoung	H. H. Haylett	E. J. Whitty

ICLAG21-04

The inaugural service on the electrified suburban lines was news in 1926, including public ceremonies at Soldier Field. Above is a print of the program cover used at the celebration. On the following page, at top, is a view of both the old steam locomotive pulled suburban cars and the new electrified commuter equipment; as to the picture, there is disagreement on its date: whether it was from the 1926 inauguration or a reenactment at the 1933 World's Fair a few years later; either way, IC #1401 had been rebuilt for the occasion. The photograph at bottom captured the dress-up of some participants, masquerading as passengers from those earlier days.

1927

In March, with China struggling with internal politics, Cantonese forces shelled American and British missions on Socony Hill in Nanking; having used Communists to aid his own ascension in government, Chiang Kai-shek now expelled them from China; Chinese Communists officially split from the Nationalist Kuomintang, and established rebel bases in the countryside. In May, Minnesota's favorite son 25-year old Charles A. Lindbergh reached Paris non-stop in 33 ½ hours, solo across the Atlantic in the single-engine *Spirit of St. Louis*, and earned the nickname Lucky Lindy; New York to Paris, Roosevelt Field to Le Bourget, no parachute and no radio, simply alone; among other awards he received the first peacetime Congressional Medal of Honor. The British Broadcasting Company – BBC – was founded. The first transatlantic telephone call was made, between the United States (American Telephone & Telegraph) and England (British Postal).

60-year old sculptor Gutzon Borglum began with a team carving with dynamite in the Black Hills of South Dakota; his son Lincoln would lead the workers who finished the Mount Rushmore monument to four U.S. Presidents in 1941. The car radio, while far from affordable by the masses, made its debut. A&W root beer became a taste sensation. Working with Harvard Medical School, Philip Drinker developed what one day would be called the iron lung; postulated 49 years earlier by Frenchman Dr. Woillez, the first practical electric respirator would be installed at Bellevue Hospital in New York City in July. In the first public demonstration, live television was transmitted intercity from Washington, D.C. to New York City, U.S. Secretary of Commerce Herbert Hoover appearing on the screen. 20-year old Idaho farm boy Philo Taylor Farnsworth of Berkeley, California applied for a patent on his "image dissector", his invention of an electronic television system; he was granted patent # 1,773,980 three years later. The first feature-length talking motion picture was released – *The Jazz Singer* with 41-year old Al Jolson. Lita Grey Chaplin and Charles Spencer Chaplin divorced. The Academy of Motion Picture Arts and Sciences was organized, electing Douglas Fairbanks as its first President. Ford replaced the Model T, having sold 15 million copies since 1908, with the Model A, 5 million of which would be produced through 1931. Formica plastic laminate arrived, as did Duncan yo-yo's. 32-year old Babe Ruth stroked 60 homers in 154 games, setting a record that would last for 70 years; Roger Maris launched 61 homers 34 years later but in a 162-game season. In August, President Coolidge surprised Washington by announcing he would not run for another Term. Italian immigrants Sacco and Vanzetti received their sentence to the electric chair in Boston in August for their 1920 crime; among others, Felix Frankfurter, Albert Einstein, H.G. Wells and Jane Addams would demonstrate against their death penalty. In September, an estimated 150,000 fight fans jammed Chicago's Soldier Field to watch Gene Tunney get up from the canvas with a 'long count' in the seventh round to defend and retain his heavyweight boxing title against former champion Jack Dempsey in a ten round decision. In January Abe Saperstein's Chicago-based Harlem Globetrotters took it on the road for the first time – to Hinkley, Illinois. The first underwater motor vehicle tunnel in the U.S., the Holland Tunnel under the Hudson River linking New York and New Jersey, opened for business in November. With the Federal Reserve policy of easy-money and a lower rediscount rate, the year kicked off the march to the speculative zenith. The Mississippi Valley experienced record floods, huge federal relief was hurried through channels. One of the first to cash in on the development of automobiles, Burma-Shave began its roadside ad jingles; the campaign would last over 30 years and produce hundreds of catchy phrases. Founded the prior year by 27-year old Juan Terry Trippe, Pan American World Airways began scheduled international flights flying a route from Key West to Havana. Boeing Air Transport was created to operate mail routes; it would form United Air Lines.

The 4-6-4 Hudson wheel arrangement was first constructed by American Locomotive; this wheel arrangement drew its name from the Hudson River, along which many of these models sped. To tap into the emerging field of air transportation, the Pennsylvania Railroad together with Wright Aeronautical, Curtis Aeroplane, and National Aviation formed Transcontinental Air Transport, which would evolve into the forerunner to TWA three years later.

In the Chicago-area the Markham Locomotive Facility was completed, it included a 48-stall roundhouse; this facility supplemented the two roundhouses at 27th Street closer in the city. Illinois Central completed its new steam locomotive facility in Paducah, Kentucky, where both maintenance and new construction would take place; 4-6-2 Pacific-type #1150 and 2-8-2 Mikado-type #1742 both claimed the title as first to enter, and 2-10-2 Central-type #2741 would be the last steam locomotive outshopped 31 years in the future; all major locomotive construction and heavy repair/rebuilding was moved from Burnside Shops on the outskirts of Chicago to the new facility. With the

IC45x35-141

The only major new equipment change on the Illinois Central in 1927 was the receipt of 15 Baldwin-built 0-8-0 (53 D; 175 BP; 221,500 TW; 49,115 TF) switch engines in the middle of the year; these engines were rostered in as series IC #3540-3554 and would be rebuilt (190 BP; 56,500 TF) in later years. Shown above is the first in the series, IC #3540; this picture was a Builder's Photograph showing the as-new condition.

addition of a net 39 miles of track, system mileage edged up to 6,612. Weeks of torrential rains caused record floods on the Mississippi River, finally breaking the levees at Mound Landing, Mississippi (on the east bank 18 miles north of Greenville) and Pendleton, Arkansas (on the west bank) on April 21st and pouring through the crevasses for the next two months; the final tally showed there were 42 major breaks in levees in Mississippi, Louisiana and Arkansas with flood waters extending over 25,000 square miles; on Illinois Central operations, portions of the Greenville division were shut down for 108 days, while parts of the Vicksburg, Shreveport & Pacific trackage were closed for 41 days; despite experiencing substantial property damage of its own, Illinois Central was active in the rescue effort, sending some 200 relief trains to transport flood victims to safety and Red Cross camps in addition to making equipment available at numerous points for temporary housing. Revenues for the year dropped to $183.0 million, less than 15 percent due to passenger traffic (38,089,266 passengers). Even with the flood conditions, freight tonnage rose to over 63.3 million. Locomotive availability dropped to 1,871 units with the addition of 16 new units (one freight and 15 switching (0-8-0's)) netted against the retirement of 109 engines; eleven engines were converted to superheaters. Chicago's Lake Front Ordinance and the Chicago terminal improvement continued with construction on the new Randolph Street suburban station. Work on the Edgewood Cutoff was nearly complete; the southern portion between Maxon and Fulton, Kentucky opened on April 4th.

The flooding Mississippi river system in 1927 set all the wrong records. The 1927 floods proved "the straw that broke the camels back", forcing Federal authorities to take responsibility for the system, one day through the Corps of Engineers.

Above, Leland, Mississippi (Cleveland District) on April 25, 1927; with the streets starting to flood, everyone began moving to high ground - oftentimes the railroad right-of-way. Below, Rolling Forks, Mississippi (Cleveland District) on May 2, 1927; with rising water, cars and trucks were sidelined and boats became the transportation mode.

Above, stretch of track used as highway near Shaw, Mississippi (Cleveland District) on April 26, 1927; commercial vehicles needed a place to go too. Below, IC continued placing cars and helping move people as on April 30, 1927; the owner of the little boat next to the roadway wrote "loaned by (Gleason)" on the side, just hoping to get it back.

ICLAG03-05

ICLAG03-06

ICLAG03-01

Above, Egremont, Mississippi (Cleveland District) on May 2, 1927 with everything stacked on the right-of-way; this picture appeared in the June, 1927 issue of the IC Magazine. Below, Greenville, Mississippi (Riverside District) on May 1, 1927 with cars set out by IC for refugees; note the new car dealership vehicles parked on the platform at right.

ICLAG03-04

Markham Yard began classifying cars in 1926; it was 1927 when the Markham Yard Locomotive Facility was completed and opened for business. The two photographs below show the progress. On top is a picture from August, 1925 showing the turntable and roundhouse under construction. The roundhouse was designed with 36 100-foot stalls and 12 120-foot stalls, yielding a 48 stall roundhouse; it was to be serviced by a 100-foot turntable. In the picture, the turntable had been poured and the roundhouse was going up. The lower view showed the facility nearing completion in June, 1926

IC45x35-254

IC45x35-253

While there were more than a few major steam locomotive manufacturers over the years, a number of railroads built their own locomotive erection and maintenance shops. For the Illinois Central, while it had operations all over the railroad and some larger facilities in McComb, Memphis, and Chicago (at Burnside Shops), the facilities built in Paducah, Kentucky would always be remembered as the major steam locomotive assembly plant. Besides being capable of maintaining every type of steam locomotive on the Illinois Central roster, this facility also had the ability to erect large steam locomotives from scratch, fabricating all its own parts, as exemplified by the Paducah-built 4-8-2 Mountains (70 D; 275 BP; 423,893 TW; 78,540 TF) of the 1940's (series IC #2600-2619).

ICLAG11-05

In the photograph at top, a previously published picture, the Illinois Central locomotive shops at Paducah, Kentucky are highlighted in an aerial view; it was obvious the facility had come a long way from the original locomotive shops built in Paducah by the Chesapeake Ohio & Southwestern in the 1880's.

On the facing page are two views of labor at Paducah shops, giving a good example of the heavy work that the shop forces could handle. In the upper view, shop floor personnel work on the cylinder casting for a locomotive. In the lower picture, flanged tires are pressed on drive wheels already mounted on axles; the drivewheel set closest to the floor are 55 1/2 inches in diameter, so these were for a freight engine.

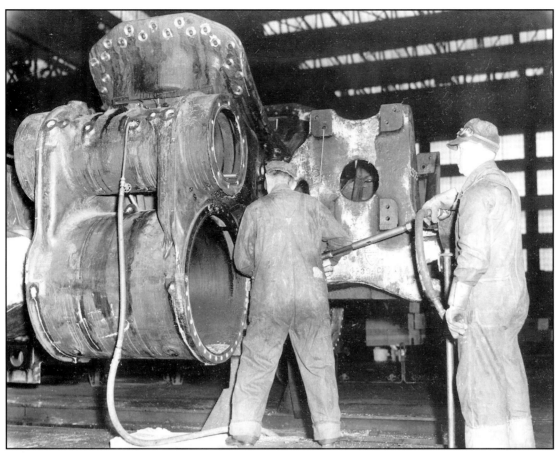

ICLAG11-03

ICLAG11-04

In the photograph shown above Illinois Central personnel gathered around to have their picture snapped with the new 250-ton overhead crane in the background. Illinois Central forces were quite proud of Paducah shops, in general, and of the high capacity crane, in particular. Note in the picture how the crane is holding up an IC 2-10-2 Central-type, whose weight exceeded 380,000 pounds. This picture (Sacra photo for the Illinois Central) was taken in 1926 when the 250-ton crane was installed in the erection room, before the shops opened for business. This view was published in the September, 1934 issue of the Illinois Central Magazine. Identified in the photograph were, left to right, E.S. Rozelle (machine shop foreman), W.H. McGann (mechanical inspector), O.L. Neisler (mechanical inspector), F.R. Judd (engineer of buildings, Chicago), C.M. Starke (master mechanic), L. Robinson (shop engineer, Chicago), O.T. Dunn (assistant engineer in charge), D.J. Jones (mechanical assistant engineer of buildings, Chicago), and H.H. McMeen (mechanical inspector). Paducah shops opened in 1927.

On the facing page is a snapshot of the erection room floor at Paducah shops. When this picture was taken there were 10 steam locomotives in various stages of construction, nine on the erection floor and one suspended in air by the 250-ton overhead crane. The four units on the bottom of the picture were large locomotives: the two closest to the bottom had their frames laid out with cylinder castings attached; the next one up had its boiler mounted; the fourth one from the bottom had its running gear and drive wheels installed, revealing it to be a 4-8-2 Mountain-type engine.

1928

47-year old Scottish bacteriologist Alexander Fleming discovered penicillin and founded the field of antibiotics; not until the 1940's would the mold be proven, perfected and produced; Fleming would share the 1945 Nobel Prize for his work. In the Soviet Union famine brought about by Stalin's modernization began to spread; the famine would claim 25 million. Leading an aerial search, Norwegian explorer Roald E. Amundsen disappeared in the Arctic. In August Naval aviator Richard E. Byrd became the first to reach the South Pole on foot, pushing off across Antarctica from his polar headquarters Little America. 41-year old Chiang Kai-shek, head of the revolutionary party Kuomintang, defeated the warlords, unified the country and became President of China; Communist leader 35-year old Mao Tse-tung built his rebel forces in the countryside. The ninth edition of the Modern Olympics Games was held in Amsterdam, Netherlands, U.S. swimmer Johnny Weismuller won more gold; the Olympics sponsored the second winter games in St. Moritz, Switzerland, 15-year old Sonja Henie of Norway won her first of three golds.

23-year old pianist Vladimir Horowitz made his American debut at Carnegie Hall. In the battle of competing film formats, George Eastman's Kodak determined a minimum of 10mm was needed for optimal image quality and an additional 6mm for perforations, thus arrived 16mm color motion picture film; GE and RCA demonstrated black & white TV for the home. The first animated talking cartoon was released - *Steamboat Willie*, in which Walt Disney introduced Mickey Mouse and performed Mickey's voice. Peter Pan peanut butter and Kellogg's *Rice Krispies* cereal arrived on shelves. Frank Henry Fleer's confection factory introduced *Dubble Bubble* gum and bubble blowing was revolutionized. Gerber baby foods were marketed on supermarket shelves for the first time. Walter Chrysler added the Dodge name to his motor company. In a June landing in South Wales, Boston settlement worker 31-year old Amelia Earhart became the 1st woman to fly the Atlantic, but only as a passenger; she would fly the route solo, in 1932. Speculative fever on Wall Street pushed the markets ahead creating enormous wealth; making money became a national pastime as the markets continued to make new highs. At the 19th Republican convention in Kansas City, lame duck President Calvin Coolidge's Secretary of Commerce, Iowa born Herbert Clark Hoover, won the nomination for President on the 1st ballot; the Party chose Senator Charles Curtis of Kansas as the nominee for Vice President. At the 25th Democratic convention in Houston, New York Governor Alfred E. Smith won the nomination for President on the 1st ballot after Ohio shifted its votes at the end of the rollcall; Senate Minority Leader Joseph T. Robinson of Arkansas was chosen the Vice Presidential nominee of the Party. The Hoover/Curtis ticket won in a landslide in November, Herbert Hoover becoming the 31st President. In local elections, Franklin D. Roosevelt won a narrow victory for the Statehouse in New York with sitting Governor Smith otherwise occupied in the race for President. Brothers Paul and Joseph Galvin acquired troubled Stewart Storage Battery Company and renamed it Galvin Manufacturing, the forerunner to Motorola Corporation. Academy Awards were handed out for the first time by the Academy of Motion Picture Arts and Sciences; the silent film *Wings* won best picture. 26-year old British physicist Paul Dirac predicted the existence of another elemental particle, the anti-electron; four years later 27-year old American Carl David Anderson would find just such a subatomic particle, much like an electron but with a positive charge – the positron.

The six-mile Moffat Tunnel on the Denver & Salt Lake fifty miles west of Denver opened in February, facilitating the connection between Denver and Salt Lake City.

With the addition of slightly over a net 118 miles of track, chiefly related to the Edgewood Cutoff, system mileage rose to 6,731. Revenues for the year dipped $179.6 million, less than 14 percent due to passenger traffic (40,473,220 passengers). Mirroring revenues, freight tonnage dipped to 61.9 million. Locomotive availability dipped for the second consecutive year as retirements outweighed additions: 49 retirements brought the roster to 1,822 engines; 12 units were converted to superheated engines and 403 Mikado-type locomotives had their steam pressure raised from 175 to 185 pounds, both projects raising tractive force. Chicago's Lake Front Ordinance and the Chicago terminal improvement continued with work started to electrify freight service within the city; a new type of locomotive would be required in the next year to utilize the coming electrification; so began the move away from coaling stations, turntables, roundhouses, water plugs, cinder pits, and other such auxiliary facilities. Work on the Edgewood to Fulton line was completed, with service begun in May; besides all the other benefits, Illinois Central's route from Chicago to New Orleans became 22 miles shorter. In June participating with the U.S. Army airship C-52 from Scott Field, Illinois near Belleville in an experiment suggested by Paramount News, mail was successfully transferred in

ICLAG21-26

While there still was money to be made, there still were trips to be taken. During the go-go 1920's, Illinois Central's popular passenger trains saw a lot of use, especially those to Florida destinations.

motion from dirigible to train (IC passenger train #225 between St. Louis and Memphis) near Lenzburg, Illinois. Following up on the record water levels of the previous year in the lower Mississippi Valley, Congress responded with the Flood Control Act; with the U.S. Corps of Engineers dropping its "levees only" attitude, one result was the authorization of a spillway 30-some river miles above New Orleans connecting the Mississippi river to Lake Pontchartrain; the two-year construction of the 5 ½ mile long Bonnet Carre spillway, with a design capacity to divert one-fifth of the Mississippi river volume at flood (250,000 cubic feet of water per second), began the next year; besides building over three miles of spur track to facilitate construction, by 1936 Illinois Central elevated its tracks over each side levee forming the spillway, just in time for the spillways first use in 1937.

1929

While Chinese President Chang Kai-shek struggled to deal with a civil war and a bankrupt Treasury, Russian troops aided by Mongol rebels crossed onto Chinese soil North of the Yangtsze River forcing government troops to fall back. Georges Clemenceau passed away at age 88. Stalin consolidated his power base in Russia; Leon Trotsky, a major player under Lenin found no such favor with Stalin, and was expelled from Russia.

54-year old Herbert C. Hoover was sworn in as the 31ˢᵗ President of the United States in March. 27-year old William S. Paley founded CBS, the Columbia Broadcasting System. Bell Labs researchers staged the first public demonstration of color television in June, transmitting between New York and Washington, D.C. Russian-born American physicist Vladimir K. Zworykin demonstrated his electronic television system in Pittsburgh, some 10 years before it would be introduced to the public; Zworykin also filed for his first patent on color television. With silent films competing against the new sound movies for the first time, the Academy Award for best picture went to the talkie *The Broadway Melody*. Motion pictures were produced with the sound recorded on the video track, rendering synchronization unnecessary. 29-year old Freeman F. Gosden and 39-year old Charles J. Correll, who debuted as *Sam 'n' Henry* in 1925, changed their name because of a legal dispute and premiered as *Amos 'n' Andy* on radio; two white guys pretending to be two black guys, for many too provocative. While frequency-modulation radio had been conceptualized, fruitless experiments with narrow-band FM were discarded in favor of research with wide-band FM, which would be patented and introduced four years later by Edwin H. Armstrong. Dunlop Rubber whipped up a batch of latex with liquid soap and invented foam rubber. Belated action by the Federal Reserve finally slowed the rage on Wall Street, but it was too little too late; on October 29ᵗʰ, the stock markets' over-leveraged, speculative buying frenzy ended with a momentous crash – Black Tuesday. While President Hoover worked to have the states speed up public works projects to keep employment levels from declining, the domino effect of the Crash over the next three years saw banks fail, life savings disappear, factories close, and employment shrink. The Great Depression was here for good, and would last throughout the 1930's. In a November flight that lasted almost 19 hours Commander Richard E. Byrd, with a crew of three (Bernt Balchen, Harold June and Ashley McKinley), became the first to fly over the South Pole and the only man to fly over both Poles. Boeing Airplane and Transport Corporation became the United Aircraft and Transport Corporation; five years later the government would force it to be split in three: United Airlines (transportation), Boeing Aircraft (manufacturing in the Western U.S.) and United Aircraft (manufacturing in the eastern U.S., primarily Pratt & Whitney). Chicago celebrated St. Valentine's Day its own way, with a massacre of six of George "Bugs" Moran's gang members and one bystander in a North Clark Street garage. 30-year old Ernest Hemingway published *A Farewell to Arms*; he would be awarded the Nobel Prize in Literature 25 years later for his body of work. Oxford, Mississippi-born William Faulkner published *The Sound and the Fury*. The Chicago Cardinals defeated the Chicago Bears 40 – 6, former Stanford football All-American and future NFL Hall of Fame member Ernie Nevers scoring all 40 points for the victors. 30-year old Robert Maynard Hutchins became president of the University of Chicago. The cartoon character Popeye premiered. A new lemon drink called 7-Up was marketed for the first time. Texas-born 22-year old Orvon Gene Autry recorded his first hit *That Silver-Haired Daddy of Mine*; the record sold over 5 million copies and Autry went on to add success in movies.

In January the Great Northern Railway completed construction and dedicated one of the longest tunnels in the world, the 7.8-mile long Cascade tunnel; this 41,100-foot long tunnel was built in the State of Washington through the Cascade mountain range on the way to Puget Sound, a crossing roughly 1,200 feet lower than the Great Northern's Stevens Pass; this tunnel replaced a shorter one (2.6 miles) opened 29 years earlier. In June the Great Northern Railway honored its founder James J. Hill in renaming the *Oriental Limited*, and thus inaugurated its *Empire Builder* service on the 2,200-some miles between Portland/Seattle and Chicago.

With a little over 18 miles of retirements, system mileage dipped to 6,712. Revenues for the year edged higher to almost $181 million, a little over 13 percent due to passenger traffic (42,712,964 passengers). Freight tonnage rose to 62.8 million. With an October Crash in the stock markets, the economy would soon feel the pressure; Illinois Central revenues inching higher in spite of it all masked what no one could foresee: revenues would be more than halved before the storm would pass. For the third consecutive year retirements outpaced additions, and locomotive availability dropped: to 1,762 units (1,761 steam and one oil-electric), with the addition of 16 units (15 8-wheeled switchers and a single oil-electric switch engine) and the retirement of 76; 8 units were converted to superheaters

IC45x35-205

During the 1920's Illinois Central passenger business fell off, a fact that IC tried to reverse. Since new bus lines were cropping up and siphoning off travelers, Illinois Central decided to venture in with its own bus service, hoping to grab a share of that market and also feed into IC's passenger trains. The Central Transportation Company was formed as a subsidiary of Illinois Central, and began operations in April, 1929. The first route established daily roundtrips between Dubuque and Waterloo with Bus #8. Shown above is Central Transportation Company Bus #10.

and 20 Mikados received increased steam pressure, from 175 to 185 pounds. Illinois Central's first steps into power alternatives to steam was not without much research: Illinois Central's first was a diesel/electric unit (# 9000) which weighed approximately 108 tons and had twin 300-horsepower diesel engines driving generators to four motors; the second was a Westinghouse-built all-electric unit (#10000) with a weight of 100 tons that produced 1,450 horsepower at the motors from the overhead electric contact system; the third unit (#11000) was a combination suggested by the Chicago electric company Commonwealth Edison - the unit weighed 85 tons with a combined 1,000 horsepower at four motors powered from the overhead catenary system, with the option of running off storage batteries that could be recharged from the overhead system or the twin 155-horsepower diesels included on the unit. Illinois Central made its first steps in offering bus service, instituting a run between Waterloo and Dubuque. A brand new Chicago Produce Terminal began operations, a joint venture of the Illinois Central and the Santa Fe; the original Produce Terminal operation began in 1925. Having held hearings for eight years on a consolidation proposal of the Nation's railroads, the Interstate Commerce Commission adopted it's Plan (Docket 12964) recommending 21 major systems, 19 in the U.S. and two in Canada; the Illinois Central anchored System 10.

IC1929-02

IC1929-01

IC1929-03

The last new steam power of any kind that Illinois Central would acquire from outside builders was a series of 15 (series IC #3555-3569) 0-8-0 (53 D; 175 BP; 231,000 TW; 49,115 TF) switch engines from Lima Locomotive in 1929; these units would be renovated (190 BP; 56,500 TF) later. This page, top to bottom, like kids lined up at the cafeteria, IC #3555 (0-8-0), IC #3668 (0-8-2) and IC #3694 (0-8-2) were captured waiting their turn at the trough; this photograph was used in a story on the Memphis Division in the April, 1950 IC Magazine. At middle, a close-up of IC #3555, the first of the new series. At bottom, IC #3561 in a Builder's Photograph. On the facing page, at top, IC #3563 was caught with three cabooses on its tail. At middle, IC #3568 was snapped with its crew posed; the tender held 9 tons of coal and 9,000 gallons of boiler water. On bottom, IC #3569, the last of the 1929 Limas, was captured in a standard side shot.

IC1929-04

ICNEGGS-18

IC1929-05

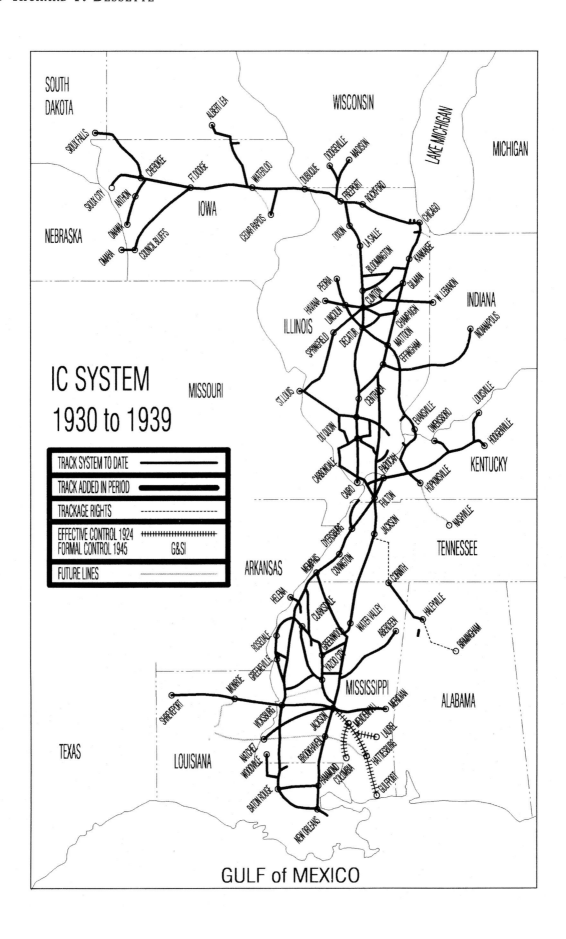

IC SYSTEM
1930 to 1939

TRACK SYSTEM TO DATE	————
TRACK ADDED IN PERIOD	━━━━
TRACKAGE RIGHTS	--------
EFFECTIVE CONTROL 1924 FORMAL CONTROL 1945	++++++++ G&SI
FUTURE LINES	·········

1850's 1860's 1870's 1880's 1890's 1900's 1910's 1920's **1930's** 1940's

The Fifteenth Census of the U.S. population was taken, finding a little over 123 million people in the U.S., a 16 percent increase from the prior census; the country would add almost 9 million people by 1940, less than ten percent through immigration. In thirty years, the U.S. population had increased 50 percent, that of California six-fold. Stalin/Hitler/Mussolini/Roosevelt/Chiang/Mao/Hirohito made preliminary moves; America remained isolationist, while Europe and Asia experienced rising fascism. With the Depression, America began its acronym government: Roosevelt's "New Deal" encompassed Reform in the FDIC, SEC, IRS, and SS; Recovery through the CCC and WPA; Relief in the NRA and AAA. On the cusp of recovery, the Dust Bowl turned the tide - drought and over cultivation; when drought forced thousands of Plains' farmers out, the winds blew across bare land. With flaws in capitalism showing, radical Communists emphasized socialist concepts; so started the red scare. The world took scant notice of the new German politician – Adolf Hitler. Talk of ending Prohibition gained momentum; the five-day workweek became more prevalent; many private golf courses turned public. Rural electrification gained momentum. With new federal highways, suburban development was helped. Art Deco arrived.

In 1930 the major line-haul rail carriers operated a little over 249,000 miles of railroad, a figure that would decline by over 15,000 miles by 1940. Since little was spent on maintaining railroad property, railroads exited the decade with a lot of deferred maintenance; war in the 1940's would exacerbate the situation. With money tight and passenger loads dropping, railroads exchanged sizzle for substance and began streamlining passenger service equipment.

IC fortunes followed the economy; after the costly electrification of suburban service came the Depression, crimping Illinois Central finances; Illinois Central would borrow $35 million from the RFC and another $15 million from the PWA. The locomotive fleet in 1932 was roughly 1,750 - but one-fourth was bad-ordered; one locomotive was repaired by stripping another. Absent funds to purchase new equipment, Illinois Central began a massive program of fleet modernization; by the end of the decade, fleet tractive force had been increased and modernized extensively, with over 1,600 units run through the shops.

GROWTH OF ILLINOIS CENTRAL RAILROAD BUSINESS

Year (1)	Tonnage (mil/tons)	Lumber (mil/tons)	Grain (mil/tons)	Coal (mil/tons)	FFV (mil/tons)	Cotton (mil/tons)	Aggregates (mil/tons)	Passengers Commuters	Miles/Fare
1930	53.6	3.2	2.7	16.7	1.4	.517	7.0	39,697,856 34,885,376	20/$0.49
1931	42.7	2.2	2.3	13.6	1.3	.382	5.9	32,048,888 28,865,360	19/$0.43
1932	33.8	1.4	2.0	13.6	1.1	.432	2.7	24,895,859 22,696,791	19/$0.37
1933	33.0	1.7	2.1	12.4	1.1	.549	2.1	29,569,329 27,434,090	18/$0.31
1934	35.7	1.6	2.1	13.3	1.2	.481	2.5	29,593,979 26,642,319	19/$0.31
1935	37.7	2.3	1.6	14.0	1.2	.635	2.4	25,177,140 22,309,110	21/$0.35
1936	44.8	3.0	2.3	14.9	1.3	.813	3.4	27,878,591 24,464,091	23/$0.37
1937	45.9	2.9	2.0	15.2	1.3	.811	3.4	32,579,109 29,177,372	21/$0.34
1938	39.0	2.0	3.0	12.1	1.2	.673	2.8	30,142,357 N/A	20/$0.33
1939	42.1	2.4	2.2	13.7	1.1	.754	2.7	30,386,365 N/A	20/$0.31

FFV = Fresh Fruit & Vegetables Passengers/Commuters = Total Ridership, and Commuter Portion
Miles/Fare = Average Passenger Trip and Charge (1) Fiscal Year N/A = Data Not Available

1930

Frenchmen Dieudonne Coste and Maurice Bellonte became the first to fly across the Atlantic non-stop from East to West, against the prevailing winds - Paris to New York in a little over 37 hours in September. With unemployment and government deficits rising in the face of decreasing taxes, Germany moved closer to political unrest; President von Hindenburg and Chancellor Bruening pushed financial reforms which various parties in the Reichstag threatened to derail. Montevideo, Uruguay became the site of soccer's first World Cup Championship, Uruguay beating Argentina in the final match for the trophy.

28-year old University of California, Berkeley Professor Ernest O. Lawrence developed the cyclotron, a machine that one day would be called the particle accelerator or atom smasher; Lawrence constructed a small instrument in 1930, and the University built a larger one the following year; Lawrence would be awarded the 1939 Nobel Prize in Physics. The first practical and affordable car radio, a development of Paul Galvin (later of Motorola) and William Lear (later of Lear Jet), premiered. Dr. Waldo L. Semon of B.F Goodrich commercialized a plasticised version of polyvinyl chloride; PVC was one of the first in a series of chlorinated plastics. 28-year old Robert T. "Bobby" Jones, Jr., the only amateur to ever win golf's Grand Slam, stroked his way into the history books and retired from competition at the end of the season. Idaho farm boy Philo T. Farnsworth of Berkeley, California was granted a patent on the *Television System*. Louis Blattner introduced his version of the tape recorder, the Blattnerphone, using a magnetized steel tape instead of a wire. The Great Depression continued as commodity and stock prices slipped once more; drought once again ravaged the West. The Bank of United States, a small New York bank with 60 branches, gained the dubious honor of being the first to close its doors because of the depression; it was only a preview of the massive failures to come. President Herbert C. Hoover struggled to pull the economy out of its tailspin. The Smoot-Hawley Act was passed by Congress, establishing some of the highest tariff rates in history; the Act was credited with deepening the depression. New York Governor Franklin D. Roosevelt was elected to his 2nd Term as Governor in a landslide. In local elections across the country, sentiment to repeal the 18th Amendment regarding prohibition gained momentum and propelled candidates into office. The flavor of politics moved decidedly Democratic with gains in both the House and the Senate. 100-year old Mary Harris (Mother) Jones was laid to rest in the Union Miners Cemetery in Mt. Olive, Illinois. Max Adler donated the Adler Planetarium to the City of Chicago. 24-year old Clyde W. Tombaugh photographed a new planet in the heavens using the Lowell Observatory in Flagstaff, Arizona; the ninth planet in our solar system would be named Pluto; Tombaugh's discovery confirmed calculations made 16 years earlier by Harvard professor Percival Lowell, who built the observatory in Flagstaff in 1894 with his own funds. A vaccine for typhus was developed. *All Quiet on the Western Front* with Lew Ayres and Louis Wolheim won the Academy Awards for best picture and best director; an antiwar movie based on World War I, France and Germany banned the film. 38-year old former Cedar Rapids high school art teacher Grant Wood unveiled his painting *American Gothic*. *Gallant Fox* won the Triple Crown of horse racing, the Kentucky Derby, Preakness and Belmont; *Gallant Fox* was the 2nd horse to accomplish this feat. Boeing Air Transport, soon to be United Air Lines, pioneered the use of stewardesses on airline flights; Ellen Church, an R.N. and graduate of the University of Minnesota, was the first. Transcontinental Air Transport and Western Air Express merged to form Transcontinental and Western Air, the progenitor of Trans World Airways; the Pennsylvania Railroad, a founder of Transcontinental Air, retained an interest in the venture for six years. *Fortune* magazine appeared on newsstands for the first time. Hostess Twinkies and Snickers candy bars appeared for the first time. 24-year old Max Schmeling became the only German to ever hold the world heavyweight championship boxing title when he defeated Jack Sharkey on a foul; this championship bout was for the vacant title, last held by Gene Tunney. St. Paul's 3M (Minnesota Mining & Manufacturing) introduced Scotch (transparent) tape; it was the invention of 44-year old Richard G. Drew, and came five years after he invented masking tape.

Roller bearings came to railroads, first being applied to steam locomotives, beginning the end of brass journal bearings and "hotboxes".

The Vicksburg toll railway/highway bridge opened, rendering the Louisiana & Mississippi River Transfer Company and its ferry boats the *Pelican* and *Albatross* unnecessary; this bridge was the first to span the Mississippi south of Memphis; after Illinois Central locomotive # 3535 pulled a trailer car of dignitaries over the bridge the day before its official opening, the first regular Illinois Central train to cross was headed by locomotive # 3968. With just

ICLAG21-14

Night shots around Congress Street in downtown Chicago became a favorite as a number of trains lined up for duty at the same time. This Kaufmann & Fabry negative (13-3579) for the Illinois Central caught five engines posed just so. Left to right, they were IC #2419 (a 1924 Lima-built 4-8-2 Mountain); IC #1889 (a 1923 Alco/Schenectady-built 2-8-2 Mikado); IC #1194 (a 1920 Alco/Schenectady-built 4-6-2 Pacific); IC #1912 (a 1923 Lima-built 2-8-2 Mikado); and IC #1613 (a 1911 Baldwin-built 2-8-2 Mikado). With the Chicago skyline fronting Michigan Avenue on the left, the overhead electric for the Illinois Central suburban service crisscrosses above the locomotives.

11 miles of net retirements, system mileage dipped to 6,701. The falloff in the economy that began the previous October gained momentum through the year, with record drought in the Mississippi valley compounding matters (nationally, below average precipitation in 40 States and record lows in half of those); revenues for the year dropped 18 percent to $148.5 million, barely 13 percent from passenger traffic (39,697,856 passengers). Freight tonnage dropped to 53.6 million. Locomotive availability edged up by two to 1,764 units (1,754 steam and 10 electric/oil-electric) with the addition of 9 switching units (4 electric and 5 oil-electric) netted against the retirement of 7 engines; 7 Mikado-type locomotives had their steam pressure raised from 175 to 185 pounds and the ten Mallet-types from 200 to 220 pounds, both projects raising tractive force. Chicago Terminal Improvement projects continued, such as the Randolph Street suburban station, albeit at a reduced pace. A 600,000-gallon water tank was erected at Markham Yard, along with almost 2 miles of 16-inch cast iron pipe to access Chicago water. Toward the end of the year, Board Chair Charles H. Markham passed away at age 69.

1931

Spanish republicans overturned the monarchy when 45-year old King Alfonso XIII, the last of the Bourbons, abdicated the throne to avoid violence and sought refuge in England; Niceto Alcala Zamora was elected the first President of the 2nd Republic of Spain. Chinese President Chang Kai-shek's Nationalist forces fought with Mao Tse-tung's Communists elements, Mao trying to rebuild the Communist party. Japanese and Chinese forces clashed over territorial claims in three eastern provinces of China, with Japan invading Manchuria; this was the beginning of a 15-year effort to triumph over China; while Japan would control much of China's coastal territory, it would never conquer the interior. Having jailed Gandhi because of civil disobedience, the British freed him after he staged a hunger strike. With financial difficulties spreading around the globe, nations began hoarding hard assets; worldwide pressure on its currency system forced England to abandon the gold standard and close its stock exchanges temporarily, Austria's largest bank - Credit Anstalt - collapsed, Germany closed its Boerses, exchanges in the U.S. remained open in spite of hundreds of bank failures; the U.S. bank panic spread, over 300 closed in September and 500 in October. Russian-born 48-year old Anna Pavlova, the most famous ballerina of her time, died of pleurisy while on tour in Holland. Italian Premier Benito Mussolini and Vatican leader Pope Pius XI were forced farther apart ideologically as Fascists repressed Catholic organizations.

Dated the last day of 1930, Pope Pius XI issued his encyclical on marriage – *Casti Conubii* – reaffirming the Church's standing on marriage, divorce and birth control. In March in Jackson County, Alabama the Scottsboro Nine were pulled off a Southern Railroad freight train, and accused of heinous crimes; tried (first trial lasted one day) and retried a number of times over the next five years, 8 of the men were sentenced to death, illuminating the condition of Southern blacks; two landmark U.S. Supreme Court decisions worked to set things straight: Powell v Alabama (right to adequate representation) and Norris v Alabama (right to racially inclusive juries); four of the Nine were released in 1936, four more in the 1940's, and the last in 1950. The 102-story Empire State Building opened as the world's tallest, a title it would hold for over 40 years. Construction on Boulder Dam began. Thomas A. Edison died in October in New Jersey at age 84, having been issued a record of over 1,090 patents during his lifetime. Knute Rockne died in a plane crash; his record at Notre Dame was 105-12-5. Schick marketed one of the first practical models of an electric razor. Chester Gould conceived the Dick Tracy comic strip. Record wheat crops in the Great Plains drove prices to all time lows. 32-year old Al Capone, the gang kingpin who rose to power during Prohibition, had a falling out with the Treasury Department; with evidence uncovered by Treasury agents led by the FBI's Eliot Ness and aided by gangster-attorney E. J. O'Hare, Capone was indicted and sentenced to 11 years in prison for income tax evasion; he was released in 1939, and withered away in 1947; O'Hare's son would become a naval aviation hero in World War II, and brand an airport years later. Boeing test flew its first monoplane bomber – the twin-engine B-9. 32-year old Wiley Post and 28-year old Harold Gatty left New York in a modified single-engine Lockheed Vega, the *Winnie May*, and circled the globe in 8 days establishing a speed record that would last until Post broke it two years later in his solo flight. Langley Research Center in Virginia achieved the record of first full-scale wind tunnel in operation in May. The George Washington Bridge over the Hudson River connecting New York's upper Manhattan and New Jersey, the world's largest suspension span, opened in October. The Marx Brothers appeared in *Monkey Business*; Adolphe Menjou and Pat O'Brien in *The Front Page*. The western *Cimarron* with Richard Dix and Irene Dunne won the Academy Award for best picture. Violinist Isaac Stern debuted. Francis Scott Key's *The Star Spangled Banner* became the official national anthem when signed into law by President Hoover. Pearl S. Buck's novel *The Good Earth* was awarded the Pulitzer Prize; she would be awarded the Nobel Prize in Literature seven years later. The heavyweight boxing champion Max Schmeling was stripped of his title when he refused a rematch with former holder Jack Sharkey. To generate income Nevada legalized gambling. Arkansas elected the first woman to the U.S. Senate, Hattie T. Caraway. Grasshoppers ravaged the farms across the country. After a three-year family war, Maranzano finally overcame Masseria, and then met the same fate; the result: New York's new crime boss 34-year old Charles "Lucky" Luciano brought organization to the Mafia, establishing families with particular territories and business specialties. 5-year old Sammy Davis, Jr. was a hit in *Rufus Jones for President*. *Bisquick* biscuit mix debuted on supermarket shelves. Four air transport companies (Varney, Boeing, Pacific and National) joined to form United Air Lines. 36-year old James Thurber's cartoons appeared in *The New Yorker*.

The Baltimore & Ohio Railroad placed the first completely air-conditioned passenger train in service.

With a public relations campaign that dated back to 1920, Illinois Central continued with advertising by having posed pictures taken for various purposes. While activity tailed off during the Depression, many excellent views have been preserved from the 25 year campaign of the Illinois Central. A number of the photographs were taken by Kaufmann & Fabry and by Hedrich-Blessing. At left is a photograph from a Hedrich-Blessing negative (10918A) shot for the account of IC.

ICLAG21-18

With Chicago Terminal Improvements, Illinois Central completed construction of its in-town passenger station for the Chicago commuter service even closer to the City center, located below grade at Randolph Street reaching almost to the Chicago River; the station was not visible from the street level of the City. With a net reduction of 13 miles of trackage, system mileage dipped to 6,688. The decline in business accelerated, fueled by drought, unemployment and bank failures; revenues for the year dropped over 21 percent to $116.8 million, just 12 percent from passenger traffic (32,048,888 passengers). Freight tonnage dropped across-the-board to 42.7 million. Locomotive availability slipped to 1,762 units (1,752 steam and 10 electric/oil-electric) with the retirement of two engines (one freight and one switching); 4 Mikado-type locomotives had their steam pressure raised from 175 to 185 pounds.

1932

Increasing their in-country forces, Japanese troops routed Chinese defenders around Shanghai. Irish Free State members refused to pay England the age-old land annuities, thus heightening tension between Irish Free State President Eamon de Valera and English Prime Minister MacDonald. Germany, continuing to reposition its geopolitical posture, threatened to withdraw from a disarmament conference in Geneva unless its demands were met, setting off yet another early warning signal.

With the resignation of the almost 91-year old Oliver Wendell Holmes from the bench, 61-year old New York State Justice Benjamin Nathan Cardozzo was appointed to the U.S. Supreme Court where he would have influence far exceeding his six-year tenure. Heart specialist A.S. Hyman developed the first practical heart pacemaker, 70 years after electric stimulation was suggested as a remedy for cardiac arrest. Unemployment reached 14 million; the Great Plains experienced drought and over-cultivation of land, resulting in a small wheat crop; crop prices dropped and compounded the small harvest; the drought exacerbated the effects of the Depression; 1932 would be the lowest of the lows encountered in the Great Depression. A new sales tax was proposed to increase funds flow into the Treasury. Sears brought out a gas lawnmower. 40-year old James Chadwick discovered the neutron, the third subatomic particle; the Englishman was awarded the Nobel Prize in Physics three years later for his work. In March, the Lindbergh baby was kidnapped. Samuel Insull, who as personal secretary to Thomas Edison was there when J.P. Morgan formed General Electric out of Edison's dynamo business, followed in the steps of Charles T. Yerkes in building a utility empire; the tightening of money crimped his leveraged companies and Samuel Insull was indicted for the collapse of his utility empire; he would be acquitted. George Eastman ended his business career and took his life at age 77. In May Boston settlement worker 35-year old Amelia Earhart flew solo across the Atlantic Ocean, the first woman to do so; in August she matched that record with a non-stop, transcontinental one – Los Angeles to Newark. It became an all-U.S. Olympic year with both summer and winter games held in the States; in July, the tenth revival of the Modern Olympics, and the first to be held in the U.S. since 1904, opened in Los Angeles with 37 countries represented; Mildred "Babe" Didrikson, in track and field, and Clarence "Buster" Crabbe, in swimming, were two of the stars; in Lake Placid, New York the third Winter Olympics were held; the U.S. won four gold medals in speed skating. Labor gained a nice victory with the passing of the Norris-LaGuardia Act, a federal anti-injunction law that made it harder to stop striking unions. At the 20th Republican convention in Chicago and maintaining a prohibition plank, incumbent President Herbert C. Hoover was nominated for re-election on the 1st ballot; Vice President Charles Curtis was nominated once again for Vice President. At the 26th Democratic convention espousing a prohibition reform plank in Chicago, New York Governor Franklin D. Roosevelt gained the nomination on the 4th ballot; Texan John Nance Garner, Speaker of the House, was chosen his running mate. Events between the nominating conventions and the election would prove critical to voters. Arguments and debate over the Patman Bill which proposed early payment of the $2.4 billion bonus due World War I veterans in 1945 dragged on; some 20,000 mostly homeless ex-servicemen, called the Bonus Expeditionary Force, camped in Washington D.C. When the Bill was passed in the Democrat-controlled House but struck down in the Republican-controlled Senate, a few spats with Capital Police soon escalated into a confrontation with Federal troops and tanks led by Army Chief of Staff General Douglas MacArthur; while the squatters were quickly routed, it was a publicity nightmare for President Hoover's Republican Party. Hoover's Administration also struggled throughout 1932 to reach a compromise between opposing bills to pass legislation approving Reconstruction Finance Corporation (RFC) loans for relief projects. The sentiment was that the Republican Party couldn't propel America out of the national quicksand of depression. As a result, the Roosevelt/Garner ticket won in a landslide in November carrying 42 of the 48 States; Democrats swept into power in both Houses, just shy of the 2/3rd majority in the Senate. With the elections, prohibition reform took a huge step forward; Congress ended the year with a joint resolution proposing an amendment to repeal national prohibition. The Tomb of the Unknown Soldier was dedicated at Arlington National Cemetery. Babe Ruth hit his debatable "called shot" home run at Wrigley Field off Chicago Cubs pitcher Charlie Root in the third game of the 1932 World Series; this was the Babe's last home run in a World Series. Chicago-born Florenz Ziegfeld who created and produced 22 editions of the *Follies* musical revue passed away in Hollywood at age 65. The *George Burns and Gracie Allen Show* premiered on radio, as did a 38-year old comic in *The Jack Benny Program*. *Grand Hotel*, a film starring John and Lionel Barrymore, Wallace Beery, Joan Crawford and Greta Garbo, won the Academy Award for

ICLAG21-16

With the City of Chicago at its feet and an Illinois Central 4-8-2 Mountain aimed for downtown, the running gear was caught "rods-down". The photograph faces north and frames the City center.

best picture. Aldous Huxley published his *A Brave New World* in the U.S. Purdue basketball star John Wooden became a three-time All-American. 30-year old Jack Sharkey regained the heavyweight boxing title from the German fighter Max Schmeling. With over 6,000 seats, Radio City Music Hall opened with the claim of world's largest movie theatre. *Zippo* lighters appeared for the first time, as did *Frito* corn chips and *Skippy* peanut butter.

Seizing the initiative during the Depression, the Southern Pacific gained majority control of the Cotton Belt, the St. Louis Southwestern Railway. Three years earlier the Interstate Commerce Commission recommended consolidation (Docket 12964) of the eastern railroads into five major systems in order to institute a new financial and economic base in the troubling times; the major carriers eventually countered with a plan which would assemble four main systems, and it was a variant of this plan that the Commission approved, establishing the New York Central, the Pennsylvania, the Baltimore & Ohio and the Chesapeake & Ohio-Nickel Plate as the four primary systems.

With a scant 12 miles of trackage retired, system mileage dropped to 6,676. After annual declines of 18 and 21 percent, the Company booked a considerable 23.5 percent reduction, revenues for the year just topping $89.3 million, barely 10 percent from passenger traffic (24,895,859 passengers). Reflecting the prevailing conditions, freight tonnage dropped to 33.8 million. Locomotive availability dipped to 1,760 units (1,750 steam and 10 electric/oil-electric) with the retirement of 2 units (one freight and one switching); the steam fleet had a total tractive force of 78,531,213 pounds, average 44,880 pounds per engine. Trapped in the credit abyss, Illinois Central's Central of Georgia subsidiary entered receivership; it would be written off the books ten years later. In an effort to further reduce expenses, an across-the-board ten percent wage reduction was put in place; this cut would be fully restored within four years.

1933

Japan continued its invasion of China (practice for a bigger conflict), the government in Nanking admitting defeat. In a series of astonishing steps, the playing field in world politics changed. 43-year old Adolph Hitler's Party came to power in Germany, Hitler was appointed Chancellor, and Germany dropped out of the League of Nations and the Disarmament Conference. Seeing Hitler's international success in establishing German independence, Irish Free State President Eamon de Valera began posturing for an Irish Republic, secession from the British Empire. Sixteen years after it was fashioned out of the ruins of World War I on the heels of the Bolshevik Revolution, the Soviet Union gained official recognition from the U.S. when diplomatic relations were resumed. With war reparation payments straining the economy, Italian Premier Mussolini and the Fascist Grand Council hinted they might withdraw from the League of Nations; Japan did so. Oil was discovered in Saudi Arabia.

In January the 20th Amendment to the U.S. Constitution was ratified, formalizing the dates of national officeholder terms and the succession rules for President and Vice President; Utah made it official when it became the 36th State to ratify the Amendment; Virginia had been the 1st to ratify, Florida the 45th and last. FM-radio broadcasting was developed by 43-year old Edwin H. Armstrong; frequency-modulation significantly reduced the static associated with amplitude-modulation. Bell Laboratories researchers made the first efforts recording music on two channels, and stereophonic sound was born; it would be seven years to a single-groove recording system. *Cavalcade* won the best picture and best director Academy Awards. *King Kong* with Fay Wray was released in Hollywood. 5-year old Shirley Temple signed with Fox Studios. 18-year old Billie Holliday (nee Eleanor Gough McKay) made her debut recording, with 23-year old Benny Goodman. With the question "Who's afraid of the big bad wolf?", Disney released the *Three Little Pigs*. *Newsweek* magazine appeared for the first time; *Sanka* coffee, *Ritz* crackers and *Windex* window cleaner all made their supermarket debut. 26-year old German-born Ernst Ruska developed an electron microscope with magnifications finally surpassing those of optical microscopes, revealing a whole new world under our noses; Ruska and Max Knoll began exploration in 1928 and demonstrated a small machine in 1931. Chrysler Motors outsold Ford. The Boeing Model 247 with seats for ten and a cruising speed of 160 mph, arguably the first modern passenger airplane, took its maiden flight at Boeing Field in Seattle; Douglas Aircraft's answer to the Boeing 247 was the DC-1, which entered service later in the year. The last rigid airship built in the U.S. was commissioned, the *USS Macon*. Wiley Post became the first to circle the globe solo, still flying his beloved single-engine Lockheed Vega, the *Winnie Mae*. Chicago's second World's Fair - the Century of Progress Exposition - opened on the lake front in May right in the middle of the Depression; 40 years after the Columbian Exposition and 100 years since Chicago was organized, the Century of Progress would span the sublime to the ridiculous: the Exposition would receive over 35 million visitors over two summers, and 29-year old Sally Rand (nee Helen Beck) would be dragged into Court for her fan dance with ostrich feathers (she won). Introduced at the same time as the Century of Progress, the last building from the 1893 Columbian Exposition, the Palace of Fine Arts, reopened as the Museum of Science and Industry. Organized to coincide with the Exposition, Comiskey Park was the site of the first All-Star Baseball game; the American League won the inaugural event 4 to 2, Babe Ruth hitting the first All-Star home run. The first national amateur softball tournament was held at the World's Fair, taking the game to a broader stage; the Amateur Softball Association was formed, bringing national organization and uniform playing rules. Chocolate chip cookies were a taste sensation. There were 90,000 housing starts. The Plains states continued to experience drought with the crop blowing away in the wind. In early-1933, Giuseppe Zingara traveled from his home in New Jersey to Miami and fired five shots in an attempted assassination of President-elect Franklin D. Roosevelt, fatally wounding Chicago Mayor Anton J. Cermak instead. In March, 51-year old Franklin D. Roosevelt became the 32nd President of the U.S. and promptly waged war on the depression with the New Deal – jobs and economic programs. With 25 percent unemployment and some 9,000 bank failures along with 24 States having declared bank holidays to date, the Great Depression was in full bloom; to fight hoarding and panic withdrawals, President Roosevelt in March ordered a four-day national bank holiday and, following England's lead two years earlier, struggled with the problems caused by a gold standard by placing an embargo on gold. In March in order to let the public know his plans concerning the bank situation President Roosevelt broadcast his first Fireside Chat. Later in the year the Federal Deposit Insurance Corporation – FDIC – was created to insure bank deposits and stem panic withdrawals. To strengthen the banking system, commercial banks were prohibited from underwriting securities issues, by the new Glass-Steagall Act – the Banking Act of 1933; this eventually forced J.P. Morgan & Company to break into two firms: Morgan Guaranty Trust Company and Morgan, Stanley & Company. The National Labor Relations Board was created to deal with labor issues. In March/April the first Civilian Conservation Corps camp opened; over the next 9 years the CCC would open over 2,500 camps and provide work for 2.5 million men under the age 25. In May Congress created the Tennessee Valley Authority, the first Federal effort at rural electrification. Congress passed the Securities Act of 1933 that required truthful statements in securities filings. In September 54-year old German physicist Albert Einstein fled Nazi Germany for the U.S., settling in Princeton, New Jersey. In December the 21st Amendment to the Constitution repealed the 18th Amendment in effect since January 1920, becoming the only amendment to repeal another when it abolished national prohibition after almost 14 years as an unsuccessful experiment; Utah was the 36th and deciding state to ratify the Amendment, Michigan the 1st, Montana the 38th and last, while South Carolina rejected the proposal and never did ratify. Milk with vitamin D added arrived on supermarket shelves. 26-year old Primo Carnera took Jack Sharkey's heavyweight boxing title with a 6th round KO in New York. Mount Holyoke graduate and Jane Addam's Hull House activist Frances Perkins became the first female cabinet member when Franklin Roosevelt named her Secretary of Labor.

With roughly 18 miles of retirements, system mileage dropped to 6,658. On the heels of three straight years of substantial declines in revenues, results steadied for the year as revenues dipped less than 2 percent to $88.0 million, just 10 percent from passenger traffic (29,569,329 passengers); passenger traffic during the year rose 19 percent, primarily due to the Chicago World's Fair business. Freight tonnage dipped to 33.0 million. Locomotive availability slid to 1,757 units (1,747 steam and 10 electric/oil-electric) with the retirement of three units and no additions. Five years after agreeing to build its newest and largest airfield on 22,000 acres of cotton outside Shreveport, the Army Air Corps' Barksdale field was formally dedicated; built as a training base and aerial range the future Barksdale Air Force Base, hard by the Illinois Central tracks, was named after Goshen Springs, Mississippi-born Lieutenant E. H. Barksdale who died at age 28 while testing aircraft.

The big news of 1933 was the opening of Chicago's second World's Fair, in the middle of the greatest depression the Country would ever experience. Coinciding with the World's Fair, Illinois Central facilitated the construction of a connecting line over its property at 12th Street; IC allowed the Chicago Surface Lines coming across 12th Street (Roosevelt Road) to build their lines right through Central Station and to vault over IC tracks; this joined the City side of its tracks with the trolleys on the Lake side of the tracks. On the next two pages are four pictures of the opening of the Chicago Surface Line tracks (August 1, 1933). Top to bottom, the first photograph shows the inaugural car approaching the ramp from the west on 12th Street. The second view shows the first trolley up close, with Chicago's Mayor Kelly leaning on the window frame next to the operator. The third picture views the new tracks from the east side of the IC property, looking back at Central Station; the Surface Line tracks through the trainshed roof are visible. The last photograph was taken from the rooftop of Central Station and shows the trolley tracks vaulting over IC lines; Soldier Field is visible on the far right, with the Field Museum to its left; the Mayor Kelly inaugural car is barely visible under the Museum.

ICLAG21-20

IC45x35-06

IC45x35-17

12 st. aug 18T 33

ICLAG21-21

1934

In Vienna in an escalating display of instability, Austrian Nazis assassinated Austrian Chancellor Engelbert Dollfuss. German President von Hindenburg, the only balance to extreme Nazism, passed away at age 86; Chancellor Hitler assumed the duties. Over 25,000 Chinese communists, the peasant Red Army under Mao Tse-tung began their long march retreat of some 6,000-miles; the Long March would end one year later. Russia joined the League of Nations, while Japan became increasingly hostile toward the U.S. and England. Italy was the host nation for soccer's second World Cup Championship, Italy defeating the team from Czechoslovakia in the final. Anastasio Somoza took control of Nicaragua, and promptly assassinated his rival former revolutionary 39-year old Augusto Sandino; 45 years later Somoza's son would be overthrown by a group known as - Sandinistas.

Federal Communications Commission was born. To further regulate trading in the securities industry Congress passed the Securities Act of 1934; the Securities Exchange Commission was created, the SEC; Joseph P. Kennedy became the first Chairman of the SEC. Arthur H. Compton at General Electric developed the first practical fluorescent light bulb, 75 years after French scientist Alexandre Edmund Becquerel produced phosphorescence. Dupont announced the invention of a new fiber, one day called nylon, by 38-year old organic chemist Wallace Hume Carothers; it would be four years before it was commercialized but the Iowa-born University of Illinois doctoral graduate never lived to see its success, dying at the early age of 41 when he took his own life. The Plains states experienced another year of drought, dust and a failed wheat harvest; Vinita, Oklahoma experienced more than 36 consecutive days of temperatures exceeding 100 degrees; the Plains States watched their land blow away, experiencing a "black blizzard". Outside the Plains states, agricultural efforts to cut production and raise prices were somewhat successful, farm incomes experiencing a temporary rise. The Douglas Aircraft DC-2 entered service. Muzak Corporation, which would later begin playing scientifically chosen music to captive audiences, was formed; originally projecting moods, it later scheduled stimuli. In 1933 the U.S. Justice Department began an intensive drive against organized crime, and results came fast: in May, 24-year old Clyde Barrow and Bonnie Parker were brought down in Illinois Central country near Gibsland, Louisiana outside Shreveport; in July, John H. Dillinger, a 31-year old from Indiana who was one of the first to earn the moniker Public Enemy No. 1, was shot as he left the Biograph Theater movie house in Chicago by agents of the Department of Justice led by Melvin H. Purvis; Purvis followed up that feat with the shooting of the new Public Enemy No. 1 Charles "Pretty Boy" Floyd in Ohio in October; proving many things come in threes, Federal Agents added the recently-promoted No. 1 George "Baby Face" Nelson to the retirement list in November in a Chicago suburb. The Chicago Blackhawks won their first Stanley Cup. The first College All-Star game was played to a tie against the Chicago Bears. 25-year old Max Baer gained Primo Carnera's heavyweight boxing title with an 11th round TKO, when the referee stopped the fight; as the third fighter to hold the title in as many years, he also would retain it for a single year. Ernest O. Lawrence received patent #1,948,384 on the cyclotron, *The Method and Apparatus for the Acceleration of Ions*. *The Bob Hope Show* premiered on radio. Frank Capra's *It Happened One Night* with Claudette Colbert and Clark Gable opened on the big screen; it swept best picture, director, actor and actress Oscars at the Academy Awards; 6-year old Shirley Temple received a special award and became the Academy's youngest winner. The Dorsey Brothers started a new band; one year later Tommy and Jimmy would split to form their own bands; they would reunite 18 years later. Kirstein and Balanchine founded the School of American Ballet. Ernest and Julio Gallo began their involvement in the wine business. Alcatraz went from being just a rocky island to a maximum-security prison. The character *Donald Duck* was rolled out by Walt Disney; *Flash Gordon* appeared in comic strips. The University of Michigan won the national championship in football; center Gerald R. Ford, who would become the only appointed U.S. President forty years later, was the team's MVP. Upon the disappearance of Wallace Fard Muhammad, 37-year old Elijah (Poole) Muhammad became the leader of the Nation of Islam.

The Chicago, Burlington & Quincy and Union Pacific pioneered the use of diesel-electric locomotives on main-line passenger trains. By improving the diesel engine, Charles Kettering invented the first lightweight, high-speed diesel locomotive; using his engine design, the Chicago Burlington & Quincy's diesel-powered, stainless steel three-car streamliner *Zephyr*, built by the Budd Manufacturing Company, set the record between Denver and Chicago, covering a little over 1,000 miles in just over 13 hours. In an experimental run Union Pacific's diesel-powered *City*

ICLAG21-15

Another view of steam engines lined up for duty, in a night shot; the units in the middle were both 4-8-2 Mountain-types (IC #2530 and IC #2516, respectively). This picture was from a Hedrich-Blessing negative (11795) taken for the account of Illinois Central.

of Portland covered the 3,258 miles between Los Angeles and New York City in 56 hours and 55 minutes, a single-train record yet to be beaten. The Milwaukee Road faced receivership yet again.

Panama Limited, stopped two years earlier during the Depression, resumed operation in December. With the retirement of 61 miles of track, system mileage dropped to 6,597. After four straight declines, a rebound was in order as revenues for the year rose to $91.1 million, a scant 10 percent from passenger traffic (29,593,979 passengers). Showing greater strength than revenues, freight tonnage rose to 35.7 million. Locomotive availability slipped to 1,754 units (1,744 steam and 10 electric/oil-electric) with the retirement of three units (one passenger and two switching) and no additions; 21 boosters were removed from Lima-type freight locomotives, decreasing tractive power 12,000 pounds each. In a supplemental contract with the Public Works Administration the Company funded the purchase of eleven diesel locomotives (for switching and transfer work in Chicago) and ordered a single diesel-powered streamlined train (the future *Green Diamond* for operation between St. Louis and Chicago); the original contract with the Public Works Administration funded, among other things, the relining of Tunnel Number 3 in Reevesville, Illinois which would be completed the following year. With the Federal Government building floodways in an attempt to manage the level of the Mississippi river, Illinois Central began construction on trestles to provide openings for the floodways; one and one-half miles of single-track trestle were planned near Sellers, Louisiana and more then 2 miles of double-track trestle near LaBranch, Louisiana. The Cairo river bridge approaches were substantially rebuilt with Public Works Administration funding; the first trains over the new construction took place early the next year.

1935

Canadian Joseph Bombardier built the first snowmobile. In February British physicists 42-year old Robert Watson Watt and colleague Arnold F. Wilkins developed the forerunner to Radio Detecting and Ranging (RADAR), which would prove decisive in the Battle of Britain in World War II. Adventurer Lincoln Ellsworth became the first to fly coast-to-coast across Antarctica, flying 2,400 miles in the Northrop Gamma *Polar Star* and within 25 miles of Commander Richard E. Byrd's abandoned polar base camp Little America. North Africa became a geopolitical point of contention as Italian Premier Mussolini began trouble for Emperor Haile Selassie by invading Ethiopia. Reza Pahlevi decided he didn't like the name Persia, and promptly became the Shah of Iran. Germany hinted at the future: breeding programs were established to create a perfect race and Nuremberg laws were passed to prevent intermarriage. 47-year old T.E. Lawrence, the once and future *Lawrence of Arabia*, died in a motorcycle accident back home in Dorset, England.

35-year old American geologist Charles W. Richter formulated a measurement to show the magnitude of ground waves generated by earthquakes, later named after him. In February Bruno Richard Hauptmann was found guilty of the Lindbergh baby murder. AEG introduced the tape recorder. In May President Roosevelt established the Works Progress Administration (WPA) creating jobs and training for the unemployed; while it could occupy roughly three million workers at any one time, over nine million would benefit from this Program over the next eight years. Boulder Dam was completed harnessing the Colorado River, creating Lake Mead and connecting Nevada and Arizona; authorized by Congress in 1928, construction began in 1931 and ended in 1935; its name would be officially changed to Hoover Dam twelve years later. The National Labor Relations Act was passed by Congress; providing for collective bargaining, it was a victory for labor. In August President Roosevelt signed the Social Security Act; the first effort to provide retirement income was based on ideas by U.S. Supreme Court Justice Louis Brandeis; fifteen days after the Social Security Act, the President signed the Railroad Retirement Act. Crops in the Plains States withered in the dust and drought; the term 'dust bowl' was coined to describe the area (consisting of parts of Colorado, New Mexico, Nebraska, Kansas, Oklahoma and Texas). Still smarting from the misery of World War I, Congress began passing a series of Neutrality Laws aimed at keeping America out of Europe's "Gathering Storm". In June Alcoholics Anonymous was organized. Humorist Will Rogers and globe circling aviator Wiley Post died in an airplane crash near Point Barrow, Alaska. In September, Louisiana Senator Huey P. "Kingfish" Long, while campaigning for the 1936 Presidential nomination in Baton Rouge, was assassinated by 29-year old doctor Carl A. Weiss. Wracked by internal strife and dissatisfied with AFL representation, the Mine Workers and Clothing Workers unions broke away, after the United Mine Worker's John L. Lewis was expelled from the AFL; they formed a more aggressive bargaining unit, the forerunner to the CIO, to expand the labor movement beyond skilled craftsmen; the AFL was arranged craft by craft, while the CIO was structured industry by industry. The DC-3 arrived in December with the first flight by American Airlines from Clover Field in Santa Monica; initially equipped with sleeping berths, it later was outfitted with 21 passenger seats and more than 10,000 were produced for assorted service; it was called variously: an RAF Dakota, a Navy R4D or an Army C-47 in military versions. Pan Am Airways inaugurated commercial aviation across the Pacific Ocean; its 'China Clipper' fleet service was 59 hours from San Francisco to the Philippines. Mississippi-brothers Algene and Fred Key set the endurance record staying aloft for 27 days in the single-engine *Ole Miss*, being refueled and supplied while in flight until landing at the Meridian, Mississippi airport. Parker Brothers came out with the board game Monopoly (patented by Charles Darrow) in a perfect example of art imitating life following the Great Depression. 28-year old James J. Braddock won the heavyweight boxing title by flattening Max Baer. After losing the championship title to Braddock, Baer went from bad to worse; working to climb back into contention and get a rematch for the title, Baer agreed to fight a little known newcomer, 21-year old Joe Louis. Jay Berwanger of the University of Chicago Maroons took home the first *Heisman Trophy*; the next year he would be the first selection in the first NFL football draft, yet he would decide against playing as a professional. The first Orange Bowl was played with Bucknell shutting out the University of Miami 36 to 0; two years earlier it was called the Palm Festival and Miami beat Manhattan College 7 to 0. In January in the first edition of the Sugar Bowl, Tulane edged Temple 20 to 14 in New Orleans. Ohio State University's Jesse Owens set four world records in a single track meet; he would win that many gold medals the next year in Berlin. Major league baseball played its first night game, in Cincinnati. Beer was marketed in cans for the first time. 39-year old Ira and 37-year old George Gershwins' musical

Porgy and Bess arrived; unbeknownst to George, he had only two creative years left. Prontosil hit the market as the first "wonder drug"; its wonder properties would later be found to be due to a chemical discovered in 1908, sulfanilamide. With the development of the three-color camera, the first full-color feature-length movie was made, *Becky Sharp*. *Mutiny on the Bounty* with Charles Laughton and Clark Gable won the best picture Academy Award. *Fibber McGee and Molly* premiered on radio. Count Basie formed a band in Kansas City. *Omaha* won the Triple Crown of horse racing, the 3rd horse to accomplish the feat, and the first son to follow in his father's footsteps (1930's winner Gallant Fox). *Real Lemon* and the *Jolly Green Giant* became fixtures on supermarket shelves. 34-year old George Horace Gallup founded the American Institute for Public Opinion, the genesis of the Gallup Poll.

Elvis Presley was born in January in Tupelo, Mississippi, hard by the Illinois Central. The long-challenged Alfred I. DuPont estate was settled after taxes at $31 million; part was used to buy 53 percent of the Florida East Coast Railroad. The 4.4-mile long (including approaches) Huey Long Bridge across the Mississippi River above New Orleans opened in December; when dedicated it was the longest steel/concrete railway-highway bridge in the U.S. The Milwaukee Road introduced 100-mph steam-powered service between Milwaukee and Chicago, the streamlined *Hiawatha*.

With the retirement of nine miles of trackage, system mileage dropped to 6,588. With the failure of the Minneapolis & St. Louis railroad, the Company negotiated with the Reconstruction Finance Corporation to acquire a 99-mile segment from Albert Lea to Hopkins, Minnesota just west of the Twin Cities with the Chicago & Northwestern; application to the Interstate Commerce Commission was filed, but Illinois Central never would gain access to this line. While still in the doldrums, the economy continued to steady as revenues for the year approached $97.5 million, a scant 9 percent from passenger traffic (25,177,140 passengers). Even with the smallest corn crop in 60 years from the harvest limiting the rebound, freight tonnage rose to 37.7 million. Locomotive availability dropped to 1,532 units (1,514 steam and 18 electric/oil-electric) with a heavy retirement program of 230 units (79 passenger, 111 freight and 40 switching) netted against the addition of 8 oil-electric switch engines purchased with Public Works Administration loans. It now had been seven years since Illinois Central purchased new steam power; as management could see the light at the end of the depression with the forecast upturn in business, the choice was to purchase new locomotives or modernize the existing fleet, and modernize was the choice of Floyd R. Mays the Company's 56-year old General Superintendent Motive Power. Thus began Illinois Central's program of fleet modernization which eventually would take in nearly every locomotive during an eleven-year program carried out at Paducah and other outlying shops; in time, modernization would encompass increased boiler pressure, mechanical stokers, new main drivers, and force-feed lubricators among other improvements; increased power was affected chiefly through higher steam pressure, which directly translated into a boost in tractive force with little increase in fuel consumption; higher steam pressure led to automatic stokers for more coal on the fire, a bigger grate on which to burn the coal, more water to use the added heat and make more steam, larger tenders to carry more water and coal supplies and strengthening and reinforcing the entire locomotive unit to sustain the increase in expansive force. In the first year of the modernization program, steam pressure was raised on 12 Mountain-type (4-8-2) and 93 Pacific-type (4-6-2) locomotives, and boosters were removed from 13 Lima-type (2-8-4) freight locomotives, lowering tractive force but simplifying maintenance. Almost four miles of trestle were completed in Louisiana to provide for the Mississippi river floodway.

1936

German engineer Dr. Heinrich Focke produced a working helicopter. In January in the 26th year of his reign, 71-year old King George V passed away in his sleep; the 41-year old Prince of Wales became Edward VIII, a throne he would renounce for Mrs. Wallis Warfield Simpson by the end of the year, whereupon his brother would ascend to the Throne. Germany repudiated the Treaty of Versailles and the Locarno Treaty. Hitler's troops entered the demilitarized Rhineland unopposed, since maintaining a demilitarized zone was an untenable position for France. Hitler followed up troop movements with an offer of a 25-year non-aggression pact. Italians conquered Ethiopia in Spring, Mussolini declaring it the dawn of the 2nd Roman Empire; on May 9th, Premier Mussolini declared a new colony, Italian East Africa. 16-year old King Farouk ascended to the throne of Egypt. Having meddled in Chinese affairs for years, including North China autonomy and Chang Kai-shek's Kuomintang (Nationalist Party), Japan withdrew most of its demands; a quiet before the storm. In Berlin at the eleventh edition of the modern world Olympics, Germany held the first Olympics to be televised, just in time for American Jesse Owens to embarrass Hitler's master race by winning four gold medals. The fourth edition of the Winter Olympic games was held in Garmisch-Partenkirchen, Germany, near Munich. Spain began its own Civil War with fascist rebels led by Generalissimo Francisco Franco warring against the elected Republican government, the socialists and liberals having won many seats in recent elections; in response, the U.S. declared nonintervention, Germany and Italy declared their support. The Soviet Union proposed a new Soviet Constitution to replace the original from 1923; among other items, the seven existing soviet republics would grow into 11, with the splitting of one into three and the addition of two new ones; with everyone's attention focused in western Europe, Stalin purged his government.

Weather concerns occupied all of the U.S., with floods swirling through the northeastern States, drought and heat scorching through the central and northwestern States; the 'Dust Bowl' years continued in the Plains and Midwest. Californian Arnold O. Beckman patented the pH meter, an instrument that measured acidity or alkalinity electronically. RCA broadcast the first television show. Price Waterhouse began its long-term relationship with the Academy Award Oscars, although the sealed envelope would not appear until 1940. 37-year old Henry R. Luce, the founder of both *Time* and *Fortune*, published the first issue of *LIFE* magazine, fashioning a new version of photojournalism in the days before regular television; *LIFE* would publish 1,800-some consecutive weekly issues before being forced to change with the times. Margaret Mitchell's *Gone With the Wind* zoomed to first place on the bestseller list; the novel earned the Pulitzer Prize the following year. Basketball became an Olympic sport. Ty Cobb, Honus Wagner, Babe Ruth, Christy Mathewson and Walter Johnson became the first members of the Baseball Hall of Fame; three years later the Hall and Museum were opened in Cooperstown, New York. Joe DiMaggio was a rookie with the New York Yankees. Viewed as another Great White Hope former champ Max Schmeling, defeated Joe Louis (at 27-0-0, his first professional loss) in a non-title fight in Yankee Stadium. At the 21st Republican convention in Cleveland, Kansas Governor Alfred M. Landon was elected the Presidential nominee on the 1st ballot; Chicago Daily News publisher Frank Knox was the unanimous choice as the Party's Vice Presidential nominee. At the 27th Democratic convention in Philadelphia, President Franklin D. Roosevelt was nominated for re-election by acclamation; Vice President John Nance Garner was accorded a similar honor. In November, the Roosevelt/Garner ticket was re-elected to a 2nd Term in a New Deal-avalanche, gaining 523 of the 531 votes of the Electoral College, winning 46 of the 48 States in the Union (missing only Maine and Vermont), and increasing majorities in both Houses of Congress. *The Chase and Sanborn Hour* premiered on radio with Edgar Bergen and Charlie McCarthy; *The Shadow* debuted with the question, "Who knows what evil lurks in the hearts of men?". *The Great Ziegfeld* won best picture and actress Academy Awards; best supporting actor and actress categories were added to the Awards. Keynesian theory began with John Maynard publishing his *General Theory of Employment, Interest and Money*. 48-year old American playwright Eugene O'Neill received the Pulitzer Prize in Literature, one of four Pulitzers he would be awarded in a distinguished career; he also received the Nobel Prize in Literature in this, one of his finest years. 31-year old American Carl David Anderson, who discovered the subatomic particle the positron four years earlier, was awarded the Nobel Prize in Physics. 46-year old Henry F. Phillips patented a new kind of screw and driver.

IC's first streamlined train, the diesel-powered *Green Diamond* 5-unit lightweight trainset, entered regular daily roundtrip service between Chicago and St. Louis on May 17th; the fully articulated trainset ran on six 4-wheel

The date was May 17, 1936; Illinois Central's first streamlined train, the Green Diamond, *began in service between St. Louis and Chicago's Central station. This photograph caught the action under the trainshed at 12th Street.*

ICLAG21-12

trucks and was capable of speeds over 80 miles per hour. MS-1 overnight merchandise freight inaugurated October 1st, 527 miles from Chicago to Memphis in under 14 hours; 12-year old Baldwin-built 4-6-2 Pacific-type #1311 headed 29 carloads on the first train. With the retirement of a little over 13 miles of track, system mileage dropped to 6,575. With signs of the economy firming, revenues for the year approached $115.0 million, less than 9 percent from passenger traffic (27,878,591 passengers). Matching the strong results in revenues, freight tonnage rose to over 44.8 million. Locomotive availability rose to 1,520 units (1,500 steam and 20 electric/oil-electric) with the addition of two oil-electric switch units netted against the retirement of 14 units (12 freight and 2 passenger). In the second year of the modernization program, steam pressure was increased on 35 Mountain-type, 96 Pacific-type, 9 Mikado-type, 2 Mogul-type and 50 6-wheel switching engines, while being reduced on 4 10-wheel passenger units; one Mikado freight engine had its booster removed, dropping tractive power by 9,250 pounds. Illinois Central western lines in Iowa and Illinois were hit with record snowfalls in early February, testing the mettle of all.

ICLAG21-10

Even though deep in the Great Depression, not all news was negative. Public Works Administration funding facilitated the construction of Illinois Central's first lightweight streamlined trainset, a diesel-powered trainset at that. Ordered in 1934, IC accepted delivery of the Pullman Standard Car Manufacturing Company product in 1936. The first run for the Green Diamond's *daily Chicago to St. Louis schedule was May 17, 1936. On the previous page, the first run was memorialized. Above, a photograph of some dignitaries at the inaugural sendoff, everyone wanting to have their picture taken with the striking head-end view. On the facing page, at top, the 5-unit trainset was snapped on the riverfront, on a promotional tour around the System. At bottom, another view of the headend of the trainset, passing by the Van Buren Street commuter station.*

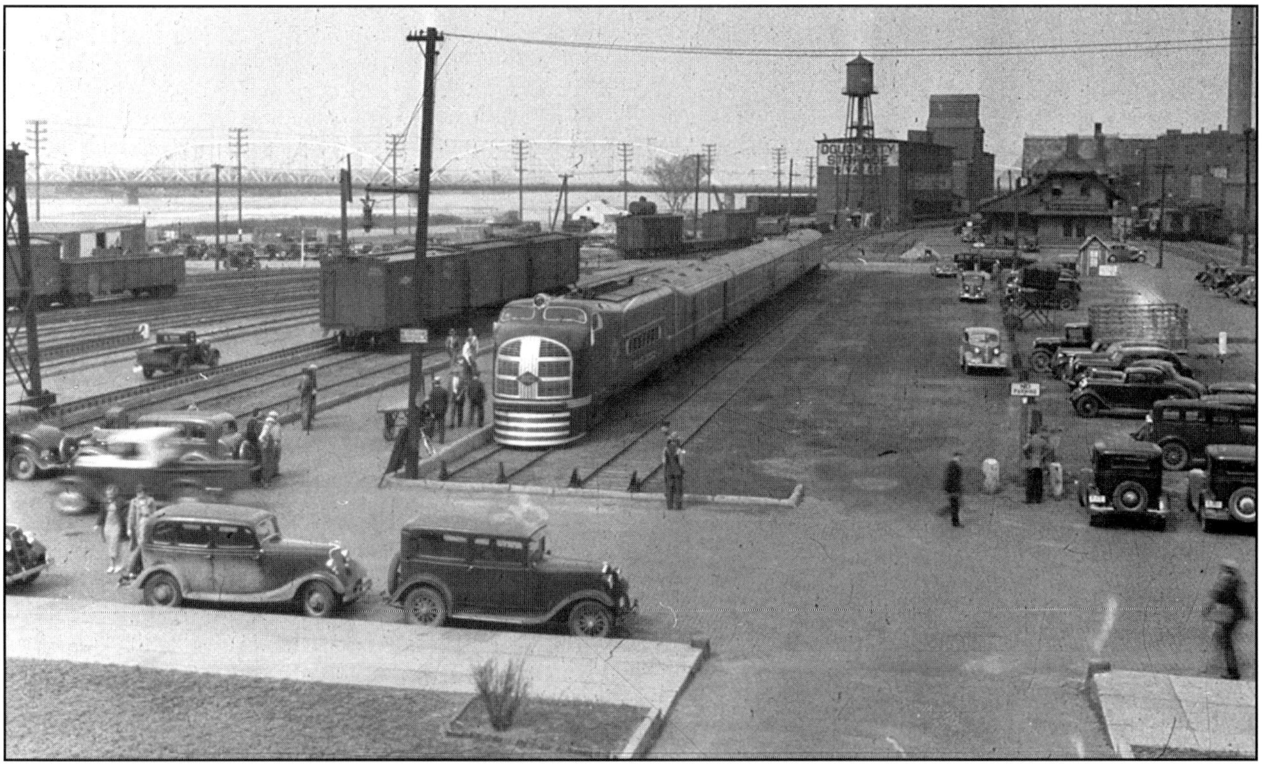

ICLAG21-13

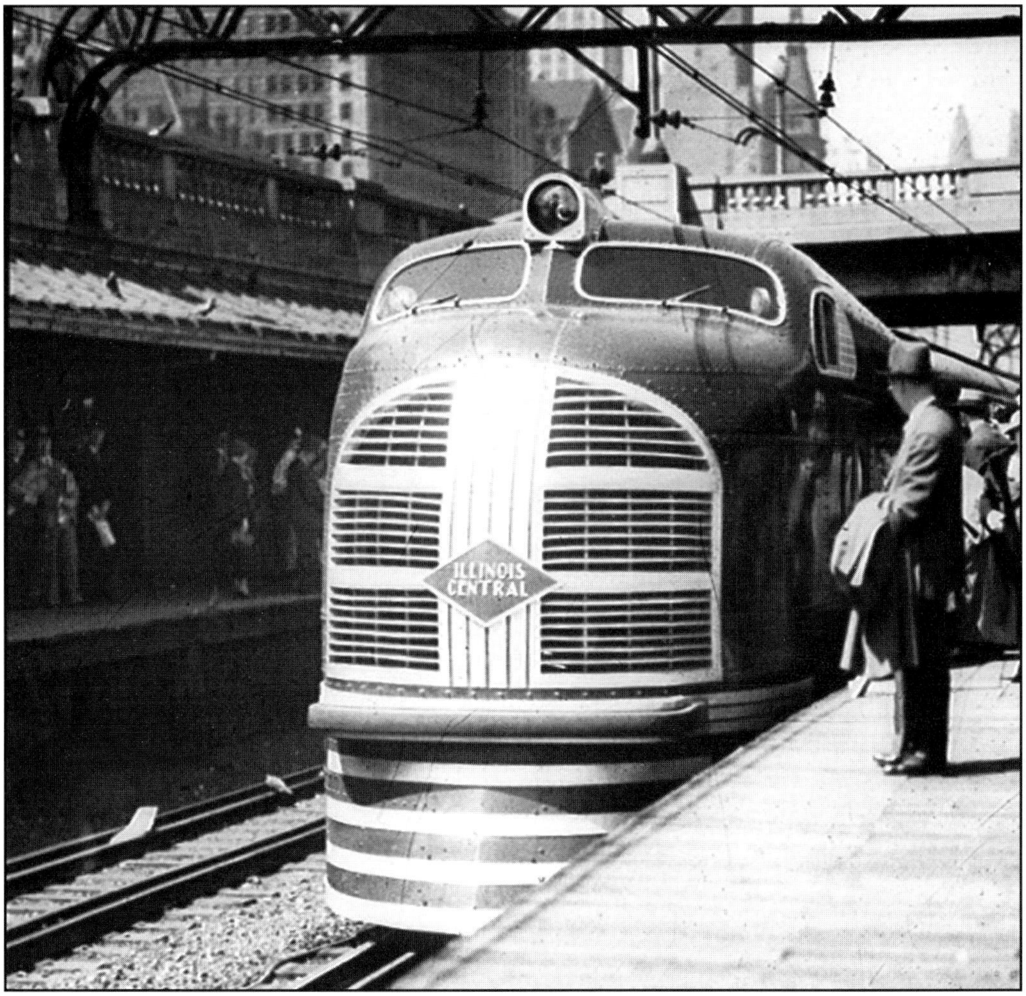

ICLAG21-11

1937

Throughout the year, Spain experienced its own civil war with anarchists fighting for control of Barcelona and Madrid; Italian Premier Benito Mussolini sent volunteers to aid the Spanish insurgents led by Franco, even though Britain and France warned Italy not to meddle in Spanish affairs. In May the Duke of York was crowned King and Emperor of the English Empire as George VI; his 11-year old daughter Princess Elizabeth watched with interest as she became heir presumptive to the throne of England. In the Sino-Japanese conflict, Japan escalated hostilities in China in what amounted to an undeclared war; Japan forged alliances with Nazi Germany to protect its expansionary efforts in Southeast Asia and the South Pacific; in December Japan sank the U.S. gunboat *Panay* in the Yangtze River 25 miles from Nanking; Nanking finally fell to Japanese forces. With an increasing number of aggressor nations, America's policy of neutrality was strained. Russian leader Stalin continued house cleaning with his purge.

The recovering economy went into a recession in 1937. The United Auto Workers organized most auto manufacturers after striking General Motors for 44 days, idling over 110,000 and causing street riots necessitating the Michigan National Guard; Chrysler Motors settled after a 30-day strike by 65,000 workers; this represented the first major organizing victory for the industry-based CIO. Steel workers struck Chicago's Republic Steel, where ten marchers were killed in confrontations with police in what came to be called the Memorial Day Massacre. Insulated window glass debuted. 23-year old Joe Louis (nee Joseph Louis Barrow), instead of Max Schmeling who had beaten Louis the year before in a battle of contenders, was allowed to fight James J. Braddock for the heavyweight boxing championship at Comiskey Park; Louis won with an 8th round knockout to become the new and disputed world champion, which title he would retain for nearly 12 years by defending it 25 times. 55-year old Franklin D. Roosevelt the 32nd President of the U.S. began his 2nd Term on being sworn into office on January 20th, the first inauguration held on a day other than March 4th (1933 Norris Amendment to the Constitution moved Inauguration Day from March 4 to January 20). In February, exasperated at what he viewed as interference by the Supreme Court in nullifying some of his New Deal measures and under the guise of revitalizing the Judiciary, Roosevelt proposed expanding the Court to 15 Justices from 9, if the six members age 70 and older refused to retire; instead of moving for a Constitutional amendment, Roosevelt's attempt to "pack" the Court was brought forward as a Bill to Congress; this was one of the few bills Roosevelt failed to carry through the Congress. In May at Lakehurst, New Jersey on the first leg of its 11th round trip between Germany and the U.S. the zeppelin *Hindenburg* gave meaning to the term crash-and-burn when its spectacular arrival was caught on video and audio; designed to float on non-explosive helium, it was filled with some seven million cubic feet of cheaper but explosive hydrogen gas; thus ended the age of rigid construction dirigibles for passenger transportation. In July the Amelia Earhart mystery was created when she and her navigator Fred Noonan in their twin-engine Lockheed Electra airplane dropped out of sight in the Pacific West of New Guinea on a leg of an attempted flight around the world. In December Walt Disney produced his first full-length animated feature film – *Snow White and the Seven Dwarfs*. In May the George A. Hormel Company rolled out a new pink luncheon meat product made from spiced ham – SPAM. Backed by Victor Bendix, the first home laundry machine made its appearance. In August 27-year old Edwin H. Land founded his Polaroid Corporation. The first Donut Day took to the streets and corners of America. A vaccine for yellow fever was developed. While short-term storage of blood had been in practice for over twenty years, Dr. Bernard Fantus at Cook County Hospital in Chicago set up the first hospital blood bank, deposits for future withdrawals. 32-year old Italian-born American physicist Emilio Segre generated the first man-made element, technetium. 67-year old chief designer Joseph B. Strauss with assistants Charles Ellis and Leon Moisseiff created an engineering masterpiece; in May the Golden Gate Bridge opened for business, suspended high over San Francisco Bay. The Cotton Bowl was inaugurated in Dallas in January, Texas Christian beating Marquette 16 to 6. *The Guiding Light* premiered on radio. *The Life of Emile Zola* with Paul Muni won the best picture Academy Award; Luise Rainer won best actress for her performance in *The Good Earth*, the first repeat winner. Glenn Miller formed a band in New York. 70-year old conductor Arturo Toscanini was coaxed out of retirement and back to work with the premier of the NBC Symphony Orchestra. Alabama Senator Hugo L. Black, a member of the KKK in his youth, was appointed to the U.S. Supreme Court amid much controversy, where he stayed for 34 years; Byron "Whizzer" White, who would be appointed to the same Court 25 years later and would be its youngest nominee, was an All-American running back and *Heisman Trophy* runner-up on Colorado's undefeated team. John D. Rockefeller died at age 98. Howard Johnson pioneered in

ICNEGGS-15

While the Illinois Central would not take delivery of new steam locomotives from outside builders in the 1930's, that doesn't mean it stopped mechanical experimentation to improve utilization and efficiency of steam power; quite the contrary, as this period proved one where the Mechanical Department would shine, from the massive rebuild programs undertaken at various shops to the cobbling together of new steam locomotive wheel arrangements from otherwise used-up engines: to wit, IC #1, Illinois Central's one and only effort at the 4-6-4 Hudson wheel arrangement. In fact, Illinois Central had a plan to convert all the 2-8-4 Lima wheel arrangements into these 4-6-4 Hudsons, and IC #1 was the test model. While the conversion went off without a hitch, the performance of the 4-6-4 wheel arrangement was less than satisfactory, and IC dropped its conversion plan. Instead, IC would renovate the 2-8-4's between 1939-1943, removing boosters and feedwater heaters, replacing them with injectors and increased boiler pressure, and renumbering the units into the series IC #8000. But for IC #1, its place in history was secure as the one and only, as pictures on the next two pages testify.

franchising motels. Popular blues singer Bessie Smith died at age 43 in a car crash shaded with controversy in Mississippi. *War Admiral* won horse racing's Triple Crown, only the 4th horse to accomplish this feat; just like his father *Man O' War*, *War Admiral* recorded only one loss in his racing career, to *Seabiscuit* in a match race the next year.

Having recently completed construction of its central gold depository at Fort Knox, Kentucky, the U.S. Treasury moved 39 trainloads of bullion valued at $6.5 billion from New York and Philadelphia to the new vault; the last leg of the trip was the 31 miles from Louisville to Fort Knox on the Illinois Central, and Illinois Central 2-8-2 Mikado-type # 1689 got the job done; Fort Knox originally was the military reservation Camp Knox, built 19 years earlier during World War I; before that, it was a flag stop and village on the Illinois Central called Stithton. Record floods caused by excessive rain in the Ohio River watershed (10 to 13 inches in 7 days), closed every gateway across the river below Pittsburgh; with rising water at Evansville, Metropolis and Cairo, Paducah Locomotive Shops was flooded with a peak of 68 inches of water in portions of the plant; it would be three weeks before water levels receded below floor level, and another three weeks of cleanup before operations could resume. With 16 miles of track retired, system mileage dipped to 6,559. The economic recovery suffered a temporary setback with a recession in the latter part of the year; closer to home, heavy floods on the Ohio River pressured results, revenues for the year falling slightly to $114.0 million, under 10 percent from passenger traffic (32,579,109 passengers). Unlike revenues, freight tonnage rose slightly to 45.9 million. Locomotive availability dipped to 1,518 units (1,497 steam and 21 electric/oil-electric) with the addition of one new oil-electric switch engine and the retirement of 3 0-6-0 switchers. In the third year of the modernization program, 63 Mikado-type 2-8-2's and 9 Pacific-type 4-6-2's received improvements such as, mechanical stokers, force/vacuum feed lubricators, higher boiler pressure, larger tenders, new type driving wheels, and balance for higher speeds; in addition, 14 Central-type 2-10-2's were converted to Mountain-type 4-8-2's and 1 2-8-4 (#7038) was converted to a 4-6-4 (#1 and then #2499), all with larger drivers and higher boiler pressure.

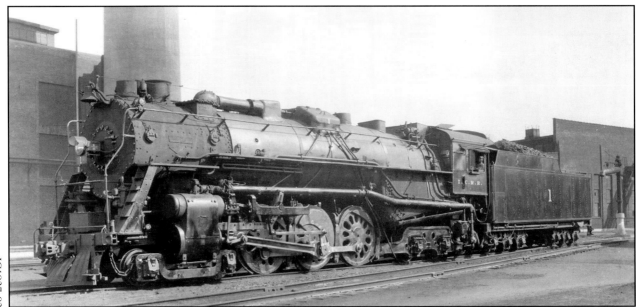

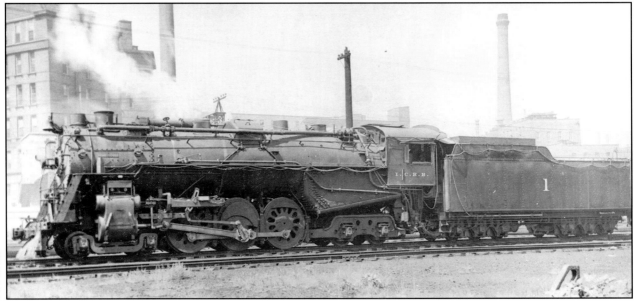

Illinois Central's 4-6-4 Hudson-type was created by removing the running gear and wheel arrangement off a 2-8-4 Lima-type (IC #7038: 63 1/2 D; 240 BP; 388,000 TW; 70,259 TF) and dropping what was left on a new 4-6-4 chassis (73 1/2 D; 265 BP; 407,050 TW; 55,186 TF; 68,826 TF with booster). The result was Illinois Central #1, which came with Walschaerts valve gear and Boxpok drivers; the tender held 20 tons of coal and 15,000 gallons of boiler water. When the initial design proved slippery, the booster was removed and the cylinder size reduced, but IC #1 would remain a single copy.

On the facing page are three views of IC #1. Top to bottom, IC #1 was captured at Markham Yard on September 14, 1939; the steam line to the booster can be seen running down the side, just above the running gear. At middle is a later view, when the steam line to the booster had been moved up top the boiler, and eventually cut out; also seen is the reduced cylinder size. The picture at bottom was taken after the unit had been renumbered to IC #2499 in 1945; this view was snapped at Fulton, Kentucky on October 8, 1946. What happened to the wheels/frame/cylinders from the 2-8-4 Lima left over after the boiler went to the Hudson-type? The running gear was used, with a boiler from IC #1549 (a 1914 Baldwin-built 2-8-2), to fashion a new 2-8-2 Mikado, IC #2020 (63 1/2 D; 225 BP; 326,500 TW; 68,330 TF); this unit had Baker valve gear, was superheated and came with a Hanna stoker; the tender held 18 tons of coal and 12,000 gallons of boiler water. This engine was renovated and renumbered to IC #2199 in 1942, and saw service until 1955.

IC1937-01

SUPERHEATER	SCHMIDT	VALVE - 12"		TEND. CAP'Y: WATER 12,000 GALS.
STOKER	TYPE B-K	CYL. 30" STROKE - 30"		TEND. CAP'Y. - COAL 16 TONS
SYPHONS	NICHOLSON			TRACTIVE EFFORT 73,768 LBS.
REVERSE GEAR	RAGONNET	STEAM PRESSURE 225 LBS.		LT. WGT. ENGINE 347,768 LBS.
VALVE GEAR	WALSCHAERT			LT. WGT. TENDER 76,600 LBS.
		GRATE AREA 88.3 SQ. FT.		

HEATING SURFACE			
ARCH TUBES 23.5 SQ. FT.		LD. WGT. ENG. TRK. 64,849 LBS.
FIREBOX 386.0 SQ. FT.		LD. WGT. DRIVERS 266,351 LBS.
FLUES & TUBES 4728.0 SQ. FT.		LD. WGT. TR. TRK. 62,568 LBS.
SYPHONS 108.5 SQ. FT.		LD. WGT. TOTAL (ENG.) 393,768 LBS.
TOTAL 5246.0 SQ. FT.		LD. WGT. TENDER 208,600 LBS.
SUPERHEATER 1285.0 SQ. FT.		

Absent funds for new equipment, Illinois Central satisfied its needs with rebuilding and renovating locomotives, oftentimes rebuilding units into new wheel arrangements. IC took boilers from 56 Lima 2-10-2 (64 1/2 D; 190 BP; 382,000 TW; 72,112 TF) Centrals (from series IC #2901-3025) and mated them to new 4-8-2 (70 D; 225 BP; 393,768/409,500 TW; 73,768 TF) Mountain-type chassis to fashion powerful locomotives (series IC #2500-2555) between 1937 and 1942. The unused chassis from the 2-10-2's was used to create heavier 2-8-2 Mikados and 2-10-0 Decapod switchers.

IC1921-01

The first of Mechanical Department genius Floyd R. Mays low-budget upgrades is shown on the facing page, IC #2500; these units could maintain horsepower at speed, even with heavier train weights. IC #2500 (from IC #2953) was the first rebuild, outshopped in 1937; this particular unit has been displayed at Centralia, Illinois since 1962. In the lower picture on the facing page the same unit is shown at work; the view was snapped as IC #2500 pounded down the line between Chebanse and Kankakee on February 4, 1943. This page, top to bottom, IC #2501 (from IC #2960) was captured working northbound through Mattoon, Illinois at 10:45 am on February 18, 1949. At bottom, IC #2502 (from IC #3006) was snapped in 1953 on the Illinois Division.

IC4x5-66

IC4x5-61

At top, IC #2503 (from IC #2954) was another 4-8-2 Mountain-type rebuild of 1937; note the extended coping on the tender, increasing capacity. Below, IC #2512 (from IC #2993) was caught being refueled, in a close-up of the head end; this view dates to October 4, 1955 at Markham Yard, when a Traffic School was being held by Management.

IC1904-15

IC1903-16

IC45x35-126

Illinois Central supplemented its switching needs by rebuilding/converting units during the Depression. A number of 0-8-0 switch engines (53 1/2 D; 220 BP; 201,600 TW; 43,160 TF) were created out of older Alco/Schenectady and Rogers-built 2-8-0 Consolidations from the series IC #651-785 (57 1/2 D; 200 BP; 199,210 TW; 32,243 TF). The two units converted in this fashion in 1937 are shown above, IC #3300 and IC #3301. These locomotives had Baker valve gear, were superheated and came with Economy steam chests; the tender held 9 tons of coal and 8,000 gallons of boiler water.

IC #3300, at top, was converted from IC #751, a 1904 Rogers-built 2-8-0. IC #3301, shown in the two lower pictures, was converted from IC #724, a 1903 Rogers-built 2-8-0.

IC1911-03

IC1911-15

IC1909-06

IC1909-02

Another group of 2-8-0 Consolidations (63 D; 200 BP; 238,200 TW; 39,180 TF) that were converted into 0-8-0 (61 D; 235 BP; 225,500 TW; 50,844 TF) switch engines (series IC #3410-3424) were 14 units from series IC #900. From top to bottom, IC #965, a 1911 Baldwin, is shown after being converted from a 2-8-0 into an 0-8-0, just before being rerostered as IC #3415; this picture is IC's Builder's Photograph of the rebuild. IC #3415 is the same engine sometime between 1937 and its 1942 renumbering to IC #3400; the tender held 12 tons of coal and 7,000 gallons of boiler water. IC #3405 (original 1909 Baldwin 2-8-0 IC #951, rebuilt into 0-8-0 IC #3420) was one of six in this series rebuilt with larger cylinders, creating a tractive force (71,615 TF) that easily exceeded adhesion limits. On bottom, IC #3418 came from IC #948, a 1909 Baldwin 2-8-0.

In its acquisition of the Alabama & Vicksburg in 1926, Illinois Central took control of five 2-10-2 Centrals (A&V #470-474); IC rostered these in as IC #3100-3104. In 1937 IC rebuilt four of these 2-10-2's (58 D; 185 BP; 274,720 TW; 51,318 TF) into 0-10-0 (55 D; 225 BP; 264,720 TW; 68,374 TF; except IC #3103/3104, 267,270 TW) switch engines; the last unit (IC #3101) was rebuilt in 1941; rostered as IC #3602/3606.

Top to bottom, IC #3104 (former A&V #474) was caught after rebuilding but before being renumbered. The second picture of IC #3104 shows it at work, and still not renumbered. IC #3604 (former IC #3102 and A&V #472) was captured in a yard, awaiting assignment. At bottom, IC #3605 (former IC #3103 and A&V #473) was snapped in another yard shot; the tender held 10 tons of coal and 7,000 gallons of boiler water.

1938

Oil was discovered in Kuwait. Civil war raged on in Spain with Loyalists fighting Rebels, monarchists/republicans against fascists/nationalists. Japan captured Canton. Italy's Mussolini increased his in-country forces in Libya. German Chancellor Adolph Hitler demanded the right to self-determination for Germans in Austria and Czechoslovakia. British Foreign Secretary Anthony Eden, at odds with Prime Minister Neville Chamberlain who sought to placate Italy and Germany, resigned his cabinet position in a policy dispute; seventeen years later, Eden would be Prime Minister. Dropping all pretense of diplomacy, three weeks after his self-determination speech Hitler gave Austrian Chancellor Kurt Schuschnigg a choice – resign or be invaded; given that his predecessor Dollfuss had been assassinated in 1934, he resigned, and a Nazi leader was installed as Chancellor and Austria was effectively annexed to the German Empire. The Sudetenland, a German populated area on the northern frontier of Czechoslovakia, became the next touchstone for self-determination; Herr Hitler stated that acquisition of the Sudetenland was the last territorial demand Germany would make in Europe. British Premier Chamberlain made two visits to German Chancellor Hitler in September in an effort to ameliorate the situation. In November in a preview of things to come, Hitler instigated violence against Jews and their business' in the infamous *Kristallnacht* – The Night of Broken Glass. The largest passenger ship ever, the *Queen Elizabeth*, was launched in England; it was over 1,000 feet long and over 100 feet wide. Soccer's third World Cup Championship was hosted by France, with participation effected by the rising war; the final match saw Italy defeat Hungary in what would be the last World Cup game for 12 years.

In a time of increasing paranoia, the House Un-American Activities Committee was formed; among others, it would investigate the ACLU and the Campfire Girls; real infamy lay in the future, when it would undertake the secret blacklisting of entertainment and media individuals. 32-year old physicist Chester F. Carlson working for a New York law firm invented the photocopier, one day to be called the Xerox; conceptualized in 1937, Carlson made his first "copy" in 1938 and he would receive patent #2,297,691 on *Electrophotography* four years later; a public demonstration lay ten years in the future while commercial success was 24 years away. Dupont's nylon yarn was marketed for the first time; while its' replacement of silk in stockings in 1940 gained it marketing fame, its use in parachutes during World War II proved crucial. Working at Dupont, 28-year old Ohio State University graduate chemist Roy J. Plunkett discovered polymerized tetrafluoroethylene (PTFE); after military use during World War II the substance became *Teflon*. Swiss chemists Arthur Stoll and Albert Hofmann discovered LSD – lysergic acid diethylamide; it wasn't until 1943 that LSD was found to be hallucinogenic. 24-year old Joe Louis avenged his loss two years earlier by crushing former champ Max Schmeling, viewed as Nazi sympathizer this time instead of a Great White Hope, in a little over 2 minutes in a fight at Yankee Stadium. Work began on the Pennsylvania Turnpike. Bugs Bunny appeared in a Warner Bros. cartoon. With the situation in Central Europe deteriorating, American tourists began to change travel plans. In October on the Mercury Radio Theatre 23-year old Orson Welles broadcast English author H.G. Wells' *The War of the Worlds* over the radio and started a panic, saying aliens landed in New Jersey. The *World News Roundup* debuted with William L. Shirer in London, Ansel Mowrer in Paris, Bob Trout in Washington, and Edward R. Murrow in Vienna; *The Green Hornet* ("Britt Reid") premiered on radio. Physicist Vladimir K. Zworykin demonstrated the first practical television. Frank Capra's *You Can't Take It with You* won both best picture and director Academy Awards; Spencer Tracy (best actor), Bette Davis (best actress) and Frank Capra were all second time winners. Having played for years with Benny Goodman and others, Gene Krupa started his own band, in New York City. Thornton Wilder's *Our Town* opened on Broadway and earned a Pulitzer Prize. 31-year old Douglas G. "Wrong Way" Corrigan took off with a broken compass from Bennett Field in New York headed home to California and landed in Dublin, Ireland a little over 28 hours later, supposedly. The Civil Aeronautics Authority was formed to regulate the burgeoning air traffic. Rome University professor 37-year old Enrico Fermi was awarded the Nobel Prize for Physics for his work with radioactive substances; he immigrated to the U.S. a short time later. The National Invitational Tournament (NIT) organized the first postseason college basketball tournament. In the second game of a three game series late in the season against Pittsburgh, Chicago Cubs player-manager Charles Leo "Gabby" Hartnett gained fame with his late inning "Homer in the Gloamin'" in the fading light. Brothers Ladislao and Georg Biro constructed the first practical ballpoint pen, a non-leaking writing stick.

With increased costs, declining business, and greater competition from trucks and barges, the railroad industry continued to report poor results and a weakening financial condition; government responded by considering plans

ICNEGGS-22

During the year Illinois Central continued its program of rebuilding/converting 2-8-0 Consolidations into 0-8-0 switch engines,
albeit at a reduced pace; above is IC #3406, the only such conversion in 1938. IC #3406 was fashioned out of IC #990, a 1911
Baldwin-built 2-8-0 (63 D; 200 BP; 238,200 TW; 39,180 TF); the resulting 0-8-0 (61 D; 235 BP; 225,500 TW; 50,844 TF)
switch engine was IC #3421; it was renumbered to IC #3406 in 1942.

to force the consolidation of rail carriers, since they weren't voluntarily doing so. The Pennsylvania Railroad's *Broadway Limited* reduced transit time between New York City and Chicago to 16 hours.

System mileage dipped to 6,556 with the retirement of a scant three miles of trackage. The economic recovery remained on the back-burner with the recession continuing during the first half of the year, Illinois Central revenues falling to $105.4 million, just over 9 percent from passenger traffic (30,142,357 passengers). Matching revenues, freight tonnage dropped to 39.0 million. Locomotive availability dipped to 1,504 units (1,483 steam and 21 electric/oil-electric) with the retirement of 14 engines (2 4-6-0 passenger, 8 2-6-0 freight and 4 0-6-0 switchers). In the fourth year of the modernization program, 62 2-8-2's received improvements such as mechanical stokers and new type driving wheels; in addition, seven 2-10-2's were converted to 4-8-2's; steam pressure was increased on those 69 units plus one 4-6-2, one 4-6-0, 27 2-8-4's and seven small 2-8-2's; one 2-8-0 was changed into an 0-8-0 switch engine; boosters were removed from 11 2-8-4 engines. In December, 39 years after hiring on as a messenger in the New Orleans freight office, McComb, Mississippi-born 51-year old John Lansing Beven was elected the 15th President of the Company, with Larry A. Downs moving up to Chairman; the location of the Annual Meeting of Directors was changed from New York to Chicago.

IC1938-01

IC45x35-114

IC1918-02

Another renovation program of the Illinois Central during this restricted-budget period was that of rebuilding small 2-8-2 (63 1/2 D; 185 BP; 282,700 TW; 54,158 TF) Mikado-types from the 1500-series into larger and more powerful (64 1/2 D; 225 BP; 336,000 TW; 74,078 TF) locomotives; while most engines had their 27" x 30" cylinders replaced with 28" x 32" cylinders, eleven of the 41 units received 30" x 32" cylinders, yielding impressive gains in tractive force (85,395 TF). In simple terms, the rebuild was one of placing the small 2-8-2's boiler on a 2-10-2 Central's cut-down chassis, with other modernizations. The rebuilt engines were rostered in as IC #2100-2140.

These two pages, five views of rebuilt 2-8-2's. On the facing page, top to bottom, IC #2102 (boiler from 2-8-2 IC #1786, a 1916 Lima) was caught in the yard, showing its 6,000-class (mallet) tender (21 tons of coal and 13,000 gallons of boiler water) and Baker valve gear. IC #2104 (boiler from 1918 Baldwin 2-8-2 IC #1815) was one of the eleven that received the oversized cylinders. IC #2105 (boiler from 1918 Baldwin 2-8-2 IC #1814) was caught at Vicksburg, Mississippi on July 9, 1941. This page, at top, IC #2106 (boiler from 2-8-2 IC #1816, a 1918 Baldwin) was snapped as it eased through Ruston, Louisiana on the Shreveport line on March 7, 1953. At bottom, IC #2111 (boiler from 1912 Baldwin 2-8-2 IC #1562) was captured at near Bloomington, Illinois on September 6, 1944.

ICNEGGS-23

IC45x35-124

Illinois Central continued its program of taking boilers from Lima 2-10-2 (64 1/2 D; 190 BP; 382,000 TW; 72,112 TF) Centrals from series IC #2901-3025 and patching them on new 4-8-2 (70 D; 225 BP; 393,768/409,500 TW; 73,768 TF) Mountain-type chassis to create more powerful locomotives, rostered in as series IC #2500-2555. These two pages, four examples of the seven units converted in 1938. On the facing page, at top, IC #2516 (from IC #3015) was photographed passing Indian Oaks, Illinois on May 23, 1950; note the auxiliary tender used in this match-up. At bottom, IC #2517 (from IC #2987) was snapped in a yard shot. This page, at top, IC #2519 (from IC #2957) was captured with a view of the auxiliary tender. At bottom, IC #2520 (from IC #2958) was snapped in a standard yard shot. There were two types of auxiliary tenders used: A500's and A600's, which held 11,200 and 13,600 gallons of boiler water, respectively; this more than doubled the water available for steam production. The tender also held 24 tons of coal.

1939

The discovery of uranium fission was announced in January. In the Spanish Civil War Generalissimo Francisco Franco's rebel forces took Barcelona and Madrid as the elected Republican government defenses collapsed; London and Paris gave official recognition to the Franco regime, and Spain's 32-month civil war came to an end; a return to democracy lay 35 years away. Pope Pius XI passed away; 63-year old Eugenio Pacelli was elected to replace him by the College of Cardinals; he chose the name Pius XII, would be the first Pope to visit the United States, and led the Church for 19 years. Hitler occupied the remnants of Czechoslovakia in March. Like the pea-under-the-shell slight-of-hand game, Hitler switched the linchpin for avoiding war to the Polish port of Danzig on the Baltic Sea. In August, Germany and Russia signed a mutual non-aggression pact, promising also not to aid the others' opponents; the pact would prove to be simply a partition of Poland. Turkey reaffirmed its pledge to the Allies; France and Britain prepared for war in earnest. In September, Hitler reinvented armored warfare; his panzer division blitzkrieg would over-run Poland in a matter of weeks. Britain and France declared a state of war with Germany existed; President Roosevelt declared a national emergency. The British liner *Athenia* was sunk off the coast of Ireland by German torpedoes; the first ship to be sunk in World War II, and a presage of the battle for the North Atlantic. Having colluded with Hitler, Russia entered Poland from the East and retook Polish Ukraine and White Russia. Russia followed up by severing diplomatic ties with Finland, then crossed the border and bombed an airfield in the capital city of Helsinki; in the end Finland traded territory to Russia to retain its independence. Having established Russia's presence on the world stage, Stalin now sat on the sidelines and watched events unfold in Europe. In one of the first naval battles, British naval forces chased the damaged German pocket battleship *Graf Spee* into neutral Montevideo harbor, where the Germans scuttled her rather than be taken. General George C. Marshall was sworn in as Chief of Staff of the U.S. Army. World War II officially began in Europe. The compound dichlorodiphenyltrichloroethane was first prepared in 1874 by German chemist Othmar Zeidler, but it wasn't until 40-year old Swiss scientist Paul Muller demonstrated its properties as an insecticide almost 65 years later that it took the world by storm; Muller was awarded the 1948 Nobel Prize for his work with DDT. In May the German ship *St. Louis* left Hamburg for Havana with over 900 Jewish refugees; it would return to Europe weeks later after being turned away by both Cuba and the United States.

26-year old William Hewlett and 27-year old David Packard started a business in their Palo Alto garage; renamed Hewlett Packard in 1942. Having already designed a binary relay calculator, a simple circuit composed of relays and switches (Model K - for kitchen), 35-year old George Robert Stibitz exploited that knowledge in the intervening two years to construct the first electric digital computer (Bell Labs Model I), foreshadowing present technology. Physics professor John V. Atanasoff at the future Iowa State University began his own experiments in computing, with vacuum tubes replacing relays and talk of binary arithmetic. Packard became the first to offer car air-conditioning. Little League baseball was founded in Williamsport, Pennsylvania. With world events simmering in the background, President Franklin D. Roosevelt dedicated the opening of the New York World's Fair in Flushing Meadows outside New York City in April; television debuted at the World's Fair. A second major fair was held, in San Francisco on a 400-acre man-made island in San Francisco Bay called Treasure Island; it was called the Golden Gate International Exposition. NBC began regular TV programming; the first major league baseball game to be telecast was the Cincinnati Reds against the Brooklyn Dodgers from Ebbets Field. Contralto Marian Anderson performed for 75,000 people on the steps of the Lincoln Memorial when refused admission to Constitution Hall by the Daughters of the American Revolution because of her race; she would return to Constitution Hall four years later and end that segregation policy with a performance. In September Russian immigrant 50-year old Igor Sikorsky managed to get his version of a helicopter two-feet off the ground for a few seconds; he didn't invent the helicopter, but made practical use of it and would demonstrate an improved model the following year. Pan American Airways instituted regular service to Europe, transatlantic flights to Lisbon. 33-year old Howard Hughes bought control of Transcontinental and Western Air, the soon-to-be Trans World Airways - TWA. New York Yankee great Lou Gehrig retired on July 4th because of ill health; Gehrig had benched himself after 2,130 consecutive games, a record that would last for 56 years. Ted Williams began his rookie year. Harvard law professor 58-year old Felix Frankfurter was appointed to the U.S. Supreme Court, the sixth and last foreign-born to sit on the Court (Wilson, Iredell, Paterson, Brewer, and Sutherland) would remain there 23 years; William O. Douglas the 40-year old chairman of the Securities

IC1939-01

Illinois Central continued its program of converting small (63 1/2 D; 185 BP; 282,700 TW; 54,158 TF) Mikados into large (64 1/2 D; 225 BP; 336,000 TW; 74,078 TF) ones by dropping the boilers on 2-10-2 chassis; eight units were renovated in this fashion in 1939. IC #2117 received its new boiler from IC #1526; IC #2118 from IC #1648.

IC45x35-106

and Exchange Commission was appointed to the Court two months later, and stayed for 36 years; in the end, President Roosevelt would have eight members appointed to and one promoted on (Stone) the Supreme Court, second only to George Washington who appointed the first Court. David O. Selznick's production of *Gone With The Wind* starring Clark Gable and Vivien Leigh premiered on the big screen, and walked off with 9 Academy Awards, the first color movie to win Best Picture; best supporting actress Hattie McDaniel broke a different color line; best director Victor Fleming also directed Judy Garland in *The Wizard of Oz*, in what had to be his finest year. *The Milton Berle Show* premiered on radio. 31-year old Edward R Murrow moved his broadcast post from Vienna to London, and kept America informed about events in Europe with his news reports. John Steinbeck's *The Grapes of Wrath* was a bestseller, and was awarded a Pulitzer Prize; he would be awarded the Nobel Prize in Literature 23 years later. The NCAA began a postseason basketball tournament; the first was won by Oregon who defeated Ohio State 46-33 in Evanston, Illinois. Albert Einstein wrote a letter to President Roosevelt pushing for nuclear research, which led to a small appropriation, which grew to a larger program, which became the Manhattan Project.

With no change in trackage, system mileage remained at 6,556. Bouncing back from the recession, revenues for the year topped $111.3 million, less than 9 percent attributable to passenger traffic (30,386,365 passengers). Mirroring revenues, freight tonnage rose to 42.1 million. Locomotive availability dipped to 1,452 units (1,426 steam and 26 electric/oil-electric) with the addition of five oil-electric switch units netted against the retirement of 57 units. In the fifth year of the modernization program, steam pressure was increased on 143 engines (17 Mountains, 2 Limas, 87 Centrals, 23 large Mikados, 5 small Mikados, 5 Consolidations and 4 six-wheel switchers); 13 Central freight engines were rebuilt as Mountain passenger units and one Consolidation was converted into an eight-wheel switcher; the running gear and tenders of seven 2-10-2 Central-type locomotives (left over from their conversion into Mountains in 1937 and 1938) were mated to the boilers of a like number of 2-8-2 Mikados to fashion 2-10-0 Decapod switch units for hump yard use.

IC4x5-67

IC4x5-68

IC1921-05

ICNEGGS-48

IC4x5-63

Illinois Central's program of dropping used Lima 2-10-2 (64 1/2 D; 190 BP; 382,000 TW; 72,112 TF) boilers on new 4-8-2 (70 D; 225 BP; 393,768/409,500 TW; 73,768 TF) chassis beds continued with 13 units (series IC #2521-2533) produced in 1939; these 13 units eventually had 240 pounds of boiler pressure applied, increasing tractive force (to 78,685 TF) yet again. On these two pages, five views of four engines, all but one coupled with auxiliary tenders. On the facing page at top, IC #2524 (from IC #2935) was captured on the line between Kankakee and Paxton on July 6, 1946. At middle IC #2525 (from IC #2927) was caught hustling down the triple main. At bottom, the second view of IC #2525 was snapped at Mays Yard outside New Orleans in 1956. This page, at top, IC #2527 (from IC #2918) was viewed on October 30, 1939 in Chicago at 27th Street, fueled and ready for assignment; this tender held 24 tons of coal and 11,000 gallons of water. At bottom, IC #2530 (from IC #2913) was snapped near Indian Oaks, Illinois on May 23, 1950; fuel efficient it wasn't, the regular tender had high coping and an auxiliary tender was included.

IC1921-06

Two views of another 4-8-2 fashioned out of a 2-10-2 boiler and a new Mountain-type chassis are shown on this page. Above, IC #2532 (from IC #2912) was captured raising steam on a cold, winter day in a photograph used in the Illinois Central Magazine in a December, 1950 story on the St. Louis Division. Below, another view of that engine was stopped in a picture taken at an unidentified location. Both views show use of the auxiliary tender.

IC4x5-69

IC1939-02

ICNEGGS-16

Another one of the many projects Floyd R. Mays took up with his Mechanical shops was the construction of 15 (series IC #3610-3624) 2-10-0 Decapod switch engines, with seven units completed in 1939. Mays had the shop forces cannibalize old 2-8-2 Mikado boilers (series IC #1500) and stitch them onto old 2-10-2 Central chassis (series IC #2900) to create powerful 2-10-0 Decapods (61 1/2 D; 225 BP; 325,000 TW; 89,560 TF). The boiler left over from the 2-10-2 went to the 2500-series 4-8-2 Mountains the Mechanical shops were producing at the same time. In the picture at top, IC #3612 used a boiler from a 1914 Baldwin (IC #1507) and a chassis from a 1921 Lima (IC #2962). IC #3615 also utilized a boiler from a 1914 Baldwin (IC #1537) and a chassis from a 1921 Lima (IC #2924). Mating short boilers to long wheel bases made interesting arrangements; note in both pictures how the rear drive wheels rest under the firebox, instead of their usual position in front. The lower photograph was from a Kaufmann & Fabry negative taken for the Illinois Central.

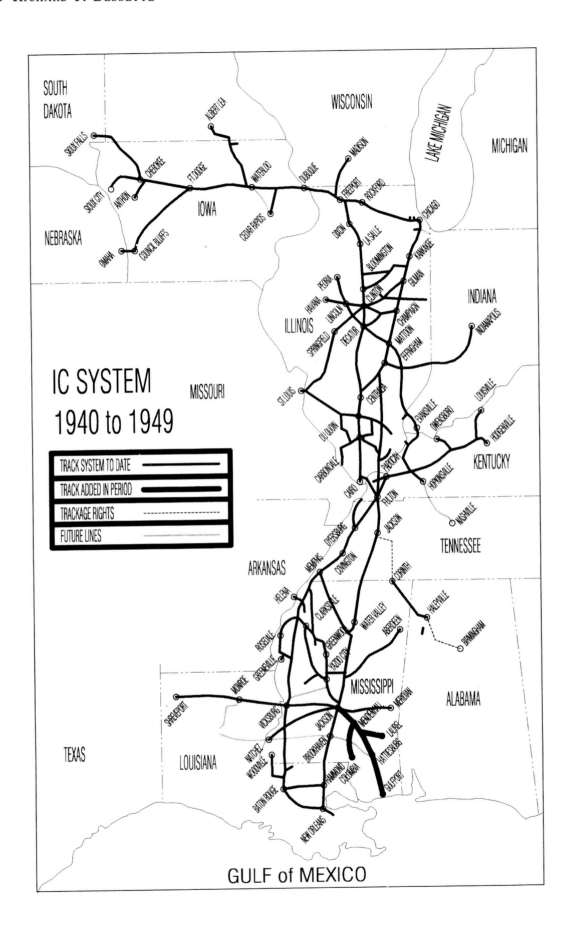

IC SYSTEM
1940 to 1949

TRACK SYSTEM TO DATE	
TRACK ADDED IN PERIOD	
TRACKAGE RIGHTS	
FUTURE LINES	

1850's 1860's 1870's 1880's 1890's 1900's 1910's 1920's 1930's **1940's**

The Sixteenth Census of the U.S. population showed a little over 132 million people in the U.S., having grown 7 percent from the prior census; the country would add over 19 million people by the end of the decade, less than ten percent through immigration. With millions of men diverted to the armed forces, another great migration of blacks from the south to the industrial north and west occurred; this migration would be spurred on by the invention of the mechanical cotton picker in 1944. After Williams and DiMaggio in 1941, the war started and professional sports dropped from view; when the war ended, sports exploded as stars returned. When France fell, the U.S. War Department reported it could field 5 divisions; Germany had 140. Penicillin, discovered in 1928, finally was proven in clinical trials in early 1940's; streptomycin quickly followed and the age of wonder drugs was born. Much of the country was rationed: deprivation during the war a badge of honor, unlike the shame it caused during the depression. At the end of the war, the Soviet Union and the United States divided Korea along the 38th parallel; the Allies divided Europe and Germany. After a brief recession (1946), the American economy soared to satisfy the pent up demand; price controls would follow. U.S. industry, untouched by the war, dominated international trade. The GI Bill of Rights would provide college education to almost eight million working-class Americans and subsidize new homes for five million veterans, helping fashion the great middle class.

In 1940 the major rail carriers operated a little over 233,500 miles of railroad, a figure that would decline almost 10,000 miles by the end of the decade. During the war railroads, already under maintained during the Great Depression, were heavily relied upon; they ended up with worn out property; the deferred maintenance had to be dealt with in the ensuing years. It was the era of speed, versus the past where train travel was luxurious and slow and comfortable; as speeds rose, amenities declined.

Illinois Central would shoulder its share during the war years to and from facilities on its lines; 22 posts, camps or forts housing some 350,000 men were sited on the Railroad. What had been a surplus of almost 700 steam locomotives would turn into a shortage with the national defense program.

Growth Of Illinois Central Railroad Business

Year (1)	Tonnage (mil/tons)	Lumber (mil/tons)	Grain (mil/tons)	Coal (mil/tons)	FFV (mil/tons)	Cotton (mil/tons)	Aggregates (mil/tons)	Passengers Commuters	Miles/Fare
1940	44.9	2.7	2.2	15.0	1.1	.776	2.4	31,146,427 N/A	20/$0.32
1941	57.0	3.6	2.4	17.5	1.1	1.1	3.2	33,172,605 N/A	24/$0.38
1942	76.1	4.0	3.2	20.7	1.0	1.1	6.4	39,605,808 N/A	31/$0.57
1943	80.4	3.4	3.8	23.5	1.1	1.2	3.5	48,466,037 N/A	41/$0.79
1944	80.3	3.0	3.4	26.0	1.5	1.1	2.1	50,703,272 N/A	43/$0.84
1945	76.7	2.7	3.3	26.8	1.6	.989	2.5	51,992,868 N/A	38/$0.72
1946	69.5	3.5	3.1	24.1	1.4	.944	3.2	54,186,193 N/A	31/$0.58
1947	72.1	3.3	4.4**	24.4	1.4	.863	3.5	52,147,754 47,067,959	27/$0.50
1948	72.9	3.0	4.0	25.7	1.1	.931	3.7	48,387,08 5N/A	27/$0.55
1949	64.3	2.2	4.2	21.1	0.9	1.0	4.2	42,333,575 37,893,715	27/$0.57

FFV = Fresh Fruit & Vegetables   Passengers/Commuters = Total Ridership, and Commuter Portion
Miles/Fare = Average Passenger Trip and Charge   (1) Fiscal Year   N/A = Data Not Available
**Includes soybeans, for the first time

1940

Claiming it a defensive move, Hitler's troops invaded Denmark and Norway, then the Low Countries - Netherlands, Belgium and Luxembourg. British Expeditionary Forces in Belgium were pushed out of Brussels back toward the North Sea. German troops opened a 60-mile front on the northern border of France; showing the advantage of mechanized forces over fixed fortifications, the Germans raced around France's "impregnable" Maginot Line. When the Germans trapped almost 500,000 soldiers against the North Sea, Dunkirk became a reality. Sensing its moment, Italy declared war on France and England and used its 250,000 troops in Italian-occupied Libya to push east and attack Egypt, England's crucial link to its eastern empire and oil supply; Greece would be next. French troops abandoned Paris, rather than watch it devastated; foreign troops entered Paris for the first time since 1871; France fell in June. Marshall Henri Philippe Petain the French hero of World War I would become a collaborator and lead the new subservient government from Vichy, while a defiant rebel General Charles de Gaulle organized the Free French resistance movement. In June Russia asserted its territorial claims in Romania; with their own vital interests in Romania, mainly the Ploesti oil fields, Germany and Italy recognized Russia's claims. Hungary massed its forces at the Romanian frontier to keep tabs on Russia; Turkey mobilized 500,000 troops to protect the Dardanelles and the Bulgarian front. In July/August, Field Marshall Hermann Goring's Luftwaffe began its air assault on Britain; a confident Adolf Hitler scheduled his invasion of England for September. Because RADAR operated as an early-warning system, England won the Battle of Britain, and Germany lost all chance of a land invasion. Field Marshall Erwin Rommel brought Germany's tanks to Africa. In November British airplanes destroyed Italian battleships anchored in Taranto Harbor at the foot of Italy, a presage of the massive aerial bombardment that would come; the British success at Taranto proved inspiration for the Japanese. In September America began its first peacetime conscription, drafting 900,000 men under the new Selective Service Act; over 16 million men received registration cards. 66-year old Winston Churchill was named Prime Minister, replacing Neville Chamberlain; Churchill gave his "Blood, Toil, Tears, Sweat" speech. General Francisco Franco, with an eye to retaking the key point of Gibraltar, leaned Spain toward Germany. While Stalin remained on the sidelines of war, his agents were busy, as exiled Soviet leader 60-year old Leon Trotsky was assassinated in Mexico City. Japan named Hideki Tojo its War Minister and silently prepared for the global conflict; Tojo became Premier the next year. A world at war again trumped the Olympic games, with the twelfth edition scheduled for Tokyo, Japan and Helsinki, Finland canceled; Wimbledon also was canceled.

Hedging its bet, Congress and the President authorized an increase in the Army, additional airplanes and the construction of over 65 warships, creating a two-ocean navy. In July Russian immigrant Igor Sikorsky demonstrated his improved-version of the helicopter, moving up and down and hovering freely. At the 22nd Republican convention in Philadelphia, former Democrat and Indiana-born Wall Street lawyer/businessman Wendell Lewis Willkie was elected the Presidential nominee on the 6th ballot; Oregon Senator Charles Linza McNary was chosen the nominee for Vice President. At the 28th Democratic convention in Chicago, incumbent President Franklin D. Roosevelt was nominated for re-election on the 1st ballot over two members of his Administration: Postmaster General James A. Farley from New York and Vice President John Nance Garner from Texas; Secretary of Agriculture Henry Agard Wallace from Iowa was chosen as the Party's Vice Presidential nominee. In November Franklin D. Roosevelt, on the promise of keeping America out of the war, was elected to an unprecedented 3rd Term, the only president to be so honored. The nation's first superhighway - the Pennsylvania Turnpike - opened in October; it was a product of New Deal job programs and utilized 50-year old half-finished railroad tunnels to conquer the mountains. The U.S. Government issued the first social security checks, the dawn of retirement income. George Halas pioneered his T-formation and the Chicago Bears with Sid Luckman demolished the Washington Redskins with Sammy Baugh 73 to 0 in claiming the NFL Championship. The University of Chicago Maroons, the original Monsters of the Midway in football, withdrew from the Big 10. Joe Louis defended his heavyweight boxing title four times, just like the previous year. Regular FM (frequency-modulation) radio broadcasting began. *Truth or Consequences* debuted on radio with Ralph Edwards. Alfred Hitchcock's *Rebecca* took the best picture Academy Award at the first presentation with sealed envelopes opened on stage, no longer announcing winners in advance; Walter Brennan became the first three-time winner. Natchez-born Richard Wright published his masterpiece *Native Son*, the story of Bigger Thomas. The Tacoma-Narrows Bridge south of Seattle collapsed into Puget Sound four short months after its completion, leading engineers into the study of aerodynamic stability. Nobel laureate 72-year old Karl Landsteiner, working with A.S. Wiener in the study of transfusion reactions, discovered Rh factors. *Morton Salt* appeared on supermarket shelves.

The Santa Fe became the first to use diesel-electric locomotives in regular freight service; diesel-electric power was now used in every type of service, numbering the days of steam power. Congress' answer to the railroads' plight of wallowing in red ink during the 1930's was the Transportation Act of 1940; this Act leveled the competitive field among the various modes of transportation and supported relief with work rule inconsistencies. The Gulf, Mobile and Ohio Railroad (GM&O) was formed in the merger of the established yet bankrupt Mobile and Ohio (M&O) with the upstart yet sound Gulf, Mobile and Northern (GM&N); long rivals for business, the Illinois Central objected to the merger unsuccessfully, and would not have the last word on the subject until 32 years later in a merger of its own.

Lawrence A. Downs passed away at age 68. Illinois Central daily passenger service between Jackson, Mississippi and New Orleans, Louisiana gained a new streamline train – the *Miss Lou*. A new seven-unit diesel-powered streamliner trainset, the original *City of Miami*, entered service on December 18 making a round trip every third day; the *City of Miami* was Illinois Central's third diesel-powered streamliner service, the *Green Diamond* the first. Having moved 39 trainloads of gold bullion to its new depository in 1937, the U.S. Treasury completed its deposit with 45 additional gold trains valued at $9.0 billion shipped to Fort Knox, Kentucky in 1940 and 1941; the Illinois Central handled the last leg of the trip, from Louisville to Fort Knox. With just 11 miles net retired during the year, system mileage dipped to 6,545. Continuing slow and steady progress, revenues for the year approached $114.3 million, under 9 percent from passenger traffic (31,146,427 passengers). Following suit, freight tonnage rose to 44.9 million. Locomotive availability dipped to 1,439 units (1,406 steam and 33 electric/oil-electric) with the addition of six oil-electric switch engines and the streamlined oil-electric diesel *City of Miami*, netted against the retirement of 20 units. In the sixth year of the modernization program, steam pressure was increased on 64 engines (1 Mountain, 23 Limas, 28 Mikados, 9 Consolidations and three six-wheel switchers); seven 2-10-2 freight engines were converted into 4-8-2's for faster service; four Mogul-type freight engines were converted into six-wheel switchers and three small Mikado-type freights into eight-wheel switchers; the running gear from 2-10-2 freight engines were reworked with the boilers and tenders from 2-8-2 freights to cobble together seven 2-10-0 Decapod switch locomotives for the hump yard.

IC1923-28

Illinois Central continued to paste old Lima-built 2-10-2 Central (64 1/2 D; 190 BP; 382,000 TW; 72,112 TF) boilers on new 4-8-2 Mountain (70 D; 225 BP; 393,768/409,500 TW; 73,768 TF) chassis during 1940, completing seven additional units; fifteen more engines would be produced (in 1942) under this program. At the top, IC #2537 (from IC #3019) is shown raising a stir as it pounds through the countryside, it's auxiliary tender along for the ride. At bottom, IC #2538 (from IC #2999) was captured in a yard shot with its six-axle tender. These two units had boiler pressure increased even higher, to 240 pounds, resulting in greater tractive force (78,685 TF).

IC45x35-112

Illinois Central #2539 was another 4-8-2 Mountain-type fashioned out of an old 2-10-2 Central boiler (from IC #2922) and a brand new chassis bed. A product of Illinois Central shops in 1940, it was pictured as above in a artist's sketch; note the streamlined, high coping on the four-axle tender.

The 0-8-0 switch engine pictured below was another product of 1940, cobbled together by Floyd R. May's Mechanical shops. This engine began its service life as a 1919 Baldwin-built 2-8-2 (57 1/2 D; 200 BP; 217,500 TW; 40,418 TF) Mikado erected for the Vicksburg Shreveport & Pacific as VS&P #354; renumbered to VS&P #364, it was acquired by the Illinois Central in the 1926 combination of roads, and was rostered in as IC #3965. With its drivers lowered and its boiler pressure boosted, it was rebuilt into an 0-8-0 (55 D; 220 BP; 211,500 TW; 46,076 TF) switch engine in 1940 and served another 12 years. It was photographed at Paducah, Kentucky on August 5, 1941.

IC4x5-83

IC1940-02

Continuing the program begun the prior year of fashioning 2-10-0 (61 1/2 D; 225 BP; 325,000 TW; 89,560 TF) Decapod switch engines from 2-8-2 Mikado boilers and 2-10-2 Central running gear, IC's Mechanical shops fashioned seven units in 1940, bringing the fleet size to 15 engines; once again, the boilers freed up from the 2-10-2 Centrals went into the 4-8-2 Mountain program (used 2-10-2 boilers and new 4-8-2 chassis).

At top, IC #3618 (IC #1644 boiler and IC #2980 chassis) was photographed in August, 1948 pulling a solid trainload of canned pineapple through Markham Yards. At bottom, IC #3619 (IC #1505 boiler and IC #2959 chassis) was captured at Markham Yards on October 15, 1948 when it participated in radio tests. On the facing page, top to bottom, IC #3621 (IC #1690 boiler and IC #2999 chassis) was caught in a yard shot. IC #3622 (IC #1570 boiler and IC #2922 chassis) was snapped at Paducah, Kentucky on August 5, 1941. IC #3623 (IC #1569 boiler and IC #2970 chassis) was viewed in a yard shot with crew and fuel aboard, ready for action.

IC1940-03

IC1940-01

IC1940-04

1941

Having dealt harshly with political prisoners and Jews and Gypsies since he rose to power in the early 1930's, Hitler now began work that would yield a Final Solution policy - the Holocaust; of the hundreds of prisons and ghettos built to handle undesirables, six specific death camps would be built with the sole purpose of implementing Hitler's plan of genocide – Auschwitz, Belzec, Chelmno, Majdanek, Sobibor and Treblinka – all located in German-occupied Poland. On the war front, Hitler bailed out Mussolini twice - in Libya and in Greece - from disastrous attempts to increase Fascist influence and independence. German Field Marshall Erwin Rommel arrived in Libya in February to retake the territory, an effort that would take his Afrika Korps 17 months. In May, the British (*H.M.S. Hood, Prince of Wales, King George V, Rodney, Dorsetshire, Norfolk*, et. al.) sank the German pocket battleship *Bismarck*, just eight days after being placed in service. Germans invaded Yugoslavia and Greece in April. In May, 47-year old Deputy Fuehrer Rudolph Hess parachuted out of a German plane over a farm in Scotland, deserting the German cause and Hitler; Spandau Prison and #7 lay just over the horizon. Claiming Russia two-faced, Germany dumped the 22-month old non-aggression pact and attacked in June, opening the offensive along a 2,000-mile front. Stalin would be pressed at Leningrad (now St. Petersburg) in the north, at Moscow in the central region and Stalingrad in the south; the war on the Eastern front would last 2 ½ years. In August the U.S. House of Representatives agreed by a single vote (203 to 202) to continue its military buildup and extend the draft, the close vote showed how deep antiwar and isolationist currents/sentiments ran. On December 7th the U.S. was forced out of its neutral stance; discerning its' moment in history, Japan - declaring war on both the U.S. and England - launched surprise attacks on Pearl Harbor naval base in Hawaii, Guam, the Philippines, Hong Kong and Singapore. Japan's Admiral Yamamoto Isoroku planned and Admiral Nagumo executed the Japanese attack on Pearl Harbor; the absence of the U.S. aircraft carriers at the Pearl Harbor attack would prove decisive. The next day, President Roosevelt presented for vote a resolution for war at a joint meeting of Congress; without debate, with a unanimous 82 to 0 vote in the Senate and a 388 to 1 vote in the House - the lone dissenting vote from 61-year old Republican Congresswoman Jeanette Rankin of Montana who also voted against the World War I declaration in 1917 - the United States formally declared war on Japan. Within days special agents of the Federal Bureau of Investigation began rounding up Japanese nationals. At the end of December, Winter stopped the German offensive just short of the Russian capital Moscow, a failure from which the German war machine would never recover on the Eastern front. British scientists 40-year old John R. Whinfield and J. T. Dickson invented a new fiber - *Dacron*. Having traveled the world for 30 years, 51-year old Ho Chi Minh returned to his homeland, set up a rebel base in the mountains and began his quest for an independent Vietnam.

Lincoln Borglum oversaw completion of the project his father began in 1927, the U.S. President monument on Mount Rushmore in southwestern South Dakota. In the first half of 1941 labor conflicts flared at steel plants in Pennsylvania, coal mines in Appalachia and shipbuilding yards in New Jersey; the unrest was over wage rates, overtime provisions and representation. Ford signed its first labor contract with a union. Ted Williams lived the words "no fear" and played on the last day of the season, raising his average from .400 to .406; Joe DiMaggio, the "Yankee Clipper", hit safely in 56 straight games, a record that still stands tall as second place on the list is a mere 44 straight games; Lou Gehrig passed on at age 37. Regular commercial TV broadcasts began. 59-year old Franklin D. Roosevelt the 32nd President of the U.S. became the only U.S. President ever sworn in for a 3rd Term in January. In June President Roosevelt restricted all German and Italian assets in the U.S., and closed their American consulates. 26-year old Orson Welles' *Citizen Kane*, based loosely on the life of William Randolph Hearst, was released in movie theatres over Hearst's best efforts to stop it. *The Red Skelton Show* premiered on radio. John Ford's *How Green Was My Valley* starring Walter Pidgeon and Maureen O'Hara walked off with the best picture and director Academy Awards; canceled because of Pearl Harbor, the Awards were actually given out in February 1942. Calumet Farm's *Whirlaway* won the Triple Crown of horse racing, becoming only the 5th horse to achieve the feat. Joe Louis took on all comers, defending his heavyweight boxing title seven times. *Cheerios* cereal appeared on supermarket shelves. Ernest Evans was born, the future Chubby Checker.

The first 4-8-8-4 "Big Boy" wheel arrangement of the Union Pacific was constructed by American Locomotive; with over 7,000 drawbar horsepower, only 25 of the 386-ton giants would be produced. The Swiss Federal Railways

IC1912-03

The impending U.S. involvement in a world at war put pressure on equipment, especially steam locomotives; the residual effects of a decade of depression left little in the way of capital investment. To reconcile these opposing forces, the Illinois Central had been in a posture of rebuilding and renovating equipment, converting wheel arrangements, and cannibalizing parts from bad ordered engines to fashion serviceable ones. These programs would continue through the decade.

Pictured above upon its release from Paducah shops in August, 1941 is IC #2050, an Alco/Brooks-built 4-6-2 (75 1/2 D; 215 BP; 245,000 TW; 39,334 TF) Pacific (original roster position of IC #1089); this unit was renovated (61 D; 215 BP; 248,733 TW; 48,683 TF) with lower drivers and other improvements to boost power; essentially, the original passenger engine was converted into a freight engine with the modifications. The picture was taken in 1941 as Illinois Central's Builder's Photograph; note the classic rods-down pose. Scores of light Pacifics were rejuvenated in this fashion.

pioneered in the use of a gas-turbine locomotive with a 2,200 hp engine. The Erie reorganized for the fourth and last time; this version would persist, until it formed part of the Erie Lackawanna 19 years later.

Land O'Corn 2-unit streamlined trainset began daily round trip service between Chicago and Waterloo on October 26. Illinois Central had its first run of the *Sunchaser*. With the retirement of 56-some miles of track, system mileage dropped to 6,489. With the recovery gaining momentum, revenues for the year surged to $142.4 million, almost 9 percent due to passenger traffic (33,172,605 passengers). Freight tonnage also moved ahead strongly to 57.0 million. With retirements again exceeding new equipment, locomotive availability dropped to 1,397 units (1,360 steam and 37 diesel) with the addition of four oil-electric engines (two switching and two transfer) and four streamlined oil-electric diesel passenger engines, netted against the retirement of 50 units (4 all-electric and 46 steam). In the seventh year of the modernization program, steam pressure was increased on 144 engines (10 Pacifics, 12 Limas, 21 Centrals, 46 Mikados, 2 Consolidations and 53 switchers); one Central-type freight was converted into an 0-10-0 switcher, 9 Mikado freights were converted into six 0-8-2 hump switchers and three 0-8-0 switchers, and ten Consolidations were converted into 0-8-0 switchers. Concrete lining of Tunnel Number 2 on the Edgewood line was begun.

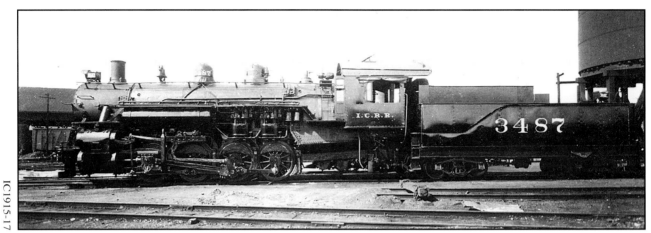

IC #3487, an 0-8-0 (55 D; 220 BP; 211,500 TW; 64,355 TF) switch engine, originally was a 1915 Baldwin 2-8-2 Mikado (57 1/2 D; 200 BP; 217,500 TW; 40,418 TF) erected for the Vicksburg Shreveport & Pacific (as VS&P #350, then #360); acquired by the IC in 1926, it was renumbered to IC #3960. The unit was rebuilt as an 0-8-0 in 1941, and renumbered to IC #3487. The tender held 8 tons of coal and 7,500 gallons of boiler water.

IC #3499 was a similar conversion of a 2-8-2 with similar dimensions. This engine was erected in 1924 by Baldwin as a 2-8-2 Mikado for the Alabama & Vicksburg (as A&V #463); when IC acquired the A&V in 1926, it received this engine and rostered it in as IC #3972. It was converted into an 0-8-0 (55 D; 220 BP; 217,300 TW; 46,076 TF) switch engine in 1941 and renumbered as shown.

IC #3624 was the last of 15 (series IC #3610-3624) 2-10-0 (61 1/2 D; 225 BP; 325,000 TW; 89,560 TF) Decapod switch engines fashioned out of 2-8-2 boilers and 2-10-2 chassis by IC's Mechanical shops. IC #3624 took the boiler from IC #1843 and the running gear from IC #2946. The spare 2-10-2 boiler went to 4-8-2 IC #2541.

In 1941 in response to the ever growing need for switching equipment, Illinois Central's Mechanical department initiated a new program that resulted in a unique wheel arrangement - an 0-8-2 switch engine. These 0-8-2 engines (62 D; 225 BP; 294,000 TW; 72,551 TF) were converted 2-8-2 Mikado-types from the IC #1500-series (63 1/2 D; 185 BP; 282,700 TW; 54,158 TF). Fifty units would be constructed, six in 1941 and the rest in 1942; initially rostered in to the IC #3450 series, they were renumbered into the IC #3650 series in 1942. Two of the six 1941 units are pictured above. IC #3651 (original IC #3451) was derived from 1914 Baldwin-built 2-8-2 IC #1519. IC #3656 (original IC #3456) was developed from another 1914 Baldwin product, 2-8-2 IC #1508. The tenders in this series (IC #3650-3699) held 11 tons of coal and 9,000 gallons of boiler water.

IC1914-10

IC1914-11

1942

In an effort to undermine Japanese confidence, Lieutenant Colonel James H. "Jimmy" Doolittle took off with sixteen B-25 Mitchell bombers from the carrier *USS Hornet* in the Pacific Ocean on a 700-mile one-way trip and dropped bombs on the Japanese mainland in April; while not causing much damage, the raid did give the Japanese people pause to contemplate what may lay in the future; 46-year old Doolittle, a PhD in Aeronautics from Massachusetts Institute of Technology, was awarded the Medal of Honor and double-stepped up to Brigadier General. After Pearl Harbor the Japanese ran amok throughout Indo-China and the South Pacific; they pushed the English under Allied General "Vinegar Joe" Stilwell out of Burma and sank their ships in the Bay of Bengal; they forced the Americans to surrender and General Douglas MacArthur to retreat from the Philippines with the fall of Bataan and the island of Corregidor; while thousands of prisoners would perish during the 60-mile long Bataan Death March, the Japanese winning streak was to end soon. South of New Guinea the Japanese and American navies met in the Battle of the Coral Sea; while losing the aircraft carrier *Lexington*, American forces under Admiral Frank Fletcher stood up to the Japanese and forestalled any invasion of Australia. Summer found Japanese attention focused on Midway Island to the west of Hawaii, a stepping-stone on the way to Pearl Harbor and the U.S. West Coast; U.S. intelligence intercepted messages concerning plans for Midway and on June 3rd the Japanese attack force was spotted nearing Midway; in the Battle of Midway, the Japanese lost all four aircraft carriers sent (*Kaga, Akagi, Soryu and Hiryu*) - the death-knell of their naval war offensive; the American Navy had to abandon the carrier *Yorktown*. After Midway, the Japanese essentially fought a defensive war, the Americans island hopping their way back to the Japanese mainland, beginning with Guadalcanal in the Solomon Islands. In the European Theatre, battles raged along three fronts; Allied air crews versus German jet engine-propelled V-1 flying bombs; the Russians in the Southern Crimea, in the Kharkov and Caucasus regions and around Stalingrad; and the English in North Africa where British General Bernard Law Montgomery would drive out Rommel's Afrika Korps at the seminal El Alamein. While Abraham Lincoln's November 1864 letter to Mrs. Bixby regarding the loss of her five sons during the Civil War gained fame, the sinking of the light cruiser *USS Juneau* during the battle for Guadalcanal 78-years-to-the-month later struck closer to home as the five sons of Illinois Central conductor T.F. Sullivan of Waterloo made their "...*sacrifice upon the altar of freedom*".

In a fit of wartime paranoia, the U.S. began detention of what eventually would total over 100,000 Japanese-Americans in internment camps. In December 41-year old Italian-born physicist Enrico Fermi and friends built an "atomic pile" and created the first controlled artificial chain reaction; the scientists secret laboratory was at the squash courts under the stands of Amos Alonzo Stagg football field at the University of Chicago. Doing their part for the war effort, Harvard University scientists led by Louis Feiser developed an inexpensive blend of naphthenic acid and palmetate to be used as a thickener for flame throwers; napalm would prove adaptable to many uses in war. Auto companies shifted production to war material. Congress gave the Office of Price Administration the power to ration hundreds of items; the War Production Board began rationing of tires and fuel, gasoline deliveries being cut back to one-half of prewar levels in some areas; most automobile drivers received only three gallons per week. As anti-inflation measures, rent control and wage/price freezes were put in effect. The AFL-CIO promised not to strike companies for the duration of the war. Maxwell House invented instant coffee. In November the Boston nightclub Cocoanut Grove started on fire; set in a time before laws mandating adequate emergency exits, there were almost 500 fatalities. William Wyler's *Mrs. Miniver* with Greer Garson opened on the big screen and took best picture, director and actress Academy Awards. Dmitri Shostakovitch's Symphony No. 7 was smuggled on microfilm out of Russia through enemy lines to the U.S. where it had its American debut with Arturo Toscanini conducting the NBC Symphony Orchestra. Glenn Miller's recording *Chattanooga Choo Choo* on the RCA Victor label sold over one million copies, the first gold record; Irving Berlin's *White Christmas* won the Academy Award as best song. Joe Louis entered the service, stopping all competition for the heavyweight boxing title after 19 title defenses. Dannon yogurt and Kellogg's *Raisin Bran* were marketed for the first time.

Needing scrap steel to support the war effort, the Southern Pacific pulled its unused track out of Promontory, Utah; thus ended the historic joining of the first transcontinental railroad.

Thirty-one years after the original steam-powered *Panama Limited* entered service, two new diesel-powered streamlined *Panama Limited* trains were placed in service between Chicago and New Orleans on May 3rd. Employment

IC1942-01

Showing a fueling operation, both coal and water, these photographs were used in the Illinois Central Magazine in an April, 1949 story.

IC #2127 was a 2-8-2 (64 1/2 D; 225 BP; 336,000 TW; 74,078 TF) Mikado, fashioned out of a smaller 2-8-2 boiler (from IC #1700) dropped on a larger 2-10-2 Central chassis. It was caught refueling on a LaSalle to Freeport trip.

IC1942-02

at Paducah Shops peaked at over 1,400. With the retirement of 135 miles of track, system mileage dropped to 6,354. Fueled by the buildup of war material, revenues grew by 50 percent and for the year set a record in topping $213.0 million, almost 11 percent due to military and passenger traffic pushed ahead by tire and gasoline rationing (39,605,808 passengers). Freight tonnage rose substantially to 76.1 million. With 10 retirements exceeding the 5 additions, locomotive availability dipped to 1,392 units (1,355 steam and 37 diesel) with five new 4-8-2 Mountains built at Paducah shops (the 2600-series were the first ever locomotives designed and built in their entirety by Paducah workers, #2600 being the first), netted against the retirement of four Pacifics, three Moguls and three switchers. In the eighth year of the modernization program, steam pressure was increased on 188 engines and 83 locomotives were converted to other classes. At the end of the year, 4,306 employees were serving in the Armed Forces. Illinois Central faced facts and wrote off its investment in the Central of Georgia, an $18.5 million hit to the books. Mays Yard, a new switching and storage facility needed especially because of the war effort, was opened with eight tracks outside New Orleans to supplement the four existing yards (Poydras, Government, Stuy Docks and Levee); expanded to 15 tracks during the next year and finished at 21 tracks in 1944 (standing capacity of 2,400 cars), it officially became an A-type saucer yard (slightly depressed in the center) with double leads; the yard was named after Floyd R. Mays, the operating vice-president who championed its construction.

IC1942-03

Illinois Central completed its small Mikes to big Mikes program in 1942; sixteen were constructed in 1942, bringing the program total to 41 units (series IC #2100-2140).

IC #2135 (64 1/2 D; 225 BP; 336,000 TW; 74,078 TF) shown above was captured in a yard, fueled and awaiting assignment. Its genesis was a boiler from IC #1616, a 1911 Baldwin product.

IC #2136 (85,395 TF), at right, was snapped at work, pulling a short string of coal cars. This unit was produced from IC #1565's boiler, a product of Baldwin in 1912.

IC1942-04

IC4x5-70

IC4x5-71

Illinois Central would complete its program (56 engines) of patching used Lima-built 2-10-2 Central (64 1/2 D; 190 BP; 382,000 TW; 72,112 TF) boilers to new 4-8-2 Mountain (70 D; 225 BP; 393,768/409,500 TW; 73,768 TF) chassis beds in 1942, with the last 15 units; many of these boilers had been freed up in the small Mikes to big Mikes program, which used only the chassis. At top, IC #2544 (boiler from IC #2941) was caught hustling its long consist over the Illinois Division on January 30, 1951. At bottom, IC #2547 (boiler from IC #2965) was snapped motoring through Danforth, Illinois on March 7, 1952. Both pictures show use of the auxiliary tender, with high coping on the regular tender.

On the facing page are two last views of the 4-8-2 Mountains built with used 2-10-2 boilers. At top is IC #2548 (boiler from IC #2947), shown headed northbound on cruise control out of Kankakee on June 25, 1947 at 8:40 in the morning. In the lower photograph, IC #2549 (boiler from IC #2909) was captured easing over the turntable at Markham Yard on October 4, 1955; this picture was taken while Traffic School was being held for Illinois Central management.

This page, two photographs of Illinois Central #2600, the first of 20 (series IC #2600-2619) Paducah-built 4-8-2 (70 D; 275 BP; 423,893 TW; 78,540 TF) Mountain-types; five units were released from the shops in 1942, the other 15 in 1943. These were the heaviest and most powerful Mountain-types on the IC, and represented the finest in steam locomotive power technology. The first view below is IC's Builder's Photograph of IC #2600 on release from the shops; this picture was published in the Illinois Central Magazine in the 1950's. Note the centipede tender which, at 24 tons of coal and 22,000 gallons of boiler water, was the largest single tender on the IC; other fuel hungry units used auxiliary tenders. The picture at bottom shows the same unit working through Gilman, Illinois on July 21, 1947.

IC1901-01

IC1901-04

Illinois Central performed many other conversions and rebuildings during the 1940's. On this page are two views of an old 2-6-0 (63 D; 200 BP; 177,750 TW; 30,222 TF) Mogul converted to an 0-6-0 (53 1/2 D; 215 BP; 181,500 TW; 40,194 TF) switch engine. IC #3738 was a Pittsburg-built 2-6-0 in 1901 (rostered in as IC #579); this unit was renumbered to IC #3738 in 1937/ 1938, and converted into an 0-6-0 switcher in 1942. It was captured at Vicksburg, Mississippi in the photograph on top just after conversion, and before renumbering into IC #392; it was renumbered one last time, to IC #352, as shown.

On the facing page are four views of 0-8-0 switchers, two each of two engines. These represent the 2-8-0 Consolidations and 2-8-2 Mikados converted by IC into 0-8-0 switch engines in 1942. In the top two views, IC #3328 is shown; this unit was developed from a 1904 Rogers-built 2-8-0 (57 1/2 D; 200 BP; 199,210 TW; 32,243 TF) Consolidation (original IC #781) into an 0-8-0 (53 1/2 D; 220 BP; 201,600 TW; 71,346 TF) with oversized cylinders, creating an adhesion nightmare; the second view of IC #3328 was snapped during a trip between LaSalle and Freeport, and used in an April, 1949 Illinois Central Magazine story. The two photographs at bottom show IC #3490, an 0-8-0 (55 D; 220 BP; 211,500 TW; 46,076 TF) that had its genesis in a 1915 Baldwin 2-8-2 (57 1/2 D; 200 BP; 217,500 TW; 40,418 TF) Mikado-type; the original 2-8-2 was erected for the Vicksburg Shreveport & Pacific (as VS&P #353); renumbered to VS&P #363, IC acquired it in 1926 and rostered it as IC #3963, then renumbered to that shown when converted in 1942.

ICNEGGS-52

IC1904-16

ICNEGGS-21

IC1915-18

IC1914-12

IC1914-13

These two pages, four views of 0-8-2 (62 D; 225 BP; 294,000 TW; 72,551 TF) switch engines that were produced by converting IC #1500-series 2-8-2 (63 1/2 D; 185 BP; 282,700 TW; 54,158 TF) Mikado units; 44 such conversions would be done in 1942, bringing the fleet (final roster position IC #3650-3699) of 0-8-2's to 50; the tenders held 11 tons of coal and 9,000 gallons of boiler water.

At the top, IC #3666 (from a 1914 Baldwin, IC #1535) was captured undergoing repairs; note the cylinder head cover removed. IC #3667 (from IC #1513, a 1914 Baldwin) was caught with hostlers in the cab and gangway, fueled and ready for assignment. On the facing page, at top, IC #3668 (from IC #1579, a 1912 Baldwin) was snapped fueling; this photograph was from one used in a story on the Memphis Division in the April, 1950 issue of the Illinois Central Magazine. At bottom, IC #3669 (from a 1911 Baldwin, IC #1609) was captured at Mays Yard outside New Orleans; note it's pulling a short consist of office car and caboose.

IC1912-14

IC1911-16

IC1912-15

IC1911-17

These two pages, six more 0-8-2 conversions. This page at top, IC #3672 (from IC #1588, a 1912 Baldwin) was captured at Markham Yard on October 4, 1955; this picture caught part of a presentation at a Traffic School put on for management. IC #3676 (from IC #1614, a 1911 Baldwin) was snapped in a typical yard shot. Facing page, from top to bottom, IC #3678 (from IC #1631, a 1911 Baldwin) was caught in a picture dated September 17, 1945. IC #3684 (from a 1912 Baldwin, IC #1665) was snapped in a yard shot. IC #3689 (from a 1911 Baldwin, IC #1612) was viewed on July 23, 1946 at Mays Yard, with the engineer in the photographic seat. IC #3699 (from IC #1609, a 1911 Baldwin) was the last 0-8-2 built; it was captured at McComb, Mississippi on February 20, 1952.

IC1911-18

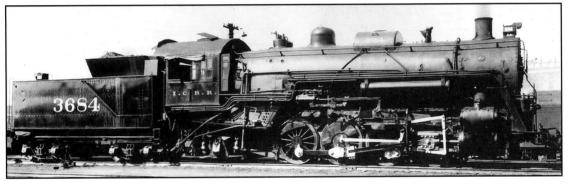

IC1912-16

IC1911-19

IC1911-20

1943

In the Pacific, General Douglas MacArthur and Admiral Chester Nimitz implemented the American war strategy in two corridors, one toward the Philippines and the other toward Japan. On MacArthur's thrust, the first island was Guadalcanal, where Japan suffered its first defeat on land, in February 1943; next to follow were New Guinea, Rabaul, New Britain, and Bougainville in the Solomon Island chain, where *PT109* earned its fame. On Nimitz's lane, the battles would lead through the Gilbert Island chain including Tarawa and Makin, which would open up the Marshall Islands and the way to the Marianas the next year. American intelligence determined that the Japanese hero of Pearl Harbor - Admiral Yamamoto - would be making an inspection trip; on April 18th off the island of Bougainville, west of Guadalcanal, American P-38's intercepted and shot down Yamamoto's airplane; a severe loss for Japanese confidence and motivation. In Europe, the Germans would surrender in Tunisia and Stalingrad. Tunisia prefaced the Italian campaign: Major General George S. Patton (Seventh Army) and English General Bernard Law Montgomery (Eighth Army) in Sicily, and General Mark W. Clark (Fifth Army) at Salerno. Mussolini was run out of office, ending 21-years of one-man rule. Italy soon ceased all military resistance and left the fight to the Germans. From Salerno, Allied forces took Naples, and then bogged down in the Apennine Mountains on the way to Rome, the stalemate lasting through the winter. At Stalingrad, the Russian Army moved from defense to counter-offense. American daylight and British night bombing raids continued; the Nazis massacred thousands in the Warsaw ghetto. 32-year old Dutch physician Willem Johan Kolff invented the kidney-dialysis machine. In January, Churchill and Roosevelt met at Casablanca in North Africa; Roosevelt, Churchill and Stalin (The Big Three) in the first of two meetings met at Tehran, Iran later in the year. A joint development of English and American researchers, the Allies began using proximity fuses on its projectiles, obviating the need for timed fuses or direct hits.

The antibiotic streptomycin was discovered by 55-year old Russian-born American microbiologist Selman A. Waksman, who would be awarded the Nobel Prize in 1952 for his discovery; created by a soil-borne mold, streptomycin won the war against tuberculosis. Completion of the U.S. Department of Defense 6.5 million square foot, five-sided, five-story headquarters – the Pentagon – occurred in January. In January Lockheed launched the 4-engine Constellation on its maiden flight; it would be used in military applications as the C-69 until the end of the war. Two U.S.D.A researchers, Lyle D. Goodhue and W.N. Sullivan, invented the aerosol can; its first application would be a spraying insecticide for the armed forces. 33-year old French Navy Commandant Jacques Cousteau perfected SCUBA gear, self-contained underwater breathing apparatus, with the simple addition of a control valve; he called it an Aqualung. The All-American Girls Professional Baseball League (AAGPBL) was formed; it began with underhand pitching; organized and supported in large measure at first by Chicago Cubs baseball owner and chewing-gum king Philip K. Wrigley, the League would last 12 years. In late March 41-year old Richard Rodgers and 48-year old Oscar Hammerstein II opened the musical Oklahoma on Broadway, for which they would be awarded a Special Pulitzer Prize Citation in Letters; they would later collaborate on Carousel (1945), the Pulitzer Prize winning South Pacific (1949), the King and I (1951) and the Sound of Music (1959). In April meats, cooking oil and cheese became rationed due to the war. In June the Internal Revenue Service began withholding income taxes, under the auspices of the Current Tax Payment Act. The American cost-of-living finally returned to 1929 pre-crash levels. Overlooking the AFL-CIO promise of one year ago, 500,000 coal miners struck in a labor dispute; the U.S. government seized control of the mines. Increasing mobilization for the war effort, the 48-hour week was mandated as minimum for war material plants. Dow Corning pioneered in the production of silicones. *Perry Mason*, the *Cisco Kid* and *The Buster Brown Gang* debuted on radio. NBC, which had formed two New York-based networks in 1927, a Blue and a Red, was forced to divest one or the other by the government's monopoly watchers; they chose to drop the Blue network, which later became a competitor in the form of ABC. *Casablanca* starring Humphrey Bogart and Ingrid Bergman took best picture and actor Academy Awards. *Count Fleet* became the 6th horse to win the Triple Crown of horse racing. After 15 years, the *Amos 'n' Andy* radio show was canceled when Campbell Soup couldn't afford to continue its sponsorship. Uncle Ben rolled out his "converted rice". In an effort to speed up sorting and delivery, the US Post Office requested addresses include city zone numbers, the forerunner to Zip codes.

Having angled and argued for wage increases for over two years, the Brotherhood of Locomotive Engineers and the Brotherhood of Railroad Trainmen scheduled a strike of their quarter million members for the last day of 1943; the strike was called off when President Roosevelt offered arbitration; the brotherhoods representing conductors,

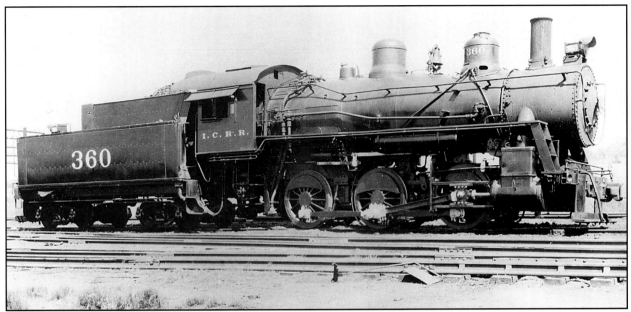

IC1901-05

Illinois Central repeated its 1942 conversions of 2-6-0's into 0-6-0's, changing over seven more units in 1943; IC #360, shown above, was one of those units. A 1901 Pittsburg-built 2-6-0 (63 D; 200 BP; 177,750 TW; 30,222 TF) Mogul (with original roster position of IC #583), it was renovated in 1937/1938 and renumbered to IC #3742; it then was converted into an 0-6-0 (53 1/2 D; 215 BP; 181,500 TW; 40,194 TF) switch engine and renumbered IC #360, and had 8 years of service. The tender held 9 tons of coal and 8,000 gallons of boiler water.

firemen and switchmen rejected arbitration, so the President ordered his Secretary of War to take possession of the railroads; settlements with labor were reached in the next few weeks, government control lasted only 22 days from December 27 until January 18.

With the retirement of but 18 miles of track, system mileage dropped to 6,336. Marching in step with the full operation of government plants, records were set as revenues for the year rose to $247.6 million, over 15 percent due to surging military and passenger traffic (48,466,037 passengers). Freight tonnage rose to 80.4 million. Locomotive availability rose to 1,407 units (1,370 steam and 37 diesel) with the addition of 15 new 4-8-2 Mountains built at Paducah shops, against no retirements. In the ninth year of the modernization program, steam pressure was increased on 192 engines and 10 locomotives were converted to other classes. At the end of the year, 7,346 employees were serving in the Armed Forces. Following Interstate Commerce Commission rules, the Company began using depreciation accounting for certain expenses, in place of the historic practice of betterment accounting.

The release of the last 15 brand-new Paducah-built 4-8-2 (70 D; 275 BP; 423,893 TW; 78,540 TF) Mountain-types was the biggest equipment news of the year, and probably the last when it came to steam locomotion.

On this page, at top, IC #2605 was caught hauling a solid train of reefers loaded with fresh bananas, north of Kankakee; this picture was published in the October, 1947 Illinois Central Magazine. At right, IC #2607 was captured getting back on the throttle as it passed a work gang.

On the facing page are three views of IC #2608. At top, a side view has a good shot of the web-spoke drivers. The two lower photographs are the same day (October 2, 1958), but from different sides; these captured the engine in local freight service at a location between Centralia and Carbondale, Illinois.

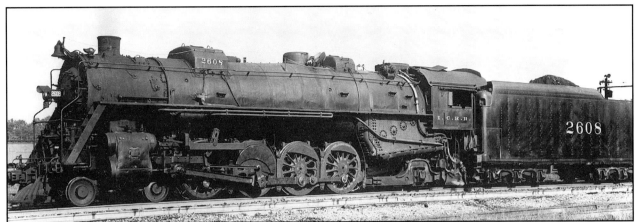

IC1943-01

ICLAG19-01

IC4x5-73

IC45x35-115

IC1943-02

IC1943-03

Illinois Central #2610 is shown in the top two photographs; uppermost is IC's Builder's Photograph, taken at Paducah, Kentucky on March 19, 1943; the shiny new engine apparently was released from the shops right after a heavy rain. The middle picture of IC #2610 was undated and from an unidentified location. At bottom, IC #2611 is shown with mixed consist, easing by the prairie grass; this photograph was published in the July, 1950 issue of the Illinois Central Magazine in a story on the East St. Louis Division.

IC1943-04

IC4x5-64

Illinois Central #2613, at top, was captured in a standard yard shot; what was significant about this engine was that it had the distinction of being the engine that moved the last excursion trains on the Illinois Central, in 1960. In the lower photograph, IC #2613 was caught hauling its consist through Indian Oaks, Illinois on May 23, 1950.

IC45x35-116

IC1943-05

IC4x5-65

Illinois Central #2615 is shown in the top two pictures; at top is the Paducah shop Builder's Photograph on release of the unit from the shops, dated June 25, 1943. The second view of IC #2615 gives a good perspective on the Boxpok drivers, which became standard equipment instead of the web-spoke drivers. At bottom, IC #2616 was captured with its centipede tender huffing through Indian Oaks, Illinois on May 23, 1950.

On the facing page, at top, is a photograph of IC #2618, the next-to-last Paducah-built 4-8-2 Mountain of 1943. The view of this unit, snapped cruising through the countryside, was preserved in a negative by Gibson. At bottom, IC #3293 was pictured at an unidentified shop on the Illinois Central; originally a 1905 Alco/Brooks-built 0-6-0 (51 D; 200 BP; 142,000 TW; 31,287 TF) switch engine (rostered as IC #69), this unit was rebuilt in 1943 into an 0-6-0T (210 BP; 34,000 TF) unit; this engine saw service until 1957.

1944

32-year old Polish-born German engineer Wernher von Braun and associates brought the liquid-fueled V-2 rocket to the war. In the European Theatre, Allied troops under General Mark W. Clark (Fifth Army) retook Rome, having flanked the enemy with an amphibious landing at Anzio. Days after Rome fell, D-Day arrived on the coast of Normandy in northern France as *Operation Overlord* on June 6, starting with over 150,000 Allied troops. The battle would lead through the French countryside, until Allied Forces retook Paris on August 24th/25th; Brussels was liberated a short time after. Hitler's Generals tried to assassinate him in July after D-Day; in retaliation Hitler purged, Rommel made an offer he couldn't refuse. The war in Western Europe would close out the year with General Omar Bradley's 12th Army Group reaching the Siegfried Line, the Germans last ditch counter-offensive in the Ardennes Forest - the Battle of the Bulge, and General Patton's Third Army relieving Brigadier General Anthony G. (Nuts) McAuliffe's 101st Airborne Division at Bastogne the day after Christmas. On the Eastern front, the Russian Army continued its relentless race to Germany, causing Romania to switch sides and Bulgaria to surrender outright; the Russian offensive relieved Leningrad (which had been under siege for 900 days) and Minsk, and entered Hungary and Yugoslavia, reaching the outskirts of Poland by year's end. In the Pacific Theatre, General Douglas MacArthur pressed from New Guinea to the Philippines (making good on his promise to return) through Mindanao, Samar and Leyte. Admiral Chester Nimitz carried on his surge through the Marshall Islands, Kwajalein, Truk, thence the Mariana Islands with Saipan falling to American forces; the Battle of the Philippine Sea took place, where the American fleet knocked out over 400 Japanese aircraft; troops landed on Guam and Tinian (it was from Tinian that Colonel Paul W. Tibbets, Jr. would fly his B-29 Superfortress *Enola Gay* with the first atomic bomb the next year). The Japanese dared everything, including Kamikaze suicide attacks; the Battle of Leyte Gulf took place, U.S. Admiral Kincaid earning a victory; U.S. Admiral Halsey defeated a Japanese carrier group in the waters off Formosa, destroying over 300 Japanese aircraft. Roosevelt and Churchill would meet in Quebec, Canada. 25-year old Richard Bong became America's all-time ace when he shot down his 27th airplane, thus exceeding World War I-Eddie Rickenbacker's tally; Wisconsin-born Bong received the Medal of Honor and finished the war with 40 confirmed kills, a U.S. record that stands. Unlucky thirteen proved true again as the thirteenth edition of the Modern Olympics, scheduled for London, was canceled due to world events. Army Chief of Staff George C. Marshall became the first wartime five-star General of the Army in December, a new grade sponsored by Congress to equal the European rank of Field Marshall; Eisenhower, MacArthur and Bradley would eventually reach this grade, as would the Air Force equivalent in Henry H. Arnold; all were graduates of West Point, with the exception of Marshall who graduated Virginia Military Institute. William D. Leahy earned the first four-star flag – Fleet Admiral – by act of Congress; he would be followed by Ernest J. King, Chester Nimitz and William F. "Bull" Halsey.

Boeing introduced the B-29 bomber. President Roosevelt signed the Servicemen's Readjustment Act (GI Bill), providing various measures to help veterans gain training, housing and education. At the Dumbarton Oaks Conference in Washington, D.C. a skeleton of a proposed United Nations was developed. At the 23rd Republican convention in Chicago, New York Governor Thomas E. Dewey was elected the Republican nominee for President on the 1st ballot; Ohio Governor John W. Bricker was selected the nominee for Vice President. At the 29th Democratic convention in Chicago, President Franklin D. Roosevelt was nominated for re-election, an unprecedented 4th party nomination, on the 1st ballot; in what would represent the 3rd change in running mate, the Party did not nominate the sitting Vice President but selected newcomer Missouri Senator Harry S Truman the nominee for Vice President; Truman would come from behind to win the Party nomination on the 2nd ballot, having finished second to the sitting Vice President on the 1st ballot. In November the Democratic Roosevelt/Truman ticket was elected by a wide electoral vote majority but a narrower popular vote margin; Franklin D. Roosevelt became the only man ever elected to four Terms. Dow Chemical invented styrofoam. Workers at Montgomery Ward & Company went on strike when their contract expired; management refused the Government order to extend the old contract, whereupon the U.S. seized control of Sewell Avery's company, carting him out of office. *The Adventures of Ozzie and Harriet, The Danny Kaye Show* and the *Chesterfield Supper Club* with Perry Como all debuted on radio. *Going My Way* with 40-year old Bing Crosby opened at the movies and won best picture, director and actor Academy Awards. 25-year old Leonard Bernstein had the opportunity to step in for guest-conductor Bruno Walter with the New York Philharmonic and made the most of it, beginning a decades-long relationship that would see his 1,000th performance 27 years later. Chiquita-brand bananas appeared on shelves.

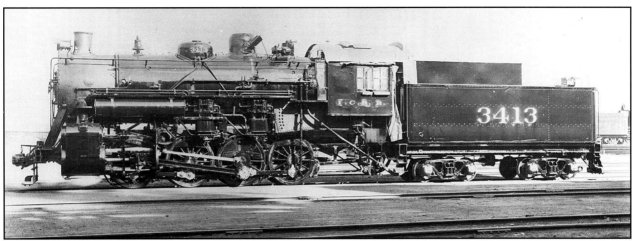

As late as 1944, Illinois Central was still converting 2-8-0 Consolidations into 0-8-0 switch engines; shown above in a Paducah shop Builder's Photograph (dated February 4, 1944) is IC #3413; this unit originated as a Baldwin-built 2-8-0 (63 D; 200 BP; 238,200 TW; 39,180 TF) as IC #974, and was converted into an 0-6-0 (61 D; 235 BP; 225,500 TW; 71,615 TF); this unit received oversized cylinders (27" x 30") which gave it tractive force exceeding adhesion limits.

Passenger ridership on railroads, already pushed higher because of wartime rationing of gasoline, reached its all time peak. The Federal Courts ruled the Pullman Car Company a monopoly and forced it to divest either the car manufacturing or sleeping car service unit; Pullman chose to lose the sleeping car service unit, and the following year sold the business and equipment to the railroads.

With no substantive changes, system mileage remained at 6,336. In the third year of the war the Company again notched performance records, as revenues for the year rose to $259.3 million, over 16 percent due to military and passenger traffic (50,703,272 passengers); through passenger service revenues were four times that of 1941. Freight tonnage edged slightly lower to 80.3 million. Locomotive availability dipped to 1,404 units (1,367 steam and 37 diesel) with no additions and three retirements. In the tenth year of the modernization program, steam pressure was increased on 88 engines and one Consolidation-type was converted into an 0-8-0 switcher. By the end of the year, a total of 9,248 employees had been inducted into the Armed Forces. Employee wages set a record at an annual average of $2,487, driven by wartime emergency overtime. Illinois Central maintenance experimented with a novel method of track stabilization – pressure grouting; initial efforts were on the levee approach to Illinois Central's bridge between Council Bluffs and Omaha.

IC1911-14

IC1924-05

IC1926-03

IC1923-17

Illinois Central received 60 (series IC #2400-2459) 4-8-2 (73 1/2 D; 230 BP; 362,500 TW; 58,389 TF) Mountain-types from Alco/Schenectady and Lima between 1923 and 1926. IC rebuilt 11 of these units in 1944/1945; two rebuild patterns were used: series IC #2300-2307 (73 D; 275 BP; 384,500 TW; 69,813 TF) and series IC #2350-2352 (70 D; 275 BP; 390,500 TW; 73,303 TF).

On the facing page, at top, IC #2300 (original IC #2428) was captured with 78 cars of southbound SN-3 at Lake Cormorant, Mississippi; this photograph was used in the July, 1952 Illinois Central Magazine. At bottom, IC #2301 (original IC #2455) was caught working through Poplar Street in Memphis, Tennessee. This page, IC #2303 (former IC #2413) was snapped hauling its consist over the 187' high Brush Creek bridge, nine miles north of Haleyville, Alabama.

IC1923-18

IC1923-19

IC1924-07

This page, two pictures at top show IC #2304 (original IC #2404); one cruising over the Brush Creek bridge and the other in a standard yard shot. At bottom on both pages, IC #2305 (former IC #2430); this page cruising down the mainline, the facing page with New York Central United States mail car in tow. At top of facing page, IC #2306 (original IC #2406) was captured hauling the Creole *southbound through a cut near Paxton, Illinois; this photograph was published in the May, 1946 issue of the Illinois Central Magazine.*

1945

In January the paradox of war: convicted of violating the 58th Article of War the prior year, 24-year old U.S. Army Private Eddie D. Slovik gained the ignominy of being the last American serviceman ever executed for desertion…while Texas-born Audie Murphy, having fought through Italy and on into France with his men, would receive the Medal of Honor and return home the most decorated U.S. serviceman. In February 1945, Stalin/ Roosevelt/Churchill met in the doomed Czar Nicholas' II Livadia Palace near Yalta to plan the peace and the shape of Europe. Allied advances revealed the atrocities of the death camps, Treblinka, Auschwitz, Dachau and others. On the Western front of the European Theatre, the Battle of the Bulge in the snows of Belgium carried on through the winter in early 1945, the Bulge finally repulsed by early February. Allied forces then pushed across the Rhine into Germany: the U.S. First Army from General Omar Bradley's 12th Army Group at Remagen, and General George S. Patton's Third Army at Oppenheim. On the Eastern front, Russian forces pressed through Poland, conquering Warsaw, Czestochowa then Danzig, and pushed right on to the German border, through the Oder River defenses and into Berlin by April. The Russian 58th Guards Rifle Division under Major General Vladimir Rusakov and the U.S. First Army's 69th Infantry Division under General Emil Reinhardt met at the River Elbe to link the eastern and western fronts on Germany's doorstep. Benito Mussolini and his mistress Clara Petacci were executed by their countrymen; 56-year old Adolph Hitler committed suicide with Eva Braun. Berlin fell and Germany surrendered unconditionally to the Allies on May 7th in a schoolhouse in Rheims, France; Victory in Europe (V-E) day was declared on May 8th. In the Pacific, the Americans continued island-hopping, to Iwo Jima in February and to Okinawa in the Ryukyu islands in April. Patterned after the heroic Samauri warriors of the past, Japanese pilots developed Kamakazi suicide attacks to stem the tide of the American fleet, but it was not to be. It proved to be a short hop from Enrico Fermi's 1942 chain reaction to an atomic-bomb; a team led by J. Robert Oppenheimer provided the technology and the U.S. tested the A-bomb, a nuclear fission device, near Alamogordo, New Mexico at a test site called Trinity in July; in August nuclear weapons were used for the first time – uranium-core *Little Boy* over Hiroshima and plutonium-core *Fat Man* over Nagasaki – which sped V-J day along on September 2nd with the surrender signed onboard the *USS Missouri* in Tokyo Bay. The steamer *USS Ancon*, the second ship with that name to gain fame, was the vessel used to broadcast the surrender proceedings around the world; the original *USS Ancon* made the first official passage of the Panama Canal in 1914. Emperor Hirohito called an end to the war after the two atomic bombs were dropped on Japan, not knowing that those were the only two atomic bombs the U.S. had in its stockpile. Over 400,000 Americans lost their lives during the War, second only to the Civil War. The war was directed by President Roosevelt and Prime Minister Churchill; the peace would be managed by President Truman and England's new Prime Minister Clement Attlee. At the end of the War, Chinese Communists under Mao Tse-tung took effective control away from the Nationalist Party led by Chiang Kai-shek; rebel leader Ho Chi Minh's followers occupied Hanoi and declared Vietnam independent; and the U.S. and the Soviet Union divided Korea, the 38th parallel used as the point of reference. In June the San Francisco Conference of 50 countries ended with the charter of a proposed United Nations approved; the charter included provisions for an eleven member Security Council, the U.S., Russia, China, Britain and France having veto power and being the only permanent members. War crimes trials would begin in Nuremberg in November. With the fall of Japan, France was unwilling to allow Vietnam independence; nine years later the French would be forced to do so.

With the war ending, American auto production returned to pre-war business, as did labor relations; in November the United Auto Workers (UAW) struck General Motors and Ford. DuPont marketed vinyl flooring. Fluoride was added to drinking water for the first time with the hope of preventing cavities. Golfer Byron Nelson set the record with 19 PGA victories in a single year. Sloan-Kettering Institute founded by namesakes. GI Bill of Rights was passed to aid returning veterans, which it would accomplish by providing college education and by subsidizing the ownership of new homes. The 32nd President of the U.S. Franklin D. Roosevelt began his 4th Term in January. Eighty-three days later, President Roosevelt passed away in April at Warm Springs, Georgia at the age of 63, less than four weeks before the surrender of Germany; the former political obscurity but straight-talking 60-year old Harry S Truman succeeded him in office as the 33rd President of the U.S. Roosevelt was the seventh President to die in Office (Harrison, Taylor, Lincoln, Garfield, McKinley, Harding and Roosevelt). Richard and Betty James invented a new toy for children based on a spring tumbling end over end; Betty named it the *Slinky*. The *Arthur Godfrey Time* show premiered on radio. Billy Wilder's *The Lost Weekend* starring Ray Milland hit the big screen and came away with the best picture, director and actor Academy Awards. George Orwell's *Animal Farm* was published in the U.S. Swanson and Sons frozen dinners debuted in supermarkets.

47-year old Wayne Andrew Johnston was elected the 16th President of Illinois Central in February, shortly after 57-year old John L. Beven died during an office car trip on January 3rd; Johnston had worked his way up through the ranks starting as an accountant in the Division Superintendent's office in Champaign; already with 27 years of Illinois Central experience, he would serve as President for the next 21. Indianapolis-Effingham passenger service ended. With effective control acquired in 1924, Illinois Central consolidated the Gulf & Ship Island into operations in December, adding just over 257 miles of trackage, bringing system mileage to 6,593. In the transition from war to peace, Company results were ratcheted down in concert with war production, revenues for the year dipped to $236.9 million, just under 16 percent due to military and passenger traffic (51,992,868 passengers, of which 1,132,775 were military). In addition to reductions in wartime traffic, heavy rains in the Mississippi Delta and labor strife in the lumber industry impacted freight tonnage, which edged lower to 76.7 million. Locomotive availability rose to 1,408 units (1,356 steam and 52 diesel) with the addition of 15 new diesel switchers netted against 11 retirements; the steam fleet consisted of 341 switching units (158 6-wheel, 126 8-wheel, 50 0-8-2's and 7 0-10-0's), 22 2-6-0 Mogul-types, 95 2-8-0 Consolidations, 458 2-8-2 Mikados, 69 2-10-2 Centrals, 50 2-8-4 Limas, 156 4-6-2 Pacific-types, 136 4-8-2 Mountains, 15 2-10-0 Decapods and 14 other hybrid types. In the eleventh and final year of the locomotive modernization program, Paducah Shop continued building steam boilers capable of carrying 275 pound steam to increase pressure and resulting tractive effort on engines, and eight units were converted from one class to another; the year signaled the end of Illinois Central's locomotive modernization program, with 1,674 units having been converted or improved in the eleven years since 1935. By the end of the year, a total of 10,634 employees had been inducted into the Armed Forces. Because of unresolved labor disputes threatening operations, the government's Office of Defense Transportation seized control of the Illinois Central on August 24th, possession they would not relinquish until the following May 27th. Illinois Central's heavy repair car shop at Centralia was converted into a freight car manufacturing facility. The 50-year old vaulted trainshed at 12th Street Central Station, through which millions had passed, also was transformed; removal and replacement began the prior year and ended in early 1945 – out with the old and in with the new.

IC1924-08

Shown above is one of three 4-8-2 Mountains given a new boiler in 1945; IC #2352 (original IC #2420) had reduced 70" drivers compared to other Mountains, generating even greater tractive force (70 D; 275 BP; 390,500 TW; 73,303 TF).

During the winter of 1944/1945 the old train shed at 12th Street Central Station was taken down and replaced with a flat roof. The Chicago Surface Line trolley tracks, which had driven through the trainshed since 1933, now would vault over the new roof. This page below, in a view facing north, showed the trainshed in the early 1940's, with the trolley tracks ramp visible. Facing page at top with the same view north, showed the train shed coming down and the trolley ramp still in place; the old train shed stood 62 1/2 feet above the rails, while the new flat roof would stand 23 1/2 feet above the rails. At bottom on the facing page, viewed from the east side of the IC tracks and looking back west at 12th Street Station, the new flat roof is visible with the trolley now running directly over it; this last picture dates February, 1949; note diesel intrusion IC #9014 at lower left.

IC45x35-18

IC45x35-07

IC4x5-11

1946

Peace in Europe and the Pacific proved easier said than done; the victors scrambled with each other for an edge, and the 'cold war' was set in motion At the Paris Peace Conference, the USSR and US disagreed on how to handle defeated Germany. Viewed as a solution to homeless Jews, 100,000 Jews were resettled into Palestine. In October, the verdicts at the Nuremberg war crimes trials were handed down on the original defendants; twelve Nazi leaders were sentenced to be hanged, three to life imprisonment, two to 20-year sentences, one to a 15-year sentence, one to a 10-year sentence, and three were acquitted. In January the United Nations General Assembly held its first regular session, 51 countries attended the inaugural in London; Trygve Lie of Norway was elected the first Secretary-General. Chiang Kai-shek and Mao Tse-tung waged war in China. 51-year old Juan Domingo Peron was elected President of Argentina. 47 years after U.S. occupation forces first took control, the Philippines were granted independence.

In February, Lockheed's 4-engine Constellation began non-military service. The first fully functional computer (programmable) – ENIAC, Electronic Numerical Integrator And Computer – was built at the University of Pennsylvania's Moore School of Electrical Engineering; it was developed by 27-year old J. Presper Eckert and 39-year old John W. Mauchly, and used a binary instead of decimal arithmetic language. International Business Machines (IBM) introduced its first electronic punch-card tabulators. The first microwave oven - the Radarange - was marketed by Raytheon. Sherwin Williams invented latex paint. 38-year old Walter P. Reuther was elected President of the United Auto Workers Union, CIO. Most price controls were ended, causing prices to soar; having foregone raises and benefits during the war, organized labor in the coal, auto, steel, and railroad industries struck during the year, achieving significant pay increases; the stage was set for inflation. A civilian Atomic Energy Commission was formed; the Manhattan Engineering District's Metallurgical Laboratory, credited with developing the atom bomb under Enrico Fermi, was renamed Argonne National Laboratory. The baby boom began, with 20 percent gains in the birth rate. Polyester fiber was invented. 43-year old Dr. Benjamin Spock published his *The Common Sense Book of Baby and Child Care*, written while he was in the Navy. The radio shows *Sam Spade* and *The Bing Crosby Show* debuted. Joe Louis picked up where he left off and defended his heavyweight boxing title, this time against Billy Conn with an eighth round KO at Yankee Stadium. William Wyler's celebrated war movie *The Best Years of Our Lives* with Fredric March and Myrna Loy won best picture, director and actor Academy Awards. Frank Capra's *It's a Wonderful Life* debuted at the movies. Robert Penn Warren's novel on politics and politicos, *All the King's Men*, took the Pulitzer Prize. Yogi Berra debuted with the Yankees. For the second year in a row, the *Heisman Trophy* went to an Army man: Felix "Doc" Blanchard in 1945, and Glenn Davis in 1946. *Assault* won the Triple Crown of horse racing, only the 7th horse to do so. The National Basketball Association was formed with 11 teams. A new Roosevelt dime, to honor the fallen president, replaced Mercury dimes issued since 1916. Timex watches appeared. The Roman Catholic Church elevated its first American to sainthood when it canonized Mother Frances Xavier Cabrini, the founder of the Missionary Sisters of the Sacred Heart of Jesus. The Juilliard Graduate School (nee 1925) and the Institute of Musical Art (nee 1905) joined to form the Juilliard School of Music.

IC commuter service from Chicago was extended to Richton Park with a single track extension. With the retirement of 11 miles of track during the year, system mileage dipped to 6,582. While higher than any prewar year, revenues still reflected a decline from war production levels, dropping to $211.1million, just under 15 percent from passenger traffic (54,186,193 passengers). With strikes in the coal and steel industries, and petroleum movements retreating to prewar patterns, freight tonnage dropped to 69.5 million. Locomotive availability dropped to 1,364 units (1,288 steam and 76 diesel) with the addition of 24 new diesels netted against 68 retirements; the steam fleet consisted of 329 switching units (1 4-wheel, 141 6-wheel, 130 8-wheel, 50 0-8-2's and 7 0-10-0's), 13 2-6-0 Mogul-types, 81 2-8-0 Consolidations, 452 2-8-2 Mikados, 69 2-10-2 Centrals, 50 2-8-4 Limas, 140 4-6-2 Pacific-types, 136 4-8-2 Mountains, 15 2-10-0 Decapods and 3 (2 4-4-2 Atlantics and one 4-6-4 Hudson) other hybrid. The Company dedicated a memorial to those who had sacrificed their lives during the war, bearing the names of 220 employees. The government's Office of Defense Transportation relinquished federal control of the railroad on May 27th. To simplify bookkeeping, the Company merged the balance sheets of 13 subsidiaries into results and dissolved their separate corporate existence.

This post-war mid-1940's photograph shows the change in locomotive power that was slowly but inevitably taking place on the Illinois Central. With steam locomotives IC #2412 (a 1923 Alco/Schenectady 4-8-2 Mountain) and IC #1166 (a 1918 Alco/Brooks 4-6-2 Pacific) shown on the far left, diesel switcher IC #9007 was caught on the far right; between these engines are A + B units of IC's streamlined diesel passenger service. The photograph was taken at Illinois Central's 27th Street shops in Chicago, shown servicing engines.

1947

Pushed in measure by worldwide horror at Nazi atrocities, the United Nations General Assembly – led by the U.S. and the Soviet Union – voted to partition Palestine and establish a Jewish state; the Arab member states walked out of the Assembly and vowed trouble. India achieved independence from Great Britain; with partitioned states for Hindus (India) and Moslems (Pakistan), the fight for independence now became a religious war; with Pakistan's territory not contiguous, some 24 years later the Bengalis would secede from West Pakistan and create Bangladesh. The USSR and U.S. continued to argue Germany's fate. Chiang Kai-shek and Mao Tse-tung battled for China; the U.S. stopped mediating their civil war.

President Truman ordered loyalty investigations of federal employees. Secretary of State George C. Marshall outlined his European Recovery Plan; the Marshall Plan was economic and technical aid aimed at getting Europe back on its feet. The Taft-Hartley Act passed over the veto of President Harry S Truman, a loss for labor unions. Congress passed the National Security Act that established the Central Intelligence Agency and the National Security Council, made the wartime Joint Chiefs of Staff permanent and established the Secretary of Defense as a cabinet post. Congress altered presidential succession, changing the order from Secretary of State next in line after the Vice President to third in line, after the Speaker of the House and president Pro Tempore of the Senate. The House Un-American Activities Committee began blacklisting entertainment and media individuals. Hungarian-born American scientist Dennis Gabor invented the technique of holography, the appearance of three dimensions in an image. B.F. Goodrich Company debuted the tubeless tire, for which it would receive a patent four years later. *Tide* synthetic detergent appeared on supermarket shelves. The ubiquitous *Tupperware*, invented two years earlier, appeared in markets. Branch Rickey and 2nd baseman Jackie Robinson made history with the Brooklyn Dodgers, officially integrating baseball in a game against the Boston Braves; Robinson won Rookie of the Year honors. The World Series was televised for the first time, and on all three major networks; the Yankees beat the Brooklyn Dodgers. In September 24-year old Air Force Captain Charles E. (Chuck) Yeager strapped on the experimental Bell X-1 rocket plane *Glamorous Glennis* and became the first to fly faster than the speed of sound, the supersonic age. Middleweight Rocky Graziano made his second title shot count with a 6th round KO of nemesis Tony Zale; Zale would win the rubber-match the next year. Joe Louis continued his dominance of the heavyweight division, a 24th title defense. Tennessee Williams' *A Streetcar Named Desire* hit Broadway, Marlon Brando playing the heavy Stanley Kowalski; it won the Pulitzer Prize in Drama the next year. *Kraft Television Theatre*, *Meet the Press* and *Howdy Doody* all debuted on television; on radio, *You Bet Your Life* with Groucho Marx, and the *The Jack Parr Show* both premiered. Elia Kazan's *Gentleman's Agreement*, which looked at anti-Semitism, took best picture and director Academy Awards. The Tony Awards debuted. *Redi Whip* whipping cream and *Almond Joy* candy bars appeared. 41-year old Howard Hughes' eight-engine *Spruce Goose*, officially an H-4 Hercules flying boat, made its only flight. In Texas City the freighter *Grand Camp* loaded with ammonium nitrate exploded in flames, starting fires in the nearby Monsanto plant, which caused another freighter to explode, the *High Flyer*; when the fires burned out a week later, over 550 were dead. Little League baseball held its first World Series in Williamsport, Pennsylvania; hometown Maynard Midget League was the victor.

The New Orleans and Mobile to St. Louis-GM&O merged with the Chicago and Kansas City to St. Louis-Alton Railroad, an end-to-end combination and parallel competitor for the Illinois Central. The *City of New Orleans* daytime streamliner service between Chicago and New Orleans made its first run in April; diesel power on the Kentucky Division (Louisville to Fulton) section of the *City of New Orleans* at times was replaced with a semi-streamlined steam locomotive because the diesel's speed couldn't be utilized given the number of restricted curves; a larger Pacific-type steam unit (IC #1146) received semi-streamlining at Paducah Shops, and maintained the replaced diesel's schedule. The Illinois Central set its record for hauling imported bananas, moving 52,250 carloads north from New Orleans; trucks cruising the State highways would eventually take all this business. With the retirement of a single mile of track, system mileage dipped to 6,581. A steady economy and rate increases approved by the Interstate Commerce Commission drove revenues almost 15 percent to $242.2 million, under 11 percent from passenger traffic (52,147,754 passengers); freight tonnage rebounded to 72.1 million. Locomotive availability dropped to 1,324 units (1,250 steam and 74 diesel) with the retirement of 40 units.

Illinois Central's program for streamlined steam locomotive power was short and sweet: IC #1146, a 1916 Alco/Brooks-built 4-6-2 Pacific (originally: 75 1/2 D; 190 BP; 278,000 TW; 41,000 TF - rebuilt to: 215 BP; 285,500 TW; 45,816 TF). With the success of the streamlined diesels, Illinois Central decided to experiment with streamlining steam in 1947, and IC #1146 was the only unit ever so equipped; with just this little experience the Company, especially Mechanical forces, felt streamlining was more trouble than the savings. The unit was used on sections of the Panama Limited; it was scrapped in 1951. The photograph, which appeared in the Illinois Central Magazine in the 1950's and 1970's, was reprinted from the 1970's issue.

IC1916-19

1948

In January, 78-year old Mohandas K. "Mahatma" Gandhi was assassinated by 37-year old religious extremist Nathuram Godse; the assassination eliminated the person most responsible for achieving India's peace and 1947 independence. In May the new State of Israel was established, David Ben-Gurion became the first Premier. Ruling white South Africans imposed a system of racial separation – apartheid. Congress approved the Marshall Plan and the USSR promptly condemned it. Still unable to agree on a German peace treaty the Soviets blockaded West Berlin, the Allies responded with a massive airlift of aid; the U.S. and USSR closed each other's consulates. Chiang Kai-shek nationalists began losing ground to Mao Tse-tung communists in China; the communists declared a republic in North China. As a counterpoint to Nuremberg, Japanese War General and Premier Hideki Tojo, taking the fall for the Emperor, and five others convicted of war crimes met the hangman in Japan. Cardinal Mindszenty was arrested and charged with treason in Hungary, eventually sentenced to life imprisonment. London hosted the fourteenth edition of the Modern World Olympics, the first in twelve years, with 17-year old American Bob Mathias winning his first Olympic decathlon; the fifth Winter Olympic games was held in St. Moritz, Switzerland.

To increase playing time, long-playing (LP) records with slower speeds went commercial in the U.S.; first was a 33 1/3-rpm (based on the Maxfield patent (#1,637,082) of 1927) 12" platter invented by 42-year old Peter Goldmark the year before and espoused by his employer CBS (Columbia Broadcasting System); the next year, a 45-rpm 7" micro-groove disk promoted by RCA (Radio Corporation of America) appeared; use of either required new playing equipment from the standard 78-rpm disks. B.F. Goodrich Company introduced tubeless tires for automobiles. Bell Laboratories announced the 1947 invention of the transistor, a replacement for radio vacuum tubes, by American physicists 38-year old William B. Shockley, 40-year old John Bardeen and 46-year old Walter H. Brattain; this invention took the 3-electrode vacuum tube and converted it into a circuit element utilizing semi-conductive materials, like crystals of germanium; the U.S. Patent Office granted patent #2,524,035 two years later; the three inventors were awarded the 1956 Nobel Prize in Physics. A 200-inch reflecting telescope, conceived of and planned for by George E. Hale in 1928, was opened on Mt. Palomar in California; Chicago-born Hale did not live to see the new telescope, missing its introduction by ten years. Edwin H. Land demonstrated his 1947 invention, the Polaroid instant camera. Swiss engineer George deMestral invented Velcro. Ten years after Chester F. Carlson made his first "copy", the Haloid Corporation showed off its newly-acquired technology by demonstrating xerography to the public; it would be another 12 years before the renamed Xerox Corporation rolled out a machine based on Carlson's ideas. In June, the "Brown Bomber" Joe Louis, trailing on points, knocked out "Jersey" Joe Walcott in the 11th round to retain the heavyweight boxing crown in Yankee Stadium; this was Louis' 25th and last defense of the crown, as he retired soon after, leaving the title vacant. At the 24th Republican convention in Philadelphia, New York Governor Thomas E. Dewey was chosen the nominee for President on the 3rd ballot; California Governor Earl Warren was chosen the Vice Presidential nominee. At the 30th Democratic convention in Philadelphia, incumbent President Harry S Truman was nominated for re-election on the 1st ballot; Senator Alben W. Barkley of Kentucky won the Vice Presidential nomination. South Carolina Governor Strom Thurmond, nominated by dissidents from 13 southern states who objected to the Democratic Party's strong civil rights platform, would run for President on the State's Rights (Dixiecrats) party slate. In November, the Truman/Barkley ticket won the election in an upset, Truman winning his first Presidential election in his own right with his platform of a "Fair Deal"; the Chicago Daily Tribune became the butt of jokes when it rushed its coverage and reported a Dewey victory. Truman's election swept Democrats into majorities in both Houses; Texas' new senator Lyndon Baines Johnson won by a disputed 87 votes. Girls Professional Baseball, the AAGPBL, switched to overhand pitching. With his New York Yankee jersey number 3 recently retired, George Herman "Babe" Ruth passed into legend at age 53. Northwestern went to its first Rose Bowl and beat California 20 to 14. The University of Kentucky notched its first NCAA basketball championship; Kentucky would win 3 more and 27 SEC titles with the 46-year old Adolph Rupp. The board game *Scrabble* arrived to entertain families; the word game was invented by Alfred Mosher Butts, who lost his job in 1931 and began designing games. *Dial* soap and *Nestles Quik* arrived in supermarkets. Honda came out with a motorcycle, Porsche with a sports car. The U.S. Supreme Court ruled religious education in public schools a violation of the 1st Amendment, thus unconstitutional. John Cameron Swayze debuted the first nightly news show on television; Perry Como, Arthur Godfrey, Allen Funt, Milton Berle and Ed Sullivan all debuted new television shows, as did Paul Winchell with Jerry

ICLAG21-17

Shop forces gather for a snapshot with their steam locomotive power, in this case Paducah-built 4-8-2 Mountain IC #2606.

Mahoney. Eve Arden premiered *Our Miss Brooks*, and Ralph Edwards debuted *This Is Your Life* on radio. Laurence Olivier directed himself in *Hamlet* at the movies, and claimed the best picture and actor Academy Awards. Calumet Farm's *Citation* became only the 8th horse to win horse racing's Triple Crown; it would be 25 years before another horse would win this prestigious series. Alfred Kinsey published his *Sexual Behavior in the Human Male*. Irv Robbins and his brother-in-law Burt Baskin franchised their first ice cream store. The World Health Organization was formed. French-based Michelin introduced the radial-ply tire in Paris.

The Chicago Railroad Fair, celebrating the 100th anniversary of the first locomotive in Chicago, opened from July 20th to October 3rd; Illinois Central was one of 37 railroad participants.

With the retirement of almost 30 miles of track during the year, system mileage dipped to 6,552. The Department of Labor reported the Cost of Living rose 70 percent in the last ten years, showing inflation was here to stay. With Interstate Commerce Commission approved rate increases making up for the past, revenues were pushed almost 11 percent to a record $268.2 million, under 10 percent from passenger traffic (48,387,085 passengers). While rate increases pumped revenues, freight tonnage had to rely on real growth edging up slightly to 72.9 million; coal business represented 34 percent of tonnage but only 17 percent of revenues. Locomotive availability dipped to 1,300 units (1,223 steam and 77 diesel) with the retirement of 27 steam units and the addition of 3 freight diesels. With locomotive engineers and firemen angling for increased wages and rejecting Emergency Board findings, the Secretary of the Army seized control of Illinois Central operations under Executive Order from May 10 until July 9, after settlements were reached; sixteen non-operating unions also sought relief but in the form of a 40 rather than 48 hour week with wages held constant, which relief they received the following year.

1949

Communist Mao Tse-tung rose to power with his Red Army in China, taking Nanking; nationalist Chiang Kai-shek resigned and was driven from China to the Island of Formosa, thus establishing two Chinas; Formosa later would be renamed Taiwan. While communists won in China, they were defeated in the Mediterranean: Allied-backed government forces retained power over Communist factions in a three-year Greek civil war; American aid to Turkey helped it achieve economic stability and fight off Russian demands for naval base sites. In May Israel was admitted to the United Nations General Assembly, the 59th country in the General Assembly; six Arab states walked out in protest; the U.S. established official diplomatic relations with the Republic of Korea (South Korea). The Soviet Union ended its land blockade of Berlin after eleven months; with a unified West Germany, a functioning government was established under Konrad Adenauer as Chancellor. The former Allies, without Soviet Russia, launched the forerunner to the North Atlantic Treaty Organization, shared security. In September, the Russians detonated their first atomic bomb, evening-up the sides in the nascent atomic age and giving rise to the term nuclear proliferation. Siam, apparently tired of its name, became Thailand. Newfoundland was added as a Province of the Dominion of Canada.

In March the first non-stop flight around the world was completed after four in-flight refuelings. The first 2-stage rocket was launched at White Sands proving grounds in New Mexico. 64-year old Harry S Truman the 33rd President of the U.S. was sworn in to his first full term as President in January. One-half million steelworkers struck. Cortisone, first isolated in the mid-1930's, was offered commercially for the first time. The National Basketball League and the Basketball Association of America joined to form the National Basketball Association. *Dragnet* with Jack Webb debuted on radio; Ted Mack's *Original Amateur Hour*, Fran Allison's *Kukla, Fran and Ollie* and *The Lone Ranger* with Clayton Moore and Jay Silverheels all premiered on television. The first daytime "soap opera" also debuted, *These Are My Children*. *All the King's Men* with Broderick Crawford as Willie Stark opened and won best picture and actor Academy Awards. Arthur Miller's *Death of a Salesman* with Willy Loman opened on Broadway to critical acclaim, being awarded a Pulitzer Prize. George Orwell published his novel *1984* in the U.S. for the first time. In June, with the title vacant, 27-year old Ezzard Charles beat "Jersey" Joe Walcott in a 15 round unanimous decision at Chicago's Comisky Park for the world's heavyweight boxing title. 27-year old "Raging Bull" Jake La Motta took the middleweight boxing crown when he TKO'd Marcel Cerdan in the 10th. 42-year old developer William Levitt began a building surge of some 10,000 homes on New York's Long Island, using prefabricated housing to beget the suburbs. The minimum wage rose from 40 cents per hour to 75 cents. Volkswagen sold cars in the U.S. for the first time. *Silly Putty*, a 1943 General Electric attempt at synthetic rubber, arrived for kids. Pillsbury began its "Bake Offs" for housewives.

Chicago held its Railroad Fair for the second consecutive year, from June 25th until October 2nd.

With the retirement of a scant nine miles of track during the year, system mileage dipped to 6,543. With the spread of the five-day 40-hour work week impacting suburban passenger traffic and labor strife cutting back freight business, revenues dropped to $253.8 million, over 9 percent from passenger traffic (42,333,575 passengers). Continued work stoppages, especially in the coal industry, trimmed freight tonnage to 64.3 million. With the retirement of steam continuing apace, locomotive availability dropped to 1,260 units (1,182 steam and 78 diesel) with the retirement of 41 steam units and the net addition of 1 diesel freight; the steam fleet consisted of 315 switching units (1 4-wheel, 136 6-wheel, 121 8-wheel, 50 0-8-2 hump switchers and 7 10-wheel), 10 2-6-0 Mogul-types, 46 2-8-0 Consolidations, 447 2-8-2 Mikado-types, 41 2-8-4 Limas, 69 2-10-2 Central-types, 15 2-10-0 Decapods, 136 4-8-2 Mountains and 103 4-6-2 Pacific-types. Dropping unprofitable passenger trains, begun the prior year, continued; a thorough review of all intercity passenger trains was undertaken. The repair and rebuilding of the Cairo river bridge crossing was begun, starting with the rehabilitation of three of the concrete piers that held up the steel spans, along with plans to construct three additional piers. On April 1st after two years of work the flat switching facility christened Johnston Yard (standing capacity of 6,000 cars with a throughput of 15,000 per day) was officially opened in Memphis (Engine #8027 headed the first train through); essentially a conversion of the 46-year old twin-hump Nonconnah Yard, employees nonetheless opted for the name change.

With not a little pomp and circumstance, Illinois Central celebrated the opening of its new classification yard in Memphis: Johnston Yard. This flat switching facility, named after former President Wayne Johnston, replaced Nonconnah Yard which had been in service almost 50 years. IC #8027 (former IC #7036), a 1926 Lima-built 2-8-4 (rebuilt: 63 1/2 D; 265 BP; 393,500 TW; 77,578 TF) wheel arrangement, had the honors. The photograph above was snapped on opening day, April 1, 1949; it captured IC #8027 with 100 cars, the first train out of Johnston Yard.

IC5x7-04

IC4x5-38

Illinois Central bridge on the Indianapolis District; this photograph appeared in the August, 1954 issue of the IC Magazine.

AFTERWORD

The Decade After The 1940's

"Heartbreak Ridge", "Triangle Hill", "Sniper Ridge" and "Punchbowl" emerged, as 50,000 Americans died before the Korean Armistice at Panmunjom. King George VI yielded to Queen Elizabeth II. Fidel Castro rose. France was outlasted at Dien Bien Phu, Vietnam partitioned along the 17th Parallel. Britain left the Suez after 74 years. Norgay and Hillary topped Mt. Everest. The Rosenbergs met the electric chair. A. Scott Crossfield flew twice the speed of sound. Pius XII died and Cardinal Roncalli became John XXIII.

The Seventeenth Census tallied 151.5 million citizens. Alger Hiss was found guilty; Joseph McCarthy was censured. John L. Lewis' United Mine Workers struck, as did steelworkers. The AFL and CIO merged, George Meany its President. Conversion from coal to oil and gas surged. The FBI's Ten Most Wanted List appeared. Puerto Rican nationalists tried to assassinate the President, and later shot five Congressmen. The 22nd Amendment passed, limiting presidential terms. The *Andrea Doria* and *Stockholm* collided.

I Love Lucy ran through 1957 with 179 episodes. Ozzie and Harriet, David and Ricky jumped to television. *TV Guide* appeared; Soaps arrived: *As The World Turns* and *The Edge of Night*. "Superman" George Reeves committed suicide. The Oscars were televised for the first time, Bob Hope the host. J.D. Salinger introduced Holden Caulfield; Ralph Ellison published *The Invisible Man*; *The Cat in the Hat* entertained children. Christine (nee George) Jorgensen went to Denmark. Harvey Lavan Cliburn, Jr. won Moscow's International Tchaikovsky Piano Competition. Charles Hardin "Buddy" Holly, Ritchie Valens and the Big Bopper ended their rock and roll career in Iowa. Diners Club heralded the credit card. Smokey the Bear made public service ads, Carl Swanson his TV Dinner, George Stephens the Weber Grill. Holiday Inns opened, in Memphis. Tylenol competed with aspirin. Elvis Presley signed with RCA, and the U.S. Army.

Kodak revisited Cyanoacrylics, *Super Glue*. Edward Teller developed a hydrogen bomb; Watson and Crick decoded DNA. John Bardeen postulated superconductivity, earning a second Nobel. Jonas E. Salk tested a killed-virus polio vaccine, Albert B. Sabin a live-virus one. Charles H. Townes built the maser, Gordon Gould the laser. Joseph E. Murray shifted a kidney between identical twins, an organ transplant. The Olympics returned; Russia fielded its first team in 40 years. Roger Bannister beat the 4-minute mile. City College of New York won the NCAA and NIT. Bobby Thomson hit the "shot heard 'round the world". Mantle, Mays and Aaron were rookies, Marciano undefeated. Don Larsen pitched a perfect game in the World Series; Brooklyn's Don Newcombe won the Cy Young award. Bill Russell went to Boston, Wilt Chamberlain to Philadelphia, the Dodgers and Giants to California. The Daytona 500 debuted.

Dwight D. Eisenhower and Richard M. Nixon ran for the White House against Adlai E. Stevenson II and John J. Sparkman; Nixon made his famous "Checkers Speech". The Census Bureau used the first commercial computer – Univac; IBM developed FORmula TRANslator. Congress set up Health, Education and Welfare. Chevrolet rolled-out the fiberglass-body Corvette; Ford, the Edsel. George C. Marshall held the Nobel Peace Prize. 59-year old Alfred C. Kinsey studied American sex habits. Russia won the space race with Sputnik I: NASA started Project Mercury with astronauts Glenn, Carpenter, Grissom, Cooper, Schrirra, Slayton and Shepard. Russia's Lunik III looked at the far-side of the Moon.

Brown vs. Board of Education ended public school segregation; its champion, 46-year old Thurgood Marshall, would rise to the Supreme Court; Federal troops went to Little Rock. 42-year old Rosa Parks just said no, 26-year old Dexter Avenue Baptist Church Pastor Martin Luther King, Jr. stepped on the national stage. Catholic Fulton J. Sheen, Baptist Billy Graham and theologian Norman Vincent Peale moved the religious revival. *Nautilus* voyaged under the North Pole. Congress added the phrase "one nation under God". South Carolina's Strom Thurmond became the first write-in senator. 44-year old James R. Hoffa took over the Teamsters. Alaska became the 49th State, Hawaii the 50th. The St. Lawrence Seaway opened.

The nations' rail system had almost 224,000 miles of track. 10,000 switchmen staged a three-day wildcat strike over wage-hour disputes; the IC's Brotherhood of Railroad Trainmen in Birmingham was the last to return to work. Threatened with strikes during Korea, President Truman seized the railroads; control lasted 21 months until May,

1952. Clint W. Murchison and Sid W. Richardson bought 1/8th of the shares of the New York Central from the Chesapeake & Ohio to help fellow Texan Robert R. Young gain control; manipulator Young won using his Allegheny holding company, ending a six-year crusade; Young would self-destruct four years later in his Palm Beach mansion, but not before he hired Alfred E. Perlman away from the Denver & Rio Grande Western. New York Central and Pennsylvania began talking merger.

Illinois Central fortunes mirrored the Country: charging ahead then caught in an inflationary spiral. The retirement of steam accelerated, with the need for scrap iron during the war and rebuilding.

Year	Revenues ($ mil)	Tonnage (mil)	Passengers Commuters	Locomotives Steam/Diesel	Mileage
1950	$276.0	71.8	39,310,551 35,443,056	1,254 1,129/125	6,539
1951	$295.1	78.1	39,246,694 34,943,599	1,230 1,066/164	6,539
1952	$306.9	76.6	36,978,574 32,893,630	1,140 926/214	6,539
1953	$308.4	75.0	35,060,865 31,086,916	1,106 847/259	6,537
1954	$276.0	71.0	30,207,967 26,836,881	1,083 774/309	6,539
1955	$294.5	79.7	30,835,799 27,148,173	945 566/379	6,531
1956	$298.4	81.6	29,507,833 25,918,254	845 395/450	6,503
1957	$289.8	75.2	27,989,493 24,645,097	813 293/520	6,497
1958	$264.9	67.3	25,649,671 22,497,595	875 274/601	6,497
1959	$271.7	69.6	23,441,524 20,186,980	831 219/612	6,500

Illinois Central celebrated its centennial year. Rebuilding of the Cairo river bridge continued, with new steel spans lifted in place while the old spans were dropped into the river; rebuilding entailed nine main channel spans replaced with twelve new structures, the old span on each end remaining. By war's end, 950 Illinois Central employees had entered military service. Simplifying its corporate structure, Illinois Central consolidated, liquidated and dissolved the Chicago, St. Louis & New Orleans, and thirteen additional subsidiaries, including the entity used to build the Edgewood Cutoff, the Southern Illinois & Kentucky. Scrap drives became the norm; at Paducah shops surplus boxcar equipment routinely was burned in the scrap yard to get rid of the wood, the left over metal frame easily reclaimed with a torch. Illinois Central sold air-rights to Prudential Insurance for the construction of a skyscraper; construction of the foundations for the 41-story Prudential building progressed, oftentimes digging through rubble from the Great Chicago Fire of 1871; it was dedicated on December 8, 1955. Illinois Central held its 2nd Management Seminar for 800 senior and junior officers; Dr. Norman Vincent Peale was the dinner speaker; Illinois Central's version of "team building". The Company negotiated with the Chicago, Rock Island & Pacific to jointly-purchase the 96-mile long Waterloo, Cedar Falls & Northern, which was done by 1956. The Company equipped 14 locomotives with experimental radios to provide constant contact between the yard office and switching crews, a sign of the future and arguably the biggest efficiency ever installed. Lining of the East Dubuque, Illinois tunnel was finished, and same begun on the Monticello, Wisconsin tunnel. Illinois Central began "piggy-back" service in 1955. During 1959 Illinois Central merged both the Alabama & Vicksburg and Vicksburg, Shreveport & Pacific into the consolidated balance sheet, having operated as subsidiaries since 1926. Steam would linger two years as 176 were retired in 1960 and the last 43 in 1961.

IC45x35-262

ICLAG08-06

ICLAG08-03

The Cairo bridge crossing over the Ohio river, which joined the north and south parts of the IC, was completely renewed in the early 1950's. American Bridge Company erected the steel on the new bridge, which consisted of six through truss spans (two - 518' 11" long and four - 400' 11 1/4" long) and six deck truss spans (each 197' 7" long), all supported on 16 masonry piers (13 original and 3 new intermediate concrete piers). Substructure work was performed by Kansas City Bridge Company and Massman Construction. This page, all views from the north side of the river: the top two pictures show the old and the renewed bridge from the same vantage point; note the light versus heavy gauge of steel. The photograph at bottom views the bridgework in perspective, from a wider angle.

ICLAG08-07

ICLAG08-05

The picture on this page at top, shows how a new span was erected in place of the old span; specifically, the photograph shows Span #9 being rolled in on the bridge piers. Falsework was erected on each side of a section, the old span rolled out and the hoisted new span rolled in; the old span would then be dropped into the river to be salvaged. The completed renewal is shown in the picture at bottom, an aerial view looking down the Ohio river toward the confluence with the Mississippi river. The two pictures on this page, as well as the lower ones on the previous page, were from the Final Report on Reconstruction, Illinois Central Railroad Cairo Bridge over the Ohio River, *published by Engineers Modjeski and Masters for the Illinois Central Railroad in June, 1953.*

Lagniappe

Illinois Central Wrecks and Miscues

A picture book on the Illinois Central railroad would not be complete without a few photographs of train wrecks and other such mishaps, such as the 2-10-2 Central # 2744 that drifted out of the roundhouse and eased its nose into the turntable pit. A derrick and number of workers were required to pull the engine's pilot out of the pit, and lucky to have nice weather for the heavy work.

ICLAG01-01

Lima-built in 1923, the 2-10-2 Central-type engine began service as #3017 (64 1/2 D; 190 BP; 382,000 TW; 72,112 TF); modernized and renumbered in 1944, it became #2744 (64 1/2 D; 240 BP; 404,500 TW; 91,088 TF).

ICLAG01-02

ICLAG01-03

IC45x35-210

Shown above is an IC engine with its cab shorn off in some kind of mishap; no other information was available. Shown below is IC # 696, a 1903 Alco/Schenectady-built 2-8-0 Consolidation that happened to be sitting at the wrong place at the wrong time. #696 was set out on a siding when IC # 804 passed by and blew up. Engine #696 was repaired and lived to see another day, being sold to Mexico in 1921 and becoming NdeM #1136.

IC1850-04

Turntables and Roundhouses

Turntables were an interesting artifact on railroads. They had the obvious duty of turning the engine into the right direction for use at the head end of a train. But as steam engines grew longer and heavier, turntables had to follow suit and become longer and stronger. A 4-4-0 American-type steam engine might register 50 to 60 feet in length over the pulling faces, a 2-8-2 Mikado-type some 70 to 80 feet long, and a 2-10-2 Central-type up to 100 feet long; weight also would be a factor as balance became an issue for turntables. In early days, turntables were simply leveling as the load was placed so as to be balanced on the disk, wheels at each end of the turntable providing direction and the center-pivot taking all the weight; later on with, for example, a loaded 4-8-2 Mountain-type with a wheelbase of around 80 feet, the engine might fit on an 85 foot turntable but be so out of balance it could not be turned, since the engine's center of gravity was different than the turntable's. In the end, turntables were changed from the leveling, balance type to the three-point suspension type; these new turntables had load-bearing wheels under each end of the table, thus providing support all along the table's length.

ICLAG02-01

Waterloo, Iowa Roundhouse on June 30, 1898. In a day before powered turntables they were called "strong arm" tables because it took a strong arm to push the handle at the end and rotate the turntable into position. This particular disk was built by Chicago Forge & Bolt in 1888; it was 54' long and built out of iron. In the roundhouse are (l to r) engines #482, an 1895 Brooks-built 2-6-0 Mogul (56 1/2 D; 165 BP; 126,000 TW; 24,500 TF); #503, an 1896 Rogers-built 2-6-0 Mogul (56 1/2 D; 165 BP; 126,000 TW; 24,500 TF) and #929, an 1891 Brooks-built 4-4-0 American (65 D; 119,400 TW); note that #929 has a link and pin coupler, while the other "newer" models have automatic couplers.

Same place, fifty years later: Waterloo, Iowa Roundhouse on August 3, 1948. New roundhouse facilities and now sporting a new turntable, this one longer and powered. In the roundhouse are (l to r) engines #1178, a 1918 Alco/Brooks-built 4-6-2 Pacific (75 1/2 D; 190 BP; 278,000 TW; 41,000 TF...later modernized to 215 BP; 285,500 TW; 45,816 TF) and #1587, a 1915 Lima-built 2-8-2 Mikado (63 1/2 D; 185 BP; 282,700 TW; 54,158 TF).

ICLAG02-05

Shown above at a pause in the action, probably break time. Note the nearest engine is IC #2499, the railroad's only 4-6-4 Hudson-type; originally 1926 Lima-built 2-8-4 #7038 (63 1/2 D; 240 BP; 388,000 TW; 70,259 TF), it was rebuilt in 1937 into 4-6-4 Hudson #1 (73 1/2 D; 265 BP; 407,050 TW; 55,186 TF); in mid-1945 it was renumbered #2499, thus dating the picture sometime after 1945. Below left illustrates a large (greater than 30 stall) roundhouse facility and turntable. Below right is a snapshot of the Freeport, Illinois roundhouse and turntable dated August, 1897; the old turntable at Freeport was an 1887 product of American Bridge Works.

ICLAG02-06

IC45x35-252

Ferry Operations

At various times in its history, usually until bridge crossings were constructed, the Illinois Central and its predecessor companies utilized ferry operations to match traffic patterns. Illinois Central had ferry operations, many short-term, between places such as: Dubuque, Iowa and Dunleith, Illinois (bridge built 1868); Evansville, Indiana and Henderson, Kentucky (bridge built 1885); Thebes, Illinois and Cape Girardeau, Missouri (bridge opened 1905); Cairo, Illinois and Fillmore, Kentucky (bridge built 1889); Paducah, Kentucky and Brookport, Illinois (C.B.&Q. bridge built at Metropolis in 1917); Helena, Arkansas and various points on the East side of the Mississippi river, such as Trotter's Point and Friar's Point, Mississippi; Arkansas City, Arkansas and Huntington, Mississippi (from 1885 to 1889); Natchez, Mississippi and Vidalia, Louisiana; and Vicksburg, Mississippi and Delta Point, Louisiana (ferry started 1885, bridge built 1930).

As needed, Illinois Central would hand-tailor individual steam locomotive units to a particular service; light track or bridge restrictions or track profile might require substitution of a special engine, such as those working the river transfer ferries. Steam locomotive #726, a 1903 Rogers-built 2-8-0 Consolidation (original #684, renumbered #726 in 1943) was used to switch carloads of freight onto and off of the ferry worked between Helena, Arkansas and Trotter's Point, Mississippi. At high water, there was no problem shuttling the twelve car capacity in a two passes (one for each ferry track), but low water increased the incline from ship to shore and forced double switches for each ferry track; retro-fitting 26-inch Pacific-type cylinders in place of the OEM 20-inch Consolidation-type cylinders plus an increase in steam pressure to 220 pounds solved the pulling power problem by almost doubling tractive force, from 32,243 pounds to 61,557 pounds.

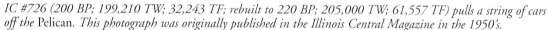

IC #726 (200 BP; 199,210 TW; 32,243 TF; rebuilt to 220 BP; 205,000 TW; 61,557 TF) pulls a string of cars off the Pelican. *This photograph was originally published in the Illinois Central Magazine in the 1950's.*

ICLAG05-02

ICLAG05-04

ICLAG05-01

Shown above and below left is the Pelican *docking at the Trotter's Point incline on the east side of the Mississippi river; note how the transfer vessel is a two-track affair, while the incline is a single; IC 2-8-0 Consolidation #726 is aboard. Above right shows a docked and unloaded* Pelican, *tethered to the incline at shore. Below right shows another IC engine working the* Pelican *- #790, an Alco/Cooke 2-8-0 Consolidation from 1903 (51 D; 190 BP; 183,100 TW; 41,946 TF). Photograph above left was originally published in the Illinois Central Magazine in 1956.*

ICLAG05-03

ICLAG05-05

The Yazoo & Mississippi Valley had the crossing to Helena, Arkansas where the Missouri Pacific interchanged traffic; this service was especially long-lived, started in 1889 it lasted for 83 years; multiple inclines or landings on the east side of the river were required, as inclines were routinely washed away by high water levels, such as the Trotter's Point incline in April, 1922. In ascending river level to match nature's vagaries, inclines eventually were located at Trotter's Point (one mile from Helena), Glendale (almost two miles from Helena) and the Mississippi state levee (three and one-half miles from Helena); connections with the Illinois Central were a short distance away at Lula (mainline connection on the old Yazoo & Mississippi Valley).

IC45x35-223

Above is a side view of the twin-paddle wheel W.B. Duncan. *Below is the 360-some foot long* Albatross.

IC45x35-226

Ferry service would use river vessels such as the *Joy* (3 car capacity), *John Bertram* (4 car capacity), *DeKoven* (5 car capacity), *Wm. B. Duncan* (10 car capacity), *Anna S. Cooper* (tug), the *Albatross* (capacity of 14 freight or 10 passenger cars) and the *Pelican* (12 car capacity with locomotive). The 201' transfer boat *Wm. B. Duncan* was built and launched at Jeffersonville, Indiana in 1881, the *DeKoven* in 1894; the *Wm. B. Duncan* was acquired by the Illinois Central in 1918, serving at Helena when sold in 1935. The *Pelican* (built in 1902 and launched in Dubuque) was a ferry boat used at Vicksburg, Mississippi to cross the Mississippi river to Delta Point, Louisiana; after the Vicksburg bridge over the river was completed in 1930, the *Pelican* transferred up river to Helena, Arkansas to ferry cars across at that point; the *Albatross* (60 feet longer than the *Pelican*) was another vessel used at Vicksburg. The *Pelican* was a little over 300-foot long all-steel ferry boat with twin 301-foot long tracks; it had 35-foot diameter twin paddle wheels that operated at an average 17 revolutions per minute and propelled the vessel at 14 miles per hour upstream and 20 miles per hour downstream; it had a registered tonnage of 1,079 and carried a crew of 10.

Upper right, the crew poses on the incline lead of the Paducah to Brookport ferry across the Ohio river; IC engine #199 was an 1888 Schenectady-built 0-6-0 (51 D; 99,000 TW) originally built as Paducah Union Passenger Depot #1; IC acquired the engine in 1896 and retained it until 1926. This photograph dates between 1896 and 1919.

IC1888-11

Middle right, same crew same engine working the 201' long, 2-track W.B. Duncan. Note the relatively high water level as the ship to shore incline is downhill; the ice on the tracks in the foreground indicates winter conditions. This photograph dates between 1896 and 1919.

IC1888-12

Below, same engine number but a different version; note the different smokebox door and the different headlamp style. This picture is thought to show #199 working the W.H. Osborn at the Paducah to Brookport incline, and is dated between 1896 and 1919.

IC1888-09

ICLAG17-08

Inclines were used for river crossings all over the Illinois Central, most for short periods of time; for example, the incline at Cairo, Illinois was rendered useless when the railroad bridge over the Ohio river was completed in 1889. The photograph above is the Mississippi river crossing at Thebes, Illinois; this incline facilitated ferry operations over to Cape Girardeau, Missouri until supplanted by a railroad bridge in 1905, replacing the Grays Point ferry service; at the time of this photograph around 1900, Thebes was considered the gateway to the southwest.

Above and at rest in dock, the W.B. Duncan *on the left and the* Albatross *on the right. Below is a view down the center of the* Albatross *showing its through track design, making it capable of loading and unloading from either end.*

IC45x35-222

Above, the bridge and decks on the W.B. Duncan, *as taken from the top of the* Albatross *which lay next to it. Below is the view straight down the center of the* W.B. Duncan, *showing the twin track, 10-car capacity.*

IC45x35-227

South Water Street Operations

Extensive operations at South Water Street were developed over a long period of time, and encompassed both passenger and freight business for a number of years.

Freight: At one time there were two large grain elevators (A and B), a number of warehouses and unloading docks – both rail and water, scales and equipment and employee facilities, and miles of track – all located in downtown Chicago on the lake front. With so much traffic being trans-loaded at the water-rail docks, plans were developed to reconfigure the slips; these plans were never put in practice. As Chicago grew, the Illinois Central's sooty rail operations on the lake front also increased, to the point of becoming a public nuisance; thus would arise a series of lake front improvement proposals.

Passenger/Commuter: The entrance to the original passenger/commuter station (Great Central) was located on South Water and, after Great Central burned down in the Great Chicago Fire of 1871, those operations were consolidated at the southern end near Randolph Street; photographs in the suburban section show commuter operations working out of the roofless, burned out station.

View of the South Water Street facilities looking straight south. In lower middle foreground was the Tribune Tower; just across Michigan Avenue to the right was the Wrigley Building. Chicago river moved left to right across lower part of picture, while the boat at dock was being serviced at IC's Water Street operations. At lower middle and far left one can just see the grain elevator that remained when this photograph was taken in the 1920's. The IC's yards extended left of Michigan Avenue in the middle half of the snapshot. Above left was Grant Park, still being filled in with material.

ICLAG07-03

To relieve congestion on the Chicago river, IC proposed a rearrangement of loading/unloading slips at its South Water Street operations in downtown Chicago. Above is the artist's conception of what the new dock facilities would have looked like; below is a photograph of the actual arrangement in the 1920's. The proposal was made to the Chicago City Council in 1916 and, after eight years of debate and delay, was dropped from consideration. The above photograph was published in the IC Magazine in March, 1922.

ICLAG07-08

ICLAG07-09

ICLAG07-05

This page above, that plank road is shown from the east side, looking west back into downtown Chicago. At the end of the road on the left side is the Chicago Public Library at the corner of Michigan Avenue. This picture dates to Chicago in 1921, a time when horses were still in use. At the extreme lower left in the snapshot, one can see a horse's head and mane and blinkers, captured by accident by the photographer.

Opposite page left, shows two close-up views of the South Water Street operations. On top is a view looking South, anchored by the grain elevator on the lower middle left in the picture; this picture shows Lake Michigan in the upper left and the still soggy future Grant Park, still being filled in during the 1920's. Underneath is a view of the facilities looking north from Michigan Avenue on the far left. Both views show how busy and congested the yards were, and only a few hundred feet from busy Michigan Avenue. In the lower photograph, the street passing beneath the building at lower middle left that advertises Chevrolet, Ben Bey cigars and Frigidaire is a plank road that provides access across the IC yards - the future Randolph Street.

Various Transportation Vehicles

Inspection cars and motor cars of all types were used over the years on the Illinois Central System. This included employee trains or vehicles used to get labor to the job site. Board members went out on the road from time to time to get a better feel for actual operations. Hospital transportation also was needed at the Company's main infirmaries in Paducah and Chicago. While time and technology have improved the modes of transportation, getting from here to there is still the object.

ICLAG13-03

IC4x5-49

ICLAG13-04

One way or another, employees had to get out on the system and check the track and roadbed, and rail cars were the usual vehicle. Over the years railcars changed with the times, but getting to oftentimes near-inaccessible places was always the rule. Opposite page shows two rail cars of the 1930's/1940's: a Buick on top and a Chrysler on bottom. Both cars were equipped with steel wheels, so there were two main ways to turn them around - on a turntable or by using the hydraulic pump underneath to jack the car up for manual rotation. This page photograph top shows the Buick (M17) being turned on a table.

Pictures right show the variations on the theme: Upper right shows a Chevrolet from the late 1920's/early 1930's, middle right shows an early Ford outfitted for rail inspection, and lower right depicts what appears to be a Model-A, but one owned by the Gulf & Ship Island, with a four-wheel lead truck and a convertible top to take advantage of the nicer climate.

The photograph opposite top appeared in the December, 1950 IC Magazine in an article on the St. Louis Division, as did the photograph at the top of this page. The picture opposite page bottom appeared in the same magazine in the April, 1950 issue, in a Memphis Division story; the railcar is shown starting its run one morning at the station in Greenwood, Mississippi.

IC45x35-238

IC45x35-240

IC4x5-15

IC45x35-234

Many other vehicles were used over the years to get around on the railroad. Clockwise from upper right, a hand operated cart that could carry and be man-handled by four; a two-man cart with gasoline powered engine; an employee transfer car, with protection from the elements (shown here in East St. Louis); a hand and foot operated three-wheeled, one man velocipede; and a larger gas operated cart, used oftentimes by management or Board members to get a close look at operations and facilities.

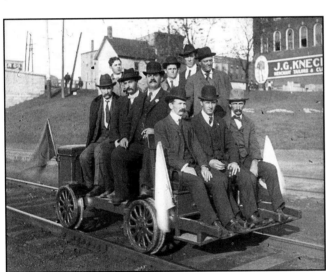

IC45x35-236

IC45x35-231

IC45x35-239

IC45x35-237

IC45x35-204

IC45x35-203

The Illinois Central Hospital Department had its own vehicles for the transportation of employees to and from its hospital facilities; the railroad had major medical operations in Chicago, Illinois and Paducah, Kentucky, as well as New Orleans, Louisiana. The Chicago operation was formalized in 1911, while the Paducah facilities came along with the purchase of Collis P. Huntington's 456-mile long Chesapeake, Ohio & Southwestern in 1893. Above are two views of an IC ambulance derived from the ever-adaptable Ford Model-T; the picture was in Chicago in 1912 (published in November, 1912 IC Magazine); note the nicely wrapped spare tires next to the driver, and the unpaved roads of the time. Shown below was the hospital ambulance in Paducah, in an undated photograph, in a time when horses were still productive.

IC45x35-247

Suburban/Commuter Operations

Commuter operations date back to the first runs of the nascent Illinois Central railroad in the 1850's. Operations, now more properly called suburban, continue through today and over the years were singularly responsible for developing the southside and suburbs of Chicago.

Photo Courtesy of Chicago Historical Society; Chicago (Alexander Hesler photograph - ICHi-05211).

Photo Courtesy of Chicago Historical Society; Chicago (J. Carbutt stereograph - DN-0009582).

ICCHS-06

Photo Courtesy of Chicago Historical Society; Chicago (J. Carbutt photograph - ICHi-35751).

ICLAG20-06

Four views of the IC's Great Central Station (W.W. Boyington, architect) at South Water Street on the Chicago River, all looking north. Clockwise from opposite page lower photograph: a J. Carbutt picture (dated 1861 to 1871) looking down Michigan Avenue from Congress Parkway, about a mile from the station; an A. Hesler picture dated 1858 from the same vantage point, but closer; this page top, another J. Carbutt view (this one circa 1866), but close to the train entrance; lastly, an R.A. Beck view showing the roofless Great Central Station, with its 3-3-2 track layout, and intact south wall. With the roof consumed by the Chicago Fire, the station was used roofless for 22 years. Captured during a snowstorm by Beck on April 22, 1893, it was torn down shortly thereafter when the new depot at 12th Street opened.

The Randolph Street suburban station showed a new look in this May 21, 1895 view. Looking north through the depot, the walls of the roofless old Great Central Station have been torn down; Randolph now boasts passenger ramps to ease entry and exit from the cars, and six tracks across are used for commuters. Three of the six engines in the photo are identified: l to r, #204, unidentified, unidentified, #219, #220, and unidentified. #204 was Rogers-built in 1883, #219 was IC-built in 1890, and #220 was IC-built in 1891; all three were 2-4-4T wheel arrangements (56 1/2 D, 140 BP, 117,200 TW and 11,862 TF). Pictures opposite page right show detail, the hurry and scurry of rush-hour traffic and the dress style of the day of the commuters.

Randolph Street station, between 1900 and 1922, as published in the July, 1922 issue of the Illinois Central Magazine. Viewed north through the depot, an overhead walkway has been added so passengers do not have to walk across live tracks. Still a six-across commuter station, engines #1409, #1429, #1408, #1422 and #1433 fill tracks 1 and 3 through 6, and stand ready for service. All engines were Rogers-built with the exception of #1409.

1893 World's Columbian Exposition

The Illinois Central planned long and hard for the 1893 Exposition, inasmuch as it would play the primary role in transporting visitors. With a major loading and unloading station at Van Buren in downtown Chicago, express trains moved directly into Terminal Station on the Fair grounds; the railroad also had local stations along the way. Illinois Central would set records in moving people quickly and efficiently.

While the express trains on the Illinois Central passed straight into Terminal Station on the World's Fair grounds, there also were a number of local stops on the railroad that accessed entrances to the Fair; above is one such entrance. The Illinois Central signage on the left notes "Trains Leave Here For Chicago" and lists times for both weekdays and Sundays. The signage in the distance announces "Visitors Entrance" and "Admission 25 cents".

ICLAG15-02

ICLAG15-04

Above and below in a R.A. Beck photograph, Illinois Central Jackson Street bridge accessing trains for the World's Fair grounds; picture views northeast, with the city on the left and the fairgrounds a few miles away on the right. Opposite page right shows two views of trains at Van Buren Street station, as published in the Illinois Central Magazine. The top picture views north back into the city, showing the Illinois Central tracks pass under the Jackson Street bridge; on the far right in the picture is a public waiting room; security can be seen on the passenger platform and on top of the ticket booths in the distance; engine #1343, an 1872 Rogers-built 4-4-0 (62 D, 66,000 TW) eases by the platform. The lower picture on the opposite page views southwest from Van Buren Street, with Lake Park (one day Grant Park) on the right; this picture clearly shows the special World's Fair cars Illinois Central built for the event; catching its breath in the foreground is engine #1376, an 1856 Rogers-built 4-4-0 (56 D, 62,000 TW) that was rebuilt in 1875.

ICLAG15-03

ICLAG15-05

SINGLE TRIP-10¢ ROUND TRIP-20¢

ICLAG15-09

Manual Labor

In a day before assembly lines, mass production and industrialization, manual labor was the rule, not the exception. Railroading was a tangible business: one you could see, feel and touch at every turn. While some employees sat behind desks in business offices, most worked in the field. Working in the field, especially in the roadway, equipment and transportation departments, was dirty, dangerous and demanding. Employees could be out on the road for a number of days in track gangs, spiking, gauging, repairing and grading roadway and track, and eating and sleeping in work trains; they might be in shops lifting, welding, riveting, torching or fabricating; they could be in a steam locomotive engine shoveling thousands of pounds of coal in a day before automatic stokers or performing grate shakedowns, boiler washes, and locomotive changes; they could just as easily be throwing a switch or taking on coal and water in the tender. Guess that's why it was called work.

ICNEGGS-04

"We've Been Working On The Railroad..." is how the song goes, and it couldn't be more true. Above is a derby-clad car-knocker connecting car and engine with the old style link and pin coupler, in September, 1891 at Weldon Yards.

Opposite page right shows two pictures of track gangs. Above right is a picture dated April 13, 1946 with a gang changing out a piece of rail at Pass Manchac; laborers wielding sledges and pry bars man-handled the rail into position. Below right shows a crew out on the Winnfield District changing out ties; note the rail jacks used to lift the rail off of the ties. These views illustrate that not every job was mechanized nor in large terminal settings.

ICLAG09-01

ICLAG09-02

Left shows a welder inside the smokebox of a locomotive performing repairs, as published in a story on the St. Louis Division in the Illinois Central Magazine. Below left is a picture from the June, 1950 issue of the Magazine in a story on the Memphis, Tennessee operations; it shows an operator utilizing the new Sperry detector to check the axle (sans drive rods) for invisible cracks. Below right shows perspective and proportion with a man next to a 56 1/2 drive wheel; this view was taken out on the Winnfield District.

Opposite page right shows two views of the interior of a steam locomotive cab. Upper right is a straight ahead view with the fireman shoveling coal, and the engineer watching the steam; it is a good perspective on the available room. From a different engine, the engineer's seat is clearly shown in the bottom right view; no one could say the right-hand seat was anything but spartan.

ICLAG12-03

Above shows a fireman performing the periodic grate shakedown to remove ash from the pan; note the ash buildup under the engine and between the rails. Below right shows a switchman working a switch for the Waterloo to Fort Dodge local freight; this picture was printed in the Illinois Central Magazine in the 1950's in a series entitled "A Day in the Life Of..."; the actual date of the picture is August 6, 1952.

The two top pictures on the opposite page right show the engine and tender for the Albert Lea to Waterloo local freight at the coal tipple taking on fuel; in a day before safety harnesses and guard rails, employees had to watch out for themselves and be careful at all times. The lower photograph shows a suburban engine taking on water at the Kensington water plug near Chicago; this previously published picture shows the surfeit of management that oftentimes accompanied simple daily tasks.

IC4x5-40

ICLAG09-03

ICLAG09-04

IC45x35-182

Predecessor Railroads

Besides its own land grant trackage, the Illinois Central System was comprised of more than 100 smaller railroads that were purchased or acquired over the years and brought into the fold. As these smaller carriers were consolidated into operations, their equipment sometimes was rostered onto the Illinois Central and oftentimes not, being simply retired or made not a part of the acquisition. Either way, a number of pictures of steam locomotives from these predecessor railroads have been preserved.

IC1907-02

Illinois Central acquired the Alabama & Vicksburg in 1926; along with the roadway came a variety of steam locomotive equipment. Shown are two of the three 4-6-0 10-wheelers that became Illinois Central's property; these 4-6-0's were Baldwin-built in 1907 (68 D; 180 BP; 146,070 TW; 25,000 TF), had Young valve gear and were superheated. These pictures were taken in July, 1926 (#406) and December, 1925 (#407), as Illinois Central audited equipment and finalized the acquisition; these engines were rostered and renumbered to IC #5063 and IC #5064, respectively. Engine #406 above, which was photographed at Cherry Street Station in Vicksburg, was published in the Illinois Central Magazine in November, 1926.

IC45x35-164

Above and right are two views of A&V #430, one of two oil-burning 0-10-0 switch engines Illinois Central acquired with the A&V; the two engines (#430 and #431) were Baldwin-built in 1922 (58 D; 185 BP; 320,000 TW; 78,082 TF; - later 220 BP; 308,300 TW; 92,855 TF); these units were built for dedicated operation on the A&V's Vicksburg to Delta Point ferry. The Vicksburg side of the service had a particularly rough incline, a 3.75% grade for 1,700 feet from the water's edge to the head of the incline. Photographed in December, 1925 A&V #430 was rostered and renumbered to IC #3400. The engine was equipped with Young valve gear; the tender held 7,000 gallons of water and 2,900 of oil.

A&V #471 below was one of five 2-10-2 Centrals that came along with the 1926 acquisition. Baldwin-built in 1919 (58 D; 185 BP; 274,720 TW; 51,318 TF), this engine was rostered and renumbered IC #3101. All five 2-10-2's were rebuilt into 0-10-0 switch engines between 1937 and 1941, and renumbered 3600 series.

Bonhomie & Hattiesburg Southern #250 shown above was a very late addition to the Illinois Central, outside even the time period of this book. When the Illinois Central merged with the Gulf Mobile & Ohio in 1972, this 27-mile long Mississippi railroad petitioned for inclusion, which was granted. The picture shows a recent, rebuilt and modernized #250 that was published in the Illinois Central Magazine around the time of the merger; #250 was a relatively rare 2-6-2 Prairie-type engine. Below, a previously published picture dated May 30, 1887, shows a much earlier Illinois Central partner. The picture captures a construction scene on the Chicago Madison & Northern, which was building the link between Chicago west to Freeport (connecting the upper ends of the Charter Line "Y"). The engine, at far left in the picture, was named the Rockford. *Note the horses employed and the visitors, out on a sunny Spring day, watching all the commotion.*

ICLAG18-09

Chicago Memphis & Gulf was acquired by the Illinois Central in 1920. CM&G #6 was a 4-4-0 American-type built by Baldwin in 1911 (62 D; 82,200 TW); it was rostered and renumbered IC #2107, and scrapped after 1924.

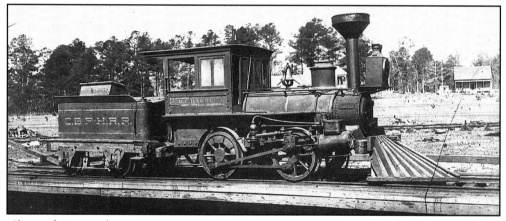

ICLAG18-05

Clinton & Port Hudson engine D.C. Hardee; this 0-4-0 switch engine operated between Ethel and Clinton, La. on what became part of the Y & M V. This R.A. Beck photo shows the 1872 unit that never was rostered on IC.

ICLAG18-19

The 44-mile long Fernwood Columbia & Gulf was another Mississippi railroad that petitioned to be included in the Illinois Central/Gulf Mobile & Ohio 1972 merger. This 2-8-0 Consolidation was never rostered on the IC.

IC1850-02

The Grand Tower & Carbondale, which evolved into the Chicago & Texas, became a part of the Illinois Central in 1897. GT&C #7 above is an old Grant-built 0-6-0 switch engine (46 D; 64,000 TW) photographed at East Murphysboro, Illinois in 1890. In a day of link and pin couplers, note the man on the far right carries a spare link. This engine was never rostered on the Illinois Central. Shown below is GT&C #9, a 4-4-0 American-type; Baldwin-built in 1891 (63 D; 80,300 TW), this engine became Chicago & Texas #9, and finally Illinois Central #1203 in 1897. This picture was taken at Mt. Carbon, Illinois (which later became Texas, Illinois) in the early 1890's. The picture of GT&C #9 was published in the Illinois Central Magazine in February, 1926 and December, 1942; the men were identified as, left to right, Robert Allan, William Fly, Frank Woolsey and Carl Mathis.

IC1891-05

With roots back to just after the Civil War, the Gulf & Ship Island was bought by the Illinois Central in 1924, and merged 21 years later. G&SI #11 above is a 4-4-2 Atlantic-type that was Baldwin-built in 1904 (72 D; 180 BP; 159,200 TW; 18,400 TF). The 2-8-0 Consolidation-type shown left was G&SI #32, Baldwin-built in 1898 (50 D; 135,000 TW). Below is #14, another 4-4-2 Atlantic-type, this one Alco/Schenectady-built in 1907 (72 D; 190 BP; 197,900 TW; 21,050 TF). Since these engines were retired or sold by the time Illinois Central assumed formal control in 1945, none were rostered on the railroad.

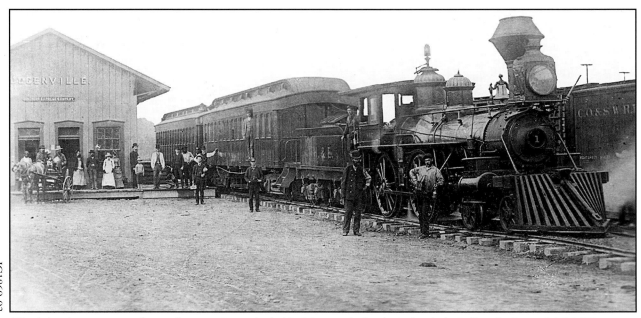

ICI1869-03

The 4-4-0 American-type shown above was Rogers-built (60 D) in 1869 for the Paducah & Gulf as the General A.M. West; *renumbered as Hodgenville & Elizabethtown #1 when that railroad opened in 1888, it was never rostered on the Illinois Central. The Hodgenville & Elizabethtown eventually became part of the Chesapeake Ohio & Southwestern. This picture dates to March 14, 1888 at the opening of the H&E; the photograph was taken at Hodgenville, Kentucky marking the first train on that branch line. The man closest to the first car was identified as J.J. Connors. This picture was published in the January, 1926 issue of the Illinois Central Magazine; the photo was credited to the LaRue County Herald News.*

Below, in a photograph published in the February, 1930 issue of the Illinois Central Magazine, is Indiana & Illinois Southern #9, a 4-4-0 American-type. While the Indiana & Illinois Southern eventually became a part of the St. Louis Indianapolis & Eastern, this engine was never rostered on the Illinois Central. This picture was thought to show the first engine acquired by the I&IS when it changed over to standard gauge. The picture dates to 1888, and was captured at Palestine, Illinois. Right to left, the men in the photograph were identified as F.P. Mills (brakeman, by pilot), Charles Parks (conductor), Perry Malloy (fireman, in gangway), and Fred Eaton (fireman, on ground and probably off duty).

ICLAGI18-08

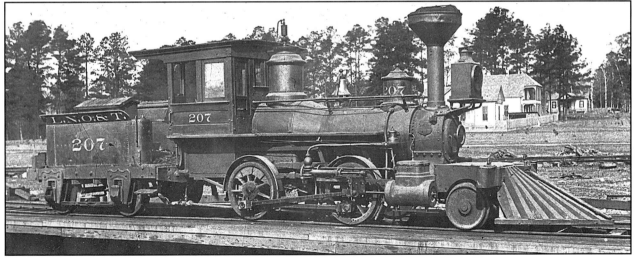

The Louisville New Orleans & Texas became a part of the Yazoo & Mississippi Valley in 1892, and eventually the Illinois Central. Photo top shows LNO&T #77, a 4-4-0 American-type built by Schenectady in 1889 (59 D; 97,000 TW). Photo middle is LNO&T #100, an 1890 4-6-0 Schenectady-built 10-wheeler (56 D; 97,000 TW). Photo bottom is LNO&T #207, an 1881 Porter-built 2-4-4. None of these engines were rostered on the Illinois Central, and R.A. Beck captured the bottom two pictures at unidentified locations.

ICLAG18-10

Above is a photograph published in the March, 1942 issue of the Illinois Central Magazine showing North Louisiana & Texas 4-4-0 American-type Richland, *an 1871 product of Rogers (60 D); this engine was a broadgauge (5'6") unit that worked out of Vicksburg on lightweight trackage (56 pound rail); the picture was taken circa 1876, and the engine was never rostered on the Illinois Central.*

Below is a picture Illinois Central published in October, 1941 showing an employee excursion train near the picnic grounds outside Peoria. Brooks-built in 1882 for the Peoria Decatur & Evansville, #23 was a 4-4-0 American-type (61 D; 80,300 TW). The picture dates August 16, 1898 at Mackinaw Falls, Illinois. Illinois Central acquired the PD&E in 1900 and renumbered this unit to IC #1220. Five men were identified in the photograph: right to left, Lee Morrison (engineer, in cab), William Pruitt (fireman, in gangway), E.E. Goff (brakeman, behind tender), Charles London (on right in baggage car door), and Conductor Butler (on left in baggage car door).

IC1882-03

IC1870-02

Hinkley-built in 1870 for the Belleville & Southern Illinois division of the St. Louis Alton and Terre Haute, B&SI #7 was a 4-4-0 American-type (68 D; 68,000 TW) snapped at DuQuoin in 1873; the engine was never rostered on the Illinois Central.

ICLAG18-18

Taunton-built in 1870 (65 D; 66,900 TW), B&SI #11 was famous for being the first engine over the Eads bridge in St. Louis. Pictured here at Belleville, Illinois some time after that event, the engine was rostered and renumbered IC #1324 in 1895. Mike Mulconnery is thought to be pictured in the cab, but 3 of his 5 sons also were engineers on the B&SI.

ICLAG18-21

St. Louis Alton & Terre Haute #49, an 1867 Norris-built 4-6-0 10-wheeler (48 D; 80,000 TW) appeared in the Illinois Central Magazine in 1945. Pictured at East St. Louis circa 1885, with engineer Ira Bookstaver and fireman Dave Hughs, it was rostered as IC #395.

ICLAG18-22

One had to be quick to find the Tennessee Central; constructed in 1903/1904, Illinois Central leased the 85-mile long Hopkinsville to Nashville line in 1905, and then chose not to renew the lease in 1908; it would be another 63 years before the line became a part of the Illinois Central. TC #605, a 2-8-2 Mikado-type, was never rostered on the IC.

IC45x35-25

The Vicksburg Shreveport & Pacific was leased in 1924 and consolidated into the Illinois Central two years later; a number of steam locomotives came along with the acquisition. Above is VS&P #32, an 1884 Schenectady-built 0-6-0 switch engine (51 D; 76,000 TW); this engine was never rostered on the Illinois Central.

Pictured opposite page right, top to bottom, are: VS&P #303, 1902 Alco/Richmond-built 4-4-0 American-type (68 D; 110,000 TW) rostered as IC #4975; a 1906 Baldwin-built 4-6-0 10-wheeler (68 D; 180 BP; 146,070 TW; 25,000 TF), VS&P #310 was later rostered as IC #5062; VS&P #332 was an 1898 Baldwin-built 2-6-0 Mogul (54 D; 102,000 TW) that was rostered and renumbered IC #530; VS&P #348, a 1911 4-6-0 Baldwin-built 10-wheeler (58 D; 144,300 TW) was rostered as IC #53; and lastly, VS&P #360, a 1915 Baldwin-built 2-8-2 Mikado (57 1/2 D; 200 BP; 217,500 TW; 40,418 TF) was rostered on the IC as #3960 and then rebuilt in 1941 into 0-6-0 switcher #3487. The first four pictures opposite right were captured on December 1, 1925 when Illinois Central personnel performed an equipment audit prior to consolidation; the last picture, posed next to a water tipple, was unidentified in time and place.

ICLAG18-15

IC45x35-161

IC45x35-162

IC45x35-163

IC1915-02

ICLAG18-06

Two views, thought to be photographed by R.A. Beck, of West Feliciana #200, the G.H. Gordon. An 1859 Norris-built 4-4-0 American-type, the pictures illustrate the old balloon-type smokestack used on wood burners; note the light duty cow-catcher on the pilot. The West Feliciana became a part of the Yazoo & Mississippi Valley and, in turn, the Illinois Central; through this lineage, the West Feliciana became the Illinois Central's oldest antecedent. WFRR #200 never was rostered on the Illinois Central.

ICLAG18-07

ICLAG18-13

The Yazoo & Mississippi Valley has roots all the way back to the earliest railroads in the South. Illinois Central acquired the 807-mile long Louisville New Orleans & Texas in 1892 and merged it into its Y&MV subsidiary; operated separately for the next 32 years, it wasn't until 1924 that the Y&MV was consolidated into Illinois Central operations. Shown above is Y&MV #7, an 1882 Rogers-built 4-4-0 American-type (63 D; 80,000 TW); scrapped in 1925, this engine was never rostered on the Illinois Central. Below, in an often published picture, is another 4-4-0, Y&MV #26, shown at Woodville, Mississippi being turned on a manual turntable. This 1884 Rogers product (57 D; 75,000 TW) was captured on the 52-foot long wooden turntable at Woodville on March 11, 1899; the unit was never rostered on the Illinois Central.

ICLAG18-14

ICLAG18-11

Shown right above and middle, are two views of
Y&MV #27, a 4-4-0 American-type that had seen
its day come and go; an 1884 Rogers product (57
D; 75,000 TW), this engine was scrapped in the
1920's and never rostered on the Illinois Central.

ICLAG18-12

Bottom is a photograph published in the Illinois
Central Magazine in May, 1933. Y&MV #37 was
a 4-6-0 Rogers-built 10-wheeler dating back to
1884 (55 D; 90,000 TW; 18,026 TF); this engine
was never rostered on the Illinois Central. The
picture was taken at Dayton, Mississippi on August
10, 1902. Julius Weber (engineer), Mr. Snow
(fireman), and Mr. Stuart (conductor) are three of
the six people in the photograph; note the jokester
coming up over the valve gear.

IC1884-02

IC1887-02

IC1889-05

IC1889-06

Y&MV #68 was an 1887 Rogers high-wheeled 4-4-0 American-type (70 D; 145 BP; 80,000 TW; 12,211 TF), shown here posed next to a turntable pit, fueled and ready for work. Y&MV #80 was a Schenectady-built (1889) 4-4-0 (59 D; 145 BP; 97,000 TW; 15,225 TF), pictured at Leland, Mississippi on August 6, 1895. Y&MV #88 was an 0-6-0 switch unit (51 D; 76,000 TW) built by Schenectady in 1889; this engine spent 13 years in yard service at Helena, Arkansas, and is pictured here at Helena in 1905; identified on the engine are J.E. Moore (fireman, sitting in the lefthand seat), B.K. Carter (engineer, in the gangway), and Wash Moore (switchman, on the running board at the head end). This picture was published in the Illinois Central Magazine in May, 1927. Y&MV #95, photographed at an unidentified time and place, was an 1890 Schenectady-built 4-6-0 10-wheeler (56 D; 97,000 TW; 17,704 TF). None of these units were rostered on the Illinois Central.

IC1890-09

Work Equipment

To maintain the Company's roadway and network of bridges, employees used pile drivers, steam shovels, and derricks among other work equipment, including inspection cars and snow plows. This equipment was located up and down the system and had to be ready for any and all work, including emergencies. While most work was planned and programmed out ahead of time, such as grading projects or bridge renewals, employees also had to be ready for derailments and other such on-call work.

IC45x35-215

Steam shovels did the heaviest of work, such as lowering grades along the right-of-way. Toledo-built steam shovel #3 is shown here with its full complement of men; the scoop on this unit swallowed 2 1/2 yards at a time.

Derricks, pile drivers and combination derrick/pile driver cars were used up and down the Illinois Central. Opposite page right shows a variety of these types. Clockwise from upper left: a Derrick car lifting poles, probably framework members, off of a flat car; Company-service car X86 in pile-driving mode; Illinois Central Pile Driver, nosed forward by an unidentified Y&MV 4-4-0 American, pounding in bridge supports; Pile Driver X7 (30-ton capacity) readied for work, pushed ahead by an unidentified 2-6-0 Mogul; and combination Derrick/Pile Driving car X25 hammering away.

IC45x35-217

IC45x35-218

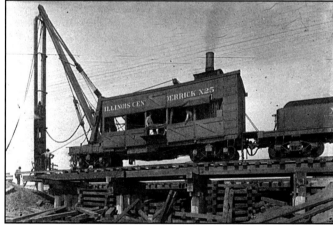

IC45x35-219

IC45x35-229

IC45x35-235

IC45x35-232

To match the work required,
derricks were built bigger
through the years. Derrick X51
(built 1902 by Industrial Works,
weight 160,000 lbs., capacity 60
tons), above, is shown posed in
the yard; derrick X54, right, is
busy pulling the boiler off of a 4-
4-2 Atlantic-type locomotive;
and derrick X90 (built by Shaw
Electric Crane in 1911, weight
208,000 lbs., capacity 100 tons)
below is shown between jobs.

IC45x35-233

IC45x35-230

RODS DOWN AND DROPPED FIRES ◆ 575

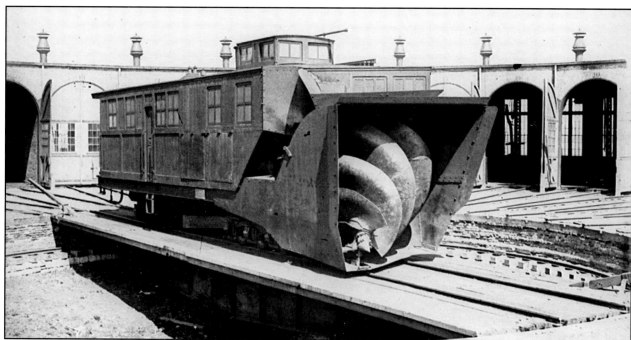

IC45x35-220

IC45x35-221

Operating a railroad in the North required snow removal equipment, and the Illinois Central could call upon a variety ranging from snowplows to flangers.

Above is an example of an early snowplow advancement - called a JULL Snow Excavator or a centrifugal snowplow, shown here on a manual turntable. The middle photograph depicts the more common push plow that waded through the snow, forcing it to either side of the right-of-way. Below, an employee works on a RUSSELL wing-elevator snow plow; this picture was featured in the Illinois Central Magazine in a story on the Iowa Division.

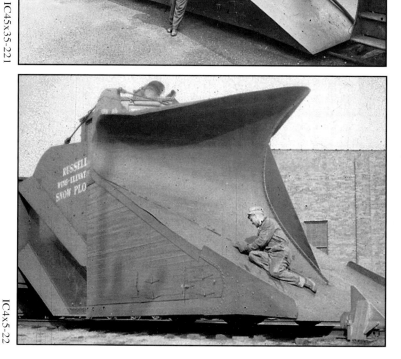

IC4x5-22

Burnside Shops

The march of Illinois Central shops in the Chicago area followed the growth of the City to the south. Early shops were located close to the city-center (Weldon) and, with early growth, moved south along the mainline (27th Street roundhouses), and then even further south along the lines for heavier repairs (Burnside). As the company grew in mileage, more centralized system-wide shops would be located at Centralia, Illinois (car shops) and Paducah, Kentucky (locomotive shops). Burnside shops were the main car and locomotive facility at the north end of the system, all shop work having been moved there at the time of the Columbian Exposition.

ICLAG10-02

Burnside shops was an extensive facility, as this aerial view facing west shows. Bisecting the upper right hand corner is 95th Street and in the foreground is the Illinois Central mainline.

IC45x35-241

These two views of Burnside shops date to 1911. The photograph above is from a vantage point facing west-northwest; the picture below faces north-northwest.

ICLAG10-01

Chicago, June, 1917

APPENDICES

Locomotives/Builders/Types

In the early years there were a number of quality builders, such as: Baldwin Locomotive Works out of Philadelphia, Pennsylvania (dates back to 1831); Cooke Locomotive Works out of Paterson, New Jersey (dates back to 1852); Seth Wilmarth of Boston, Massachusetts; Hinkley Locomotive Company of Boston, Massachusetts (dates back to 1841); William Mason Machine Works of Taunton, Massachusetts (dates back to 1852); Rogers Locomotive Works of Paterson, New Jersey (dates back to 1837); Brooks Locomotive Works formed out of the old Erie Railroad shops in Dunkirk, New York in 1869; Norris & Company locomotive works in Philadelphia, Pennsylvania; Niles Locomotive Works of Cincinnati, Ohio; Fairbanks Morse; Ross Winans of Baltimore, Maryland; and Vulcan of San Francisco, California and Wilkes Barre, Pennsylvania. Mimicing mergers and takeovers of the current day, after a time the locomotive business concentrated in the hands of a few powerful corporations. The big three were Baldwin, ALCO, and Lima.

Baldwin Locomotive Works (named after Matthias Baldwin) was on Broad Street in Philadelphia, Pennsylvania and later at Eddystone 12 miles outside of Philadelphia; Baldwin built over 65,000 units between 1831 and 1954. Baldwin built it's first successful locomotive in 1832 and dubbed it *Old Ironsides*, it's first 6-wheel driver design in 1842, it's first 2-8-0 Consolidation in 1866, it's first 2-6-0 Mogul in 1867, it's first 2-10-0 Decapod in 1885, its first Vauclain (named after former Superintendent and President) compound in 1889, it's first 4-4-2 Atlantic in 1895, and it's first 2-8-2 Mikado (first sold to Nippon Railway) in 1897; Baldwin introduced it's 2-6-2 Prairie in 1901, it's ten-wheeled locomotive with Vanderbilt Boiler and Tender (circular) in 1901 on Illinois Central, it's first 4-6-2 Pacific in 1901, it's 2-10-2 Santa Fe (Central on Illinois Central) in 1903, and in 1905 introduced Walschaerts valve motion.

ALCO-American Locomotive Company was formed by financier Pliny Fisk through merger in 1901; it began with Schenectady Locomotive Works (1847 to 1948) from Schenectady, New York and built in seven other locomotive manufacturers: Manchester (1849 to 1913); Cooke (1852 to 1926); Dickson Manufacturing (1862 to 1909); Rhode Island (1866 to 1907); Pittsburg (1867 to 1919); Brooks (1869 to 1928); and Richmond (1886 to 1927). In 1904 ALCO added the predecessor to Montreal Locomotive Works; in 1905 Rogers (1837 to 1913) came into the fold. With this impressive assemblage, consolidation soon followed. While only 25 copies were produced, ALCO was famous for its 4-8-8-4 "Big Boys" built for the Union Pacific. ALCO came out with it's first 4-6-2 Pacific in 1910, it's first 4-8-2 Mohawk/Mountain in 1911, it's first 4-6-4 Hudson and it's first 4-8-4 Niagra in 1927; ALCO built the streamlined *Hiawatha* for the Milwaukee.

Lima Locomotive Works started in the geared-locomotive business, not building a steam locomotive for railroads until 1911; in 1924/1925 Lima entered the "big leagues" when it began production of its "superpower" engines with the classic A-1 Demonstrator, the Berkshire-type 2-8-4 wheel arrangement. Based in Lima, Ohio, the company would be considered an innovator in the field and was formidable competition after introducing its new line of steam locomotive engines. Illinois Central eventually would own the A-1 demonstrator (# 7050, renumbered to # 8049).

Besides commercial builders, many railroads had major locomotive facilities for construction or overhaul, such as: the Pennsylvania's Altoona (Juniata) shops in Pennsylvania, the Illinois Central's Paducah shops in Kentucky, the New York Central's Elkhart shops in Indiana, the Santa Fe's Albuquerque shops in New Mexico, the Southern Pacific's Sacramento shops in California, the Baltimore & Ohio's Mount Clare shops in Maryland, the Union Pacific's Cheyenne shops in Wyoming, the Norfolk & Western Roanoke shops in Virginia, and the Nickel Plate's Bellevue shops in Ohio.

Major Locomotive Types
BY WHYTE CLASSIFICATION
(*Found on IC)

*	0-4-0	4-wheel switch
*	0-6-0	6-wheel switch
*	0-8-0	8-wheel switch
*	0-10-0	10-wheel switch
	0-10-2	Union type
	0-4-4T	Forney 4-Coupled-Tank
	0-6-4T	Forney 6-Coupled-Tank
*	2-4-4T	4-Coupled-Tank
*	2-4-6T	4-Coupled-Tank
*	2-6-4T	6-Coupled-Tank
*	2-6-6T	6-Coupled-Tank
*	2-6-0	MOGUL – successful in 1860's
*	2-6-2	PRAIRIE
	2-6-4	
*	2-8-0	CONSOLIDATION (Stripped wartime version = PERSHING)
*	2-8-2	MIKADO or MACARTHUR
*	2-8-4	BERKSHIRE or LIMA (1st appeared in 1925)
*	2-10-0	DECAPOD
*	2-10-2	SANTA FE (1st used on Santa Fe in 1903) CENTRAL on IC
	2-10-4	TEXAS – Selkirk (CPR) (1st appeared in 1919)
*	4-4-0	AMERICAN or 8-WHEEL
*	4-4-2	ATLANTIC
	4-4-4	READING - Jubilee (CPR)
*	4-6-0	TEN WHEELER (Casey Jones)
*	4-6-2	PACIFIC
*	4-6-4	HUDSON or BALTIC
*	4-8-0	12-WHEEL
*	4-8-2	MOUNTAIN + MOHAWK
	4-8-4	NORTHERN + NIAGRA + GREENBRIER + POCONO + Confederation (CN)
	4-10-0	MASTODON
	4-10-2	SOUTHERN PACIFIC
	4-12-2	NINES or UNION PACIFIC
	0-6-6-0	
*	2-6-6-2	IC's only mallets, from Central of Georgia
	2-6-6-4	
	2-6-6-6	ALLEGHENY
	2-8-8-2	
	2-8-8-4	YELLOWSTONE (1st one a 1929 ALCO product)
	2-8-8-8-2	ERIE TRIPLEX – six 36" x 32" cylinders (only 3 copies)
	2-8-8-8-4	VIRGINIAN TRIPLEX (only 1 copy)
	4-4-4-4	DUPLEX
	4-6-6-4	CHALLENGER
	4-8-8-2	Cab-forward on the SP
	4-8-8-4	BIG BOY

Select Illinois Central Train Names

NAME	TRAIN
SINNISSIPPI	Day train between Chicago and Ft. Dodge
CREOLE	Between Chicago and New Orleans, plus Louisville and St. Louis connections
LOUISIANE	*CREOLE* companion trains
PLANTER	Between Memphis and New Orleans via Y & MV
IOWAN	Between Chicago and Omaha, and western points
HAWKEYE	*IOWAN* companion trains, overnight
SEMINOLE	Year-round train Chicago to Birmingham to Florida resorts
FLORIDAN	Seasonal train Chicago to Birmingham to Florida resorts
PANAMA LIMITED	Between Chicago and New Orleans
CITY OF NEW ORLEANS	Between Chicago and New Orleans
CHICKASAW	Overnight train between Memphis and St. Louis
DAYLIGHT	Day train between Chicago and St. Louis
DIAMOND	Night train between Chicago and St. Louis
GREEN DIAMOND	Streamliner between Chicago and St. Louis
CITY OF MIAMI	Streamliner between Chicago and Miami
SUNCHASER	Seasonal train between Chicago and Miami
MISS LOU	Streamliner between Jackson, Miss and New Orleans
ILLINI	Streamliner between Chicago and Champaign
LAND O' CORN	Streamliner between Chicago and Waterloo
MICHIGAN BOULEVARD	St. Louis to Chicago
WORLD'S FAIR SPECIAL	Between Memphis and Chicago
IRVIN S. COBB	Between Louisville and Fulton
KENTUCKY CARDINAL	Between Louisville and Fulton

Interesting Illinois Central Suburban Station Names

LATEST NAME	FORMER NAMES
Randolph Street	Central Depot
12th Street	Park Row/Roosevelt Road/Central Station
14th Street	Weldon
26th Street	Car Works
36th Street	Fairview/Douglas
39th Street	Oakland
43rd Street	Reform School
47th Street	Kenwood
53rd Street	Hyde Park
57th Street	Woodville, previously Wood Pile
63rd Street	Woodlawn
67th Street	Oak Woods
70th Street	Brookdale
72nd Street	Essex
75th Street	Grand Crossing
79th Street	Chatham
82nd Street	Avalon Park
87th Street	Woodruff
90th Street	Dauphin Park
91st Street	Chesterfield
95th Street	Burnside
111th Street	Pullman
115th Street	Kensington
130th Street	Wildwood Yard
137th Street	Riverdale

South Chicago Branch

75th Street	Windsor Park
79th Street	Cheltenham
91st Street	South Chicago

Photographers

Any work with an historical perspective relies on the efforts of many people, in this case early photographers. A number of company photographers, in addition to many individuals, receive credit for creating and preserving the visual history of the Illinois Central railroad. While in no way a comprehensive list, following is a short acknowledgment to a few of the early photo-documentarians in this field, the people who created the original negatives and glass-plates from which most of these photographs are reproduced.

Independent Photographers:

R. A. Beck
Gerald M. Best
C. W. Witbeck
Otto C. Perry
John Carbutt

Illinois Central Company Photographers:

E.B. Adams
C. J. Corliss
G.R. Hurd
C.B. Medin
J.K. Melton
Luther Paul

Contracted Photographers:

Hedrich - Blessing
Kaufmann & Fabry

Each photograph reproduced in this volume has a code noted in the margin of the picture; this code was the author's way of tracking the source of the scanned view from the Illinois Central files. The code description key follows.

45x35 = 35mm negatives copied onto 4x5 sheet film
4x5 = 4x5 negatives
5x7 = 5x7 prints
CHS = Chicago Historical Society 8x10 prints
DPL = Denver Public Library 8x10 prints
LAG = Miscellaneous negatives and prints
NEGGS = 35mm positives
NEW = Newberry Library 8x10 prints
Year = 8x10 and 5x7 prints

Notes On Basic Locomotive Composition

There is certainly no way one can craft into this book a detailed history of locomotive development, and indeed there already are many outstanding volumes on that subject, such as *The Steam Locomotive* by Ralph P. Johnson, Chief Engineer of the Baldwin Locomotive Works to name just one. But while not here to explain the history of steam locomotives, this book must, to an extent, establish a few guide posts so the casual reader will have some understanding of the differences in the locomotives pictured, which will give clues why they were included in the first place. To that end, following is a review the *Whyte* System of classifying steam locomotive engines, and in the slightest of detail an explanation of what gave rise to the various arrangements.

The *Whyte* System is a notation that profiles the wheel arrangement of steam locomotives. A wheel arrangement of 2-6-4 refers to a steam locomotive with a total of 12 wheels, arranged 6 on each side; 2 wheels on a single axle in the front of the engine (pilot or lead truck), three pair of wheels arranged in the middle (drive wheels or drivers), and 4 wheels arranged on two axles in the rear position (rear or trailing truck).

The pilot truck is load-bearing (2-wheel pilot truck or 4-wheel bogie truck; the more lead wheels, the more stability and support) and guides the locomotive into curves and supports the front end of the locomotive; the faster the service and the more precious the cargo, the greater the use of lead trucks.

The drive wheels are the point at which the horsepower generated by the steam locomotive is converted into the driving force that turns the wheels and moves the engine along the rails. Regarding drive wheel physics, the larger the diameter of the drive wheel the faster the top speed of the engine but the lower the power for pulling (tractive force); conversely, the smaller the driver the higher the pulling power and the lower the top speed. Not all drive wheels need be flanged...ten-coupled drivers sometimes had the 1st, 4th and 5th pair flanged and the other two without flanges to ease around curves.

The trailing truck wheel set helped support a larger firebox for the locomotive; with the firebox carried on the rear wheels, instead of over or between the driving wheels, this arrangement allowed bigger fireboxes and resulted in higher steam production. While trailing trucks generally were non-powered, on some designs the rear truck was powered with a small steam engine boosting tractive effort, to help get started and on inclines; the booster would cut out over a set speed limit. A trailing truck also improved the locomotive's stability in reverse, when pushing freight equipment.

Switching engines generally had all drive wheels, such as 0-4-0 or 0-8-0, centering all the weight of the locomotive on the drivers and generating maximum pull and push power; no lead trucks were required because no high speed curves would be encountered, and rear trucks were not required because a larger firebox wasn't needed in this slow-speed service.

The 4-4-0 American-type had excellent tractive effort for pulling but slow speed, which wasn't important at that time; they had deep but narrow fireboxes between the drivers and were used in both freight and passenger services. Growth went along freight lines (2-wheel lead trucks) and passenger lines (4-wheel lead trucks); the Mogul 2-6-0 with its extra pulling power for freight, the longer 4-6-0 and the 4-8-0 for passenger; next came the Mogul's cousin the 2-8-0 Consolidation. The Atlantic 4-4-2 came along with a bigger firebox, and then the Pacific 4-6-2 which gave both a bigger boiler and bigger firebox; the well-balanced Pacific gained huge acceptance. The 4-6-4 Hudson followed the Pacific, then the 4-8-2 Mountain and the 4-8-4 Northern. The 2-8-2 Mikado was the next evolution with its wide and deep firebox, below and behind the driver wheels. World War I held up locomotive development for a period. The next area of improvement was in raising the temperature of the steam itself, thus creating more power with more expansive steam - the age of superpower and superheaters; the 2-8-4 Berkshire was the leader, with a much bigger firebox (12 ½ feet by 8 feet for a 100 square foot grate area), supported on a 4-wheel rear truck; the bigger firebox and bigger boiler made more steam at a higher pressure, generating more horsepower. The next iteration was 2-10-0 Decapods, which were like a big Consolidation, then the 2-10-2 Santa Fe's and the 2-10-4 Texas'. World War II slowed steam development, which reactivated after the war; while some impressive new steam engines were built after World War II, the rising cost of coal was the last straw as steam power gave way to diesel engines.

Steam locomotive construction always tried to balance the engine on the pilot, drive and trailing wheels. There was a limit to how much weight one could place over the drive wheels before the engine simply sank into the mud. While greater weight might yield higher tractive effort on paper, it often would require stronger rails and greater roadbed preparation. In the development of steam locomotives there were hundreds of improvements and advances over the years, such as: force-feed lubricators, which allowed longer runs before an oilman had to check moving parts; superheaters, which provided more efficient use of steam; and stokers, which allowed the bigger fires' 6,000 pounds-of-coal-per-hour appetite to be fed, a rate hand-firing could not maintain. Heavy freight units like the 4-8-2 Mountain-type 2500-Class could consume up to 6,000 gallons of water and 4 tons of coal per hour.

The boiler was key, because the rate at which it turned water into steam regulated everything else…and the superheater was a major advance in boilers. Superheaters heated saturated steam (the point where water changes into steam at a given pressure) to an even higher temperature; with saturated steam the temperature dropped below vaporization as it hit the cylinder heads, losing some expansive force; with superheaters, the temperature was so high that even with the temperature loss it remained above the vaporization level, so no expansive force was lost. A key but originally unintended attribute of superheated boiler steam was that the pressure could be dropped while the temperature was raised, thus generating a savings on coal and water usage while maintaining efficiency.

The typical locomotive was a single-expansion engine and utilized only high-pressure cylinders. Tractive force could be raised by increasing steam pressure or increasing the diameter of the cylinder; higher boiler pressure oftentimes required strengthening the boiler, while increasing the diameter of the cylinders simply gave more surface for the steam to push against and thus more horsepower; both methods were subject to diminishing returns (physics) as the expense to accommodate the change eventually exceeded the benefit derived. Frenchman Anatole Mallet invented articulated compound expansion engines, which used both high-pressure and low-pressure cylinders; boiler steam passed through high-pressure cylinders, which exhausted it into low-pressure cylinders where it was utilized a second time; compounds were popular for a while because they burned less fuel for the power and were more efficient; the advent of superheated steam proved even more effective, with fewer mechanical gadgets, halting the growth of compound expansion engines.

Tractive Force is a calculated number, and subject to manipulation; the calculation is:

$$\text{Tractive Force} = (K \times P \times C^2 \times S) / D$$

K = the percentage factor of steam pressure which adjusts for the pressure drop from boiler to cylinder;

P = Pressure, in pounds per square inch;

C = Cylinder diameter, in inches;

S = Stroke, in inches;

D = Diameter of drive wheels, in inches.

Thus an engine such as IC #2600, a Paducah-built 4-8-2 Mountain, which had 28 inch cylinders with a 30 inch stroke, 70 inch drive wheels, and 275 pounds of boiler pressure would calculate out to 78,540 pounds of tractive force when using an 85 percent factor; it would yield 83,160 pounds of tractive force with a 90 percent factor.

$(.85 \times 275 \times 28^2 \times 30) / 70 = 78,540$ pounds of tractive force

$(.90 \times 275 \times 28^2 \times 30) / 70 = 83,160$ pounds of tractive force

Illinois Central Historical Roster

Nationally, between 125,000 and 150,000 steam locomotives were built during the age of steam; maybe 70,000 were in operation on the road during the peak years immediately following World War I; Illinois Central steam topped out at about 1,964 units in 1926. In almost 110 years of steam, it is impossible to precisely state how many steam locomotives were officially rostered on the Illinois Central; with some engines rebuilt from one type to another (for example, a 2-6-0 into an 0-6-0), some units acquired through consolidations and never rostered into the Illinois Central fleet, other units put together from two or more different types to form a third type (for example, the running gear and tenders of Central-type locomotives mated to the boilers of Mikados to fashion Decapod switch units), and other such operations in the machinery department; close is possible, precise isn't. Following is an approximation of the Illinois Central fleet as officially rostered through the years; much of this material was drawn from *Illinois Central Steam Finale* by Lloyd E. Stagner and Stephen A. Lee.

Type	Wheel Arrangement	Number Rostered	1st Use On IC	Notes
Mogul	2-6-0	337	1880	
Prairie	2-6-2	1	1902	Cnvtd to 4-6-2
Consolidation	2-8-0	359	1891	
Mikado	2-8-2	605	1911	
Lima	2-8-4	51	1926	also, Berkshire
Decapod	2-10-0	15	1939	Switchers
Central	2-10-2	137	1916	also, Santa Fe
American	4-4-0	503	1852	
Atlantic	4-4-2	26	1902	80" drivers
10-Wheel	4-6-0	245	1877	Casey Jones
Pacific	4-6-2	180	1905	heavy + light
Hudson	4-6-4	1	1937	rebuilt 2-8-4
Mountain	4-8-2	60 and 76	1923-1937	2400+2500/2600
Switch	0-4-0	50'ish	1856	Shop swx
Switch	0-6-0	295	1889	
Switch	0-8-0	131	1921	
Hump Switch	0-8-2	50	1941	former 2-8-2's
Switch	0-10-0	7	1926	Ala. & Vicks.
Mallet	2-6-6-2	10	1926	Cent. of Georgia
Suburban	2-4-4T, 2-4-6T	56	1880	Tea Kettles

Biggest Drivers on Illinois Central Steam = 80" on the 4-4-2 Atlantics
Highest Boiler Pressure on Illinois Central Steam = 2800-Class rebuilt 2-10-2 Centrals @ 275 lbs. (1)
Heaviest Engines on Illinois Central Steam = 2-6-6-2 Mallets from the C of G @ 438,000 lbs.
Highest Tractive Force on Illinois Central Steam = 2800-Class rebuilt 2-10-2 Centrals @ 104,322 lbs. (2)
Largest Tenders on Illinois Central Steam = 2600-Class 4-8-2 Mountains @ 24 tons and 22,000 gallons

(1) Other types also. Some higher, but only experimental units.
(2) Depends on tractive force calculation factor, 85% or 90%, yet these were the highest.

INDEX OF LOCOMOTIVES

PHOTO Nº	BUILDER	CLASS	CYLINDERS	WEIGHT	BUILT	NUMBER OF ENGINES OWNED									
						1883	1884	1885	1886	1887	1888	1889	1890	1891	1892
1	ROGERS	CONSOLIDATION	21"X24"	137300	1891									22	22
2	SCHENECTADY	10 WHEEL	19"X24"	123500	1889-90							3	6	6	6
3	COOKE	DO	19"X24"	120000	1890-91								20	26	26
4	BALDWIN	DO	16"X24"	70000	1871	1	1	1	1	1	1	1	1		
5	BROOKS	MOGUL	18"&19"X24"	98000	1883 &c	1	1	1	6	31	45	49	49	49	
6	HINCKLEY	DO	19"X24"	94000	1888						10	10	10	10	10
7	I.C.R.R.	DO	18"X24"	94000	1880 &c	25	32	36	46	55	61	62	62	62	62
8	SCHENECTADY	DO	18"X24"	94100	1889							14	14	14	14
9	ROGERS	8 WHEEL	18"X24"	110000	1892										
10	BROOKS	DO	18"X24"	107000	1890-91								8	25	25
11	I.C.R.R.	DO	18"X24"	96100	1888						4	4	4	4	
12	BROOKS	DO	17"X24"	70000	1875	2	2	2	2	2	2	2	2		
13	I.C.R.R.	DO	17"X22"	70000	1862 &c	95	95	90	89	89	86	86	80	75	
14	I.C.R.R.	DO	17"X24"	70000	1868 &c	30	32	36	38	42	44	45	51	55	
15	BROOKS	DO	16"X22&24"	66000	1875	3	3	3	3	3	3	3	3		
16	ROGERS	DO	16"X22"	62000	1855 &c	84	86	87	87	84	84	87	86	83	
17	ROGERS	DO	15"X22"	56000	1854 &c	68	65	59	53	49	45	47	46		
18	I.C.R.R. & ROGERS	SUBURBAN	16"X22"	70700	1880 &c	8	8	10	13	17	17	17	19	21	
19	BROOKS	6 WHEEL SWITCH	18"X24"	84000	1889 &c							3	18		
20	HINCKLEY	DO	15"X24"	62000	1875	4	4	4	4	4	4	4	4		
21	I.C.R.R.	4 WHEEL SWITCH	16"X24"	62000	1881 &c	10	14	14	18	22	27	31	31	31	
22	ROGERS	DO	15"X22"	50000	1856	1	1	1	1	1	1	1			
23	ROGERS	DO	13"X22"	40000	1857	1	1	1	1						
					TOTALS	334	346	346	363	402	436	470	516	567	

ICLAG21-25

INDEX OF CARS

PHOTO Nº	CLASS OF CAR	BUILT	LENGTH	NO OWNED 1883	1892
1	1ST CLASS PASSENGER COACH, VESTIBULE	1891	51'-6"		16
2	1ST CLASS PASSENGER COACH	1890	51'-6"	65	119
3	2ND CLASS PASSENGER COACH & SMOKER	1864	47'-10"	89	45
4	CHAIR CAR	1889	54'-0"		19
5	BAGGAGE & EXPRESS CAR	1890	50'-0"	15	58
6	BAGGAGE CAR	1857	41'-2"	24	
7	POSTAL CAR	1890	60'-1⅛"		102
8	POSTAL CAR	1872	41'-3½"	14	
9	SUBURBAN COACH	1887	45'-1"	41	125
10	SLEEPING CAR	1857	50'-5½"	5	
11	FURNITURE CAR	1890	40'-0"		100
12	BOX CAR, 25 TON	1881	35'-0"		384
13	BOX CAR, 20 TON	1887	35'-0"		3454
14	BOX CAR, 14 TON	1868	26'-0"	3827	3318
15	COAL CAR, 30 TON	1888	35'-0"		1620
16	COAL CAR, 15 TON	1869	28'-6"	1976	814
17	FRUIT CAR, 25 TON	1891	35'-0"		102
18	FRUIT CAR, 14 TON	1881	28'-6"	188	711
19	STOCK CAR, 20 TON	1887	35'-0"		596
20	STOCK CAR, 14 TON	1864	28'-6"	730	429
21	ENGINE SNOW PLOW				24
22	JULL SNOW EXCAVATOR	1891			
23	STEAM SHOVEL	1890			

ICLAG21-24

From an Illinois Central in-house publication discussing the Company's progress between 1883 and 1892.

Illinois Central Locomotive Index

Works Consulted

Bibliography:

Abbott, Shirley. <u>The National Museum of American History</u>. 1981. New York: Smithsonian Institution, Abrams, 1987.

Ackerman, William K. <u>Early Illinois Railroads</u>. Fergus Historical Series, No. 23. Chicago: Fergus Printing, 1884.

————. <u>Historical Sketch of the Illinois Central Railroad</u>. Chicago: Fergus Printing, 1890.

Adams, John Winthrop. <u>Great Railroad Photographs</u>. Philadelphia: Courage Books, 1994.

Alsop, Joseph. <u>FDR – A Centenary Remembrance</u>. New York: Viking, 1982.

Association of American Railroads. <u>Railroads and Railroading</u>, Washington, D.C.: AAR, September 1963.

Bell, William Gardner. The United States Army Center of Military History – OnLine: <u>Commanding Generals and Chiefs of Staff, 1775-1995</u>. Washington, D.C.: Center of Military History, 1997. <http://www.army.mil/cmh-pg/books/cg&csa/CG-Intro-II.htm>

Berkman, Pamela, ed. <u>The History of the Atchison, Topeka & Santa Fe</u>. New York: Bonanza Books, 1988.

Best, Gerald M. <u>Iron Horses to Promontory</u>. San Marino, California: Golden West Books, 1969.

Brownson, Howard Gray. <u>History of the Illinois Central Railroad to 1870</u>. Urbana, Illinois: U of Illinois, 1915.

Bryan, C.D.B. <u>The National Air and Space Museum</u>. 2nd ed. New York: 1988, Smithsonian Institution, Abrams, 1988.

Cahill, Marie and Lynne Piade, eds. <u>The History of the Union Pacific</u>. New York: Crescent Books, 1989.

Carnegie Library of Pittsburgh, eds. <u>The Handy Science Answer Book</u>. Detroit: Visible Ink Press, 1994.

Cochran, Thomas C. <u>Railroad Leaders 1845-1890</u>. Cambridge, Massachusetts: Harvard UP, 1953.

Congressional Quarterly. <u>National Party Conventions</u>, Washington, D.C.: Congressional Quarterly, 1979.

Corliss, Carlton J. <u>Mainline of Mid-America</u>. New York: Creative Age Press, 1950.

————. <u>Trails to Rails</u>. 2nd ed. Chicago: Illinois Central Railroad, 1937.

Crowson, George M. <u>A Lifetime of Service – Wayne Johnston and the Illinois Central Railroad</u>. Chicago: Illinois Central Railroad, 1968.

Cruise, David and Alison Griffiths. <u>Lords of the Line</u>. New York: Penguin-Viking, 1988.

Daily Democratic Press. <u>The Railroads, History and Commerce of Chicago</u>. Chicago: Daily Democratic Press, 1854.

Davis, William C., editor and Bell I. Wiley, senior consulting editor. <u>The Image of War, 1861-1865</u>, 6 vols. New York: National Historical Society, Doubleday, 1981-1989.

De Bono, Edward, ed. <u>Eureka</u>. London: Thames and Hudson, 1974.

DeGolyer, Everett L., Jr. Text. <u>The Track Going Back</u>. Fort Worth: Amon Carter Museum, 1969.

Edson, William D., ed. <u>Railroad History No. 140</u>, Boston: The Railway and Locomotive Historical Society, 1979.

Federal Writers' Project of the Work Projects Administration. <u>Illinois – A Descriptive and Historical Guide</u>. Chicago: A.C. McClurg, 1939.

Garden, J.F. <u>Nicholas Morant's Canadian Pacific</u>. Revelstoke, British Columbia, Canada: Footprint Publishing, 1991.

Gates, Paul Wallace. <u>The Illinois Central Railroad and Its Colonization Work</u>. Cambridge, Massachusetts: Harvard UP, 1934.

Gilbert, Paul and Charles Lee Bryson. <u>Chicago and its makers</u>. Chicago: Mendelsohn, 1929.

Gordon, Lois and Alan Gordon. <u>American Chronicle</u>. New York: Atheneum-Macmillan, 1987.

Greenberg, Dolores. <u>Financiers and Railroads 1869-1889</u>. Newark: U of Delaware P, 1980.

Hellemans, Alexander and Bryan H. Bunch. <u>The Timetables of Science</u>. New York: Simon, 1988.

Illinois Central Railroad. <u>Illinois Central Electrification Banquet</u>. Palmer House. Chicago: Gentry Printing, 1926.

Jacobs, Timothy, ed. <u>The History of the Baltimore & Ohio</u>. New York: Crescent Books, 1989.

Jacobs, Timothy. <u>The History of the Pennsylvania Railroad</u>. New York: Bonanza Books, 1988.

Kinert, Reed. <u>Early American Steam Locomotives</u>. Seattle: Superior Publishing, 1962.

Klein, Aaron E. <u>The History of the New York Central System</u>. New York: Bonanza Books, 1985.

Lausanne, Edita. <u>The Great Trains</u>. Ed. Bryan Morgan. New York: Crown, 1973.

Lavallee, Omer. <u>Van Horne's Road</u>. Toronto: Railfare Books, 1974.

Leech, Margaret. <u>Reveille in Washington 1860 - 1865</u>, New York: Harper, 1941.

McGrew, Edward W. <u>Corporate History of the Illinois Central Railroad Company</u>. Chicago: Illinois Central Railroad.

Mika, Nick and Helma. <u>Railways of Canada</u>. Montreal: McGraw-Hill Ryerson, 1972.

Modelski, Andrew M. <u>Railroad Maps of North America</u>. Washington, D.C.: Library of Congress, 1984.

Rehor, John A. <u>The Nickel Plate Story</u>. Waukesha, Wisconsin: Kalmbach Publishing, 1965.

Research and Development Bureau, eds. <u>Organization and Traffic of the Illinois Central System</u>. Chicago: Illinois Central Railroad, 1938.

Richardson Fleming, Paula and Judith Luskey. <u>The North American Indians</u>. New York: Harper, 1986.

Sautter, R. Craig and Edward M. Burke. <u>Inside the Wigwam</u>. Chicago: Wild Onion Books, 1996.

Schmidt, Barbara with Dave Thomson. <u>Samuel L. Clemens' Mississippi Steamboat Career</u>. <http://www.twainquotes.com/Steamboats/SteamboatsCareer.html>

Shapiro, Larry. <u>A Book of Days in American History</u>. New York: BOMC, Scribners, 1987.

Smithsonian Exposition Books. <u>The Smithsonian Book of Invention</u>. New York: Smithsonian Institution, Norton, 1978.

Stagner, Lloyd E. and Stephen A. Lee. <u>Illinois Central Steam Finale 1936-1960</u>. David City, Nebraska: South Platte Press, 1994.

Stover, John F. <u>History of the Illinois Central Railroad</u>. New York: Macmillan, 1975.

————. <u>Iron Road to the West</u>. New York: Columbia UP, 1978.

Swanson, Stevenson, ed. <u>Chicago Days</u>. Wheaton, Illinois: Cantigny First Division Foundation, 1997.

Tindall, George Brown and David E. Shi. <u>America: a narrative history</u>. 4th ed. New York: Norton, 1996.

United States Postal Service. <u>Celebrate the Century Decade Panes</u>. Issued by U.S.P.S. various U.S. cities: 1998 through 2000.

Viola, Herman J. <u>The National Archives of the United States</u>. New York: Abrams, 1984.

Wallechinsky, David and Irving Wallace. <u>The People's Almanac</u>. New York: Doubleday, 1975.

Weber, Thomas. <u>The Northern Railroads in the Civil War 1861-1865</u>. 1952. Bloomington, Indiana: Indiana UP, 1999.

Westing, Fred. <u>The Locomotives that Baldwin Built</u>. New York: Bonanza Books, 1966.

Wilner, Frank R. <u>Railroad Land Grants</u>. Washington, D.C.: AAR, revised August 1984.

Yenne, Bill. <u>The History of the Southern Pacific</u>. New York: Bonanza Books, 1985.

Ziel, Ron. <u>The Long Island Railroad in Early Photographs</u>. New York: Dover Publications, 1990.

Libraries & Historical Societies:

The Chicago Historical Society. Chicago, Illinois.

Illinois Central Historical Society. Paxton, Illinois.

The Smithsonian Institution. Washington, D.C.

Richard J. Daley Library. University of Illinois at Chicago. Chicago, Illinois.

Deering Library. Northwestern University Transportation Library. Evanston, Illinois. Illinois Central Magazine, various from Volume 1, Number 1 in July 1912 through the 1970's. Chicago: Illinois Central Railroad.

The Newberry Library. Chicago, Illinois. Illinois Central Railroad Company Archives, various materials 1851-1906.

Periodicals:

The New York Times Company. New York Times. Various 1860 through 1955.

Poor, Henry V. Poor's Railroad Manual. New York: H.V. & H.W. Poor (later Poor's Publishing Company), various from 1868 to 1940.

Moody, John. Moody's Analyses of Railroad Investments (later, Moody's Transportation Manual). New York: John Moody & Company (later, Moody's Investors Service), various from 1909 forward.

Web Sites:

Nobel Prize information: <http://www.almaz.com/nobel/>

Obscure Politics facts: <http://www.politicalgraveyard.com/index.html>

Olympic Games records: <http://www.olympic.org/uk/games/index-uk.asp>

Otto C. Perry memorial collection of IC photographs: <http://www.gowest.coalliance.org> Western History/Genealogy Department at the Denver Public Library. Over 15,500 photographs on-line, almost 250 of which are Illinois Central.

Pulitzer Prize information: <http://www.pulitzer.org/Archive/archive.html>

Steam Locomotive information: <http://www.steamlocomotive.com/>

ABOUT THE AUTHOR

ICLAG21-31

Richard P. Bessette was born and raised in Chicago. Fresh out of college in 1970, the author accepted a job with the Illinois Central Railroad in Marketing; this was followed by stints in Corporate Planning in 1983 and Finance in 1985; the author left the Railroad in 1990, at the end of the financial roller-coaster of the 1980's: the Railroad was taken public in 1988, returned private in 1989 and went public once again that same year. While at the Illinois Central, the author saw it merge with the Gulf, Mobile & Ohio, spend hundreds of millions during the Railroad Recovery and Revitalization period, and lead the line sale revolution in the industry. The author is married with two children and lives in a Chicago suburb.

Text and titles were typeset in Adobe Garamond.
Folios were typeset in Cheltenham.